CHILD BEHAVIOR THERAPY

Child
Behavior
Therapy

Edited by David Marholin II

Gardner Press, Inc., New York

Distrubuted by Halsted Press
Division of John Wiley & Sons, Inc.

New York · Toronto · London · Sydney

GARDNER PRESS, INC.
19 Union Square West
New York, New York 10003

Distributed solely by the Halsted Press Division
of John Wiley & Sons, Inc., New York

Library of Congress Cataloging in Publication Data
Main entry under title:

Child behavior therapy.

    Includes bibliographical references and index.
    1. Behavior therapy. 2. Child psychotherapy.
I. Marholin, David.
RJ505.B4C45   618.9′28′914   77–23929
ISBN 0–470–99277–8

Printed in the United States of America

To my parents, Bun and Evelyn

Preface

The American Psychiatric Association issued a "Task Force Report" on behavior therapy in July, 1973, and concluded as follows: "The work of the Task Force has reaffirmed our belief that behavior therapy and behavioral principles employed in the analysis of clinical phenomena have reached a stage of development where they now unquestionably have much to offer informed clinicians in the service of modern clinical and social psychiatry" (p. 64)[1]. In the late 1960's "behavior modification," as it was then called, began to achieve acceptance as a viable tool mainly with severely retarded, psychotic, and autistic children. The techniques of shaping, positive reinforcement, and punishment were employed chiefly in state institutions, experimental laboratories, and special school programs.

We are today witnessing an exponential increase in what is now more commonly referred to as "behavior therapy." While behavior modification emphasized the consequences of one's overt observable behavior in teaching appropriate social, self-help, and academic behaviors, behavior therapy has broadened the concept of behavior modification to include various emotional, psychosomatic, and cognitive realms.

Behavior therapy now is carried out in the child's home and regular classroom. It has helped children control epileptic seizures; it has helped to teach delinquent adolescents how to negotiate conflict situations with their parents; it has alleviated children's fears of dentists, hospitals, and surgery; and it has provided teachers with ways to modify inappropriate behaviors of students as well as showing students how to modify inappropriate behaviors of teachers.

Behavior therapy has had a profound professional impact. Psychologists, psychiatrists, and social workers increasingly label themselves behavior therapists, and the professional and public demand for professionals and paraprofessionals trained in behavior therapy techniques continues to mount.

This book is designed to inform the reader about the nature of behavior therapy. It is not intended as a "how-to-do-it" manual. In fact, it is the author's contention that no book can teach one how to use behavior therapy. One of the primary leaders in the field of child behavior therapy, Dr. Sidney W. Bijou, has continually emphasized that behavior therapy does not offer a touchstone. Because the approach has an apparent simplicity that can be deceptive, Dr. Bijou has suggested that there are two requirements for those interested in using behavior therapy techniques. First, one should "learn with precision the nature of the concepts and principles, the methodology of practical application and the basic literature on the behavioral technology of teaching, the individual research methodology" (p. 69)[2], and the assumptions of behavior therapy and their implications for therapeutic practices. Second, the prospective child behavior therapist should obtain experience in applying these principles. Those who would wish to use the approach should arrange to observe demonstrations in actual clinical settings and should seek out opportunities to practice the techniques under the close supervision of a competent behavior therapist.

Given Dr. Bijou's suggestions, one may ask, "Why produce another book on child behavior therapy?" It is this writer's observation that, although there are numerous books describing the basic principles of behavior therapy with presenting empirical evidence to support the notion that "behavior therapy works," there is a need for a volume which presents a clinical picture of the varied assumptions, applications, and sophistications of behavior therapy. This book intends to fill that need. This book is not intended as a substitute for Dr. Bijou's two requirements. It is intended as a valuable adjunct to the practicing clinician who has either met the requirements or is currently completing them.

This volume is organized into three major sections. The first part provides the conceptual bases of the behavioral therapies. It includes chapters devoted to theoretical foundations of behavior therapy, behavioral assessment, program design, and program evaluation. The second part deals with applications of behavior therapy to child psychopathology. Chapters are devoted to treating conduct-problem children in group settings, family therapy, mental retardation, delinquency, treatment of anxiety states and avoidance behaviors, somatic disorders, and community group home treatment models. Finally, the last four chapters are devoted to current issues in behavior therapy including generalization, ethical and legal considerations, staff training, and intra-institutional roadblocks to behavior modification programming.

I owe much to my colleagues and mentors whose writing, teaching, and modelling so significantly shaped my behavior and ultimately made this volume possible: Sidney Bijou, Don Freedheim, Tom Heads, Fred Kanfer, Liz McInnis, Carl Miller, Bill Redd, Don Shannon, and Warren Steinman. I would also like to express my gratitude to the contributors of this volume.

NOTES

1. American Psychiatric Association Task Force Report, Behavior therapy in psychiatry. July, 1973, American Psychiatric Association, Washington, D.C.
2. Bijou, S. W. What psychology has to offer education—now. *Journal of Applied Behavior Analysis*, 1970, *3*, 65–72.

Contents

xi

Part III
Current Issues

CONTRIBUTORS

Sidney W. Bijou, Departments of Psychology and Special Education, University of Arizona, Tucson, Arizona

Jay S. Birnbauer, Dejarnette Center for Human Development, Staunton, Virginia

Curtis J. Braukmann, Achievement Place Research Project, Department of Human Development, University of Kansas, Lawrence, Kansas

Tom B. Heads, Department of Psychology, Central Connecticut Regional Center, Meriden, Connecticut

Alan E. Kazdin, Department of Psychology, Pennsylvania State University, University Park, Pennsylvania

Kathryn A. Kirigin, Achievement Place Research Project, Department of Human Development, University of Kansas, Lawrence, Kansas

Robert P. Liberman, Department of Psychiatry, UCLA School of Medicine and Camarillo Neuropsychiatric Institute Research Center, Camarillo, California

Elizabeth T. McInnis, Los Niños Center, San Diego, California

Titus McInnis, Vista Hill Foundation, San Diego, California

David Marholin II, Department of Special Education, Boston University, Boston, Massachusetts

Edward K. Morris, Department of Human Development, University of Kansas, Lawrence Kansas

W. Robert Nay, Department of Psychology, University of Illinois at Urbana-Champaign, Champaign, Illinois

William H. Redd, Department of Psychology, University of Illinois at Urbana-Champaign, Champaign, Illinois

C. Steven Richards, Department of Psychology, University of Missouri at Columbia, Columbia, Missouri

Lawrence J. Siegel, Department of Psychology, University of Missouri at Columbia, Columbia, Missouri

William S. Sleator, Boston, Massachusetts

Paul E. Touchette, Department of Neurology, Harvard Medical School and Eunice Kennedy Shriver Center for Mental Retardation, Waltham, Massachusetts

Lawrence R. Weathers, Florida Mental Health Institute, Tampa, Florida

Alan G. Willner, Achievement Place Research Project, Department of Human Development, University of Kansas, Lawrence, Kansas

Montrose M. Wolf, Department of Human Development, University of Kansas, Lawrence, Kansas

Part I
Conceptual Bases
of the Behavioral Therapies

The Theoretical Foundations of Behavior Modification

William H. Redd and William S. Sleator

Modern psychology has delivered to us an incredibly powerful tool: behavior modification. By means of a deceptively simple strategy of changing how the social environment responds to our actions, long-standing habits and patterns of behavior are being radically altered. Self-destructive autistic and schizophrenic children who in the past have been drugged or kept in straightjackets can now be freed of their violent behavior and participate in meaningful activities; severely retarded children are being taught to care for themselves and even to engage in productive work; individuals are developing ways to eliminate migraine headaches; obese people are learning how to get thin and then actually *stay* thin; classrooms of unruly students can be handled in specific ways that promote better learning. Without a doubt, behavior modification is one of the important developments in the history of psychology and education.

Behavior modification begins with the straightforward assumption that human behavior is lawful. This idea is certainly *not new*. Anyone who presumes to study the world or any of its parts begins with the premise that things are lawful. Freud, Aristotle, and Locke all viewed man as an orderly creature. If we did not behave according to basic principles, however complex, then all of psychology, education, sociology, and economics would fall apart. These efforts would be totally useless.

Following a trend toward a more scientific approach in psychology, people working in the areas of clinical psychology and education started reformulating their theories in terms of the principles of learning. The notion was that perhaps many of man's problems involve his having learned maladaptive and undesirable patterns of behavior. If the problem behaviors were *learned*, so the thinking went, then they could be *unlearned*.

Although we could spend a great deal of time listing these principles, we limit our discussion here to the two principles that are most crucial in behavior modification. The first is the Law of Effect. It states that all organisms, both human and animal, are influenced by the consequences of their behavior. If a behavior leads to negative (unpleasant) ends, or to nothing at all, then it will cease. But actions that produce positive consequences (pleasure) will be repeated. A child keeps putting food into his mouth because it tastes good, but he quickly takes his hand away from the hot stove because it hurts. It would be a strange world indeed if man continued to do things that brought him personal pain and destruction. In fact, when society sees someone violating this principle, it usually identifies him as neurotic or even crazy, a danger to himself or society, and, often it institutionalizes him. In common-sense terms, we do things that feel good, and we refrain from doing things that hurt. When you think about it, it is clear that this principle is crucial to the survival of mankind. If our earliest ancestors did not eat when they were hungry, protect themselves from wild beasts and from the cold, or make love when they felt like it, we would not be around today.

In more scientific terms, then, the Law of Effect states that behavior will increase or decrease in frequency according to the effect it has on the individual. The probability of a certain behavior being repeated is directly related to the consequences that behavior produces.

Another principle of human learning that is important in behavior modification came from the famous Russian physiologist Pavlov and involves the effect of events and stimuli that *precede* an individual's behavior. Working with dogs in a scientifically regulated laboratory, Pavlov discovered that stimuli which reliably predict another event will come to have an effect similar to the events they predict. The dogs were held still in a harness and given small amounts of meat powder directly into their mouths. Immediately before the powder was delivered a bell would ring, signaling the presentation of the powder. After many such pairings of bell and food, the dogs started salivating at the sound of the bell, even when the food did not follow. The sound of the bell produced the same reaction as the meat powder. A human example of this principle is the competitive swimmer's reaction to the starter's saying "On your mark, ready, set." The starter's words elicit many of the same feelings of excitement and anxiety as the sound of the starting gun. Of course, the reactions of the swimmer are far more complicated than those of Pavlov's dogs, but according to learning theory, the same principle applies in both cases.

To see how these principles have been applied to human problems, we can turn to a classic case study. In 1924, Mary Culver Jones treated a 3-year-old boy who was terrified of rabbits. No one knew why, but when in the presence of a variety of furry objects, including small animals, fur coats, wool rugs, feathers, and especially rabbits, he would exhibit severe anxiety, often breaking into tears. Jones did not use the Freudian approach of deep and lengthy probing into the child's unconscious in an effort to try to discover the hidden origin of his fears. Instead, she took the basic learning principles we have described and simply taught him not to be afraid.

She started out by presenting him with the rabbit in a way that did *not* frighten him. While he was eating some of his favorite foods in a comfortable situation, she had the rabbit placed, in a cage, far enough away from him so that although he was aware of its presence, it was not alarming enough to interfere with his enjoyment of the food. Every day the rabbit was moved just a little bit closer, but never close enough to be frightening. Eventually it was let out of the cage and gradually brought close to the child. By the end of treatment he was even able to play with it affectionately.

What had happened was that he learned to associate the rabbit with the pleasurable stimulus of eating. He learned that the rabbit was not going to hurt him, he saw other children playing happily with it, and his fear was simply wiped out—as was also his fear of other furry objects. This procedure is straightforward, really nothing more than a systematic application of common sense, the idea being to introduce the feared object very gradually, making sure that at all times the fearful person is calm and relaxed.

Another interesting early example of the application of learning principles to psychological problems involves the treatment of enuresis, or bed-wetting. Two early behaviorists, Hobart and Molly Mower, dispensed with the popular psychodynamic theories of enuresis and treated it as merely the child's inability to control his bladder. Whatever the reason, he just had not learned how to control it, and their objective was to teach him to do so.

What they did was to design a pad that was placed on the bed or in the child's pants that sounded a buzzer when any moisture touched it. In other words, as soon as he began to urinate, the buzzer would sound and would continue until the child awoke and turned it off. The idea was that through repeated associations of the distended bladder and awakening the child would learn to awaken rather than void in response to the sensation of a full bladder. This method was very successful in "curing" enuresis to the point that the child learned to hold his urine through the night. Moreover, the procedure worked very fast and was inexpensive. In fact, a similarly designed apparatus is available in the Sears catalogue. The original technique has been slightly modified in the last 35 years, but the principles involved have not.

Although the basic learning principles we have been describing have been so well demonstrated that no psychological theory rejects them, there is still much controversy about their relevance to psychological problems and conflicts. The major difference between the behavioral approach and more traditional conceptualizations of psychopathology is that *the behavioral approach rejects the notion that "disturbed" behavior is a manifestation of some deeper psychological state or conflict*. This point of view is, of course, the shocker that makes many people regard behaviorism with contempt, if not horror, as a cold and inhumanly scientific view of the nature of man. Because of the great effect Freud has had on contemporary thought, many of us have grown up with the notion that our behavior is the manifestation of conflicts between our id and superego, upon which our sanity depends. Freud maintained that our fears, our motivations, and our problems with other people are all part of a complex, interwoven saga, much of it deeply buried, like a lost civilization. According to this view we must probe our psyche carefully, pulling away the layers in order to understand ourselves. Only by doing this can we change.

The behaviorist tells us that what we have to do is change those things in the social environment that influence our behavior. The proponents of more traditional theories insist that this approach cannot work, because our outward behaviors are merely *symptoms* of the conflicts going on within us. You may be able to eliminate a particular symptom, they argue, but if the conflict is still there the symptom will only reappear in another form—this is what is known as symptom substitution. According to this formulation, only when the inner conflict has been resolved can the unwanted behavior be eliminated for good.

The concept of symptom substitution is perhaps the most widely posed refutation of behavior theory. But the behaviorist's answer to this criticism is on a purely empirical basis: symptom substitution rarely, if ever, occurs. It just does not happen. In their review of the literature, psychologists Ullmann and Krasner (1975) concluded that symptom substitution is the exception rather than the rule.

Behaviorists argue that new symptoms do not appear because all behaviors, both normal and "pathological," are not symptoms at all.

Rather, they are merely the individual's response to particular aspects of his environment. Particular maladaptive responses may have developed over a long period of time or may be reactions to immediate situations.

We can see how problem behaviors are developed by looking at the very simple example of parents picking up their crying child. Since they do not like to hear the child cry, they pick him up when he does, because picking him up usually makes him stop. According to learning theory, the child's quieting is a positive event for the parents and, therefore, it will reward their picking him up. But since being picked up is also a positive event for the child, his own *crying* will be rewarded because they pick him up when he does it. It is a vicious cycle. The child strengthens his parents' behavior by ceasing to cry when they hold him, and the parents strengthen the child's crying by picking him up when he does it.

Of course it often is not as simple as that example, and the behavior modifier does not claim he always knows or is able to determine why we do what we do. One can be pretty sure that the child learns to avoid the hot stove when he touches it, but one may not know why the child plays with blocks. It could be because his parent gives him a piece of candy whenever he plays quietly, or because his parent scolds him for *not* playing with the blocks, or simply because he finds them interesting. Who can be sure? What the behavior modifier does believe is that the child plays with his blocks because such play yields positive consequences which are referred to as *reinforcers*, events that increase the likelihood that the behaviors they follow will be repeated.

The method of the behavior therapist, it then follows, is to alter his client's *environment*, rather than trying to change the client's behavior directly. The theory is that the environment, by reinforcing some behaviors and not reinforcing others, is what is bringing about the particular behavior; and that a change in the way the environment responds will in turn bring about a change in behavior.

With this brief account of the underlying assumptions of behavior modification, we can really get to the question of just exactly what it is that the behavior modifier does when he's practicing behavior modification.

To start with he determines the problem, in the obvious way of talking to the client, or in the case of young children to their parents or teacher. The behavior modifier tries to be as specific as possible—exactly what are the problem behaviors, and how often do they occur. Unlike the more traditional methods, the behavior modifier's questions are straightforward, with no subtle, hidden meanings. He is not trying to delve into the unconscious—in fact, he goes in the opposite direction.

He may also observe the client in his natural, every-day environment. If the client is a child with disruptive classroom behavior, the behavior modifier might simply go into the classroom and watch what happens. Of course, this is not always possible, as in the case of an adult who complains that he "can't get along with anybody." In such a case the behavior modifier can ask the client himself to observe carefully just what is going on when the problem occurs, perhaps even to keep a written record of it; or the client can ask his family or friends to observe.

Once the specific problem is determined, the next step is to find out what the client hopes to get out of the program. Here we come to an important distinction between responsible behavior modification and other forms of treatment. The behavior modifier does not approach his client with any a priori notion of "mental health" or of the "true nature of man." He is not trying to get his client to become what *he*, the therapist, thinks a person should be. His aim is not necessarily to rid him of "neurosis," or to "self-actualize" the client, nor to make the client more social or more competitive, nor even to get the client to live up to any of the norms or standards imposed by society (unless, of course, the client is a threat to society). The therapist's function is to help the client solve what *he*, the client, feels are his own particular problems. For the behavior modifier, the direction comes from the client.

Although the decision as to the goals of the therapy are not the therapist's, sometimes there are cases the therapist will not take because the client's goals are incompatible with the therapist's personal ethics. An example might be a situation in which a teacher comes to the behavior modifier and wants him to devise a program to provide the teacher with a classroom of docile children who remain quietly seated throughout the day. But if the behavior modifier feels that such a goal is not good for the child and, in fact, might be harmful, he would say so. And if they could not agree on an appropriate goal, the behavior modifier would most likely refer the teacher elsewhere.

But, assuming that a clear set of goals has been established and agreed on by both parties, the therapist turns his attention to the meticulous assessment of the problem. The behavior modifier determines the environmental conditions (events) that are associated with the problem behavior. The object here is to discover what happens immediately preceding the problem behavior, and might therefore be eliciting it, and what events happen right after it, which might be reinforcing it. The therapist also attempts to determine the antecedents and consequences of any adaptive, positive behavior that might relate to the long-range goal the client is trying to achieve. The specific goal of assessment is to determine what situations in the environment are reinforcing the problem behaviors and what situations are reinforcing any instances of the desired behaviors. Assessment consists essentially of studying the client's social environment. Only when the antecedents and consequences are determined can the behavior modifier know how to alter the environment in a way that will discourage the problem behavior and encourage the desired behavior.

To see how this careful assessment works, let us review an actual case. It involves a 20-year-old woman who suffered from long-standing, painful inflammation of the skin on the back of her neck. Endless medical treatments, including ointments, pills, lotions, and X-ray therapy, did not do much to help her, mainly because she insisted on persistently and vigorously scratching the back of her neck. This naturally negated any of the effects of the treatment, actually increased the inflammation, and was probably what had started the skin condition in the first place.

When a behavioral assessment of her environment was made, it turned out that her brother had always been the darling of her parents. Recently, in fact, he had been receiving most of their attention. They did not have much money, but what they had was being spent on him. And even more than ever, the daughter had been treated as an inferior, if not virtually ignored. And that was when the skin condition developed.

When she became ill, of course the whole situation changed. Now they were spending money on her doctor bills, not on her brother. She was getting all kinds of concerned attention from her family, and her fiancé as well became especially solicitous, frequently helping her apply her various ointments. And so she kept on scratching like mad.

She was, in other words, being abundantly reinforced for the scratching. The behavior modifier instructed her family to ignore the skin condition and the fiancé to stop helping her apply the ointment. What the therapist was doing was altering the environment so that the scratching would no longer be reinforced. His assessment of the situation had, indeed, been accurate, because in 3 months the dermatitis had completely disappeared. When a follow-up study was made 4 years later, she was happily married, in a situation presumably more naturally reinforcing than her family environment had been, and the skin condition had not returned.

We can go to a typical classroom for another example of the importance of assessing which environmental events reinforce the problem behavior and which events reinforce good behavior and how they can be altered. A teacher might come and tell the behavior modifier that he has a boy in class who is incorrigible. He cannot do anything with the child, who shows off, sasses the teacher in front of his classmates and does not do his work. He is driving the teacher up the wall. To make an accurate assessment of the situation the behavior modifier goes to the classroom to observe. He notes what the teacher and classmates do when the child acts up or is aggressive. He also determines what things precede these outbursts. Equally important, the behavior modifier looks to see what happens when the child works quietly at his desk or raises his hand to be called on. What he finds is unfortunately typical of many classrooms. Every time the boy makes a daring wisecrack that sends the teacher into a tizzy, the class goes wild. The boy is their hero. Not only does he get all the attention, he earns the respect of classmates, especially the other boys. However, when he is quietly reading at his desk, nothing happens; he is ignored. And when he raises his hand the teacher never calls on him, probably assuming that he is going to make another wisecrack or give the wrong answer.

The social environment of the classroom is clearly reinforcing his bad behavior and giving him absolutely no reinforcement for doing well. He may be driving the teacher up the wall but the teacher is certainly not doing much to encourage him to do otherwise. After making his observations, the behavior modifier has a discussion with the teacher and explains how he might be contributing to the problem. Chances are that if he ignores the child's wisecracks, praises him for reading at his desk, and calls on him when he raises his hand, things will turn around. Good behavior should replace his disruptive antics. As in many cases, the solution does not really involve implementing a detailed program, it merely involves reordering the way the social environment responds to the child.

But sometimes this reorganization is formalized into a program in which the contingencies of reinforcement are clearly specified. In a classroom the teacher might give special treats for improvement in academic subjects or deportment. The parent might give the child extra spending money for completing his weekly chores. And if the child misbehaves he would be required to forfeit certain opportunities or privileges for a specified period of time. Often this involves removing the children from the source of rewards for a few minutes. This period of time out might mean going to his room until he settles down or sitting in the corner of the classroom for a brief time. The general tendency among behavior modifiers is not to recommend the use of punishment, because many fear that bad side effects will result.

In some classrooms and residential treatment facilities programs have been systematized into what is called a token economy. As the name suggests, the classroom is run on a carefully designed economy in which plastic poker chips or some type of point (i.e., tokens) are the medium of exchange. Tokens are given to the children contingent on their performance and can be traded for privileges, trinkets, and treats. It is just like the system we all live under–we are paid with money and use the money to buy what we want. Chips are given out to each child when he completes an assignment or behaves in a certain way. Then at some future time (perhaps each day, or once or twice a week) the chips can be traded for goodies at a store or canteen set up in the classroom. Regardless of how simple or elaborate a program is, the basic principle is that good behavior must be rewarded.

In some cases the behavior modifier discovers during the initial assessment that he is not the professional who is needed. Let us take another example of a disruptive child. During the behavior modifier's observation he noted that things were fine as long as the child was studying at his desk with the materials directly in front of him. But when assignments were written on the blackboard he was less well behaved. He appeared to become uninterested and disruptive. It seemed that his bad behavior was associated with how the materials were presented—near or far. Based on the hunch that the child might have difficulty seeing the blackboard, a visit to an eye specialist was suggested. Glasses corrected most of the behavior problems.

Because most behavior modification programs involve rearranging how the person is reinforced in his daily life, it is of paramount importance to determine what events or "things" the individual likes. There are, of course, certain basic things that are reinforcing to almost everyone—food, sex, love, attention, and appreciation—but nevertheless we are all unique in our personal preferences, and any effective program must be sensitive to the preferences of the client. A 14-year-old boy may find the ear-splitting sound of hard rock very pleasant; whereas his 40-year-old father may find it aversive. For the boy the music is a reinforcer, but for the father it is a punisher. A good behavior modification program would certainly take these differences in taste into account.

There are still two more important aspects of an effective behavior modification program, both of which become critical when the problems that are to be solved by the program become more complicated. The first is the specification of *short-term* behavioral goals. Most problems are not simple enough to be solved in one fell swoop, and therefore, the program must be organized in stages. Intermediate goals must be devised, starting with the most easily attainable and progressing by gradual stages toward the final objective. An optimal arrangement of this series of goals would eliminate the possibility of failure at any point in the program, so that the client is being continually reinforced for his progress.

The last aspect of a program that we must mention is one that has been a critical part of all the programs we have discussed—constant monitoring. The therapist keeps a continuing record of how the client and the environment are doing. Thus if more appropriate behaviors are not increasing in frequency and maladaptive behaviors are not dropping out, he knows something is wrong with his program and will change it accordingly. If the girl with dermatitis we discussed earlier stopped scratching her neck and began pulling out her hair instead, the therapist would know something was wrong and make a change in the treatment program. In the same way that he is not trying to make all his clients live up to an arbitrary image of what the "normal" person should be, he also does not expect one particular program to work for everybody, and will modify his treatment of each individual as necessary.

As stated at the outset, behavior modification is nothing more than a tool. Like airplanes, like lasers, like atomic power, it can be used both destructively and constructively. There is nothing about behavior modification itself that controls how it is applied. It is the practitioner who makes these important decisions.

REFERENCES

Bandura, A. *Principles of behavior modification.* New York: Holt, Rinehart & Winston, 1969.

Bijou, S. W., & Redd, W. H. Child behavior therapy. S. Arieti (Ed.)., *American handbook of psychiatry*, vol. 5. New York: Basic Books, 1975, pp. 319–344.

Brown, B. S., Wienckowski, L. A., & Stolz, S. B. Behavior modification: Perspective on a current issue. *American Psychologist, 1975, 30,* 1027–1048.

O'Leary, K. D., & Wilson, G. T. *Behavior therapy: Application and outcome.* Englewood Cliffs: Prentice-Hall, 1975.

Sulzer, B., & Mayer, G. R. *Behavior modification procedures for school personnel.* Hinsdale, Ill.: The Dryden Press, 1972.

Ullmann, L. P., & Krasner, L. *A psychological approach to abnormal behavior.* Englewood Cliffs, N. J.: Prentice-Hall, 1975.

Yates, A. J. *Theory and practice in behavior therapy,* New York: Wiley, 1975.

2

Behavioral Assessment
LISTEN WHEN THE DATA SPEAK

David Marholin II and Sidney W. Bijou

Before making decisions about specific therapeutic interventions, a comprehensive functional analysis should be undertaken, regardless of the presenting problem (Hersen & Bellack, 1976; Kanfer & Grimm, 1977; Kanfer & Saslow, 1969; Marholin & Kanfer, Note 1) The major steps include objectively defining target behaviors, identifying antecedents and consequences of those target behaviors, selecting and testing potential reinforcers, and devising a reliable method to observe, record, and graphically display the occurrence of selected behaviors (Gottman & Leiblum, 1974; Holland, 1970; Wolpe, 1973). This rule of thumb applies to all populations, settings, and behaviors.

INDIVIDUAL ASSESSMENT

This chapter is concerned with those assessment strategies that have evolved from a functional analysis of behavior. Before progressing further toward this aim, it is useful to examine the traditional conceptualizations of "personality" or human behavior on which most assessment techniques are based. Historically, the concepts used by personality theorists for understanding human behavior have been dispositional in nature, including such concepts as "instincts," "needs," "drives," and "traits" which have been assumed to operate as motivational determinants of behavior in a variety of situations. This conceptualization of human behavior, which might be described as following the "M" or mental model, has led the clinician to ask: "What is there about the client's developmental history and personality structure which is causing him to have certain problems, and what aspects of his personality should be altered in order to eliminate or minimize these problems?" Furthermore, traditional assessment has previously consisted of assigning the client to given categories. In psychopathology or special education these are frequently called "diagnoses." The client is also placed at a specific point on an arbitrary continuum. This procedure allows for a comparison of the individual's score (e.g., intelligence quotient) or profile (e.g., MMPI) to the population mean. Finally, success during and after treatment is predicted from test results. In general, these practices have been found to be of little value. Other than the stigmatizing and dehumanizing aspects of such a labeling process (Farina, Holland, & Ring, 1966; Laing, 1967; Schwartz & Skolnick, 1962; Szasz, 1960), criticisms of the traditional mental model of assessment have been leveled on purely practical grounds (Cautela & Upper, 1975; Ferster, 1966; Phillips & Draguns, 1971). First, the reliability of psychiatric and educational classification systems is dubious at best (Goldfried & Kent, 1972; Kanfer & Saslow, 1975; Stuart, 1970). Second, classification systems derived from psychiatric nomenclature are not based on any one consistent classificatory principle; rather, they mix together categories based on behavior, age, severity, etiology, and the like (Lorr, Klett, & McNair, 1963; Zigler & Phillips, 1961). Third, they are not based on meaningful and observable behaviors. Finally, a dispositional diagnosis not only fails to provide information relative to the most appropriate type of treatment (Bannister, Salmon, & Leiberman, 1964; Kanfer & Phillips, 1970; Stuart, 1970), but it does not prognosticate a client's behavior during and after treatment (Kanfer & Saslow, 1969; Stuart, 1970).

In contrast with the "M" model, there is the "I" or interactional model of human behavior which is based on a functional analysis of behavior. Although the mental model focuses on the characteristics an individual "has," the interactional model of human behavior emphasizes what a person "does" in various situations (Mischel, 1968). According to the "I" model, the two most important clinical uses of assessment data are to (1) specify clearly those areas in which behavior change should take place and

(2) determine the conditions that would probably lead to such behavior changes, or the modification of the problem behavior. The "I" model suggests a parsimonious approach to assessment which includes only such information as is necessary for effective decision making about the treatment program. Because knowledge about a child's past history is often unnecessary in the sense that treatment or education cannot undo or redo this history, the emphasis of a functional analysis point of view is solely on those conditions responsible for the maintenance of undesirable behaviors or the conditions necessary for the development of new repertoires. In summary, assessment from the point of view of the "I" model consists "neither of placing a child in a diagnostic category, nor of a search for hypothetical underlying causes, neurological or otherwise" (Bijou & Grimm, 1975, p. 164). Diagnosis or assesment is, instead, oriented toward obtaining the kinds of information or data that can be directly used to *develop and guide a treatment program.* In their extensive review of the status of psychotherapy, Strupp and Bergin (1969) comment on the behavioral diagnostic approach:

A new philosophy and methodology of diagnosis is developing within the behavioral school. It is being complemented by the work of an increasing number of eclectically-oriented psychiatrists who tend to focus upon pragmatic, behavioral criteria such as being in or out of school, maintaining marriage or becoming divorced, frequency of arrest, being in or out of the hospital, etc. While still in its infancy, this approach is having an increasing impact upon clinical assessment and upon the specification of outcome criteria for research purposes (p. 60).

Assessment, as a component of treatment, may be viewed as consisting of several distinct tasks (Bijou & Peterson, 1971; Kanfer, 1972). The first involves an initial analysis of the problem situation to ascertain what services the client may require and whether the program or agency can provide these services. During this period an initial attempt is made to identify those behaviors to be increased or decreased in frequency or changed in form. (The question of which of several problematic behaviors to change is addressed more fully in chapter 13 by Heads.) When the problem has been identified, the staff are in a position to make an "accept— not accept" decision based on whether their particular program is equipped to deal with the problem. Assuming that the child is accepted into the program, the second task involves a functional analysis to identify the environmental conditions that elicit, prompt, reinforce, or punish particular problem behaviors and to specify what conditions might be manipulated to alter the child's behavior. The third and fourth tasks deal with progress during and after treatment.

INTAKE EVALUATION

In assessing the nature of the presenting problem, one may conceptualize it as falling into one or more of four general categories (Bijou, 1976). The first consists of *behavioral excesses* (Bijou & Peterson, 1971; Ross, 1972; Sherman & Baer, 1969). These include a class of related behaviors which occur and are described as problematic because of excess(es) in (1) frequency, (2) intensity, or (3) duration. Hyperactive children, aggressive youngsters, and children who engage in prolonged tantrums are examples of children who possess behavioral excesses along one or another of these dimensions. This class usually includes children who are labeled as conduct problems, or youngsters who are in continual conflict with their parents or siblings. The second category consists of problems including *shy*, *withdrawn*, and *fearful* behavior. It includes children with specific or generalized phobias (Lazarus, Davison, & Polefka, 1965), children traditionally described as adjustment problems (Ross, 1972), or personality problems (Quay, 1972) in which shy or timid behavior is an overriding feature. The third category relates to *behavioral deficits*. This type of behavior is described as problematic because it fails to occur (1) with sufficient frequency, (2) with adequate intensity, or (3) in appropriate form. Here we find children who are not performing well in school; children who have few, if any, friends or do not know how to get along with their peers; and youngsters who do not talk. Children who are retarded in the development of skills would also be included in this group. Problems that involve behaviors under *inappropriate stimulus control* make up the fourth group. The behavior may be satisfactory in content but occurs, from the point of view of society, in the wrong place or at the wrong time. The largest number of childhood behavior problems probably fall into this group. Here we find enuretic children, who suffer from neither an excess nor a deficit of behavior; they simply make a response at an inappropriate time and place. As examples of minor infractions we find in this group children who engage in persistent laughing in church or running in the house. The problem in each of these cases may not be to reduce the frequent occurrence of behavior but to allow it to occur at a time and place more appropriately matched to the behavior, such as laughter at a birthday party or running on a baseball diamond. Certain cognitive problems also belong in this category, such as children who know their multiplication tables but are unable to respond when called upon by the teacher.

Assessment prior to intervention provides some of the information necessary for preparing child-specific programs for behavioral change. Data for these purposes are derived from (1) interviews and reports, (2) direct observation whenever possible, (3) inventories and behavioral surveys, and (4) projective techniques and psychometric tests.

Regardless of one's theoretical bias, the interview has been and continues to be the universal device to obtain information about the behavior of children and their environments. Unfortunately, even Freud (1946) came to the regretful conclusion that client's accounts of past events tended to be based more on fantasy than fact. Furthermore, the information obtained from an interview may be biased, especially if informants (e.g., parents) consider themselves to blame for a child's behavior or when they are dissatisfied with prior treatment attempts. However, if the interviewer keeps the shortcomings of the interview in mind, it might provide useful information as a basis for further examination of the problem behavior(s) and environmental conditions.

The major objectives of an interview depend on the problem(s) presented but, in general, consist of developing testable hypotheses about factors that are contributing to the child's current problems and may be relevant for the subsequent planning of a treatment program. In listening to complaints of significant others and the target child, the behavior analysist attemps to elicit a specific description of the events that constitute a problem so that he can evaluate which of the varied components of the situation are amenable to change. Rather than global descriptors such as "disrespectful," "lazy," and "obstinate," behavioral and situational specifics are required for a functional analysis.

A search for specifics leads the behavior-analytic interviewer to ask such questions as: (1) What behavioral repertoires does the child have that can be used to build a treatment program? (2) What aversive or unpleasant conditions are currently in the child's environment? (3) What reinforcers are functional for the child? (4) What conditions maintain the problem behavior(s)? (5) Should the problem be attacked? (6) What methods and resources are needed for intervention and are they available? (7) What additional information is needed to make a tentative decision?

In addition to information gathering and hypothesis testing the interview allows for the development of a language system that allows the interviewee to communicate more effectively with the interviewer (Bijou & Redd, 1975). It is important, for example, to develop a language system emphasizing discrete and observable behavior. This allows the interviewer to more effectively construct a complete behavioral analysis of particular situations, and it helps the one being interviewed to monitor and con- sequate particular discrete behaviors.

It is important to search for more than a single cause or maintaining variable of problem behavior, because changing one aspect of the child's environmemt may be equally as effective as changing another in reducing the client's difficulty. For example, truancy may be the result of insufficient attention from parents at home, lack of an academic repertoire to perform at the expected level at school, excessive support from a peer group, or merely lack of positive consequences for attending school (Kanfer & Grimm, 1977). Because the reduction of one or several of these problem areas may be sufficient to alleviate the problem behavior (Baer, 1975), it is important to attempt to identify as many of the maintaining conditions as possible (Peterson, 1968).

The interview may be conceptualized in three stages (Becker & Wagner, Note 2). In the initial stage one might ask the informants "how they see the problem." It is most often necessary to question for specifics. This is especially true when jargon or vague terms are used (e.g., "You say he is mad. Tell me more about that. When is he mad? How does he show it?"). Often it is important to explore for problems other than those first presented. This may be accomplished with the aid of a checklist of behavior problems (Quay & Peterson, Note 3; Wahler & Cormier, 1970) or a survey of behavioral competencies such as the Vineland Social Maturity Scale, AAMD Adaptive Behavior Scale and the Development Skill Age Inventory (Alpen & Boll, 1972). Although the data derived from checklists or surveys do not provide direct information about functional relationships, they may help indicate problem areas or behavioral strengths that may have otherwise gone unnoticed (Lazarus, 1971).

In the second stage of the interview it is important to explore for situations in which behaviors are more or less probable and simultaneously to ask for specification of consequences of problem behaviors ("What happens after the child does so and so?") and antecedents ("What happened before the child does so and so?"). It may be useful to ask the parents or informants what strategies have been tried relative to the problem behavior. Finally, the problem behaviors are summarized for the parents or guardians.

The final stage of the interview concentrates on the identification of behavioral strengths and potential reinforcers for the child. The following questions are useful: "What does the child do well?", "What does the child like to do?", and "What will the child work for?"

Interviews with children, particularly young children, are often difficult and provide limited information about specific problem areas. Nonetheless, some time should be spent with the child or with the child and his parent(s) together. Observing the child and his parent(s) together allows the therapist to make some assessment of the child's general physical and social demeanor, the child's behavior in the presence of his or her parents, and the parents' reactions to particular behaviors of the child. Often with very young or nonverbal children, therapists have used toys such as dolls, play trucks, and paints to form initial impressions of the child's motor development, activity level, and sex-role behaviors (Rekers & Lovaas, 1974). However, even when children are verbal, one should be cautious about drawing general conclusions from impressions gained from the interview situation. A child might be a superb impression manager, appearing delightfully appropriate during an interview, yet be a hellion in school, home, or neighborhood. Whenever possible, observations should be made in the setting(s) in which the problem behavior exists, for example, the home, school, and day-care center (Johnson, Christensen, & Bellamy, 1976). Although the presence of an observer may alter a child's behavior, the chances are that information obtained under these circumstances will be more meaningful than information obtained from retrospective interviews as well as psychometric tests or projective devices (Bijou & Grimm, 1975; Bijou & Peterson, 1971; Bijou & Redd, 1975).

Recent innovations in technology have aided the behaviorally oriented therapist in collecting interactional assessment data in the natural environment. For example, several investigators have developed relatively inexpensive procedures for direct observation, including the use of audio recording (Bernal, Williams & Pesses, 1971; Johnson & Bolstad, 1975) and radio transmitters (Purcell & Brady, 1965; Soskin & John, 1963). In a recent advance, Johnson, Christensen, and Bellamy (1976) employed a radio transmitter and two reel-to-reel tape recorders in the home of a disturbed family during pre-intervention assessment. The transmitter broadcast to a receiver-recording apparatus in the home. The target child wore a radio transmitter on his belt, and the apparatus was activated by an interval timer at predetermined "random" times or by parents at predetermined "picked" times. The "picked" times were situations selected by the parents during which problems typically occurred (e.g., bedtime). Although the parents and target child were aware of the "picked" times, they were unaware of the "randomly" selected times, thus partially overcoming the problems of subject reactivity as a result of knowledge of observation times (Jones, Reid, & Patterson, 1975; Lipinski & Nelson, 1974). As described, the equipment costs approximately $650.00, and a minimum of technical expertise is needed for its operation. The unobtrusive use of audio recordings has proven to be of considerable utility for assessment in the home (Johnson et al., 1976).

Projective tests have been widely used in different ways and to different degrees by child psychiatrists, clinical and school psychologists, and social workers. Although over 2000 articles have been written concerning projective techniques, projective devices simply do not warrant the time for their administration, scoring, and interpretation (Stuart, 1970). When comparing Rorschach and TAT test results with clinical diagnosis, the validity coefficients are so low that projective devices are probably of little use for individual treatment decisions (Crombach, 1949; Fisher, 1967). In fact, the clinician who would use a projective technique should answer the question, "Am I doing better than I could do by flipping pennies?" (Meehl, 1954). An honest answer to this question would be an unqualified, "No" (Stuart, 1970).

Standardized or norm referenced tests such as the Stanford-Binet Intelligence Scale (Terman & Merrill, 1960) and the Wechsler Intelligence Scale for Children (Wechsler, 1967) have been employed in assessment to indicate (1) a child's aptitude for work in regular public school classes as they are presently constituted, organized, and conducted and (2) provide data for school personnel, particularly principals, who are interested in comparing a child's school aptitude with children of a similar age. Current testing practices with norm-referenced tests may be criticized on three grounds. First, almost all "intelligence tests are particularly unfair to children who are disadvantaged in one way or another, and are, because of their emphasis on school type experiences, less than adequate as measures of intelligence even for so-called normal children" (Bijou & Grimm, 1975, p. 170). Second, norm-referenced tests reveal what a child can or cannot do in comparison to his peers, but what is needed is information about what he can do in relation to an explicit program of instruction or training (Ribes-Inesta, 1972; Risley, Reynolds, & Hart, 1970). Finally, the results of currently available psychometric tests provide practically no data useful for program planning. Tests provide only indirect information about the conditions that caused a child to be referred for treatment and, in general, have proven wholly abortive (Yarrow, Campbell, & Burton, 1968). "Although one might test a child to survey his abilities and skills, such tests do not indicate behavioral contingencies that have *actually* caused his parents to seek professional assistance. Nor do current psychometric tests identify the conditions that may be responsible for the development and maintenance of deviant behavior" (Bijou & Peterson, 1971, p. 65).

POST-INTAKE ASSESSMENT
FOR TREATMENT PROGRAMMING

Once the problem has been evaluated and a decision has been reached to develop a particular treatment program, the behavior(s) to be changed must be clearly identified. Often there is some general agreement among significant others as to the behavior problems of a child and the global goals to be achieved. However, global problem definitions are insufficient to initiate a program. For example, it is insufficient to select as a treatment goal the alteration of aggressiveness, hyperactivity, bickering, social skills, or self-esteem. Problem behaviors presented in terms of traits, personality characteristics, and labels are too general and open to idiosyncratic interpretation to be of much utility. Global terms should be defined so that they can be observed, measured, and agreed on by those planning and administering the program. If behaviors are defined in objective terms, few or no inferences are necessary to detect behaviors when they occur. For example, "aggressiveness" was inferred from predelinquent boys' use of comments which threatened others (Phillips, 1968). "Aggressive" comments including threats of destruction of an object, person, or animal were defined as the problem behaviors to be changed. It was noted that "hyperactivity" exhibited by young children in classroom settings usually was inferred from the number of times they got out of their seats. Therefore, "getting-out-of-seat" was denoted as the behavior to be changed (Quay, Werry, McQueen, & Sprague, 1966). In one program a "poor attitude toward school" among females in a large group-home setting was the primary goal of intervention (Marholin, Plienis, Harris, & Marholin, 1975). A "good attitude toward school" was defined as arriving at classes promptly and achieving passing weekly school grades. These examples demonstrate that objective behavioral definitions can profitably replace general terms such as aggressiveness, hyperactivity, and poor attitude.

Formal assessment, which usually takes place following a clear definition of the problem to be treated, serves two purposes. First, such assessment establishes the frequency of occurrence of a particular behavior prior to intervention, commonly referred to as the baseline performance. Data from direct observation of a child's behavior are usually the primary source for baseline information. When properly carried out, systematic observation and recording of a child's behavior provide objective data and clearly show many of a child's behavioral strengths and weaknesses. It has been shown that reliance on human judgement in the absence of objective assessment may distort the extent to which the behavior is actually occurring (Kazdin, 1973; Kent, O'Leary, Diament, & Dietz, 1974; Schnelle, 1974). For example, a situation involving physical blows between two residents of a treatment setting may be so intense that counselors recall them as occurring very often. Because fights are so noticeable, they may seem more frequent than they actually are. In contrast, some children may engage in so many fights that counselors become somewhat accustomed to their high rate. Thus fights may be perceived as being of greater or lesser frequency than are shown by the objective data.

Second, precise behavioral pre-treatment data are required to reflect, accurately and objectively, changes in the child's behavior after treatment is initiated. Because the aim of treatment is to alter problem behavior, behavior during treatment is usually compared to behavior before treatment or during the baseline period.

In behavioral analysis, the assumption is that a child's progress in treatment is a function of the adequacy of the specific contingency conditions prescribed for him; hence continuous assessment takes on a special importance. If running accounts provided by systematic observations indicate that the child is not making reasonable advancement, the program should be scrutinized and modified accordingly. Therefore, program evaluation and program modification are directly and continuously inter-related.

Before one need concern himself with program evaluation, the problem of selecting appropriate reinforcers must be considered. Because the best prepared treatment program will not produce change in the child unless he is motivated to respond as required, emphasis must be placed on assessing which stimuli (e.g., praise, activities, privileges, and special food) are functional reinforcers for the child, that is, which ones will increase the frequency of desired behaviors when presented contingently on their occurrence. This may be accomplished by a functional test involving the presentation of a "potential reinforcer" immediately following a particular response. If the response in question increases, a functional reinforcer has been identified. Conversely, if the response fails to increase in rate over baseline measures, the potential reinforcer is *not* a functional reinforcer for that particular child. Potential reinforcers may also be identified by (1) asking the child (e.g., Homme's Reinforcement Menu; Homme, Csanyi, Gonzales, & Rechs, 1970), (2) watching what he does, or (3) asking the parents or others who know him well. Another useful method for locating potential reinforcers is to provide a sample or portion of an event to an individual noncontingently to see if he likes it, that is, reinforcer sampling (Ayllon & Azrin, 1968). For example, a child who has never gone to a zoo may not be motivated to work to have the opportunity to go to the zoo. If the child is noncontingently taken to the zoo and likes it, the zoo may then become a functional reinforcer which might aid the therapist in modifying behavior in the future.

Recording the occurrence of the particular behaviors to be altered is likely to provide a great deal of useful information in planning and carrying out a treatment program. In observing specific behaviors it is likely that particular antecedent and consequent events will be systematically related to the occurrence of the behaviors being observed. The recording of "antecedent-behavior-consequence" relationships may lead to hypotheses of which environmental events control behavior and thereby can be changed to alter the very same behavior. These hypotheses must be subsequently tested by altering the events to determine their influence on behavior. For example, in observing the number of times a child in a group home setting swears at his houseparent following routine requests to complete particular tasks, it may be noticed that the houseparent consistently responds by stopping whatever he is doing and delivering a short lecture on the inappropriateness of obscene language. Such an observation provides information about the stimulus conditions controlling the problem behavior, noncompliance and swearing at an adult in this case. Observing consequences is exceedingly important in a behavior modification program, for it is likely that some consequence is maintaining undesirable behavior. On the other hand, if certain appropriate behavior is lacking from a child's behavioral repertoire, it is likely that the behavior is not reinforced when it occurs. In the example of the child swearing at his houseparent, it is highly probable that positive reinforcement (i.e., attention in the form of a lecture) consistently follows and subsequently reinforces swearing, whereas more appropriate verbal inter-actions with the houseparent generally go unnoticed and unreinforced. Because in most behavior modification programs consequences which follow problem behavior(s) are altered in some way, they must be carefully assessed. In the previous example, it is likely that treatment will involve instruction in some new behaviors, for example, complying with requests in an appropriate manner. These behaviors are usually broken down into steps so that the child will learn them, such as (1) complying with simple requests with the accompanying verbal response ignored, (2) simple requests without swearing, (3) simple requests preceded by an appropriate verbal response (e.g., "OK"), and finally, (4) more difficult requests preceded by an appropriate verbal response. Regardless of the precise steps in a treatment program, it is necessary to determine what is maintaining the child's undesirable behavior (e.g., houseparent's attention) in order to select appropriate consequences to produce desired behavioral changes, that is, by ignoring swearing or noncompliance and attending to successive approximations to compliance.

In addition to assessing the consequence side of the "antecedent-behavior-consequence" model of behavior, careful attention should be given to assessing the antecedent component. For example, it is often reported that individuals may successfully prevent epileptic seizures, diminish their severity, or stop them once they have begun by recognizing antecedents of the seizures and engaging in various incompatible behaviors (Zlutnick, Mayville, & Moffat, 1975). Examples include a patient's report that she is able to stop a seizure by vigorously shaking her head from side to side. Another patient reports that he can successfully "talk himself out of having a seizure" by saying such things as, "Oh, no, I am not going to have a seizure," or "You can't get the best of me" (Mostofsky & Balaschak, 1977). Using video replay, Feldman and Paul (in press) report seizure reduction in five individuals, ranging in age from 13 to 40. The authors assert that recordings of the seizures and specification of the antecedent events "provided a means by which the patients could acquire otherwise unrecognized or forgotten information. Once equipped with the identity of the specific emotional trigger, the patient could avoid the kinds of events which might be expected to induce a seizure and be better able to cope with threatening environmental cues when encountered in the future."

MONITORING BEHAVIOR CHANGE

An important step in assessment involves the practice of objectively recording behavior during as well as prior to intervention. In this way, nonfunctional practices may be replaced by effective ones. Although agents (therapists, teachers, etc.) are responsible for monitoring the relative occurrence of behaviors,

they cannot state the rate accurately and therefore, deprive themselves of the means for determining if a change in procedure is being effective. Subjective measurement systems are gross and insensitive to small changes. Hence the agent receives no reinforcement except when there is a whopping change in a subject's behavior. She tries method A and since the subject is just as bad as yesterday on her subjective measuring rod, she tries B, C, D, and E within the next 2 weeks and concludes that the subject is hopeless. Since there are no magical techniques, a look at the rate at the end of each day for several days in succession is necessary. If the objective is a decrease and there has been no decrease over several days in which the method has been applied consistently, then institute method B. If there has been a decrease, continue method A for a while longer. There may be indications of improvement in data collected objectively when improvement is not at all apparent to subjective impression (Birnbrauer, Burchard, & Burchard, 1970, p. 32).

The first step in devising a monitoring system to assess selected behavior change is the development of a code (Bijou, Peterson, & Ault, 1968). The specific stimulus and response categories that make up a code are selected from a survey of interactions in the treatment setting and usually include behaviors of the target child and the change agent. The most difficult task in defining behaviors for inclusion in the code is preparing criteria so unequivocal that two or more observers will be in total agreement almost all the time. For example, if one wishes to record the number of times a child talks, talking must be defined so specifically that observers can easily discriminate talking from grunting, sneezing, laughing, or whistling. Similarly, if one wants to count the number of times a child complies with an adult request, the criteria for compliance must be specified so that it is not confused with similar but noncompliant actions.

There are several approaches to defining problem behaviors. One consists of developing a specific observational code for each problem behavior studied. For example, if a program to reduce the frequency of hitting alone were developed, an observational code that distinguished hitting from similar behaviors (e.g., patting, shoving, or pushing) might be devised. A second method of defining and recording target behaviors is to develop a general observational code. The general observational code allows for the simultaneous recording of more than one target behavior. For example, in a study designed to evaluate the effects of chlorpromazine on the behavior of five retarded individuals, a general behavioral code was developed which provided for the simultaneous recording of eye contact, standing, walking, touching, being within 5 feet of another adult, being in bed, and talking (Marholin, Touchette, & Stewart, Note 4). If any one of these seven behaviors occurred within a 10-second interval it was checked in a box corresponding to the appropriate behavior and interval.

Once clearly defined, behavior may be systematically assessed by recording the frequency of its occurrence (e.g., number of swear words), the length of time (duration) it occurs (e.g., time spent doing homework), the magnitude of the response (e.g., loudness of voice) or its latency (e.g., time between request and compliance). In most behavior modification programs a frequency and/or duration measure is employed. For comprehensive discussions of assessment strategies in treatment see Hall (1971), Hersen and Barlow (1976), Kazdin (1975), Nay (in press), and Wahler, House, and Stambaugh (1976).

A frequency count, perhaps the simplest procedure, is particularly useful when the response to be changed is discrete and its duration is relatively constant. The number of times a child hits someone, throws an object, uses a verbally threatening statement, refuses to comply with a request, and attends an activity are examples of behaviors amenable to frequency recording. On the other hand, less discrete ongoing behaviors such as sitting in one's seat, talking, playing a game, and sleeping are difficult to count, because each response may occur for vastly differing amounts of time. For example, if a child studies for 10 minutes before going to school and 2 hours after dinner, these occurrences might.be counted as two instances of studying. However, a great deal of information would be lost if a frequency measure were used to assess the amount of studying. Frequency measures are generally expressed in terms of a response rate, that is, the frequency response divided by the number of minutes observed each day. Frequency measures, whether expressed as absolute numbers or rates, have several advantages over other recording procedures including simplicity in scoring, availability of inexpensive counting devices (e.g., golf counters), and sensitivity to change over time. Finally frequency measures are instances of the actual behavior performed. Because in most cases the goal of behavior therapy is to decrease or increase the frequency of a specific behavior, a frequency count of its occurrence provides the best measure.

The second most common measurement employed is interval recording. With this strategy, behavior is observed for certain periods of time only. For example, a 30-minute block of time may be set aside each day to observe some particular behavior(s). The block of time is subdivided into 10- or 15-second intervals. the specified behavior is observed during each interval and scored as having occurred or not occurred. Interval recording procedures are flexible, because virtually any behavior can be recorded. Behaviors that are not discrete (i.e., difficult to determine their beginning or end) are particularly amenable to this type of recording procedure. Moreover, with this procedure, several behaviors or individuals may be simultaneously observed. Finally, the observations resulting from interval recording can be easily converted into a percentage score by dividing the number of intervals in which the behavior occurred by the number of intervals observed and multiplying by 100. The percentage of time devoted to various activities such as studying, working, and socially interacting lend themselves well to interval recording.

Behavior may also be recorded by time sampling. This procedure is similar in most respects to interval recording, except that it does not require continuous observation. Therefore, time sampling is more practical in many clinical settings where staff time is at a premium. In time sampling, the observer records the occurrence or nonoccurrence of behaviors only at the end of a specific time interval. For example, a counselor in a group home may want to measure the average time a particular child interacts with his peers during a 12-hour day. The time available for observation would be divided into intervals. In the example below, a 12-hour observation period was divided into 12, 1-hour intervals. The observer recorded the behavior only at the end of the intervals, that is, once every hour. At the end of each hour the counselor located the subject and recorded whether he was interacting with his peers at that instant.

In Table 1 the time sample record shows that the child was socially interacting at 10 A.M., 11 A.M., and at noon, again at 5 P.M., and finally at 8 P.M. and 9 P.M. At 1, 2, 3, 4, 6, and 7 P.M. he was not interacting. Thus the time sample record shows that the child was interacting 6 out of 12 (or 50%) of the times that the counselor sampled his behavior.

In recording the frequency of time the child spent studying, a parent might use a combined time sampling and interval recording method. The parents might decide that they wished to sample studying behavior from the time the child returned from school until bed time. Therefore, they decided to record behavior in 10-second intervals over 10-minute observational periods once every hour from 6 P.M. to 10 P.M. or four times daily. Every hour the parents recorded whether the child was in his room working quietly. If the child remained in the room working for long periods

Table 1

Hour	10 a.m.	11 a.m.	12 noon	1 p.m.	2 p.m.	3 p.m.	4 p.m.	5 p.m.	6 p.m.	7 p.m.	8 p.m.	9 p.m.
Behavior	I	I	I	N	N	N	N	I	N	N	I	I

I = Interacting
N = Not interacting

of time, many intervals would be scored as studying. Because the child might be working for 5 seconds of a particular 10-second interval, the parents might decide that he must be working for 8 seconds out of any 10-second interval to be scored as "working." At the end of each 10-minute observation period the parents totaled the number of 10-second intervals in which the child was scored as working and divided by the total number of 10-second intervals observed (i.e., 60). The result would be a measure of the percentage of time the child studied in a particular 10-minute observation period. At the end of the day the parents would add the percentage scores for the four observations and divide by four to arrive at a daily percentage of the child's studying.

A recording technique described by Hall (1971) called "placheck" (planned activity check) is a practical technique to use when the behavior of a group of children is to be assessed. It is similar to a time sampling technique, except that at the sampling times the observer counts all the persons engaging in the behavior being recorded. The number of individuals engaged in the behavior is then divided by the total number of individuals present. By multiplying the quotient by 100, the observer is able to determine the percent of children engaging in a behavior at any particular time. Placheck may be useful when assessing children's behavior in a classroom or work setting.

Reliability of Observations

No matter which assessment method is chosen, it is important that the observers agree on the occurrence of the behavior, because assessment can only by useful when it has been demonstrated that the behavior itself is being measured. If one person does the recording, any recorded change in behavior may result from a change in his definition of the behavior rather than a change in the behavior. For this reason, it is useful on occasion to have two independent observers record the target behavior at the same time to determine whether the definition of the behavior has been inadvertently changed by one of them. Employing several observers periodically is also helpful in determining whether the behavior being observed is sufficiently well defined. If a response can be observed consistently, it is likely that it can be reinforced or punished consistently. The contrary is also true; that is, if the behavior is not consistently observed, it is unlikely that it will be consistently treated.

Reliability is determined in different ways, depending upon the assessment strategy employed. Regardless of its manner of calculation, reliability provides an estimate of how consistently the behavior is observed and scored. Reliability of frequency measures is determined by dividing the smaller of two frequency measures by the larger frequency count of the second observer (if the observers differ) and multiplying the total by 100. For interval recording, reliability is determined by dividing the number of intervals in which both observers marked the behavior as occurring (agreements) by the total number of intervals either observer marked the behavior as occurring and multiplying by 100 (c.f. Hawkins & Dotson, 1975, for a thorough discussion of the reliability calculation). Although there is no absolute criterion for acceptable reliability, values greater than 80% are considered acceptable. Reliability under 80% indicates that response definitions require further refinement.

Presenting Data

Finally, it is helpful to present graphically data collected during baseline and treatment. This type of transformation provides a visual, long-range account of the course of treatment. The form of graphic representation employed such as a bar chart, frequency graph, or cumulative curve is a matter of convenience and of appropriateness for the data.

In summary, there are five crucial steps in assessing or evaluating a behavioral treatment program: (1) specification of the treatment situation (e.g., child's home, residential setting, classroom), (2) the establishment of a reliably defined set of stimulus and response categories (e.g., antecedents, behaviors, consequences), (3) an objective procedure to record behavior, (4) an estimation of the reliability of the recording procedures, and (5) a means of presenting the data graphically for easy assessment of progress.

The five crucial steps in assessing a behavioral treatment program are presented in a program for a 14-year old girl, Shirley, who was referred to a residential, community-based treatment center because of an "extreme negativistic attitude" in the presence of adults, noncompliance, and "depression" (Marholin *et al.*, 1975). Her "negativistic attitude" was redefined as the occurrence of the following:

(1) Pouting: frowning, griping, crying, or sobbing, sitting off to the side in a group situation, whispering to peers.

Conversely, a "positive attitude" was defined as:

(1) Positive verbal statements to a child or adult about what they were doing, overt conversation with peers.

"Noncompliance" was defined as:

(1) Not following through within a 5-minute period with a task-specific request of an adult staff member and yelling "No" following a request. Conversely, compliance was defined as:

(1) Following through within 5 minutes the initiation of a task requested by an adult.

"Depression" was defined as:

(1) Ignoring questions or verbal prompts by walking away from a child or adult.

(2) Negative statements about herself (e.g., "I'm ugly."), pessimistic statements about the future (e.g., "I'll never get to go home.").

"Negative-positive attitude" and "depression" behaviors were recorded in each 15-second interval of observation during two 30-minute time blocks each day. Reliability checks made on five occasions showed interobserver reliability to average 86%. Compliance was recorded as the percentage of follow-throughs following five task-specific adult-delivered requests during each of two 75-minute time periods each day. Each behavior was recorded on a frequency graph posted in the staff office which allowed all staff to follow Shirley's day-by-day progress. Details of the entire treatment program are too numerous to report here. However, noncompliant, depression like, and pouting behaviors were reduced, whereas compliance and positive statements were increased.

Further details and examples of this method of assessing progress in treatment may be found in Bijou, Peterson, & Ault (1968), DeRisi and Butz (1975), and Phillips, Phillips, Fixsen, & Wolf (1974).

ASSESSMENT OF BEHAVIOR
AFTER TREATMENT

The literature on treatment outcome or post-treatment behavior of individuals has been scrutinized in recent years (Marholin, Siegel, & Phillips, 1976; Paul & Lentz, in press; Stokes & Baer, 1977). Its importance has been highlighted by the recent financial crisis which has been felt by various mental health delivery systems. Typically, post-treatment behavior is measured by means of standardized tests. "When the findings are positive, the treatment program is praised; when negative, it is roundly condemned. Negative findings are generally accorded one or two interpretations: (1) the children were incapable of learning from the treatment program and perhaps from any other program, or (2) the children were capable of learning but the program was ineffective because of time limitations or poor instructional technique, or both" (Bijou, 1974). Unfortunately, such interpretations presuppose that the post-treatment behavior is a function of some component of the treatment program per se, rather than the child's situation at the time of the follow-up evaluation and his history since the intervention. However, the fate of modified behavior is largely dependent on the contingencies in operation during the period after treatment (see Marholin & Siegel, Chapter 11). For this reason it may be argued that "the evaluation of therapy involving operant behavior requires a procedure that differs markedly from the medical model. It is this: the behavior of the individual should be monitored throughout the treatment program, and the data obtained at the end of treatment (terminal behavior compared to the operant level of that behavior) is the basic measurement of effectiveness of that program" (Bijou & Peterson, 1971, p. 76). In other words, generalization and maintenance of behavior change following treatment is a function of the child in relation to post-treatment conditions rather than of the treatment procedures themselves. Hence, "a disadvantageous post-treatment history can make the most effective treatment appear worthless; a favorable post-treatment history can cast a halo over a mediocre or even an inferior program" (Bijou, 1974).

One may argue that because treatment or educational behaviors taught in the clinic, school, or residential setting *must* occur in at least one other setting if they are to have any utility for the individual (Marholin, et al., 1976), the clinician's responsibility must extend beyond the end of the formal treatment program. Follow-up assessment is the first step needed to indicate whether the behavior(s) assessed have been weakened, maintained, or extended by the contingencies in the natural environment. If they have been maintained or extended, the therapist has an opportunity to provide a vital clinical function by reinforcing those involved (child, parents, siblings). On the other hand, if appropriate behavior has not been maintained, it is the responsibility of the clinician to determine what contingencies in the post-treatment environment are lacking or mediating against the maintenance of desired behavior. For example, following an application of home-based reinforcement procedures to weekly grades received in public school settings by female residents of a community-based facility, post-checks were taken at irregular intervals upon the adolescent's return to the community (Marholin et al., 1975). When the post-checks revealed that the youngster's grades remained at approximately the same level as that observed prior to her return to the community, the youngster and her family were heartily socially reinforced. On the other hand, when a particular youngster's grades were found to have deteriorated at follow-up, remedial procedures were immediately instituted, including training and subsequent monitoring of the parents in devising contingency programs aimed at specifying weekly grade requirements for specific privileges at home and in the community. In this manner, follow-up assessment as part of an overall treatment program may provide the difference between failure and success of any intervention attempt.

SUMMARY

This chapter presents a functional analysis of children's behavior disorders. A functional analysis approach is based on observable and measurable behaviors, rather than underlying psychopathic states or mental processes. Assessment should be oriented toward obtaining the kinds of information or data that can be directly used to develop and guide a treatment program. In this regard there are four tasks involved in a functional assessment of children's behavior. The first involves an analysis of the problem that brings the child to the attention of an agency or professional person. Presenting problems are conceptualized as falling into one or more of four categories: behavioral excesses, behavioral deficits, behavior under inappropriate stimulus control, and shy, withdrawn, and fearful behavior.

Data for preparing child-specific programs for behavioral change derived from (1) interviews and reports, (2) direct observation, (3) inventories and behavioral surveys, and (4) projective and psychometric tests are discussed from the point of view of utility in the treatment program. Although interviews may introduce a certain amount of bias or distortion, they may be employed initially in an effort to discover functional relationships to further explore by means of direct observation. Checklists and surveys are sometimes useful as an interview aid. Standardized tests of intelligence, school achievement, and personality as well as projective devices provide only indirect information about the conditions that caused a child to be brought for treatment and practically no data relative to treatment programing.

The second aspect of assessment involves a functional analysis of environmental factors that elicit, prompt, reinforce, or punish particular problem behaviors and an identification of those which might be manipulated to alter the child's problem behavior. Behaviors are defined in objective terms so that they might actually be observed, measured, and agreed on by those administering the program. The collection of data prior to intervention is stressed. In this way alone can treatment techniques be objectively evaluated. Consideration is given to those conditions, antecedent and consequence, that function to maintain the child's behavior in the treatment program. Furthermore, functional reinforcers are selected and tested to provide proper motivation for the child to change his behavior.

The third aspect of the functional approach to assessment involves objectively recording and evaluating behavior during treatment. Continuous monitoring allows for the discarding of ineffective treatment strategies and the systematic testing of new ones. The technique for monitoring progress during treatment involves: the specification of the situation in which the treatment takes place, the use of a stimulus-response code to record objectively behavior change, a recording procedure using rate or duration of response occurrences, and graphic presentation of the data.

The fourth and final aspect of a functional analysis of assessment concerns the evaluation of behavior after formal treatment. Because behaviors acquired in the treatment setting should occur in at least one other setting if they are to have any utility at all for the individual, the clinician's responsibility extends beyond the end of formal treatment. Although behaviors observed during the post-treatment period indicate the operation of post-treatment contingencies, follow-up data are useful. They provide information on the need for further changes in the child's environment to recover or maintain the behavior established in treatment.

REFERENCE NOTES

1. Marholin II, D., & Kanfer, F. H. A functional analysis of a phobia of the Catholic Host: A case study. Manuscript submitted for publication, 1977.
2. Becker, W. C., & Wagner, B. A behavioral interview schedule. Unpublished manuscript. University of Illinois at Urbana-Champaign, 1969.
3. Quay, H. C., & Peterson, D. R. Manual for the Behavior Problem Checklist. Mimeo, University of Illinois at Urbana-Champaign, 1967.
4 Marholin II, D., Touchette, P. E., & Stewart, R. M. An experimental analysis of the effects of chlorpromazine withdrawal on the behavior of retarded adults. Manuscript submitted for review, 1977.

REFERENCES

Alpern, G. D., & Boll, T. J. Developmental Skill Age Inventory. Indianapolis: Psychological Development Publications, 1972.

Ayllon, T., & Azrin, N. The token economy: A motivational system for therapy and rehabilitation. New York: Appleton-Century-Crofts, 1968.

Baer, D. M. In the beginning, there was the response. In E. Ramp & G. Semb (Eds.), Behavior analysis: Areas of research and application. Englewood-Cliffs, N. J.: Prentice-Hall, 1975, pp. 16–30.

Bannister, D., Solomon, P., & Leiberman, D. M. Diagnosis-treatment relationships in psychiatry. British Journal of Psychiatry, 1964, 110, 726–732.

Bernal, M. E., Gibson, D. M., Williams, D. E. & Pesses, D. I. A device for automatic audio tape recording. Journal of Applied Behavior Analysis, 1971, 4, 151–156.

Bijou, S. W. Focus. Journal of Applied Behavior Analysis, 1974, 7(1).

Bijou, S. W. Child behavior treatment. In S. W. Bijou (Ed.), Child development: The basic stage of early childhood. Englewood-Cliffs, N. J.: Prentice-Hall, 1976, pp. 133–163.

Bijou, S. W., & Grimm, J. A. Behavioral diagnosis and assessment in teaching young handicapped children. In T. Thompson & W. S. Dockens (Eds.), Applications of behavior modification. New York: Academic Press, 1975, pp. 161–180.

Bijou, S. W., & Peterson, R. F. The psychological assessment of children: A functional analysis. In P. McReynolds (Ed.), Advances in psychological assessment, Vol. 2. Palo Alto, Cal.: Science and Behavior Books, 1971, pp. 63–78.

Bjou, S. W., Peterson, R. F., & Ault, M. A method to integrate descriptive and experimental studies at the level of data and empirical concepts. *Journal of Applied Behavior Analysis*, 1968, *1*, 175–191.

Bijou, S. W., & Redd, W. H. Child behavior therapy. In S. Arieti (Ed.), *American handbook of psychiatry, Vol. 5*. New York: Basic Books, 1975, pp. 319–345.

Birnbrauer, J. S., Burchard, J. D., & Burchard, S. N. Wanted: Behavior analysts. In R. H. Bradfield (Ed.), *Behavior modification: The human effort*. San Rafael, Cal.: Dimensions Pub. Co., pp. 19–76.

Cautela, J. R., & Upper, D. The process of individual behavior therapy. In M. Hersen, R. M. Eisler, & P. M. Miller (Eds.), *Progress in behavior modification, Vol. 1*. New York: Academic Press, 1975, pp. 275–305.

Cronbach, L. J. Statistic methods applied to Rorschach scores: A review. *Psychological Bulletin*, 1949, *46*, 393–429.

DeRisi, W. J., & Butz, G. *Writing behavioral contracts: A case simulation manual*. Champaign, Ill.: Research Press, 1975.

Farina, A., Holland, C. H., & Ring, K. Role of stigma and set in interpersonal interaction. *Journal of Abnormal Psychology*, 1966, *71*, 421–428.

Feldman, B. G., & Paul, N. G. Identity of emotional triggers in epilepsy. *Journal of Nervous and Mental Diseases*, 1977, in press.

Ferster, C. B. Classification of behavioral psychology. In L. Krasner & L. P. Ullmann (Eds.), *Research in behavior modification*. New York: Holt. Rhinehart, & Winston, 1966, pp. 6–26.

Fisher, S. Projective methodologies. In R. R. Farnsworth, O. McNemar (Eds.), *Annual review of psychology, Vol. 18*. Palo Alto, Cal.: Annual Reviews, 1967.

Freud, S. *An autobiographical study*. London: Hogarth Press and Institute of Psychoanalysis, 1946.

Goldfried, M. R., & Kent, R. N. Traditional vs. behavioral personality assessment: A comparison of methodological and theoretical assumptions. *Psychological Bulletin*, 1972, *77*, 409–420.

Gottman, J. M., & Leiblum, S. R. *How to do psychotherapy and how to evaluate it*. New York: Holt, Rhinehart, & Winston, 1974.

Hall, R. V. *Behavior modification: The measurement of behavior, Vol. 1*. Lawrence, Ka.: H & H Enterprises, 1970.

Hawkins, R. P., & Dotson, V. A. Reliability scores that delude: An Alice in Wonderland trip through the misleading characteristics of interobserver agreement scores in interval recording. In E. Ramp and G. Semb (Eds.), *Behavior analysis: Areas of research and application*. Englewood Cliffs, N. J.: Prentice-Hall, 1975.

Hersen, M., & Bellack, A. *Behavioral assessment: A practical handbook*. New York: Pergamon Press, 1976.

Holland, C. J. An interview guide for behavioral counseling with parents. *Behavior Therapy*, 1970, *1*, 70–79.

Homme, L., Csanyi, A. P., Gonzales, M. A., & Rechs, J. R. *How to use contingency contracting in the classroom*. Champaign, Ill.: Research Press, 1970.

Johnson, S. M., & Bolstad, O. D. Reactivity to home observation: A comparison of audio recorded behavior with observers present or absent. *Journal of Applied Behavior Analysis*, 1975, *8*, 181–185.

Johnson, S. M., Christensen, A., & Bellamy, G. T. Evaluation of family intervention through unobtrusive audio recordings: Experiences in "bugging" children. *Journal of Applied Behavior Analysis*, 1976, *9*, 213–219.

Jones, R. A., Reid, J. B., & Patterson, G. R. Naturalistic observations in clinical assessment. In P. McReynolds (Ed.), *Advances in psychological assessment, Vol. 3.* San Francisco: Jossey-Bass, 1975, pp. 42–95.

Kanfer, F. H. Assessment of behavior modification. *Journal of Personality Assessment*, 1972, *36*, 418–423.

Kanfer, F. H. & Grimm, L. G. Behavioral analysis: Selecting target behaviors in the interview. *Behavior Modification*, 1977, *1*, 7–28.

Kanfer, F. H., & Phillips, J. S. *Learning foundations of behavior therapy.* New York: Wiley, 1970.

Kanfer, F. H., & Saslow, G. Behavior analysis: An alternative to diagnostic classification. *Archives of General Psychiatry*, 1965, *72*, 529–538.

Kanfer, F. H., & Saslow, G. Behavioral diagnosis. In C. M. Franks (Ed.), *Behavior therapy: Appraisal and status.* New York: McGraw-Hill, 1969, pp. 417–444.

Kazdin, A. E. Methodological and assessment considerations in evaluating reinforcement programs in applied settings. *Journal of Applied Behavior Analysis*, 1973, *6*, 517–531.

Kazdin, A. E. *Behavior modification in applied settings.* Homewood, Ill.: The Dorsey Press, 1975.

Kent, R. N., O'Leary, K. D., Diament, C., & Dietz, A. Expectation biases in observational evaluation of therapeutic change. *Journal of Consulting and Clinical Psychology*, 1974, *42*, 774–780.

Laing, R. D. *The politics of experience.* New York: Ballantine Books, 1967.

Lazarus, A. A. *Behavior therapy and beyond.* New York: McGraw-Hill, 1971.

Lazarus, A. A., Davison, G. C., & Polefka, D.A. Classical and operant factors in the treatment of a school phobia. *Journal of Abnormal Psychology*, 1965, *70*, 225–229.

Lipinski, D., & Nelson, R. Problems in the use of naturalistic observation as a means of behavioral assessment. *Behavior Therapy*, 1974, *5*, 341–351.

Lorr, M., Klett, C. J., & McNair, D. M. *Syndromes of psychosis.* New York: Macmillan, 1963.

Marholin II, D., Plienis, A. J., Harris, S., & Marholin, B. L. Mobilization of the community through a behavioral approach: A school program for adjudicated females. *Criminal Justice and Behavior*, 1975, *2*, 130–145.

Marholin II, D., Siegel, L. J., & Phillips, D. Treatment and transfer: A search for empirical procedures. In M. Hersen, R. M. Eisler, & P. M. Miller (Eds.), *Progress in behavior modification, Vol. 3.* New York: Academic Press, 1976, pp. 291–342.

Meehl, P. E. *Clinical versus statistical prediction.* Minneapolis: University of Minnesota Press, 1954.

Mischel, W. *Personality and assessment.* New York: Wiley, 1968.

Mostofsky, D. I., & Balaschak, B. A. Psychological control of seizures. *Psychological Bulletin*, 1977, *84*, 723–750.

Nay, W. R. *Behavioral assessment strategies.* New York: Gardner Press, 1977, in press.

Paul, G., & Lentz, R. J. *A comparative study of mileu versus social learning programs.* Cambridge, Mass.: Harvard University Press, 1977, in press.

Peterson, D. R. *The clinical study of social behavior.* New York: Appleton-Century-Crofts, 1968.

Phillips, E. L. Achievement Place: Modification of the behaviors of predelinquent boys within a token economy. *Journal of Applied Behavior Analysis*, 1968, *1*, 213–233.

Phillips, E. L., Phillips, E. A., Fixsen, D. L., & Wolf, M. M. *The teaching family handbook*. Lawrence, Ka.: University of Kansas Printing Service, 1974.

Phillips, L., & Draguns, J. G. Classification of the behavior disorders. *Annual review of psychology, Vol. 22*. Palo Alto, Cal.: Annual Reviews, 1971 pp. 447–482.

Purcell, K., & Brady, K. Adaption to the invasion of privacy: Monitoring behavior with a minature radio transmitter. *Merrill-Palmer Quarterly*, 1965, *12*, 242–254.

Quay, H. C. Patterns of aggression, withdrawal, and immaturity. In H. C. Quay & J. S. Werry (Eds.), *Psychopathological disorders of childhood*. New York: Wiley, 1972, pp. 1–29.

Quay, H. C., Werry, J. S., McQueen, M., & Sprague, R. L. Remediation of the conduct problem child in a special class setting. *Exceptional Children*, 1966, *32*, 509–519.

Rekers, G. A., & Lovaas, O. I. Behavioral treatment of deviant sex-role behaviors in a male child. *Journal of Applied Behavior Analysis*, 1974, *7*, 173–190.

Ribes-Inesta, E. Discussion: Methodological remarks on a delinquency prevention and rehabilitation program. In S. W. Bijou, & E. Ribes-Inesta (Eds.), *Behavior modification: Issues and extensions*. New York: Academic Press, 1972, pp. 85–97.

Risley, T., Reynolds, N., & Hart, B. The disadvantaged: Behavior modification with disadvantaged preschool children. In R. Bradfield (Ed.), *Behavior modification: The human effort*. San Rafael, Cal.: Dimensions Pub. Co., 1970, pp. 123–158.

Ross, A. O. Behavior therapy. In H. C. Quay, & J. S. Werry (Eds.), *Psychopathological disorders in childhood*. New York: Wiley, 1972, pp. 273–315.

Schnelle, J. F. A brief report on invalidity of parent evaluations of behavior change. *Journal of Applied Behavior Analysis*, 1974, *7*, 541–543.

Schwartz, R. D., & Skolnick, J. H. Two studies of legal stigma. *Social Problems*, 1962, *10*, 133–142.

Sherman, J. A., & Baer, D. M. Appraisal of operant therapy techniques with children and adults. In C. M. Franks (Ed.), *Behavior therapy: Appraisal and status*. New York: McGraw-Hill, 1969, pp. 192–219.

Soskin, W. F., & John, V. P. The study of spontaneous talk. In R. G. Barker (Ed.), *The stream of behavior*. New York: Appleton-Century-Crofts, 1963, pp. 228–281.

Stokes, T. & Baer, D. An implicit technology of generalization. *Journal of Applied Behavior Analysis*, 1977, *10*, 349–367.

Strupp, H. H., & Bergin, A. E. Some empirical and conceptual bases for coordinated research in psychotherapy: A critical review of issues, trends, and evidence. *International Journal of Psychiatry*, 1969, *7*, 18–90.

Stuart, R. B. *Trick or treatment: How and when psychotherapy fails*. Champaign, Ill.: Research Press, 1970.

Szarz, T. S. The myth of mental illness. *American Psychologist*, 1960, *15*, 113–118.

Terman, L. M., & Merrill, M. *Stanford-Binet Intelligence Scale. Manual for the Third Revision: Form L-M*. Boston: Houghton-Mifflin, 1960.

Wahler, R. G., & Cormier, W. H. The ecological interview: A first step in out-patient child behavior therapy. *Journal of Behavior Therapy and Experimental Psychiatry*, 1970, *1*, 279–289.

Wahler, R. G., House, A. E., & Stambaugh, E. E. *Ecological assessment of child problem behavior: A clinical package for home, school, and institutional settings.* New York: Pergamon Press, 1976.

Wechsler, D. *Wechsler Preschool and Primary Scale of Intelligence Manual.* New York: Psychological Corporation, 1967.

Wolpe, J. *The practice of behavior therapy,* (*2nd Ed.*). New York: Pergamon Press, 1973.

Yarrow, M. R., Campbell, J. D., & Burton, R. V. *Child rearing.* San Francisco: Jossey-Bass, 1968.

Zigler, M., & Phillips, L. Psychiatric diagnosis : A critique. *Journal of Abnormal and Social Psychology,* 1961, *63,* 607–618.

Zlutnick, S., Mayville, W. J., & Moffat, S. Modification of seizure disorders: The interruption of behavioral chains. *Journal of Applied Behavior Analysis,* 1975, *8,* 1–12.

3

Some Guides to Designing Behavioral Programs

J. S. Birnbrauer [1]

This chapter is about the decision making that precedes and accompanies applications of behavioral procedures. The best we can expect from a science of behavior are principles that apply in general and guidelines for making them apply in particular situations. These guidelines come from one's own experience and that of others, but inevitably a certain amount of trial and error will be necessary to adapt procedures to the problem and circumstances at hand. I hope to assist you to plan more successfully than you might have done on your own, and to assist you in organizing your self-instruction. The real learning for you, just as for clients, takes place as one tries, stumbles and gains, and keeps trying. Learning behavior analysis, in other words, results from *applying* behavior analysis, which has been described as a "self-examining, self-evaluating, discovery-oriented research procedure for studying behavior" (Baer, Wolf, & Risley, 1968, p. 91).

The basic principles of behavioral psychology, summarized by Redd and Sleator in Chapter 1, are few in number and relatively easy to remember. Many find them commonsensical, and at the same time, wanting. They seem insufficient to solve complex personal and social problems. Be assured that there is more to it and there are no easy ways. With some success, better organization of time and resources, and tricks of your own, behavior analysis will become easier. You will be able to anticipate problems, change your tactics to prevent problems from becoming crises, and, therefore, have many fewer difficulties. Indeed, since behavior principles refer to change in behavior over time and do not tell one what to do in emergencies in the absence of prior assessment and a total treatment plan, the time to plan and instate programs is *before* matters reach the boiling point. For that reason, it simply will not do for these principles to be practiced only by "experts" when they are needed. They should be learned and used by everyone, including clients.

In this chapter I refer to you—parent, teacher, nurse, volunteer, group-home counselor, supervisor, therapist, etc.—as the agent (from "therapeutic agent" or "agent of change"), the person responsible for planning and conducting programs to bring about improvements in behavior. I refer to the child or children, e.g., son/daughter, class, residents, and employees, as the client. One may, of course, be both the agent and client, and as part of your preparation, I strongly urge you to design a program to effect some change in your own behavior or within your family. Some possible targets are: losing 10 pounds, exercising 15 minutes per day, smoking no more than 10 cigarettes per day, pleasantly acknowledging/complimenting your son's (daughter's, spouse's) cooperative and thoughtful behavior at least twice a day, cessation of interruption of your spouse or offspring during conversations, indeed, accumulating 5 minutes of conversation per day with spouse and/or offspring, and there are always those annoying little habits to eliminate like nail-biting, forgetting to switch off lights or flush the toilet, and whistling off key.

OVERVIEW OF BEHAVIOR ANALYSIS

Behavior analysis may be divided into three stages—planning (assessment), intervention, and consolidation—but in reality, these are continuous, for planning never ceases and consolidation is a continuation of intervention with altered objectives. The objectives of the planning phase are: (1) definition of problem(s), (2) definition of target behavior and priorities, (3) hypotheses about antecedent and consequent conditions within agent control that should be changed, (4) a method of recording, (5) baseline data, and (6) an intervention plan that one has reason to believe will be feasible and effective.

Intervention continues until *n* hours (periods, days or weeks) of presence of target behavior that you have selected for strengthening ("acceleration targets"), and/or absence of behavior that you have designated for weakening ("deceleration targets"), have been recorded. In other words, intervention continues until objective criteria for success have been met. One also needs "revise program" criteria, that is, *n* units of time without observing a promising trend in the desired direction or *n* applications of selected procedures without a promising change in frequency.

When the criteria for success have been reached, agents move on, usually imperceptibly, to consolidate what has been achieved. The objectives of consolidation are to ensure that behavior continues not only within the home or facility, but also in varied conditions much like the client will encounter when the agent is not present. Obviously, consolidation refers to follow-up. Follow-up, however, conveys steps which are passive and taken after programs. We now know, as Marholin and Bijou indicate in Chapter 2 that maintenance of gains must be planned for—hence, the more active term, consolidation. If intervention is not successful according to the preset criteria, then agents ask, "What was wrong with the program?" and implement the changes that seem advised.

I hope your reaction to my overview is along the lines of, "That's what everyone does or should do," because behavior analysis is just applying good management principles. (See Mager & Pipe, 1970, a short, amusing reference which includes flow charts and checklists that agents will find very helpful.) The distinguishing feature is the precision with which objectives are defined (emphasized by the expression "target behavior"), intervention is carried out, and effects are measured. Some prefer the term "precision teaching" to convey this essential difference (Kunzelmann, 1970).

Rules of accountability and behavior analysis require that decisions be based on explicit and recorded assessments of the requirements for success—in multiplication, on open units, on a week-end pass—and an explicit evaluation of the client's level of functioning vis-a-vis those requirements. Goals are defined by the requirements of social, vocational, and academic "tasks"; these global goals are in turn broken down into their components, and programs are designed to teach those components (target behaviors) that assessment of the client reveals is necessary.

The agents' task is to choose the approach that is a best fit, given their abilities and other demands on them, and yet will result quickly in measurable progress. Since the importance of reinforcement of *agent* behavior cannot be overstated, a small-step-by-small-step plan on one problem or one part of a problem is recommended in the beginning. That way you will be reinforced sooner by progress and perhaps receive bonus unanticipated side-effects. I find that, as a rule, people get themselves into trouble because they try to do too much at one time *without appreciating that they are*, and consequently are disappointed by the outcome. Indeed, in many situations problems disappear simply as a result of agents' focusing on fewer problems at a time and organizing their time and resources more efficiently.

To review, the steps are (1) defining problem(s) and arranging them hierarchically in order of importance (establishing priorities), (2) conducting task analyses, (3) defining target behavior, (4) counting and keeping a record of target behavior, (5) selecting time and place for instruction, (6) selecting reinforcers, negative consequences, and instructional aids, and (7) testing for generalization and continuing to observe to ensure that gains are maintained. Each of these steps is discussed in detail.

SOURCES OF INFORMATION

Let me consider first the kind of information needed for planning and how agents go about gathering it. Much of it is already available. Teachers routinely do thorough studies of each pupil's competencies in the subject matter areas for which they are responsible and will be aware of conduct, social skills, reactions to failure, criticism and praise, and relationships with peers. Now group homes and other residential facilities also are required to assess routinely and to keep progress records. Although parents do not record behavior and progress, they, too, can complete most sections of an inventory when asked to do so. Thus, it is a matter of gathering together available information, updating it, checking its accuracy, and answering additional questions that occur while completing the inventory. Have faith: pertinent questions will come to mind as a direct consequence of beginning to think in terms of target behavior and present and specific environmental reasons for difficulties.

All the usual sources of information—direct observation, task and situation analyses, skills assessments, interviews with client and others, records of past performance, and medical and other specialist's (psychologists, speech, occupational and physical therapists, etc.) examinations—may be employed usefully. A major difference between assessment in behavior analysis and other approaches is that agents play the most significant role and specialists, if needed at all, supply "finishing touches".

Generally, I recommend looking at past records and seeking consultations after observing, conducting task analyses, and interviewing.

I delay consulting past records mainly because they may bias in wrong directions. Whenever looked at, agents should bear in mind that records are often of doubtful reliability and may well be out of date. The reason I suggest waiting before seeking specialists' examinations is that the helpfulness of consultants is directly related to the specificity of referral questions and the information about client and situation that agents supply. I am not suggesting that agents go it alone. To the contrary, they should *not*; they should consult others freely. I am merely suggesting a way of deriving maximum benefit from consultants.

Direct Observation, Skills Assessment and Task Analysis

Direct observation, by which I mean observation of interactions in uncontrolled situations such as dining rooms, classrooms, and playgrounds, serves two purposes. The first purpose is to aid in problem definition, hypothesis generation, and every aspect of program planning, including what behavior and events should be recorded. The second purpose is evaluation of progress. In this section, I have in mind primarily direct observation as it pertains to the first purpose. Methods of recording baselines are considered in the section on target behavior. (See also Marholin and Bijou, Chapter 2.)

Direct Observation. The kind of observation required in behavior analysis is somewhat new. First, it is very detailed. Second, it retains the sequence of events—antecedent-client behavior-consequences. Bijou, Peterson, & Ault (1968) in their helpful paper on narrative recording and collecting quantified data suggest dividing recording sheets into four columns to aid in maintaining order of events. The first column is time; the other three, antecedents, client behavior, and consequences. Third, agent behavior is attended to as carefully as client behavior. Fourth, behavior and events, not interpretations thereof, are recorded and communicated.

Most of us are not aware that we continually categorize, interpret, and infer rather than report "the data." For example, we showed a workshop group a picture of a boy pulling a girl's hair and asked, "What's going on?" The answers included: "The boy is teasing his sister." (SISTER?) "The boy is angry with the girl." "The boy is trying to get his sister angry, possibly to get his mother's attention." "The boy is pulling the girl's hair." The first three replies clearly are hypotheses about why the boy was pulling the girl's hair and do not say a word about what the boy did. It is not just splitting hairs to emphasize recording behavior rather than hypotheses, because if agents do not realize they are guessing at reasons for behavior, they may base their reactions and programs unwittingly on their incorrect hypotheses.

Additional reasons are to protect against forgetting and miscommunication. Only the person who wrote the shift note, "Mary was disturbed all morning" knows what Mary did and in time will forget what it was. Even "Mary refused to participate in any activities this morning" leaves many possibilities, and there is not an inkling about possible precipitating and consequent events. On the other hand, "8:30—Mary and Ella were assigned to the dining room cleanup. They got into a loud verbal battle, Mary stormed to her room, slammed the door, told me to get lost and other things when I went to her. At 10 and 11, same thing happened. She came to lunch, ate in silence. We left her alone. She went to school with the others at 1" is a more helpful summary. In following up this note, fewer questions need to be asked, and personnel would be better able to answer them with the information in the note to remind them.

We often categorize agent behavior as well. If I were to tell you, "I reinforced her coming to lunch on time," I am telling you what I intended to do or hoped I was doing. You would have to ask, "What did you do?" If that question is necessary, the report is not describing behavior, that is, acts and words others can see, hear, and agree on.

There are limits, of course, on how much detail can be included and even observed. For that reason, along with the fact that narrative records are difficult and time consuming to quantify, behavior analysts rather quickly devise event and response counting systems to obtain a more accurate description of the extent of problems and to evaluate progress.

Although agent observations are invaluable, it is highly desirable to employ independent observers as well. Most people agree with this view now, but because of financial constraints are not able to hire observers. A solution is volunteers—students, other clients, and retired persons. They can be found, if they are sought, and many studies in the literature have, in fact, relied on volunteers. Agents will need, however, to take care that volunteers are reinforced in other ways, such as showing appreciation, inviting them to unit and staff social gatherings, including them in planning conferences (unless you want to keep them "blind" to your purposes), and demonstrating to them that they are making vital contributions to client welfare. Look on maintaining observer behavior as you would on maintaining client and staff behavior.

Sometimes selecting the most profitable times to observe is a problem. The obvious rule, to observe when behavior is most likely to occur and when it should occur, may not *seem* applicable, because, for example, the behavior occurs very infrequently or the client behaves "like an angel" when observers are present. Persist for awhile if you find yourself in this position, because if other things remain the same, clients adapt quickly to observers. More importantly, observation while things are going smoothly is just as important as observing misbehavior. The smooth times, after all, are the very times agents should be teaching and reinforcing appropriate behavior, talking and planning with clients, negotiating contracts, and so on. It is thus instructive to see if agents are making the most of moments of good behavior and how they are going about it. I make a point of observing at times that are supposed to be the best as well as the worst. By contrasting these two situations, agents can get good clues about what is wrong at the bad times and what might be done to make them like the good times.

As often as not, atypical behavior by clients in the presence of observers is a result of changes in agent behavior. Teachers and counselors often will do what they think observers want them to do or try to avoid unpleasant incidents. *They* need time to adapt. Of course, if what they do is working better, then the problem may have been solved and they should be encouraged to continue their new practices.

Skills Assessment. Often, clients have difficulties in a particular activity such as reading, athletics, speech, and dressing. Direct observation of performance of activities in the area of concern are, to me, an essential first step. The agent should arrange to have an observer present when instruction in the activity is scheduled. A simple rating scale or checklist may be constructed to aid in recording instructions, client responses, and consequences. These assessments should be conducted in the usual conditions and also in what you think are ideal conditions, for example, when agent and client are ready, when there is sufficient time, and when you are using what you suppose are strong reinforcers. The point is to determine whether the desired behavior has been learned but is not being evoked at appropriate times or the behavior is not "in the client's repertoire" and instruction in the activity is needed. Another part of skills assessment is to try to correct a known particular deficit, for example, reversal of the letters "d" and "b" or noncompliance with a particular command. "Tests" such as these give valuable clues about client reinforcers and errors in agent presentation of instruction. On the other hand, it may be that you have a much better idea of what the problems are, but do not know what you can do about them. Thus skills assessment reveals that you should seek the advice of experts in the area.

Task and Situation Analyses. Direct observation is often the only method that will reveal precisely what an academic, vocational, or social "task" requires of clients. Task analysis and skill assessment are opposite sides of the same coin and usually proceed together with the former supplying the basis and justification for teaching particular responses. The task may be specific such as shoe-tying and buttoning a shirt or as broad as finding or keeping a job or "making" it outside the training facility. As part of our preparation of youngsters for transfer from our special unit to the regular school program, we spent some time observing in the school in order to understand the behavior required for success in that situation (Birnbrauer, 1971).

Interviews of Clients

A course in interviewing in this chapter is obviously not possible. I include this section simply to correct any remaining misimpression that behavior analysts do not talk to their clients—if their clients will talk with them. By all means consult your clients and seek their perceptions of their problems and possible solutions, but in doing so heed these words of advice: (1) Wait until you and the client are likely to talk and listen to each other. (2) Make certain clients do not have to act up in order to have conferences with you. (Regularly scheduled individual and group meetings is one solution, but even so, agents can fall into the trap of calling such meetings short when there are no problems or rule infractions to discuss.) (3) Believe what clients say, although the client, you, and I know that we do not always know either what is wrong or what is best for us. (4) Try to effect some change as a result of the meeting. That is, reinforce clients for talking with you.

**Initial Interview of Important Others
and Self-Referred Clients**

Because most people are not accustomed to observing and reporting behavior in the detailed, sequential fashion that behavior analysis requires, an important objective of initial interviews with agents or self-referred clients is to teach them these skills. Interviews typically begin with statements like, "She's impossible, will never do what she is asked, sasses back, flies into rages, and isn't doing too well in school either. Her teacher says she isn't doing her school work, although she has the ability." The need is clearly present to go through those broad statements again more slowly. Usually, I ask the agent to recite a detailed account of today and/or yesterday from the time the child awakened (arrived in school) until bedtime (left school) with a word of explanation about why. The narration gives rough estimates of problem frequency, how the agent reacts to problems, what the client does, and what happens when the client is not presenting difficulties (which almost invariably turns out to be most of the time), and what precipitates difficulty. Through questions like "Excuse me, and *then* what did you *do*?", "Describe what Suzy did during that 'rage' this morning.", "Is that her usual way of 'raging'?", agents are sensitized to observe their own behavior, others' behavior, and physical arrangements more closely. I ask also about agent feelings and agent reasons for behaving in the way described to begin a tentative list of what is reinforcing and punishing to the agent.

By contrasting the circumstances present when behavior is appropriate and when it is not, I begin to generate hypotheses about precipitating and maintaining events. Indeed, it is not uncommon that asking agents to stand back and recite events slowly in sequence leads them to discover solutions without my saying a word.

A final step I try to include is to develop a simple recording system for counting salient behavior, knowing that it is tentative. I am rarely so lucky as to hit on the best one right off, but agents will need the practice. Moreover, most agents appreciate being given specific assignments to complete and will do so, especially if they have shared in the design of the system and the hour has produced some order out of the chaos described at the beginning. Considerable progress toward completing the imposing list of objectives of the planning phase can be made in an hour of discussion, and nothing prevents agents from doing the same thing on their own, that is, record retrospectively the events of the day in their own shorthand and by themselves with questions. It is an excellent way to begin. Accounts of recollections are then followed up with further observations and independent verification as needed to settle on target behavior, method of recording progress, and intervention procedures.

TARGET BEHAVIOR AND RECORDING

The consensus is that the clearer objectives are, the better. Taken to the logical extreme, objectives should be expressed as: the behavior to occur, the circumstances in which it is to occur, and the rate of occurrence (Mager, 1962). Some target behaviors of a course in behavior analysis might be: (1) reporting orally in behavioral and event terms, in sequence three 5-minute episodes of social interaction with no more than 10 errors of omission and commission per episode; (2) defining the key terms—target behavior, reinforcer, punishment, and prompt—giving five examples of each from one's own experience, and identifying each with 90% accuracy in three sample sequences of behavior in diverse situations such as an office, a playground, and a dining room; and (3) in less than 1 hour per skill, shaping skills of three different kinds so that client behavior occurs at twice the baseline rate, representing the data graphically, and describing the graph in words. These three targets when attained do not make a behavior analyst. What does? One answers that by analyzing what agents must *do*, and the conditions in which they will be called upon to perform.

Behavior analysts have been criticized for their choice of target behaviors (e.g., Winett & Winkler, 1972). Objectives should indeed be questioned. Behavior analysis requires only that objectives be measurable and justified in terms of task and situation requirements. Much of the difficulty with target selection has arisen because task analyses have not been conducted and behavior analysts, along with others, accepted on faith that target responses were justified. If, for example, reading is a desirable skill to teach children, then sounding out new words is a justified target, if it can be shown that sounding is an essential component of reading. Having decided that enrollment of Alice in the Happy Hours Day Care Center will be beneficial for her and the family, the target behaviors are those required for admission. Thus the parents may have to give priority temporarily to toilet training over equally important objectives such as creative play. Some retarded and emotionally disturbed children have not learned to learn by observation, that is, by imitation. If it is to their benefit to learn to imitate, the targets would be to copy particular, in and of themselves possibly useless, responses (Baer, Peterson, & Sherman, 1967; Lovaas, Berberich, Perloff, & Schaeffer, 1966). As one reduces objectives to specific target responses, it is true that they appear less important on their face. A final example comes from Howe and Howe's (1975) description of the "values clarification" approach to education. They advocate pupil-controlled, open classes and outline a program to teach the behavior necessary for success in such learning environments. Although they do not enumerate the prerequisite behaviors in detail or use the expression, target behavior, they would agree that teachers need to know what they are. To sum up: "Relevance of Behavior Rule: Teach only those behaviors that will continue to be reinforced after training" (Ayllon & Azrin, 1968, p. 49).

I know of no alternative but to ask what skills are necessary for success in the situations clients will encounter, using the answer as one's justification, exposing it to others for their reactions, and working toward the ends in a step-by-step fashion. The alternatives I have seen strike me as excuses for inaction or as rationalizations for avoidance behavior. So: (1) conduct task and situation analyses; (2) select target behaviors as client response and client needs for effective living indicate; (3) keep the targets small and few in number to start with; and (4) concentrate on a particular time and/or place, for example, evening meals, math periods, or group meetings. You may record at only those times, although recording at other times as well obviously is preferable.

Of course, agents should choose times when they are not under tight limitations. Thus it probably will be necessary to "create time" by looking carefully at the activities and obligations that are packed into certain time slots and eliminating those that can be completed later. We always can be more efficient than we are and often place demands on ourselves and others for no good reason. Just drop those pointless activities and requirements out. In addition, it is wise to choose a target behavior and times with which you can expect assistance from others. In my judgement, it is best to select targets and keep records on the basis of what you can do and will do well, after establishing the importance of a broad objective, such as increasing cooperative behavior around the home, and the relevance of a particular response, such as doing one chore each evening, to the overall goal of greater cooperation.

Agents often express concern about the apparently slow pace of behavioral interventions; for example, they want to do more than just change their style of instruction during math periods. In reply, I point out, first, that the agent probably is underestimating the difficulty of the program. Second, I ask, "Why turn everything upside-down before you have some good clues that the changes will be effective?" Third, the chances are good that simple changes (in the eyes of agents) will have more general effects than anticipated.

A second frequently encountered problem is agent uncertainty about objectives. This problem is particularly acute when agents believe some prerequisites and practices are wrong, unnecessary, or unjust. One simply has to make hard decisions as to what seems best for the client. At the same time, agents should teach skills that will enable clients to effect changes in rules. Client participation in goal setting and program planning through unit or family meetings and contract negotiations is one way of accomplishing this end. It is no good if clients "fight the system" head on and it is equally undesirable if they just accept things as they are.

I think at this point it would be wise to supplement this background on target behavior selection with reference to any issue of the *Journal of Applied Behavior Analysis* (1968–) or a collection of studies (e.g., Becker, 1971; O'Leary & O'Leary 1977; Worell & Nelson, 1974). Compare the description of the problem in Introduction and Subjects with the responses recorded and dealt with in the study. While doing that, take note also of how the responses were recorded, because others' studies are the best source of ideas about how to record in your situation. Practice and revision, unfortunately, are necessary, even for experienced persons.

Recording (Counting) Behavior

A recording system that yields numerical estimates of problem frequency per unit time is necessary to assess progress objectively. This fact has been accepted in the educational establishment for some time, as evidenced by the use of tests, both teacher constructed and standardized. In the mental health field, where social and personal characteristics are of concern, measurement has lagged far behind except in research. The need, nevertheless, is clearly present if we are to avoid arbitrary and capricious decisions about commitment, promotion, and release.

The major difference between measurement as it is used in traditional education today and behavior analysis is frequency of assessment. Instead of weekly, monthly, and term ratings and tests, behavior analysis calls for objective assessment continuously, hourly, by period, or daily, depending on the baseline rate of behavior and frequency of opportunities to emit target behavior. The reason should be obvious: one needs information as soon as possible about the efficacy of programs. If one is on the correct track, the program is continued; if not, it can be revised sooner rather than later. Some argue that subjective rating is sufficient: they *know* if things are better or not. They are in error. In the workshop I mentioned earlier, after the participants became better at reporting behavior and events, we asked, "How often did that response occur?" The answers ranged from about 5 to 20. Replay with everyone counting amazed all of us. The actual number was 42.

The fact that during baseline the average number of tantrums was 10 per day and the average was five for the first 5 days of intervention usually will not be detected by agents who count subjectively, and it makes the difference between continuing and abandoning an effective program. Caught up with having to cope with something like tantrums, agents need the reinforcement that objective counting provides. Another particularly good example is in the practice of carefully measuring the size of the spot of urine during the use of the "buzzer and pad" apparatus to teach nocturnal continence. If used faithfully long enough, this procedure has a very high success rate (Collins, 1973; Yates, 1975), but since it requires parents to get up during the night, see that the child goes to the toilet, change the linen, and reset the buzzer and pad carefully, it is hardly a procedure that parents and children enjoy. A sizeable reduction in accident-free nights may not occur for 1 to 4 weeks, but the size of the urine spot diminishes more quickly, indicates that the child is constricting the bladder control muscles sooner, and it is a good predictor of success. Thus parents will be encouraged to continue. Getting agents to stick with programs is a continuing problem which frequent data recording helps solve.

Three types of target behavior are now described: behavioral products, events, and self-reports.

Behavioral Products. These are the easiest to record since they can be counted at convenient times and may not require second observers to establish reliability, assuming reasonable care and honesty. Behavioral products refers to the permanent records left by client behavior rather than behavior itself. Some examples are problems (pages, units of work) completed per lesson, size of spots of urine, chores like bedmaking and lawn mowing completed, money missing from purse, alchohol/tobacco on breath, and weight lost (gained). Where quality of work needs assessing, such as in bathroom cleaning, checklists and establishing recorder reliability will be necessary, but the fact that agents may choose when to record is still an immense advantage. Such records are also more easily justified, and clients may be taught to do the checking not only to assist agents but also to determine if they can distinguish correct from incorrect products. Achievement Place, a community-based home for pre-delinquents, uses client-managers for these purposes, and being a manager turns out to be a valued reinforcer (Phillips, Wolf, & Fixsen, 1973).

Other types of behavior products are reinforcers earned and administrations of punishments such as "time-out" and tokens taken away. These data have to be recorded anyway. I have set them apart, however, because independent observers will need to verify that criteria for giving reinforcers, taking them away, and administering other punishments are constant across agents and time.

Events. This category refers to recording behavior itself by either the frequency or interval method described by Marholin and Bijou in Chapter 2. Common examples are time spent out of seat (in the right or wrong place) per hour; number of tantrums per hour; number of oral questions answered correctly per opportunity; frequency of lateness at work (meals, classes, meetings) and perhaps number of minutes late; bladder and bowel accidents; and "disruptions," "appropriate behavior," and other composite measures.

The alternative ways of recording events are numerous, and if there is a rule to follow in making one's choice, it is to choose a method that you think will be followed accurately and will yield a high enough range of scores to detect small changes. Then let experience guide from that point. A day or so will usually tell you if you are recording too frequently or infrequently. For example, suppose Willy is "highly disruptive" in a day care center. By that the agents mean: (1) he takes objects away from other children and wrecks their block buildings, etc.; (2) he assaults other children and staff when instructions to cease or change activities are given; and (3) he wanders away from and makes noises during group activities. Assaultive behavior, being salient and requiring some form of intervention, would be recorded as it occurs and tallied up each day. Obtaining the *actual* number of times Willy disrupts group activities and engages in other responses would not only take too much staff time but also be unnecessary. Recording Yes (he did disrupt) or No (he did not) every hour (range 0–8 per 8 hour day) or preferably at natural breaks in the day, for example, from arrival to snack, after snack to lunch, and so forth, might suffice to start with. Alternatively, the staff could select two 15-minute times per day to record every minute, e.g., during a morning and afternoon group activity (range: 0–30 per day). If the hourly method is chosen and Willy is disruptive in bursts, his daily totals might be on the order of 1 or 2 "yeses." Thus his behavior would have to become perfect before change could be noted with that scoring system. On the other hand, with intensive scoring of group sessions, improvement from disrupting one-half of the time to one-third of the time would be seen and be reinforcing.

Client Self-Reports. These reports are necessary, of course, when the aims of intervention include changing client feelings and thoughts, for example, the amount of anxiety experienced in social situations, anger felt or perceived in others' actions, and repetitive disturbing thoughts. Because only the client can attest to these private events, agents are in the uncomfortable position of not being able to verify their accuracy. Thus they should obtain event and/or behavior product records as well. That way, agents can determine whether client reports of feeling better are accompanied by changes that would support these statements, for example, the number of social events participated in for the person anxious about crowds, the amount of work completed for the depressed person, and the reactions of other persons to the client's appearance and behavior. Often, self-reports of feelings are advisable to show that the agent cares about client feelings and to permit clients to tell agents what they think of the agent, the program, and the progress being made.

For assistance in setting up recording systems, see Bijou, Peterson & Ault (1968), Hall (1970), and thumb through published work. It might help to conclude this section by reminding that initial recording systems represent best guesses about measures that will both reflect progress in the behavior of interest and be feasible. Except in continuing programs, the recording systems reported in the journals invariably are the products of several revisions. You will be in good company when you find you have to revise the system.

In selecting target behavior, use all of the information that is available and that you think worth gathering. This step is, of course, not unique to behavior analysis. The unusual aspects of target behavior selection is our emphasis upon verifying information through objective recording and actually counting behavior and events surrounding behavior. The second unusual aspect is that target behaviors are very specifically defined. In the remainder of this chapter I will discuss how to go about deciding what to do now that you know what the problems are and know what your objectives are.

SELECTION OF REINFORCERS

Definition of Reinforcement

It may not be an exaggeration to say that anything that can be felt, smelt, tasted, seen, or heard serves to reinforce the behavior of some people some of the time. Consider the behavior of persons in mental hospitals and prisons, or observe your children, preferably the adolescents, or contemplate what maintains your spouse's behavior as he/she refinishes old furniture, jogs, campaigns for this or that cause, tends the baby, cleans a perfectly clean room, or your neighbors who have knockdown-dragout fights daily and yet stay together and profess love for each other. That peoples' behavior is reinforced and punished in different ways is hardly news to anyone. Nevertheless, many agents persist in treating clients as if clients like what the agents like or clients like what they should like. In planning behavioral programs, a basic step is to discover the individual client's hierarchy of reinforcers, accept it, and work from that starting point.

Psychologists have not been successful in stating general rules for selecting reinforcers. The textbook way of determining if an event is reinforcing is to present it after a selected response on several occasions. If the response increases in frequency, or speed of occurrence, the event functioned as a positive reinforcer. If the response decreases in frequency, the event was punishing, aversive, or a negative consequence. If neither occurs, the event was neutral. The last conclusion is not so simply drawn, however, because strengthening and weakening behavior with response consequences depend on several factors. Among the most important are (1) immediacy, the time between response and event being tested, (2) frequency of response—event correlation, (3) quantity (magnitude) of event being tested, (4) difficulty of the response, (5) availability of other reinforcers for other behavior concurrently, (6) fatigue and the state of the person's health at the time of testing, and (7) how much or how little of the event has been sampled before testing (satiation-deprivation).

Fortunately, although the foregoing test is the ultimate way of defining reinforcers and each of these factors must be considered in designing and implementing a reinforcement program, agents may make good guesses in the following ways. First, social and verbal events (praise, smiles, expressions of appreciation, affection and physical contact) have been found to be effective in such a variety of situations that they should be tried first and must be controlled in any event for reasons that I will discuss shortly. Second, token or point systems, in which the immediate consequence, a token or point, symbolizes opportunities to choose from a range of activities and objects later, also have widespread applicability. Third, three rules of thumb that agents commonly employ are applicable: (1) asking clients what they want to work for, (2) observing how clients spend their free time, and (3) introducing clients to new events.

Asking Clients What They Want

Before interviewing clients, I suggest constructing a list of illustrative items from which the client may choose, a "reinforcer menu" (Addison & Homme, 1966). The list should contain only those items that (a) are economical, (b) are ethical and safe, (c) can be given frequently and quickly (points/tokens provide a way of meeting this criterion), and (d) can be controlled, that is, given when correct behavior has occurred *and* withheld when it has not. (There are two facets to this last criterion. First, agents must check laws and regulations pertaining to clients rights to receive items and opportunities regardless of their behavior. Second, if it is ethical to withhold a reinforcer until certain behavior occurs, it may be practically very difficult.) Reinforcement menus typically include: activities (movies, playing records, time alone, talking with agents for 15 minutes, etc.), privileges or honors (entering the cafeteria first, assisting agents, "manager for the day," choosing which television programs will be watched, etc.), and tangibles (edibles, money, hobby and sporting equipment, clothing, toiletries, etc.). The list is advisable to avoid having to deny clients their choices because they do not meet the four criteria previously listed.

As you know, people often say they want something, but change their minds when the time comes to work for it. Thus, this method may not be as reliable as the one to follow, but there is no harm done, for the matter can be renegotiated. Furthermore, including the client from the outset is highly desirable, if not required by rules pertaining to client consent.

Observing How Clients Spend Free Time

"Observe what the individual does when the opportunity exists. Those activities that are very probable at a given time will serve as reinforcers" (Ayllon & Azrin, 1968, p. 60). Essentially, this method replaces the reinforcement menu with a buffet; instead of asking for clients' orders, one observes what they help themselves to. The way this is done is to set up free activity times (at the end of work/study periods), allow the clients free access to any of several choices, such as painting, carpentry, reading, table games, and television, and note the activities chosen and the length of time. The clients should be free to switch activities at will (otherwise time data will be meaningless), and observation should be repeated about five times. Access to a frequently chosen activity can then be used to strengthen behavior.

Note that free choice periods, themselves, may be used quite effectively as reinforcers for completing assignments, earning 100 points, and so on, making it unnecessary to find the preferred activities of each individual in the group (Wasik, 1970). Occasionally, a client will engage in none of the available activities or flit from one to another in which case, agents may inquire about possible additions to the buffet or try the next method.

Introducing Clients to New Reinforcers

Sometimes called "reinforcer sampling" (Ayllon & Azrin, 1968; Kazdin, 1975, pp. 136–138), the idea of this third method is to induce the client, by hook or by crook, to "try it, you might like it." Agents might, for example, prompt a client to play a particular game with them and/or preferred peers or pay tokens or cash for participation once or twice. Taking clients on excursions to places they have never been or to do novel things also illustrates reinforcer sampling. Of course, if after sampling the activity is not chosen verbally or when made available, it still is non-reinforcing.

Social Reinforcers

Constructing a list of possible reinforcers is not so difficult as choosing events which are not only reinforcing but also meet practical and ethical requirements. Moreover, one has to be mindful of continuation of the behavior outside the program which leads to a preference for commonly employed reinforcers and "natural" consequences.

Social reinforcers meet all of the requirements: they are cheap and safe; the supply is unlimited; they can be dispensed immediately, anywhere; they can be controlled, because they belong to each of us. Social reactions are ideal except that they require special circumstances to gain and maintain reinforcement value. Although the analogy does not seem entirely correct, social events are like points, tokens, and money: they are effective reinforcers if they symbolize good things or avoidance of bad things in the future. It is essential to remember that in practice, regardless of theoretical arguments. The reason should become clear by asking yourself, "Why should anyone be reinforced by *my* approval, attention, etc., when he/she can get it from others with whom he/she interacts?" The answer is, "because there are some things for which my approval is essential—that only I can provide in the client's life for the time being at least." Those "things" hopefully include other social events such as comfort when hurt or ill, good advice and instruction, interesting conversation, and good listening. In addition, agents' approval derives value by virtue of the fact that they can provide opportunities, for example, recommend a pass, and that they are relatively more wealthy, for example, can give allowances and keys to the car.

Difficulties arise because it is not sufficient just to say "good." Nor is it sufficient to say "goods" and give clients the things they want. Agent approval must be given if, and only if, desired appropriate behavior on the part of the client occurs first *and* the back-up reinforcers are withheld until that behavior occurs. If agents give away the back-up reinforcers for free, they nullify the effectiveness of their social reinforcers, because they have given away the source of their power. That is why learning to control attention is so important.

Individuals who are not reinforced by contact with others, affection, and attention are rare. Thus usually the issue is, will my reactions be reinforcing, and how do I make certain they will be? Teachers, foster parents, and group workers are Johnnies-come-lately in clients' lives and will have to establish the value of their approval and affection. Clients, for their part, come equipped with a variety of ways of gaining these and have a vested interest, as it were, in preventing agents from learning to use reinforcers contingently. Clients display behavior that agents feel must be responded to, such as threats, destructive, assaultive, and self-injurious behavior. They engage in amusing and interesting behavior that is harmless enough, if it were not out of place and effective in avoiding studying, work, and punishment. They may be skilled in verbal behavior that evokes guilt or doubt and places agents in the role of "bad guys." Despite these difficulties, it is remarkable the number of times problems are solved by agents instituting control over their *own* social behavior.

Tokens and points supplement social events. They are concrete reminders of the back-up reinforcers that have been earned and how much longer clients must behave before they have met the criteria for cashing them in.

Token/Point Systems

The forms of tokens used, the back-up reinforcers used, target behaviors selected, and the type of clients have been quite varied without affecting success. With young severely retarded children, Birnbrauer and Lawler (1964) used poker chips backed up by edibles, and cheap trinkets. Each chip was accompanied by praise and affectionate touch and was given at first after each instance of appropriate social or correct academic behavior, for example, saying a word correctly, raising hand, hanging up coat, and writing one pencil stroke on the paper, depending on the child's level of competence. In an academic classroom, the pupils received checkmarks ($\checkmark$) for correct responses. These were entered on specially prepared sheets of paper much like trading stamps used to be saved (Birnbrauer, Wolf, Kidder, & Tague, 1965). Burchard (1967) used "slugs" imprinted with the client's own number with his adolescent offenders. They received tokens for participation in vocational activities, and chores as well as academic and social behavior and these were backed up by the time outside the locked unit, better living accommodations, personal items, cigarettes, and excursions. Perhaps numerical points are most common now (Phillips, Phillips, Fixsen, & Wolf, 1972). Token/point systems are, in short, very versatile. For additional information see reviews by O'Leary and Drabman (1971) and Kazdin and Bootzin (1972).

In setting up a token or other reinforcer system, heed the following rules: (1) control praise and other reactions (don't, e.g., make the common mistake of lapsing back into nagging the client about earning his points); (2) set realistic requirements so that the reinforcers will be obtained frequently; (3) despite client enthusiasm, set short-term (hourly, daily, to no longer than weekly) "agreements" so that point earning does not extinguish; (After the time has elapsed, clients should be given the option of obtaining something small now, e.g., an hour of skating, or something larger later, e.g., a weekend trip or motor bike; some agents have offered interest to encourage continued work toward longer-term backups. Written, unwritten, points or tangibles, the situation is not unlike exacting a promise from a child to care for a puppy forever and ever; the novelty wears off; agents must be prepared to vary reinforcers as they go.); and (4) be certain that you can live with the rules set or agreed on.

The only drawbacks of token or point systems of reinforcement are that they lack "naturalness" and they can become an administrative headache. Their advantages are: (1) they can be delivered quickly and in any denomination thus frequently and inexpensively; (2) to the extent that they are backed up by a variety of valued objects and opportunities, points will be reinforcing to most members of the group and they are less subject to the effects of satiation; (3) they can be obtained only from agents, although one has to take precautions to prevent their being obtained "illegally"; and (4) once their value is established, they can be taken away or deducted if a form of punishment seems necessary. An unexpected benefit of tokens is that they seem to be a good way of teaching agents to control their social reactions, for the instructions to give tokens apply also to approval and attention. It seems as if the specificity and concreteness considered necessary for client learning also facilitates agent learning. It makes sense when you think about it.

The problem of token systems being atypical and thus their effects limited to the situation(s) in which the system operates has been known to exist for a decade (Birnbrauer, et al., 1965). Consequently, several methods of making the transition to more natural conditions have been tried. Essentially, they amount to gradually "fading" tokens and back-up reinforcers and eventually substituting an "honor," "merit," or self-recording and self-administration scheme that does not use tokens at all (Birnbrauer, 1971; Phillips, Phillips, Fixsen, & Wolf, 1972; Santogrossi, O'Leary, Romanczyk, & Kaufman, 1973). In addition, other agents, such as parents and employment supervisors, usually are encouraged to report back to the program and to follow similar procedures.

Tokens have been used for entire groups, that is, ward, class, or group home, and then "faded out" individually and for particular targets with particular children on an as needed basis. The former use does entail considerable bookkeeping and gets one into problems similar to managing any economy such as adjusting prices when tokens become plentiful or scarce. Extensive preparation is required to set up a unit-wide system. The second way is quite simple in contrast. Agents are well-advised to try a point system with a particular target behavior with one client or themselves to start with. A system for the group could be developed from experience with one client at a time or agents may continue to employ tokens individually.

Most anything can serve to strengthen, that is, reinforce, behavior that precedes it. The trick is to find things that function in that way for each client and that can be employed differentially. Some agents need to learn to be less stingy with their praise and tangible or token reinforcers, whereas others need to learn to be more selective in giving approval and tangibles to achieve the aim of providing the consistent *relationships* between client behavior and social and other consequences that is necessary for client learning of desired behavior to take place.

CHOOSING METHODS OF WEAKENING BEHAVIOR

Five general methods of decreasing the frequency of undesired behavior employed by behavior analysts are: (1) extinction—eliminating positive reinforcement of undesired behavior; (2) *d*ifferential *r*einforcement of *o*ther behavior (DRO)—extinction of undesired behavior while prompting and reinforcing other behavior; (3) *t*ime-*o*ut from positive reinforcement (TO)—temporarily preventing access to positive reinforcement; (4) response cost, overcorrection, fines and restrictions; and (5) physical pain.[2]

The first decision is whether the behavior warrants any intervention other than extinction, that is, ignoring the behavior, on the assumption that attention will strengthen or maintain the behavior. If more active steps are required because weakening the behavior has high priority, the next decisions pertain to DRO—how to arrange the environment and instruction to prompt alternative behavior, reinforce it, and make certain that reinforcement of incorrect behavior does not occur. DRO *must* be a part of every plan to weaken behavior, for it is the means of teaching alternative behavior. The third step in planning is to decide if procedures in addition to DRO will be necessary. This decision can await the outcome of trying just DRO, unless the behavior is imminently dangerous to client or others. If DRO is not safe or not being successful, the final decisions are about what form and quantity of punishment to use. The last three methods above are forms of punishment within behavior theory.

I begin with a view of punishment. Then, I list factors to be considered in choosing a method of weakening behavior, and finally I comment briefly on the five methods listed above.

Definition of Punishment

In behavioral psychology, an event is punishing if it decreases the frequency of behavior that precedes it (Azrin & Holz, 1966). "No, that's wrong" is punishing, if its effect is to decrease the wrong behavior it follows (refers to). The grinding of the gears of a car is punishing, because it results in diminution of incorrect operations of clutch and accelerator. Taking away points, the bite of a dog, a hot stove, live electrical socket, and smack on the hand are punishing, if the individual avoids them subsequently. Although events that hurt, frighten, and anger often will weaken behavior and thus be punishing in the behavioral sense, hurting neither defines punishment nor is a necessary or sufficient element in achieving the aim. For individuals, an event will function in different ways; it may weaken or strengthen behavior or do neither.

One uses negative consequences in behavioral interventions to accomplish particular educational and therapeutic purposes. In general terms, the purposes are: (1) to prevent positive reinforcement of incorrect behavior and (2) to stop behavior and to delay its recurrence long enough to gain opportunities to teach—to gain time for reinforcement of other behavior to have its effect. Rarely, and then only temporarily, do we want people to just avoid dogs, stoves, other people, learning situations, and the like. We want to teach them to treat them appropriately and to acquire discriminations about when and where to emit and not emit certain behavior. Acquisition of the right way depends on the quality of instruction about the right way, the consequences of the right behavior, and opportunities to practice. The same or similar negative consequences when used in the absence of a plan to teach alternative behavior is simply misguided or intended to serve other purposes such as preventing recurrence of behavior and deterring others from behaving likewise. Often, we seem to have no alternative than to expel from school, imprison, and restrain for extended periods of time, but we should be aware that these purposes are distinct from therapeutic and educational ones, and are admissions of failure.

General Considerations

Everything that applies to the selection of positive reinforcers applies also to selection of a method of weakening behavior. (1) What will be maximally effective varies with individuals. (2) The procedure selected must be (a) sufficiently intense and (b) capable of being administered quickly and as frequently as the misbehavior occurs, for, like positive reinforcement, it seems that the important factor is a consistent relationship between behavior and negative consequence. (3) People adapt to negative consequences just as they satiate to positive reinforcers, necessitating that agents take advantage of the moment and induce and reinforce alternative behavior. (4) The strength of social and symbolic negative consequences must be maintained. (Surely you have observed a parent saying "No" repeatedly and ineffectually and noted that there was no follow-up. You would be right to conclude that was why the child ignored the "No's.") (5) The oft-cited temporary effects of punishment have their parallel in reinforcement programs. In either case a consolidation plan is required. (6) Even the undesirable "side-effects" that follow from improper use of negative consequences also can be obtained by improper use of positive reinforcers.

To a large extent, clues about effective punishment procedures will be obtained in the course of selecting positive reinforcers for clients. Taking away and preventing temporary access to (a) what clients say they like, (b) what clients choose to do in their free time, (c) points/tokens, and (d) social reinforcers are likely candidates. The ultimate test, however, is that the procedure decreases the strength of behavior that precedes it.

More and more, behavioral agents ask clients to nominate negative consequences and consult the peer group as well. Such discussions provide chances for client and agent to explain their behavior and to rehearse ways clients may avoid punishment in the future. Although waiting for a residents' meeting to select the punishment violates the immediacy of punishment rule, a period of uncertainty often is punishing, in itself, and the potential gains from including the client and group seem to outweigh whatever risks the delay entails. Consistency and immediacy from that time forward should, of course, be adhered to.

Agents planning family or unit meetings to select a punishment are reminded to (a) have a "punishment menu," (b) to record the decisions exactly, and (c) to set an early date, for example, 3 days later, for review of progress. If daily meetings are held routinely, then the client's progress should be noted at these. Gains should be recognized enthusiastically. If further instances of misbehavior have occured in the interim, encouragement to keep trying, expressions of confidence, and advice should be given, with revision of the program, as a rule, reserved for the date agreed on. We are not, after all, dealing with miracle cures so repeated trials should be allowed before making changes.

I do not know any rules for setting the severity of negative consequences, because it is so much an individual matter (Burchard & Barrera, 1972; White, Nielsen, & Johnson, 1972). Generally speaking, time-out from reinforcement (TO) is shorter than most might suppose necessary; 15 seconds to 15 minutes encompass the TO intervals in most studies in the literature. Shorter intervals are desirable so that more opportunities to practice appropriate behavior will be available. On the other hand, token and other losses, because they should be based on the client's "wealth," might be quite high, and if physical punishment is employed, it should be intense enough to startle the client and *stop* the behavior. One does want to avoid adaptation, which can happen if the severity of negative consequences is increased gradually with repeated offenses. One relatively mild, loud smack on the hands for a first "offense" may suffice on one trial whereas levels far above that might be required later, if built up to gradually.

You may have noted that the foregoing assertion is contrary to common practice. Our criminal justice system and other authorities typically do set penalties according to number of previous offenses. Whatever the precedents for this practice are, they are not psychological research on punishment. Another common basis for selecting a punishment, that of "fitting the punishment to the crime," also is not derived from research. It is a legacy of punishment as revenge and is thought to enhance deterrent value.

Extinction, DRO, and TO

Extinction. This procedure consists of allowing behavior to occur without positive reinforcement. The most common example is ignoring behavior that one presumes is reinforced by attention such as putting the baby down and steadfastly refusing to reply to its crying and calling (Williams, 1959). One also sees extinction operating when a child rapidly ceases playing with a light switch after the bulb has burnt out, when people "lose interest in" card games with a series of bad hands, and when ex-cigarette smokers gradually stop reaching for packs that are no longer in their shirt pockets.

DRO and Extinction Compared. DRO incorporates extinction and is, by far, the more sensible procedure with priority targets. Imagine you have entered a reception area and the receptionist does not look up from her work. You wait, shuffle, clear your throat, and finally say "excuse me." She does not look up. So you call more loudly, move closer, and perhaps get to the point of tapping her on the shoulder. Imagine your reaction if she still does not reply and also what it is like for the receptionist to ignore your shouting and tapping! That's the position in which extinction alone places client and agent. The client's behavior is apt to get worse before it ceases, and nothing is done to prompt what should be done instead. The addition of prompts and reinforcement of alternative behavior converts extinction alone into DRO. (Technically, one does not have to prompt other behavior to apply DRO, but it seems foolish not to. Also, sometimes the other behavior reinforced is anything but the undesired behavior. I use DRO to include this form and reinforcement of a prescribed alternate behavior, and emphasize the latter because it shows more careful planning.) How much simpler and more efficient for the receptionist and you, if she had said, "Please wait a minute; take a seat." Teachers will say, "I will answer your question when you return to your desk," (DRO), rather than ignore the child until he/she returns to the desk (extinction). But then, ignoring behavior until the correct alternative occurs is necessary. Returning to the example, you might have replied, "I only have a quick question" or asked your question. At that point, the receptionist either will have to ignore your reply and attend to the work that needs to be completed or give in. The latter reinforces your persistence. Clients very often are taught to persist, contrary to instructions, in just this manner.

A fair amount of quick thinking, re-arrangement of physical conditions, and instruction is required in DRO, but numerous teachers and other agents have been successful in a number of situations with just differential reinforcement of other behavior with attention as the reinforcer (e.g., Allen, Hart, Buell, Harris, & Wolf, 1964, to encourage peer play of a nursery school child; Broden, et al., 1970, to increase studying of a primary school child and found that the child's neighbor also improved; and Peterson & Peterson, 1968, to decrease self-injurious behavior of a retarded boy). It is probably the best-documented finding within the behavior modification literature.

Although these illustrations employ agent attention as the reinforcer, DRO also applies with token and other tangible reinforcers. I have focused on attention, because one of the ticklish aspects of DRO is making certain reinforcers are withheld until the right behavior occurs. When tangibles are being used, they can be placed out of reach, and it is clear that they are being withheld. It takes experience, on the other hand, for agents to know whether they are withholding attention. Another important part of DRO is to choose alternatives that have high probability of occurrence and/or to arrange conditions so that the desired behavior will occur. Verbal instructions may not be applicable or the best way of doing the latter. Parents often use DRO quite smoothly when they remove a valuable or dangerous object and place another in the child's hands, while carrying on a conversation. Seconds later, they may be observed smiling or making a funny face at the child. "Re-directing" activities is identical to DRO, if reinforcement of the other activities is included.

TO. Because of difficulties in withholding reinforcers, notably but not exclusively social reinforcers, the procedure known as time-out from positive reinforcement (TO) is extremely useful. TO is DRO with the addition of procedures that (a) signal no reinforcement and (b) *ensure* that behavior will not be reinforced for a set period of time. Reinforcement is prevented by restraining the client, by placing the client in an area in which reinforcers are not available, or by removing the reinforcers or the reinforcing person from the client. Some examples are (a) placing the client in his room every time a tantrum occurs for a minimum of 10 minutes or until the tantruming has ceased (Wolf, Risley, & Mees, 1964); (b) saying "No," recovering stolen food, and removing the client from the dining room for 5 minutes whenever the client steals food from a neighbor; (c) saying "No," removing object, and withholding it for 15 seconds each time destructive play occurs; (d) saying "time-out" and sending client to TO bench for 5 minutes or 30 minutes immediately if fighting or other aggressive behavior occurs (Burchard & Barrera, 1972); (e) saying "No" followed by 15 seconds away from group instruction and token reinforcement (Zimmerman, Zimmerman, & Russell, 1969); and (f) saying "NO," firmly holding the client's arms to his/her sides for 10 seconds or until the client has ceased struggling after each instance of destructive, self-injurious, or assaultive behavior. The receptionist could have applied TO if the office was so arranged that she could have continued her work out of view. Indeed, abruptly turning or walking away from the client may function quite effectively as time-out.

The steps in applying TO as it is employed most commonly are as follows: First, the undesired behavior is followed (preferably *interrupted*) by a verbal signal to stop. Second, if the client stops, the agent praises the client and continues the activity or lesson. If the client does not, the behavior is stopped physically and restraint or separation is instated for the duration of time selected. Third, when the interval has elapsed and the client's behavior has subsided, the activity or lesson resumes with the client receiving reinforcers just like nothing has happened. (Some agents ask if the client is ready to return to the activity. I see no reason not to, so long as the answer is honored, the client's "sulking" is not given undue attention, and agents question the reinforcement value of the activity.) Agents must be careful to avoid protracting punishment further by excluding the client or decreasing opportunities for reinforcement. If anything, reinforcement should be increased. Finally, the TO procedure is repeated as soon as it is necessary. Agents should not be dismayed if the undesired behavior is repeated within seconds of return to the group. It is common, because many clients have been taught that adults do not persist very long with their intervention procedures. A series of trials in the course of 1 hour, although tiring, may be virtually all that is needed to eliminate some responses.

The choice of procedure depends upon the behavior, physical arrangements, availability of staff, and type and frequency of reinforcement in the situation. Some clients will not present further difficulties when told to sit away from the group; others will, thus requiring a separate room or being attended by an adult (Zimmerman, et al., 1969). Food stealing could be responded to equally well by restraint or exclusion whereas self-stimulatory behavior requires restraint. Burchard and Barrera (1972) were able to use just a TO bench even though their clients were adolescent offenders, because of the value of the tokens which TO cost them and the still greater cost of going to seclusion. Birnbrauer, et al., (1965) used TO, that is, 10 minutes in an empty room adjacent to their classroom for serious misbehavior, both while a token system was in use (TO meant no opportunity to earn tokens) and while it was not. During the phase in which tokens were not being used, TO was necessary much more often. Two members of one class actually vied to see who would be placed in TO first. Solnick, Rincover, & Peterson also have shown that the effectiveness of TO varies with the rate of reinforcement during an activity.

To sum up, extinction, differential reinforcement, and time-out are on a continuum of degree of intervention to prevent reinforcement of undesired behavior. Extinction is basic to each and by itself is invaluable to weaken or at least not strengthen many low-priority responses that are not worth making an issue of, for example, some tantrums, grumbling, swearing, threats, and "cute" behavior. If agents do not ignore such behavior, the dangers are that they will be distracted from their major purpose, reinforce inconsistently, and thus slow down the learning of target behavior. Something I have observed frequently is an agent's expecting a client to comply with an instruction cheerfully, quickly, and perfectly. That is obviously a bit too much to expect. The chances are excellent that if compliance is reinforced and muttering, objectionable language, slow pace, and pained expressions are ignored, they will disappear. The first tantrum, if ignored and not given in to, will be the last one.

DRO supplements extinction with a deliberate plan to strengthen other response patterns and TO is a way of ensuring that reinforcement is withheld following inappropriate behavior. I hope there is no doubt that time-out from positive reinforcement is quite different from isolating, expelling, and restraining clients as these have been employed characteristically in the past.

Response Cost, Overcorrection, Fines, and Restrictions

I now discuss three approaches to weakening behavior in this section. The first, response cost, refers to the immediate taking away of a valued object or privilege after each act of misbehavior occurs. The second, overcorrection, involves loss and cost and also is applied immediately and on a one offense to one loss ratio. The third—fines, restrictions, loss of status, and the like—bear superficial similarity to response cost procedures, but within behavioral programs are used sparingly and as backup punishments.

Response Cost. Probably the most common and best way to employ response cost is within a point/token system. The procedure consists simply of taking away one, five or 1000 points (the number depending on the client's wealth and earning rate, that is, the value of each point) immediately after each instance of incorrect behavior. If the points are reinforcers, then deducting them should be punishing. It is similar to saying "no" or "wrong" in that the loss of points and "no" symbolize some loss in the future unless the client starts behaving correctly. The advantages, thus, are speed and ease; taking away can be done with virtually no interruption of ongoing activities; clients may begin immediately to recoup their losses; and it may be applied to the group or a number of individuals at one time.

Taking away something that has little reinforcement value, of course, is useless and one has to be prepared to withhold the back-up reinforcers when the time comes if the client has insufficient points. A difficulty that arises frequently at the time of deducting tokens is that clients argue, complain, and cajole. While these reactions are good signs in that they suggest the tokens are valuable, agents nevertheless will need to ignore the argument and enter the debit matter of factly, perhaps restating the reason. Of course, if the client is correct, then it is appropriate for the agent to apologize and correct the mistake. If it is not clear who is correct, then my preference would be to use the opportunity to clarify the rules for the future or defer to a group decision, in either case not deducting for that particular instance. Sometimes clients will simply refuse to give over their points and dare agents to take them away. Agents should be prepared for that eventuality with a back-up procedure such as 10-minutes of isolation. (I would apply the back-up even if the client were correct, because of the objective to teach peaceful means of settling disputes.) Agents must behave consistently with the rules and be willing to listen to the client's side. In short, peaceful solutions must be available and reinforced.

Ways of avoiding hassles at the time of deduction are to: (1) announce and record the loss then, but deduct at the time of token exchange; and (2) do not give points/tokens directly to clients, but instead post them on a chalkboard or deposit them in banks (Kaufman & O'Leary, 1972). As a rule, if agents are firm from the outset, certain of the rules that have been agreed on, and opportunities to regain tokens are plentiful, disputes and hassles disappear rapidly. With any form of punishment, if clients escape or avoid the punishment by inappropriate behavior, the intervention plan is in trouble.

Response cost may be applied without going to the trouble of setting up a token system under limited circumstances. Agreements may be made of a simple nature that draw direct lines between some behavior that should or should not occur in a period or day and a short-term loss or low-cost penalty at the end of the period of time in question. For example, failure to complete the dishes or homework costs the client an evening of television— the evening of the offense—or the use of the car that night; failure to complete assignments means last in line for the movie, and so on. I wish to emphasize that the loss is relatively immediate and small. Parents commonly try to use this procedure and get into trouble, because of long delays between behavior and penalty. With greater time, clients may react with a "what the hell" attitude and act up further in the interim and unlike token loss, all of the delay is wasted time. What sometimes happens to aggravate matters is agents will then heap penalty upon penalty until the child has lost television for a month, a penalty which will be exceedingly difficult to enforce. When clients are building up losses in this way, it is time to revise the program.

For further information on response cost with delinquents, see Burchard and Barrera (1972) and Phillips, et al., (1972), and with mental patients, Upper (1973).

Overcorrection. Foxx and his colleagues (Foxx, 1976; Foxx & Azrin, 1972, 1973; Foxx & Martin, 1975; Webster & Azrin, 1973) have demonstrated the effectiveness of procedures which they call overcorrection. Overcorrection consists of requiring (with graduated guidance if necessary) the client to repeatedly practice behavior for a period of time. Some examples are 2 hours of bed rest immediately after assaultive behavior; 10 minutes of arm exercise after client emits self-stimulatory behavior; 5 minutes of neatly arranging all of the furniture in a room after knocking over a chair; and 5 minutes of apologizing to every person present after speaking abusively to a cottage parent. The activities chosen are of two general types: (a) positive incompatible behavior, for example, walking slowly and quietly if the inappropriate behavior is running noisily, and (b) restitution, that is, restoring the environment to better than its original condition.

The important features of overcorrection seem to be: (a) preventing the client from engaging in inappropriate behavior during the preselected period of time, and (b) requiring the client to practice other behavior that is aversive to the client. Thus, overcorrection is time-out from positive reinforcement with the client's behavior during TO specified. The fact that the behavior required of the client is positive or restorative means that the procedure can be explained more credibly to clients and it is often more acceptable to agents and advocates. On the negative side, the one-on-one attention required can be tiring to agents. Finally, overcorrection can not be applied with clients who are so uncooperative with the procedures that agents would have to use force to apply them.

The range of offenses to which overcorrection has been applied is large and the behavior one might have the client engage in during the overcorrection period is diverse. Before using overcorrection, be sure to read the articles cited above.

Fines and Restrictions. Fines, resrictions, isolation, restraint, exclusion, demotion to a locked unit or lower status, and unpleasant work details all are commonly employed in society at large and have been part of behavioral programs as well. Response cost is a fine, but, as I described it, it is a procedure that agents apply immediately and often. TO may employ a seclusion room, but it, too, is applied immediately, for a short time, and repeatedly as necessary to aid in teaching alternative behavior.

Larger fines, lengthy periods of exclusion, deprivation of visitor and grounds privileges, and the like, in behavioral programs, perform two valuable, but different, functions. One is to establish and maintain the effectiveness of other punishing events. They are, in other words, back-up punishments that clients are to be helped and taught to avoid through the use of procedures like those described above: DRO, TO, and response cost. The second is protection of client and others.

If client behavior meets the criteria for back-up punishment, it must be applied. At the same time, agents should look carefully at their total program—the target behaviors, the frequency and nature of reinforcement of alternative behavior, and their instruction and guidance. It may be that nothing should be changed, because punishment of this nature probably has to be experienced by at least some clients occasionally to, if you like, convince them that they will be imposed. Frequent use, on the other hand, is a definite sign to revise the program. Aside from the fact that lengthy confinement and repayment precludes opportunities to practice with reinforcement, they also present enforcement problems that change the role of agents from teacher/counselors to guards.

A possible way of offsetting the disadvantage of wasting training time and of avoiding agents becoming guards is to offer clients the option of either working off a fine or "serving time," for example, 3 days of confinement which is, purely and simply, confinement, or some other negative consequence. If a work option, such as collecting 10 bags of litter from the roadside or scrubbing the floor once a day for 10 days, is offered, it should be done with a clear understanding about when the work will be completed, the quality of work expected, and the cost of not meeting the terms. This way, clients may continue in programs at all other times and possibly learn something while fulfilling the terms of the penalty as well. Agents who oversee the work option are, in addition, retaining their role of helping clients to avoid the back-up punishment. (I might point out here that options to even participate in training programs or merely "serve time" are becoming more common and likely will be required by legislation. Translating these good intentions into practice with clients who cannot give informed consent in any meaningful way will be difficult, but well worth the effort because it requires us to think about practices and procedures and to develop alternatives.)

One final word is that restrictions and fines with any delay whatsoever have little chance of effecting desired changes in the behavior of clients who do not understand verbal explanations of the relationship between their behavior and the penalty, for example, young children and many retarded and emotionally disturbed persons. They will need to be taught this relationship and the meaning of verbal and symbolic negative consequences ("No," token loss) through experiencing them immediately along with experiencing positive reinforcement of other behavior. For them, time-out from positive reinforcement, overcorrection, or negative consequences involving physical pain is necessary.

Physical Pain

The rules now are such that the use of physical pain to weaken behavior, for example, spanking and response-contingent electric shock, is severely limited or prohibited. To obtain approval of physical punishment (and any form of punishment in some facilities), rules typically require the following: (1) consideration of, and trials with, alternative methods; (2) justification of the aim; (3) a program of which physical punishment is just one component; (4) nomination of persons who will oversee and conduct the program, stating their qualifications; and (5) provisions for internal and external monitoring of effectiveness. I have no quarrel with these requirements, for they are the same as the steps that define program planning within behavior analysis. Thus, agents should impose them on themselves whether or not physical punishment is under consideration.

I think it a pity that physical punishment has been proscribed and we have had to develop elaborate procedures to weaken behavior that are only marginally, if at all, more humane, and not as effective as a loud smack on the hand *might be*. When I compare a short, intense physical consequence with the criteria for an effective and practical way of weakening behavior, I cannot help but conclude that physical punishment is high on the list for inclusion in the rearing of young children—average, retarded, or emotionally disturbed. Detrimental side-effects will be minimal if agents *behave* in accordance with rules, that is, are consistent, precede the smack with a verbal signal, reinforce alternative behavior generously, and display willingness to solve problems by compromise at the appropriate times. Inflicting pain, however, must be severely restricted because some people are unable to keep it within reasonable bounds. There is also the real danger that the child will learn to use similar procedures in solving his or her problems with peers and other children who are smaller and less able to defend themselves.

In selecting a procedure to weaken behavior, agents should ask: (1) Will extinction suffice? (2) What alternative behavior should be taught and what procedures will be most efficient? (3) Does the client's behavior, or experience with this client, indicate a need for more active intervention such as TO or response cost? (4) What alternative, at what intensity is both likely to succeed and be feasible? Having answered those questions, then implement the program, record data to monitor progress, and revise the program accordingly. (It should be noted that very low criteria for revising a punishment program should be set, because TO, response cost, and physical pain tend to decrease behavior, and to show signs of working, within a few (3–5) applications. The signs are hesitation before emitting the behavior again, looking at the agent "warily," or just looking more alert. Then, the client should successfully avoid the punishment, that is, respond to "no" or its equivalent, on a trial, although the undesired response will recur before it is suppressed completely. The most common faults in applying punishment are delivering it too slowly (the best time being when the response begins), missing responses, and not giving the warning sharply and clearly. Signal in your best "I mean it" tone of voice and show the client that you do by intervening quickly and at every possible opportunity.) If this outline is followed, agents will be doing all that they can expect themselves and others to do.

PROMPTING APPROPRIATE BEHAVIOR

In the preceding sections on selecting consequences with which to strengthen and weaken behavior, I repeatedly mentioned making use of prompts to make appropriate or near-appropriate behavior more likely and inappropriate behavior less likely. Some agents are exasperated by talk about reinforcement, because they see their greatest problem as that of getting clients to do ANYTHING for them to reinforce. Although such statements usually are exaggerations, as agents will admit or become aware of after a series of observations, if agents still believe that, the first important change is to lower the requirements of reinforcement. There are also simple and numerous changes in physical arrangements, in instructions and demonstrations, in teaching materials, and in scheduling that may induce appropriate behavior and sometimes eliminate problem behavior entirely.

Starting Off on the Right Foot

The time to begin prompting appropriate behavior is the first day of a term or the day of admission. That day is an unexcelled opportunity, because people usually are very sensitive to the behavior of important others and on their "very best behavior" in strange environments. Therefore, I think many problems can be avoided by treating clients as normally (as defined by the school or facility) as possible from the outset. Agents should have schedules like those they intend to follow throughout the program or school term and introduce the schedule by following it in a somewhat relaxed fashion while being ready to assist, explain and answer questions as needed along the way. The reinforcement system should begin, for example, give clients their point cards with a brief explanation, give points frequently for appropriate behavior, and afford an early opportunity for them to exchange their points. (Such experience will be far more efective than a lot of talk about the system.) If "chore-for-the-week" is part of the routine, the clients should be asked to select, and so on, leaving natural break times for clients to be alone and to become aquainted with each other.

In this way, clients will learn expectations earlier and easier rather than later the hard way because the chances are they will comply and thus be reinforced for compliance in novel ways by novel persons. Simultaneously, agents' reactions will gain reinforcement value because they will be providing the structure and assistance people usually seek under these circumstances. There is much truth in the old sayings about the "importance of first impressions" and "starting off on the right foot."

Many teachers and facilities make such mistakes as beginning by "reading the riot act," explaining how good the place is and how nice everyone is, overloading clients with information, following special schedules consisting of assemblies and "fun and games," and allowing time for clients to adjust and become oriented, with the "real" program beginning 3 days or a week hence. Since common experience is that clients find orientations boring and will disbelieve them and/or forget what is said, the better way is simply to begin the "real" program. Some programs assign orientation to another resident, a buddy or big sister, the rationale being in part that such assignments are reinforcers and instructive for the older residents. For those reasons, it is a good idea, but the responsibility should be shared by staff and schedules adhered to as well. From the client's perspective, being assigned to another resident and being given a period of adjustment may be like visiting friends and spending the first day quietly with the butler.

On admission, some clients will be sullen, negative, sarcastic and verbally threatening. They too are best treated by introducing them to the program and reinforcing participation. Their questions may be answered factually, but their manner should be ignored. Agents should not strengthen negativism, sarcasm, and the like by paying attention to it, consoling, or trying to cheer the client up.

The clients who react to the first day with tears and requests to be left alone, should be, with gentle inquiries and invitations when they are quiet and on such occasions as meals. The remaining clients who are assaultive and fight the system in highly disruptive ways, of course, should be treated as necessary to stop the behavior, for example, by exclusion from the group or seclusion. Clients in each of these categories should be given the opportunity two or three times a day to begin participating in the program from that time forward as if they had just arrived.

On this first day and thereafter, agents should behave deliberately with an air of confidence that the clients will comply and learn, if not now, later. That is pretty nonbehavioral language, but if it corrects any impression that I may have given that agents should be bound to their schedule, stern, distant, and the like, I am satisfied. The cues for when and how to prompt and reinforce must be taken from client behavior. Therefore, agents should not be so absorbed by prior plans that they do not attend to client reactions.

This description of the first day gives an overall picture of the kind of atmosphere agents should strive to create and maintain. Within that, one needs, of course, to prompt specific behavior on specific occasions.

Instructions and Demonstrations

The first, most familiar way is verbal instructions. These should be short and clear, posted, supplemented by demonstrations, and followed quickly with opportunities for clients to act or participate to avoid losing their attention either because they do understand or they do not understand what is being asked of them. The only way for agents to judge what, if any, additional instruction is needed is to observe client behavior. The DISTAR programs (Engelmann & Bruner, 1974) carry this idea through to an extreme. DISTAR instructors give instructions loudly and crisply, elicit student responses immediately, and praise and dispense other reinforcers enthusiastically at a rate approximating that of a machine gun. Lulls in instruction provide opportunities to be distracted (Carnine, 1976). Avoid them.

Shaping and Fading

If instructions and demonstrations are not effective in evoking the desired behavior, there is little point in repeating them unless they might not have been heard or seen. Try a variation based on how much of the desired behavior was emitted. If the client behaves partly correctly, reinforce that, ignore the incorrect parts, and build or "shape" from that point. Shaping behavior or reinforcing approximations to desired behavior is a generally applicable and necessary set of skills to learn. It is the answer to agents who observe no correct behavior to reinforce. Shaping consists of breaking tasks down into their component parts, prompting one component by instruction, demonstration, and/or physical guidance, reinforcing the component response, and gradually dropping out the instructional aids one by one. Then, repeat the procedure with another component plus the one already established, and literally create task performance response by response. Teachers shape behavior when they break a word into the sounds which comprise it, prompt first one sound, then another, and finally blend them into the word. It may be necessary for the teacher to form the client's mouth with his/her fingers to produce the sound correctly, that is, prompt the behavior physically.

Another way to prompt correct behavior is to repeat an instruction or question immediately after you or another student have given the correct answer. "Johnny, how much is $2+2$?" "Four! Good! Bill, how much is $2+2$?" "Four! Right!" It does not matter at this point that Bill is copying Johnny. The aim is that Bill succeed, be reinforced, and thus will try again. Bringing the answer under control of "$2+2 = $?" is a subsequent objective that is achieved by "fading" prompts over repeated trials. It sounds terribly time-consuming and tedious no doubt, but shaping and fading do work and in the long run are worth the investment.

Repeating a question or instruction immediately after the correct behavior has been demonstrated may not work, because the client did not hear or see it. Many clients do need to be taught to "pay attention." Continuing with the "$2+2 = $?" example, if no response or an incorrect one was obtained, the agent could follow with the very direct instruction, "Say 4." "Four, good. How much is two plus two?" "Four, very good!" If that does not succeed, the agent might whisper "four" or give a hint such as the sound of the initial letter after "two plus two is?". Having obtained the right answer, the agent repeats the question with a slightly longer pause before prompting the answer. Chances are good that on the next day or even minutes later the client may not "remember" the correct response— your cue to re-instate a minimal prompt and go through the process again. Each repetition of the sequence will be shorter and faster. For good descriptions of teaching children to pay attention and to imitate, see studies of "generalized imitation," e.g., Baer, et al. (1967) and Lovaas, et al. (1966).

Physical Arrangements

Correct behavior may also be prompted by limiting the number of choices of behavior, placing the correct object nearest to hand, eliminating distracting items by putting them away, or placing the client away from them and/or nearer to you, and separating children. Reducing the distance between agent and client has the additional advantage of making immediate and frequent reinforcement more convenient.

In training retarded, emotionally disturbed or any child who is easily distracted, the standard practice is to conduct training in a bare quiet room with instructor and child seated face to face, so close together that the child is actually held in his/her chair by the instructor's knees. It is difficult for the child not to hear and see the prompts under these circumstances and easy for the trainer to reinforce promptly. Circular arrangement of desks or chairs with instructor in the middle accomplishes similar purposes with groups and saves steps, although obviously they can be achieved by moving around the room during instruction.

Use the physical environment and your own skills to the degree necessary to make appropriate behavior almost inevitable and incorrect behavior almost impossible and gradually remove these conditions. The cues for when to move to more difficult tasks are provided by the client's behavior. Likewise, clients tell agents when instruction is moving too rapidly and when reviews of preceding steps are necessary. Shaping and fading are reciprocal relationships and like any social relationships the outcome depends upon the sensitivity of each party, their goals, and their abilities to apply the rules of behavior change.

CRITERIA FOR PROGRAM REVISION

Having planned as best as you can, taking into consideration the physical, ethical, and financial constraints on you, and having prepared yourself and others for the program, the next step is to implement the plan. Intervention remains in effect until the criteria for success or until the "revise program" criteria are reached.

How long a program should be stuck with is difficult to say in general terms, for the decision varies with frequency of behavior, opportunities to administer procedures, and unit of recording. If instruction is intense, such as 30-minute sessions in imitating motor behavior or instruction-following, and recording is fine grain, improvements should be detectable within the first session or two, bearing in mind that sometimes procedure changes result immediately in worse behavior and that counting of trials should start from the point of applying procedures correctly. That is, it usually takes time for agents to become accustomed to new procedures; counting begins after that settling down period. On the other hand, the first session may be an absolute joy and the second and third might not be. In any case, be prepared to review ground covered in preceding sessions and base decisions about procedural changes on the *trend* in correct responding over sessions or opportunities. A program that yielded just one measure per day, such as completing an assigned chore or returning home before curfew, might require as long as 2 weeks to see if compliance were increasing. On the other hand, if compliance and concompliance were being recorded at other times during the day *and* the agent was faithfully applying the program, whether or not the program was working would be evident in a few days.

Punishment programs, as mentioned earlier, should reveal positive trends quickly—within about five consistent applications of the procedure. Furthermore, if there are no signs of hesitation before emitting the inappropriate behavior or actual avoidance of punishment by response to "No" or other signal within three to five administrations, the program probably will need revising.

I am ambivalent about saying even as much as I have about how long to continue programs without knowing to whom I am speaking. Some people tend to give up quickly, even abandon programs after one trial or no trials. They should set longer times and higher number of administrations than they feel are enough. Other people will do the opposite and hang on to programs for much too long, especially if there is some success in the beginning. If partial success is obtained, but improvement ceases, that is, you reach a plateau, the program needs revision. (The analogy of reaching a plateau, resting and then climbing to the next plateau seems to appeal to many people, but is inappropriate. In the context of therapy and education with clients who would not have reached the first plateau without intervention, it is more appropriate to assume they need further assistance to continue the climb.) Consulting persons with more experience and reference to studies using similar procedures probably are the best sources for setting criteria for program revision.

CONSOLIDATION

Unfortunately, successful intervention often is not the end; consolidation of gains is necessary. For students of behavior analysis, the final examination might consist of designing and implementing three behavioral programs from top to bottom. High scores would say that intervention, the course of instruction, was effective. The ultimate test, how well students perform on the job, remains. Consolidation for students of behavior analysis consists of taking steps during and after programs to make success as behavior analysts more likely. Consolidation for clients is the same, i.e., building in methods and tests so that there is greater assurance that they will "make it" outside the program—in the community, a nursing home, a sheltered workshop, and the like.

Concern about follow-up begins during the planning stage and influences selection of target behavior, training site, reinforcement and negative consequences, and amount of agent control (see also Marholin & Siegel, Chap. 12). Maintenance and generalization are facilitated by procedures applied during intervention itself such as varying the instructions, fading, teaching clients to monitor their own behavior and design self-management programs, and finally after intervention by re-programming other environments, and offering continued support.

Considerations During Planning

Target Behavior. You will recall Ayllon and Azrin's "relevance of behavior" rule to teach responses that are likely to be reinforced after the program. The expression, "survival skills" (Risley & Twardosz, 1976) summarizes the idea nicely. Work toward skills that will pay off for the clients in their lives, for example, teaching monetary values, adding and subtracting dollars and cents rather than mathematics or abstract arithmetic computations and why not the use of pocket calculators since they are so inexpensive now? (if time allows more math, other equally useful skills could follow); how to apply for a job; how to address police officers and other authority figures to avoid hassles; skills that enhance popularity with peers; skills that are instrinsically reinforcing once acquired like bike riding; and skills that enhance opportunities like use of public transportation and asking for assistance when needed.

Instructional Site. Generally, training conditions should be as much like those in which individuals will apply their training as possible. Open classrooms, community—based group homes, intervention in classrooms and homes, on-the-job training, and training in skills throughout the day rather than in special lessons are just a few of the many examples of how this rule is being applied. Since the idea is so commonplace, I wish to make only two cautionary statements. First, very often, "natural" training conditions will have to be worked toward by means of structured programs and the procedures listed below. They cannot be the starting point of instruction, hence the qualification, *as much like* conditions "out there" as possible. (My pet illustration—peeve—is open education, which I think an excellent goal but one for which most children and teachers need a good deal of preparation.) Second, it is easy to delude oneself about how well the rule of natural or normal conditions of training is being applied. If residents in a community home, for example, are regimented from reveille to taps, they might just as well be living in a training school in the country.

Reinforcement and Negative Consequences. Although it is true that behavior theory emphasizes employing the reinforcers client behavior indicates is necessary, try first to find effective reinforcers that are simply applied and commonly used, good candidates being social reinforcers backed up in natural ways, for example, going to the store with you. Points exchangeable for something special and pertaining to a particular target at a time are preferable to instituting a point system that applies to numerous behaviors or the entire day. Procedures along the lines of the "good behavior game" (Barrish, Saunders, & Wolf, 1969) might suffice. Strengthening negative and positive social reinforcers is always a desirable aim. Since response contingent exclusion from an activity so often is a consequence peers, teachers, and parents apply to disruptive behavior, this form of time-out may be used with the expectation that others will not need specific instructions to employ it, if needed subsequently. It is also a procedure that others, for example, store managers and restaurant diners, will approve of.

Agent Control. Since everything agents take unto themselves to do will have to be faded out during consolidation, agents should ask how much prompting will be necessary? What restrictions are essential? To what extent can clients be included in selection of reinforcers, administration of reinforcers, and all decision making? How can the group, or particular members, be employed to assist in programs? Instruction often turns out to be unnecessary, for many clients do not exhibit certain behaviors simply because they are not given opportunities to do so. Parents and teachers will complain of children who never do anything without being told or "Yea, Johnny works fine as long as I'm there looking over his shoulder." Try *not* telling Johnny what to do and *not* looking over his shoulder and see what happens. Allow clients to make decisions and encourage them to do things on their own—for themselves. During skills assessment, pause a bit before giving instructions and other prompts.

In sum, during planning look beyond immediate objectives and design programs that minimize the need for your presence, special equipment, and physical conditions. Don't overlook the simple and obvious.

Facilitating Consolidation During Intervention

Varying Instructional Conditions and Reviewing. Some tactics for facilitating maintenance and generalization of behavior are familiar: varying instructions, illustrations, problems, and general physical conditions and reviewing earlier lessons in differing contexts. I think the only thing I need to suggest about these is to hold conditions fairly constant until correct behavior has been observed three to five times in succession before introducing changes. Changes in instructions, materials, and type of problem, although not great in our eyes might constitute significant changes for the client, retard progress, and hence reduce reinforcement rates. There is, however, no harm in testing occasionally to see if you are proceeding with unnecessary caution. Client boredom with repetition of one instruction can be handled by keeping lessons shorter than the client's "boredom span" and intermingling very different types of instruction, for example, alternating 5 minutes of imitation training and 5 minutes of block building. (The latter may actually be the back-up reinforcer for points earned in imitation.) In short, I recommend *not* varying conditions from the beginning of instruction, but instead *reviewing* earlier learning in varying contexts.

Scheduling Reinforcers. Fortunately, behavior does not have to be reinforced every time it occurs for behavior to continue in the absence of reinforcement. To the contrary, behavior will continue longer if reinforcers are scheduled gradually to occur after longer periods of work/study or more units of work/study. One reinforcer ("Good" & token) per response is essential in teaching *new* skills efficiently, but very quickly, the agent should give a token after every other response, then every third, every fifth, and so on, while continuing to say "good" after every correct response. If reinforcement is being "thinned out" too quickly, the client's attention and cooperativeness will wane, thus signalling that the reinforcement rate should be increased. As in shaping behavior, thinning reinforcement requires that agents be sensitive; if they are, there is no problem.

Other changes in reinforcement scheduling to facilitate consolidation are increasing gradually the length of time between symbolic/social reinforcers and back-up reinforcement and the length of time between behavior and symbolic/social reinforcement. For example, if 5 minutes of free play is the back-up reinforcer, it may be scheduled after 15 minutes of "work" at first, then 30 minutes, and then 1 hour, at which point it is close enough to the schedule of recesses in schools that the delay need not be extended further. If praise is the immediate symbolic reinforcer, "good," "right," and the like, should follow each correct problem at first. Then, the teacher would say "Do all of these." With two problems on the page, step back, prompt again if necessary and wait until "all" had been completed, continuing in this fashion until the child is completing assignments of reasonable length with no agent approval before completion. As you can see, when both of these are accomplished the children will be working under conditions that prevail in most classes, and thus they have greater chance of being successful after transfer.

In sum, reinforcement programs are designed as client behavior suggests is necessary to teach efficiently and then changed gradually until they look very much like the systems families, employers, and other teachers typically use. If appropriate behavior withstands the changes made within the program, it has greater likelihood of holding up afterward.

Fading Prompts. Initially, in addition to reinforcing every response, agents may need to tell clients precisely what to do step by step with instructions, demonstrations, and other instructional aids. Yet, the aim is that complete chains of behavior will occur at the right times and in the right places with no assistance from you. Fading is analogous to thinning reinforcement schedules and refers to the gradual removal of social and contextual aids at a pace slow enough to ensure that correct behavior continues. It should begin early in instruction to prevent the development of undue reliance upon artificial prompts. I used "$2 + 2 = ?$" in the section on prompting behavior to illustrate fading. Space only permits my reminding that we very often fail to recognize the necessity for testing clients under less controlled conditions and applying fading. Supervisors may give *a* demonstration, ask "Do you understand?", the eager new employee says, "yes," and the supervisor leaves only to find later that the demonstration was not sufficient. Obviously, a better approach is to ask, "Understand?", "Good, I'll watch while you do just one to be sure. Go ahead," and the supervisor watches, giving hints only as they prove necessary. Hints in the form of "Does that look right?", "What was the rule I told you?" are examples of fading—making the transition from doing as agent directs to doing as the task and client directs. Test rather than assume and thereby avoid client embarrassment and frustration. The wise supervisor would finish instruction by saying, "Complete one and come to me to check it out." Clients, for their part, often need to be taught to say, "I'm not sure I understand completely. Let me do one to make sure," and ask questions of clarification. And they should be taught not to be offended by thorough instruction.

   Training in Behavior Analysis, Decision Making and Self-Management. Although in very important ways, agents will be teaching decision making, self-management, and behavior analysis by modeling, fading prompts, and scheduling reinforcers, recently behavior analysts have, in addition, begun to include specific programs to teach these skills. By instruction in behavior analysis, I mean to suggest that clients be taught about reinforcement, punishment, extinction, and prompting appropriate behavior with particular reference to how they can change other people's reactions to them in socially acceptable ways. Basically, this instruction is done by having clients note their own behavior, that is, self-record, and the reactions that behavior produced, having them discuss and rehearse other ways of behaving in such situations with group and agent feedback and/or videotape playback, and having them play the role of others, for example, parent, prospective employers, teachers, and police officers, as well. In a recent study, a "therapist" taught adolescent offenders to record their own behavior on the job and to prompt their supervisors to reinforce improved behavior (Seymour & Stokes, 1976). The client might, for example, after recording good performance, say on leaving, "I got a lot done today." The hope, of course, was that the client's improved behavior would convert essentially negative client-supervisor interactions into more positive ones that would be self-perpetuating. Supervisors might not always reply as therapists and clients might like, but therapist reinforcement and aperiodic reinforcement from others might make such plans effective nevertheless. Graubard, Rosenberg, & Miller (1971) went somewhat further and taught their retarded pupils to carry out such interventions as extinguishing peer ridicule by ignoring it and increasing their teacher's positive reactions by increased eye-contact, asking questions, and other "attentive" responses. As a group, the special class worked to improve their image within the school. Procedures like these have promise for any community facility, since rarely are they welcome neighbors. Prompting the residents to work together to improve relations with the neighbors would seem an excellent set of exercises to teach behavior analysis and self-management.

Client government and family or unit council meetings also serve as opportunities for clients to plan, talk through, and experience, by role-playing, the effects of their decisions on their future and that of others. Negotiating contracts is a good vehicle for teaching along these lines. Finally, there is no reason why members of the group could not assist each other in their self-management programs. The ultimate step is small residential groups that manage themselves entirely with the aid of counselors, paid or voluntary, who drop by regularly.

Obviously, the first step towards self-management is that clients have opportunities to do so and to experience the consequences of their decisions. Many agents have great difficulty in loosening the reins and sometimes are not aware of how tightly and unnecessarily they control client behavior. There are risks, but these can be minimized by careful study of client competencies, shaping the behavior required, and fading agent controls over the course of the program.

Follow-up. The final steps are to arrange for objective feedback about client performance in post-treatment environments, train or advise others in the procedures that you found effective ("reprogram other environments"), expose clients to these environments in stages, and arrange continuing support. With respect to follow-up data, agents in other environments such as teachers, parents, and employers may be induced to continue recording as you have been, although probably less often, and/or to share data that they routinely gather on their classes or employees together with that of the group for comparision, for example, attendance, grades, and incidents data. In addition, you will wish to observe directly, interview agents and "graduates," and so on. Supplementing data obtained from others is highly desirable both to establish reliability and to gain further information about their practices and expectations. How often and how long follow-up will need to continue varies greatly among types of problems. Therefore, you will have to refer to the relevant relapse data to determine these.

Reprogramming other environments and gradual release proceed together and may, of course, begin quite early in intervention, particularly with parents. Ideally, other agents should be trained thoroughly in behavior analysis. I have been surprised by the number of parents and professionals that have welcomed such training. (Others who refuse it at first often change their minds after seeing changes in client behavior in a behavioral training program and experiencing difficulties themselves on trial visits.) At any rate, the aim is that outside agents be helped as much as possible to change their behavior so that it supports the program. Coupling training with gradual release, for example, one unsupervised hour away from the training facility (30 minutes in a regular class), a day with a relative, a day on own, a week end with relatives, and so on, obviously will increase the likelihood of continued success by the client. Volunteers— students, big brothers and sisters, other clients, and groups like AA—may be very helpful during this stage. Finally, you may wish to make it clear to clients and others that they may visit and telephone at any time—that you are there to help if needed.

I did not promise that behavior analysis is easy, only that it becomes easier with practice, provided improvements in client behavior are highly prized reinforcers. Long-term success rates, however, will continue to be disappointingly low so long as the environments which clients come from and enter remain unchanged. One way to proceed is to make each class, group home, and institution with which we are associated a better place, as measured by realization of client potential and, thus, a model for the larger community to imitate. Why not begin with that objective in mind?

REFERENCES

Addison, R. M., & Homme, L. The reinforcing event (RE) menu. *National Society for Programmed Instruction Journal,* 1966, *5,* 8–9.

Allen, K. E., Hart, B. M., Buell, J. S., Harris, F. R., & Wolf, M. M. Effects of social reinforcement on isolate behavior of a nursery school child. *Child Development,* 1964, *35,* 511–518.

Ayllon, T., & Azrin, N. H. The measurement and reinforcement of behavior of psychotics. *Journal of the Experimental Analysis of Behavior,* 1965, *8,* 357–383.

Ayllon, T., & Azrin, N. H. *The token economy: A motivational system for therapy and rehabilitation.* New York: Appleton-Century-Crofts, 1968.

Azrin, N. H., & Holz, W. C. Punishment. In W. K. Honig (Ed.) *Operant behavior: Areas of research and application.* New York: Appleton-Century-Crofts, 1966, pp. 380–447.

Baer, D. M., Peterson, R. F., & Sherman, J. A. The development of imitation by reinforcing behavioral similarity to a model. *Journal of the Experimental Analysis of Behavior,* 1967, *10,* 405–416.

Baer, D. M., Wolf, M. M., & Risley, T. R. Some current dimensions of applied behavior analysis. *Journal of Applied Behavior Analysis*, 1968, *1*, 91–97.

Barrish, H. H., Saunders, M., & Wolf, M. M. Good behavior game: Effects of individual contingencies for group consequences on disruptive behavior in a classroom. *Journal of Applied Behavior Analysis*, 1969, *2*, 119–124.

Becker, W. C. (Ed.) *An empirical basis for change in education*. Chicago: Science Research Associates, 1971.

Bijou, S. W., Peterson, R. F., & Ault, M. H. A method to integrate descriptive and experimental field studies at the level of data and empirical concepts. *Journal of Applied Behavior Analysis*, 1968, *1*, 175–191.

Birnbrauer, J. S. Preparing "uncontrollable" retarded children for group instruction. In W. C. Becker (Ed.) *An empirical basis for change in education*. Chigago: Science Research Associates, 1971, pp. 213–218.

Birnbrauer, J. S., Burchard, J. D., & Burchard, S. N. Wanted: Behavior analysts. In R. Bradfield (Ed.) *Behavior modification: The human effort*. Palo Alto: Science and Behavior Books, 1970, pp. 19–76.

Birnbrauer, J. S., & Lawler, J. Token reinforcement for learning. *Mental Retardation*, 1964, *2*, 285–289.

Birnbrauer, J. S., Wolf, M. M., Kidder, J. D., & Tague, C. Classroom behavior of retarded pupils with token reinforcement. *Journal of Experimental Child Psychology*, 1965, *2*, 219–235.

Broden, M., Bruce, C., Mitchell, M. A., Carter, V., & Hall, R. V. Effects of teacher attention on attending behavior of two boys at adjacent desks. *Journal of Applied Behavior Analysis*, 1970, *3*, 199–203.

Burchard, J. D. Systematic socialization: A programmed environment for the habilitation of anti-social retardates. *The Psychological Record*, 1967, *17*, 461–476.

Burchard, J. D., & Barrera, F. An analysis of timeout and response cost in a programmed environment. *Journal of Applied Behavior Analysis*, 1972, *5*, 271–282.

Carnine, D. W. Effects of two teacher-presentation rates on off-task behavior, answering correctly, and participation. *Journal of Applied Behavior Analysis*, 1976, *9*, 199–206.

Collins, R. W. Importance of the bladder-cue buzzer contingency in the conditioning treatment for enuresis. *Journal of Abnormal Psychology*, 1973, *82*, 299–308.

Engelmann, S. E., & Bruner, E. C. *Distar reading I*. Chicago: Science Research Associates, 1974.

Foxx, R. M. Increasing a mildly retarded woman's attendance at self-help classes by overcorrection and instruction. *Behavior Therapy*, 1976, *7*, 390–396.

Foxx, R. M., & Azrin, N. H. Restitution: A method of eliminating aggressive-disruptive behavior of mentally retarded and brain damaged patients. *Behaviour Research and Therapy*, 1972, *10*, 15–27.

Foxx, R. M., & Azrin, N. H. The elimination of autistic self-stimulatory behavior by over-correction. *Journal of Applied Behavior Analysis*, 1973, *6*, 1–14.

Foxx, R. M., & Martin, E. D. Overcorrection as an effective treatment of the scavenging behaviors of coprophagy and pica. *Behaviour Research and Therapy*, 1975, *13*, 153–162.

Graubard, P. S., Rosenberg, H., & Miller, M. B. Student applications of behavior modification to teachers and environments or ecological approaches to social deviancy. In E. A. Ramp & B. L. Hopkins (Eds.) *A new direction for education: Behavior analysis* (Vol. I), Lawrence, Ka.: The University of

Kansas Support and Development Center for Follow Through, 1971, pp. 80–101.

Hall, R. V. *Behavior modification—The measurement of behavior.* (Vol. I), Lawrence, Kansas: H & H Enterprises, 1970.

Howe, L. W., & Howe, M. M. *Personalizing education: Values clarification and beyond.* New York: Hart, 1975.

Journal of Applied Behavior Analysis, 1968–

Kaufman, K. F., & O'Leary, K. D. Reward, cost, and self-evaluation procedures for disruptive adolescents in a psychiatric hospital school. *Journal of Applied Behavior Analysis,* 1972, *5,* 293–310.

Kazdin, A. E. *Behavior modification in applied settings.* Homewood, Ill.: Dorsey, 1975.

Kazdin, A. E., & Bootzin, R. R. The token economy: An evaluative review. *Journal of Applied Behavior analysis,* 1972, *5,* 343–372.

Kunzelmann, H. P. (Ed.) *Precision teaching.* Seattle: Special Child Publications, 1970.

Lovaas, O. I., Berberich, J. P., Perloff, B. F., & Schaeffer, B. Acquisition of imitative speech by schizophrenic children. *Science,* 1966, *151,* 705–707

Mager, R. F. *Preparing instructional objectives.* Belmont, Calif.: Fearon, 1962.

Mager, R. F., & Pipe, P. *Analyzing performance problems or "you really oughta wanna."* Belmont, Calif.: Fearon, 1970.

O'Leary, K. D., & Drabman, R. Token reinforcement programs in the classroom: A review. *Psychological Bulletin,* 1971, *75,* 379–398.

O'Leary, K. D., & O'Leary, S. G. (Eds.) *Classroom management: The successful use of behavior modification.* New York: Pergamon, 1977.

Peterson, R. F., & Peterson, L. R. The use of positive reinforcement in the control of self-destructive behavior in a retarded boy. *Journal of Experimental Child Psychology,* 1968, *6,* 351–360.

Phillips, E. L., Phillips, E. A., Fixsen, D. L., & Wolf, M. M. *The teaching-family handbook.* Lawrence, Ka.: University of Kansas Press, 1972.

Phillips, E. L., Wolf, M. M., & Fixsen, D. L. Achievement Place: Development of an elected manager system. *Journal of Applied Behavior Analysis,* 1973, *6,* 541–563.

Risley, T. R., & Twardosz, S. The preschool as a setting for behavioral intervention. In H. Leitenberg (Ed.) *Handbook of behavior modification and behavior therapy.* Englewood Cliffs, N.J.: Prentice-Hall, 1976, pp. 453–474.

Santogrossi, D. A., O'Leary, K. D., Romanczyk, R. G., & Kaufman, K. F. Self-evaluation by adolescents in a psychiatric hospital school token program. *Journal of Applied Behavior Analysis,* 1973, *6,* 277–288.

Seymour, F. W., & Stokes, T. F. Self-recording in training girls to increase work and evoke staff praise in an institution for offenders. *Journal of Applied Behavior Analysis,* 1976, *9,* 41–54.

Solnick, J. V., Rincover, A., & Peterson, C. R. Determinants of the reinforcing and punishing effects of time-out. *Journal of Applied Behavior Analysis,* in press.

Upper, D. A "ticket" system for reducing ward rules violations on a token economy program. *Journal of Behavior Therapy and Experimental Psychiatry,* 1973, *4,* 137–140.

Wasik, B. H. The application of Premack's generalization on reinforcement to the management of classroom behavior. *Journal of Experimental Child Psychology,* 1970, *10,* 33–43.

Webster, D. R., & Azrin, N. H. Required relaxation: A method of inhibiting agitative-disruptive behavior of retardates. *Behaviour Research and Therapy*, 1973, *11*, 67–78.

White, G. D., Nielsen, G., & Johnson, S. M. Timeout duration and the suppression of deviant behavior in children. *Journal of Applied Behavior Analysis*, 1972, *5*, 111–120.

Williams, C. D. The elimination of tantrum behavior by extinction procedures. *Journal of Abnormal and Social Psychology*, 1959, *59*, 269–270.

Winett, R. A., & Winkler, R. C. Current behavior modification in the classroom: Be still, be quiet, be docile. *Journal of Applied Behavior Analysis*, 1972, *5*, 499–504.

Wolf. M. M.. Risley. T. R.. & Mees. H. Application of operant conditioning procedures to the behavior problems of an autistic child. *Behaviour Research and Therapy*, 1964, *1*, 305–312.

Worell, J., & Nelson, C. M. *Managing instructional problems: A case study workbook*. New York: McGraw-Hill, 1974.

Yates, A. J. *Theory and practice in behavior therapy*. New York: Wiley, 1975.

Zimmerman, E. H., Zimmerman, J., & Russell, D. Differential effects of token reinforcement on instruction-following behavior in retarded students instructed as a group. *Journal of Applied Behavior Analysis*, 1969, *2*, 101–118.

NOTES

1. This chapter was meant to be a revision of "Wanted: Behavior Analysts" (Birnbrauer, Burchard, & Burchard, 1970). Although 6 years have resulted in numerous changes, surely I am still very much indebted to John and Sara Burchard. I wish also to thank Robert B. Cairns, Elaine Morrow, and other members of the Program in Developmental Psychology at the University of North Carolina at Chapel Hill for providing me with a comfortable and congenial environment in which to work, and David A. Eckerman, Gary (Josh) Haskett, Christa R. Peterson, and Jay V. Solnick who struggled through drafts and made many helpful suggestions.

2. This classification is unorthodox. I offer it with the hope that it will enhance practical understanding and that you will not be distracted because you would have classified procedures differently or do not think the classification exhaustive, and so forth. For what it is worth, in earlier drafts I had six and eight categories. The present scheme seemed clearest and most succinct.

4

Program Evaluation
in Clinical
and Community Settings

Alan E. Kazdin and David Marholin II

Traditionally, treatment, rehabilitation, and educational practices have been well separated from research (Weiss, 1970). Unfortunately, in many areas of mental health this is still the case. Practitioners and researchers often are separate individuals whose interests are as far apart as their offices. "Program staff have rarely liked researchers and/or evaluators who, seemingly, poke their noses into the operations of programs for measuring outcomes; peruse learned journal articles; think critical thoughts; collect a minimal amount of data; converse over the phone with research colleagues about the use of nonparametric regression equations significant at the .05 level; and negotiate for promotions, annual salary increases, and employee benefits, all from the sanctity of an isolated research or evaluation department" (Ricks, 1976, p. 399). Recently, however, attempts have been made to combine practical applications to effect behavior change in treatment settings with the research methods and evaluation techniques used by researchers.

In behavior therapy, applied behavior analysis is an area where clinical applications and research are combined. Applied behavior analysis consists of applying techniques to change behaviors of social, educational, and therapeutic significance. Usually, the techniques used to change behavior in applied behavior analysis are derived from operant conditioning. However, this is *not* an essential feature. Rather,the defining characteristic of this area is an approach toward altering behavior and evaluating treatment effects, whether the treatment happens to be called transactional analysis, gestalt therapy, or behavior modification (Kazdin, 1975c).

Most practitioners are concerned with effecting change in their clients and are much less concerned with understanding the reason for the change. Thus determining the cause of a particular change in a client's behavior is accorded a much less important role than is implementing a treatment program designed to help the client. To many individuals, systematically determining the cause of behavior change interferes with conducting treatment. There is some justification for this view of evaluation. Examining the effects of treatment adds to the task that staff members are called on to perform. Not only must treatment be implemented, but also the client's behavior before, during, and after treatment must be carefully assessed. Finally, treatment has to be presented in such a way that its effects can be separated from the influence of incidental or ancillary changes in the setting.

IMPORTANCE OF PROGRAM EVALUATION

The goal of achieving changes in clinical populations is not necessarily incompatible with determining the cause of those changes. Indeed, determining the cause of behavior change contributes a great deal to changing client behavior in many important ways. Initially, a goal of treatment is not only to change the behavior of a given client but also to understand the reasons for the change. It is one thing to change behavior, but quite another to understand why this change occurred. Throughout the history of psychology, psychiatry, and medicine, diverse treatments have been used to alter deviant behaviors and physical disorders (cf. Shapiro, 1971). Many of the treatments have consisted of now implausible "cures" for the disorders to which they were applied. The treatments occasionally may have cured the ailments. Yet, the lack of understanding of what produced changes thwarted major advances in treatment in general. Thus in the application of treatment techniques the importance of understanding why behavior has changed should not be accorded a secondary role. On the contrary, it is as important as achieving the change itself. Failure to understand why change has occurred, that is, the failure to evaluate treatment, has important practical consequences.

If a treatment is evaluated and shown to be responsible for behavior change, it can be used again when needed. When the active ingredient that caused change is known, it can be reapplied with some assurance that it may work again. For example, if delivering praise is shown to increase the appropriate behaviors of a disruptive child, praise can be used later if disruptive behavior recurs, or praise can be used to alter other behaviors that have not been focused on previously. However, if praise was not shown to be the key therapeutic ingredient, it may not have been responsible for change. When treatment is needed again, the reapplication of praise may not be effective. Aside from treating a single individual, it is important to understand what caused behavior change so that treatment can be applied to other individuals. Once a treatment is well understood, it can be applied with some assurance that it will influence behavior. In general, the evaluation of treatment has long-term benefits, both for the individual client and for all other subsequent individuals who might need treatment.

Many individuals have raised questions about the ethics of evaluating treatment (Stolz, 1976). If evaluation or applied research means sacrificing some of the beneficial aspects of treatment for a given client, there certainly is justification for this concern. Obviously, there is an ethical and, in many situations, even legal commitment to provide treatment (Freidman, 1975; Goldiamond, 1975). Evaluation should not interfere with this goal. On the other hand, it is important to mention briefly the ethical question raised by not evaluating treatment. If the goal of treatment is to provide the best possible treatment, that is, the one that effects the most marked and durable changes, evaluation is essential. Without carefully evaluating treatment effects and determining whether treatment was responsible for change, there is no real way of knowing what the most effective treatment is and no way of accumulating knowledge about how to change behavior in the future.

In the area of applied behavior analysis, treatment per se, monitoring of target behaviors before, during, and following treatment, and evaluating treatment are intertwined. It is clear that two of the three factors are necessary for any clinical intervention program. That is, as stated previously by Marholin and Bijou in Chapter 2, target behaviors must be defined in objective terms so that they might actually be observed, measured, and agreed on by those responsible for administering the program. Furthermore, data must be collected prior to initiating treatment to establish a baseline to which treatment can be compared. In addition, target behaviors must be continuously monitored during treatment. Continuous monitoring allows for discarding ineffective treatment strategies and testing of new ones. Finally, behavior after treatment must be monitored so as to assure proper maintenance. Meeting these requirements of treatment satisfy minimal clinical and ethical responsibilities to the client.

For example, a child's behavior might be assessed prior to treatment. A treatment program might then be developed to teach new behaviors and/or to reduce problem behaviors. The child's behavior might also be assessed during treatment to demonstrate that his or her behavior is changing in the desired direction. If it is, treatment would be continued. If it is not, a new treatment program would be developed. Finally, the child's behavior is assessed after treatment to determine if his appropriate behavior had been maintained. Although such an assessment approach assures the clinician that the child's behavior has changed, it says little about why it has changed. In fact, a child may improve after receiving some specific treatment or while treatment is in effect, yet his improvement may have nothing to do with the treatment. To determine whether the treatment *caused* the observed change in behavior, evaluation strategies derived from applied behavior analysis may be used. The purpose of the present chapter is to provide an overview of some of the evaluation strategies used to determine the precise role of treatment in changing behavior. The strategies refer to ways of structuring the treatment situation so that the influence of treatment on the client can be unambiguously determined. These strategies are referred to as *experimental designs*.

PROGRAM EVALUATION
AND EXPERIMENTAL DESIGN

The purpose of experimental design is to determine what accounts for behavior change. It might seem unnecessary to discuss this in the context of treatment, because when a client's behavior changes, the reason usually seems clear. Yet, experimental design is needed to rule out the influence of other factors that might have led to a therapeutic change. For example, treatment might be carried out at home to increase the cooperative social interaction of a "behavior problem" child with his sibling. The child may ordinarily fight with the sibling and avoid all cooperative contact. The child's cooperative play might be observed for a baseline (pretreatment) period. After several days of observation, the parents may provide points to both children whenever they are playing cooperatively in an attempt to increase positive social interaction. The points might be exchangeable for small toys or special privileges such as staying up beyond bedtime for a few minutes. Behavior may change when treatment is introduced. The main question is whether treatment is responsible for change.

A variety of alternative interpretations might be advanced to explain behavior change other than the influence of positive reinforcement. First, extraneous events at school that coincidentally were associated with the onset of the reinforcement program may have improved performance of the disruptive child at home. Second, the physical health of the child may have improved at the time of treatment onset and made him less irritable and obstreperous in general. Third, problems between the parents may have decreased with the onset of treatment and may have led to increases in cooperative play. Fourth, it is possible that the child's initial rate of cooperation was the lowest it had ever been. If the decision to seek treatment was based on that low rate, the rate would almost certainly increase because of the statistical phenomenon termed regression. That is, when things are the worst, they must get better. All sorts of explanations other than the effect of the reinforcement program might be advanced (e.g., an impending birthday or holiday, making new friends, joining a Little League baseball team). The purpose of evaluation is to rule out explanations other than treatment that might account for behavior change. There are several different experimental designs that can be used to identify whether some treatment intervention and not other events occurring in time led to change. In the present chapter reversal, multiple-baseline, and simultaneous-treatment designs are discussed.[1]

ABAB or Reversal Designs

ABAB or reversal designs demonstrate the effect of treatment by alternately presenting and removing treatment over time. As usually conducted, the design begins with assessment of baseline rates of behavior (referred to as the A phase). The purpose of baseline measurement is two-fold. First, baseline data provide an objective measure of the pretreatment level of the behavior that is to be changed. Second, baseline data predict what the level of behavior is likely to be in the immediate future if no treatment were provided. After baseline, treatment is implemented (referred to as B phase). Treatment is continued until behavior changes and reaches a stable level. At this point, treatment usually is withdrawn, and baseline conditions (A phase) are reinstated. Typically, behavior returns or approaches baseline levels of performance. At this time, treatment (B phase) is provided again, which usually results in a return of behavior to the level obtained during the original treatment phase.

The purpose of alternating phases is to determine the cause of behavior change. This is accomplished by assessing behaviors under different conditions (baseline and treatment). The data in each phase serve to describe what behavior is like under a particular set of conditions and to predict what behavior would be like if these conditions remained in effect.

When the conditions are changed, behavior usually deviates from this predicted or projected level of performance. This suggests that the change in conditions from baseline to treatment or from treatment to baseline led to change. To check this, the original conditions in which the prediction was made are reinstated. If the original level of behavior is recovered, this clearly suggests that the intervention led to change. The more frequently behavior is altered as the A and B phases are alternated, the clearer the demonstration.

The ABAB design can be illustrated in a study by Wahler (1969) which focused on the behavior of a 6-year-old boy, named Billy, who consistently failed to comply with the requests of his parents. Routine parental requests to go to bed or to eat certain foods simply were not followed. Observations in the home revealed that both parents responded to Billy's noncompliant behavior by reasoning, arguing with or threatening him. Initially, observers recorded whether Billy was cooperative (complied with a parental request) or was oppositional (did not comply). After 4 days of baseline, treatment was implemented. Treatment consisted of isolating Billy for 5 minutes whenever he failed to comply and providing attention and approval whenever he complied. After 5 days, oppositional behavior decreased. To determine whether treatment was responsible for change, isolation and approval were discontinued for 2 days. Finally, the treatment was again introduced. The results of the program are presented in the upper portion of Figure 1. As shown in the figure, oppositional behavior clearly varied as a function of the introduction and withdrawal of treatment.

As an additional feature of this program, the value of parental praise was measured by having parents praise Billy for dropping marbles into one of two holes in a wooden box. This task was devised to measure the reinforcing value of parental praise. If marble dropping was influenced by praise, this indicated a relatively great value of praise. As evident in the lower portion of Figure 1, the effectiveness or value of praise was higher during treatment than during the baseline and reversal phases.

Variations of the ABAB Design. The ABAB design refers to the manner in which a causal relation between treatment and behavior change is demonstrated. The design is not restricted to four phases in which baseline (A phase) and treatment (B phase) are each administered twice. The design refers merely to reinstating either the baseline or treatment phase at some point in the design. For example, in some cases the design might include only three phases (e.g., ABA). The ABA design might be very convincing, depending on the extent of differences in the level of behavior across phases and whether the second A or reversal phase recovers the original level of baseline performance. The ABA design represents the minimal number of phases needed to meet the requirements of this experimental design.

There are several other variations of the basic reversal design, many of which are beyond the scope of the present chapter (see Barlow & Hersen, 1973; Browning & Stover, 1971). The variations differ along several dimensions, such as how many different treatments are used, what phases begin the study, and what happens during the second A phase. For example, sometimes more than one treatment is implemented. Different treatments might be implemented in cases in which the first treatment (B) does not change behavior or does not achieve the extent of change desired. Rather than implement a return-to-baseline phase, another treatment (C) may be added. Eventually, at some point in the design either baseline or one of the treatment interventions must be reinstated to determine a causal relationship.

Another variation of the design depends on which phase is implemented first. In some cases, the behavioral problem needs to be altered immediately and for practical reasons cannot await baseline assessment. In these cases, the first phase might be treatment, and the design might be represented as a BAB design. The design qualifies as a reversal design, because one of the phases is reinstated.

The final type of variation of this design to be discussed here is determined according to what takes place during the second A phase (baseline). In most cases the treatment is simply withdrawn during this phase so that the original conditions of baseline are restored. During the

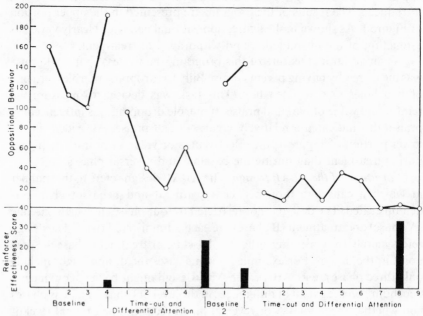

Figure 1

Number of Billy's 10-second oppositional units and parental reinforcer effectiveness scores over baseline and treatment periods.

second A phase it is possible to provide the consequences delivered during treatment on a noncontingent basis. For example, if compliance of a child is reinforced with praise during treatment, in the second A phase praise could be continued, but delivered noncontingently (i.e., independent of behavior). Without contingently praising compliance, behavior is likely to return to baseline or near baseline levels.

Limitations of the ABAB Design. The ABAB design and its variations are used more than any other design in applied operant research (Kazdin, 1975b). Nevertheless, the design has distinct limitations. Initially, and of the greatest importance to practitioners, is the fact that after behavior change has been achieved, baseline conditions must be restored. Thus after treatment has been associated with an improvement in behavior, treatment is withdrawn. When treatment is withdrawn, behavior is likely to revert to its pre-treatment rate. This requirement in the design makes it unappealing in applied work, and rightly so. Often, therapeutic change is obtained only after difficult programming, and staff members do not want to jeopardize the beneficial effects achieved. Moreover, with some behaviors such as self-injury and acts of violence one does not want to increase behavior after improvement has been achieved. The acts may be so dangerous that increasing their performance is to be avoided at all costs. Aside from the practical problem of making behavior worse, there are ethical considerations as well. Moreover, even with less crucial behaviors such as social interaction skills, compliance, and academic achievement, one might prefer not to see behavior get worse after it has improved. If positive behavior changes are achieved, it is difficult to justify withholding treatment for a period when treatment might just as easily be continued.

Aside from practical and ethical considerations, there are other problems with attempting to return behavior to baseline levels. Occasionally, when treatment is withdrawn and baseline conditions are reinstated, behavior does not revert to baseline levels. Without showing a reversal of behavior, one cannot be sure that treatment was responsible for change. It may be that some extraneous event that coincided with the onset of treatment led to change and continued in its control of behavior after treatment was withdrawn.

Of course, there are several reasons why behaviors might be maintained even when treatment is withdrawn. The most obvious one is that when certain behaviors are performed, they may be followed by naturally reinforcing consequences. For example, developing reading skills in children might be maintained because of the reinforcing consequences inherent in the materials themselves (e.g., reading a comic book, baseball cards, or *Playboy Magazine*). Even if treatment were withdrawn, reading might continue at a high rate. Similarly, developing conversation in a withdrawn child might be maintained by peer attention even after a training program was withdrawn. When some behaviors are developed, they seem to be "trapped" or naturally maintained by the environment (Baer & Wolf, 1970). Unfortunately, this turns out to be the exception rather than the rule. Typically, behaviors revert to or approach their baseline level once treatment is withdrawn (cf. Kazdin, 1977c; Marholin, Siegel, & Phillips, 1976; Stokes & Baer, 1977). Overall, the possible problems surrounding the use of a return-to-baseline phase restricts the utility of this design for applied purposes. By requiring a reversal of behavior after improvement has been achieved, the design competes with effecting clinical change (Hartmann & Atkinson, 1973). Fortunately, there are other designs that can demonstrate a causal relation and do not depend on withdrawing treatment.

Multiple-Baseline Designs

The multiple-baseline designs demonstrate a causal relation without withdrawing treatment and returning to baseline levels of performance. The effect of treatment is shown by introducing treatment at different points in time across different baselines. The variations of the design depend on whether treatment is introduced across different behaviors, different individuals, or different situations.

The design is referred to as a multiple-baseline design because data are gathered across two or more baselines. For example, one version of the design is the multiple-baseline across behaviors. In this version of the design, baseline data are gathered across two or more behaviors of a single individual or group of individuals. After each baseline has stabilized, treatment is implemented to change the first behavior. Data continue to be gathered across all behaviors, including those that remain in baseline conditions. When behavior under the treatment condition stabilizes, treatment then is applied to change the second behavior. Data continue to be gathered on all behaviors. Eventually, each of the behaviors are included in treatment in a sequential fashion. Ideally, each behavior changes only as it is included into the experimental contingency and not before. The demonstration depends on showing changes in behavior across two or more baselines. However, the larger the number of baselines across which treatment is implemented, the more convincing the demonstration.

The multiple-baseline design across behaviors is nicely illustrated in a report by Pierce and Risley (1974, Exp. 2) who evaluated the effect of punishment in a community recreation center located in an economically deprived urban area. The participants at the center (over 400 during the course of the project) were primarily male teenagers. The problem at the center was a failure to maintain the facility, as evident in frequent littering of materials, misplacing equipment, and damaging property. Rules were devised by the recreation director that, when violated, resulted in closing the center early for a predetermined period of time. For example, there was a 15-minute loss of time for breaking ping-pong balls or paddles and similar penalties for other undesirable acts. Frequent checks of different violations were made so that the time toward early closing would accumulate on a given day. Although the rules and consequences decreased violations, the director did not consistently enforce the rules.

Pierce and Risley evaluated the effect of consistently enforcing the rules on three undesirable behaviors. Each of these behaviors (littering on the game floor, misplacing the pool rack, and littering in the hall) was assessed daily. During baseline, the director continued to enforce the rules occasionally or only when violations were especially severe. The treatment phase consisted of enforcing the rules consistently so that each infraction resulted in the time loss, as originally planned. Treatment was introduced to alter each behavior at different points in time to meet the requirements of the multiple-baseline design across behaviors. As shown in Figure 2, each of the undesirable responses decreased when the intervention was introduced and not before. A causal relation between the treatment and behavior change is apparent, because behavior change was so clearly associated with the onset of treatment.

Variations of the Multiple-Baseline Design. The multiple-baseline design need not be across behaviors for a given individual or group of. individuals. Baseline data can be gathered for a particular behavior across two or more individuals. In this version, referred to as the *multiple-baseline design across individuals,* baseline data are gathered across several individuals. After the rates of behavior stabilize, treatment is introduced to alter the behavior of one individual while baseline conditions continue for the remaining individuals. Over time, treatment is extended to each individual at different points in time until each one is included in treatment. A causal relation is shown when the behavior of each individual changes when and only when treatment is introduced.

Baseline data also can be gathered for a particular behavior of an individual or group of individuals across two or more situations. For example, obstreperous behavior of a child might be observed across different situations such as in class, on the playground, and at home. In this version, referred to as a *multiple-baseline design across situations or settings,* the intervention is introduced to control behavior in different situations in a sequential fashion. As with the other versions of the design, treatment is extended to control each baseline at different points in time. And, a causal relation is demonstrated if behavior in each situation changes when and only when treatment is introduced.

Limitations of the Multiple-Baseline Design. The multiple-baseline designs are ideal in many situations, because no reversal of behavior is necessary. Thus the designs are well suited to situations in which a return to baseline would be undesirable or perhaps might have no influence on behavior. Also, in many situations the goal is to alter several behaviors or a given behavior across several individuals or situations.

Yet, the designs have problems of their own in evaluating treatment (see Kazdin & Kopel, 1975). The main problem is that implementing treatment to alter one of the baselines may have a generalized effect and carry over to other baselines. Thus baseline data may change before treatment is introduced. For example, in the multiple-baseline design across behaviors, changing one behavior may lead to changes in other behaviors, even though these latter behaviors are not included in treatment (e.g., Maley, Feldman, & Ruskin, 1973; Wahler, 1975). Essentially, there is a generalized

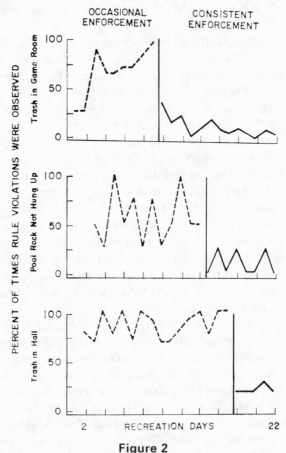

Figure 2
The percentage of time during each 2-hour recreation period that rule violations were observed. (Dashed lines show the period when the recreation director only occasionally enforced rule violations. Solid lines show when every violation was enforced.)

effect across behaviors. This militates against showing that treatment produced change when it was introduced to alter only one behavior.

A similar problem can arise in the design across individuals. Implementing treatment for one individual can alter the behavior of other individuals whose behaviors have not been included in treatment. In many programs there are vicarious effects of reinforcement, so that viewing others receive reinforcing consequences changes one's own behavior (e.g., Christy, 1975; Kazdin, 1973, 1977d). Finally, in the design-across situations it is possible that changing a given behavior in one situation leads to changes of that same behavior in other situations (e.g., Bennett & Maley, 1973; Kifer, Lewis, Green, & Phillips, 1974). Essentially, improvements associated with treatment of behavior in one situation generalize across other situations.

From a practical standpoint, the problems with multiple-baseline designs probably are much less serious than the problems of reversal or ABAB type designs for different reasons. First, extensive research utilizing multiple-baseline designs suggests that a generalized effect of treatment across different baselines is not a frequent problem (Kazdin, 1975a). Many reports have shown that relatively specific effects of treatment occur and that causal relations are readily demonstrated. Second, demonstrating a causal relation does not jeopardize the interests of the client and the goals of achieving clinical change. The design does not create a conflict of improving the client versus demonstrating the influence of treatment, as is usually the case with ABAB designs.

There is another practical advantage that is associated with a multiple-baseline design. The design allows a staff member to introduce treatment on a small scale (e.g., for one behavior or for one individual) and gradually extend treatment to other baselines. This provides an initial test of the effects of treatment and its overall practical feasibility before it is extended on a larger scale. If treatment works on the initial baseline (e.g., behavior), it can be extended to other baselines. If treatment does not change behavior, it can be altered before the program has been widely extended.

Simultaneous-Treatment Design

A major limitation of both reversal and multiple-baseline designs is that they do not easily allow the comparison of different treatments with an individual client. In both designs, two or more treatments can be implemented to change behavior in different phases. Yet, it is difficult to compare these treatments, because one always precedes the other. For example, in an ABCA design, one treatment (B) is implemented before the other (C). It is difficult to determine which is more effective, because they are given in a particular sequence. It may be that C is more (or less) effective than B just because it was the second treatment administered. The order of the different treatments interferes with any conclusions about their relative efficacy.

Occasionally, it is desirable to compare several treatments with a given individual to determine what technique works the best in changing behavior. The goal may be to determine the most effective treatment as quickly as possible and then to implement that treatment to control behavior. One design that is used to compare different treatments with the same individual is called the simultaneous-treatment design (Browning & Stover, 1971; Kazdin, 1977b; McCullough, Cornell, McDaniel, & Mueller, 1974).

The design begins with a baseline phase. After the baseline rate of behavior stabilizes, two or more treatments are implemented in the same phase. Although the treatments are implemented in the same phase, they are implemented under different conditions. For example, two different treatments might be implemented on a given day to alter a child's behavior. One treatment might be implemented in the morning, while the other might be implemented in the afternoon. If a child performed the desired behavior, it might be followed with one intervention (e.g., praise) in the morning and another (e.g., tokens) in the afternoon for that day. Of course, it may be that different rates of behavior are associated with mornings and afternoons independently of the treatments. Thus the different treatments must be distributed or balanced across morning and afternoon periods. Hence on the second day of the treatment phase the order of the treatments might be reversed (i.e., praise in the afternoon and tokens in the morning).

Throughout the treatment phase the treatments must be balanced across all conditions of administration so that the different effects of the two (or more) treatments can be separated from influences such as time of the day and staff members who administer treatment (e.g., Kazdin, 1977a). The treatment phase is continued while the conditions under which different treatments occur are varied. When behavior stabilizes under the separate treatments, this phase can be terminated. Sometimes a final phase is used in which the more (or most) effective treatment is implemented all of the time.

The simultaneous-treatment design is illustrated in a project designed to improve the classroom behavior of a 7-year old retarded child (IQ = 78), named Max, enrolled in a special education classroom (Kazdin & Geesey, 1977). Max was inattentive in class and infrequently focused on the in-seat work assigned to him. After baseline observations of attentive behavior were made during two separate periods each day, two variations of a reinforcement program were compared in improving attentive behavior. During both treatments Max received points for working on his in-seat assignments and attending to the lesson. The differences in the treatments were in how the reinforcers were dispensed. One treatment consisted of exchanging the points for back-up reinforcers (e.g., special privileges at lunch) for *himself*. Whenever his point card achieved a predetermined point total, he could cash them in for a back-up reinforcer. The other treatment consisted of exchanging the points for the same back-up reinforcers for *himself and the entire class*. Whenever his point card reached a predetermined total, he could cash the points in for reinforcers that everyone in the class received. Max earned points on each card during the two separate periods each day. The periods were varied daily so that he earned for himself or the entire class at different times throughout the treatment phase. After several days, it appeared that earning for the class as a whole led to greater attentiveness. Thus this procedure was implemented across each of the observation periods for all of the remaining days of the project.

The results of the program on Max's attentive behavior can be seen in Figure 3. The upper portion of the figure shows the overall effect of the program without separating the effects of the different treatments. Behavior improved in the treatment phase independently of the different treatments. The lower portion of the figure shows the effects of the two different treatments during the treatment phase. The results show that when Max earned reinforcers for the entire class his attentive behavior was higher than when he earned only for himself. These results suggest that earning for the class was more effective. This conclusion is supported further in the final phase, when earning for the entire class during each period improved behavior further.

Limitations of the Simultaneous Treatment Design. There are few limitations of this design. First, although the design can examine any number of treatments during the treatment phase, it is difficult for practical reasons to study more than two or three interventions. The different interventions must be balanced across all the conditions of administration (e.g., time of the day, staff members). This requires an extremely large number of days. Second, and related, if there are a large number of treatments, it may be difficult for a client to make a discrimination across the interventions. The client may not respond to the different contingencies simply because of the complexity of the program and because it is difficult to discern which treatment is occurring under the different conditions.

A third potential limitation concerns the effects of different interventions. Because the different treatments are administered concurrently (i.e., in the same phase), their effects may be somewhat different from what they would be if they were administered by themselves. Thus differences between two treatments studied concurrently may partially result from being administered together.

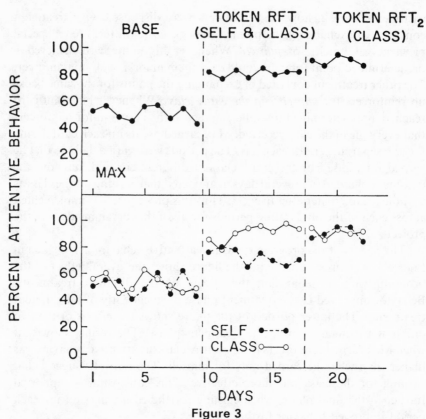

Figure 3

Attentive behavior of Max across experimental conditions. Baseline (base)—no
treatment intervention. RTFT—implementation of the token program where
tokens earned could purchase events for himself (self) or the entire class (class).
RFT$_2$—implementation of the class exchange intervention across both time
periods. (The upper panel presents the overall data collapsed across time
periods and interventions. The lower panel presents the data according to the
time periods across which the interventions were balanced, although the
interventions were presented only in the last two phases.)

WHEN TO CONDUCT PROGRAM EVALUATION

Program evaluation has and continues to be an integral compenent of
many leading child-treatment programs such as Achievement Place (see
Willner, Braukmann, Kirigin, & Wolf, Chapter 9), the Camarillo-
Neuropsychiatric Institute at UCLA (Ulmer, 1976), the Center at Oregon
for Research in the Behavioral Education of the Handicapped (Patterson,
Cobb, & Ray, 1973), the Wisconsin Child Treatment Center (Browning &
Stover, 1971), Spaulding Youth Center (Hively & Duncan, 1975), the
Kansas Neurological Institute (e.g., Guess & Baer, 1973), Project MORE

(Lent, 1975), Father Flanagan's Boy's Home (e.g., Fixsen, Note 1), and several others. However, the question often arises in service agencies about the necessity of systematically evaluating every program to determine cause-and-effect relationships.

As noted earlier, program evaluation is necessary to reapply treatment techniques that have been demonstrated as effective with a particular individual with some assurance that they may work again. Moreover, it is important to understand what caused behavior change so that treatment can be applied to other individuals. Given unlimited resources, it would be ideal, of course, to evaluate systematically every treatment program by using either one or a combination of the reversal, multiple-baseline, or simultaneous-treatment designs. Unfortunately, in service programs the ideal is far from reality. Therefore, systematically evaluating every treatment program may be impossible. When it is impractical to evaluate a treatment using an appropriate experimental design, one may choose treatment techniques that have been systematically evaluated previously by consulting various applied journals such as the *Journal of Applied Behavior Analysis, Behavior Therapy, Journal of Behavior Therapy and Experimental Psychiatry, Behaviour Research and Therapy*, and *Behavior Modification*. Of course, after selecting a specific treatment technique, one would still have to meet the criterion of assessing the client's behavior before, during, and after treatment. Monitoring treatment progress would not demonstrate conclusively that the selected treatment technique caused a change in the client's behavior, but at least would verify that change occurred.

Admittedly, evaluating every treatment program by using an experimental design may prove difficult. On the contrary, it is important to evaluate systematically as many different treatment procedures in a program as possible. Although selecting sound treatment procedures that have proven effective by others may be effective in most situations, it also may lead to serious problems. For example, a token economy program may be selected as the treatment of choice in a community-based, residential program for delinquent children. A client might enter the program on Monday. A baseline might then be taken on the number of aggressive statements on Tuesday, Wednesday, and Thursday. On Friday, an individualized token economy might be instituted for the client, with heavy emphasis on reinforcing appropriate nonaggressive language. The frequency of aggressive statements may then decrease. The treatment staff would undoubtedly attribute the client's reduced aggressive language to the token economy. However, it is possible that the other students in the program impressed on the newly admitted youth that aggressive language would lead to the staff's deciding to reject the youth from the program and result in his being sent to a state training school. Therefore, the youth might refrain from using aggressive language in the presence of program staff to avoid a highly negative consequence. In other words, the aversive contingency and not the token economy would be responsible for the change in the youth's behavior. Rather than teaching more desired behavior, the program would merely be temporarily suppressing undesirable behavior. Unfortunately, without systematically evaluating the effects of the treatment program (i.e., token economy), program staff would be unaware of the cause of behavior change. Moreover, since the changed behavior would be desirable from their viewpoint, it is likely that the staff would continue to follow the ineffective token economy procedures even though they were unrelated to client behavior.

In addition to fulfilling immediate individual clinical responsibilities, periodic program evaluation is important for a service program's growth and maintenance. Many well-structured, data-based service programs often seem to "burn-out" after several years of operation. Frequently, innovative programs appear as an adjunct to various federal and state research projects. In their initial stage of development, various program components are carefully assessed, using experimental designs as discussed earlier. After the research grant runs out and/or the developers of the program leave, those remaining often tend to follow dogmatically the procedures last developed. Program evaluation ceases, while clinical service continues. This often results in a static program.

Any clinical program should continually change as its clients, problems, and society changes. A program lacking adequate and continuous evaluative components is unlikely either to recognize the need for change or to know the proper direction change should take. In addition to providing the most effective treatment, program evaluation can become highly reinforcing to the staff involved in the applied research effort. In contrast to the dynamic program emphasing continuous program evaluation, the static program, in which staff tend to carry out rote programming tends toward extinction of appropriate program staff and client behavior alike.

EVALUATING BEHAVIOR CHANGE

The experimental designs help determine whether treatment is responsible for behavior change. It is important in applied work to know the events that led to change for many reasons, as noted earlier. There are, of course, additional questions of interest in applied work. A major question, once behavior change is achieved, is whether change is important. It is quite possible to change behavior and to show that treatment led to change. Yet, the effects of treatment may not be very important. For example, a child who hits himself or others 100 times per day may receive treatment such as the delivery of reinforcing consequences for periods of nonhitting. The effects of treatment might be evident by showing that hitting decreased to 75 times per day. Although this change is easily seen in the data, the question arises whether this change is clinically important.

In applied behavior analysis an attempt is made to alter behavior to such an extent that the client is noticeably improved and that his or her functioning in the "real world" is altered (Marholin & Phillips, 1976). This is a difficult dimension to measure. Whether someone's behavior has been sufficiently improved to affect their daily functioning may be a matter of opinion. Individuals who normally interact with the client (e.g., parents, teachers, peers) may need to judge whether the client's behavior is changed and no longer requires treatment.

In many programs, assessment of the target behavior is supplemented by the opinions solicited of other individuals who have not been involved in the program. The opinions are solicited to determine whether the behaviors studied or the changes achieved are important (e.g., Briscoe, Hoffman, & Bailey, 1975; Maloney & Hopkins, 1973; Quilitch, 1975). For example, in one program conversational skills of predelinquent girls were increased (Minkin, Braukmann, Minkin, Timbers, Timbers, Fixsen, Phillips, & Wolf, 1976). More specifically, the program was designed to increase the frequency with which these girls asked questions and provided positive feedback to others with whom they were conversing. These specific behaviors changed. Of course, change in these behaviors may not necessarily be important. Yet, adults not involved in the project judged the overall conversational ability of the girls before and after treatment and showed the latter to be superior. Thus the program affected the evaluations of overall conversational skills.

Occasionally, the importance of behavior change is measured by comparing the behavior of the client after treatment with the behavior of peers who are within normative levels of performance. For example, Patterson (1974) demonstrated that behavioral intervention in the home and at school altered deviant child behavior. Programs with individual families and teachers decreased aggressive and disruptive behavior (e.g., hitting, whining, yelling, and negativism) and improved appropriate behaviors (e.g., studying and complying with instructions). To answer the question whether the changes achieved were important, additional data were collected on the level of disruptive behaviors of individuals who were *not* identified as behavior problems but were similar in other respects (e.g., socioeconomic status, age). The results revealed that the levels of deviant behavior of the treated group fell within normative levels. Prior to treatment, however, the deviant behavior of the treated group had surpassed (i.e., was worse than) their peers. These results show that the changes made were of applied importance. Several other studies have assessed normative levels of behavior to determine whether treatment improves a client to bring him within these limits (e.g., Minkin et al., 1976; Stahl, Thomson, Leitenberg, & Hasazi, 1974; Street, Walker, Greenwood, Todd, & Hops, Note 2).

SUMMARY

This chapter describes methods of program evaluation utilized in applied behavior analysis. Applied behavior analysis combines the application of techniques to change behaviors of social, educational and therapeutic significance with a methodology for understanding the reasons for the subsequent changes in behavior. Although a thorough functional analysis of behavior provides the empirically-minded clinician with an opportunity to assess whether a change in client behavior has occurred when treatment is initiated, it does not provide information about whether the treatment itself caused the observed behavior changes. Understanding the cause of behavior change is important for two reasons. First, it allows for the application of the active ingredient of treatment at a latter time if problem behavior recurs. Second, aside from treating a single individual, it is important to understand what caused behavior change so that treatment can be applied to other individuals.

Three major experimental designs have been presented which can be used to identify whether some specific treatment intervention and not other events account for client behavior change. The reversal or ABAB design demonstrates the effect of treatment by alternately presenting and removing treatment over time. If the reversal design is successful in altering behavior as baseline (A) to treatment (B) conditions are alternated, it has demonstrated that the treatment caused behavior change. Problems with using ABAB designs include ethical considerations of returning to baseline conditions after behavior improved and the failure of behavior to return to baseline levels during the reversal phases.

The multiple-baseline designs demonstrate a causal relationship without withdrawing treatment and returning to baseline levels of performance. A multiple-baseline design relies on introducing treatment at different points in time to demonstrate a causal relationship between treatment and behavior change. There are three commonly used multiple-baseline designs: multiple-baseline across behaviors, individuals, and settings. The primary problem with multiple-baseline designs is that treatment effects may generalize to other as yet untreated behaviors, individuals, and/or settings. However, a practical advantage of the multiple-baseline design is that it allows a staff member to introduce a specific treatment technique on a small scale (e.g., for one behavior) and gradually extend the treatment to other behaviors if treatment is initially successful. If the treatment does not prove successful, it can be altered before it has been widely extended.

The final design discussed was the simultaneous-treatment design. It provides for the comparison of different treatments with an individual client. The design begins with a baseline phase. After the baseline phase, two or more treatments are implemented in the same phase but under different conditions. For example, one treatment (e.g., token reinforcement) might be implemented in the morning, while the other treatment (e.g., primary reinforcement) might be implemented in the afternoon. The order of presentation of treatment conditions (i.e., morning and afternoon) would then be systematically varied, and the child's performance compared under both treatment conditions.

Although ideally program evaluation should accompany every treatment program to ensure the client that he is receiving the best possible treatment, practical considerations often make this difficult. When careful evaluation is not feasible, treatment procedures may be selected from the growing literature that has shown specific techniques to be effective across several individuals. Of course, after choosing a specific treatment technique, it is still necessary to monitor client behavior before, during, and after treatment. Although monitoring treatment progress would not demonstrate conclusively that the selected treatment caused a change in the client's behavior, it would, however, show that the client's behavior did, in fact, change. In sound clinical practice as many treatment programs as possible should be systematically evaluated. Furthermore, a systematic program evaluation is an important component of a dynamic service program; a lack of evaluation often leads to a static and ineffectual program. Finally, in addition to determining if treatment is responsible for behavior change, it is essential to ascertain whether the change is an important one to the individual. This may be done by asking individuals in the client's environment if a significant change has occurred. Also, posttreatment levels of behavior may be compared with the normative level of behavior of the client's peer group.

REFERENCE NOTES

1. Fixsen, D. L. Personal communication (with second author), May 1975.
2. Street, A., Walker, H. M., Greenwood, C. R., Todd, N. R., & Hops, H. Normative peer interaction rate as a baseline for follow-up evaluation. Paper presented at meeting of the American Psychological Association, Washington, D. C., September 1976.

REFERENCES

Baer, D. M., & Wolf, M. M. The entry into natural communities of reinforcement. In R. Ulrich, T. Strachnik, & J. Mabry, (Eds.), *Control of human behavior* (*Vol. 2*). Glenview, Illinois: Scott, Foresman, 1970.

Barlow, D. H., & Hersen, M. Single-case experimental designs. *Archives of General Psychiatry*, 1973, *29*, 319–325.

Bennett, P. S., & Maley, R. S. Modification of interactive behaviors in chronic mental patients. *Journal of Applied Behavior Analysis*, 1973, *6*, 609–620.

Briscoe, R. V., Hoffman, D. B. & Bailey, J. S. Behavioral community psychology: Training a community board to problem solve. *Journal of Applied Behavior Analysis*, 1975, *8*, 157–168.

Browning, R. M., & Stover, D. O. *Behavior modification in child treatment: An experimental and clinical approach*. Chicago: Aldine-Atherton, 1971.

Christy, P. R. Does the use of tangible rewards with individual children affect peer observers? *Journal of Applied Behavior Analysis*, 1975, *8*, 187–196.

Friedman, P. R. Legal regulation of applied behavior analysis in mental institutions and prisons. *Arizona Law Review*, 1975, *17*, 39–104.

Goldiamond, I. Singling out behavior modification for legal regulation: Some effects on patient care, psychotherapy, and research in general. *Arizona Law Review*, 1975, *17*, 105–126.

Guess, D., & Baer, D. M. An analysis of individual differences in generalization between receptive and productive language in retarded children. *Journal of Applied Behavior Analysis*, 1973, *6*, 311–329.

Hartmann, D. P., & Atkinson, C. Having your cake and eating it too: A note on some apparent contradictions between therapeutic achievements and design requirements in $N = 1$ studies. *Behavior Therapy*, 1973, *4*, 589–591.

Hersen, M., & Barlow, D. H. *Single case experimental designs: Strategies for studying behavior change*. New York: Pergamon, 1976.

Hively, W., & Duncan, A. D. Reciprocal and self-management in educational communities. In T. Thompson & W. S. Dockens III (Eds.), *Applications of behavior modification*. New York: Academic Press, 1975.

Kazdin, A. E. The effect of vicarious reinforcement on attentive behavior in the classroom. *Journal of Applied Behavior Analysis*, 1973, *6*, 71–78.

Kazdin, A. E. *Behavior modification in applied settings*. Homewood, Ill.: Dorsey Press, 1975a.

Kazdin, A. E. Characteristics and trends in applied behavior analysis. *Journal of Applied Behavior Analysis*, 1975b, *8*, 332.

Kazdin, A. E. The impact of applied behavior analysis on diverse areas of research. *Journal of Applied Behavior Analysis*, 1975c, *8*, 213–229.

Kazdin, A. E. The influence of behavior preceding a reinforced response on behavior change in the classroom. *Journal of Applied Behavior Analysis*, 1977a, *10*, 299–310.

Kazdin, A. E. Methodology of applied behavior analysis. In T. A. Brigham & A. C. Catania (Eds.), *The handbook of applied behavior research: Social and instructional processes*. New York: Irvington Press/Halstead Press, 1977b.

Kazdin, A. E. *The token economy: A review and evaluation*. New York: Plenum, 1977c.

Kazdin, A. E. Vicarious reinforcement and direction of behavior change in the classroom. *Behavior Therapy*, 1977d, *8*, 57–63.

Kazdin, A. E., & Kopel, S. A. On resolving ambiguities of the multiple-baseline design: Problems and recommendations. *Behavior Therapy*, 1975, *6*, 601–608.

Kazdin, A. E., & Geesey, S. Simultaneous treatment design comparisons of the effects of earning reinforcers for one's peers versus for oneself. *Behavior Therapy*, 1977, *8*, 682–693.

Kifler, R. E., Lewis, M. A., Green, D. A., & Phillips, E. L. Training predelinquent youths and their parents to negotiate conflict situations. *Journal of Applied Behavior Analysis*, 1974, *7*, 357–364.

Lent, J. R. Teaching daily living skills. In J. M. Kauffman & J. S. Payne (Eds.) *Mental retardation: Introduction and personal perspectives*. Columbus, Ohio: Charles E. Merrill, 1975.

Maley, R. F., Feldman, G. L., & Ruskin, R. S. Evaluation of patient improvement in a token economy treatment program. *Journal of Abnormal Psychology*, 1973, *82*, 141–144.

Maloney, K. B., & Hopkins, B. L. The modification of sentence structure and its relationship to subjective judgments of creativity in writing. *Journal of Applied Behavior Analysis*, 1973, *6*, 425–433.

Marholin II, D., & Phillips, D. Methodological issues in psychopharmacological research: Chlorpromazine—A case in point. *American Journal of Orthopsychiatry*, 1976, *46*, 477–495.

Marholin II, D., Siegel, L. J., & Phillips, D. Treatment and transfer: A search for empirical procedures. In M. Hersen, R. M. Eisler, & P. M. Miller (Eds.), *Progress in behavior modification, Vol. 3*. New York: Academic, 1976.

McCullough, J. P., Cornell, J. E., McDaniel, M. H., & Mueller, R. K. Utilization of the simultaneous treatment design to improve student behavior in a first-grade classroom. *Journal of Consulting and Clinical Psychology*, 1974, *42*, 288–292.

Minkin, N., Braukmann, C. J., Minkin, B. L., Timbers, G. D., Timbers, B. J., Fixsen, D. L., Phillips, E. L., & Wolf, M. M. The social validation and training of conversational skills. *Journal of Applied Behavior Analysis*, 1976, *9*, 127–139.

Patterson, G. R. Interventions for boys with conduct problems: Multiple settings, treatments, and criteria. *Journal of Consulting and Clinical Psychology*, 1974, *42*, 471–481.

Patterson, G. R., Cobb, J. A., & Ray, R. S. A social engineering technology for retraining the families of aggressive boys. In H. E. Adams & I. P. Unikel (Eds.), *Issues and trends in behavior therapy*. Springfield, Ill.: C. C. Thomas, 1973.

Pierce, C. H., & Risley, T. R. Recreation as a reinforcer: Increasing membership and decreasing disruptions in an urban recreation center. *Journal of Applied Behavior Analysis*, 1974, *7*, 403–411.

Quilitch, H. R. A comparison of three staff-management procedures. *Journal of Applied Behavior Analysis*, 1975, *8*, 59–66.

Ricks, F. A. Training program evaluators. *Professional Psychology*, 1976, *7*, 339–343.

Shapiro, A. K. Placebo effects in medicine, psychotherapy, and psychoanalysis. In A. E. Bergin, & S. L. Garfield (Eds.), *Handbook of psychotherapy and behavior change: An empirical analysis*. New York: Wiley, 1971.

Stahl, J. R., Thomson, L. E., Leitenberg, H., & Hasazi, J. E. Establishment of praise as a conditioned reinforcer in socially unresponsive psychiatric patients, *Journal of Abnormal Psychology*, 1974, *83*, 488–496.

Stokes, T. F., & Baer, D. M. An implicit technology of generalization. *Journal of Applied Behavior Analysis*, 1977, *10*, 349–367.

Stolz, S. B. Evaluation of therapeutic efficacy of behavior modification in a community setting. *Behaviour Research and Therapy*, 1976, *14*, 479–481.

Ulmer, R. A. *On the development of a token economy mental hospital treatment program*. New York: Halstead Press, 1976.

Wahler, R. G. Oppositional children: A quest for parental reinforcement control. *Journal of Applied Behavior Analysis*, 1969, *2*, 159–170.

Wahler, R. G. Some structural aspects of deviant child behavior. *Journal of Applied Behavior Analysis*, 1975, *8*, 27–42.

Weiss, C. H. The politicization of evaluation research. *Journal of Social Issues*, 1970, *26*, 57–68.

NOTE

1. The present chapter provides an overview of select experimental designs in applied behavior analysis. For greater detail, the reader is referred to other sources (Hersen & Barlow, 1976; Kazdin, 1977b).

Part II
Applications
to Child Psychopathology

Treating Children in Group Settings
TECHNIQUES FOR INDIVIDUALIZING BEHAVIORAL PROGRAMS[1]

David Marholin II and Elizabeth T. McInnis

Although all psychologists, social workers, and other child care professionals profess interest in their clients as individuals, in practice, many tend to apply the same treatment procedures to individuals displaying very diverse problems (Emery & Marholin, 1977). This may be especially true when children are treated in group settings.

One of the most salient features of a behavior modification approach to treatment is the emphasis placed on a very careful analysis of the individual's problem(s), along with a tailoring of treatment procedures to specific problem(s) presented by that individual (Bijou & Redd, 1975; Hersen, 1976; Marholin & Bijou, 1977). This is not to say that commonalities among people do not exist or that there are not general principles that serve to generate similar treatment strategies. The behavior therapist, however, takes the position that before a treatment strategy can be formulated and subsequently tested, an individual analysis of the client's problem must occur (see Marholin & Bijou, Chapter 2).

Unfortunately, group treatment settings such as residential centers, group homes, and special schools tend not to gear their programs to the development of individualized treatment strategies. This is true even for many that label themselves as behavior modification programs (Emery & Marholin, 1977). The practical realities of group settings make it difficult to operate individual programs. Undoubtedly, it is much easier to administer, train, and supervise staff if the program procedures are uniform and limited in number. Unless staff are really committed to the clinical necessity of treating individuals rather than groups, practical demands will prevail, and group treatment procedures will likely result. The fact that individualized programs are difficult to manage in group settings does not mean they are impossible. The thrust of this chapter is to outline procedures involved in generating individual programs and discuss how they might be carried out in a group setting. Specific examples of actual programs are included.

Regardless of the type of setting in which treatment is to take place, plans for child behavior therapy generally include four steps: (1) setting the behavioral objectives to be achieved, (2) preparing to begin treatment at the child's present level of competence (baseline), (3) devising a record-keeping or data-collection procedure, and finally, (4) applying the therapeutic technique (Bijou & Redd, 1975). Steps (1) and (2) are discussed thoroughly by Marholin and Bijou (Chapter 2) and Heads (Chapter 13). Regarding step (3), we need only to reiterate that record-keeping or monitoring procedures utilizing objectively defined units are an indispensible part of this type of therapy. As described by Marholin and Bijou, if the data from running accounts of the treatment program should indicate little or no change in behavior toward desired goals, the therapist is cued to modify his procedures. "Typically, procedural alterations mean adjustment of some component of the program, not its abandonment for a new one" (Bijou, 1976). Systematic monitoring of progress provides information on when the behavioral goals have been attained. Step (4), applying the therapeutic techniques to individual behaviors, is the main substance of this chapter.

The treatment of a child's problem(s) usually involves one or more of the following strategies: (1) weakening inappropriate behavior that may be aversive to others and strengthening alternative prosocial (appropriate or desirable) behavior; (2) substituting shy, withdrawn, or phobic behavior with prosocial behavior; (3) extending and elaborating skills and abilities; and (4) bringing behavior under appropriate stimulus control.

Discussions with the child regarding identification of problems and communication of expectations for behavioral change have not generally proved sufficient to bring about desired changes in behavior (Levitt, 1963). Although discussion may prove to be an important component of treatment, it must be accompanied by a carefully arranged behavioral intervention program. The techniques and procedures of the actual program will vary, of course, depending on the target behavior(s), age and functional level of the child, treatment setting, and staff-to-child ratio. These might include such techniques as shaping, prompting, modeling, role-playing, behavioral rehearsal, systematic desensitization, and training in self-management skills. These methods have been presented in numerous articles (cf., Bijou & Redd, 1975; Birnbrauer, Burchard, & Burchard, 1970) and books (Gelfand & Hartmann, 1975; Nay, 1976; O'Leary & Wilson, 1975; Rimm & Masters, 1974; Ross, 1974) and are not described here. Instead, our focus is on the individually selected motivational techniques (contingent reinforcement and punishment) which are the basis for any adjunctive therapeutic procedure. To bring about behavior change successfully, a child must learn that certain behaviors, when performed at the right time and place, will lead to positive consequences (reinforcement), and that other behaviors will either not result in any positive consequence or in some cases may lead to an undesirable consequence (punishment). The reinforcement and punishment components of a treatment program function as the motivational mechanism leading to the desired change in behavior. This represents another application of an old friend, the Law of Effect.

Structuring a treatment program so that the consequences of desired behavior are consistently reinforced is critical. In too many cases an a priori assumption is made regarding the reinforcing properties of particular events intended as reinforcers. Certain consequences such as praise, candy, and recess are generally regarded as being positive or reinforcing consequences for most children. It cannot, however, be assumed that they will function that way for any given child. In fact, many children are referred for treatment because they do not seem to be motivated by those events that function as motivators for most children (Herbert, Pinkston, Hayden, Sajwaj, Pinkston, Gordua, & Jackson, 1973; Marholin, Siegel, & Phillips, 1976; Wahler, 1969). A mechanism for individualizing the reinforcing consequences must, therefore, be built into any behavior modification system. In group settings this has generally been achieved by employing a "token economy" system (Ayllon & Azrin, 1968; Kazdin, 1975, 1977; Kazdin & Bootzin, 1972; O'Leary & Drabman, 1971). In a token system, some tangible but neutral item, such as a strip of plastic, poker chip, coin, star, point, or checkmark, is earned for the performance of desired behaviors. These "tokens" are then used as a medium of exchange, enabling the child to obtain those things which are most desirable, that is, motivating.

Technically speaking, tokens are generalized reinforcers, because they can be exchanged for a variety of reinforcing events often referred to as back-up reinforcers (Ferster, Culbertson, & Perrott-Boren, 1975). In a token economy program, tokens function in a manner similar to money in a national economy (Kagel & Winett, 1972). Tokens are earned and used to purchase various back-ups, including goods and services. There are two things one must consider in developing a token economy for therapeutic purposes. First, it is vitally important to make the target behavior(s) on which tokens are contingent as explicit as possible. Second, it is necessary to specify the rate of exchange of tokens for back-up reinforcers so it is clear how many tokens are required to purchase various reinforcers. Since tokens have no reinforcing property of their own, they need to be *established* as conditioned reinforcers. For some populations (e.g., normal-intelligence adults, adolescents, and school-aged children) it is sufficient merely to inform them that tokens can be exchanged for various back-ups. Following an explanation, the tokens take on immediate reinforcing value as long as they are periodically exchanged for other reinforcers. For individuals whose behavior is not controlled by instructions about the value of the tokens, it is necessary systematically to teach them the relationship between tokens and various back-up reinforcers. This may be accomplished by first presenting several tokens noncontingently and allowing the individual to trade his tokens immediately for some back-up reinforcer. For example, a retarded child may be given a few tokens before "cookie and milk time." A few seconds after receiving the tokens he might give them to his teacher in exchange for cookies and milk. By consistently pairing the tokens with back-up reinforcers, their value is established.

Token systems of reinforcement offer several noteworthy advantages over other types of reinforcement delivery systems, especially when employed in a group treatment milieu. First, tokens are "potent reinforcers and can often maintain behavior at a higher level than other conditioned reinforcers such as praise, approval, and feedback" (Kazdin, 1975, p. 129). A second advantage of tokens is that they bridge the time period between the desired response and back-up reinforcement. In other words, if a reinforcer (e.g., an activity) can not practically be delivered after a particular desirable behavior, tokens can be delivered immediately and used to purchase a back-up reinforcer later. Third, tokens being exchangeable for a variety of things are not apt to lose their reinforcing power through repeated administration (satiation effect). Fourth, since tokens are not consumed (e.g., as with food) or do not require performance of behaviors that may be incompatible with the target response (e.g., participating in a special activity), they may be easily administered without interrupting the target behavior. Fifth, and perhaps most important for group applications of behavior modification, tokens permit administering a single reinforcer to individuals who have different reinforcer preferences. Sixth, tokens permit parceling out other reinforcers (e.g., activities and privileges) which might have to be otherwise earned in an all-or-none fashion. That is, a number of tokens can be earned toward the purchase of a large back-up reinforcer.

Although most token economy programs allow individual selection of reinforcers, they are generally organized on a group-wide basis. The group system is generally adopted to handle some of the economic issues which confront a token system. For example, to set a rate of exchange for the tokens (prices) the economy may be established as a closed one, that is, the number of tokens which can be earned are limited so that prices may be established. Since it is generally easier for the staff if there is a single price for a given item or activity (e.g., a candy bar = 5 tokens, a television program = 10 tokens), the number of tokens each child can earn during the day is generally standardized. If this were not the case, some children would have less purchasing power (be poor) in relation to others. In fact, many token systems go one step further and specify that all children will earn tokens for certain behaviors (e.g., everyone gets a token for doing homework and tooth brushing). However, this does and perhaps should not have to be the case. Indeed, if one assumes that children are referred for specific problem behaviors, one would expect that at least some behaviors required for token earnings would be individualized (Emery & Marholin, 1977).

One thing is certain: the most motivating treatment program will not produce change in the child unless the program is carefully designed. In designing the program, one may select components from three basic procedures: (1) Reinforcement may be employed to increase desired behavior. (2) One of three punishment procedures may be used to decrease problem behaviors: (a) extinction or ignoring, (b) time out from reinforcement, and (c) response cost or loss of a reinforcer. (3) A clear, fair, and honest contingency contract in the form of a consequence agreement between the behavior therapist and the client may be written.

In subsequently carrying out the program, the following principles of effective usage should be kept in mind: (1) Identify prerequisite skills and remediate deficits. In progressing toward a treatment goal, it is important to select a prerequisite behavior to build on. (2) Shape in small steps. Reinforce approximations of desired behavior ("Shape, don't rape!") (3) Deliver reinforcing and punishing consequences as close in time as possible to the behaviors responsible for them. (4) Prompt and model appropriate behaviors. Demonstrate and reinforce approximations to the desired behavior. (5) Gradually raise requirements for reinforcement to occur. Reinforce small improvements. When a behavioral criterion is infrequently met, it should be broken down into smaller steps so that the child can be successful about 90% of the time. (6) Require mastery at one level before proceeding to the next. (7) Employ aversive punishment procedures (e.g., time out, response cost) as a last resort. *Never* use any aversive punishment technique without a simultaneous reinforcement program. (8) Attend to the consequences of the child's behavior at all times and in all situations.

Since the principles listed are far from exhaustive, the reader is referred to Birnbrauer (Chapter 3), Nay (1976), Tharp and Wetzel (1969), and Whaley and Mallot (1971) for additional coverage of the basic principles for developing and carrying out an individualized treatment program.

Consistency in implementing any reinforcement system is a critical component of these principles and an important variable in the success of any behavior change program. Programs implemented on a group-wide basis have the advantage of being readily implemented in a consistent fashion. The fact that consistency is sometimes achieved at the cost of individualization (e.g., selected group target behaviors, standardized token earning and pricing) is the price that many clinicians feel they must pay when children are treated in group setting. Although it is not easy, it is possible to achieve an almost totally individualized program that can be consistently implemented by the treatment staff (Browning & Stover, 1971; Marholin, Plienis, Harris, & Marholin, 1975; Monkman, 1972; Wagner & Breitmeyer, 1974). To implement such a system, some mechanism must be established to communicate program information effectively (individual behavioral criteria, verbal prompts, time-out and extinction procedures) to the staff. Since individualized programs are constantly changing, written instructions in the form of case notes or treatment plans prove unwieldly because they need frequent updating and require that staff constantly "memorize" changing procedures. One solution to the problem of conveying individualized treatment information was developed on a 15-bed residential unit for behavior-problem children (aged 5–14) operated by the Herman Adler Center in Champaign, Illinois (McInnis, Note 1; McInnis & Marholin, 1977). Central to this system is the use of a "mark sheet" which provides both a means of communicating program information as well as a method for reinforcing individual target behaviors. A "mark sheet" is simply a piece of paper that contains (in abbreviated form) all the information necessary to implement a child's individual program. The sheet indicates the target behaviors the child must perform to receive a unit of reinforcement (a mark), how many units of reinforcement can be given for each behavior (the number of boxes on the sheet), the prices he must pay for various back-up reinforcers, and any spending restrictions, such as marks earned for helping another person being exchanged only for home visits.

Whenever the child performs one of the specified target behaviors, a mark is placed in the appropriate box on the sheet and the child is praised for his accomplishment. The number of boxes appearing in each of the target areas indicates the number of marks that can be earned for that behavior. This enables the system to be structured in an individualized closed manner and provides a mechanism whereby schedules of reinforcement (the frequency with which a behavior is reinforced) can be taken into account.

Every child is given a new mark sheet each morning and is responsible for keeping it with him all day. Loss of the sheet results in a loss of the opportunity to earn and spend the reinforcers. Experience indicates that even the youngest (5 years old), lowest functioning (IQ = 30) child on the unit quickly learned to assume this responsibility. Staff responsible for implementing the program are not assigned to specific children but rather to groups of children or activities. For example, a staff member assigned to supervise a meal would ask to see each child's mark sheet and then carry out the program as indicated on each sheet. One child might receive mark reinforcement for using utensils properly, another might be reinforced for not stealing food, a third for appropriate conversation, and perhaps the others might not receive specific reinforcement for any meal behavior. Specification of mark reinforcement for target behaviors does not limit staff interaction to these activities alone. The staff member would also be able to praise any appropriate behavior and interact socially with all of the children.

Whenever marks are spent, they are blocked out with a felt-tip pen, and a notation is made on the sheet indicating what items or privileges were purchased. At the end of the day the sheets are collected, leaving a complete record of which behaviors were reinforced, how often they were reinforced, how many marks were spent, and what reinforcers were purchased. The information, thus provided, enables staff to monitor all 'facets of the program. The earning data can be used as a rough index of behavior change, and the combined earning and spending records indicate whether the economy is balanced. Mark earning should not be the only source of information related to behavior change, because they are not independent of staff behavior and do not reflect the actual frequency of the child's behavior. Direct observation of client behavior should be carried out as often as possible to supplement mark-earning data. When the information from various sources indicates that the program should be modified, the mark sheet is simply altered to take account of the changes, and the staff working with the children need only to look at the mark sheets to be informed of the program changes. Since the program information is in the child's possession, he does not allow the staff to remain uninformed, calling any changes immediately to their attention. This provides for constant accountability of both staff to child *and* child to staff. Besides conveying program information, the system also possesses some advantages for the child. The mark sheet provides a concrete means of communicating behavioral expectations to the child. Even those who cannot read can point to the different segments of their mark sheets and verbalize what they must do to earn marks in particular boxes. Since the child keeps the mark sheet with him, it provides continuous feedback regarding his performance in specific target areas. In addition, the presence of empty boxes on the sheet frequently functions as a prompt for the desired behavior. Empty boxes also provide a cue for staff to prompt and subsequently reinforce those specific behaviors on the part of the child. In addition to serving as the vehicle for immediate tangible reinforcement, the mark sheet provides an opportunity for delayed social reinforcement, in the same manner as a child bringing home papers from school. Staff members on the evening shifts are able to praise and express approval for the child's performance during the day when the child shows them his mark sheet.

The Adler program includes three levels. Following a brief orientation period, a treatment program formulated for each child is put into effect at the time he enters Level I. Level I programs are characterized by a high frequency of contingent mark and social reinforcement. New behaviors learned while a child is on a Level I program are shifted to Premack (see Touchette, Chapter 7) for a reduced schedule of mark reinforcement when a child moves to Level II. Remaining problem behaviors are broken down into groups of target behaviors, which are set up so that they may be handled sequentially. When a child finally graduates to Level III, most of the goals set for the child's individual program have generally been met. At this stage marks are faded, and the child's behavior is brought under the control of Premack contingencies and social reinforcement.

Figure 1 illustrates a Level I program generated for Terry, a 12-year-old boy who had been referred for treatment after having been expelled from school because of his antisocial and aggressive behavior.

In the treatment setting, Terry was verbally abusive, ignored adult requests, continually whined, disrupted group activities with negative attention-getting behaviors, ridiculed or otherwise ignored his peers, and took no responsibility for his clothes or belongings. Thus the thrust of his program was to require and reinforce positive interactions with others, particularly his peers. "Good conversation" (saying something positive during the course of a meal), "sunshine" (any expression of positive affect), "accepting group decisions" (without whining or tantruming), and "sharing" were all designed to reinforce positive interactions with others. "Listening to adults and accepting teacher decisions" enabled the staff to reinforce Terry when he attended and followed through with their requests. Responsibility for his belongings was reinforced when Terry made his bed, picked up his room, and put his things away. Paying three marks for breakfast did not mean that Terry missed breakfast if he could not pay. When a child was required to pay for a meal, it meant that he was buying the privilege of sitting with the group and receiving second helpings and dessert. A child who could not pay sat by himself at the "free table" and received the basic meal (meat and vegetables) without seconds, extras, or dessert (see Chapter 13 by Heads). In school Terry received marks for task completion and responding to the teacher's requests.

Garron (Figures 2–5), a 7-year-old boy, was referred for treatment because of his severe tantrums, which often involved destruction of property. These tantrums occurred most frequently in school situations, where Garron had become frustrated with the task or failed to receive immediate attention in response to his demand for it. He was not achieving

UNIT MARK SHEET

ID# 0051   NAME: TERRY   DATE: _____

I. MAB'S

   BED MADE

   ROOM NEAT   PAY 3 FOR BREAKFAST (OTHERWISE NOT SPENDABLE)

   CLOSETS & DRAWERS

II. MEALS

   GOOD CONVERSATION
   BREAKFAST

   Pay 3 for Store Ticket (Otherwise not Spendable)
   GOOD CONVERSATION
   LUNCH

   Pay 3 for Store Ticket (Otherwise not Spendable)
   GOOD CONVERSATION
   DINNER

   Pay 3 for Store Ticket (Otherwise not Spendable)

III. P.E.

   A. BEGINNING THE ACTIVITY

      1. POSITIVE ATTITUDE

      2 LISTENING TO THE TEACHER

PRICES:

   Game Room - 5
   Evening Activity - 15
   Bikes - 5
   Snacks - 5
   TV - 5
   Up Late - 5

B. GOOD SPORTSMANSHIP AND ACCEPTING TEACHERS DECISIONS

(One mark - per ten minutes)
   6/7 = Cold Drink

IV. SCHOOL

NO SCHOOL TIME OUTS

If Yes, please check box   Store = Ticket

V. ANYTIME MARKS

   1. SUNSHINE

   2. LISTENING TO ADULTS FIRST TIME

   3. ACCEPTING GROUP DECISIONS

   4. SHARING

SAVINGS:

1

5

10

Figure 1
Terry's Level I unit mark sheet

at grade level, even though he tested in the superior range. Peer relationships were also difficult for Garron, since he attempted to dominate and direct others in a negative way. His quick temper and negative approach to others resulted in frequent fights with his peers.

Garron's Level I program (see Figure 2) was structured to heavily rein-

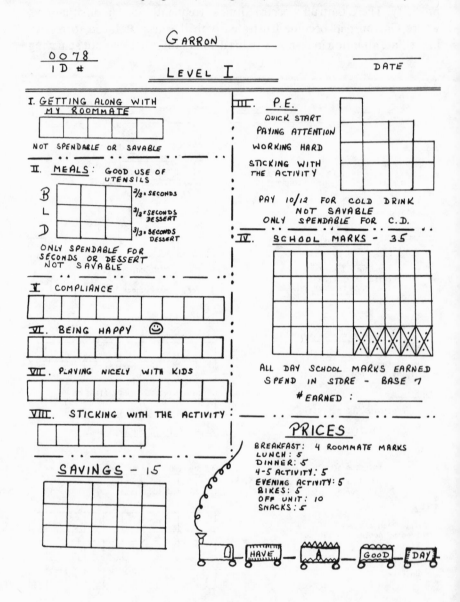

Figure 2
Garron's Level I unit mark sheet

force positive interactions with his peers, such as "getting along with my roommate," "playing nicely with others" (sharing, taking turns, not bossing or fighting), and "being happy" (expressions of positive affect: smiles, friendly gestures, positive statements). Task completion ("sticking with the activity") was also specifically reinforced, especially in the school setting where he was reinforced for both working independently and completing assigned work.

Tantrum behavior was punished by using a time-out procedure. Although the emphasis of the mark sheet program is on positive reinforcement of adaptive or desired behaviors, there are systematic punishment procedures to weaken undesirable behaviors incompatible with the target behavior(s). For example, to increase a child's following directions, it is often necessary to weaken or eliminate tantrums that might follow an adult-delivered request. Inappropriate behavior may be weakened by extinction or by aversive contingencies, the latter including time out (TO) from positive reinforcement opportunities and response cost (RC). When extinction or nonreinforcement procedures are used in conjunction with positive reinforcement to strengthen desirable behavior, the behavior selected to be strengthened is usually one that is incompatible with the inappropriate behavior. For example, if compliance to adult requests is the target behavior for a child who consistently responds to requests by systematically naming five reasons why he can not, shall not, and will not do what he is asked (e.g., "I don't know how", "I'm not your slave!", "Make me!") it might be necessary to ignore (extinguish) his verbal rationalizations consistently, while at the same time positively reinforcing successive approximations to following through with the request. If the same child reverts to a tantrum following a request by an adult, a brief time out involving the removal of the child from a reinforcing situation immediately following the tantrum might be implemented. The time-out procedure could consist of escorting the child to an adjacent room devoid of toys and objects that might otherwise provide reinforcement. After he remains quiet for a preset brief period (e.g., 2 minutes), he might be returned to the group, where he can once again be reinforced for appropriate behavior. As the frequency of his inappropriate tantrums decreases, the therapist may begin to reinforce him for progressively more complete attempts at compliance.

To demonstrate in more concrete terms how an individualized mark reinforcement program might actually work, Garron's Level I and II programs are reproduced in full (see Figures 2–5). The text that follows is taken directly from the program description made available to and followed by all treatment staff. Information regarding each child's program is contained in a cardex file. Each section of the program is described on a separate card, and thus alterations can be made in one portion without having to rewrite the entire program. The programs were written by the child's counselor in consultation with all program staff (e.g., counselors, teachers, psychologist).

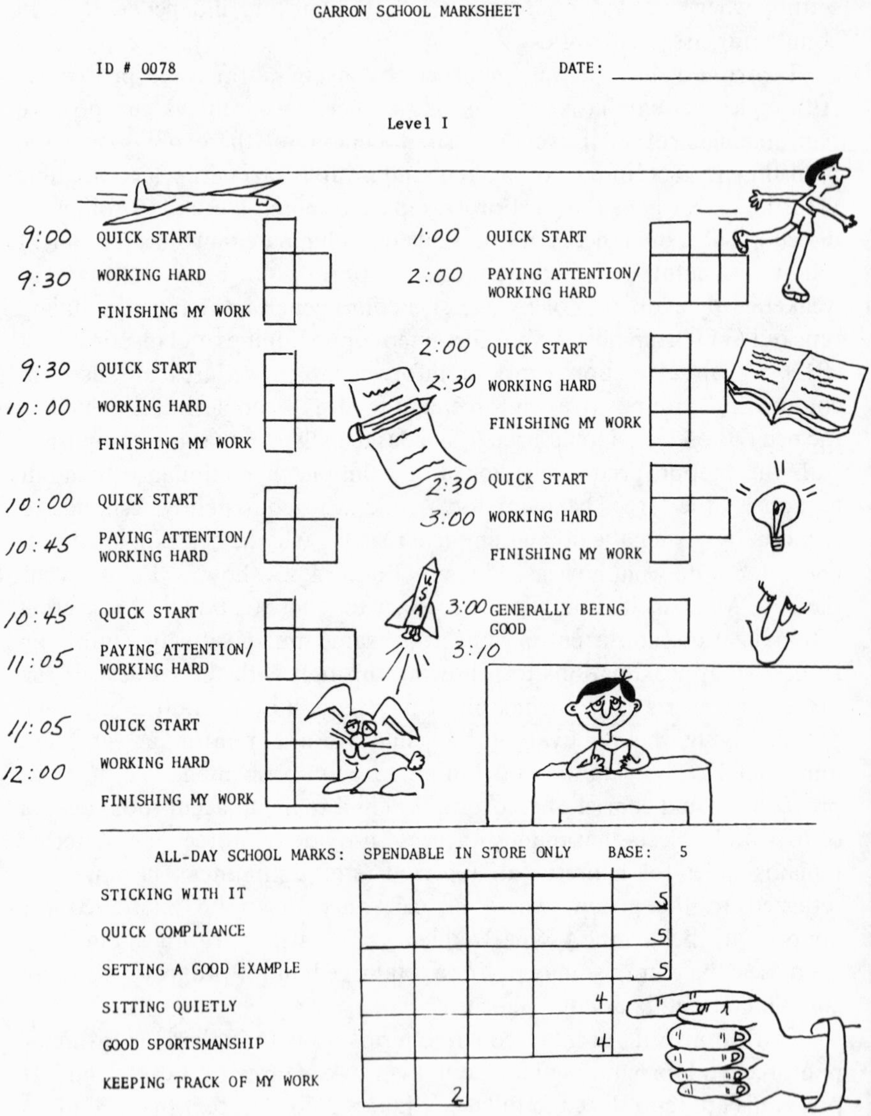
GARRON SCHOOL MARKSHEET

ID # 0078 DATE: ____________

Level I

9:00 QUICK START
9:30 WORKING HARD
FINISHING MY WORK

9:30 QUICK START
10:00 WORKING HARD
FINISHING MY WORK

10:00 QUICK START
10:45 PAYING ATTENTION/ WORKING HARD

10:45 QUICK START
11:05 PAYING ATTENTION/ WORKING HARD

11:05 QUICK START
12:00 WORKING HARD
FINISHING MY WORK

1:00 QUICK START
2:00 PAYING ATTENTION/ WORKING HARD

2:00 QUICK START
2:30 WORKING HARD
FINISHING MY WORK

2:30 QUICK START
3:00 WORKING HARD
FINISHING MY WORK

3:00 GENERALLY BEING GOOD
3:10

ALL-DAY SCHOOL MARKS: SPENDABLE IN STORE ONLY BASE: 5

STICKING WITH IT 5
QUICK COMPLIANCE 5
SETTING A GOOD EXAMPLE 5
SITTING QUIETLY 4
GOOD SPORTSMANSHIP 4
KEEPING TRACK OF MY WORK 2

Figure 3
Garron's Level I school mark sheet.

Garron — Level I Program
Effective 3/20 — Monday

I. GETTING ALONG WITH MY ROOMMATE–5 MARKS: NOT
    SPENDABLE
    When Garron and his roommate are in their room (without other kids or
    staff present) playing nicely together ... or simply on peaceful terms ...
    generally for a period of 10 minutes, Garron can receive a mark in this
    category. These marks will go toward a "special" treat (e.g., trip to
    McDonalds, ride in the car, etc.).

II. APPROPRIATE TABLE MANNERS–9 MARKS   Garron 3/20
    Breakfast (B) = 3 marks–must earn 2 before having seconds.
    Lunch   (L) = 3 marks–must earn 3 before having dessert.
    Dinner   (D) = 3 marks–must earn 3 before having dessert.

    This category is to reinforce Garron for eating appropriately (does not
    include social behavior). He could earn marks for correct usage of utensils,
    sitting nicely, not eating with fingers, small bites, etc. Initially, you may wish
    to prompt him and give him examples of what appropriate table manners
    entail.

    If Garron displays inappropriate social behavior, such as singing, humming,
    or whistling at the table, he should be prompted to stop. If the behavior
    occurs again during the meal, Garron should be sent to the free table.

III. P.E.–12 MARKS   Garron 3/20
     Garron can earn: Quick Start   – 1 mark
                       Paying Attention   – 3 marks
                       Working Hard   – 4 marks
                       Sticking with Activity – 4 marks

     Garron must pay 10 marks for Cold Drink.

IV. COMPLIANCE–10 MARKS   Garron 3/20
    He should receive a compliance mark for quickly and cheerfully following
    directions or requests. If he delays at all or gives some verbal retort, he should
    not receive a mark.

V. BEING HAPPY–10 MARKS   Garron 3/20
    Garron can earn a mark for having a positive attitude toward an activity
    and/or enjoying the company of other kids. He should generally maintain a
    cheerful attitude toward activity or kids for about 15 minutes. He will not get
    marks (on cottage) for positive statements per se. However, reinforce his
    positive statements with lots of social praise.

VI.   PLAYING NICELY WITH OTHER KIDS–10 MARKS   Garron 3/20
      Garron can earn a mark for sharing toys, being a good sport during games,
      helping other kids during play periods, cooperating with kids, etc. Please be
      explicit when telling him how he earned a mark.

VII. STICKING WITH THE ACTIVITY–5 MARKS   Garron 3/20
      This is to reinforce Garron for generally participating in activity for its
      entirety. He can receive a mark at the end of the period. Garron will need to be
      socially reinforced during the activity for sticking with it. If he steps out of the
      activity briefly yet comes back and stays with it, he can still earn the mark.
      Continual stepping out of an activity would cause Garron to miss the mark.

VIII. SCHOOL–35 MARKS   Garron 3/20
      All day school marks earned: Sticking with it, First Time Compliance,
      Raising My Hand, and Saying Nice Things—Encouraging Others—should
      be recorded on unit mark sheet. He can spend only those marks in the store—
      base 7.*

IX.   SAVINGS—LIMIT 15 MARKS   Garron 3/20
      Marks which can be saved:
      1. Compliance
      2. Being Happy
      3. Playing Nicely with Other Kids
      4. Sticking with the Activity

X.   PRICES   Garron 3
      Breakfast with
      Group   = 4
      Lunch with Group   = 5
      Dinner with
      Group   = 5
      Bikes   = 5   Free time periods (after breakfast and
                                   lunch)
      Cold Drink   Pay 10 P.E. marks
      4:00 – 5:00   = 5   (Special Recreation Activity)
      Phone Call   = 10   Can only be placed after dinner
      6:00–7:00   = 5   (Special Recreation Activity)
      7:00 – 8:00   = 10   (Special Recreation Activity)
      Snacks   = 5
      Bed Time Story   = 5
      Recovery Charge   = 14   (If mark sheet is lost)

XI.   MAB'S (Minimum Appropriate Behavior, i.e., self-help skills)
      Garron has shown some inconsistency in performing morning MAB'S. To
      deal with any problems, premack Garron. Example: you may join the rest of
      the group for free time before breakfast when you finish cleaning your room.

* A store which stocked various toy and food items was maintained on the unit. Pricing of
items in the store was done in terms of "store units." Each child's program established how
many of his marks would be required to buy one store unit. In Garron's case he had to pay 7
marks (base 7) for each store unit, so if he wanted to buy an item which cost 5 store units, he
would pay 35 of his marks. This system enabled the store to establish and "advertise" a single
price for all items, and at the same time handle the individualized purchasing power of each
child's program.

XII. PUNISHMENT–TIME OUT (TO)   Garron 3/20
   Minor – Moderate Tantrums (5 minutes in TO)*
   1. Screaming – shreiking (in response to staff decisions, requests, or another
      kid's behavior directed toward Garron)
   2. Stamping Feet
   3. Pounding on Things
   4. Throwing Things on the Floor
   5. Stomping Off to Room and Shutting Door with Unnecessary Force
   6. Others
   * Relatively mild intensity and of a short duration.

   Severe Tantrum Behavior (10 minutes in TO)
   In response to staff decision, requests, or another kid's behavior directed
   toward Garron:

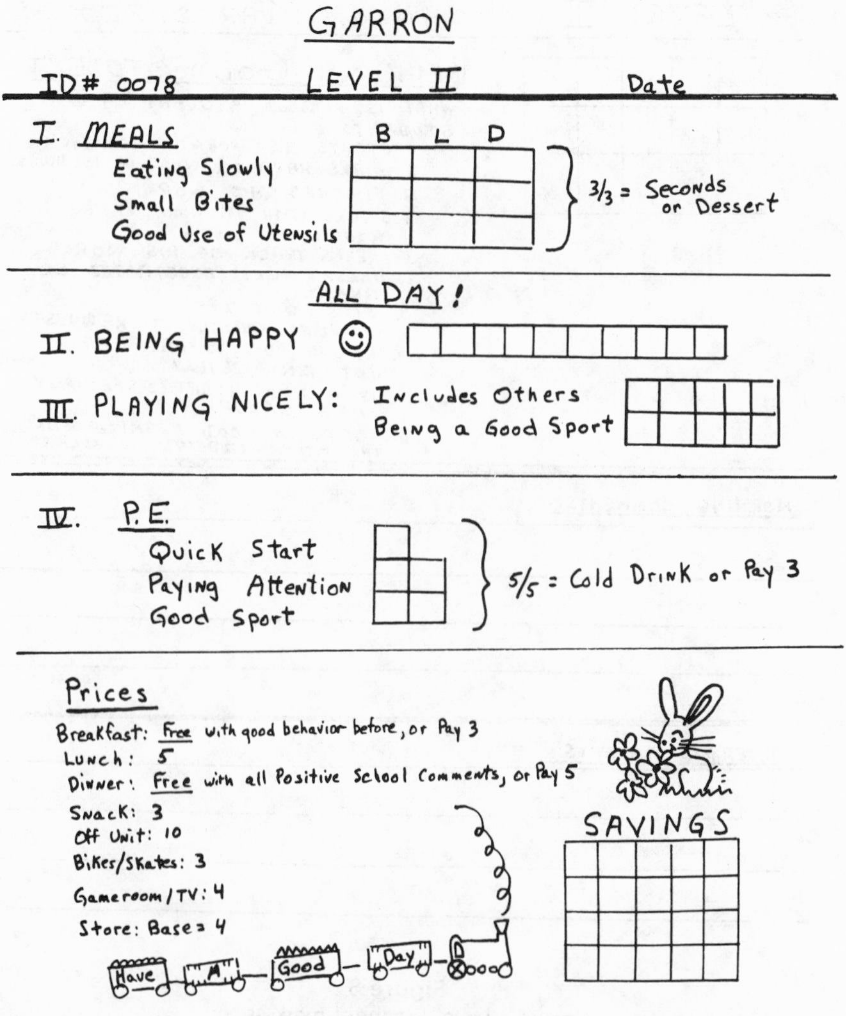

Figure 4
Garron's Level II unit mark sheet.

1. Screaming – shreiking = high intensity, long duration
2. Throwing Chairs
3. Slamming Door as Hard as He Can
4. Others

Any tantrum of high intensity and long duration is a major tantrum.

If major destruction accompanies a tantrum, he should be sent to TO for 20 minutes (i.e., plaster falling off the walls, etc.).

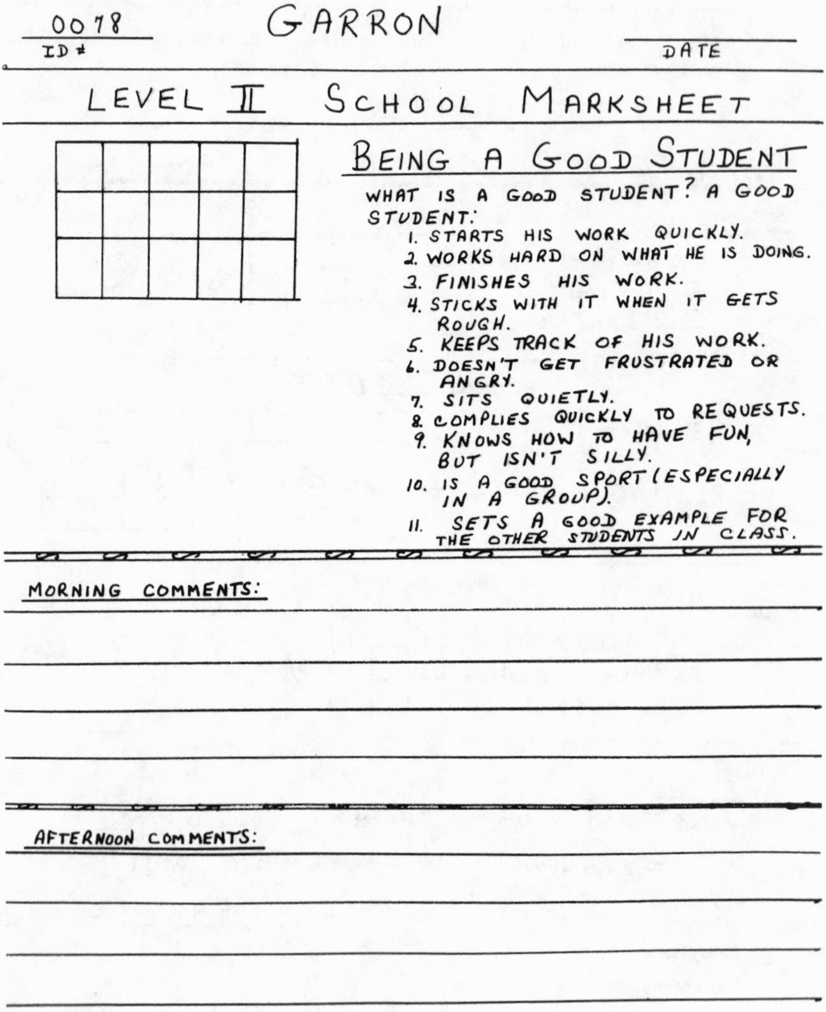

0078   G A R R O N
ID #   DATE

LEVEL II   SCHOOL MARKSHEET

BEING A GOOD STUDENT

WHAT IS A GOOD STUDENT? A GOOD
STUDENT:
1. STARTS HIS WORK QUICKLY.
2. WORKS HARD ON WHAT HE IS DOING.
3. FINISHES HIS WORK.
4. STICKS WITH IT WHEN IT GETS ROUGH.
5. KEEPS TRACK OF HIS WORK.
6. DOESN'T GET FRUSTRATED OR ANGRY.
7. SITS QUIETLY.
8. COMPLIES QUICKLY TO REQUESTS.
9. KNOWS HOW TO HAVE FUN, BUT ISN'T SILLY.
10. IS A GOOD SPORT (ESPECIALLY IN A GROUP).
11. SETS A GOOD EXAMPLE FOR THE OTHER STUDENTS IN CLASS.

MORNING COMMENTS:

AFTERNOON COMMENTS:

Figure 5
Garron's Level II school mark sheet.

NOTE: When invoking TO for tantrum behaviors DO NOT label his behavior as a tantrum. Inform him of what behavior is being punished (i.e., screaming loudly, slamming his door, throwing books on the floor, etc.) and how much time he needs to serve.

Garron – Level II
Effective June 27

INTRODUCTION
Garron has improved considerably in the $3\frac{1}{2}$ months that he has been at Adler. His tantrums have decreased to the point that they are relatively infrequent, of mild intensity, and of short duration. Garron's cooperation with staff requests and his following of cottage rules has also improved greatly. In the area of peer relations, Garron is now an accepted member (sometimes leader) of the group; in general, he has been interacting appropriately with the group and often times exhibits concern for group members (for their feelings, their welfare, their rights). Garron has also learned how to handle failure and frustration in competitive situations much better. The school situation has also shown marked improvement. Garron is no longer the disruptive element he once was; his self-control has increased so that now he is approaching model student behavior.

All this is very encouraging. My [Garron's counselor] goals now are to maintain this good behavior on Garron's Level II, to continue teaching Garron appropriate interactional tools, to reward Garron in a special way for the absence of all deviant behaviors in a given time period, and to gradually wean him off marks and onto a totally social, premacked program in preparation for his return home.

I.	**EARNING MEALS**	Garron 6/27
	A. Breakfast	If Garron has caused no problems before breakfast (i.e., been in time out or creating a disturbance), he can have breakfast free — otherwise he must pay 3 marks. This would be a good time to premack Garron, e.g., "if you're cooperative about getting your room together, you can have free breakfast," "if you get along with other kids before breakfast, you can have it free."
	B. Lunch	Pay 5. In the near future, this will probably also be premacked.
	C. Dinner	If Garron receives *all* positive comments on his school sheet, he may eat dinner free — otherwise he must pay 5. Please praise Garron liberally whenever he gets dinner free (e.g., "It looks like you had a super day!" "You should be proud of how well you did in school — I am," etc.).
II.	**MEALTIME BEHAVIORS**	
	A. Good Table Manners	9 marks. This category is set up to reinforce Garron for eating appropriately. He earns three marks per meal for:
	1. eating slowly	not gobbling his food, remembering to swallow before talking, chewing his food correctly.

2. taking small bites

Garron knows by now what constitutes a small bite; *he needs no prompting* for this category. If Garron takes a bite you feel is too large or if he takes a bite from a large hunk held on his fork, he should immediately miss this mark.

3. using utensils properly

This category is geared primarily toward Garron's use of his knife. Garron should remember to cut his food into proper sized bites. If he uses his fingers when a utensil is in order, Garron should immediately miss this mark.

B. Social Behavior at Meals

Please remember to reinforce Garron verbally for good social behavior at meals (e.g., sitting nicely, good conversation, waiting patiently, not being silly, etc.). If Garron displays inappropriate social behavior (e.g., singing, whistling, humming, being silly, etc.) at the table, you should prompt him once to stop (if the behavior is not purposefully attention getting), and if the behavior occurs again, he should be sent to the free table. If you feel Garron is deliberately doing someting inappropriate to get attention from the kids, (Garron will usually cue you subtly with a look or a statement, before he intentionally does something inappropriate), he should be sent directly to the free table *without prompting*.

C. Seconds and/or Dessert

If Garron earns all three of his meal marks, he may have seconds and/or dessert free. Initially, you may wish to remind him of this "good deal." If he fails to earn all three marks, he must pay two marks if he wants to have seconds and/or dessert.

D. Free Table

If Garron eats at the free table (by choice or necessity), he may still receive his meal marks, but, of course, seconds and dessert are unavailable.

If Garron is silly at the free table (making faces or noises, playing with another free table customer, trying to get attention from the good table, etc.), invoke a 10-minute TO. You may prompt him *once* to settle down, if you feel it is necessary. However, limit your prompts to *one*, for Garron is quite aware of when he is exhibiting silly behavior.

III. BEING HAPPY   Garron 6/27

Garron can earn a mark for having a positive attitude toward an activity, for enjoying the company of other kids, or for having a sunny, cheerful disposition. This sunny attitude should generally last for 15 minutes in order for Garron to receive a mark. Be generous with social praise in this category; let Garron know you enjoy being around him when he is cheerful and how much fun it is to be with him.

IV. PLAYING NICELY   Carron 6/27
We will continue to reinforce Garron socially for sharing toys, cooperating
with others, taking turns, helping others during play periods, accepting
decisions, keeping his cool, etc. Garron will also receive marks in two sub-
categories of playing nicely:

A. Including others in games/activities

Garron can receive a mark in this category whenever he makes a serious
effort to include someone in a game or activity who would not normally be
included at the outset of the game/activity.

B. Being a Good Sport

Garron can receive this mark whenever he accepts defeat or failure
cheerfully, accepts a group decision (not of his choice), accepts second or
third choice, perserveres in the face of provocation or failure, etc. (Be on
the lookout for minor tantrums in this area.)

V. P.E.   Garron 6/27
Garron can earn:

A. Quick Start	1 mark — on time, ready to participate when the teacher is ready to start the class and following through on the teachers's first directions.
B. Paying Attention	2 marks — listening to what the teacher is saying as evidenced by the ability to repeat and carry out directions or attending to the ongoing activity.
C. Working Hard/Good Sport	2 marks — depending upon the activity, reinforce Garron for sticking to the activity, trying hard, accepting defeat, having team spirit, etc.
D. Cold Drink	If Garron earns all 5 of his P.E. marks he receives a cold drink free, otherwise he must pay 3. Reinforce him verbally for his excellence in P.E. which entitled him to a *free* cold drink.

VI. SCHOOL   Garron 6/27

A. Being a Good Student
The number of marks Garron can receive in school has been cut in half
and specific categories have been eliminated from his school program. He
will now receive marks for being a good student, which includes: quick
starts, working hard/on task, finishing work, sticking with it, keeping
track of work, not getting frustrated or getting angry, sitting quietly,
complying quickly, not being silly, exhibiting good sportsmanship, and
setting a good example. These marks should be coupled with social
reinforcement; please be explicit with Garron when you are reinforcing
him—tell him exactly what it was that was good.

B. Morning and Afternoon Comments

In a few words record how Garron did in a specific class or during the time period overall. Don't hesitate to put down negative comments; it is important that Garron receives feedback, both positive and negative, on how he is doing. Eventually marks will be eliminated altogether in favor of a school comment sheet (such as is feasible to use in a public school). If Garron receives *all* positive comments on his school sheet, he earns another *good deal* – free dinner.

VII. SAVINGS*   Garron 6/27
All marks are spendable and savable.

VIII. PRICES   Garron 6/27
Breakfast   Free with good behavior before breakfast, otherwise pay 3.
Lunch   Pay 5.
Dinner
Free if Garron receives
all positive school com-
ments, otherwise pay 5.
Seconds and /or Dessert Free if all 3 meal marks are earned, otherwise pay 2.
Cold Drink   Free with 5 of 5 P.E. marks, otherwise pay 3.
Snacks   Pay 3.
Evening Activity   Pay 10.
Bikes/Roller Skates   Pay 3 per period.
Game Room   Pay 4 per $\frac{1}{2}$ hour period.
TV   Pay 3 per $\frac{1}{2}$ hour period.
Everything Else   (phone, non-pay 4–5 or 6–7, office supplies, bedtime story) — free with good behavior.
Store   Base 4.
Recovery Charge   Pay 10.

IX.   PUNISHMENT   Garron 6/27
Same as Level I.

Individualized treatment programs that utilize a point system motivational approach may be seen in the recent development of a number of behavior modification group homes for predelinquent and delinquent youth. These programs are based on the teaching-family model of Achievement Place, a community-based, community-controlled group home model developed at the University of Kansas (see Willner, Braukmann, Kirigin, & Wolf, Chapter 9). The treatment program is carried out by teaching-parents (generally a married couple) in a small (6–8 youth) family-style setting located in a home in the troubled youth's local community. The most important role of the teaching-parents is that of

* If any earned marks are not spent, they are to be recorded in the savings section of the next day's mark sheet.

teacher. They educate the youths in a variety of areas in order to equip them with alternative, more adaptive skills, thereby increasing their chances of survival and success in the community.

The point system at Achievement Place begins by having the target behaviors followed immediately by positive or negative consequences. The positive or negative consequences take the form of points that can be earned for appropriate behaviors or lost for inappropriate behaviors. Points are given (reward) and taken away (fines) for a variety of social (e.g., appropriate language with peers, appropriate language with adults, pouting and sulking, fighting, defiance, manners, promptness, limit testing, and rowdiness), self-help (e.g., room clean, weekly house jobs, volunteering, hygiene, and neatness), academic (e.g., grades in school, social behavior in school), and other relevant behaviors (e.g., calls or reports by public, legal offenses, home visit reports by parents). Like the Adler program, the youth at Achievement Place carry a sturdy, 5 × 7 inch "point card" on which point rewards and fines are recorded. The card is divided into halves, a "made" side and a "lost" side. When a youth earns points, he writes the value in the column marked "no. of points made," and gives a brief description of the behavior in a "description of behavior" column.

As opposed to the token economy employed by the Adler program, the teaching-family system is a positive (points or tokens *given* for certain specified behaviors) *and* negative (points or tokens taken *away* for certain behaviors) economy. Moreover, Achievement Place employs a flexible economy, allowing for an unlimited opportunity to earn as well as lose tokens for target behaviors. In an inflexible economy there is no way to make up unearned tokens. However, in a flexible economy tokens that are unearned or lost do not necessarily mean the loss of privileges, only that additional effort will have to be made in order to earn tokens to buy the desired privileges (use of tools, television, recreation room, attending extra-curricular activities at school) and other back-up reinforcers (allowance, snacks, clothes, gifts).

Although the teaching-family token economy depends partially on mild punishment through contingent loss of points in addition to contingent positive reinforcement for its effectiveness, the flexibility in the economy means that, in reality, the youth seldom suffer the loss of their privileges. In fact, in one 13-week period, only one of seven boys at Achievement Place failed to earn a sufficient number of points to purchase all the major privileges offered (Phillips, Phillips, Fixsen, & Wolf, 1974, p. 57). A very important advantage of a system that includes point fines is the opportunity they present to teach the participants of the program how to react appropriately to criticism. The fining of inappropriate behaviors provides the teaching parent an excellent chance to observe and teach alternative responses to aggressive, defiant, and belligerent behavior which often follows any form of even mild criticism directed at the youth by parents, teachers, or employers.

THE TEACHING INTERACTION

The point system or token economy is crucial in treatment programs, because earning points or marks strengthens appropriate behavior, and fines or other punishment techniques reduce inappropriate behavior. In this manner the token economy provides motivation for a child to change. Although the token economy may be very helpful, one must be warned of the danger of misusing or abusing the great power of the token economy to modify unwanted behavior alone, thereby neglecting the essential function of teaching new skills and strengthening alternative behaviors to replace the maladaptive behaviors that led to referral for treatment (McInnis & Marholin, 1977). "This can make a program suppressive rather than educational" (Phillips et al., 1974, p. 58). Most children referred for treatment need to learn new skills to better deal with situations at school, home, or in the community. The token economy *alone* will not do an adequate job of teaching those *new* behaviors. A technique that has been referred to as the "teaching interaction" (Phillips, Phillips, Fixsen, & Wolf, 1974) used in conjunction with tokens is helpful in teaching new behaviors. The teaching interaction consists of 10 separate components, including the expression of affection, praise for work already accomplished, descriptions of inappropriate and appropriate behavior, the rationale for the appropriate behavior, request for acknowledgement that the youth understands, practice, feedback, and rewards such as social praise and/or points or marks for a "job well done."

An example of the teaching interaction is presented below. The teaching interaction described begins with a teaching-parent from Achievement Place assigning a youth the task of cleaning the kitchen sink and counter top for the first time. The teaching interaction presented occurred when the teaching-parent returned to see how the youth was progressing.[2]

Teaching Interaction Component	Example	Reason the component may be important
1. Expression of affection (a smile, special greeting, joke, physical contact)	Teaching-parent smiles and says "Hi. Are you having any problems?" He places his hand on the youth's shoulder.	Indicates to the youth that the teaching-parent is pleased to see him, likes to interact with him and is concerned about any problems he may be having.

Teaching Interaction Component	*Example*	*Reason the component may be important*
2. Praise for what has been accomplished.	"Say, that sink looks fine."	Indicates to the youth that teaching-parent is aware of what he has already accomplished.
3. Description of the inappropriate behavior.	"But you haven't gotten this counter top clean."	Instructs the youth about what he did incorrectly or hasn't yet done.
4. Description of the appropriate behavior. (A demonstration may be necessary.)	"So why don't you get a damp, soapy rag and wipe off the counter. Be sure that you rub hard on these spots of stuck-on food. (Teaching-parent points to them.) Let me show you what I mean." (Teaching-parent demonstrates.)	Instructs the youth about what is expected of him. The task often should be broken into small steps. Demonstration may be needed in order to clarify the verbal instruction.
5. Rationale for the appropriate behavior.	"We want you to know how to take care of a kitchen so that when you have your own apartment it will look nice. And, you'll be able to help around your house if your parents ask you to. Also, we need to keep the kitchen clean so we can keep the germs away. Also, if we have visitors they won't get a bad impression of us."	Instructs the youth why it is important that he engage in the behaviors, i.e., the potential future consequences.
6. Description of the present consequences.	"As soon as you finish cleaning the counter top you can have your points."	Instructs the youth about the immediate rewards for his appropriate behavior.
7. Request for acknowledgement.	"Do you understand?" or "Ok?"	Prompts the youth to ask any questions he may have. Also, the youth's acknowledgement provides feedback to the teaching-parent that the youth was

Teaching Interaction Component	Example	Reason the component may be important
7. Request for acknowledgement.	"Do you understand?" or "Ok?"	attending to the instructions and understands them. (It is quite aversive for the teaching-parent if the youth is completely unresponsive throughout the teaching interaction.)
8. Practice	"Now, why don't you try to clean these spots?"	Practice is a very important component because it gives the teaching-parents immediate feedback whether the appropriate behavior is in the youth's repertoire and he understands the instruction.
9. Feedback during practice: Praise and correction.	"That looks good. How about rubbing this spot a little harder. That's right."	Provides positive feedback for those behaviors the youth is performing correctly and provides further instruction and practice for the behaviors that are not yet appropriate.
10. Reward: Praise and points	"Give yourself 1,000 points. That is a fine job."	Gives the youth immediate consequences for the appropriate behavior.

Obviously, all 10 components of the teaching interaction are not necessary in every situation. For example, if the youth had had prior experience cleaning the sink at Achievement Place there would have been no need for describing the appropriate behavior, rationale, consequences, practice, or feedback during practice. Rather, the teaching-parent might only be required to praise the youth for the work accomplished, describe the specific work left, request an acknowledgement, and praise the final product or completion of the task. Such a teaching interaction might be as shown in the table on page 131.[3]

Another illustrative example of a teaching interaction focuses on teaching negotiation skills to youths and their parents. A problem faced by many adolescents involves conflict situations with authority figures such as

1. Praise for what has been accomplished.   "Say, that sink looks fine."

2. Description of in-appropriate behavior.   "But, why don't you try to clean this counter top right here."

3. Request for acknow-ledgement.   "Ok?"

4. Reward: Praise only.   "Hey, that is a fine job."

parents, teachers, and bosses. The conflict situation is an interpersonal situation in which the youth and authority figure have opposing desires. For example, the youth wants to go to a party, but his parents demand that he stay home. Although the youth frequently makes an inappropriate response to a conflict situation (e.g., running away, using abusive language, breaking furniture), in many of these situations negotiation is possible that might allow both parties to acquire more acceptable consequences. The following example presents a type of teaching interaction that successfully taught two mother-daughter and one father-son pair effective interpersonal negotiation skills (Kifer, Lewis, Green, & Phillips, 1974). To evaluate the effectiveness of their teaching program, each of the three pairs were observed in their home before and after the teaching sessions. The home observations consisted of collecting sample data regarding each subject pair's behavior in discussing actual conflict situations in their natural home environment. The actual text describing the training sessions is reprinted below.[4]

The purpose of this experiment was to determine (a) if negotiation skills could be simultaneously taught to youths and their parents, and, if so, (b) the effect of these skills on mutually agreeable solutions to conflict situations, and (c) the extent to which these skills would generalize to discussions of real conflict situations at home.

METHOD

Subjects

Two mother-daughter pairs and one father-son pair served as subjects. The youths (aged 13, 16, and 17) had at least one contact with the County Juvenile Court. The boy and one girl were in Achievement Place homes (Phillips, 1968), and the other girl was a candidate for Achievement Place. Only one parent was involved in each case because two of the youths were living with only that parent and the father of one of the girls declined to participate. All subjects were volunteers for this project and freely signed informed consent forms.

Setting

All training procedures were conducted in a small (12 by 15ft. — 3.6 by 4.5 m) windowless classroom containing a table and chairs, videotape recording equipment, and a cassette tape recorder.

Procedures

Overview. Each parent-child pair experienced three main phases of this study. The first was a *home observation* conducted one week before classroom sessions and consisted of collecting sample data regarding each subject pair's behavior in discussing actual conflict situations in their home. The second phase consisted of *classroom sessions.* The third phase was another *home observation* to measure generalization of trained behaviors into the home. The first two authors functioned as trainers and made all experimental contacts with subjects.

Home observations. Trainers visited subjects' homes and asked them to identify " the three most troublesome problem situations between the two of you at this time." Any conflict situation identified by both parent and youth were discussed. In case different situations were identified, at least one selected by the parent and one by the child were discussed.

Subjects were instructed to discuss each situation for 5 min without help from trainers and were told to "try to reach a solution acceptable to both of you." At the end of the first discussion, trainers gave brief general praise for discussing the situation, restated the next conflict situation, and repeated the instructions.

Classroom sessions. Each parent-child pair attended their own weekly session. The same three-step format was used in all sessions: (a) presession simulation, (b) discussion and practice simulations, and (c) postsession simulation.

    1. *A presession simulation* was conducted as soon as subjects arrived. Trainers described a hypothetical parent-child conflict situation and instructed them to role play that situation to the best of their ability. No other instructions were given. This and all other simulations were stopped by trainers after 5 min unless subjects indicated they were finished before that time.

2. *Discussion and practice* followed a standard procedure known as the Situations – Options – Consequences – Simulation (S.O.C.S.) model originated by Roosa (Note 2). After the presession simulation, trainers passed out copies of a sheet (see Figure 6 for an example) containing a description of the same situation that subjects had just simulated, a list of response options, and a list of consequences.

First, this situation was read again by trainers. Then trainers and subjects took turns matching each option with its probable consequences. Additional options and consequences were added if they occurred to anyone. After all options were related to their probable consequences, the parent and the child selected the consequences that were most desirable to them. By noting which options led to desired consequences, subjects selected the best response to the situation. Finally, practice simulations were conducted in which each subject practised their selected option. Typically, the child played the role of the youth for the first few times; then subjects switched roles. The trainers rarely took part in these practice simulations. They

Situation

You have worked all summer for money and your mother insists that you spend it on clothes, but you want to spend it on something else.

Options

1. Tell her it is your money and it is none of her business what you spend it on.
2. Spend it on ugly clothes you know she hates.
3. Since she will not let you spend it the way you want, give it to charity.
4. Do not spend it on anything; put it in savings and let it collect interest.
5. Spend some on clothes she wants you to get and some on what you want.
6. You buy clothes if she will buy what else you want.
7. Sell them to a friend after you buy them.
8. It is easier to buy the clothes than hassle with mother.

Consequences

1. Get her mad at you and maybe have money taken away.
2. You have to wear the clothes you bought.
3. Feel good in helping a worthy cause.
4. End up with more money than you originally had.
5. Find out the clothes were a good thing.
6. Be miserable about the whole thing.
7. Never learn how to negotiate.

Figure 6

Sample sheet used in classroom sessions. From "Training predelinquent youths and their parents to negotiate conflict situations" by R. E. Kifer, M. A. Lewis, D. R. Green, and E. L. Phillips, *Journal of Applied Behavior Analysis*, 1974, 7, 357–364. Copyright 1974 by Society for the Experimental Analysis of Behavior, Inc. Reprinted by permission.

functioned like directors of a film, providing instructions before simulations, quietly observing simulations, signalling the beginning and end of simulations, and providing feedback.

3. Finally, a *postsession simulation* was conducted exactly like the presession simulation.

The same pool of hypothetical situations was used for each parent-child pair, but situations were counterbalanced across pairs. Negotiation was a possible option in all situations. Subjects were encouraged to use their own real-problem situations, but these were never volunteered except by the father-son pair during their last two classroom sessions.

All simulations were videotaped unless subjects preferred not to use the equipment that day. Videotapes were not replayed after each simulation because of the extra time involved. Replays were made only to check the occurrence of a behavior if there was any doubt, or to show subjects an especially good performance.

Behavior definitions. Two response classes were measured: negotiation behaviors and agreements. Negotiation was separated into three component behaviors: Complete Communication, Identification of Issues, and Suggestion of Options.
  1. *Complete Communication*: statements that indicate one's position (what one thinks or wants) regarding the situation being discussed and that are followed in the same verbalization by a request for the other person to state his position or respond to the position just expressed. Examples: (a) "I want to spend my summer job money on a bike. Is that O.K. with you?" (b) "I want you to run for Student Council. What do you think about it?"

2. *Identification of Issues*: statements that explicitly identify the point of conflict in the situation. This statement may contrast the two opposing positions, or try to clarify what the other's position is if this is unclear, or identify what one thinks the conflict is really about. Examples: (a) "You want me to buy clothes, but I want to buy a bike." (b) "The real issue is that I want you to learn responsibility." Subjects were encouraged but not required to use the word "issue" when performing this behavior to make its occurrence more explicit.

3. *Suggestion of Options*: statements that suggest a course of action to resolve the conflict, but not merely restatements of that person's original position. Examples: (1) "How about if I spend some on clothes and use the rest to buy a bike if you'll help me pay for it?" (b) "I could get a part-time job and learn responsibility that way." Subjects were encouraged but not required to pose options in the form of questions to increase the likelihood of receiving an answer to the option.

4. *Agreements*, the end result of negotiation, were recorded as one of two types: Compliant or Negotiated.

1. *Compliant Agreements*: agreements by one person to the original position of the other. Example: "All right, I'll spend all my money on clothes."

2. *Negotiated Agreements*: agreements to a suggested option that is not merely the original position of either person. Such agreements can take the form of a compromise, a deal (A gets his way but must in turn do something for B), or a new alternative (a different course of action). Example: "O.K., I guess a job would be fine." Agreements need not restate the course of action agreed upon. This was done in the examples to preserve the identity of situations.

Training procedures. Instructions, practice, and feedback were used to train subjects to use all three negotiation behaviors in practice simulations. Instructions consisted of telling the subject to perform all three behaviors; e.g., "Use Complete Communication, remember to Identify the Issue, and Suggest some Options." Practice involved each subject rehearsing all three negotiation behaviors in practice simulations. Feedback consisted of social reinforcement such as praise, smiles, and head nods. Instructions were given during these simulations, and verbal praise occurred after these role plays.

First one subject was instructed, then practiced these behaviors until he performed all three in the same simulation. Then, the other subject went through the same procedure. Subjects were taught to use the negotiation behaviors in the order in which they were defined. A typical sequence occurred as follows. First, trainers instructed the youth before his first practice simulation to use all three negotiation behaviors. Then, trainers signalled subjects to begin the simulation and smiled or nodded approval after any negotiation behavior used by the youth. Usually, the youth did not use all three behaviors in the first attempt, so he was praised for those behaviors he did use and reminded to use the behaviors he did not use. Next, the youth was instructed to use all three behaviors and the second practice simulation was started. This sequence occurred until the youth performed all three negotiation behaviors in the same practice simulation. At that point, subjects switched roles and the parent went through the same sequence. After the parent met the criterion of all three behaviors in the same simulation, that session was ended and the postsession simulation was conducted.

Figure 7 shows the percent of the three component negotiation behaviors emitted during the pre- and post-session classroom simulations by the three parent-child pairs.

As may be seen in the figure, a multiple-baseline design (as described by Kazdin and Marholin in Chapter 4) across child-parent pairs reveals a substantial increase in the use of the negotiation behaviors over baseline levels in post-treatment simulations. Figure 8 presents pre- and post-training data from the homes of the youth-parent pairs. "Post-training home observations of all three subject pairs showed substantial increases over pre-training observations in both performance of negotiation behaviors and agreements reached" (Kifer et al., 1974, p. 363).

Teaching packages including the use of instructions and rationale, demonstration, practice, and feedback coupled with proper reinforcement contingencies have proved successful and practical in demonstrating behavior change with various groups of youngsters. For example, teaching interactions have been used to teach job interview skills to predelinquent adolescents (Braukmann, Maloney, Fixsen, Phillips, & Wolf, 1974),

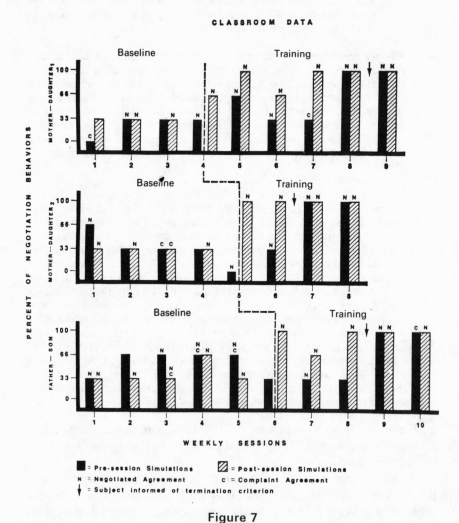

Figure 7

Percentage of negotiation behaviors emitted by each parent-child pair during pre- and post-session classroom situations. From "Training predelinquent youths and their parents to negotiate conflict situations" by R. E. Kifer, M. A. Lewis, D. R. Green, and E. L. Phillips, *Journal of Applied Behavior Analysis*, 1974, *7*, 357–364. Copyright 1974 by Society for the Experimental Analysis of Behavior, Inc. Reprinted by permission.

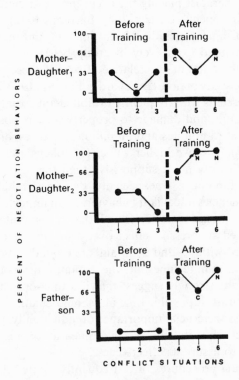

Figure 8

Percentage of negotiation behaviors emitted by each parent-child pair during pre- and post-session classroom situations. From "Training predelinquent youths and their parents to negotiate conflict situations" by R. E. Kifer, M. A. Lewis, D. R. Green, and E. L. Phillips, *Journal of Applied Behavior Analysis*, 1974, 7, 357–364. Copyright 1974 by Society for the Experimental Analysis of Behavior, Inc. Reprinted by permission.

conversation skills to junior high-school students (Minkin Braukmann, Minkin, Timbers, Timbers, Fixsen, Phillips, & Wolf, 1976), and important police-youth interaction behaviors to court-adjudicated delinquent youths (Werner, Minkin, Minkin, Fixsen, Phillips, & Wolf, 1975).

AVERSIVE FORMS OF PUNISHMENT

Individually devised response-cost and time-out procedures have been increasingly used in group treatment programs to suppress deviant behavior. The time-out procedure is a response-contingent event that involves reinforcer withdrawal (Leitenberg, 1965). In applied settings the procedure involves the therapist discontinuing the administration of reinforcement or the therapist placing the client in a restricted, allegedly less reinforcing environment (Burchard & Barrera, 1972). Although various forms of punishment including both time-out and response-cost procedures have been used extensively in group behavior modification programs, little is known about the relative effects of these procedures (Kazdin, 1975). In one study of note (Burchard & Barrera, 1972) a group of mildly retarded adolescents who frequently exhibited antisocial behaviors such as swearing, assault, and damage to property were exposed to two parameters of time out (5 minutes and 30 minutes) and response cost (5 tokens and 30 tokens). The two higher values (30 tokens and 30-minute time out) were significantly more suppressive than the lower values (5 tokens and 5-minute time out). Unexpectedly, the lower values actually lead to increased frequencies of deviant behavior. In an important finding, White, Nielson, and Johnson (1972) found that a 1-minute time-out duration had a marked suppressive effect over a no time-out condition unless it was contrasted with 15- and 30-minute time-out durations. When contrasted with the 15-minute time out, the 1-minute time out became ineffective. These results strongly suggest that if a time-out contingency must be applied, the shortest possible time out should be utilized initially. The findings also stress the crucial importance of individually monitoring the suppressive effect on behavior of any time-out or response-cost contingency in order to assure its effectiveness.

Although time-out procedures are frequently quite effective in suppressing various undesirable behaviors, it is the opinion of these authors that it be used only after all other conceivable positive treatment procedures have been applied. First, punishment alone does not teach new behavior. Second, although administering tokens appears to increase the frequency of staff social approval of clients, removing tokens or time out does not affect the frequency of approval (Bailey & Iwata, 1973). Third, the use of various time-out procedures often results in undesirable side effects, including avoidance behavior and an aroused emotional state (Johnston, 1972; Kazdin 1973b). Fourth, time out is extremely negatively reinforcing (termination of aversive event, which increases response that terminated the event) from the point of view of program staff. That is, time out quickly suppresses various client behaviors that are aversive to the staff (e.g., fighting, swearing) and thus negatively reinforces the staff's use of punishment. Because strong punishment procedures are so effective, the use of time out is often inadvertently abused. Abuse may take the form of using time out as seclusion for long periods of time, which is neither time out from reinforcement nor legal or ethical treatment (Martin, 1975). Furthermore, punishment is frequently used to the exclusion of teaching new adaptive behavior. Finally, punishment may reinforce adults for attending to children's undesirable behavior rather than selecting some desirable behavior to encourage and respond to positively.

Before deciding on the use of any punishment procedure, a program should be devised in which reinforcement is delivered for behavior that is incompatible with or displaces the undesirable response. Take, for example, the problems of delinquents. Delinquent behaviors per se might be directly suppressed. Delinquent behavior is a response or a series of responses that are aversive to society as a whole. If they are reduced in frequency by some punishment procedure such as time out (Burchard, 1967), one social problem might temporarily be alleviated. However, if delinquent behaviors are directly suppressed, there may be no alternative way for the previously delinquent youth to gain other more socially approved reinforcers. For example, "if stealing and property damage are reduced in delinquents, but no alternative skills exist in them for gaining the same reinforcers, then they can only become examples of no response; and, although we may no longer consider them a delinquency problem, we will surely find that they are now a welfare problem or a retardation problem" (Baer, 1975, p. 28). A preferred strategy might involve targeting behaviors that are believed to be incompatible with delinquency (Emery & Marholin, 1977). These would include social/interpersonal, vocational, and school behaviors. That is, if the desirable skills to gain relevant reinforcers in other than illegal means are taught well enough, then no direct suppression of stealing and property destruction would be necessary. "Those undesirable responses may simply fall into disuse, displaced by the desirable (and more profitable) skills" (Baer, 1975, p. 28).

USE OF PEERS

Individualized programming creates a problem as far as manpower shortages caused by individual program requirements (e.g., program writing, data collection, decision making). However, a recent advance in the area of group behavior modification programs using peers in roles such as data collection (Siegel & Steinman, 1975), reinforcement delivery (Axelrod, Hall, & Maxwell, 1972; Graubard, Rosenberg, & Miller, 1971; Solomon & Wahler, 1973), or participants in group contingencies (Marholin et al., 1975; Medland & Stachnik, 1972; Patterson, Cobb, & Ray, 1972), have demonstrated one means of supplementing treatment staff. Moreover, young clients have been called upon to make decisions about matters related to their own treatment (Fixsen, Phillips, & Wolf, 1973; Phillips, Phillips, Wolf, & Fixsen, 1973).

For example, Patterson, Cobb, and Ray (1972) describe a direct classroom intervention program for a deviant child. Additional time at recess for the entire class was made contingent on the total number of points earned by a target child. The contingencies are initially tailored in such a manner that on the first trial the child will obtain the requisite points to earn extra recess time for all of his classmates. Gradually the contingencies are altered to require greater amounts of appropriate behavior from the target child. Similar procedures making reinforcement for a group contingent on the performance of a single child (e.g., Barrish, Saunders, & Wolf, 1969; Walker & Buckley, 1972), a part of the group (e.g., Harris & Sherman, 1973), or the entire group (Packard, 1970) have been successfully employed. In such a situation each menber of the peer group may encourage the desired response of the target child or children in order to obtain reinforcers (Patterson, 1965). On the contrary, peers may occasionally employ censure and reprimands in order to control their peers' behavior (Axelrod, 1973; Schmidt & Ulrich, 1969). The adult therapist must, therefore, be careful to prompt and reinforce peers to encourage and reinforce appropriate behavior of their colleagues and discourage repeated censure and strong reprimands. If children are sucessful in modifying their peers through direct reinforcement procedures, they are likely to become cues for appropriate behavior when the therapist or adults are not around. Thus the likelihood of generalization beyond the therapy situation is increased. This notion gains some support from a comparison of group reward and individual reward during a 4-week treatment and a 4-week maintenance period with two groups of hyperactive elementary school children (Rosenbaum, O'Leary, & Jacob, 1975). Results indicated that children in the group-reward condition showed better maintenance than those in the individual-reward condition.

Perhaps the most interesting and functional use of peers is in the direct administration of treatment programs (Drass & Jones, 1971; Long & Madsen, 1975; Surratt, Ulrich, & Hawkins, 1969; Ulrich, Louisell, & Wolf, 1971). In one dramatic example, predelinquent peers residing at Achievement Place served as speech therapists for their peers who had articulation problems (Bailey, Timbers, Phillips, & Wolf, 1971). Using a treatment procedure including modeling, peer approval, delivery of contingent points, and verbal feedback, peers sucessfully trained correct word pronunciation of their own peers. Positive results were obtained, although the peers had no specific speech training and very little adult supervision. Moreover, the effects of the speech training generalized to novel words not included in the training sessions and were maintained up to 2 months following formal treatment.

In another program it was shown that not only could peers successfully use reinforcement procedures to modify the behavior of another child, but that observing and administering reinforcement had desirable effects on the peer-therapist himself (Siegel & Steinman, 1975). Two 10-year-old children (Brad and Jimmy), residing at the Adler Center previously described, participated. The two boys were chosen by their teacher because of the severity and similarity of their behavior problems in the classroom. Both children were noncompliant, and neither child exhibited a great deal of on-task or independent seat work. To evaluate the effectiveness of the program, a multiple-baseline procedure was used in which three classes of behavior were measured concurrently for each child (i.e., on-task behavior, independent behavior, and compliance). Following a baseline collected during 10 30-minute reading and spelling classes, Brad was selected to be the behavior modifier or "observer," and Jimmy was chosen as the target or "model." Jimmy was selected as the target child because he exhibited a slightly higher frequency of appropriate classroom behavior during the baseline sessions and, therefore, would provide Brad with a greater opportunity to observe and reinforce appropriate classroom behavior (see Figures 9 and 10).

Program procedures were in effect during the first 15 minutes of each class session. During the final 15 minutes of the class session, the program procedures were dropped to assess the degree of generalization. The procedures were as follows: First, Brad was taught to count the number of 10-second intervals Jimmy was on task and/or engaging in independent work. Brad recorded these behaviors during the first 15 minutes of the class period. He was given his daily classroom assignments and instructed by the teacher to begin his classwork at the beginning of the second 15 minutes of the class session. Brad received points for accurately scoring Jimmy's behavior during the first 15 minutes of the class session. Beginning with session 16, Brad was instructed to place a white plastic token in a container on Jimmy's desk each time he had observed that Jimmy was on task for a complete 10-second interval. In a second reinforcement condition, Brad continued to deliver white tokens to Jimmy for his on-task behavior. In addition, he was instructed to place a black token in a second container on Jimmy's desk each time he observed Jimmy to be working independently throughout the 10-second interval. In the third reinforcement condition, Brad continued to reinforce Jimmy with white and black tokens for on-task and independent behavior. However, the teacher now reinforced Jimmy for compliance (a behavior which had not been reinforced before) by placing a yellow token in a third container on Jimmy's desk. In the fourth reinforcement condition, Brad and the teacher traded behaviors to reinforce. Brad continued to record and reinforce Jimmy for working independently, but instead of recording and reinforcing on-task behavior, Brad now recorded and reinforced compliance. The teacher reinforced on-task behavior instead of reinforcing compliance. In the final phase of this program, Brad became the target or "model." Jimmy recorded Brad's on-task and independent behavior and reinforced him with tokens for each 10-

second interval in which Brad remained on-task or worked independently. Jimmy also received points for accurately recording Brad's on-task and

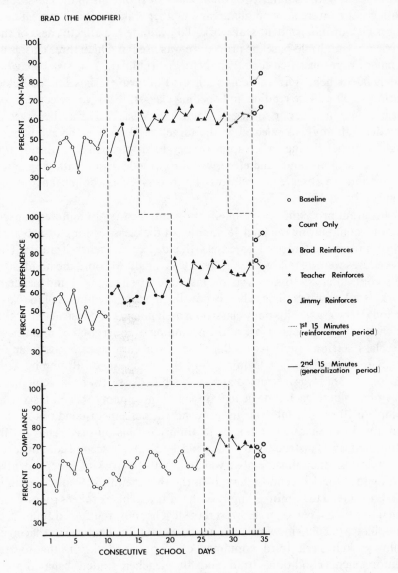

Figure 9
Summary of on-task, independent, and compliant behaviors of the child serving as peer modifier (Brad). From "The modification of a peer-observer's classroom behavior as a function of his serving as a reinforcing agent" by L. J. Siegel and W. M. Steinman. In E. Ramp and G. Semb (Eds.), *Behavior analysis: Areas of research and application*. Englewood Cliffs, N.J.: Prentice-Hall, 1975, pp. 329–340. Copyright 1975 by Prentice-Hall, Inc. Reprinted by permission.

independent behavior. Neither Jimmy nor the teacher recorded or reinforced Brad's compliance.

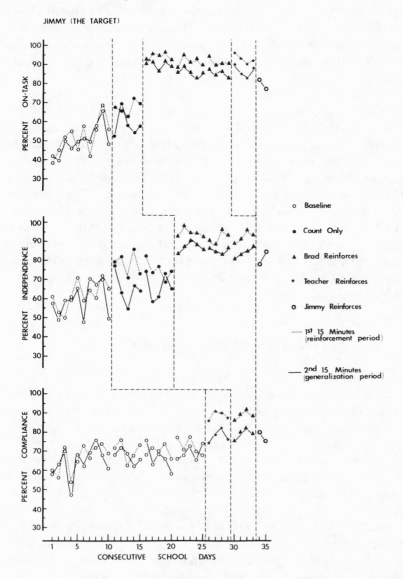

Figure 10
Summary of on-task, independent, and compliant behaviors of the target child (Jimmy). From "The modification of a peer-observer's classroom behavior as a function of his serving as a reinforcing agent" by L. J. Siegel and W. M. Steinman. In E. Ramp and G. Semb (Eds.), *Behavior analysis: Areas of research and application.* Englewood Cliffs, N.J.: Prentice-Hall, 1975, pp. 329–340.
Copyright 1975 by Prentice-Hall, Inc. Reprinted by permission.

As can be seen in Figures 9 and 10, each child's behavior increased rapidly when it was reinforced by his peer. Moreover, a small but reliable improvement in a specific behavior of the peer modifier was noted when he was reinforcing that specific behavior. That is, not only did Jimmy's on-task behavior increase dramatically when Brad recorded and reinforced Jimmy's on-task behavior, but Brad's on-task behavior increased also. Thus, the results of this program indicate that peers not only can function as effective observers and behavior modifiers of other children, but they also may acquire beneficial behaviors themselves when they do so.

In summary, the use of peers in reinforcement programs may provide "less restricted stimulus control over patient performance (which may result from complete reliance upon staff-administered contingencies)" (Kazdin, 1975, p. 249), more frequent reinforcement for desirable behaviors occurring during staff absences (Kazdin, 1973a), beneficial effects for the peer modifier, and enhanced generalization (Johnston & Johnston, 1973; Marholin et al., 1976). The importance of these findings to the development of individualized programs lies in the fact that use of peer modifiers may free staff for supervisory functions allowing more efficient use of their time for program evaluation, program modification, and counseling (Kazdin, Note 3).

CONCLUDING REMARKS

This chapter presents examples of methods to individualize treatment programs in group settings. The core of the treatment is the motivational system. Motivation is provided through individualized token or mark systems of reinforcement aimed at prompting and strengthening adaptive behaviors. Some form of mild punishment is often used along with the motivational system in order to weaken competing, less desirable behaviors. Although the token system itself is seen as necessary to motivate change, the "teaching interaction" is seen as a key to teaching new behavior. The teaching interaction includes the expression of affection, praise for work already accomplished, descriptions of inappropriate and of appropriate behavior, the rationale for the appropriate behavior, request for acknowledgement that the child understands, practice, feedback, and rewards such as social praise and/or points, tokens, or marks for a "job well done." Finally, peers may be utilized in a treatment milieu to monitor and directly consequate the other's behavior. Not only may peer treatment effectively modify the target peer's behavior, but it may also modify in a desired direction the "peer modifier's" own behavior.

The techniques presented are only as good as the creativity of the therapist, consistency of the program, and cooperativeness of the natural environment in which the child will ultimately reside. That is, the techniques discussed are merely tools which may be used to shape a successful treatment program, an unsuccessful program, or no program at all, depending on the training and motivation of the staff. However, the techniques described do not offer a touchstone. It is up to the motivated therapist to acquire the skills necessary to effectively utilize the techniques by "learning with precision the more specific aspects of the approach" from first hand sources (e.g., Ferster, Culbertson, & Perrott-Boren, 1975; Miller, 1975; Skinner, 1953, 1966, 1968; Whaley & Mallot, 1970), "observing demonstrations in actual educational and clinical settings, and seeking out opportunities to practice the techniques under supervision" (Bijou, 1970, p. 69–70). One thing is clear: the procedures, when used skillfully, do work.

REFERENCE NOTES

1. McInnis, E. T. An individualized program for behavior-problem children. Paper presented at the Annual Meeting of the Association for the Advancement of Behavior Therapy, New York, September, 1973.
2. Roosa, J. B. SOCS: situations, options, consequences, and simulation: a technique for teaching social interaction. Unpublished paper presented at American Psychological Association, Montreal, August 1973. (Reprints may be obtained from Dr. Jan Roosa, Suite 107, 3700 W. 83rd., Prairie Village, Kansas 66206).
3. Kazdin, A. E. Implementing token programs: the use of staff, patients, and the institution of maximizing change. Paper presented at the Annual Meeting of the Association for the Advancement of Behavior Therapy, New York, October 1972.

REFERENCES

Axelrod, S. Comparison of individual and group contingencies in two special classes. *Behavior therapy*, 1973, *4*, 83–90.

Axelrod, S., Hall, R. V., & Maxwell, A. Use of peer attention to increase study behavior. *Behavior Therapy*, 1972, *3*, 349–351.

Ayllon, T., & Azrin, N. H. *The token economy: A motivational system for therapy and rehabilitation.* New York: Appleton-Century-Croft, 1968.

Baer, D. M. In the beginning, there was the response. In E. Ramp & G. Semb (Eds.), *Behavior analysis: Areas of research and application.* Englewood Cliffs, N. J.: Prentice-Hall, 1975, pp. 16–30.

Bailey , J. S., & Iwata, B. A. Reward versus cost token systems: An analysis of effects on students and teacher. *Proceedings of the 81st Annual Convention of the American Psychological Association*, 1973, *8*, 887–888.

Bailey, J. S., Timbers, G. D., Phillips, E. L., & Wolf, M. M. Modification of articulation errors of predelinquents by their peers. *Journal of Applied Behavior Analysis*, 1971, *4*, 265–281.

Barrish, H. H., Saunders, M., & Wolf, M. M. Good-behavior game: Effects of individual contingencies for group consequences on disruptive behavior in a classroom. *Journal of Applied Behavior Analysis*, 1969, *2*, 119–124.

Bijou, S. W. What psychology has to offer education—now. *Journal of Applied Behavior Analysis*, 1970, *3*, 65–71.

Bijou, S. W. *The basic stage of early childhood development*. Englewood Cliffs, N.J.: Prentice-Hall, 1976.

Bijou, S. W., & Redd, W. H. Child behavior therapy. In S. Arieti (Ed.), *American handbook of psychiatry, Vol. 5*. New York: Basic Books, 1975, pp. 319–345.

Birnbrauer, J. S., Burchard, J. D., & Burchard, S. N. Wanted: Behavior analysts. In R. H. Bradfield (Ed.), *Behavior modification: The human effort*. San Rafael, Cal.: Dimensions Publishing Co., 1970, pp. 19–76.

Braukmann, C. J., Maloney, D. M., Fixsen, D. L., Phillips, E. L., & Wolf, M. M. An analysis of a selection interview training package for predelinquents at Achievement Place. *Criminal Justice and Behavior*, 1974, *1*, 30–42.

Burchard, J. D. Systematic socialization: A programmed environment for the habilitation of antisocial retardates. *Psychological Record*, 1967, *17*, 461–476.

Burchard, J. D., & Barrera, F. An analysis of time-out and response cost in a programmed environment. *Journal of Applied Behavior Analysis*, 1972, *5*, 271–282.

Drass, S. D., & Jones, R. L. Learning disabled children as behavior modifiers. *Journal of Learning Disabilities*, 1971, *4*, 418–425.

Emery, R. E., & Marholin II, D. An applied behavior analysis of delinquency: The irrelevancy of relevant behavior. *American Psychologist*, 1977, *32*, 860–873.

Ferster, C. B., Culbertson, S., & Perrott-Boren, M. C. *Behavior principles* (*2nd ed.*). Englewood Cliffs, N. J.: Prentice-Hall, 1975.

Fixsen, D. L., Phillips, E. L., & Wolf, M. M. Achievement Place: Experiments in self-government with predelinquents. *Journal of Applied Behavior Analysis*, 1973, *6*, 31–47.

Gelfand, D. M., & Hartmann, D. P. *Child behavior analysis and therapy*. New York: Pergamon Press, 1975.

Graubard, P. S., Rosenberg, H., & Miller, M. B. Student applications of behavior modification to teachers and environments or ecological approaches to social deviance. In E. Ramp and G. Semb (Eds.), *New direction in education: Behavior analysis 1971*. Lawrence: The University of Kansas Support and Development Center for Follow Through, 1971.

Harris, V. W., & Sherman, J. A. Effects, of peer tutoring and consequences on the math performance of elementary students. *Journal of Applied Behavior Analysis*, 1973, *6*, 587–598.

Herbert, E. W., Pinkston, E. M., Hayden, M. L., Sajwaj, T. E., Pinkston, S., Cordua, G., & Jackson, C. Adverse effects of differential parental attention. *Journal of Applied Behavior Analysis*, 1973, *6*, 15–30.

Johnston, J. M. Punishment of human behavior. *American Psychologist*, 1972, *27*, 1033–54.

Johnston, J. M., & Johnston, G. T. Modification of consonant speech-sound articulation in young children. *Journal of Applied Behavior Analysis*, 1972, *5*, 233–246.

Kagel, J. H. & Winkler, R. C. Behavioral economics: Areas of cooperative research between economics and applied behavior analysis. *Journal of Applied Behavior Analysis*, 1972, *5*, 335–341.

Kazdin, A. E. Issues in behavior modification with mentally retarded persons.

American Journal of Mental Deficiency, 1973a, *78,* 134–40.

Kazdin, A. E. Time out for some considerations on punishment. *American Psychologist,* 1973b, *28,* 939–941.

Kazdin, A. E. Recent advances in token economy research. In M. Hersen, R. M. Eisler, & P. M. Miller (Eds.), *Progress in behavior modification, Vol. 1.* New York: Academic Press, 1975, pp. 233–275.

Kazdin, A. E. *The token economy.* New York: Plenum, 1977.

Kazdin, A. E., & Bootzin, R. B. The token economy: An evaluative review. *Journal of Applied Behavior Analysis,* 1972, *5,* 343–372.

Kifer, R. E., Lewis, M. A., Green, D. R., & Phillips, E. L. Training predelinquent youths and their parents to negotiate conflict situations. *Journal of Applied Behavior Analysis,* 1974, *7,* 357–364.

Leitenberg, H. Is time-out from positive reinforcement an aversive event? A review of the experimental evidence. *Psychological Bulletin,* 1965, *64,* 428–441.

Levitt, E. E. Psychotherapy with children: A further evaluation. *Behaviour Research and Therapy,* 1963, *1,* 45–51.

Long, J., & Madsen, C. H. Five-year-olds as behavioral engineers for younger students in a day-care center. In E. Ramp and G. Semb (Eds.), *Behavior analysis: Areas of research and application.* Englewood Cliffs, N. J.: Prentice Hall, 1975, pp. 341–356.

Marholin II, D., & Bijou, S. W. A behavioral approach to assessment of children's behavioral disorders. *Child Welfare,* 1977, *56,* 93–106.

Marholin II, D., Plienis, A. J., Harris, S., & Marholin, B. L. Mobilization of the community through a behavioral approach: A school program for adjudicated females. *Criminal Justice and Behavior,* 1975, *2,* 130–145.

Marholin II. D., Siegel, L. J., & Phillips, D. Treatment and transfer: A search for empirical procedures. In M. Hersen, R. M. Eisler, & P. M. Miller (Eds.), *Progress in behavior modification, Vol. 3.* New York: Academic Press, 1976, pp. 293–342.

Martin, R. *Legal challenges to behavior modification: Trends in schools, corrections, and mental health.* Champaign, Ill.: Research Press, 1975.

McInnis, E. T., & Marholin II, D. Individualizing treatment programs for children in group settings. *Child Welfare,* 1977, *56,* 449–463.

Medland, M. B., & Stachnik, T. J. Good-behavior game: A replication and systematic analysis. *Journal of Applied Behavior Analysis,* 1972, *5,* 45–51.

Miller, L. K. *Principles of everyday behavior analysis.* Belmont, Cal.: Wadsworth, 1975.

Minkin, N., Braukmann, C. J., Minkin, B. L., Timbers, B. I., Fixsen, D. L., Phillips, E. L., & Wolf, M. M. The social validation and training of conversation skills. *Journal of Applied Behavior Analysis,* 1976, *9,* 127–139.

Monkman, M. M. *A milieu therapy program for behaviorally disturbed children.* Springfield, Ill.: Charles C. Thomas, 1972.

Nay, W. R. *Behavioral intervention: Contemporary strategies.* New York: Gardner Press, 1976.

O'Leary, K. D., & Drabman, R. Token reinforcement programs in the classroom: A review. *Psychological Bulletin,* 1971, *75,* 379–398.

O'Leary, K. D., & Wilson, G. T. *Behavior therapy: Application and outcome.* Englewood Cliffs, N. J.: Prentice-Hall, 1975.

Packard, R. G. The control of 'classroom attention': A group contingency for complex behavior. *Journal of Applied Behavior Analysis,* 1970, *3,* 13–28.

Patterson, G. R. An application of conditioning techniques to the control of a hyperactive child. In L. P. Ullmann & L. Krasner (Eds.), *Case studies in behavior modification.* New York: Holt, Rinehart, & Winston, 1965, pp. 370–375.

Patterson, G. R., Cobb, J. A., & Ray, R. S., Direct intervention in the classroom: A set of procedures for the aggressive child. In F. Clark, D. Evans, & L. Hamerlynck (Eds.), *Implementing behavioral programs for schools and clinics.* Champaign, Ill.: Research Press, 1972, pp. 151–201.

Phillips, E. L. Achievement Place: Token reinforcement procedures in a home-style rehabilitation setting for predelinquent boys. *Journal of Applied Behavior Analysis,* 1968, *1,* 213–223.

Phillips, E. L., Phillips, E. A., Fixsen, D. L., & Wolf, M. M. *The teaching family handbook.* Lawrence: University of Kansas Printing Service, 1974.

Phillips, E. L., Phillips, E. A., Wolf, M. M. & Fixsen, D. L. Achievement Place: Development of the elected manager system. *Journal of Applied Behavior Analysis,* 1973, *6,* 541–561.

Rimm, D. C., & Masters, J. C. *Behavior therapy: Techniques and empirical findings.* New York: Academic Press, 1974.

Ross, A. O. *Psychological disorders of children: A behavioral approach to therapy.* New York: McGraw-Hill, 1974.

Rosenbaum, A., O'Leary, K. D., & Jacob, R. G. Behavioral intervention with hyperactive children: Group consequences as a supplement to individual contingencies. *Behavior Therapy,* 1975, *6,* 315–323.

Schmidt, G. W., & Ulrich, R. E. Effects of group contingent events upon classroom noise. *Journal of Applied Behavior Analysis,* 1969, *2,* 171–179.

Siegel, L. J., & Steinman, W. M. The modification of a peer-observer's classroom behavior as a function of his serving as a reinforcing agent. In E. Ramp & G. Semb (Eds.), *Behavior analysis: Areas of research and application.* Englewood Cliffs, N. J.: Prentice-Hall, 1975, pp. 321–340.

Skinner, B. F. *Science and human behavior.* New York: Macmillan, 1953.

Skinner, B. F. What is an experimental analysis of behavior? *Journal of the Experimental Analysis of Behavior,* 1966, *9,* 213–218.

Skinner, B. F. *The technology of teaching.* New York: Appleton-Century-Crofts, 1968.

Solomon, R. W., & Wahler, R. G. Peer reinforcement control of classroom problem behavior. *Journal of Applied Behavior Analysis,* 1973, *6,* 49–56.

Surratt, P. E., Ulrich, R., & Hawkins, R. An elementary student as a behavioral engineer. *Journal of Applied Behavior Analysis,* 1969, *2,* 85–92.

Tharp, R. G., & Wetzel, R. J. *Behavior modification in the natural environment.* New York: Academic Press, 1969.

Ulrich, R., Louisell, S. E., & Wolf, M. M. The Learning Village: A behavioral approach to early education. *Educational Technology,* 1971, *11,* 32–48.

Wagner, B. R., & Breitmeyer, R. G. PACE: A residential, community oriented behavior modification program for adolescents. *Adolescence,* 1975, *10,* 277–286.

Wahler, R. G. Oppositional children: A quest for parental reinforcement control. *Journal of Applied Behavior Analysis,* 1969, *2,* 159–170.

Walker, H. M., & Buckley, N. K. Programming generalization and maintenance of treatment effects across time and across settings. *Journal of Applied Behavior Analysis,* 1972, *5,* 209–224.

Werner, J. S., Minkin, N., Minkin, B. L., Fixsen, D. L., Phillips, E. L., & Wolf, M. M. "Intervention package": An analysis to prepare juvenile delinquents for encounters with police officers. *Criminal Justice and Behavior*, 1975, *2*, 55–84.

Whaley, D. L., & Mallot, R. W. *Elementary principles of behavior.* Englewood Cliffs, N. J.: Prentice-Hall, 1970.

White, G. D., Nielson, G., & Johnson, S. M. Time-out duration and the suppression of deviant behavior in children. *Journal of Applied Behavior Analysis*, 1972, *5*, 111–120.

NOTES

1. The authors would like to thank Dr. Eric Ward for his invaluable comments on an earlier draft of the manuscript.

2. From *The teaching family handbook* by E. L. Phillips, E. A. Phillips, D. L. Fixsen, and M. M. Wolf. Achievement Place Project, Department of Human Development, University of Kansas, Lawrence, Kansas, 1974. Reprinted by permission.

3. From *The teaching family handbook* by E. L. Phillips, E. A. Phillips, D. L. Fixsen, and M. M. Wolf. Achievement Place Project, Department of Human Development, University of Kansas, Lawrence, Kansas, 1974. Reprinted by permission.

4. From "Training predelinquent youths and their parents to negotiate conflict situations" by R. E. Kifler, M. A. Lewis, D. R. Green, and E. L. Phillips, *Journal of Applied Behavior Analysis*, 1974, *7*, 357–364. Copyright 1974 by the Society for the Experimental Analysis of Behavior, Inc. Reprinted by permission.

6

Modification
of Family Behavior

Lawrence R. Weathers and Robert Paul Liberman

Although initial efforts at family therapy, derived from the psycho-analytic model, engaged the interest of many professionals in a new systems approach to treatment, the techniques were ambiguously described, time-consuming, expensive, and required patients who were reflective and psychologically minded (Framo, 1965). To make services available to a large number of families at a more reasonable cost, professionals began to enlist the help of the parents as co-therapists in family therapy.

The use of parents' assistance in the modification of a child's behavior dates back to at least Freud's "Little Hans." Freud used Little Hans' father as the primary therapeutic agent. As we have learned more about the technology of behavioral change in human beings and the dynamics of family interaction, methods for modifying family behavior have been developed that are more easily transmittable to the nonprofessional, including the parent. The directness and the simplicity of behavioral approaches make it feasible for parents and other family members to become the rightful owners of the control of each other's behavior. This "power to the people" strategy makes sense when one considers that parents and other family members who are responsible for setting values, standards, and goals for their children spend 24 hours a day with their child, whereas a professional usually can spend no more than an hour a week. There are not enough mental health professionals to spend an hour a week in an office with all the children who are in need of treatment. Besides, the office or clinic is an artificial place to learn how to behave at home or school.

The impact of this dissemination to families is often broader than one would expect. These techniques are often transferred from parent to parent within the community setting, as parents teach their neighbors the child management techniques that they have come to use and believe in themselves (Parrish, Note 1). Parent training has not been limited to behavioral approaches. Over 300,000 parents have been trained in Thomas Gordon's Rogerian-based Parent Effectiveness Training since 1970. This popular approach trains parents in child management techniques such as active listening, negotiation, "I messages," etc. ("Reassessing the Power," 1976).

Four conceptual tributaries converge in modification of family behavior: the *systems* view of family problems, the *triangular* model of family contingencies, the *exchange* model, and *developmental* considerations. Each of these is discussed with respect to the change and maintenance of family behavior.

The Systems Model of Family Behavior

The systems model provides a structure within which to understand family behavior, whether pathological or healthy. The family is an interactive syatem in which each member serves to maintain the behavior of all other family members, whether the behavior is desirable or not. The behavior of individuals within the system is a product of modeling and the reinforcement contingencies among family members and not just the characteristics of the individual. Within the family system each individual's behavior is functional for him, even though it may be disturbing to others. The individual's behavior serves to get him what he wants.

Each family member's behavior tends to be complementary to other family members. They fit together like pieces in a puzzle, each supporting and hanging on to the others. For instance, if one has a hyperactive child, one probably has a hyperreactive parent or at least a parent who ignores quiet, purposeful activities and reacts to noisy and restless activity. If one has an aggressive child, one has parents who reinforce, and perhaps model that behavior.

In moving beyond the "identified patient" conceptualization to a systems view, it is apparent that an individual problem is a family problem, an intervention for the individual is an intervention for the family, and a change in the individual reflects a change in the family. If a desirable change in an individual is to become permanent, the whole family system must accommodate the new contingency patterns as behavioral norms. That is, a new interpersonal balance in the family which supports these new norms of behavior and exchange must be established.

Intervention systems that look at the family as a whole and intervene on the reinforcement exchanges between individuals hold a better chance of changing the system than approaches directed at the identified problem person. This often means intervening at multiple and often disparate points in the system, so as to adjust the interplay throughout the family, rather than focusing on the problem person.

The Triangular Model

The triangular model is an elaboration of Tharp and Wetzel's (1969) groundbreaking triadic model of the family change process. The triadic model is a description of a unidirectional relationship among the consultant, the parent, the target child. The parent controlling the child's natural reinforcers is the primary contingency manager of the child, with guidance from the consultant. What this model does not do, but the "triangular" extension of it can do, is to elaborate on the contingencies interrelating all three members, as a system. The flow of influence and reinforcement of behavior is not unilateral, it is interactional. Each family member has very clear and powerful controls over the other's behavior. If these are not understood and taken into consideration when developing and maintaining a change program for family, then it can very easily go awry. For the relationship among consultant-parent-child to promote desirable changes, it is necessary for each participant to be adequately and systematically rewarded for his efforts. If mutual rewards are not forthcoming, the triadic relationship will become dysfunctional and terminate. The triangular model, depicted in Figure 1, is a vehicle for elucidating the interactive complexities of the contingencies that the consultant, parent, and the child have with each other. Of great import are the reinforcement contingencies and behavioral control that both the parent and the child have over the mental health consultant. He is not "above" their changing his behavior. His behavior will certainly change as a product of engaging in a "reinforcement system" with them. By making explicit and planning for the reinforcement the consultant needs to receive from his engagement with the family, he is more likely to remain motivated, systematic, and effective in his relationship with the family.

The triangular model illustrates the contingencies maintaining the triad as a system directed toward altering family behavior. The child, who is usually the identified target of the system, can tolerate the least delay of reinforcement (as indicated by the short line "B"). For a child, the rewards such as attention, food, and privileges must initially be given immediately in order to shape the behavior. Over time the delay of reinforcement can usually be increased substantially, though it must begin with short delays. The parent, being more mature, is usually able to tolerate a somewhat longer delay of reinforcement from the consultant (medium length line "A"). Parental reinforcers are usually dispensed on an approximately weekly basis via praise or attention from the consultant. The consultant has to satisfy himself with a very delayed reinforcement (long dotted line "E," medium length dotted line "C") from changes in both the child's and the parent's behavior, along with attention from the family, publications, and fees.

These differences in acceptable length of reinforcement delay must be clearly recognized. Many parents imitate the consultant's reinforcement of their own behavior in their consequation of their child's behavior. A child simply cannot tolerate the delay of reinforcement under which adults typically operate. These differences must be made explicitly clear to parents

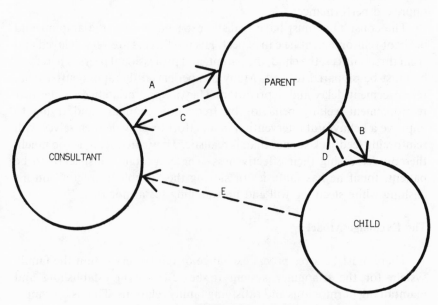

Figure 1
Reinforcement exchange in triangular model.

so that their tendency to duplicate the consultant's role does not entrap them into trying to make "little adults" out of their children.

Parents are often not responsive to some of the potential reinforcements supplied by their child to them (dashed line "D"). Many parents do not respond to their child's improved behavior as if it were reinforcing to them, even though they may articulate their desire to have a child who is better behaved. This may occur because the parent anticipates termination of their consultant's reinforcing social attention (solid line "A"), when they achieve success in their role as mediator and change agent for their problem child. Therefore, the child's improvement threatens the parent's reinforcement. The consultant has to carefully correct this notion so that the parent understands that the consultant's continued attention and contact is maintained by the parent's improved performance (dotted line "C") and from the child's improved performance (dotted line "E"). This must be done both verbally and behaviorally. One example of this is a procedure used by the authors in training groups of parents as behavior therapists for their children. The authors give those parents who have done their homework exercises approximately 10 minutes of their undivided attention in front of the whole training group. Parents are passed by in the group discussion when they indicate that they have not done their homework. In addition, when their child makes an improvement they are given extra time to tell the group and the leaders about it. The leaders model and encourage group approval for parents' reporting on their child's improved performance.

The consultant must have realistic expectancies for the amount and delay of reinforcement he can expect. His reinforcers are very delayed and from three sources, the child, the parent, and professional peers. Therefore, he must be prepared to wait. Many inexperienced therapists suffer from reinforcement delay and deprivation. They inappropriately escalate their reinforcement-seeking behavior by frequently changing and trying to improve a behavioral intervention in an effort to provide themselves with reinforcing feedback sooner than is realistic. They can intervene too much, thereby decreasing their effectiveness. The consultant must learn to be patient, for if he has fantasies of slaying the "problem dragon" on his dashing white steed, he will end up watching his armor rust.

The Exchange Model

There must be a reciprocal exchange of reinforcers within the family system for the triangular system to be effective in establishing and maintaining harmonious and satisfying family relations. That is, one must expect to provide reinforcers to others in the family for whatever is received from others. There are no gifts or Santa Claus bringing something for nothing. The value of relating to another person and remaining in that relationship is dependent on the amount, type, and rate of reinforcement one gets out of relating with him (Stuart, 1972). Parent training, contingency contracts, and behavioral family therapy are media through which the exchange of reinforcers can be systematically applied to family interactions. The exchange model spells out exactly how one may earn reinforcement, produces an opportunity to assure that the exchanges of reinforcement are equitable, and enhances the range, rate, and magnitude of reinforcement. As a result of applying this model to therapy, the value of interpersonal relationships within a family should become richer and more satisfying.

Developmental Model

To round out the conceptual underpinnings of family behavior therapy, we need to look at the effects of the development of the target child on the choice of behavioral interventions. Parents need to be taught to listen to the desires and needs of their children, even young ones. Information on maturation is given through behavioral workshops so that parents can know how at all stages to involve their child appropriately and actively in the change process.

One of the crucial points in this development of participation is at about 11 years, the transition point between Piaget's concrete operations to formal operation stages of intellectual development. The developmental change makes the child much more facile in participating in adult abstractions and values. At this juncture it becomes critical for children to begin to have an active and participatory role in targeting the behaviors to be changed, selecting methodolgies for changing them, and determining the reinforcers to be involved. Before 11 years of age it is generally acceptable for parents to target behaviors and develop behavioral programs unilaterally, only consulting the child in terms of reinforcers for which he will work. In the following discussion, parent training as generally a unilateral approach, is discussed for children less than 11 years old. In the latter part of the chapter contingency contracting will be explicated as a more appropriate intervention for children greater than 11 years of age.

During preadolescence and adolescence, peer reinforcers become more important or even dominant. Effective programs for these children must include this dimension, particularly if behavior changes are to be durable after the intervention is withdrawn.

Parent Training

Training parents as behavior therapists is much more than it appears to be. It is a way to modify the whole family interaction system, without being

Table 1
General Dimensions of Parent Training

Advantages	MODELING	
	Office (Usually Group)	*Community (Usually Individual)*
Transfer of Training	Good Practice specific implementation skills which are necessary to change child's behavior in An artificial setting which is *not optimal* for transfer. (This leads to ⏐)	Excellent The actual setting where the behaviors will have to function, which is ideal for transfer. (This leads to ⏐)
Speed of Results	Fast ↓ The practice of the actual behaviors improves the speed of results in proportion to how similar the practice situation is to the implementation situation Some situational translation is necessary here so the results are a little slower than ⟶	Very fast ↓ When the practice situation is identical to the implementation situation as is the case here.
Diagnostic Opportunity	High Being able to observe the parent/child interaction can offer the clinician many valuable insights, The artificiality of the office situation limits this when compared to ⟶	Very high The natural environmental determinants of behavior found in the home.
Disadvantages	*Office (Usually Group)*	*Community (Usually Individual)*
Cost/ effectiveness	Good These approaches tend to be time-consuming and difficult whether done individually or in a group	Fair The added transportation and time costs of community application are extensive
Staff Skill to Implement	High Substantial clinical skill is necessary to demonstrate and shape parent behaviors	Very high Particularly when done in the family home where the therapist is not the most comfortable and all the situational determinants of disfunctional behavior are present.
Parent as an Independent Problem Solver	Low Parents are usually given specific descriptions of how they are to behave with little conceptual information on how to problem solve family behaviour problems. The family continues to be dependent on the professional, for future problem solving.	Low

	Moderate	Low
Parent Resistence to Demonstrating Their Skill	Parents tend to see their demonstration of their skill in front of the therapist as an aversive and evaluating situation--	They tend to feel more comfortable in the familiar surroundings of their home.
	Low	Moderate
Motivation of Parent	The active involvement required in this approach tends to be threatening and high in response cost. Special motivational procedures such as doing it in the family home helps.	

DYDATIC

Advantages	*Office (Usually Group)*	*Community (Usually Individual)*
	Excellent	Good
Cost/ effectiveness	Since these are easy to do in a group format and applicable to a wide range of child problems and parent capabilities but	Community groups are more difficult to organize.
	Moderate	Moderate
Staff Skill to Implement	Workers with little specific experience in parent training can utilize this approach because they can be "preprogrammed" with the aid of cassettes, leader's guides, manuals, texts, etc.	
	Potentially very high	Potentially high
Parents as an Independent Problem Solver	Since parents are trained to understand the procedures and concepts of behavior analysis and modification they can *potentially* continue to analyze and modify family behaviors after treatment has been terminated (but there are no good data on this supposition). This may allow parents to take the responsibility for earlier recognition and remediation of family problems.	
Motivation of Parents	The group setting can be used as a differential social reinforcer.	The individual contact and attention can be used as an effective motivator.

Disadvantages	*Office (Usually Group)*	*Community (Usually Individual)*
	Very Slow	Very Slow
Speed of Results	Many concepts must be learned before interventions begin (if immediate results are important modeling must be used).	
	Difficult	Difficult
Transfer of Training	The behaviors and stimuli tend to be very different from those required for implementation of behavioral programs. This can be a major roadblock to the effectiveness of Dydactic programs; this is often due to ulterior payoffs the parent receives as a function of the child's pathology.	

explicit about it. Explicitly the parents are trained as behavior therapists, or as "stand-ins" for the professional. Since the explicit focus is on the child, and changes in parent behavior are "to manage the child," there tends to be much less resistance and defensiveness on the part of the parents. Implicitly the parents' behavior toward the child and other family members are changed in order to modify the child's behavior. These changes in parents' behavior may have more lasting importance on the child's development.

Parent training as a mode of modifying family behavior has many practical features to recommend it. There are not enough qualified therapists to deal with all the problem children who need help. Not only can parent training relieve therapists from having to treat children directly, but it also has the potential for building competance in the parents, who can be on the "front line" for early intervention when new problems first present themselves. Early intervention can greatly reduce the costs and difficulties correcting a behavior problem, since well-trained parents are likely to "nip it in the bud" versus waiting for it to become big enough to invest the money and energy to consult a professional. Thus, parent training is a vehicle for moving child mental health from intervention to prevention.

Prevention of behavior problems is much easier for a parent to do than for a mental health consultant, because the parent naturally controls the major reinforcers for the child. Many reinforcers, such as social reinforcement from a parent, simply and obviously are not transferrable to another person, such as the therapist. Also, training the parent makes it much easier for the child to utilize the new behaviors he learns, because he does not have to transfer stimulus control from a therapist to the people he has to respond to on a day to day basis.

Since transfer of training is a major problem in generalization of any new learned behavior, avoiding the whole issue pays off handsomely in quicker and more durable changes in family behavior. Training the parents as behavior therapists also serves to modify their behavior toward the child, and not just the child's behavior. Therefore, parent training serves as a way of intervening in the family contingency system at more than one point. This increases the probability that the intervention will be durable after the mental health consultant has withdrawn, because the system itself has been intervened by not just one target individual.

There are many approaches to parent training, each with its own advantages and disadvantages. Table 1 graphically depicts some general dimensions of parent training along with their merits and liabilities. For discussion purposes, major dimensions can be broken down into four factors: modeling versus didactic approaches, and office versus home implementation (which are usually group versus individual, respectively).

Probably a combination of the didactic and the modeling approaches is most effective. Actual training programs tend to combine both, since they tend to complement each other in terms of their strengths and weaknesses. The didactic behavioral training seems to be an excellent, inexpensive approach for the first line of intervention on a wide array of problems. This can be effectively backed up with specific skill training taught by modeling approaches in areas that were not adequately remediated by the broader spectrum didactic techniques.

At the Oxnard Community Mental Health Center in California, groups of 12 parents have been participating in 8–10 week workshops in child management led by paraprofessionals and social workers. These group workshops sprouted from a community need since schools, parents, welfare and probation departments, and family doctors flooded the Center with referrals of children who had behavorial, emotional, and academic problems. Over 400 parents have obtained training during the past 5 years, and the Parent Workshop has become a mainstay of the Center's program and the first line of service for all child psychiatry.

The Workshop Leaders. Leaders are selected on the basis of interest, commitment to work with the problems of children, and willingness to work one night per week. One psychiatric social worker and several mental health technicians form the core leadership pool. Potential leaders learn how to train parents in child management by serving in a trainee or assistant leader's role in actual workshops. Generally, trainees need to assist with three Workshops before they are ready to take primary leadership repsonsibility. Initially, the group leader acts as the primary consultant to the parents, but as the workshop proceeds, parents are encouraged and reinforced for taking active roles in giving suggestions and feedback to each other.

The Curriculum

Since a major focus on this parent training effort is the remediation of presenting problems specified at the clinical intake, the Workshop format includes approximately one hour of general didactic material and one hour of individual case consultation and intervention for each meeting. Both general and specific interventions are presented through a combination of lecture, discussion, and behavioral rehearsal with modeling and feedback.

The general curriculum is summarized in outline form in Table 2. At the first meeting, the social learning model of child behavior is presented and comparisons are drawn with other orientations or "schools" of psychotherapy. The concept of "a behavior" is operationalized in lay terms and parents are taught to specify and pinpoint the *observable* dimensions of their children's behavior. Parents also learn that normal and abnormal behaviors are on a continuum, and have similar causes and explanations in the social learning model.

Table 2
Outline of Curriculum

I. Purposes and rationale
    A. Ground rules and deposit
    B. Readings and assignments
    C. Our consulting contingent on home-recorded data

II. The causes of behavior and how behavior can be changed

III. The social learning model

IV. What is "a behavior"?
    A. Observation and specification
    B. Normal versus abnormal (disturbing) behavior
    C. Assign parents to begin thinking about one behavior to work on

V. What is learning?
    A. The ABC's of behaviors (antecedents, behavior, consequences)
    B. Reinforcement and motivation; increasing rates of desirable behavior
       1. Types (social, nonsocial) of reinforcers
       2. Advantages of social reinforcers
       3. Behavioral components of effective social reinforcement (role playing)
    C. Modeling
    D. Shaping techniques; the importance of reinforcing approximations to your
       expectations

VI. Ways of decreasing undesirable behavior
    A. What is punishment?
       1. Punishment is not defined by type of pain inflicted
       2. Functionally punishment is defined by its suppressing effect on behavior
       3. Pain and aggression are unnecessary; thus reducing parental guilt and
          anxiety
    B. The forms of punishment
       1. Ignoring
       2. Mild social punishment
       3. Time-out from reinforcement
    C. When and where to use each type
    D. Behavioral components of effective punishment (role playing)
    E. Special problems in the use of punishment

VII. Combining reinforcement and punishment to effectively change behavior
     A. Special motivational systems
        1. Tokens, points, stars
        2. Contingency contracting

VIII. Forecasting behavioral problems as a parent and how to handle the future
      relationship between parents and child

Parents are guided to specify a behavior which not only is of major concern to them, but also appears to offer the parents a potentially successful experience in dealing with their child's problem. If at all possible, parents are guided into pinpointing an appropriate behavior which they would like to accelerate, since this requires some form of positive parent-child interaction rather than criticism, ignoring, or punishing.

In subsequent workshop sessions, parents bring in a daily count of the behavior they have specified and are observing. After 1–2 weeks of baseline record-keeping, the leader suggests ways for parents to change the targeted behavior in a desired direction. The in-home observations and data records by the parents are continued on a daily basis, until a successful intervention strategy is found. When a parent is satisfied with the behavior change obtained, a second behavior problem is pinpointed and the intervention process begins again.

In the workshop, parents cover the antecedents and consequences of behavior, the importance of reinforcing consequences for behavior, types of reinforcers available to parents, reinforcer fading, bribes versus rewards, social modeling, shaping, the role of punishment, kinds of punishment and how to use each.

Throughout all topics, parents read homework assignments in advance from texts on child management (Patterson & Guillion, 1974; Becker, 1971). At the beginning of each meeting, a brief quiz on the reading assignment is administered to encourage parents to complete their assignments. Parental discussion and cathartic ventilation is not a major component of their training process.

A series of role-playing experiences teach parents skills in the use of social reward (reinforcement), mild social punishment, ignoring, and time-out procedures. For each of these child management techniques a number of specific behavioral dimensions for effective delivery have been isolated. For example, when giving praise to their children, parents practice smiling and leaning toward their children, and delivering the approval in a warm tone of voice *immediately* after the appropriate behavior has occurred. Parents practice each of these procedures using scenes reflecting common household situations. Group leaders model appropriate interactions and give specific feedback to each parent on the non-verbal and verbal behavioral components of their performance.

Population Served

Of all those participating, 72% were mothers and 28% fathers. Completion of high school was the mean educational level for all participants. Seventy-two percent of the parents were married and 28% were divorced, separated or widowed. Of the married parents, 19% brought their spouses to at least half of the meetings. Each family had an average of three children. The mean age of the children who were considered to have problems by the parents was 7 with a range of 1 to 15 years. Sixty percent of the "problem children" were male and 40% female.

At the time of intake and orientation, each of the parents filled out a Behavior Severity Checklist to indicate the behavioral problems exhibited by their children. In Table 3 is shown the percent of parents reporting the 15 most common problems as "severe and of great concern." Of all the parents, 41% reported that their children's behavior was troublesome only at home, 57% reported troubles at home and at school, and only 2% reported that problems existed at school alone. Only 4% of the children viewed as deviant had previously received psychiatric treatment. Less than 3% of the children were autistic or psychotic. The great majority of the deviant children could be diagnosed as "adjustment reaction of childhood," "unsocialized aggressive reaction of childhood," and "hyperkinetic reaction of childhood."

At the Oxnard Mental Health Center, attendance at Parent Workshops has been a helpful measure of program progress for changing the program structure. When the workshops began, attendance for the eight weekly sessions was under 30% of those coming to at least the first session. This dismal response prompted the institution of an avoidance contingency with the parents: A $10.00 "good faith" deposit is now required at the first session which is returned in full if one or both parents (or a surrogate sent by them) attend each and every session. In the 39 workshops held since that contingency was established, attendance has averaged over 75%. Forty-

Table 3
Behavior Problems Reported as "Severe" by Parents Participating in the Workshop

Behavioral Problem	Percentage Rating as "Severe"
Disobedience; difficulty in disciplinary control	52
Disruptiveness; tendency to annoy and bother others	49
Fighting	45
Talking back	43
Short attention span	42
Restlessness; inability to sit still	40
Irritability; easily aroused to intense anger	37
Temper tantrums	35
Attention-seeking; "show-off" behavior	35
Crying over minor annoyances	33
Lack of self-confidence	33
Hyperactivity; "always on the go"	33
Distractability	33
Specific fears; phobias	17
Bed wetting	16

two percent of parents attending the first Workshop session completed the nine sessions with perfect attendance. Eighty-four percent of the enrolled parents completed the Workshop with only 1–2 "excused" absences. An "excuse" was given if the parent(s) sent in their homework assignment and behavioral data by proxy and completed the quiz which covered the assigned reading material. Regarding the most important criterion of participation, parents brought to the meetings the behavioral data on their children when it was expected and assigned 86% of the time.

Attempts to involve poverty-level, Mexican-American parents of pre-delinquent junior high school students in Workshops failed to achieve more than a 10% attendance beyond the first session. Poor attendance occurred, despite such efforts as calling the parent(s) on the phone reminding them about the Workshop session, sending messages about the Workshop home with their children, offering them transportation to the evening Workshop at the mental health center, and in some cases, having a Spanish-speaking teacher's aide talk to the parent face-to-face. Difficulties were also encountered in attempts to enlist these parents' cooperation in setting up school-home contingency contracts for their children, even when home visits by indigenous non-professionals were utilized. When Workshops were held more conveniently in public housing projects and were *led* by indigenous and Spanish-speaking leaders, attendance increased to 35%. While this is an improvement, an adequate technology to promote the attendance and participation of parents from poverty and multi-problem families is yet to be developed.

Program Outcome

The outcomes of the Parent Workshop Program have been measured by evaluating the conceptual and behavioral skills of the parents, the behavioral changes produced in the children of the Workshop participants, and the generality of training effects at follow-up made 12 and 24 months after the termination of each Workshop. Since the Workshop curriculum has focused on the intellectual and cognitive education of the parents through lectures, reading assignments, demonstrations, and verbal discussion of the effects of parental interventions guided by the Workshop leaders, program outcome can partially be determined by changes in pre-post tests of conceptual knowledge about child management procedures. Conceptual knowledge was assessed using a 50 item true-false test of basic social learning principles and behavioral intervention procedures. Over the past four years of administering the test, parents have shown a 61% mean increase in correct answers on the post-test taken at the end of the Workshop.

Because of the expense and inconvenience of sending observers into the homes to directly assess changes in children's behaviors, the self-reports of parents and their data graphs have served as indirect measures of change in the children. These graphs contained the parents' recorded observations of the behaviors targeted for change in their children during baseline and treatment periods. A parental intervention or treatment was considered "successful" if it changed the specified behavior by 30% or more in the desired direction from the average frequency recorded during the baseline period. Sixty-two percent of the targeted problem behaviors responded to treatment by either desirable increases or decreases in frequency. To substantiate parental reports, observers have been sent directly into homes on five occasions, and have verified the data brought in by the parents. Less than 2% of parents did not complete at least one child management intervention. In almost every case, these individuals were attending the Workshop by order of the court, and avoided active participation in the parent training program.

After the parents were guided to specify target problems in their child and to record their observations of the problem behavior (or its alternative, desirable, complementary behavior) during a baseline period, a treatment intervention was chosen after joint consultation among the parent, the Workshop leader, and the supervising psychologist. Parents utilized a variety of reinforcing strategies to accelerate desirable behaviors, and extinction and punishment strategies to decelerate problem behaviors. In Table 4 are listed the interventions which were reported as being successful by the parents. In general, parents were already using punishment and deprivation, mostly incorrectly and with poor results, in attempting to control their children when they joined the Workshop. It was easier for parents to learn to apply punishment techniques correctly, than to develop and consistently use positive reinforcement approaches. Parents were more likely to identify, focus on, and specify problem behaviors rather than

Table 4
Treatment Interventions Reported by Parents
to be Successful in Modifying Problem
Behavior in Their Children

Intervention	Percentage of All Successful Interventions
Social reinforcement	20
Token reinforcement	19
Activity reinforcer	13
Time-out from reinforcement	19
Extinction	14
Enuresis alarm	8
Mild social punishment	5
Other interventions	2

operationalizing desirable behavioral goals which might be incompatible with the problem behaviors. The Workshop leaders, therefore, were sensitized to this parental proclivity for orienting toward and punishing undesirable, disturbing behaviors. The leaders emphasized positive reinforcement strategies from the start, attempting to steer the parents toward accelerating desirable behaviors during their first efforts at developing an intervention.

Although project data strongly suggest a relationship between parents' level of educational attainment and success of outcome, the relationship was not statistically significant. In addition, the relationship between number of parents in the home and success of outcome was not significant.

The most meaningful measure of outcome in parent training efforts, should be in the performance or behavior of the parents themselves as they attempt to carry out child management procedures which they have learned. Behavioral measures of what parents *do* with their children are more rigorous criteria of outcome than are tests of conceptual knowledge or what parents talk about doing with their children. Role-playing or behavioral rehearsal is a step toward more realistic and direct measurement of the changes that occur in parents' abilities to manage their children's problem behaviors. A series of twelve brief scenes of parent-child interactions have been developed for evaluating parenting skills before and after participation in the Parent Workshop Program. For example, a parent is told, "Jamie and Todd are fighting with each other again. Despite your repeated requests that they stop, the brothers continue to fight and argue. What would you do in this situation?" This introduction is followed by a role-played scene in which two of the staff from the Workshop Program portray children fighting with each other. The parent is instructed to behave as he or she might in trying to handle this type of sibling conflict. A third Workshop staff person assesses the adequacy of the parent's intervention using a pre-determined set of evaluative criteria on a checklist.

For each of the role-played scenes, one or two child management strategies are previously chosen as most appropriate; for the fighting example above, mild social punishment or time out are most effective. If in a role-played scene a parent began delivering mild social punishment to the "fighting children," he or she would be given "correct" checkmarks for each of the following behavioral components:

1. looks at the children
2. moves to within 3 feet of children (physical proximity)
3. exhibits "disapproving" facial expression
4. gives brief verbalization (less than 3 sentences)
5. verbalizes with low volume and slow, fluent pace
6. makes a non-verbal gesture consistent with disapproval
7. early delivery of punishment (within 5 seconds of start of "fight")

8. tracks children's behavior to positively reinforce the first sign of
   desirable change.

A similar series of evaluative criteria is used for each of the parenting
strategies required by the role-played scenes. Preliminary results, using the
role-playing format for evaluating the Workshop Program, indicate that
the pre- and post-tests are sensitive to changes in the parents' child
management skills, and to different types of Workshop curricula. Twenty-
eight parents were consecutively assigned to two groups receiving a
standard Workshop curriculum limited to didactic presentations, and to
two groups receiving the standard approach plus 30 minutes of behavioral
rehearsal with modeling and feedback on intervention strategies such as
social reinforcement, time-out, ignoring, and mild social punishment.

Using the twelve scenes in pre- and post-tests, comparisons between the
standard didactic approach and the role-playing training indicate that the
role-playing group members showed significantly greater improvements in
their parenting responses after training ($p < 0.01$, $t = 4.51$, $df = 15$).

Behavioral rehearsal with modeling can be effectively augmented by the
use of a "bug-in-the-ear" device so that instructions and feedback
(Weathers & Liberman, 1973) can be given to the parent covertly while he
is attempting to manage the child's behavior or the person in the Workshop
taking the role of the child. Parents tend to learn extremely quickly with the
aid of this prompting and reinforcing device. If the direct approach to
training is carried out in the home, the therapist and parent usually
continue to alternate roles in managing the child's behavior until the parent
becomes proficient. When these techniques are adapted and implemented
within the home they become even more effective since this limits the
amount of transfer of training that is necessary.

Follow-up telephone interviews tap two additional dimensions of
program outcome: generalization or durability of improvements over time,
and consumer satisfaction. Parents are contacted by phone at 6, 12, and 24
months following their completion of a Workshop. Each follow-up
consists of up to three phone call attempts, in the morning, afternoon, and
evening. If a parent is not contacted after three calls, no further follow-up
is attempted. At the six month point, 73% of Workshop graduates have
been contacted; at 12 months, 42%; and at 24 months, 23%.

When contacted, parents are asked a series of questions designed to
determine their use of techniques and procedures learned in the Workshop:
current problem behaviors and how they were managed; their children's
progress in school; and their interim use of other professional services to
assist them in managing their children's behavior.

Parents in the control group came to the mental health center with
child-related complaints and were placed on a six-month waiting list for the
Workshop. These parents had not yet entered a Workshop by the time they

were interviewed, six months after their initial intake. The major differences between the control and Workshop parents at the six month follow-up interview were, a significantly higher proportion of children of the control group having special school conferences for behavioral disturbances or academic deficiencies (p <0.001, $x^2 = 16.20$), and twice as many control parents than Workshop parents who consulted a pediatrician because of their child's behavior.

Very few of the parents who completed the Workshop continued to keep records or graphs of their children's behavior. Those that were recording behavior at the six month follow-up, were doing so within home token economies that had been set up during the Workshop. By the 12 month follow-up, no parents were maintaining records, although almost half stated that they were using child management strategies which they learned during the Workshop. As the time between the end of the Workshop and the follow-up interview increased from six to 24 months, the number of parents who consulted a pediatrician for help with their children's behavioral problems increased from 10 to 25%. On the other hand, as time between Workshop and follow-up increased, the number of school conferences for problems steadily decreased.

Consumer satisfaction, another level of program outcome, was high for particpants of the Workshop Program. Between 90 and 100% of the parents claimed that the Program was helpful, that they liked it, and that they would recommend it to a friend or relative. In fact, many of the referrals to the Parent Workshop Program came from satisfied participants of previous Workshops.

Cost Effectiveness

As a group treatment procedure, the Parent Workshop Program provided a large number of parents with consultation and training in child management at a low cost. Costs of the Workshop have been computed for each parent, each child with designated problem behaviors, and each problem behavior. The bases of the computation were 392 participating parents and their 446 children with targeted problems.

Therapists or Workshop leaders spend an average of 20 hours to conduct a workshop, including preparation and supervision. They were paid a mean of $4.94 per hour. Assistant leaders, who were volunteers from outside the Mental Health Center undergoing training for subsequent leadership of similar groups, were not paid. Supervision by the psychologist averaged five hours per workshop at $10.00 per hour. The mean workshop enrollment was 13 parents. Using these figures, the average cost to train each parent was $11.42; the average cost per "problem child" was $9.90; and the cost for each targeted behavior was $5.19. Since

62% of the problem behaviors were satisfactorily modified, the cost for each successfully changed behavior was $8.40.

If child psychiatric services had been provided on an individual basis at the Mental Health Center, the cost for a psychiatrist to see each child for nine hours would have been $119.88. The cost for a psychologist to spend nine hours with each child would have been $77.94. In the traditional child guidance format where parents are seen separately by a social worker, an additional cost of $61.11 for nine hours would have been incurred.

Case Examples

The parent training approach can be illustrated by the following case examples. They are exemplary, not for their successful outcomes, but because of the types of problems and interventions which were involved.

Case 1. Shawn, a very bright 9-year-old boy, had been participating in a

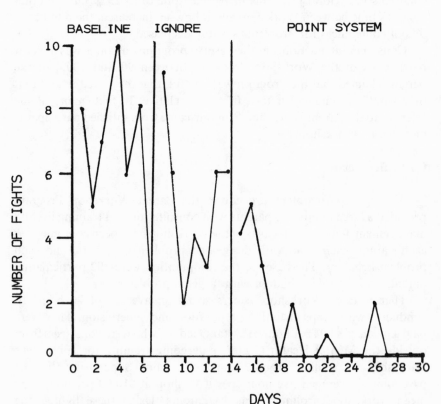

Figure 2
Daily mean frequency of fights.

day treatment school program for some time because of his severe behavior problems at school and at home. In a weekly parent workshop, Shawn's parents identified his inciting fights with his older brothers as behavior they wished to change. Shawn would taunt his brothers by stealing or destroying small items in his brothers' rooms while they were watching. As soon as the brother would come to the defense of his property, Shawn would scream for help from his parents. When the parents arrived, Shawn would claim the item was his and that he was being physically abused.

The parents tried to extinguish the behavior by ignoring Shawn's calls for help. The behavior initially was reduced from a baseline of about 7 fights to only about 4, but the taunting subsequently increased until his brothers (age 17 and 18) were no longer able to restrain themselves and became violent with Shawn. This, of course, elicited the parents' intervention on Shawn's behalf, since he was much younger and smaller than his brothers.

The second intervention employed a broader systems approach. The brothers were given points which they could award to Shawn every hour he did not irritate them. The points were exchangeable at the end of the day for two minutes each, doing an activity of Shawn's choice with his father. The program reduced the number of fights to near zero. Within a week, the parents were generalizing the points to other situations and thinning out the original payoff ratio.

This case illustrates the use of interventions at several points in the family system to modify a negative behavior. By using both brothers and the father as positive reinforcers, the family was able to develop a more pleasurable interaction with Shawn, while reducing the unwanted behavior.

Case 2. Dick was 9 years old when his parents joined the workshop. He was described by his parents as "having a learning disability" and being "demanding and rude" toward them. During the first session they translated these problems in measurable goals of (1) increasing Dick's rate of reading and (2), increasing the frequency of his saying "Please" and "Thank You" at the dinner table. During the baseline period (two weeks), Dick's parents counted the (1) number of pages he read in daily homework assignments, and (2) the number of times he said "Please" and "Thank You" at the dinner table. The parents were instructed to react to the reading and the dinner situation as they had done in the past and not to begin offering encouragement or rewards. The graph that Dick's parents kept is shown in Figure 3. During the baseline period, Dick read between 0–7 pages per day and rarely issued any polite phrases.

On the 15th day, Dick's parents began an incentive or positive reinforcement program for his behaviors. For each page of reading completed, Dick received one cent. As can be seen from the graph, positive

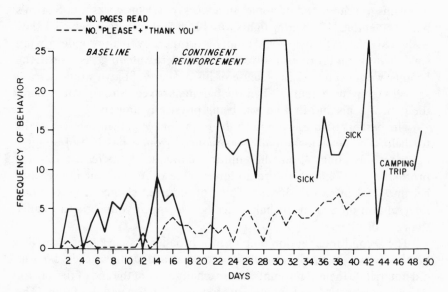

Figure 3

The use of a home reinforcement program implemented by the parents of Dick, a 9-year-old boy referred to a mental health center for a learning disability and rudeness. During the baseline period, Dick's parents simply recorded the number of pages he read in homework assignments and the number of times he said "please" and "thank you" at the dinner table. During the contingent reinforcement phase, his parents rewarded Dick with one cent for each page read and with compliance with his dinner table requests if they were preceded by "please."

reinforcement more than doubled Dick's reading rate. It should be noted that almost a week went by before Dick really responded to the incentive. This lag period is due to a testing out by the child of the seriousness and consistency of the parents. It is important to prepare parents for the testing out and to encourage them to remain believable.

The contingency which was put into effect to increase Dick's politeness was to have the parents comply with Dick's requests only when they were preceded by "Please." This simple and natural reinforcer—parental compliance—was sufficient to increase Dick's rate of saying "Please" and "Thank You" to very acceptable levels. A six month follow-up revealed that Dick had improved his reading to the point where he was actually beyond his class level and that his "Please's" and "Thank You's" were now automatic. His parents said that they were using these principles with their other children and were serving as child management "advisors" to their friends.

Time-out is a frequently used form of punishment aimed at reducing undesirable behavior. Brief (2–10 minutes) periods of social isolation are made immediately contingent upon the child's misbehavior; hence, the child does not experience the emotional, social, and verbal consequences (reinforcers) that his misbehavior generates in others.

Case 3. Alfred, age three, was brought into the mental health clinic by his mother because he was "unhappy and emotionally unstable." This presenting complaint was behaviorally specified in the workshop as "Alfred has a high rate of crying." He cried when it was time for bed, when he wanted a bedtime story, when he wanted a toy in the supermarket, and when he was left at his nursery school. Figure 4 shows that Alfred cried between 6–20 times a day during baseline counts.

The first intervention tried by his parents was extinction; whenever Alfred cried, they tried to ignore him. There was a moderate decrease in the crying, but the family had difficulty being consistent about ignoring him. This accounts for the tremendous variability in the frequency of crying during the second week. At the next workshop session, we suggested that they use time-out by placing Alfred in his room for five minutes (or until he stopped crying), contingent upon the crying episodes. As can be seen in the

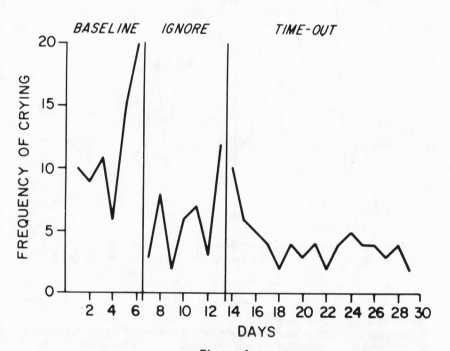

Figure 4

Daily mean frequency of crying during baseline, ignoring, and time-out conditions.

graph kept by Alfred's parents, time-out effectively reduced crying to an age-appropriate level of about twice daily.

Case 4. Martha was a three year old who regularly threw temper tantrums. Her mother would respond by "climbing the walls" and shouting at her to stop. The mother counted 3 to 33 tantrums per day during a two week baseline period as can be seen in Figure 5. Instructing the mother to ignore the tantrums led to a gradual but satisfactory reduction in their frequency which persisted at a six month follow-up.

Case 5. Mrs. F. complained that her boys would not mind her—they refused to comply with her requests. During the first week of baseline, Mrs. F. counted the number of requests made of all the boys; responses were divided into immediate compliance, delayed compliance, and noncompliance. Table 5 shows the frequency of each category during baseline. As a therapeutic intervention, the Workshop leader designed a token system. Points were accumulated on a wall chart posted at home in

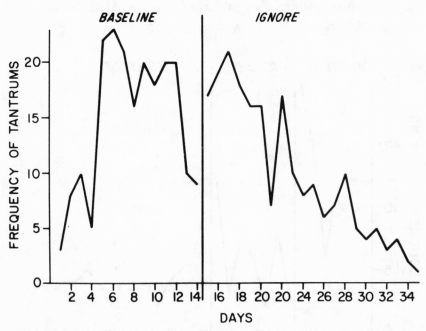

Figure 5

The use of an extinction program in the home by the parents of a 3-year-old girl with temper tantrums. After the baseline period, the parents were instructed by the group leader to simply ignore and turn away from Martha during her temper tantrums. Note that the end point is not a complete elimination of tantrums (which would be unreasonable to expect for a 3-year-old), but rather a reduction to a tolerable, low, and developmentally appropriate frequency.

the following way: Immediate compliance (within 1 minute of request) earned 6 points, delayed compliance (by the end of the day) earned 2 points, noncompliance earned no points. These points could be exchanged as follows: 4 points for $\frac{1}{2}$ hour of TV viewing, 4 points for $\frac{1}{2}$ hour of outside play, or 1 point for 15¢. This token system was in effect for two weeks when the "token system data" in Table 5 was determined.

Table 5
Mean Percentage of Immediate Compliance,
Delayed Compliance, and Noncompliance during 2
Weeks each of Baseline and a Token System for
Three Brothers

	Baseline	Token System
Immediate Compliance	7.0	41.7
Delayed Compliance	49.0	36.8
Noncompliance	44.0	21.5

A very clear shift in the relative percent of compliance occurred when the token system was initiated. A six-fold increase in the rate of immediate compliance occurred and the rate of noncompliance was more than halved.

Case 6. Mr. and Mrs. B. were very concerned that their children were communicative and their youngest son in particular was showing a high rate of temper tantrums. An ititial behavioral goal was to increase the rate at which Mr. B. dispensed social reinforcers, since it was felt that if the father modeled more positive verbal behavior and praised the family members more often, then communication would increase and tantrums diminish. Figure 6 shows Mr. B.'s rate of compliments to (1) his wife, Mrs. B.; (2) to his tantrumming son; and (3) to the other two children. Individual contingencies of self-reinforcement were applied by Mr. B. A predetermined rate of compliments directed to his wife and children were required for specific consequences to occur. Shaving, ice cream, naps, watching television, a special breakfast, and bowling were the reinforcers used by Mr. B. to increase successfully his rate of complimenting others. Concurrently, the communication within the family improved and the youngest son's tantrums decreased.

These case studies are representative and not highly selected from the 62% of families that reported success in their workshop experience. Although the quality of the data is open to question, their progress in acquiring meaningful and satisfying parenting skills is well documented. It should be noted that the parents uniformly reported a much improved atmosphere at home, with more positive family relationships and interaction after gaining competence in the use of behavioral principles such as reinforcement.

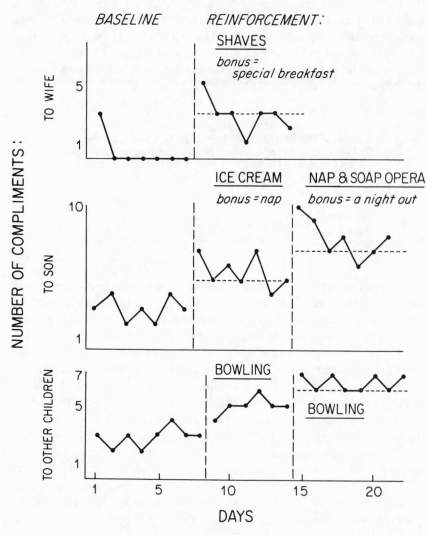

Figure 6

Daily mean frequency of compliments to household members during baseline and self-reinforcement contingencies. *Top graph:* Three compliments per day to his wife earns the right to shave the next morning; more than three earns a special breakfast. *Middle graph:* Five compliments to his son earns his favorite dish of ice cream in the evening; more than five earns nap time. A contingency requires a minimum of seven compliments per day. *Bottom graph:* Five compliments per day to each of the other children earns his weekly bowling night; a later contingency changed the measurement frequency to weeks.

Contingency Contracting

There has been a great deal of recent popularity in contingency contracting with families for community-based intervention strategies. The face validity of the approach makes it seem to be a simple and expedient way to harness the natural reinforcers in the family and in the community to shape more pleasing family interaction patterns. Contracting is particularly popular in working with children 11 years and older, since they can more readily participate and understand the contract negotiation process. By specifying who does what to whom and when, contracts can restructure the implicit agreements family members tend to develop among themselves. The contract serves as a vehicle to make these implicit assumptions, norms, and agreements explicit and consistent across different family members. Contracts serve to reduce the ambiguity between family members' perceptions of what rewards and expectancies they have for each other. They allow interpersonal exchanges to be carefully structured in families that are so disorganized and conflict orientated that formalized and explicit rules are necessary to elicit change. Both parent and child behaviors may be pinpointed for change and attached to positive and negative consequences that can be clearly understood by all. More important than the actual renegotiation of the reinforcement contingencies within the family may be the actual learning of the negotiation processes itself. Many troubled families lack the ability to communicate their needs and feelings to each other. They tend to interact through coercion, manipulation, and hostility. The negotiation process during contracting is often the first time family members have ever discussed their mutual needs, much less negotiated ways of satisfying them.

Family contracts are an effective vehicle to accomplish three interrelated objectives: (1) They clarify the contradictory and ambiguous communications characteristic of many dysfunctional families, so that each member is aware of what is expected of him and what rewards are available upon meeting these expectancies. (2) They are useful to systematically supplement the naturally available reinforcers with extrinsic reinforcers while undesirable behaviors are being unlearned and desirable behaviors are being relearned. (3) Contracts also serve to help parents re-establish their control of some of the major reinforcers for adolescents, rather than leaving these rewards under the control of the deviant peer group.

Translating these three objectives into practice can be facilitated by observing some procedural guidelines. From Stuart's (1972) exchange model we can develop four criteria or guidelines for developing contingency contracts:

1. The negotiation of a contract must be open, honest, and free from

overt or subtle coercion. The discussion and negotiation process may be the most important therapeutic element in contingency contracting.

2. The terms of a contract should be expressed in simple, explicit and clearly understood words. Responsibilities and rewards should be described in terms of a specific, observable behavior. The contract should state, for example, "a C grade or better on the weekly quiz" rather than "do better in class." "Doing better in class" means different things for different parents and children. Novices in contracting are inclined to write in vauge, general terms, using the ambiguity to ease the negotiation between parent and adolescent. Each party can interpret a vague statement in ways agreeable to himself. This only serves to postpone the conflict until someone believes he has fulfilled the contract, as he interpreted it, and is challenged and confronted by the other party. It is important to review and clarify each clause of the contract with all participants immediately after the contract has been negotiated. Every person involved in the contract must know specifically what is expected of him and what may be gained in return.

3. For a contract to be effective it has to provide an opportunity for each participant to optimize his reinforcement or minimize his cost or losses in the area of life covered by the contract. The contract must provide advantages to each party over the status quo. A family member should be able to get more for his social and material investments than he is currently getting. It often requires ingenuity to discover privileges or reinforcers that can be suitably exchanged to provide each party with a gain.

4. The behaviors contracted for must be in the repertoire of the person agreeing to them. It is easy to make the mistake of asking too much. The level of performance or responsibilities required in a contract must be within the grasp of the contractors. A contract should be an opportunity for accomplishment, success, and reward. Contracts are written so that all parties are highly likely to be reinforced for improvement they make in their behavior. The criterion for reinforcement can be increased in small steps as the performance level increases. Eventually the terminal goals are reached by approximations.

Elements of Contingency Contracting

Contingency contracts, as a tool to shape more appropriate family behavior systematically, specifies who does what to whom and when. The basic elements in a contract are (1) Responsibilities are the goals for new behaviors of specific family members at specific times and places. (2) Privileges are rewards made contingent upon the performance of responsibilities. They increase the frequency with which more appropriate family behaviors are learned and integrated into the family norm of reciprocity. (3) Bonuses are given for consistent fulfillment of contract terms, as a first step in establishing long-term stability of new behaviors. (4) Penalties are made for failure to adhere to the contract. They give parents a limited and prescribed response to adolescent behavior, which is often less drastic than has been customary. (5.) Record keeping on the contract serves to signal when responsibilities are completed, privileges have been earned, bonuses have been earned, penalties have been earned, and the success or failure of the contract itself.

Note that the child's responsibilities are the parents' priveleges (reinforcers) and the parents' responsibilities are the child's reinforcers. It provides the grist for milling out future contract updates. These characteristics of contracts become clearer when one can relate it to a particular family. Janice was a 14-year-old girl who was referred to the first author because of her marginal academic performance and truancy along with a variety of behavior problems at home. Both parents worked as semi-skilled laborers and spent little time with Janice, who in turn spent little time at home. At the second hour the therapist negotiated a contract, using the Family Contracting Exercise (Weathers & Liberman, 1975b), between Janice and her parents. This first contract focused on a few of the higher priority issues. The contract was implemented as follows:

Janice's Responsibilities *Parent's Privileges*	*Janice's Privileges* *Parent's Responsibilities*
Attend school each day	Each day at school earns $1.00 to be spent for new clothes
Bring weekly math quizzes home	Each quiz brought home with a "D" or better grade earns Janice a ride in the family car to a point of Janice's choice not more than 10 miles from home.
Be out of bed and dressed by 7:10 A.M. on week days	Breakfast of Janice's choice will be on the table at 7:10. After that it will be thrown out and she will not be allowed to cook anything else.

Bonus Clause: If Janice attends 3 days or more of school she will earn a shopping trip with her mother for 2 hours on Saturday afternoon.

Penalty Clause: Janice's use of the phone shall be contingent upon her having been to school that day.

Procedures for Generating Contingency Contracts with the Family

Writing a contingency contract can be extremely difficult with highly disorganized, conflicted, and distressed families. The net result of attempting to negotiate a contract with such a family can be an explosive and destructive interaction, and an incomplete contract that cannot be implemented. Traditionally, contracts have been neogiated within the general format of family therapy. The therapist typically announces that he thinks a contract would help family interactions, then he explains the concept and procedures. He begins by asking family members what they want from each other and what they would be willing to give in exchange. To negotiate the contract with such an approach often takes a very skilled counselor and many hours of emotional strain for himself and the family. The experience can be so explosive and aversive that the family will soon terminate therapy, because it seems to them that this procedure just exacerbates rather than ameliorates the family problems.

The emotionality, anger, guilt, and frustrations of such sessions have prompted some family therapists to develop more structured approaches (Haley, 1973; Ivey, 1971; Minuchin, 1974). Such techniques serve to structure the family counseling session so that only manageable amounts of affect are handled at any one point.

There are at least two structured exercises that have been developed to generate family contracts, the Family Contracting Exercise (Weathers & Liberman, 1975b), and the Family Contract Game (Blechman, 1974). The principles underlying these two techniques are very similar though their structure is somewhat different. The structure of these exercises reduces the skill required of the therapist to develop a contract, since each step is carefully laid out for both the family and the therapist. Since the Family Contracting Exercise is the more comprehensive and detailed of the two, along with providing a detailed flow of the contracting steps (Figure 7) that any contract must go through, it will be described more comprehensively (cf. Weathers & Liberman, 1975b, for complete details for fabricating your own exercises). The exercise is a structured learning experience that leads family members in a step-wise fashion from identifying personal needs to constructing a contingency contract. The steps in the process are purposely kept very small and mechanical so that sensitive issues can be effectively probed at a low emotional arousal and threat level. Through this procedure an adolescent and his parent can develop a mutually acceptable contract. An inexperienced helper can usually develop a contract of three to five clauses in $1\frac{1}{2}$ to 2 hours. The exercise, which is introduced and facilitated by a therapist leads family members in a step wise fashion through: (1) identifying their needs and desires (rewards) for themselves and each other; (2) setting priorities and rewards for self; (3) empathizing with each other; (4) setting costs on providing rewards to others, and (5) bargaining and compromising.

These steps, outlined in Figure 7, are based on a systematic analysis of the procedures that any contract development must go through. The contracting exercise provides systematic practice in interpersonal

CONTINGENCY CONTRACTING EXERCISE

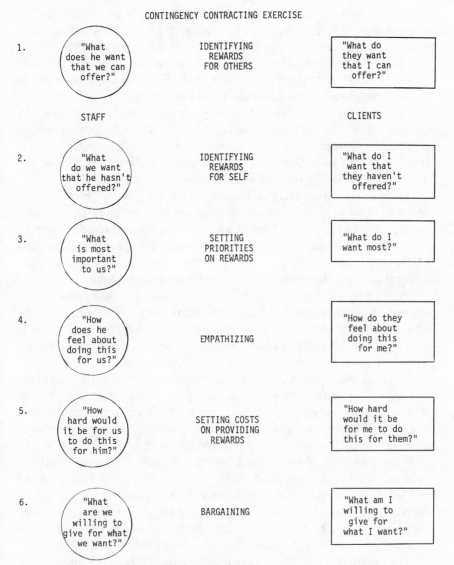

Figure 7

Steps in contingency contracting exercises.

negotiation skills. These may be used by the family on a more informal basis to develop informal interpersonal contracts, after the family crises and the need for formal contracts have passed.

For many families doing the exercises is the first time they have systematically thought about what they want from each other, much less expressed this to each other. The process provides diagnostic information to the consultant about family interaction patterns, social skill deficiencies, and specific survival skills necessary in the particular family. It also teaches interpersonal negotiations, empathy, compromising, and specification of needs and behaviors. Generalization of a therapeutic effect of the procedure beyond the duration of the contract is very dependent on how well the family learns these negotiation skills. This learning may often be augmented by role playing, feedback, and prompting.

The decision of the data-gathering system within the contracting exercise allows the contract to be left with the family immediately after negotiation. A weekly checkstrip/postcard, located on the contract form, is checked off by each family member contracted. This is mailed to the therapist on a weekly basis to keep him aware of the family's progress.

The Family Contracting Game is a somewhat simpler "board game" designed to develop one contract clause in about 15 minutes. By moving a marker around the "board" family members are taken through a series of steps that help them systematically negotiate a single-clause contract. Unlike the exercise, the game requires that family members enumerate rather than select the behaviors they want from one another and what they are willing to give in exchange. The game also has somewhat larger sequential steps. Because of these two disadvantages the game could be difficult to implement with very seriously dysfunctional families. The game does offer the advantage of being quicker to negotiate a contract clause, when implemented with moderately disturbed families.

The effectiveness of contingency contracts are not well supported in the literature (Stuart, 1972; Weathers & Liberman, 1975a). For example, one study utilizing six predelinquent adolescents left the efficacy of contracting in doubt (Weathers & Liberman, 1975a). The contracts were developed with the aid of a structured exercise (Weathers & Liberman, 1975b). In addition, prompting (Weathers & Liberman, 1973) and videotape feedback were used to shape negotiation skills. Of the three behaviors per subject (curfew compliance, school attendance, and verbal abusiveness) that were evaluated in a multiple-baseline design, only the latter showed any systematic impact by the contract; and this was questionable because the data were solely from the subjective reports of parents.

The failure of contracting may be due to many therapists being seduced by the contract's face validity, relying too heavily on it, and expecting too much from a contract. True, if family members would, in fact, uphold the clauses of the contract, contracts would be extremely effective. Unfortunately, this is very seldom the case. Family members can be helped to implement a contract if therapists are willing to use other techniques in conjuntion with the contract. Contingency contracts can serve as powerful motivators and diagnostic and structuring devices to coordinate a whole range of family interventions into one systematic, logical, comprehensive whole. Unless these added support and multiple interventions strategies are implemented, most contingency contracts are worth just about as much as the paper which they are printed on.

Discussion

Both parent training and contingency contracting represent two facets of the application of the triangular model to the modification of family behavior. Parent training has enjoyed greater popularity, both in terms of research effort and clinical application. The results, at least for the behavioral approaches, have been very encouraging. Reported success rates vary between 41% and 100% depending on criteria used (Eyberg & Johnson, 1974; Mira, 1970; Patterson, 1974; Rinn, Vernon, & Wise, 1975; Rose, 1974; Wahler, 1969).

In Table 6 a comparison of the outcomes of parent training in child management as reported by programs is presented. Improvements in children's behavior are usually accompanied by positive changes in parent's attitudes toward their children, and by a high level of consumer satisfaction.

The cost of parent-training programs is much less than more traditional, longer-term psychotherapeutic approaches in child psychiatry with only 25 man-hours of paraprofessional and professional time for each

Table 6
Outcome of Parent Training Programs
Reported in the Literature

Authors	Ss	Outcome Criteria	Success Rate
Eyberg & Johnson [1974]	17	Parents reported data; better than 30% reduction in deviant behavior	94%
	17	Parent attitudes & checklist	88%
	17	Home observations; better than 30% reduction in deviant behavior	41%
Rinn, Vernon & Wise [1975]	639	Parent reported data; 68–100% goal attained	92%
	154	Parent reported data, 68–100% 17 month follow-up	54%
Rose [1974]	58	Parent reported data, "effective modification" of 1 or more behaviors	76%
Patterson [1974]	14	Parent reported data, "marked reduction	66%
	27	Home observations, better than 30% reduction in deviant behavior	66%
Wahler [1969]	5	Home and clinic observations, better than 50% reduction in deviant behavior	100%
Mira [1970]	100	Parent reported data, modification of 2 problem behaviors	50%

group at the Oxnard Mental Health Center. A group educational program for parents at the Huntsville (Alabama) Mental Health Center has reported a cost per problem child of $19.44, somewhat higher than the cost of the program at the Oxnard Mental Health Center, but still much lower than the estimated cost of $121.77 to treat each family in individual, outpatient psychotherapy.

Although much data have accumulated to suggest strongly that the behavioral approach to parent training is effective, there is a critical need for additional studies that employ multiple outcome criteria with follow-up, that report the results with successive versus "selected" cases, and that compare different models or "schools" of parent education. The Oxnard study, with a large number of successively referred parents, indicates that a structured group format sustains a high level of attendance and participation and results in improvements in conceptual knowledge and parent and child behaviors. However, the study does not shed light on the *relative* effectiveness, efficiency, and durability of the improvements in children and parents as compared to other modes of intervention, such as reflective methods of counseling that focus on feelings and understanding (Tavormina, 1974).

Not every parent successfully applies the social learning techniques taught in the workshop; however, experiences with "failures" in training can be used to advantage. A study of cases and conditions in which difficulty and failure occur can point the group leaders and program managers toward making the critical changes in the workshop necessary for greater effectiveness. Resistances and failures among parents stem from both philosophical antipathy and personal problems.

Changes can be made in the workshop format to improve the success rate. Contingency deposits (Eyberg & Johnson, 1974) have been demonstrated to increase the following through with "homework" assignments, especially among lower-class families. On-the-spot, immediate instructions, advice, feedback and support can be provided in the home to advantage with parents who do not have the personal resources to bridge the gap between the workshop sessions and applications in the home. In this case, training is tailored to the unique domestic circumstances and to the particular behavioral problems shown by the child. Supplementing a group workshop with home interventions increases parental confidence and rapport when a helper is accessible when needed. Another way to facilitate generalization of workshop instructions is through the liberal use of telephone prompts and checks. This can be done by a clinic secretary who is orientated and trained in the kinds of interactions needed to prompt and reinforce parents as they attempt to use the social learning principles outlined in the workshop.

There are many potential applications of a parent workshop approach to child mental health problems. Parents of battered children can benefit from instruction in the tangible and step-by-step methods of child management as well as from professional and peer-conducted group therapy (Savino & Sanders, 1973). Problems have been described with parent training components that have enabled severely retarded and autistic children to live at home in the community and attend special classrooms (Salzinger, Feldman, & Portnoy, 1970). Workshops can be offered to parents of children who are a high risk for delinquency. Studies have shown that a large proportion of children referred to child guidance clinics subsequently develop criminal and other antisocial behavior (Robins, 1966). Speculatively, the parent workshop might prevent disorders in children's behavior from escalating into adult problems. This is an empirical question that could be answered with a large sample of parents and children plus a suitably long follow-up period. This approach is currently being used with a delinquency prevention program in the Chicano barrio of Oxnard where community workers have been trained in the use of social learning principles (Aitchison & Merrill, 1974). The parent workshop model can also be used with gatekeepers in the community who screen and refer children and adolescents for psychiatric services. Family doctors, paramedics, nurse practitioners, and probation officers could relieve the overburdened mental health system by acquiring skills to intervene more effectively and confidently with problems that they encounter in their daily work.

Contingency contracting with adolescents and their parents has been used as a therapeutic method since the late 1960s. It is rooted in solid learning principles, and considerable early success has been reported with its use (Cantrill, Cantrill, Huddleston, & Woodridge, 1969; Tharp & Wetzel, 1969). However, there are problems and limitations with contingency contracting that should be amplified. The best results with contracting have come in studies where only one reliably measured behavior—such as school attendance or weight loss—was the discrete focus of that intervention (Cantrill et al., 1969). Feasible and enforceable contracts, even if focused on limited, small-scale behavioral changes for adolescents and parents, will pay handsome dividends in outcome.

Record keeping is central to maintaining the fulfillment of contingency contracts. Many families have major problems and resistances in keeping faithful and accurate records. The record-keeping function prompts family members to carry out their responsibilities and honor the awarded privileges, but it is not always used that way by families. Many families, especially those who have impulsive and capricious life styles, will fail to maintain records. Therapists must solve this problem or else expect noncompliance with contracts.

Several interventions can increase the likelihood of record keeping.

Regular phone calls from a secretary or the therapist can effectively prompt and reinforce recording of progress, and special reinforcement contingenicies can be developed to increase the incentive for keeping records. For example, "good faith" deposits of money have been required prior to entering the therapeutic program (Eyberg & Johnson, 1974). The families earn the money back as refunds contingent upon their providing the therapist with completed progress records and homework assignments.

Dropout rates are often very high. In a recent, controlled study of contracting, only 8 of 28 families initially referred by the probation department completed the baseline period for evaluation, and only 6 completed the full series of three home treatment sessions and follow-up (Weathers & Liberman, 1975a). Many families will reject contracting, because it forces them to re-evaluate their status quo and ongoing value system. Contracting also opens up communication within the family system, and there is often resistance to this openness that can be viewed as a kind of invasion of family privacy.

Although it is inviting to speculate that the type of interventions, the frequency and duration of contact, and the therapeutic support with family members can improve treatment results, previous research indicates that the duration of therapist-client contact is not an important variable in the outcome of contingency contracting (Jayaratine, Stuart, & Tripoli, 1974; Stuart & Tripoli, 1972). Contracts often do bring about immediate and temporary improvements in the family situation and the behavior of the troubled adolscent.

In the case of families with dysfunctional adolescents, the parents have often lost much of their reinforcement control over their offspring. Contracting with parents who do not control significant reinforcers for the adolescent is ineffective, and without some attempt to engage the peer group in the intervention strategy, little can be gained by family therapy alone. With less deviant and disorganized families, contingency contracting may be shown to be an effective, desirable behavior change agent.

REFERENCE NOTE

1. Parrish, V. Director Regional Intervention Program, Nashville, Tennessee. Personal communication, 1972.

REFERENCES

Aitchison, R. A., & Merill, J. M. Emphasis on environment: The partnership between home, mental health services and school. *exChange*, 1974, *2* (5), 13–19.

Becker, W. C. *Parents are teachers: A child management program.* Champaign, Ill.: Research Press, 1971.

Blechman, E. A. The family contract game: A tool to teach interpersonal problem solving. *Family Coordinator*, 1974, *23*, 269–281.

Cantrill, H., Cantrill, C., Huddleston, B., & Woolridge, R. Contingency contracting with school problems. *Journal of Applied Behavioral Analyses*, 1969, *2*, 215–220.

Eyberg, S. M., & Johnson, S. M. Multiple assessment of behavior modification with families: Effects of contingency contracting and order of treated problems. *Journal of Consulting and Clinical Psychology*, 1974, *42*, 594–606.

Framo, J. Rationales and techniques in intensive family therapy. In I. Boszormenyi-Magy & J. C. Framo (Eds.), *Intensive family therapy.* New York: Harper and Row, 1965.

Haley, J. *The uncommon therapies.* New York: Norton, 1973.

Ivey, A. E. *Microcounseling: Inovations in interviewing training.* Springfield, Ill.: Charles C. Thomas, 1971.

Jayaratine, S., Stuart, R. B., & Tripoli, T. Methodological issues and problems in evaluating treatment outcomes in the family and school consultation project 1970–1973. *Evaluating social programs in community, residential, and social settings: Proceedings of the 5th Banff International Conference on Behavior Modification.* Champaign, Ill.: Research Press, 1974, pp. 141–174.

Koch, S. Reassuming the power of a parent. Part IV, View. *Los Angeles Times*, October 3, 1976.

Minuchin, S. *Families and family therapy.* Cambridge: Harvard University Press, 1974.

Mira, M. Results of a behavior modification training program for parents and teachers. *Behaviour Research & Therapy*, 1970, *8*, 309–311.

Patterson, G. R. Interventions for boys with conduct problems: Multiple settings, treatments, and criteria. *Journal of Consulting and Clinical Psychology*, 1974, *42*, 471–481.

Patterson, G. R., & Gullion, M. E. *Living with children.* Champaign, Ill.: Research Press, 1974.

Rinn, R. C., Vernon, J. C., & Wise, M. J. Training parents of behaviorally-disordered children in groups: A three years' program evaluation. *Behavior Therapy*, 1975, *6*, 378–387.

Robins, L. N. *Deviant children grown up: A sociological and psychiatric study of sociopathic personality.* Baltimore: Williams & Wilkens, 1966.

Rose, S. D. Group training of parents as behavior modifiers. *Social Work*, 1974, *19*, 156–162.

Salzinger, K., Feldman, R., & Portnoy, S. Training parents of brain-injured children in the use of operant conditioning procedures. *Behavior Therapy*, 1970, *1*, 4–32.

Savino, A. B., & Sanders, R. W.: Working with abusive parents: Group therapy and home visits. *American Journal of Nursing*, 1973, *73*, 482–484.

Stuart, R. B. Behavioral contracting with the families of delinquents. *Journal of Behavior Therapy and Experimental Psychiatry*, 1972, *3*, 161–169.

Stuart, R. B., & Tripoli, T. Experimental evaluation of three time-constrained behavioral treatments for predelinquents and delinquents. In R. D. Rubin, J. P. Brady, & J. D. Henderson (Eds.), *Advances in Behavior Therapy* (Vol. 4). New York: Academic Press, 1973, pp. 1–12.

Tavormina, J. B. Basic models of parent counseling: A critical review. *Psychological Bulletin*, 1974, *81*, 827–835.

Tharp, R., & Wetzel, R. *Behavior modification in the natural environment.* New York: Academic Press, 1969.

Wahler, R. G. Oppositional children: A quest for parental reinforcement control. *Journal of Applied Behavior Analysis*, 1969, *2*, 159–170.

Weathers, L., & Liberman, R. P. Contingency contracting with families of delinquent adolescents. *Behavior Therapy*, 1975a, *6*, 356–366.

Weathers, L., & Liberman, R. P. The family contracting exercise. *Journal of Behavior Therapy and Experimental Psychiatry*, 1975b, *6*, 208–214.

Weathers, L., & Liberman, R. P. The Porta-Prompter—A new electronic prompting and feedback device: A technical note. *Behavior Tharapy*, 1973, *4*, 703–705.

7

Mental Retardation
AN INTRODUCTION TO THE ANALYSIS
AND REMEDIATION OF
BEHAVIORAL DEFICIENCY

Paul E. Touchette

INTRODUCTION

Learning may fail to occur because a child has not yet come into contact with an environment which has the characteristics necessary to produce it, or because neurological malfunctions make it impossible. We always assume the former, accepting the latter conclusion only if every possible intervention technique has been exhausted. Although it is often clear that children with severe learning disorders have serious physical damage, the extent to which those physical problems interfere with, or preclude learning is usually less clear. The nervous system, once damaged, has limited capacity to repair itself. There is, however, no justification for coming to the conclusion that behavioral remediation or improvement is impossible because physical restoration is unlikely. On the contrary, it has been repeatedly demonstrated that special training procedures can make desirable behavior much more likely and can dramatically expand the adaptive behavioral repertoire of virtually all retarded individuals (Birnbrauer, 1976).

This chapter is not concerned with children who are technically retarded by virtue of lower than average IQ scores and who are otherwise unremarkable. The children for whom intensive programs of behavior therapy are designed are those who will remain completely dependent on others throughout their lives unless something dramatic happens. These children fail to adapt to the group processes of public educational and caretaking systems. They require individual care and attention. They learn little from ordinary encounters with parents, peers and classrooms. They are not, however, unchangeable. Seguin (1907) demonstrated that prior to the beginning of this century. More recently Skinner (1968), Bijou (1966) and their colleagues brought the laboratory based experimental analysis of behavior to bear and produced even more convincing data. Finally, the past few years have seen an explosion of applied field studies and demonstration projects which have made the condition necessary for positive behavior change in retarded young people very concrete and replicable.

Behavior therapists can now point to this susbstantive and growing body of data (Lovaas & Bucher, 1974) which indicates that retarded children can behave in more socially acceptable ways and acquire more skills when behavioral intervention techniques are properly applied. Parents, physicians, educators and other relevant decision makers are becoming convinced. More imaginative and scientific approaches to behavioral deficiency are at hand. Still, there are problems. The number of individuals who appreciate the order of magnitude of behavior change which can result from competent therapy, and the conditions required to produce such changes, are few. Even among these devoted researchers and therapists, quantifying and predicting behavioral outcomes precisley, is beyond current techniques. The fact that we cannot state accurately how rapidly a given child will progress, or what that child will eventually accomplish, presents problems to those who must set service priorities and allocate funds.

This chapter will point out some of the ways in which behavioral intervention can improve the intellectual and social prospects of children with learning disorders. I hope you will conclude that the way to determine what a handicapped child can accomplish is to bring every possible resource to bear and to observe the results.

Expectations

We expect behavior patterns to emerge spontaneously at certain ages as a child matures: sitting up at 4 to 6 months, standing at 9 to 10 months, naming familiar objects and people intelligibly before the second birthday, and a host of more complex social and physical skills that succeed these. The learning handicapped child may lag behind in any or all activities which normal children reliably engage in. It is easy to conclude that a child who does not emit behavior which other children of the same age have acquired is incapable of it. With the overwhelming evidence that social and physical environments affect what is learned and when (Bijou & Baer, 1967), we must consider the possibility that the child can learn to behave in the desired way under different circumstances. It is unreasonable to conclude that the child's unknown learning history has produced the best performances which the child is capable of.

Precursers of desirable behaviors appear spontaneously in most children. Toddlers reach for, touch, and grasp almost every object within range, often to the dismay of their parents. Exploratory grasping and manipulations which occur at suppertime suggest to parents that the toddler is "ready" to be taught to eat independently with the spoon currently being waved in the air. The observation is an accurate one. It is the result of the child demonstrating skills and motivation which make the teaching of self-feeding a probable success. The ordinary course of interaction between parent and child may change drastically when "readiness" signs do not occur at the expected times. Most parents expend a lot of effort getting the child to do the things which he or she appears ready to do and being delighted when a new achievement comes along. Standing, walking, the first few words, early naming of objects and pets, etc., are accomplishments which parents report with pride. Without assistance and advice, the parent of the learning disordered child may spend little time instructing the child and attempting to provoke new behavior, and may instead "care for" the disabled child in ways which offer fewer and fewer opportunities to learn. The danger is that the parents will adapt themselves and the home environment to the child's current level of behavior, rather than engaging in the types of interactions most likely to help the child to learn.

The current level of competence or range of behavior exhibited by a retarded child may be of little use in predicting potential accomplishments. Until systematic training efforts have been carried through, all we know is that the child has not yet acquired behaviors in the repertoire of most children. If a child is not progressing, it is because something less than optimal contingencies of reinforcement prevail. If a child is not learning, it is because the environment has not been arranged to meet that child's needs. Rate and course may vary widely, but measurable progress can always be achieved.

REINFORCEMENT

Reinforcement is the only way to build and maintain behavior. As Redd and Sleator pointed out in Chapter 1, reinforcement is any event which increases the probablity of the behavior which it follows. Reinforcers differ from one person to the next, and the same person will find different events more or less reinforcing at different times. Even reprimands intended as punishment may involve an attention component that some find reinforcing.

When the topic is behavioral deficiency, we must be concerned with the quantity, appropriateness and character of the retarded learner's reinforcers. You and I can make good guesses about what will be reinforcing for most children. If we are wrong, it matters little, the selection is vast, familiar, and readily at hand. Finding a reinforcer which has characteristics suitable to use in a behavior change program may, however, be a problem if the child has a major learning disorder.

You can count on the retarded child's having fewer acquired tastes than normal. We tend to forget, if we have ever considered it, how many of our reinforcers and those to which we expect children to respond, are the result of extensive learning histories. Our lives and those of our children are filled with activities whose payoffs have no intrinsic value. The culture determines the details of sysmbols of social distinction and success for which we all strive in one way or another. They are real reinforcers; but they have been acquired through learning.

Learning handicaps may interfere with the acquisition of subtle discriminations whether they concern letters of the alphabet, or signs of social distinction and success. Taste and style are terms which point to the learned values which permeate our selection of desirable clothing, entertainment, living arrangements, decor and even food. The reinforcing properties of a school grade, a teacher's approval, or the opportunity to wear a cap and gown in June are learned. Retarded children cannot be assumed to be motivated by events like these.

Some children who suffer from major learning handicaps are unresponsive even to ordinary social reinforcers. They avoid social contact with adults and peers altogether, preferring to be left alone. Verbal praise, hugs, smiles, affection and approval are major influences on the behavior of most children. When they have no effect, or are actively shunned, it creates a frustrating and disarming problem for parents and teachers who are accustomed to using attention and approval as powerful, reliable and always available reinforcers. When they are shunned, they have a tendency to interact less with the child.

Reliable reinforcers are prerequisite to any program of constructive behavior change. Without them, the child's prognosis is not good. In the absence of social reinforcers, we generally turn to the most primitive reinforcer, food. Some change agents resist the use of "edible" reinforcers, even though a child may be responsive to little else. The attitude is easy to understand. Providing a bit of food after a response appears unnatural. The training environment may, to some, more closely resemble a trained seal act than a nursery, home or school. The passive acceptance of a massive deficit in social responsiveness is not an acceptable alternative. Most children are capable of responding appropriately to some social reinforcers, though they may not yet have done so. Using food as a reinforcer may be a brief but necessary first step.

A common approach takes advantage of the fact that neutral stimuli which predict reinforcement, themselves acquire reinforcing properties. An exaggerated predictive correlation between a neutral social event (praise) and a primitive reinforcer (food) can serve as a first step toward socialization (Lovaas, Freitag, Kinder, Rubenstein, Schaeffer & Simmons, 1966). In the intitial instance a single, readily discriminated, statement, "very good" for example, will reliably precede a bit of food. When this statement has demonstratable reinforcing properties, food will follow it intermittently, and another statement "that's nice" or "well done" may be added. How far the process can be carried toward the normal subtle distinctions with no explicit backup must be empirically determined.

Less severe problems of reinforcer selection can be the result of impoverished experience in institutional or overprotective environments. We may find that a child does not seek access to toys, playgrounds, dolls auto rides, special clothing and other things simply because he or she has had little or no experience with them. All that is required to expand the number and type of experiences which motivate the child, is to bring her or him into contact with the target events on a regular basis so that their intrinsic reinforcing properties may come to bear. Rides in the school bus or walks in the park may be causes for apprehension until the child discovers that they are often associated with playgrounds, balloons, snacks and happy people. In order to establish those first walks or rides, it may be necessary to provide a high density of food or social reinforcement for coming along. The general strategy is to make currently effective reinforcers contingent on involvement with unfamiliar events, things, people and places which will themselves become attractive once familiar (Ayllon & Azrin, 1968).

Frequently Occurring Behaviors

Parents, guardians, teachers and other change agents may be unaware of less conventional reinforcers which they have at their disposal. We have learned that any active organism can be readily reinforced. Gerbils, hamsters, and other laboratory rodents make frequent use of a running wheel if it is available to them. A recent series of studies pointed out that making the avilability of running contingent on other behavior would increase the strength of that other behavior (Premack, 1965). The analogy is easy to make and it has been empirically validated (Homme, de Baca, Devine, Steinhorst & Rickert, 1963; Wasik, 1970). All children engage in some behavior. Many learning disabled young people engage in repetitive hand, face, and body movements. These apparently undesirable behaviors, which occur at high frequency, can be a resource. By making frequently occurring behaviors contingently available after less likely but more desirable behavior, even profoundly unresponsive children can be reinforced.

If Joey rocks when left alone, he may learn to improve performance of an eye-hand coordination exercise in order to get access to the rocking chair or hobby horse where his rocking is neither grotesque nor disapproved. Our experience with the use of repetitive "self-stimulatory" behaviors as an initial reinforcer, is that careful programming will result in Joey's eventually finding other learned activities more reinforcing than rocking. We have never had to actively eliminate a "self-stimulatory" behavior which was used as a reinforcer for other readily acquired behavior. When rocking ceases to be a reinforcer, behaviors and events which rocking helped to build can be applied as consequences to build another layer of behavior.

Tokens

When reinforcers are plentiful, a system for making them contingent on appropriate behavior is a necessity. While casual and imprecise association of reinforcers with accomplishments may suffice for the normal child, explicit and readily understood pairings are essential for the child with a major learing disorder. The effectiveness of reinforcement is a function of the frequency and immediacy with which it follows the desired response.

Small, immediate, frequent reinforcers effect more rapid changes in behavior than do large, delayed, infrequent events. Most reinforcers, however, do not fit well into this ideal pattern. There is no way to dispense access to a playground, toy, game, book, music, or whatever, often and precisely. Even food has its problems unless resticted to "bite size" portions and used only when the child is hungry. The resolution is a medium of exchange which can be conveniently handled and which is a reliable reinforcer. Poker chips, points, or some other readily dispensed token can be made contingent on behavior immediately and frequently. Tokens that mediate access to a number of effective reinforcers, with time and repeated use, themselves acquire reinforcing properties. If widely and frequently applied, they may "generalize," becoming effective at all times, because there is always something which the child wants to which they provide access. Tokens make the delivery of reinforcement quantifiable, concrete and recordable. The individual who "pays off" behavior with tokens is less likely to need personal charm to effect the child's behavior in a positive way. Tokens can be dispensed in large numbers. In a training session lasting 30 minutes, 100 or more tokens may be dispensed contingent on small improvements in articulation. One can hardly conceive of any "natural" reinforcer which would be usable in this way. Contractual arrangements may range from requiring a child to fill a small bucket with poker chips in order to get a snack, to complex contractual arrangements covering weeks of behavior and mediating almost any conceivable reinforcer. The use of token reinforcerment systems in residential facilities and training environments has been comprehensively reported elsewhere (Ayllon & Azrin, 1968; Kazdin & Bootzin, 1972; Lent, Le Blanc & Spradlin, 1970).

There are problems with token economies (Kuypers, Becker & O'Leary, 1968). The name itself is a clue to what often goes wrong. In setting up awkward miniatures of the national economy, many projects have focussed on arbitrary and complex negotiated exchanges which cast the trainees and staff in an adversary relationship. Anything beyond a primitive token economy can generate a furor in the staff implementing it because it is too good a replica of the real world. Given the opportunity, each staff member has strong ideas about fairness in the distribution of wealth and the arranging of costs, which tend to obliterate basic considerations of providing a generalized reinforcer for training purposes.

It takes skill, careful design, and reliable systematic operation to make a token economy work and keep working. There are few consequences built into the system to maintain the appropriate behavior of the staff. Probably the most important detractor is that there are more familiar and expeditious ways to get things done. The rules and bookkeeping inherent in a token economy have long-range benefits, but are always a short-term nuisance. Few of the well known token economies, reports of which popularized the approach, are still in operation.

NEW BEHAVIORS

Primary advice for the behavior change agent is to reinforce desirable behavior and ignore undesirable behavior. This simple prescription has produced dramatic effects and is acquiring widespread practice. It is generally inadequate as a guiding principle for therapeutic intervention with the retarded.

Reinforcing appropriate or desirable behavior while ignoring less desirable behavior is a strategy designed to *shift* rather than *create* behavior patterns. It presumes that the desired behavior is likely to occur in a reasonable period of time and that it will be readily strengthened relative to competing responses. In the case of a retarded individual with a limited repertoire and stereotyped response patterns a frequent concern is how to get the desired behavior to occur at all. The defining characteristic of the retarded child is broad behavior deficit. This simple fact is readily forgotten while attempting to cope with the responsibilities inherent in supervising the well being of behaviorally deficient children. New behavior, explicitly identified as such, should be the objective of therapeutic programming more often than it is in common practice.

Guided Learning

Reinforcement strengthens the behavior which it follows. It is very likely that a retarded child will emit certain desirable behaviors very infrequently or not at all. In that case, the change agent is faced with the problem of the first instance, how to get the behavior to occur so that it can be reinforced.

Desired responses which are unlikely to occur spontaneously within a reasonable period of time can be expedited by guidance (Kozloff, 1974). In this context, guidance is anything which makes the response highly likely. If we want the child to grasp a spoon or writing utensil properly, we might manually guide his or her hand into correct posture. Holding the instrument properly can then be reinforced. The desired behavior, however, is not holding a spoon while someone holds the child's hand. Rather it is holding and using the spoon or whatever, unaided. That is accomplished by gradually withdrawing the guidance in tolerably small steps while continuing to reinforce the child for appropriate behavior.

More sophisticated tasks and more sophisticated learners make possible the use of an almost endless variety of guides. Verbal instructions as well as physical guidance might be employed in teaching shoe tying, as well as subtler prompts such as wiggling the end of the shoelace to attract the child's attention to it when it should be grasped. A child with advanced observing skills and a fairly broad response repertoire can be guided by providing a model performance which he can imitate (Hingtgen, Coulter & Churchill, 1967; Steinman, 1970; Lovaas, Berberich, Perloff & Schaeffer, 1966). Written instructions, pictures and various other prompts can guide the behavior of even more sophisticated learners (Bijou, Birnbrauer, Kidder & Tague, 1966).

Gradual elimination of guidance can result in a transfer of stimulus control. Stimuli controlling the child's behavior in the assisted phase are those provided by the therapist. When guidance has been successfully withdrawn, the stimuli controlling that same behavior will be features of the natural environment. Control of the behavior is said to have transferred from prosthetic guides to the natural stimuli. In the case of the child with a serious learning handicap, assistance must be withdrawn slowly, in steps which the child can tolerate without making errors. Errors would disrupt and possibly destroy the performance (Stoddard & Sidman, 1967; Touchette, 1968).

All guidance procedures used by behavior therapists are designed to bring behavior under the control of naturally occurring stimuli and naturally occurring contingencies of reinforcement as well. The child learning to tie her shoes is dependent on the instructor for physical assistance, prompts and reinforcement for success. If the program meets its objectives, the day will come when she will tie her shoe because it is untied whenever and wherever that may occur. Contol will have transferred to appropriate stimuli. The reinforcement contingencies associated with neatness and not tripping or losing a shoe are the natural consequences which are likely to maintain the behavior.

Appropriate stimulus control can be achieved only after a careful analysis of both training procedures and the events which will be relevant when guidance has been withdrawn. Consider, for example, a non-ambulatory child who is about to be taught to walk. As with many things retarded children must be taught, this is something which everyone has observed a normal child learning. Most children learn to walk near their first birthday. Often a parent or other participant in the game stands in front of the toddler offering support with both hands and backing slowly away. When the child moves forward with some degree of confidence and with little pressure on the adult's hands, the "instructor" may release the child's hands momentarily. Toddlers fend for themselves, finding substitute supports in the form of chairs, stools, ottomans, tables or other objects to move about the edges of or to push along. These commonplace events come to mind when the retarded child appears to be ready to learn independent walking. The objective of a guidance program is to transfer control from external supports to the child's own muscular and vestibular systems. That transfer may occur spontaneously in the normal child. It is less likely to in the retarded young person. It is desirable if not essential, therefore, that guidance and support be provided in a way which makes it very likely that natural stimuli and reinforcers will acquire control of independent walking. One simple approach is to support the child from behind rather than in front. The child will tend to move toward interesting places, objects, and people rather than toward the person to whom he is clinging. The "instructor" will find it easy to gradually withdraw support without making the fact visually obvious, a likely source of disruption. A series of small reductions usually results in the child's walking independently literally before he realizes that he has done it. Even a commonplace and familiar problem like this one calls for a careful analysis of the conditions which will support and maintain the behavior after guidance has been withdrawn. Anything less reduces the probability of success.

While the examples used here may suggest it, this method is not restricted to simple self-help skills. Programmed instructional materials make use of the same principles to teach academic and vocational subject matter (Holland, 1960). A skillful group leader will gradually withdraw guidance of role playing, modeling or discussion sessions, transferring control to the members of the group. Examples of stimulus control transfer can be found in many well executed teaching and therapy programs.

Errors

If, in response to the statement, "find the picture of the kitten," a child touched a picture of a Pontiac station wagon, that behavior would accurately be described as an error. Typically you would make some effort to correct it. Rarely would any effort be made to discover or eliminate the cause of the error. The assumption at work in this example is that errors are a natural or even necessary part of learning. They are not.

Errors are the result of imperfect instruction. They occur when the child has been misled or when the training program requires discriminations and other behaviors which the child does not have available. A sequence of tasks which gradually increases demands on the learner can maintain perfect response accuracy while teaching new behavior. If the proper form of guidance is used and withdrawn at the optimal rate, the child will learn to perform a new task without ever making an inappropriate response (Touchette, 1968).

Learning with few or no errors presents special opportunities for children with major learning disorders. Laboratory evidence indicates that those instructed errorlessly recall what they have learned better than those who have made errors prior to learning. More importantly, tasks which prove impossible presented in a trial and error format are readily learned when the performance is built up in small steps which maintain appropriate responding (Touchette, 1968). It would be a mistake to conclude that eliminating errors makes things easier to learn; rather making things easier to learn eliminates errors.

A careful reading of the preceding section on guidance will have led you to conclude that the design of this type of instructional program is difficult and time consuming. The benefits to the child, however, can be commensurate. The effects of learning are generally cumulative. Each thing that the child learns makes learning more likely from unprogrammed sources (Touchette, 1971). The consistent success which errorless instruction produces tends to ameliorate anxiety and fragile motivation produced by prior failures and frustration. Major changes in the child's and guardian's expectations can result.

Generalization

It is unreasonable to assume that new behavior, learned under nearly ideal circumstances will be available in other places, with other people. Behavior is to some extent dependent on the environment in which it was established. It is no surprise to the experienced behavior therapist when a child who has made substantive progress in the context of a training program, shows little or no progress elsewhere (Rincover & Koegel, 1975). This familiar problem is called a failure to generalize. Almost any change may disrupt fragile new performances. The child who has just learned to walk may fall to the floor when a door is slammed in an adjacent room. He or she will almost surely regress in new surroundings, on a different type of floor, outdoors or amidst bustling floor traffic. A recent graduate of a self-feeding program may become an incompetent source of embarrassment on her visit to a restaurant. The best circuit board assembler in the prevocational workshop may be unable to produce an acceptable product when the supervisor is changed.

No learned response pattern will generalize spontaneously to all situations. There are circumstances which can disrupt the best of us. Generalization is a matter of degree. Being able to count change in a quiet room with your tutor under no time pressure is a far cry from having to count your change after buying a token for the subway at rush hour. To the extent that they are known, stressful environments can be gradually approximated in a training program in order to raise the probability of generalization. Limitations on what the therapist has control over, and the practical impossibility of introducing features of the real world gradually make this an approach with limited application.

The only guarantee of generalization is to retrain the behavior in the new, disruptive environment. This is not quite as bad as it sounds. Since the child has the behavior available, it can be re-established using an abbreviated version of the program which originally taught it. Each time a behavior pattern is re-established in a new environment, the probability that it will appear spontaneously and appropriately in the next new setting is increased (Stokes, Baer & Jackson, 1974). Since technical expertise is not as critical to retraining as it is to original learning, this is an area in which parents, siblings, relatives, friends and more advanced or less handicapped retarded individuals can make a major contribution.

DISTRESSING BEHAVIOR

So far I have dealt with operations which potentiate absent skills or extend behavioral repertoires. Observing school, group home, or institutional facilities for the retarded, will often reveal behaviors which are undesirable and should be eliminated rather that nurtured. Undesirable behaviors vary widely in sophistication and frequency. In young children repetitive hand, head or body movements, facial contortions, tantrums, apathy, avoidance of eye contact, odd noises, drooling and incontinence are often observed. Older children may in addition display worrisome aggressive, destructive or self-abusive behaviors. These behaviors are distressing. Making a mess at mealtime, being clumsy, wandering off when unattended, and failing to follow simple verbal instructions can constitute a real threat to the child. When they are frequent occurrences, behaviors like those above can retard, if not rule out, the learning of new skills.

Replacement

A functional analysis does not differentiate between distressing and pleasing behaviors, although any observer would. Disgusting and delightful are judgements, descriptions of an observer's behavior, not that of the child. Functionally, behavior is behavior. Difficult though it may be to accept, undesirable behaviors are present for the same reasons as desirable behaviors. They are followed by reinforcement. Distressing behavior may be looked on as a direct result of a paucity of desirable behavior which achieves the same ends.

Behavior cannot be considered independent of its consequences (Skinner, 1938). If we substitute punishment for reinforcement, we may discourage the distressing behavior, but the absence of reinforcement will serve as a standing motivation to engage in the undesirable behavior which once produced it. If, on the other hand, we provide the same reinforcement for an easily emitted and desirable response, there will be no reason to engage in the previous behavior. Replacement is therefore a more permanent solution.

We cannot assume that the retarded child has appropriate behavior with which to replace less desirable behavior currently at high strength. The simplest form of positive intervention makes this assumption. The schedule of reinforcement known as DRO, *d*ifferential *r*einforcement of *o*ther behavior, arranges the delivery of positive consequences whenever the undesirable response has not occurred for some specified period of time. Any behavior other than the distressing behavior is increased in probability. This simple contingency has produced rapid and dramatic decreases in undesirable behavior in some cases (Repp & Deitz, 1974). A more constructive approach is to guide the establishment of desirable alternative behaviors. A desirable, readily accessible, and densely reinforced behavior will then become part of the child's social repertoire. There is, in fact, no good alternative to replacement as a way of eliminating undesirable behavior. Reinforcing sitting is a way to get rid of too much running around. Punishing running around will not have the same result.

Distressing behaviors impose on us in a way that desirable behaviors do not. For this reason, the well behaved child is often ignored while the child who is a source of irritation receives the lion's share of attention. That attention may not be "pleasant," but it is intense and reliable. The natural anger which irritants provoke, does not prompt us to do anything pleasant for the child who is the source of the problem. It is important, therefore, that the replacement approach emphasizes reinforcement as a means of promoting adaptive behavior. Such programs enhance rather than violate the legal and human rights of the child, while effectively eliminating many unacceptable response patterns.

Retarded children can exhibit a bewildering array of frustrating and difficult to deal with behaviors. In extreme cases, violent acts may threaten the physical well-being of the child and those around him or her. Drugs, restraint and punishment have the potential to eliminate these child-produced aversive events rapidly. In the majority of cases these are exactly the techniques applied. It does not require a sophisticated behavioral analysis to see that expeditious elimination of this type of behavior is a reinforcer for the child's guardians. Drugs, punishment and restraint may solve the immediate problems of those who must care for the child, but they do not alleviate the problem of the child. That problem is, and will continue to be, behavioral insufficiency. There is a real danger that procedures which suppress undesirable behavior and accomplish nothing else, will delay or prevent any constructive solution to the child's problems. The continued effectiveness of these methods is dependent on their continuous application. Constructive alternatives take time, discipline, well trained staff and careful planning, but they can, and often do, result in permanent, unobtrusive solutions.

Drugs

Drugs which are prescribed because of their effects on behavior are called psycho-active or pyschotropic. Those that tend to eliminate agitated behavior are called sedatives or tranquilizers. The names suggest non-debilitating, even pleasant effects. In fact, the effects of these drugs are poorly understood. One thing is clear, no psycho-active drug expands limited behavioral repertoires. These agents have no direct beneficial effect on the problem of behavioral insufficiency. On the contrary, initial research indicates that tranquilizing drugs interfere with learning in odd and subtle ways (Sprague, Barnes & Werry, 1970). Since learning inefficiencies are the defining problem of the retarded child, agents which add to or complicate the problem are an inappropriate choice for long-term therapy.

Clinical researchers are currently attempting to determine what value psycho-active drugs may have as a temporary measure to facilitate the initiation of behavioral intervention (Greenberg, Altman & Cole, 1975). Drugs which supress emotional or aggressive outbursts may make it easier to get a program of developing alternative behavior underway. Even in this format, caution is in order. Cases of severe behavioral disorder among retarded young people are rarely alleviated when tranquilizing agents are applied in reasonable dosages. Dramatic changes occur only at doses which virtually immobilize the child. Because expansion of access is always the goal of behavioral intervention programs, the extended unproductive restriction of a child's behavior, whether physical or pharmacologic, is unacceptable.

Punishment

Punishment can effect immediate reductions in the frequency of undesirable behavior (Risley, 1968). Birnbrauer's chapter in this volume deals with aversive consequences applied in behavior change programs in some depth. I shall not do so here. It is argued that mild forms of punishment can serve to break up ritualistic or repetitive behaviors which might go on for an extended period of time, reducing opportunity to effect a positive change. Any stimulus which startles the child will have this effect, and it need not be punishing. Severe punishment in the form of painful but nondamaging electric shock has been shown to be effective in reducing or eliminating self-mutilation and extreme aggressivity (Lovaas & Simmons, 1969). This form of intervention, combined with reinforcement of incompatible behaviors has been touted as cost and time effective. There is evidence to suggest that positive, constructional alternatives alone, though slower and more costly, are equally effective, more humane and possibly more permanent (Peterson & Peterson, 1968; Vukelich & Hake, 1971).

At issue here is the question of what to do about behaviors which are impossible to ignore and threaten serious harm. They must be dealt with before any constructive intervention is contemplated. The reality of the situation is that few programs for the retarded have the luxury of making any choice at all in this arena. An experimental analysis will show that the problem behaviors, even those of extreme severity, are in most cases maintained by contingencies of reinforcement. Rarely are agencies which serve the retarded in a position to alter the consequences of behavior. They do not have the expertise or facilities necessary to carry out a program of systematic environmental manipulation. Few parents or staff are equipped to deal with crisis level problems of aggressive, self-mutilative, or destructive behavior in constructive ways. The cheapest and most accessible solutions are suppressive. Sedative medication, punishment, and physical restraint are the techniques most commonly employed to prevent self-mutilation and damage to others. The problem is disturbing to behavior analysts who know that there are more humane, constructive procedures available. For most children in this sad condition, those alternatives remain only a theoretical possibility.

Escalation

The crux of the matter is a struggle for control which has been called variously "escalation" (Goldiamond, 1974) and "the extinction-coercion deviant behavior syndrome" (Patterson & Reid, 1970). Some children who are not socially skillful have no acceptable way of responding to the sudden cessation of reinforcement. When reinforcement is cut off, intentionally or incidentally, a behavioral disaster may ensue.

You will recognise the termination of reinforcement as extinction, a procedure which reliably reduces or eliminates behavior. The sudden omission of reinforcement in a context where it has been reliably available can produce a temporary but dramatic intensification of the relevant behavior. This effect is especially reliable when the situation allows no alternative access to the reinforcer. Accompanying the increase in intensity there is likely to be an emotional outburst.

Most children have extensive repertoires of social behavior. When one strategy stops producing the desired consequence, they shift to an alternative which has worked in the past. Retarded children may have such limited social repertoires that when reinforcement is not forthcoming they have no other behavior which is likely to work. Options which provide alternative paths to reinforcement are the only reason why escalation does not occur in every instance of extinction.

Consider Mary, an 11-year-old victim of Down's syndrome (mongolism), who accompanies her older sister on shopping trips to the neighborhood supermarket. There, skillfully displayed by the management, she finds many edible treats which she would like to have. Mary is overweight and may be diabetic. Her physician recently warned against giving her sweets. In previous trips, Mary has always been able to wheedle a bag of candy from her sister by whining and threatening to become a source of embarrassment. This time, the older sister is steadfast, it is for Mary's own good, and it is time to let her know who is boss. Mary begins to cry when her usual requests are refused. Her sister becomes firmer and tells Mary that this is childish behavior. If she keeps it up, she will never get any more candy. Mary becomes more distraught, eventually becoming completely unmanageable, rolling in the aisle, screaming! Her older sister wishes she had planned ahead, as a crowd gathers. She knows that she must give in and console Mary, reinforcing the whole unfortunate episode.

Mary might not have gotten her candy, but she certainly was the center of attention. Attention is a powerful reinforcer for most young people, and it is one which is especially difficult to withhold if undesirable behavior escalates. It is often the case that the item under dispute between adult and child is not the real source of the problem, rather it is the undivided attention from the adult which the child receives near the termination of an escalation episode. Attention of equivalent intensity is not generally given to a child behaving in desirable ways.

Eliminating this sort of unproductive struggle is really quite easy, though not what we appear to be instinctively predisposed to do. The socially inept child simply cannot be relied on to find an acceptable alternative on his or her own. It is necessary to reassure him or her that reinforcement is available, and to guide the child to an easy, acceptable way to obtain the desired reinforcer. Neither of these steps necessitates "backing down" or otherwise reinforcing the child's attempts at coercion, kicked off by the threat of being cut off from attention or some other important event.

Recently, Michael, an 8-year-old boy, diagnosed as retarded and autistic, came to us for visual attention tests. This sort of testing is carried out in a laboratory which houses automated apparatus to which the children may respond in various ways, receiving tokens for their efforts. It is designed to be fun and interesting, and it is. Michael approached the laboratory with my assistant, Jeanne. He took one look through the open door, shouted "NO" loudly and braced himself for a struggle. Michael began mumbling, and seemed to be working himself up into a tantrum. Jeanne waited. When Michael paused briefly, she gave him a few raisins and some verbal reassurance. Next she asked Michael to hold her hand, he did, and he received a few more raisins as well as praise for his cooperation. Soon, they were walking up and down the hall together, and eventually in and out of the testing room. Michael was receiving an occasional raisin and being praised frequently for being cooperative as he responded appropriately to Jeanne's requests. Reinforcement was delivered usually in or near the testing area. Jeanne and Michael entered the testing room. She asked him to sit with her in front of the testing apparatus. Our usual testing procedure began as Michael received a token from the apparatus and was shown that it could be traded for raisins, toys, etc. As Michael began to work at the testing tasks, Jeanne moved slowly away, returning occasionally to exchange things which Michael selected, for the tokens.

It had taken Jeanne six minutes to get Michael in front of the apparatus eager to work. She dispensed about two dozen raisins and a lot of verbal praise. Initially, she reinforced Michael for being quiet and looking at her, then for following her physical guidance, and eventually for sitting, waiting and exchanging tokens.

Michael was a major problem to his parents and teachers because of his "negativism." He resisted anything new, and might become very emotional for hours if things did not go as he wanted. They struggled with Michael. We did not. He was readily reinforced both with raisins and praise. That made him especially easy to work with. Another child might have been handled differently, Michael put up another brief fuss when it was time to leave. He wanted to keep at it and get more tokens. He did, for leaving.

There are lots of young people like Michael who are more effective at getting attention for being obnoxious than for being cooperative. Alternative behavior may be available, but it is a low probability event. Both learner and instructor benefit from the approach used above. The only reasons for not using guidance withdrawn in rapid gradual steps to establish desired behavior, is because you don't know how, or because it is physically impossible.

Environments which the child is in for only a few hours, the supermarket, the barber's, a hospital or physician's office, the dentist's, a neighbor's home, the bank, etc. are generally thought to offer little opportunity to arrange contingencies of reinforcement. A common approach is to "placate" the distressed child. This potentiates an arrangement whereby the child may receive social and tangible reinforcers for behaving badly in any new place. Some forethought and rapidly withdrawn guidance, as in our example above, repeated a few times, can strengthen a pattern of cooperation and anticipation.

BEHAVIORAL OBJECTIVES

Selection and specification of objectives is the first, and often the most important step in therapeutic intervention. Well stated, the objectives communicate precisely what the change agent and the client are trying to accomplish. They reflect an analysis of the client's current and future needs. The quality of that analysis and its predictive validity determine whether the program will significantly expand the client's options and autonomy.

The two areas in which program objectives may be inadequate are the relevance of content and the specificity of criteria.

Intervention procedures cannot be selected until goals are clearly identified. Carefully stated objectives can make the intervention procedures of choice apparent to all concerned. Yet, it is not uncommon to find change agents expending large quantities of their time and the child's working toward casually selected and poorly specified goals. Training programs for severely retarded adolescents which deal exclusively with vague academic objectives, traditional and irrelevant, are a case in point.

Specification

An adequate statement of behavioral objectives describes what the child will be able to do when intervention is complete; how often, where, and under what circumstances. Anyone who has seriously attempted a rigorous analysis and description of this sort will agree that it is no easy task.

Child and parents should be involved in the development of specifications where possible. This may be obvious to some of you, still it is rarely done. Agreeing formally to contribute to the program will increase the likeihood that all parties understand the objectives and the criteria for their accomplishment. In identifying objectives together, client and guardian may for the first time attend to the specific relevant behaviors and their consequences. The awareness of the problem thus engendered often results in substantive progress. It is not uncommon to find that both parent and child are surprised at what the problem really amounts to in a functional behavioral analysis. The awareness of the problem thus engendered can result in positive change.

When goals are communicable to the child, he or she may participate actively as data collector, observer, and ally to the therapist, often making strides toward self-management in the process. If the idea of a retarded child "taking data" seems unlikely to you, consider how simple the procedure can be made. Little skill is required when the record is in the form of pegs in a board or beads moved from left to right on a string. The ability to observe and record his or her own activities is an important part of the self-discipline which leads to independence (Kanfer, 1970).

Observable behaviors, which all concerned agree to accept as evidence that an objective has been achieved, constitute terminal behavior specifications. These specifications form a simple contract with the client. They identify accomplishments which guardians and change agents have agreed in advance to honor, often in the form of increased autonomy. It is essential that terminal behavior specifications be carefully worked out in advance. Precise and comprehensive specifications are the key to eliminating disagreements as to whether objectives have or have not been met.

Care must be exercised to avoid specifying terminal behaviors which exceed levels of competence with which we are satisfied in each other. Social behavior of "normal" children and adults is not 100% free of mistakes. Individuals who have acceptable table manners occasionally drop or spill something. Well behaved children are not always attentive. No one is clean and neat at all times. There are no well identified standards for table manners, neatness and attentiveness. In their absence it may be necessary to observe and record the behavior of ordinary people in the environments in which the child's program predicts he or she will eventually reside. The results of such a survey are sometimes surprising.

Goals set near the current level of behavior are more likely to be met quickly. This is not always the choice, however, as persistence in the pursuit of long range goals may be relevant. The arbitrary nature of goal setting means that terminal behavior specifications fall, broadly, into two categories: stepping stones and final performances. In the first instance an intermediate goal provides evidence of progress and perhaps indicates a point at which some substantive change in the intervention program is called for. The program moves on to the next goal as soon as its predecessor is achieved. The accomplishment is a prerequisite for the next step, not an objective in itself. A final performance, on the other hand, is something which should take place in the child's permanent behavioral repertoire. Here, the behavior may be learned beyond a simple criterion of accomplishment in order to stabilize, perfect, and increase the probability of transfer. An effort will be made to bring the behavior into contact with "natural" contingencies of reinforcement which are usually at a lower density and of a different type than those used in training (Baer & Wolf, 1970). This type of activity would not only waste time and effort if it were applied to an intermediate goal, it would inhibit progress by making the behavior difficult to modify. Any behavior or skill may be a stepping stone or a final performance according to the child's capacities and the specific features of his or her program. I will let you conjure up your own example of each.

Precisely specified terminal behaviors are the most frequently overlooked component of intervention plans for children with special needs. One critical function which they serve is to prevent us from adapting the environment to the child, rather than expanding the child's behavioral repertoire. Larry is quite clumsy and seems to be accident prone. His terminal behavior objective is to be accident free on the stairs and in the hallways without reminders or supervision for five consecutive days. His supervisor had to point this out to the special education department head at the school who had decided to solve the problem by putting Larry in the self-contained classroom on the ground floor. Eliminating the opportunity to use the stairs and walk in the hallways might reduce the probability of accidents, but it restricts rather than expands Larry's potential autonomy and allows no possibility that he will meet the stated objectives of his program.

In general, terminal behavior specifications keep change agents and clients on track. They help to avoid decisions based on length of time in the program, staff availability, funding and other influences which are not reflections of the child's accomplishments. It is also important to note that when terminal behavior specifications have been met, they represent a very special and precise record of the child's accomplishments. They are not inferred from small samples of behavior or test results but are recorded as having occurred reliably and observably in the specified environment(s).

Selection

Critics sometimes complain that behavioral intervention goals lack breadth. Therapists counter that it is delimitation which keeps the program relevant, manageable and likely to reach completion expeditiously. There is, additionally, an element of protection for the client in narrowly defined behavioral objectives. They prevent intrusion into areas which are not intervention targets. Perhaps Marie dresses sloppily, but she is involved in a behavior change program in order to learn to use the telephone and to tell the time. A clear statement to that effect excludes contingencies designed to produce fastidiousness.

What is included? What is excluded? Which skills are priority targets? What is the long range plan of habilitation? Who will decide? Jerry cannot sign his name, he walks unsteadily and slouches, his shirt is rarely buttoned properly, he manipulates and arranges small objects compulsively, he doesn't smile, he tends to be aggressive toward smaller children, he is profoundly afraid of being embarrassed before strangers, he cannot tell what day of the week it is, and he calls all animals "doggie". Jerry's most pressing problem cannot be identified empirically. It is a matter of judgement. What distresses Jerry may not be what distresses others about Jerry, and neither of those priorities may be high for a vocationally oriented program. There is no way to resolve these dilemmas except to hope that an informed child, parent or guardian, and therapist can come to reasonable and reasoned decisions (Hawkins, 1975).

The basic question is, who benefits? When the child does not profit from meeting the program's objectives, the program is not a good one. Unacceptable objectives benefit only the guardians or institutions which are responsible for the child's welfare. It is, of course, possible for behavior changes to profit both the child and supervisors. If this is the case, as it often is, so much the better. When there is a conflict of interests, however, the child's interest must prevail. Profit is subjective. How do we know when the child has profited? The best we can do is to estimate whether new behavior which is contemplated will extend his or her options, access and autonomy.

As advocacy for the rights of the handicapped becomes commonplace, justification of behavioral intervention goals has taken on new importance. Traditionally, objectives were chosen by the staff of the therapeutic agency or the individual therapist on the basis of personal judgement and philosophy. In an effort to substantiate the competency of goal selection, some have turned to the developmental scales of Cattel (1940), Bayley (1969), Gessell (1940), Doll et al. (1953). It is a simple matter to identify the current level of functioning by using these scales, and target whatever comes next. This apparently reasonable approach has major flaws. Developmental scales are not exhaustive lists of behaviors which children display at various ages. They are, rather, a selection of behaviors which are well correlated with physical maturation. As the child grows older, these behaviors tend to emerge in sequence. Skills which emerge whenever they are taught or whenever the opportunity to learn them is presented, are intentionally eliminated from developmental checklists, as they will correlate poorly with age. The small, biased sample of behaviors which these lists contain were selected on bases which hardly recommend them as guides for remedial programs. Unchallenged acceptance of developmental milestones as determinants of goals for retarded children can lead to ineffective or irrelevant programs.

The suggestion that "typical" sequences of skill development are "preferred" or "necessary" generally lack empirical foundation. Environmental, motivational, experiential and maturational factors contribute to the acquisition of skills in children. What comes before is not always a prerequisite for what follows; it is even less often the cause of its successor. Must a 13-year-old cerebral palsied child who has never been ambulatory crawl before walking? Must babbling precede speech production in a mute 8-year-old victim of Down's Syndrome? Is it necessary for any child to scribble before some more disciplined use of a writing utensil is attempted? The intuitive and empirical answer to these questions is "no."

Objectives and goals are things that have not yet happened. Their likelihood, appropriateness and facilitative effects are always a guess; their selection an art. We are not graced with tests of their rightness or wrongness of objective selection, only opinions. Behavior therapists use a functional approach. Goals are suggested after an examination of the child's current skills under the prevailing contingencies of reinforcement. The therapist then attempts to determine what new or altered behavior patterns would provide a significant increase in the child's access to information, social contact, reinforcers and options. This may not require any reference to the behavior of "normal" or "typical" children, as the retarded child is rarely in a "normal" or "typical" environment.

Changes are underway in the generic nature of care for retarded and physically handicapped children and adults. It appears that they will be more and more likely to remain members of the communities into which they were born. No one really knows what the future will bring in terms of employment, entertainment, living, loving and learning opportunities for those people stigmatized by their behavioral inadequacies. No "cures" are on the horizon. Behavioral intervention programs for the retarded young which are comprehensive in scope and have continuity are still some way off. We will for some time yet, be setting goals and objectives which can be accomplished quickly with immediate benefits.

GENERAL COMMENTS

All children start out naive, vulnerable and dependent. As they grow and learn, the responsibility for avoiding danger becomes more and more theirs, and less and less a matter of parental intercession. The 3-year-old who has walked off alone is cause for great concern, the 11-year-old less so, and the 15-year-old is expected to display a certain amount of independence. When are the risks small enough to remove restrictions and direct supervision? This question is the bane of every adolescent, the dilemma of evey parent.

We know roughly what to expect in the case of a normal child. There will be mistakes, accidents, embarrassed requests for assistance and separation traumas. Eventually, inexorably, independence will come. Even hesitant parents allow their children autonomy in the face of risks. The goal is the knowledge that the child will eventually have to handle matters of personal safety unaided. The child in turn seeks autonomy which allows him or her to pursue personal interests more closely. For the retarded child, the future is less clear. He or she may remain dependent on others even as an adult. The goads to achieve independence may be missing.

Risks and Restrictions

The two components of risk taking are awareness and decision. We are little concerned with the individual who decides to take a risk unless he or she is unaware of the true probabilities. Our social system for deciding about competence hinges on this distinction. Those who are aware of danger and go ahead nonetheless are often admired. Those who are unaware of danger are judged incompetent, and their access may be restricted. Intellectually disadvantaged children are assumed to be incompetent in matters of personal safety until proven otherwise (Perske, 1972). It can be exceedingly difficult for them to establish their right to make decisions in matters which involve real or perceived risk.

Autonomy is not inevitable for a child with a major learning handicap. Parents and guardians who must enlist or at least approve of programs directed toward self-management are often threatened by the prospect, judging it to represent increased exposure to danger. Special training to increase mobility and self-reliance is often late in coming, unenthusiastic or altogether absent.

In the interest of safety, hazards are made physically inaccessible to normal and learning handicapped children alike. For the retarded they are much more likely to remain inaccessible, exaggerating naivety and vulnerability. Extended protection can, and often does, reduce opportunity to learn appropriate caution in the presence of dangerous but commonplace objects. To focus on risks without approaching them constructively is to preclude the growth of adaptive behavior.

Traditionally children with major learning disorders have been dealt with as invalids to be cared for. The result has been demeaning, often in the extreme (Wolfensberger, 1972). Close supervision, little mobility, few options and dramatically restricted access to people, places and things do not add up to a rich and rewarding daily existence. They should not be a part of any individual's life. The behavior therapy model suggests that a decision to restrict a child because risks exceed his or her current capacity, carries with it a commitment to specify and attempt to produce those changes in behavior which would reverse that decision.

Simple "care" is not the answer. It is inimical to progresss in self-reliance. Providing the basic necessities of life in a danger-free environment is an unlikely strategy for generating new adaptive response patterns. The "protective custody" approach to the retarded child offers dramatically reduced long-range prospects as compared to systematically executed programs of therapeutic intervention.

Parents, guardians, institutional staff and other caretakers to whom decisions fall, must examine carefully the areas in which their interests and the interests of the retarded child conflict. They must weigh the debilitating effects of limited access to events, their normal consequences and contexts against the reduced probability of accident or embarrassment which restrictions may offer.

Why We Are Optimistic

The extension of behavior therapy to the remediation of severe behavioral insufficiencies is a relatively recent occurrence. Most of the literature reporting case studies, technique development and basic research has accumulated over the last 10 to 12 years. Severe learning disorders have been around much longer than that. The result of this discrepancy has been that children who were refractory to traditional, established treatment were those with whom behavior therapists first dealt. Those cases were not the easy ones. The results have been encouraging nonetheless.

Clinic, hospital and institutional staff have referred for treatment their incorrigible, untrainable, projectile vomiting, seizing, nude, incontinent, speechless, aggressive, multiply handicapped, grotesques from back wards and isolation. When staff did not present them, therapists have gone looking for problems which test the power of their techniques and provoke development of new methods. Substantive positive changes in behavior have been reported in case after case, over a wide range of learning handicaps (Barrett, 1977). Each child is unique. Although there are some for whom we can as yet do little, the accumulation of carefully documented reports suggests that these are few among many.

Behavior therapy derives from the experimental analysis of behavior carried out in laboratories throughout the world. The clinical techniques which have evolved from this science are relatively free from dogma and theory. New data, analyses and procedures can therefore be assimilated with equanimity. The basic commitment of behavior therapists is to results rather than a prescribed set of procedures. Without a theory to validate, the discipline continues to collect and examine data which relate outcomes to procedures and other relevant variables. More expeditious service and more complete analyses are the inevitable result.

REFERENCES

Ayllon, T., & Azrin, N. H. Reinforcer sampling: A technique for increasing the behavior of mental patients. *Journal of Applied Behavior Analysis*, 1968, *1*, 13–20.

Ayllon, T., & Azrin, N. H. *The token economy: A motivational system for therapy and rehabilitation*. New York: Appleton-Century-Crofts, 1969.

Baer, D. M., & Wolf, M. M. The entry into natural communities of reinforcement. In R. Ulrich, T. Stachnik, and J. Mabry (Eds.), *Control of human behavior*, Vol. 2. Glenview, Ill,: Scott, Foresman and Company, 1970, pp. 319–324.

Barrett, B. Behavior analysis. In J. Wortis (Ed.), *Mental retardation and development disabilities*, Vol. 9. New York: Brunner-Mazel, 1977.

Bayley, N. Bayley scales of infant development: Birth to two years. New York: Psychological Association, 1969.

Bijou, S. W. A functional analysis of retarded development. In N. R. Ellis (Ed.), *International review of mental retardation*, Vol. I. New York: Academic Press, 1966, pp. 1–19.

Bijou, S. W., & Baer, D. M. (Eds.). *Child development: Readings in experimental analysis*. New York: Appleton-Century-Crofts, 1967.

Bijou, S. W., Birnbrauer, J. S., Kidder, J. D., & Tague, C. Programmed instruction as an approach to teaching of reading, writing, and arithmetic to retarded children. *Psychological Record*, 1966, *16*, 505–522.

Birnbrauer, J. S. Mental retardation. In H. Leitenberg (Ed.), *The handbook of behavior modification and behavior therapy*. Englewood Cliffs, N.J.: Prentice-Hall, 1976, pp. 361–404.

Cattell, P. *Infant intelligence scale*. New York: Psychological Corporation, 1940.

Doll, E. A. *Measurement of social competence: A manual for the Vineland Social Maturity Scale*. Circle Pines, Minnesota: American Guidance Service, Inc., 1953.

Gesell, A. *Gesell Development Schedules*. New York: Psychological Corporation, 1940.

Goldiamond, I. Toward a constructional approach to social problems. *Behaviorism*, 1974, *2*, 1–84.

Greenberg, I., Altman, J., & Cole, J. Combination of drugs with behavior therapy. In M. Greenblatt (Ed.), *Drugs in combination with other therapies*. New York: Grune and Stratton, 1975, pp. 135–156.

Hawkins, R. Who decided THAT was the problem? In S. Wood (Ed.), *Issues in evaluating behavior modification*. Champaign, Ill,: Research Press, 1975, pp. 195–214.

Hingtgen, J. N., Coulter, S. D., & Churchill, D. W. Intensive reinforcement of imitative behavior in mute autistic children. *Archives of General Psychiatry*, 1967, *17*, 36–43.

Holland, J. Teaching machines: An application of principles from the laboratory. *Journal of the Experimental Analysis of Behavior*, 1960, *3*, 275–287.

Homme, L., deBaca, P., Devine, J., Steinhorst, R., & Rickert, E. Use of the Premack principle in controlling the behavior of nursery school children. *Journal of the Experimental Analysis of Behavior*, 1963, *6*, 544.

Kanfer, F. Self-regulation: Research, issues and speculations. In C. Neuringer and J. Michael (Eds.), *Behavior modifications in clinical psychology*. New York: Appleton-Century-Crofts, 1970, pp. 178–220.

Kazdin, A. E., & Bootzin, R. R. The token economy: An evaluative review. *Journal of Applied Behavior Analysis*, 1972, *5*, 343–372.

Kozloff, M. A. *Educating children with learning and behavior problems*. New York: John Wiley and Sons, 1974.

Kuypers, D. S., Becker, W. C., & O'Leary, D. How to make a token system fail. *Exceptional Children*, 1968, 35, *2*, 101–109.

Lent, J., LeBlanc, J., & Spradlin, J. Designing a rehabilitative culture for moderately retarded, adolescent girls. In R. Ulrich, T. Stachnik, and J. Mabry, (Eds.), *Control of human behavior*, Vol. 2. Glenview Ill,: Scott, Foresman and Company, 1970, pp. 121–135.

Lovaas, O. I., Berberich, J., Perloff, B., & Schaeffer, B. Acquisition of imitative speech by schizophrenic children. *Science*, 1966, *151*, 705–707.

Lovaas, O. I., & Bucher, B. (Eds.). *Perspectives in behavior modification with deviant children*. Englewood Cliffs, N.J.: Prentice-Hall, 1974.

Lovaas, O. I., Freitag, G., Kinder, M. I., Rubenstein, D. B., Schaeffer, B., & Simmons, J. Q. Establishment of social reinforcers in two schizophrenic children on the basis of food. *Journal of Experimental Child Psychology*, 1966, *4*, 109–124.

Lovaas, O. I., & Simmons, J. Q. Manipulation of self-destruction in three retarded children. *Journal of Applied Behavior Analysis*, 1969, *2*, 143–157.

Patterson, G., & Reid, J. Reciprocity and coercion: Two facets of social systems. In C. Neuringer and J. Michael (Eds.), *Behavior modification in clinical psychology*. New York: Appleton-Century-Crofts, 1970, pp. 133–177.

Perske, R. The dignity of risk and the mentally retarded. *Mental Retardation*, 1972, *10, 1*, 24–26.

Peterson, R. F., & Peterson, L. R. The use of positive reinforcement in the control of self-destructive behavior in a retarded boy. *Journal of Experimental Child Psychology*, 1968, *6*, 351–360.

Premack, D. Reinforcement theory. In D. Levine (Ed.), *Nebraska symposium on motivation*. Lincoln, Neb.: University of Nebraska Press, 1965, pp. 123–180.

Repp, A., & Dietz, S. Reducing aggressive and self-injurious behavior of institutionalized retarded children through reinforcement of other behaviors. *Journal of Applied Behavior Analysis*, 1974, *7*, 313–325.

Rincover, A., & Koegel, R. L. Setting generality and stimulus control in autistic children. *Journal of Applied Behavior Analysis*, 1975, *8*, 235–246.

Risley, T. R. The effects and side effects of punishing the autistic behaviors of a deviant child. *Journal of Applied Behavior Analysis*, 1968, *1*, 21–34.

Seguin, E. *Idiocy: Its treatment by the physiological method*. New York: Teachers College, Columbia University, 1907.

Skinner, B. F. *The behavior of organisms*. Englewood Cliffs, N.J.: Prentice Hall, 1938.

Skinner, B. F. *The technology of teaching*. New York: Appleton-Century-Crofts, 1968.

Skinner, B. F. *Contingencies of reinforcement: A theoretical analysis*. New York: Appleton-Century-Crofts, 1969.

Sprague, R., Barnes, K., & Werry, J. Methylphenidate and thioridazine: learning, reaction time, activity, and classroom behavior in disturbed children. *American Journal of Orthopsychiatry, 1970, 40*, 615–628.

Steinman, W. M. Generalized imitation and the discrimination hypothesis. *Journal of Experimental Child Psychology*, 1970, *10*, 79–99.

Stoddard, L. T., & Sidman, M. The effects of errors on children's performance on a circle-ellipse discrimination. *Journal of the Experimental Analysis of Behavior*, 1967, *10*, 261–270.

Stokes, T., Baer, D., & Jackson, R. Programming generalization of a greeting response in four retarded children. *Journal of Applied Behavior Analysis*, 1974, *7*, 599–610.

Touchette, P. E. The effects of graduated stimulus change on the acquisition of a simple discrimination in severly retarded boys. *Journal of the Experimental Analysis of Behavior*, 1968, *11*, 39–48.

Touchette, P. E. Transfer of stimulus control: Measuring the moment of transfer. *Journal of the Experimental Analysis of Behavior*, 1971, *15*, 347–354.

Vukelich, R., & Hake, D. F. Reduction of dangerously aggressive behavior in a severely retarded resident through a combination of positive reinforcement procedures. *Journal of Applied Behavior Analysis*, 1971, *4*, 215–225.

Wasik, B. H. The application of Premack's generalization on reinforcement to the management of classroom behavior. *Journal of Experimental Child Psychology*, 1970, *10*, 33–43.
Wolfensberger, W. *Normalization.* Toronto: National Institute on Mental Retardation, 1972.

8

A Brief Review
of Legal Deviance
REFERENCES IN BEHAVIOR ANALYSIS
AND DELINQUENCY

Edward K. Morris[1,2]

Behavior analysis has made a significant contribution to the effective treatment of a wide variety of childhood problems. Some of the advances have been theoretical in nature, but the most important contributions have been the positive effects that the approach to behavior change has had on the day-to-day lives of children. We know, of course, that today's children are tomorrow's adults: this also means the problems of today's children will affect them as adults, unless some important changes can be made. Research and application in child behavior therapy has shown that it is possible to make some of these important changes.

One special problem that quite profoundly affects children, adults, and our society, is "legal deviance." Legal deviance refers to those behaviors that are labeled "illegal;" in the case of children, they are called delinquency, and for adults they are called criminality. However, these latter terms are deceiving, because the problems are not different in two important ways: (1) they are a function of similar principles and may be analyzed by them and (2) both problems can be changed by the application of this set of principles. The term legal deviance implies no moral qualifications, nor does it necessarily imply that other behaviors falling either within or outside the category are easier or more difficult to treat. Some behaviors are labeled delinquent that perhaps should not be (e.g., truancy, runaways), and some "legal" behaviors are actually more serious than much delinquency (e.g., autism and developmental retardation). These issues are important, but are better left for discussion elsewhere. As used here, legal deviance simply serves as a useful tool to describe a specific subset of problems that children and adults have with society today, and have had for years.

Only recently has a concerted effort been made to apply the principles and concepts of behavior analysis to understanding children's legal deviance or delinquency, and to alter some of the conditions that generate these problems. As with the wide impact of child behavior therapy in other areas, portions of this new delinquency literature have been theoretical in nature (e.g., Burgess & Akers, 1966; Hindelang, 1970; Jeffery, 1965)[3], but again the primary emphasis has been placed on ways to affect meaningfully the lives of children (e.g., Braukmann & Fixsen, 1975; Davidson & Seidman, 1974; Milan & McKee, 1974; O'Leary & Wilson, 1975; Stumphauzer, 1973).

This chapter provides a short introduction to the literature on the theoretical background, issues, and the variety of applications that have been made in behavioral analysis and delinquency. It then lists references for the major published discussion and research articles and texts in these areas so that the reader may fully sample the thought and work thus far accomplished. Special note should be made, however, that the behaviors which have led many of the youths to be labeled delinquent or predelinquent and placed in programs are not in the realm of serious crime. The youths are more often "unmanagable" at home, at school, and in the community rather than serious law breakers; this does not mean, though, that the problems might not in the future lead to more serious crime.

THE PROBLEM: SOCIETY OR THE INDIVIDUAL

The notion that a particular set of behaviors—delinquency in this case—is "operant" behavior (i.e., behavior controlled ultimately by its consequences), and that it may be analyzed as such, has become a familiar cliché. This analysis is not entirely wrong, but such thinking can, unfortunately, result in a narrowed appreciation of delinquency and the complex conditions by which it is developed and maintained. In addition, a thorough and broad analysis of legal deviance cannot be accomplished by modifying a behavior here or behavior there in a limited number of restricted settings (although this may be a start); the conditions that promote delinquency will never be directly changed by such an approach.

Along this line of thinking, other people concerned with these issues have suggested that few differences exist between those children and youths who are placed in correctional rehabilitation programs and those who are not. Sometimes the only important distinguishing characteristic seems to be that the former are apprehended (and processed), whereas the latter are not (Erickson, 1972; Murphy, Shirley, & Witmer, 1946; Short & Nye, 1957). The juvenile justice system can be injudicious at times. This point indicates that not only do individuals and their acts of delinquency need to be analyzed, but that a community's law enforcement, judicial, and correctional systems must also be understood in order to gain fuller appreciation of legal deviance. Analyzing delinquents and their behavior alone often results in too limited a perspective; the larger contexts in which the individual lives must also be taken into account. The problem of delinquency then becomes as large as society itself and should be analyzed as such (see Davidson & Seidman, 1974).

Analyzing the social and economic contexts that generate the conditions affecting individual children, thus promoting and maintaining delinquency, is not an easy feat. And, as difficult as that analysis is, imagine the problems involved in altering those conditions in order to provide positive and meaningful change. If the problem of delinquency is as large as society itself, and should be analyzed as such, then the obvious solution lies in the reorganization of specific conditions or contingencies that exist in the real world of daily living. Not only are these conditions social and economic, they may also be legal. Indeed, an analysis of the legal standards themselves might lead to modifications and deletions which would prove beneficial for both youths and the communities in which they reside (i.e., Stachnik, 1972).

But enough. Though some of the means for effective social change may be within our grasp, we are still far from being able to implement the perfect program. However, the situation need not be entirely bleak; there is still evidence indicating that important changes may be made on the individual and small group levels. No doubt individual delinquency and the social, economic, and legal contexts in which it occurs go hand-in-hand. But, a thorough behavior analysis and positive behavior change programs for individuals will begin to give us the upper hand in dealing with these latter social problems. As mentioned earlier, this may be the place to start. Certainly, the data are suggestive.

The following list of references in behavior analysis and delinquency has been divided into four major categories. The first category presents general *concepts, issues, and discussion* of behavior analysis in delinquency theory and treatment applications. The information in these articles and books includes theoretical analyses of delinquency (i.e., Burgess & Akers, 1966; Jeffery, 1965) and the correctional process (i.e., Hindelang, 1970), the application of principles and procedures to managing the behavior of delinquents (e.g., Shah, 1966), general reviews of research on these applications (e.g., Braukmann & Fixsen, 1975), critiques of behavior therapy research with delinquents (e.g., Davidson & Seidman, 1974), and legal and ethical concerns regarding behavior therapy with delinquents (e.g., *APA Monitor*, 1974, Kimbles, 1973; Martin, 1975; Wexler, 1973).

The remaining three categories list the actual research studies on applications of behavior therapy with delinquents. These references are divided according to the specific contexts or settings within which the research has been conducted: (1) *total institutions*, (2) *community treatment centers*, and (3) the *natural environment*. Total institutions (after Goffman, 1961) refer to those settings in which children and youths are held in 24-hour confinement (i.e., prisons, reform schools, and other residential treatment centers); community treatment centers refer to locally designated settings that still allow youths some continued participation in local educational, vocational, and recreational activities (e.g., group homes); and the natural environment refers to home and educational settings in which no physical constraints are placed on youths as they continue to reside in their own community.

SERVICE DELIVERY PLANNING

The above division of correctional environments suggests how a well-functioning rehabilitation system could be designed to deal best with the problems a particular community defines as unacceptable—or perhaps better yet to prevent them. The basic structure of this system would be an integrated and hierarchical arrangement of the treatment settings just described: the natural environment, community treatment centers, and total institutions.

Two of the basic aims of this service planning approach would be (1) to maximize the use of local community resources at each level and (2) to emphasize treatment of the problems in the contexts in which they developed and continue to occur. Obviously, confining youths to far-away institutions precludes the likelihood of efficient or effective changes. A third important concern here is ethics. A hierarchical approach to delinquency treatment is preferred, not just because "obvious" coercion in correctional programs will be minimized, but also because the system would be more humane and probably more effective; in addition, it would maximize prevention strategies. A specific description of the system can illustrate some of these points.

The Natural Environment. The first level of this rehabilitation system would be the local community, where programs could be carried out in the natural environment. This approach would require enlargement and improvement on current probation (Thorne, Tharp, & Wetzel, 1967), parole, and social casework models (Fischer & Gochros, 1975; Swartz & Goldiamond, 1975). In addition, the community would have to make a thorough analysis of the conditions that promoted the problem in the first place. This analysis would have to include both larger community structures (e.g., juvenile justice, employment, education, and welfare systems) and smaller ones (e.g., the neighborhood and family).

Community Treatment Centers. If thè problem interactions that arise between children and these two community structures can be effectively dealt with in the natural environment, then the altered conditions could be made permanent, perhaps constituting a prevention strategy for other youths. Or, the program could be phased out with planned generalization to the contingencies likely to exist in that natural environment (see Marholin & Siegel, Chapter 12). However, if all reasonable programs should fail, then the next step would be placement in a community treatment setting (e.g., Fixsen, Phillips, & Wolf, 1973; Phillips, Phillips, Fixsen, & Wolf, 1973). At this level, more intensive social, academic and/or vocational programs could be implemented; however, the youths could at the same time have considerable access to the local community. In this way, more effective programs may be made available, but not at the expense of losing positive and important ties with family, friends, and the community. The continued use of local educational, vocational, and recreational resources would promote continuity with the natural environment and avoid the expensive duplication process that is inherent in total institutions.

Total Institutions. Individual successes in the community treatment center level of the hierarchy would return the youths to programs in the natural environment. Failure, however, would result in a move to the total institution, where more intensive rehabilitation programs could be implemented (Cohen & Filipczak, 1971; Jesness & DeRisi, 1973; Nay, 1974). Recent evidence indicates that total institutionalization may rarely be necessary with delinquents when treatment programs in the natural environment and community treatment centers are provided with the necessary resources for effectively conducting their programs (National Advisory Commission, 1973; National Council on Crime and Delinquency, 1972). However, some serious aggressive delinquency, criminality, and varieties of nondelinquent deviant behavior (e.g., childhood psychoses, developmental retardation) may warrant this final program level in a service delivery plan. Success at this level would lead to the return of youths to the next lowest program level—the community treatment center—from which they can be reintegrated into the natural environment of the local community. Again, the emphasis in this approach to a rehabilitation service delivery system is on maintaining youths in closest possible contact with their local communities from whence the problems began. In the final analysis, this is the only place the problems will likely be solved.

Service Delivery Steps. In this hierarchical approach to structuring a delivery system—be it services for delinquents or the developmentally retarded, psychotic, or behavior-problem child—skipping levels will probably not be in the best interest of maximum therapeutic change or change maintenance. Omitting a step on the way up the ladder to total institutionalization forces treatment to occur in a setting one step removed from the original source of the problem.

In a properly run system it would seem a rare case when a youth would need to be sent directly to a community treatment or total institution setting from the juvenile court and not first provided with programs in the natural environment. The skip from programs in the natural environment to total institutions would be even more unnecessary. Aside from not dealing with the problems where they exist, skipping a level on the way up would also be a costly decision; certainly, the more restrictive the therapeutic environment, the higher the cost per individual (Phillips, Phillips, Fixsen, & Wolf, 1973; President's Commission 1967). Public funds can be more effectively and efficiently spent for programs in the natural environment and community treatment centers. In addition, monies can be recouped by reducing the costly operation of total institutions for delinquent youths or other populations.

Looking in the other direction, skipping levels on the way down the ladder might also not be in the best interests of the youths or the community. Moving directly from total institutions to a program in the natural environment, or to no program at all, does not allow for the development of intermediate procedures for behavior maintenance. The same is true for moving from the community treatment setting to outright release to the natural environment. Behavior gains made in one setting do not necessarily maintain when the settings are drastically changed (see Marholin & Siegel, Chapter 12), and the greater the setting change, the less the likelihood that new and meaningful behaviors will continue to occur. Intermediate programs will most often be necessary to bridge these gaps; without them, or by skipping them, we do a disservice to the community and to the youths who are unprepared to enter into it. Indeed, omitting a program level on the way down will, more likely than not, lead to further behavior problems. Behavior excesses and deficits that cannot be expressed because of restrictions in one environment may suddenly become painfully obvious in another. For example, one does not see poor work-interview skills in a total institution, nor does one necessarily see inappropriate parent-child interactions in a community treatment center. By allowing a gradual transition between settings, we also allow for the gradual emergence of behavior excesses and deficits. These difficulties are much easier to handle when they are minimally rather than maximally disruptive or debilitative and when the environment can still offer the necessary support to assist in transitions.

This hierarchical arrangement of treatment environments may appear simplistic and the gaps between the levels too large; in addition, a variety of assessment problems will present themselves. But these problems reflect (1) the current structure of the mental health and juvenile justice systems and (2) the current state of assessment methodology. However, nothing prohibits the closing of these gaps, and for the former problem, new programs (e.g., work, educational, and furlough release) are beginning to do this.

ETHICS

Questions regarding ethics are now commonly raised concerning the application of behavior analysis principles to individuals or groups residing in institutional settings or in the custody of other people (*APA Monitor*, 1974; Martin, 1975; Trotter, 1974). Criticism of the application is partly warranted, but some of the concern may actually be misplaced, while obscuring other important social problems and the ultimate well-being of the individual. The focus in these matters should be shifted from the philosophical issue of "determinism" and "free will" to the practical difficulties surrounding the interactions between delinquents and the communities in which they reside. Some decreased focus on delinquents and increased focus on the community's involvement in the development of delinquent behavior would help balance the current overemphasis of behavior-change procedures on the individual alone. Too often we fail to consider the local context in which individuals must live and work.

One commonly heard criticism is that it is coercive to apply behavior analysis principles to institutionalized individuals. Cases exist where this may be so, but a more important question might be raised as to why so many youths are placed under such strong institutional constraints in the first place. If youths are institutionalized when more appropriate programs in the natural environment or community treatment settings are available, then the use of *any* behavior change procedure is unethical, behavior modification included. The use is unethical not because it is coercive and changes behavior, but because youths are being unnecessarily restrained and because the total institution is not the context in which the most effective and positive treatment can occur. The issue of unresolved ethics and coercion lies, first, with the excessive restraint imposed by the juvenile justice system, and later with individuals implementing behavior modification programs. The problem would be largely resolved if alternatives to incarceration were more widely used.

By not providing the resources for effective treatment in the natural environment or community treatment settings, the justice system is engaged in the unethical, and maybe unconstitutional, practice of unnecessary restraint. Implementing alternatives would mean that fewer youths would be institutionalized. This change would result in better and more humane treatment for those in the community-based programs *and* for those few who would have to remain in the institutions; certainly, the latter would benefit from decreased crowding and increased individual programs.

In the broader context, by shifting the focus of blame from the youth, and modification of youth behavior, and moving the focus to the interactions between individuals *and* communities, we begin to move the accusation of unethical practices from the behavior therapist to the "unethical" practices of the community. This argument is not intended to throw out a smokescreen to hide abuses in behavior modification; unfortunately, they have occurred and will continue to. The suggestion is being made that current operation of the juvenile justice system may obscure the important issues and move rightful blame away from itself.

However, even if total institutionalization must be employed, another argument presents itself; and very interesting questions are raised. Let us look at the problem of ethics from another perspective. Is it not more unethical to use "punishment" (i.e., the current practice of institutionalization) without effectively altering the behavior in need of change than to set about positively improving more effective behavior? Or, put another way, is it not more ethical to provide an individual with the abilities, skills, and knowledge necessary for effective community interaction than to lock away someone who has already shown some behavioral excesses and deficits and then return him or her to the community with even more problems? Of course, we should be concerned with how children in institutions are treated, but they do not have a right *just* to be cared for. They have a right to lead effective, meaningful lives. When we turn the issue around, perhaps current practices are unethical, not programs that can humanely help people.

A better behavior analysis of the entire array of conditions involved in delinquency and of the alternatives for treatment will resolve some of the concern over ethics. Some of the issues will outright disappear, some will be placed in proper context. However, abuses will proably remain, and we must be on guard for them; we must be critical of our own excesses and deficits.

APPLICATIONS TO BEHAVIOR
IN TREATMENT SETTINGS

After providing the general introduction to concepts, issues, and discussions of applied behavior analysis and delinquency, the primary correctional contexts—total institutions, community treatment centers, and the natural environment—are presented and divided into three parts. The first part in each case is a more specific presentation of *concepts, issues, and discussions* of behavior analysis applications. The second part covers research in which *personal-social* interactions (e.g., self-care, social skills) are improved, and the third section covers research in which *academic-vocational* behaviors are enhanced. Studies presenting data relevant to both of these latter categories at the same time received multiple classification.

Sometimes the distinctions between personal-social and academic-vocational behaviors are difficult to make. Academic behaviors are prerequisite and necessary for effective social interaction, and social behaviors are prerequisite and necessary for effective educational and vocational participation. In addition, what may be considered academic behavior in one setting may be considered a social behavior in another, for example, appropriate grammar (Bailey, Timbers, Phillips, & Wolf, 1971). When categorizing these particular articles, the primary function or purpose of the behavior, as defined by the researcher or therapist, served as the basis for classification.

Total Institutions. The concepts, issues, and discussion portion of total institutions includes reviews of the research (e.g., Sandford & Bateup, 1973), overviews of major programs (e.g., Johnson & Geller, 1974; Nay, 1974), a critique of behavior therapy application in institutions (Reppucci & Saunders, 1975), and an outcome comparison study with another treatment approach (Jesness, 1975). Several studies are included that point to the destructive role peer-peer social interaction patterns can play in group setting applications (Buehler, Patterson, & Furniss, 1966; Duncan, 1974). Finally, some information is supplied on staff training (Bishop & Blanchard, 1973; Hubbard, 1973; Nay, 1974).

Research in the area of personal-social interactions covers a variety of behaviors: aggression (e.g., Burchard & Tyler, 1965), attendance (Hanson, 1971), disruptive peer group control (e.g., Brown & Tyler, 1968), stealing (Wetzel, 1966), and general socialization (Burchard, 1967; for a critique of socialization programs see Lackenmeyer, 1969). In addition, a variety of behavior therapy treatment procedures are also analyzed, including token economies (e.g., Hobbs & Holt, 1976; Karacki & Levinson, 1970), contingency management (e.g., Cohen & Filipczak, 1971; Jesness & De Risi, 1973; Willner, 1975), time out and response cost (e.g., Burchard & Barrera, 1972; Tyler & Brown, 1967), modeling (e.g., Sarason, 1976) and an innovative use of a self-recording procedure (Seymour & Stokes, 1976).

The literature on academic programs ranges from large, general programs (e.g., Cohen & Filipczak, 1971; McKee, 1966) to specific academic curricula (e.g., Halstead, 1970), and to specific educational procedures (e.g., Clements & McKee, 1968; Tyler, 1967). Research in the area of vocational training is sparse.

Community Treatment Centers. The most exhaustive application of behavior analysis principles in community treatment centers has been conducted by the Achievement Place program (see Willner et al., Chapter 9). General reviews of this research are available (e.g., Fixsen, Phillips, & Wolf, 1973; Phillips, Phillips, Fixsen, & Wolf, 1973; Phillips, Wolf, Fixsen, & Bailey, 1976), as are articles on staff training (e.g., Kirigin et al., 1975; Maloney, Phillips, Fixsen, & Wolf, 1975; Phillips, Phillips, Fixsen, & Wolf, 1974). In addition, some interesting data are available on the positive attitudes of delinquents generated by this program (Eitzen, 1974, 1975).

A wide variety of personal-social skills have been effectively altered in this program (Phillips, Wolf, Fixsen, & Bailey, 1976) and replications of it (Liberman, Ferris, Salgado, & Salgado, 1975), both within the group home and in the local school setting (Bailey, Wolf, & Phillips, 1970). Other applications have been in the areas of interview training (Braukmann et al., 1974), self-and peer-reporting (Phillips, Fixsen, & Wolf, 1972), self-government (Fixsen, Phillips & Wolf, 1973; Phillips, Phillips, Wolf, & Fixsen, 1973), conflict negotiations (Kifer, Lewis, Green, & Phillips, 1974), and conversation skills (Maloney et al., 1976; Minkin et al., 1976); all of these have subtle but important implications for subsequent outcome. The remaining research has generally dealt with the effects of token economies and contingency management on school grades (e.g., Bailey, Wolf, & Phillips, 1970; Phillips et al., 1971).

The Natural Environment. The concepts, issues, and discussion section of research in the natural environment contains few references. Most interesting, perhaps, are those suggesting (Jamieson, 1965) and presenting procedures (Tharp & Wetzel, 1969) for how behavior analysis might be applied to probation and parole programs. Additionally, some recent texts on behavioral approaches to social casework are valuable (Fischer & Gochros, 1975; Swartz & Goldiamond, 1975).

The literature on personal-social interactions covers important topics. Some of the research describes general strategy approaches to community intervention programs (Burchard et al., 1976; Cohen, 1976; Rose et al.,

1970); however, a large part of the research relates specifically to the application of contingency contracting procedures in modifying individual behavior (e.g., Alexander & Parsons, 1973; James; 1975; Stuart, 1971c) and to critical evaluation of those procedures (Stuart & Lott, 1972; Weathers & Liberman, 1975).

Several other research projects present approaches to delinquency problems that also have significant implications. Family training programs (Christophersen, Barnard, Ford, & Wolf, 1976; Patterson, Cobb, & Ray, 1973; Wiltz & Patterson, 1974) will probably have an increasing impact in this area, because they can work with many problems directly where they start. A second project has worked on providing youths the social skills they need in order to function within local community standards (Werner et al., 1975). Finally, a third project has begun to apply the powerful analytical techniques of the behavioral approach to assess the impact of local law enforcement practices (Schnelle, Kirchner, McNees, & Lawler, 1975).

The direct application of behavior analysis to academic achievement and vocational training in the natural environment is not yet a well-developed area. Positive results have been generated (e.g., Cohen, 1972; Tharp & Wetzel, 1969), but there also seem to be some problems (Jeffery & Jeffery, 1970).

SUMMARY

What sort of evaluation should be given to programs and research on the application of behavior analysis to legal deviance? In some cases the programs and research are exemplary; in other cases the work has been neither creative nor well conducted. Perhaps it is too early yet to answer the question; so much remains to be done, and done well.

The approach offers a meaningful alternative to current practices in family therapy and juvenile corrections. However, as mentioned earlier, even though these new programs may be effective when applied on a limited and immediate basis, we must not fail to realize that the problems with delinquents are not theirs alone. Though individual programs of application may be effective, ultimately the analysis and application must be taken to the larger arena of the community as a whole.

REFERENCES

Erickson, M. L. The changing relationship between official and self-reported measures of delinquency: An exploratory predictive study. *Journal of Criminal Law, Criminology, and Police Science*, 1972, *63*, 388–395.

Goffman, E. *Asylums*. Garden City, N.Y.: Anchor, 1961.

Murphy, F. J., Shirley, M. M., & Witmer, H. L. The incidence of hidden delinquency. *American Journal of Orthopsychiatry*, 1946, *16*, 686–696.

President's Commission on Law Enforcement and Administration of Justice. *Task Force Report: Corrections*. Washington, D.C.: U.S. Government Printing Office, 1967.

National Council on Crime and Delinquency, *Policies and Background Information*. Hackensack, N.J.: NCCD, 1972.

Short, J. F., & Nye, F. I. Reported behavior as a criterion of deviant behavior. *Social Problems*, 1957, *5*, 207–213.

Stachnik, T. J. The case against criminal penalties for illicit drug use. *American Psychologist*, 1972, *27*, 637–642.

The National Advisory Commission on Criminal Justice Standards and Goals. *Report on Corrections*. Washington, D.C.: U.S. Government Printing Office, 1973.

NOTES

1. This manuscript is a version of a paper prepared in 1973 while the author held a USPHS Traineeship (HD–00244) at the University of Illinois at Urbana-Champaign. Since that time, another reviewer (Burchard & Harig, 1976) has independently made a similar analysis of concepts and research in this area.

2. I would like to express my appreciation to David Marholin II, Curt Braukmann, Alan Willner, Mike Jones, and Frank Kuehn for their helpful suggestions regarding this manuscript.

3. Articles cited in this text that refer to publications listed in the major reference section of this chapter have not been referenced again at the end of this introduction.

CONCEPTS, ISSUES, AND DISCUSSION

Adams, R. Differential association and learning principles revisited. *Social Problems*, 1973, *20*, 458–470.

Akers, R. L. *Deviant behavior: A social learning approach*. Belmont, Calif.: Wadsworth, 1973.

APA Monitor. Psychology briefs: START unconstitutional. 1974, *5*, 12.

Braukmann, C. J., & Fixsen, D. L. Behavior modification with delinquents. In M. Hersen, R. M. Eisler, & P. M. Miller (Eds.), *Progress in behavior modification*, Vol. 1. New York: Academic, 1975, pp. 191–231.

Braukmann, C. J., Fixsen, D. L., Phillips, E. L., & Wolf, M. M. Behavioral approaches to treatment in the crime and delinquency field. *Criminology*, 1975, *13*, 299–331.

Brodsky, S. L. *Psychologists in the criminal justice system*. Marysville, Ohio: American Association of Correctional Psychology, 1972, pp. 69-75.

Burchard, S. L. Behavior modification with delinquents: Some unforeseen contingencies. In J. S. Stumphauzer (Ed.), *Behavior therapy with delinquents*. Springfield, Ill.: Charles C Thomas, 1973, pp. 66–74.

Burchard, J. D., & Harig, P. T. Behavior modification and juvenile delinquency. In H. Leitenberg (Ed.), *Handbook of behavior modification and behavior therapy*. Englewood Cliffs, N.J.: Prentice-Hall, 1976, pp. 405–452.

Burgess, R. L., & Akers, R. L. A differential association-reinforcement theory of criminal behavior. *Social Problems*, 1966, *14*, 128–147.

Cautela, J. R., Kastenbaum, R., & Wincze, J. P. Use of the fear survey schedule and the reinforcement fear schedule to survey possible reinforcing and aversive stimuli among juvenile offenders. *Journal of Genetic Psychology*, 1972, *121*, 255–261.

Conger, R. D. Social control and social learning models of delinquent behavior: A synthesis. *Criminology*, 1976, *14*, 17–40.

Costello, J. Behavior modification and corrections: Current status and future potential. The National Institute for Criminal Justice, Law Enforcement Assistance Association, Washington, D.C. National Technical Information Service # (PB-223-629/AS). 1972.

Davidson, W., & Seidman, E. Studies of behavior modification and juvenile delinquency: A review, methodological critique and social perspective. *Psychological Bulletin*, 1974, *81*, 998–1011.

DeRisi, W. J., & Butz, G. *Writing behavioral contracts: A case simulation practice manual*. Champaign, Ill.: Research Press, 1975.

Gelder, M. Can behavior therapy contribute to the treatment of delinquency? *British Journal of Criminolgy*, 1965, *55*, 365–376.

Gerber, K. Behavior modification with juvenile delinquents in nonclassroom settings: A selective review. *J.S.A.S. Catalog of Selected Documents in Psychology*, 1974, *4*, 83.

Hindelang, M. J. A learning theory analysis of the correctional process. *Issues in Criminology*, 1970, *5*, 43–58.

Holden, H. M. Should aversion and behavior therapy be used in the treatment of delinquency? *British Journal of Criminology*, 1965, *5*, 377–387.

Holland, J. G. Behavior modification for prisoners, patients, and other people as a prescription for the planned society. *Mexican Journal of Behavior Analysis*, 1975, *1*, 85–95.

Hutchinson, M. J. Behavior theory, behavior science, and treatment. *Canadian Journal of Criminology and Corrections*, 1968, *10*, 388–392.

Jeffery, C. R. Criminal behavior and learning theory. *The Journal of Criminal Law, Criminology, and Police Science*, 1965, *56*, 294–300.

Jones, H. G. The techniques of behavior therapy and delinquent behavior. *British Journal of Criminology*, 1965, *55*, 355–365.

Kimbles, S. L. Behavior therapy with the black delinquent. In J. S. Stumphauzer (Ed.), *Behavior therapy with delinquents*. Springfield, Ill.: Charles C Thomas, 1973, pp. 49–53.

Martin, R. *Legal challenges to behavior modification*. Champaign, Ill.: Research Press, 1975.

McConnell, J. V. Criminals can be brainwashed—now. *Psychology Today*, 1970, *3* (June), 14.

McConnell, J. V. Rook review: Menninger, *The crime of punishment. UCLA Law Review*, 1969, *16*, 645–659.

Milan, M. A., & McKee, J. M. Behavior modification: Principles and applications in corrections. In D. Glaser (Ed.), *Handbook of criminology*. New York: Rand McNally, 1974, pp. 745–776.

O'Leary, K. D., & Wilson, G. T. *Behavior therapy: Application and outcome.* Englewood Cliffs, N.J.: Prentice-Hall, 1975, pp. 195–218.

Parsonson, B. S. The modification of delinquent behaviors. *Australian and New Zealand Journal of Criminology*, 1972, *5*, 49–56.

Quay, H. C. What corrections can correct and how? *Federal Probation*, 1973, *38*, 3–5.

Ribes-Inesta, E. Discussion: Some methodological remarks on a delinquency prevention and rehabilitation program. In S. W. Bijou & E. Ribes-Inesta (Eds.), *Behavior modification: Issues and extensions.* New York: Academic, 1972, pp. 85–92.

Ribes-Inesta, E. & Bandura, A. (Eds.), *Analysis of delinquency and aggression.* Hillsdale, N.J.: Lawrence Earlbaum, 1976.

Sarason, I. G. Verbal learning, modeling, and juvenile delinquency. *American Psychologist*, 1968, *23*, 254–266.

Sarason, I. G. A modeling and informational approach to delinquency. In E. Ribes-Inesta & A. Bandura (Eds.), *Analysis of delinquency and aggression.* Hillsdale, N.J.: Lawrence Earlbaum, 1976, pp. 71–93.

Sarason, I. G., & Ganzer, V. J. Modeling and group discussion in the rehabilitation of juvenile delinquents. *Journal of Counseling Psychology*, in press.

Sarri, R. C., & Selo, E. Evaluation process and outcome in juvenile corrections: Musings on a grim tale. In P. O. Davidson, F. W. Clark, & L. A. Hammerlynck (Eds.), *Evaluation of behavioral programs.* Champaign, Ill.: Research Press, 1974, pp. 253–302.

Schwitzgebel, R. K. Learning theory approaches to the treatment of criminal behavior. *Seminars in Psychiatry*, 1971, 328–344.

Schwitzgebel, R. K. Limitations on the coercive treatment of offenders. *Criminal Law Bulletin*, 1972, *8*, 267–320.

Shah, S. A. Treatment of offenders: Some behavioral concepts, principles, and approaches. *Federal Probation*, 1966, *30*, 29–38.

Silber, D. E. The place of behavior therapy in correction. *Crime and Delinquency*, 1976, *22*, 211–217.

Stuart, R. B. Behavioral control of delinquents: Critique of existing programs and recommendations for innovative planning. In L.A. Hammerlynck & F. W. Clark (Eds.), *Behavior modification for exceptional children and youth.* Calgary: University of Calgary Press, 1971.

Stumphauzer, J. S. Modifying delinquent behavior: Beginnings and current practices. *Adolescence*, in press.

Stumphauzer, J. S. Behavior modification with juvenile delinquents: A critical review. *Federal Correctional Institution Technical and Treatment Notes*, 1971, *1*, 1–22.

Stumphauzer, J. S. *Behavior therapy with delinquents.* Springfield, Ill.: Charles C Thomas, 1973.

Vieter, W. P. Conditioning as a form of psychotherapy in treating delinquents: Some data from the literature. *Exerpta Criminologica*, 1967, *7*, 3–6.

Wexler, D. B. Token and taboo: Behavior modification, token economies, and the law. *California Law Review*, 1973, *61*, 81–109.

Wright, J., & James, J. *A behavioral approach to preventing delinquency.* Springfield, Ill.: Charles C Thomas, 1974.

Zimberoff, S. J. Behavior and modification with delinquents. *Correctional Psychologist*, 1968, *3*, 11–25.

TOTAL INSTITUTIONS

Concepts, Issues, and Discussion

Bishop, C. H., & Blanchard, E. B. *Behavior therapy: A guide to correctional administration and programming.* Athens, Ga.: Institute of Government, University of Georgia, 1973.

Buehler, R. E., Patterson, G. R., & Furniss, J. M. The reinforcement of behavior in institutional settings. *Behaviour Research and Therapy*, 1966, *4*, 157–167.

Deluca, K. T., Tanz, H. A., & Suarez, J. M. Toward an optimal incentive system in an adult correctional system. *Corrective Psychiatry and Journal of Social Therapy*, 1972, *18*, 22–31.

Duncan, D. F. Verbal behavior in a detention home. *Corrective and Social Psychiatry and Journal of Behavior Technology Methods and Therapy*, 1974, *20*, 38–42.

Hubbard, D. R. The correctional worker's role in behavior change: Some key principles. *Georgia Journal of Corrections*, 1973, *2*, 11–22.

Jesness, C. F. Comparative effectiveness of behavior modification and transactional analysis programs for delinquents. *Journal of Consulting and Clinical Psychology*, 1975, *43*, 758–799.

Johnson, D. F., & Geller, E. S. Operations manual for a contingency management program in a maximum security institution. *J.S.A.S. Catalog of Selected Documents in Psychology*, 1974, *4*, 23.

Nay, W. R. Comprehensive behavioral treatment in a training school for delinquents. In K. S. Calhoun, H. E. Adams, & K. M. Mitchell (Ed.), *Innovative treatment methods in psychopathology.* New York: Wiley, 1974.

Parsonson, B. S. The modification of delinquent behaviors. *Australian and New Zealand Journal of Criminology*, 1972, *5*, 49–56.

Reppucci, N. D., & Saunders, J. T. Social psychology in behavior modification. *American Psychologist*, 1975, *29*, 649–677.

Roberts, A. R. *Sourcebook on prison education.* Springfield, Ill.: Charles C Thomas, 1971, pp. 70–96.

Sandford, D. A. Use of an operant model to analyze officer control procedures in a borstal. *Australian and New Zealand Journal of Criminology*, 1973, *6*, 158–166.

Sandford, D. A., & Bateup, D. E. Learning how to behave: A review of the application of reinforcement in prison management. *Howard Journal of Penology and Crime Prevention*, 1973, *13*, 278–284.

Trotter, S. ACLU scores token economy. *APA Monitor*, 1974, *5* (8), 1, 7.

Trotter, S., & Warren, J. The carrot, the stick, and the prisoner. *Science News*, 1974, *105*, 180–181.

Wagner, B. R., & Breitmeyer, R. G. PACE: A residential, community oriented behavior modification program for adolescents. *Adolescence*, 1975, *10*, 277–286.

Williams, V. L., & Fish, M. The token economy in prison: Rehabilitation or motivation. *Journal of Correctional Education*, 1972, *24*, 4–7.

Personal-Social Interactions

Bassett, J. E., Blanchard, E. B., & Koshland, E. Applied behavior analysis in a

Penal setting: Targeting "free world" behaviors. *Behavior Therapy*, 1975, *6*, 639–648.

Bednar, R. L., Zelhart, P. E., Greathouse, L., & Weinberg, S. Operant conditioning principles in the treatment of learning and behavior problems with delinquent boys. *Journal of Counseling Psychology*, 1970, *17*, 492–497.

Brown, G. D., & Tyler, V. O. Time-out from reinforcement: A technique for dethroning the "duke" of an institutionalized delinquent group. *Journal of Child Psychology and Psychiatry*, 1968, *9*, 203–211.

Burchard, J. D. Systematic socialization: A programmed environment for the habilitation of antisocial retardates. *Psychological Record*, 1967, *17*, 461–476.

Burchard, J. D. Residential behavior modification programs and the problem of uncontrolled contingencies. *Psychological record*, 1969, *19*, 259–261.

Burchard, J. D., & Barrera, F. An analysis of time-out and response-cost in a programmed environment. *Journal of Applied Behavior Analysis*, 1972, *5*, 271–288.

Burchard, J. D., & Tyler, V. O. The modification of delinquent behavior through operant conditioning. *Behaviour Research and Therapy*, 1965, *2*, 245–250.

Cohen, H. L. Behavior modification in education. In C. E. Thorenson (Ed.), *The seventy-second yearbook of the national society for the study of education*. Chicago: University of Chicago Press, 1973, pp. 291–314.

Cohen, H. L., & Filipczak, J. *A new learning environment*. San Francisco: Jossey-Bass, 1971.

Colman, A. D., & Baker, S. L. Utilization of an operant conditioning model for the treatment of character and behavior disorders in a military setting. *American Journal of Psychiatry*, 1969, *125*, 101–109.

Dinsmoor, J. A. Comments on Wetzel's treatment of a case of compulsive stealing. *Journal of Consulting Psychology*, 1966, *30*, 378–380.

Dominguez, B., Rueda, M., Makhlouf, C., & Rivera, A. Analysis and control of activities in custodial human groups. In E. Ribes-Inesta & A. Bandura (Eds.), *Analysis of delinquency and aggression*. Hillsdale, N.J.: Lawrence Earlbaum, 1976, pp. 51–70.

Ellsworth, P. D., & Colman, A. D. The application of operant conditioning principles to group work experience. *American Journal of Occupational Therapy*, 1969, *13*, 495–501.

Fineman, K. R. An operant conditioning program in a juvenile detention facility. *Psychological Reports*, 1968, *22*, 1119–1120.

Fodor, I. E. The use of behavior modification techniques with female delinquents. *Child Welfare*, 1972, *51*, 93–101.

Gerard, R. Institutional innovations in juvenile corrections. *Federal Probation*, 1970, *34*, 37–44.

Hanson, G. W. Behavior modification of appointment attendance among youthful offenders. *Federal Correctional Institution Technical and Treatment Notes*, 1971, *3*, 1–20.

Hauserman, N., Zwebeck, S., & Plotkin, A. Use of concrete reinforcement to facilitate verbal initiations in adolescent group therapy. *Journal of Consulting and Clinical Psychology*, 1972, *38*, 90–96.

Hayes, S. C., Johnson, V. S., & Cone, J. D. The marked item technique: A practical procedure for litter control. *Journal of Applied Behavior Analysis*, 1975, *8*, 381–386.

Hobbs, T. R., & Holt, M. M. The effects of token reinforcement on the behavior of delinquents in cottage settings. *Journal of Applied Behavior Analysis*, 1976, *9*, 189–198.

Ingram, G. L., Gerard, R. E., Quay, H. C., & Levinson, R. B. An experimental program for the psychopathic delinquent: Looking in the "correctional wastebasket." *Journal of Research in Crime and Delinquency*, 1970, *7*, 24–30.

Jesness, C. F., & DeRisi, W. J. Some variations in techniques of contingency management in a school for delinquents. In J. S. Stumphauzer (Ed.), *Behavior therapy with delinquents*. Springfield, Ill.: Charles C Thomas, 1973, pp. 196–235.

Karacki, L., & Levinson, R. B. A token economy in a correctional institution for youthful offenders. *Howard Journal of Penology and Crime Prevention*, 1970, *13*, 20–30.

Kaufman, L. M., & Wagner, B. R. Barb: A systematic treatment technology for temper control disorders. *Behavior Therapy*, 1972, *3*, 84–90.

Kendall, P. C., Nay, W. R., & Jeffers, J. Time-out duration and contrast effects: A systematic evaluation of a successive treatments design. *Behavior Therapy*, 1975, *6*, 609–615.

Kuhl, C. A. Operant conditioning at Fricot. *Youth Authority Quarterly*, 1969, *22*, 20–23.

Lachenmeyer, C. W. Systematic socialization: Observations on a programmed environment for habilitation of antisocial retardates. *Psychological Record*, 1969, *19*, 247–257.

Lang, P. J. The transfer of treatment. *Journal of Consulting Psychology*, 1966, *30*, 375–377.

Lawson, R. B., Greene, R. T., Richardson, J. S., McClure, G., & Podina, R. J. Token economy program in a maximum security correctional hospital. *Journal of Nervous and Mental Diseases*, 1971, *152*, 199–205.

Levinson, R. B., Ingram, G. L., & Azcarate, E. "Aversion" group therapy: Sometimes good medicine tastes bad. *Crime and Delinquency*, 1968, *14*, 336–339.

McKee, J. M., Smith, R. R., Wood, L. F., & Milan, M. A. Selecting and implementing an intervention approach that employs correctional officers as behavior change agents. In M. A. Bernal (Ed.), *Training in behavior modification*. Belmont, Calif.: Brooks/Cole, in press.

Meichenbaum, F. H., Bowers, K. S., & Ross, R. R. Modification of class behavior of institutionalized female adolescent offenders. *Behaviour Research and Therapy*, 1968, *6*, 343–353.

Rhoades, W. J. A rehabilitation program for maximum security segregation units. *Journal of Correctional Education*, 1970, *22*, 21–23.

Rice, R. D. Educo-therapy: A new approach to delinquent behavior. *Journal of Learning Disabilities*, 1970, *3*, 16–25.

Sandford, D. A. An operant analysis of control procedures in a New Zealand borstal. *British Journal of Criminology*, 1973, *13*, 262–268.

Sarason, I. G. A modeling and informational approach to delinquency. In E. Ribes-Inesta & A. Bandura (Eds.), *Analysis of delinquency and aggression*. Hillsdale, N.J.: Lawrence Earlbaum, 1976, pp. 71–93.

Seymour, F. W., & Stokes, T. F. Self-recording in training girls to increase work and evoke staff praise in an institution for offenders. *Journal of Applied Behavior Analysis*, 1976, *9*, 41–54.

Sloane, H. N., & Ralph, J. L. The grant dormitory: A case history. *Journal of Offender Therapy*, in press.

Tyler, V. O., & Brown, G. D. The use of swift, brief isolation as a group control device for institutionalized delinquents. *Behaviour Research and Therapy,* 1967, *5*, 1–9.

Wellner, A. M. Project ACE (Applied Contingency Management): Maryland training school for boys. In J. L. Khanna (Ed.), *New treatment approaches to juvenile delinquency.* Springfield, Ill.: Charles C Thomas, 1975, pp. 114–124.

Wetzel, R. Use of behavioral techniques in a case of compulsive stealing. *Journal of Consulting Psychology,* 1966, *30,* 367–374.

Williams, V. L., & Fish, M. The token economy in prison: Rehabilitation and motivation. *Journal of Correctional Education,* 1972, *23,* 4–7.

Academic-Vocational Training

Bednar, R. L., Zelhart, P. E., Greathouse, L., & Weinberg, S. Operant conditioning principles in the treatment of learning and behavior problems with delinquent boys. *Journal of Counseling Psychology,* 1970, *17,* 492–497.

Clements, C. B., & McKee, J. M. Programmed instruction for institutionalized offenders: Contingency management and performance contracts. *Psychological Reports,* 1968, *22,* 957–964.

Cohen, H. L. Educational therapy. *Arean,* 1967, *82,* 220–225.

Cohen, H. L. Behavior modification in education. In C. E. Thorenson (Ed.), *The seventy-second yearbook of the national society for the study of education.* Chicago: University of Chicago Press, 1973, pp. 291–314.

Cohen, H. L. Motivationally oriented designs for an ecology of learning. In A. R. Roberts (Ed.), *Readings in prison education.* Springfield, Ill.: Charles C Thomas, 1973, pp. 142–154.

Cohen, H. L., & Filipczak, J. *A new learning environment.* San Francisco: Jossey-Bass, 1971.

Cohen, H. L., Filipczak, J. A., & Bis, J. S. CASE project. In J. Schlien (Ed.), *Research in psychotherapy* (Vol. 3). American Psychological Association, 1968, pp. 34–41.

Cohen, H. L., Filipczak, J. A., & Bis, J. S. A study of contingencies applicable to special education: CASE 1. In R. Ulrich, T. Stachnik, & J. Mabry (Eds.), *Control of human behavior* (Vol. 2). Glenview, Ill.: Scott, Foresman, 1970, pp. 51–69.

Cohen, H. L., Filipczak, J. A., Bis, J. S., Cohen, J., & Larkin, P. Establishing motivationally oriented educational environments for institutionalized adolescents. In J. Zubin & A. M. Freedman (Eds.), *The psychopathology of adolescence.* New York: Grune and Stratton, 1970.

Cohen, H. L., Goldiamond, I., & Filipczak, J. A. Maintaining increased education for teenagers in a controlled environment. In A. R. Roberts (Ed.), Readings in prison education. Springfield, Ill.: Charles C Thomas, 1973.

Dominquez, B. Rueda, M., Makhlouf, C., & Rivera, A. Analysis and control of activities in custodial human groups. In E. Ribes-Inesta & A. Bandura (Eds.), *Analysis of delinquency and aggression.* Hillsdale, N.J.: Lawrence Earlbaum, 1976, pp. 51–70.

Halstead, L. M. A new approach to teaching retarded children to read. *Corrective Psychiatry and Journal of Social Therapy,* 1970, *16,* 59–62.

McKee, J. M. The Draper experiment: A programmed learning project. In G. D. Ofiesh & W. C. Mcierhenry (Eds.), *Trends in programmed instruction.* National Education Association, 1966, pp. 91–97.

McKee, J. M. The use of programmed instruction in correctional institutions. *Journal of Correctional Education*, 1970, *22*.

McKee, J. M. The use of contingency management to affect learning performance in adult institutionalized offenders. In R. Ulrich, T. Stachnik, & J. Mabray (Eds.), *Control of human behavior* (Vol. 3). Glenview, Ill.: Scott, Foresman, 1974, pp. 177–186.

McKee, J. M., & Clements, C. B. A behavioral approach to learning: The Draper model. In H. C. Rickard (Ed.), *Behavioral intervention in human problems*. New York: Pergamon, 1975.

Rice, R. D. Educo-therapy: A new approach to delinquent behavior. *Journal of Learning Disabilities*, 1970, *3*, 16–25.

Tyler, V. O., Application of operant token reinforcement to academic performance of an institutionalized delinquent. *Psychological Reports*, 1967, *21*, 249–260.

Tyler, V. O., & Brown, G. D. Token reinforcement for academic performance with institutionalized delinquent boys. *Journal of Educational Psychology*, 1968, *59*, 164–168.

Yahraes, H. The reeducation of criminals. In R. A. Roberts (Ed.), *Readings in prison education*. Springfield, Ill.: Charles C Thomas, 1973, pp. 180–195.

COMMUNITY TREATMENT CENTERS

Concepts, Issues, and Discussion

Braukmann, C. J., Fixsen, D. L., Kirigin, K. A., Phillips, E. A., Phillips, E. L., & Wolf, M. M. Achievement Place: The training and certification of teaching parents. In W. S. Wood (Ed.), *Issues in evaluating behavior modification*. Champaign, Ill.: Research Press, 1975.

Eitzen, D. S. Impact of behavior modification techniques on locus of control of delinquent boys. *Psychological Reports*, 1974, *35*, 1317–1318.

Eitzen, D. S. The effects of behavior modification on the attitudes of delinquents. *Behaviour Research and Therapy*, 1975, *13*, 295–299.

Fixsen, D. L., Wolf, M. M., & Phillips, E. L. Achievement Place: A teaching family model of community-based group homes for youth in trouble. In L. A. Hamerlynck, L. C. Handy, & E. J. Mash (Eds.), *Behavior change: Methodology, concepts, and practice*. Champaign, Ill.: Research Press, 1973, pp. 241–268.

Hoefler, S. A., & Bornstein, P. H. Achievement Place: An evaluative review. *Criminal Justice and Behavior*, 1975, *2*, 146–168.

Kirigin, K. A., Ayala, H. E., Braukmann, C. J., Brown, W. G., Minkin, N., Phillips, E. L., Fixsen, D. L., & Wolf, M. M. Training teaching-parents: An evaluation of workshop training procedures. In E. Ramp & G. Semb (Eds.), *Behavior analysis: Areas of research and application*. Englewood Cliffs, N.J.: Prentice-Hall, 1975, pp. 161–174.

Maloney, D. M., Phillips, E. L., Fixsen, D. L., & Wolf, M. M. Training techniques for staff in group homes for juvenile offenders: An analysis. *Criminal Justice and Behavior*, 1975, *2*, 195–216.

Marholin, D., & Hall, C. H. From institution to community: A behavioral approach to contracting, advocacy, and staff training. *Adolescence*, 1978, in press.

Phillips, E. L., Phillips, E. A., Fixsen, D. L., & Wolf, M. M. Behavior shaping works with delinquents. *Psychology Today*, 1973, *6*(1), 75–79.

Phillips, E. L., Phillips, E. A., Fixsen, D. L., & Wolf, M. M. *The teaching family handbook*. Lawrence: University of Kansas Printing Service, 1974.

Phillips, E. L., Wolf, M. M., Fixsen, D. L., & Bailey, J. S. The Achievement Place model: A community-based, family-style, behavior modification program for predelinquents. In J. L. Khanna (Ed.), *New treatment approaches to juvenile delinquency*. Springfield, Ill.: Charles C Thomas, 1975, pp. 34–86.

Phillips, E. L., Wolf, M. M., Fixsen, D. L., & Bailey, J. S. The Achievement Place model: A community-based, family-style, behavior modification program for predelinquents. In E. Ribes-Inesta & A. Bandura (Eds.), *Analysis of delinquency and aggression*. Hillsdale, N.J.: Lawrence Earlbaum, 1976, pp. 171–202.

Wolf, M. M., Phillips, E. L., & Fixsen, D. L. The teaching family: A new model for the treatment of deviant child behavior in the community. In S. W. Bijou & E. Ribes-Inesta (Eds.), *Behavior modification: Issues and extensions*. New York: Academic, 1972, pp. 51–62.

Personal-Social Interactions

Bailey, J. S., Wolf, M..M., & Phillips, E. L. Home-based reinforcement and the modification of predelinquents' classroom behavior. *Journal of Applied Behavior Analysis*, 1970, *3*, 223–233.

Braukmann, C. J., Maloney, D. M., Fixsen, D. L., Phillips, E. L., & Wolf, M. M. An analysis of a selection interview training package for predelinquents at Achievement Place. *Criminal Justice and Behavior*, 1974, *1*, 30–42.

Fixsen, D. L., Phillips, E. L., & Wolf, M. M. Achievement Place: The reliability of self-reporting and peer reporting and their effects upon behavior. *Journal of Applied Behavior Analysis*, 1972, *5*, 19–30.

Fixsen, D. L., Phillips, E. L., & Wolf, M. M. Achievement Place: The reliability of self-reporting and peer reporting and their effects upon behavior *Journal of Applied Behavior Analysis*, 1972, *5*, 19–30

Fixen, D. L., Phillips, E. L., & Wolf, M. M. Achievement Place: Experiments in self-government with predelinquents. *Journal of Applied Behavior Analysis*, 1973, *6*, 31–47.

Kifer, R. E., Lewis, M. A., Green, D. R., & Phillips, E. L. Training predelinquent youths and their parents to negotiate conflict situations. *Journal of Applied Behavior Analysis*, 1974, *7*, 357–364.

Liberman, R. P., Ferris, C., Salgado, P., & Salgado, J. Replication of the Achievement Place model in California. *Journal of Applied Behavior Analysis*, 1975, *8*, 287–299.

Maloney, D. M., Harper, T. M., Braukmann, C. J., Fixsen, D. L., Phillips, E. L., & Wolf, M. M. Teaching conversation skills to predelinquent girls. *Journal of Applied Behavior Analysis*, 1976, *9*, 371.

Minkin, N., Braukmann, C. J., Minkin, B. L., Timbers, G. D., Timbers, B. I., Fixsen, D. L., Phillips, E. L., & Wolf, M. M. The social validation and training of conversation skills. *Journal of Applied Behavior Analysis*, 1976, *9*, 127–139.

Phillips, E. L. Achievement Place: Token reinforcement procedures in a home-style rehabilitation setting for predelinquent boys. *Journal of Applied Behavior Analysis*, 1968, *1*, 213–223.

Phillips, E. L., Phillips, E. A., Fixsen, D. L., & Wolf, M. M. Achievement Place: Modification of the behavior of predelinquent boys within a token economy. *Journal of Applied Behavior Analysis*, 1971, *4*, 45–59.

Phillips, E. L., Phillips, E. A., Wolf, M. M., & Fixsen, D. L. Achievement Place: Development of the elected manager system. *Journal of Applied Behavior Analysis*, 1973, *6*, 541–561.

Wasik, B. H. Janus House for delinquents: An alternative to training schools. In J. L. Khanna (Ed.), *New treatment approaches to juvenile delinquency*. Springfield, Ill.: Charles C Thomas, 1975, pp. 96–113.

Academic-Vocational Training

Bailey, J. S., Timbers, G. D., Phillips, E. L., & Wolf, M. M. Modification of articulation errors of predelinquents by their peers. *Journal of Applied Behavior Analysis*, 1971, *4*, 265–281.

Bailey, J. S., Wolf, M. M., & Phillips, E. L. Home-based reinforcement and the modification of predelinquents' classroom behavior. *Journal of Applied Behavior Analysis*, 1970, *3*, 223–233.

Harris, V. W., Finfrock, S. R., Giles, D. K., Hart, B. M., & Trosie, P. C. The effects of performance contingencies on the assignment completion behavior of severely delinquent youths. In E. Ramp & G. Semb (Eds.), *Behavior analysis: Areas of research and application*. Englewood Cliffs, N. J.: Prentice-Hall, 1975, pp. 309–316.

Kirigin, K. A., Phillips, E. L., Timbers, G. D., Fixsen, D. L., & Wolf, M. M. Achievement Place: The modification of academic behavior problems of youths in a group home setting. In B. C. Etzel, J. M. LeBlanc, & D. M. Baer (Eds.), *New developments in behavioral research: Theory, method, and application*. Hillsdale, N.J.: Lawrence Earlbaum Associates, 1977, pp. 473–488.

Marholin, D., Plienis, A. J., Harris, S., & Marholin, B. L. Mobilization of the community through a behavioral approach: A school program for adjudicated females. *Criminal Justice and Behavior*, 1975, *2*, 130–145.

Phillips, E. L. Achievement Place: Token reinforcement procedures in a home-style rehabilitation setting for predelinquent boys. *Journal of Applied Behavior Analysis*, 1968, *1*, 213–223.

Phillips, E. L., Phillips, E. A., Fixsen, D. L., & Wolf, M. M. Achievement Place: Modification of the behavior of predelinquent boys within a token economy. *Journal of Applied Behavior Analysis*, 1971, *4*, 45–59.

THE NATURAL ENVIRONMENT

Concepts, Issues, and Discussion

Deibert, A. W., & Golden, F. Behavior modification workshop with juvenile offenders: Brief report. *Behavior Therapy*, 1973, *4*, 586–588.

Fischer, J., & Gochros, H. L. *Planned behavior change: Behavior modification in social work*. New York: Free Press, 1975.

Jamieson, R. B. Can conditioning principles be applied to probation? *Trial Judges Journal*, 1965, *4*, 7–8.

Ribes-Inesta, E. Discussion: Methodological remarks on a delinquency prevention and rehabilitation program. In S. W. Bijou & E. Ribes-Inesta (Eds.), *Behavior modification: Issues and extensions.* New York: Academic, 1972, pp. 85–92.

Schwitzgebel, R. L. Private events in public places. In E. Ribes-Inesta & A. Bandura (Eds.), *Analysis of delinquency and aggression.* Hillsdale, N.J.: Lawrence Earlbaum, 1976, pp. 35–50.

Swartz, A., & Goldiamond, I. *Social casework: A behavioral approach.* New York: Columbia University Press, 1975.

Tharp, R. G., & Wetzel, R. J. *Behavior modification in the natural environment.* New York: Academic, 1969.

Yule, W. A book review of *Behavior modification in the natural environment. Behaviour Research and Therapy,* 1971, *9,* 304.

Personal-Social Interactions

Alexander, J. F., & Parsons, B. V. Short-term behavioral intervention with delinquent families: Impact on family process and recidivism. *Journal of Abnormal Psychology,* 1973, *81,* 219–225.

Alexander, R. N., Corbett, T. F., & Smigel, J. The effects of individual and group consequences on school attendance and curfew notations with predelinquent adolescents. *Journal of Applied Behavior Analysis,* 1976, *9,* 221–226.

Burchard, J. D., Harig, P. T., Miller, R. B., & Amour, J. New strategies in community-based intervention. In E. Ribes-Inesta & A. Bandura (Eds.), *Analysis of delinquency and aggression.* Hillsdale, N.J.: Lawrence Earlbaum, 1976, pp. 95–122.

Cohen, H. L. BPLAY—A community support system, phase one. In E. Ribes-Inesta & A. Bandura (Eds.), *Analysis of delinquency and aggression.* Hillsdale, N.J.: Lawrence Earlbaum, 1976, pp. 147–169.

Christophersen, E. R., Barnard, J. D., Ford, D., & Wolf, M. M. The family training program: Improving parent-child interaction patterns. In E. J. Mash, L. A. Hamerlynck, & L. C. Handy (Eds.), *Behavior modification and families.* New York: Brunner/Mazel, 1976.

Eyberg, S. M., & Johnson, S. M. Multiple assessment of behavior modification with families: Effects of contingency contracting and order of treated problems. *Journal of Consulting and Clinical Psychology,* 1974, *42,* 594–606.

Fitzgerald, T. J. Contingency contracting with juvenile offenders. *Criminology,* 1974, *12,* 241–248.

Fo, W. S. O., & O'Donnell, C. R. The buddy system: Relationship and contingency conditions in a community intervention program for youth with non-professionals as behavior change agents. *Journal of Consulting and Clinical Psychology,* 1974, *42,* 163–169.

Fo, W. S. O., & O'Donnell, C. R. The buddy system: Effect of community intervention on delinquent offenses. *Behavior Therapy,* 1975, *6,* 522–524.

James, R. E. Contingency management of delinquent behavior in the community. In J. L. Khanna (Ed.), *New treatment approaches to juvenile delinquency.* Springfield, Ill.: Charles C Thomas, 1975, pp. 24–33.

Jayaratine, S., Stuart, R. B., & Tripodi, T. Methodological issues and problems in evaluating treatment outcomes in the family and school consultation project, 1970-1973. In P. O. Davidson, F. W. Clark, & L. A. Hamerlynck (Eds.), *Evaluation of behavioral programs*. Champaign, Ill.: Research Press, 1974, pp. 141–174.

Madsen, C. K., & Madsen, C. H. Music as a behavior modification technique with a juvenile delinquent. *Journal of Music Therapy*, 1968, *5*, 72–76.

Martin, M., Burkholder, R., Rosenthal, T. L., Tharp, R. G., & Thorne, G. L. Programming behavior change and reintegration into school minieu of extreme antisocial deviates. *Behaviour Research and Therapy*, 1968, *6*, 371–383.

Parsons, B. V., & Alexander, J. E. Short-term family intervention: A therapy outcome study. *Journal of Consulting and Clinical Psychology*, 1973, *41*, 195–201.

Patterson, G. R. Interventions for boys with conduct problems: Multiple settings, treatments, and criteria. *Journal of Consulting and Clinical Psychology*, 1974, *42*, 471–481.

Patterson, G. R., Cobb, J. A., & Ray, J. S. A social engineering technology for retraining the families of aggressive boys. In H. E. Adams & J. P. Unikel (Eds.), *Issues and trends in behavior therapy*. Springfield, Ill.: Charles C Thomas, 1973, pp. 139–210.

Patterson, G. R., & Reid, J. B. Intervention for families of aggressive boys: A replication study. *Behaviour Research and Therapy*, 1973, *11*, 383–394.

Ray, E. T., & Kilburn, K. L. Behavior modification techniques applied to community behavior problems. *Criminology*, 1970, *8*, 173–184.

Reid, J. B., & Hendriks, A. F. C. J. Preliminary analysis of the effectiveness of direct home intervention for the treatment of predelinquent boys who steal. In L. A. Hamerlynck, L. C. Handy, & E. J. Mash (Eds.), *Behavior change: Methodology, concepts, and practice*. Champaign, Ill.: Research Press, 1973, pp. 209–219.

Reid, J. B., & Patterson, G. R. The modification of aggression and stealing behavior of boys in the home setting. In E. Ribes-Inesta & A. Bandura (Eds.), *Analysis of delinquency and aggression*. Hillsdale, N.J.: Lawrence Earlbaum, 1976, pp. 123–145.

Rose, S. E., Sundel, M., Delange, J., Corwin, L., & Palumbo, A. The Hartwig Project: A behavioral approach to the treatment of juvenile offenders. In R. Ulrich, T. Stachnik, & J. Mabry (Eds.), *Control of human behavior* (Vol. 2). New York: Scott, Foresman, 1970, pp. 220–230.

Schnelle, J. F., Kirchner, R. E., McNees, M. P., & Lawler, J. M. Social evaluation research: The evaluation of two police patrolling strategies. *Journal of Applied Behavior Analysis*, 1975, *8*, 353–365.

Schwitzgebel, R. K. A new approach to understanding delinquency. *Federal Probation*, 1960, *24*, 31–35.

Schwitzgebel, R. K. Delinquents with tape recorders. *New Society*, 1963, *18* (Jan. 16), 14–16.

Schwitzgebel, R. K., & Covey, T. H. Experimental interviewing and youthful offenders. *Journal of Clinical Psychology*, 1963, *19*, 487–488.

Schwitzgebel, R. K., & Schwitzgebel, R. L. Reduction of adolescent crime by a research method. *Journal of Social Therapy*, 1961, *7*, 213–215.

Schwitzgebel, R. L. *Streetcorner research*. Cambridge: Harvard Press, 1964.

Schwitzgebel, R. L. Short-term operant conditioning of adolescent offenders on socially relevant variables. *Journal of Abnormal Psychology*, 1967, *72*, 134–142.

Schwitzgebel, R. L. Preliminary socialization for psychotherapy of behavior-disordered adolescents. *Journal of Consulting and Clinical Psychology*, 1969, *33*, 71–77.

Schwitzgebel, R. L. A belt from big brother. *Psychology Today*, 1969, *2*, 42–47, 65.

Schwitzgebel, R. L., & Kolb, D. A. Inducing behavior change in adolescent delinquents. *Behaviour Research and Therapy*, 1964, *1*, 297–304.

Shah, S. A. A behavioral approach to out-patient treatment of offenders. In H. C. Rickard (Ed.), *Behavioral intervention in human problems*. Elmsford, N.Y.: Pergamon, 1974, pp. 233–266.

Slack, C. W. Experimenter-subject psychotherapy: A new method for introducing intensive office treatment for unreachable cases. *Mental Hygiene*, 1960, *44*, 238–256.

Stuart, R. B. Assessment and change in the communicational patterns of juvenile delinquents and their parents. In R. D. Rubin, A. A. Lazarus, & L. M. Franks (Eds.), *Advances in behavior therapy*. New York: Academic, 1971a, pp. 183–195.

Stuart, R. B. Situational versus self-control in the treatment of a problematic behavior. In R. D. Rubin (Ed.), *Advances in behavior therapy*. New York: Academic, 1971b.

Stuart, R. B. Behavioral contracting within the families of delinquents. *Journal of Behavior Therapy and Experimental Psychiatry*, 1971c, *2*, 1–11.

Stuart, R. B., & Lott, L. A. Behavioral contracting with delinquents: A cautionary note. *Journal of Behavior Therapy and Experimental Psychiatry*, 1972, *3*, 161–169.

Stuart, R. B., & Tripodi, T. T. Experimental evaluation of three time-constrained behavioral treatments for predelinquents and delinquents. In R. D. Rubin, J. P. Brady, & J. D. Henderson (Eds.), *Advances in behavior therapy* (Vol. 4). New York: Academic, 1974, pp. 1–12.

Tharp, R. G., & Wetzel, R. J. *Behavior modification in the natural environment*. New York: Academic, 1969.

Thorne, G., Tharp, R., & Wetzel, R. Behavior modification techniques: New tools for probation officers. *Federal Probation*, 1967, *31*, 21–27.

Weathers, L., & Liberman, R. P. Contingency contracting with families of delinquent adolescents. *Behavior Therapy*, 1975, *6*, 356–366.

Werner, J. S., Minkin, J., Minkin, B. L., Fixsen, D. L., Phillips, E. L., & Wolf, M. M. What should kids say to cops? An analysis of an "intervention program." *Criminal Justice and Behavior*, 1975, *2*, 55–84.

Wiltz, N. A., & Patterson, G. R. An evaluation of parent training procedures designed to alter inappropriate aggressive behavior of boys. *Behavior Therapy*, 1974, *5*, 215–221.

Academic-Vocational Training

Burchard, J. D., Harig, P. R., Miller, R. B., & Armour, J. New strategies in community-based intervention. In E. Ribes-Inesta & A. Bandura (Eds.), *Analysis of delinquency and aggression*. Hillsdale, N.J.: Lawrence Earlbaum, 1976, pp. 95–122.

Cohen, H. L. Programming alternatives to punishment: The design of competence through consequences. In S. W. Bijou & E. Ribes-Inesta (Eds.), *Behavior modification: Issues and extensions*. New York: Academic, 1972.

Cohen, S. I., Keyworth, J. M., Kleiner, R. I., & Brown, W. L. Effective behavior change at the Anne Arundel Learning Center through minimum contact interventions. In R. Ulrich, T. Stachnik, & J. Mabry (Eds.), *Control of human behavior* (Vol. 3). Glenview, Ill.: Scott, Foresman, 1974, pp. 124–142.

Jeffery, C. R., & Jeffery, I. A. Delinquents and dropouts: An experimental program in behavior change. *Journal of Corrections*, 1970, *12*, 1–12.

Martin, M., Burkholder, R., Rosenthal, T. L., Tharp, R. G., & Thorne, G. L. Programming behavior change and reintegration into school milieu of extreme antisocial deviates. *Behaviour Research and Therapy*, 1968, *6*, 371–383.

Staats, A. W., & Butterfield, W. H. Treatment of non-reading in a culturally deprived delinquent: An application of reinforcement principles. *Child Development*, 1965, *36*, 925–942.

Tharp, R. G., & Wetzel, R. J. *Behavior modification in the natural environment*. New York: Academic, 1969.

9

Achievement Place
A COMMUNITY TREATMENT MODEL
FOR YOUTHS IN TROUBLE

Alan G. Willner, Curtis J. Braukmann,
Kathryn A. Kirigin and Montrose M. Wolf

The dismal failure and expense of inhumane institutional treatment programs for children have been documented by many social scientists and writers (Goffman, 1961; James, 1971; Stuart, 1970; & Wolfensberger, 1970). These reports have helped to provide impetus for the development of community-based treatment as an alternative to institutional programs for youths. One direction of the community-based treatment movement has been the development of group homes designed to offer a variety of services to troubled children who are in danger of institutionalization, yet who seem to need more individualized help and contact than probation services or weekly counseling often provide (Empey, 1967; Keller & Alper, 1970). Unlike institutional programs—where day-to-day activities often bear little relationship to the outside world, where children's contacts are usually confined to members of their own sex, where they are taught to live in and become dependant on a depersonalized, hospital-like routine, and where few opportunities exist to learn skills that are useful outside of the

239

institution—treatment in a community-based setting would seem to provide a greater opportunity for normalized, practical, pleasant, and humane treatment alternatives.

During the past few years we have attempted to develop Achievement Place as one model of group-home treatment. The objectives of the program have been to develop a community-based, family-style, group-home treatment model for youths that is effective, economical, humane, and useful to a variety of communities differing in service needs and setting characteristics.

ACHIEVEMENT PLACE:
THE TEACHING-FAMILY MODEL

The Treatment Program

The treatment program developed at Achievement Place is called the Teaching Family Model (Phillips, Phillips, Fixsen & Wolf, 1974). The treatment program is administered by a married couple referred to as *teaching-parents*. The title of teaching-parents is given to distinguish them from more traditional, untrained, custodial house-parents or foster parents. In many residential settings the highly trained professional staff (i.e., social workers, psychologists, psychiatrists) have a great deal of administrating responsibility and only minimal contact with the youths in the program, whereas the "on line staff" (i.e., house-parents, aids, cottage staff) who have daily responsibility for the youths are largely untrained and lack the authority to make decisions about the treatment needs of the youths. The teaching-parent model seeks to combine these roles by preparing professional staff personally to administer, direct, and carry out the operation of a treatment program. In this model the teaching-parents receive a year of professional training, which includes classroom instruction, supervised practicum experience, and formal evaluation by the social service agencies in their community, their board of directors, the juvenile court, school personnel, the youths in their program, and the parents of the youths.

As trained professionals, the most important role of the teaching-parent is one of developing positive relationships with their youths and teaching them the social, interpersonal, academic, vocational, and self-care skills that are necessary to help these children increase their chances of survival and success in the community. Because the nature of the program is that of a small family-style setting (i.e., with six to eight children per home), the teaching-parents can develop a close relationship with each youth and can tailor their teaching to the individual needs of each child.

Teaching-Family Model (i.e., Achievement Place) group homes are usually older renovated homes located in the residential areas of the local community. The community provides direction for the group-home program through an independent board of directors composed of community representatives. The board is responsible for the financial, personnel, and policy aspects of the program—thus helping to assure the sensitivity and responsiveness of the program to its own unique community service needs.

Being a community-based program also has certain treatment advantages for the youths. It permits a child to return to his natural home during the week and/or on weekends and to continue to attend the same schools in which he had behavioral and academic problems before entering the group home. This arrangement provides for the opportunity to work closely with the youth's parents, school teachers, and school administrators in an effort to help the youth learn how to deal effectively with his problems in those settings. Another advantage of being community based is that it allows the staff to be more aware of how the youth is doing in the community. If a youth is having problems either during treatment or following his return to the natural home, the staff is in a better position to respond to these difficulties. Perhaps additional counseling, meditation, advocacy in the court, or some other form of intervention is necessary. Staying in touch with the youth and the community is an important part of treatment and aftercare and facilitating of the transition between the two.

The treatment program at Achievement Place is based on a behavior deficiency model of deviant behavior. According to this model, the behavior problems displayed by the youths reflect the absence of certain essential social and interpersonal skills, and are a probable consequence of inadequate training, personalized instruction, and encouragement. This suggests an educational model for correcting deviant behavior. In contrast with the traditional medical model, which portrays deviant behavior as indicative of "illness" and symptomatic of underlying psychopathology, the behavior deficiency model takes as a primary assumption that the youth lacks certain social and relationship-forming skills necessary to function effectively in a wide spectrum of social settings. Therefore, the goals of the treatment program would be to remediate those deficiencies through personalized demonstration, instruction, encouragement, and practice of well-specified, community survival skills. The intended outcome of this intensive teaching effort is that the children acquire those skills which result in their success at home and in school. As a result of these changes in their behavior, it is also more likely that they will achieve greater acceptance by their families and community, and will avoid future incarceration or institutionalization.

In the Teaching-Family Model an extremely important focus of treatment is one of establishing strong, positive relationships between the teaching-parent couple and their youths. Relationships based on mutal respect, concern, honesty, and affection are critical if the teaching-parents are to help their youths begin to try to change their behavior. Many of the youths coming into Achievement Place homes have long histories of painful, punishing relationships with adults. Many have been neglected, threatened, or physically abused. Early in the development of the treatment program, it became clear that if the youths were to be positively influenced by the suggestions, feedback, and efforts of the teaching-parents, or affected by them as a positive role model (i.e., learning and accepting their rationales, methods of problem-solving, and modes of positive social interaction), a mutually rewarding relationship first had to be established. These relationships begin to form as a child first enters a group-home program. The teaching-parents welcome the child, introduce the child to the others in the home, and express an interest and concern for him.

Counseling and private talks with each child is another important aspect of the Teaching-Family Model. These talks are usually held privately in an atmosphere of support, concern, and reassurance. Counseling can provide a means of helping a youth examine personal problems and seek meaningful solutions to them. It can also be an important medium through which to begin to facilitate a closer relationship between youth and teaching-parent.

Perhaps the most important role of teaching-parents is their teaching role. Teaching-parents use a variety of interaction styles to enhance their effectiveness as teachers. Much of this effectiveness depends on developing good relationships, trust, and understanding. However, requesting and teaching alternative behaviors also requires that the youth understand *why* these requests are being made. This involves the use of rationales. Rationales are explanations of the natural consequences (i.e., effect) of behavior (i.e., both for the youth and for others), and are offered in what is hoped to be a reasonable, convincing manner. For some youths, however, a discussion of natural consequences may be insufficient to change self-injurious behavior, and destructive consequences of the behavior may be so severe that more potent intervention is necessary if the youth is to avoid removal from the community (for example, when another physical assault would lead to institutionalization). In such cases a variety of other motivational techniques may be useful in helping the youth learn alternative behaviors. These motivational techniques allow the youth to earn points for learning, practicing, and applying appropriate adaptive behavior to problem situations as well as lose points for engaging in inappropiate, maladaptive behavior. Points are exchanged for privileges, first on a daily and later on a weekly basis. As the youth succeeds in learning and employing new behaviors, he advances to the merit system, in which points are no longer required for privileges. This gradual change from a more to a less structured learning environment coincides with an increase in the youth's awareness and responsiveness to subtle social interactions and expectations. The subtle, contextual aspects of the youth's natural environment now begin to have more meaning for him. Although initially points were useful to make explicit and clarify expectations, and help to make progress, achievements and verbal appreciation more tangible for the youths, this artificial means of motivition gradually becomes less important. In the final phase of in-home treatment, known as Homeward Bound, the youth begins to spend increasingly long periods of time with the natural family each week until the transition is complete, the youth has "graduated" from the program and is back home permanently.

Self-governement is an important aspect of the treatment program. It serves in helping youths develop effective personal decision-making skills, and provides a mechanism for youth involvement in the direction and operation of the treatment program. Self-government is composed of family conferences and the manager system. In family conference, the youths and teaching-parents all participate each day in discussing and deciding issues which arise in the home. These may involve making or changing rules, planning an activity in the home, or handling a particular behavior problem that a youth may be having. In this manner, family conference encourages family members to be actively involved in making decisions concerning the operation of their program. This notion of shared input, involvement and participation is important if the program is to be considered fair by its residents (Fixsen, Phillips, & Wolf, 1973). But in addition to assuring fairness, youth interest and motivation, and the opportunity to preserve and enhance individual expression and opinion, family conference also serves as an extremely important teaching technique. Through the medium of family conference, the teaching-parents can begin to teach the youths the skills involved in presenting rational and convincing arguments to one another, making group and personal decisions, problem solving, reaching mutually satisfactory compromises, knowing when to compromise and when to be assertive, and negotiating with others for what they want.

In the manager system the youths democratically elect one of the youths each day to supervise and teach the routine social, self-care, and job skills to new youths in the program (Phillips, Phillips, Wolf, & Fixsen, 1973). The manager system helps to teach the youths responsibility for leading and supervising peers. In addition, the youths learn important skills involved in developing positive relationships with peers such as how to give constructive corrective feedback in a positive nonconfronting manner and how to accept such feedback from others as well.

Working with the youth's natural family is another important aspect of the program. The youths spend most weekends with their natural or foster parents. These visits provide an opportunity for the youth to try out his new behaviors with his family. For example, instead of running away, the youth may now try to negotiate with his parents or try to find out exactly what they want from him and in the process describe his own needs and views. In this manner, they may develop a more mutually acceptable and enjoyable home life. This process, of course, is not an easy one to develop. Meetings and family counseling sessions are held each week with the youth and his family to try to iron out differences and reach mutually satisfactory conclusions. In these meetings the teaching-parents together with the youth and parents evaluate the recent weekend visit, discuss any problems which may have occurred, and plan for the next visit.

The youths who come to Achievement Place often have long histories of serious problems in school. Their teachers, principals, and parents report many difficulties with social and academic behavior in the classroom. Many youths have repeatedly failed their classes and have been suspended from school. Thus, it is not at all unusual for youths at Achievement Place to be two to three years below their age level in school. For these reasons, teaching-parents typically place great emphasis on academic remediation and school success. They often focus the afternoon activity in the home on learning academic, homework, test taking, and study skills. They work closely with teachers and school administrators to help remediate each youth's specific school problems. The public school teachers provide helpful feedback (i.e., information) to the teaching-parents in the form of daily or weekly school notes (Bailey, Wolf, & Phillips, 1970). These school notes are basically report cards that quickly but systematically describe the youth's social and academic behavior in the classroom. The school notes are composed of a series of questions relevent to a particular youth's specific problems (e.g., Did he talk out of turn? Did he disturb other students? Did he turn in his homework? Did he work on his in-classroom assignment?). School notes are usually answered by a simple "yes" or "no" for each question, and they are initialled by the teacher (with space provided for additional written comments). The school note is a useful treatment aid for keeping close communication going with teachers in that it helps the youth and teaching-parent become aware of difficulties as soon as they arise and allows for immediate attention to the problem (rather than having to wait for midsemester grades or a notice of expulsion). This important feedback also allows the youth to become aware of his progress and the value of his efforts. (A similar "home note" has been adapted for use on weekend home visits with parents). School notes and home notes also carry important in-home consequences for the youth to assist him in maintaining a high level of academic effort. In addition to the tangible benefits of success (i.e., points leading to extra privileges and goodies), the school note also provides an opportunity for teaching-parent to interact with the youth about his school progress and to give him the encouragement, positive attention, and peer prestige that his efforts and accomplishments truly deserve.

Effective teaching-parents are not only teachers, positive role models, and troubleshooters for their youths, but are also strong advocates for their youths. The advocacy role of the teaching-parents is an ongoing part of their work in the community. As they begin to meet and establish good working relationships with various community agencies (such as the juvenile court, the police, the schools, and the social welfare department), they can anticipate direct (and often informal) contact from these agencies at the first sign of complaint or trouble with one of the youths. This relationship network not only provides an invaluable opportunity for the teaching-parents to respond quickly to problems and issues that arise in the community, but it also serves an important diversionary function, in that the agency personnel and the parents who have the services of a teaching-parent become less dependent on the formal juvenile justice system for help with a problem.

The advocacy role of the teaching-parent does not terminate when the child leaves the group-home program, but is maintained on a long-term, follow-up (i.e., aftercare) basis. If a youth is later having difficulties at home, in school, on the job, or with the police, the teaching-parents are generally available and prepared to assist in solving the problem or working with the youth. This aftercare advocacy work may involve talking to the judge, helping the youth find a new job (or keep his present one), negotiating with the family, or perhaps even re-admitting the youth to the group home for a brief period of time. An attempt is made to maintain the positive relationships between the youth and his teaching-parent and between the youth and his peer group in the home long after the youth has physically left the home. Often a youth will continue to visit the home, drop by in the afternoon or for guest night, perhaps eat an occasional meal there, or even spend the night. These informal, youth-initiated or teaching-parent-initiated visits and talks help to preserve their positive relationships and help the teaching-parent remain sensitive to the needs of the youth.

Youth advocacy, however, goes beyond working for and with a young person in a personal relationship or problem-solving sense. In the Teaching-Family Model it also implies an active role in preserving and protecting the legal and human rights of the youths. As participants in treatment, youths in residential treatment face a variety of potential dangers, including mistreatment, no treatment (i.e., neglect) and overtreatment. In an attempt to avoid any of these abuses, teaching-parents are guided by four principles (some of which, in fact, may be emerging as legal trends in child/patient/residential care). The first of these is becoming known as the "principle of least restrictive treatment" (Edwards, 1972). According to this principle, treatment should be provided in as short a duration as possible and in as natural an environment as possible while still achieving therapeutic goals. This principle would argue for providing treatment within the community setting (as opposed to removal from the community), relatively free access to normalized, natural resources and activities (i.e., public schools, family and friends), and a respect for the privacy, opinions, and preferences of the individual. Teaching-parents endeavor to provide for these during treatment and advocate for them later at any judicial proceedings.

A second principle guiding the protection of children's rights is known as volunary informed consent. *Informed* consent implies that before a youth enters a Teacher-Family Model program, alternative treatment options and settings must be explained to the youth and to the parents of the youth. The teaching-parents also describe the Achievement Place treatment program, and review in detail information concerning all aspects of the program, including its potential risks and benefits to the youth. Youth and parental consent must be *voluntary* as well as informed. This suggests that admission into the program, and continued participation within requires both *initial* and *ongoing* consent. Withdrawal from treatment can occur at any time the youth or his parents choose to terminate treatment. Similar, but separate, voluntary, informed consent is requested of parents and youths for any additional participation in activities that are not strictly (and previously) defined as treatment. This includes participation in treatment-related research and data collection (Wolf, Fixsen, & Phillips, Note 1).

A third principle guiding youth paticipation relates closely to the previous one. It deals with youth involvement and consent at the level of individualizing treatment selection, and establishing and agreeing upon specific treatment goals and techniques. Treatment goals and techniques are defined (both initially on admission and periodically reviewed and redefined) by the youth and teaching-parents in concert. Rationales for the choice of goals and techniques are offered, discussed and negotiated until a mutually acceptable approach becomes defined. This process helps to ensure that the youth maintains interest and satisfaction with treatment as well as views participation as meaningful (i.e., important to him), fair, and desirable. This review and negotiation process takes place frequently in private counseling and within the context of family conference.

A final principle rigorously followed in an attempt to protect the youths from potential abuse is the participation of all Teaching-Family programs in public review and evaluation. Each program is carefully evaluated by soliciting the comments, opinions, and views of a variety of program consumers. These consumer groups are composed of individuals who are in direct contact with the program and are in an excellent position to evaluate its effectiveness and its sensitivity to the needs of the children that it serves. These consumers include the personnel in the juvenile court, social welfare department, and schools, as well as the parents of the youths in the program and the youths themselves. Their evaluations of the concern, fairness, helpfulness, pleasantness, and effectiveness of the teaching-parents help to ensure the protection of the youths' rights and the quality of the program.

A more thorough discussion of the evaluation procedure is offered later in the chapter.

Populations Served

The Teaching-Family Model was originally developed for youths 12 to 16 years old who were in serious trouble with the law, had been adjudicated by the juvenile court, and were in danger of being institutionalized. Additionally, these youths had often previously failed to respond to less restrictive forms of treatment intervention within the community (e.g., probation, treatment at the mental health center). With time a number of program variations and adaptations have developed from the original program for boys. Group-home treatment programs have been developed for girls, for coed youths, for younger children, and for retarded adults. Some of these programs are now located in both small town and large, urban, community-based settings. A few Teaching-Family programs have been developed for campus-style settings and applied to a large institutional setting (i.e., Baron, Daly, Fixsen & Phillips, Note 2).

Along with these adaptations to varied problems, age groups, and settings by many talented individuals who independently developed and administered these programs in their own settings, the treatment model began to be individualized to the needs and problems of each unique population. The motivation system, for example, was simplified and in some instances almost entirely eliminated to meet the needs and characteristics of the setting. Other treatment variations evolved to respond to the specific needs of younger children (i.e., predelinquent, behaviorally disordered, and dependent-neglected), developmentally disabled adolescents and adults and longer term residents who were preparing for independent living in the community (rather than a return to the natural family). Still others have adapted the model for use with specific cultural or ethnic populations (e.g., native American Indian youths) and children with unusual problem behaviors (e.g., autistic children). Perhaps the most recent variation of the model is a proposal to adapt the treatment program to the needs of older youths (ages 16–19). This program would emphasize the development of vocational skills and independent group-living skills.

There are approximately 60 group homes in the nation (16 of which are in Kansas) currently employing the Teaching-Family Model. These couples have been trained at one of several training centers in various parts of the country.[2] Many of these programs include variations which are only in the very earliest stages of development and pilot study. The eventual application and breadth of the model remain to be discovered.

Evaluation of the Teaching-Family Model

The development and evolution of the Teaching-Family Model continues to be a result of an ongoing process of exploration, trial, error, and refinement. This learning process through research and evaluation has been supported through grants from the National Institute of Mental Health, Center for Studies of Crime and Delinquency. The role of research and evaluation in program refinement has been central to and of primary importance in specifying problems, correcting them, and upgrading the delivery of social services. Scientific investigation and careful self-evaluation, although often painful, have helped us to develop numerous refinements in program operation, teaching-parent training, and child treatment care.

The primary purpose of our research has been to develop an effective, pleasant, and humane community-based group-home program that would offer an alternative to institutionalization for those youths who are in danger of being removed from their community. Evaluations of this treatment model have also attempted to asses the extent to which these youths and their communities have benefited from the services of the group-home program.

The research conducted at Achievement Place perhaps can be best understood in terms of an effort to answer several important questions: Are the program components, procedures, and techniques used in Teaching-Family Model homes effective in bringing about corrective behavior change for the youths? Are the teaching-parents operating these programs meeting the needs of their youths and community? What is the relative cost and effectiveness of the program in comparison to other treatment alternatives? In addressing these questions, we shall refer to three areas of research. These include procedural research, program evaluation, and treatment outcome research, respectively.

When a treatment procedure or program component is introduced into the Teaching-Family Model, it is often pretested to determine if it is effective in teaching meaningful skills and if it is likely to be acceptable to the youths in the program. For example, procedural research has been conducted on various aspects of the motivation system (Phillips, 1968; Phillips, Phillips, Fixsen & Wolf, 1971); the teaching procedures (Timbers, Timbers, Fixsen, Phillips, & Wolf, Note 3); the family conference (Fixsen, Phillips, & Wolf, 1973); and the use of rationales (Braukmann, Kirigin, Braukmann, Willner, & Wolf, Note 4). In this manner the development and gradual refinement of the treatment program has been systematically investigated using the dual criteria of effectiveness of and youth preference for the procedures.

As in the case of procedural research, program evaluation and treatment outcome research also play a critical role in the development and refinement of the treatment model. By identifying specific program goals and assessing the degree of success achieved in reaching these goals, many extremely useful suggestions and methods of program improvement have resulted.

To briefly review these goals and objectives, the Teaching-Family program has endeavored to provide a community-based program which: (1) functions as an *alternative* to institutionalization for youths in serious danger of being removed from their community, (2) is effective in reducing further involvement in the juvenile justice system, (3) is responsive to the needs of the youths and the community it serves, and (4) is economically viable as a treatment option.

To determine whether a group home is providing the community with an alternative to institutionalization, it is necessary to follow the progress of those candidates who were eligible for the program, but who did not participate for lack of available space. As with many group homes, there are usually more referrals to the program than openings available. When this occurs, a random selection procedure can be used to determine which of the candidates will enter the program. This method of selecting candidates ensures that each eligible youth will have an equal opportunity to be selected (i.e., reducing the likelihood of selection bias on the basis of a youth's "bad reputation," race, or other personal characteristic). In addition, the selection procedure allows for an assessment of the youths (randomly) not selected to determine what happens to them.

The results of a preliminary investigation (Kirigin, Braukmann, Fixsen, Phillips, & Wolf, Note 5) indicate that 56% of the youths (randomly) not selected into the original Achievement Place program were institutionalized within 2 years following the selection opportunity (in comparison to 12% of the youths who had been selected into the program). This suggests that the majority of the youths considered for admission were genuinely in danger of institutionalization and that the program provided an alternative to institutionalization for many of the youths who participated.

In assessing the effectiveness of the Achievement Place program, measures of police and court contact, school attendance and grades, and rates of institutionalization prior to, during, and following treatment were collected and compared to the same measures for youths who participated in other programs. Although the results of these investigations are still quite preliminary (because of practical difficulties in achieving random selection and the statistically small number of youths who have thus far reached 2 years posttreatment status), Kirigin et al., (Note 5) report the following tentative conclusions based upon the data collected thus far:

(1) The youths who participated in the Achievement Place program were much less likely to be institutionalized within 2 years after treatment (i.e., 22%) than similar youths (i.e., 47%) who were originally treated in institutional programs (i.e., Boys School State Reformatory).

(2) During treatment in Achievement Place there was a pronounced reduction in police and court contacts and an increase in school attendance.

(3) In the second year following treatment, the Achievement Place youths had fewer police and court contacts than before treatment. However, equivalent aged youths who had been treated in an institution had a similar reduction.

(4) The Achievement Place youths were more likely to remain in school following treatment (i.e., 56%) than comparison youths who were treated in an institution (i.e., 33%).

Another important aspect of treatment effectiveness relates to the attitudinal changes of the children receiving treatment. Eitzen (1975) conducted an independent evaluation of the Achievement Place program to assess what effect, if any, exposure to the behavioral treatment program might have on the attitudes (i.e., responses to questionnaires) of program recipients. Comparisons were made to youths attending the same junior high school as the Achievement Place youths. The preliminary results of this investigation offered tentative but impressive support for the group-home treatment experience. Eitzen reported greatest shifts in attitudes from poor to good self-esteem and from external locus of control to internal locus of control. These changes were very dramatic in the sense that prior to treatment the Achievement Place youths were much more negative on these dimensions than the comparison group, whereas following treatment they scored much more favorably. Smaller changes were also observed for positive orientation to authority figures (i.e., parents, judges, and teaching-parents) and toward achievement motivation. The latter, however, was still less than that of the comparison group. An interesting "no difference" finding was that the children participating in Achievement Place, a behavioral program, did not become more "Machiavellian" as a result of being in treatment and did not differ from the comparison children (i.e., the norm) on this dimension.

To determine the impact of the program on the community and its responsiveness to the agencies and individuals it serves, program evaluation procedures have been developed. Program evaluation consists of both consumer and professional evaluation components. In the consumer evaluation questionnaires are sent to the juvenile court, the public schools, the social welfare department, the board of directors of the group home, and the parents of the youths. These consumers are asked to complete the questionnaire by commenting on and rating the program on a number of dimensions, including effectiveness in correcting the youths' problems, cooperation of the teaching-parents, serving community needs, and the pleasantness of the home environment. The second aspect of the program evaluation is the professional evaluation component. This component involves an on-site visit to the home by a member of the training staff and a private interview with each youth in the program. During this interview the youth is asked to complete and discuss a questionnaire concerning his or her satisfaction with the program. The youth is asked to rate the program staff on the basis of their fairness, pleasantness, concern for the youths, effectiveness in helping them with their problems, and so on. The combined ratings of the various consumer groups provide rather immediate and detailed feedback about whether the program is having a positive impact on the community and the youths it serves. The feedback gives the training staff information concerning their training effectiveness as well as suggests areas where immediate, additional training and consultation with program staff are needed.

Our experience with the consumer evaluation has shown it to be a measure that is sensitive to differences both within and between programs. In addition, preliminary findings suggest that the ratings' of the consumer may correlate with more objective outcome measures of treatment effectiveness.

The cost of a program is an important aspect of program evaluation. It is possible that a program could be very effective and well-liked by the community yet impractically expensive to establish or operate. The cost of operating the Achievement Place program was compared to that of an institutional program in the same state (Kansas). This comparison revealed that it was about three times more expensive to operate the institutional program. In 1974 it cost $15 per day per youth in the Achievement Place program and $44 per day per youth in the Boys State reformatory.

In addition to the differences in operating costs, there are also clear differences in the cost of construction (i.e., purchase, renovation, and furnishing) of the two types of facilities. The construction of a new state institution in 1971 was estimated at approximately $20,000 per bed. In the same year, however, the cost of purchasing and renovating an Achievement Place style home for eight youths was only about $6000 per bed.

The comparative costs of building and operating these two types of facilities offer a compelling argument for the support of community-based programs. Community-based programs have the additional distinct advantage of not having to duplicate many existing facilities and resources such as the educational, medical, and recreational facilities already available to the youths in their community.

The Teaching-Parent

The discussion of the Teaching-Family Model thus far has centered around the treatment program, the population it serves, its cost and effectiveness. But central to the integrity of this model is the teaching-parent couple who provides these services. Who are they? Where do they come from? How are they trained?

The couples who direct and administer the operation of the Teaching-Family programs are recruited, selected, and employed by their own local group-home board of directors. Each board independently selects a couple who they believe best meets the needs of their community with its own unique characteristics. Although the training center at the Achievement Place Project does not actively recruit or hire couples for any specific program, it can provide the board with a list of interested applicants. Boards advertise the availability of their positions in local newspapers, local college and university placement offices, and in the *Teaching-Family Newsletter*, a monthly publication with a circulation of approximately 1,000.

Once hired, arrangements are made for the couple to attend the initial training workshop, the first step in a 1-year intensive training sequence. As it turns out, the couples who enter the training program are usually young, energetic people in their mid-twenties to mid-thirties. Many have been married for several years and have young children of their own. Often the couples have had previous experience in working with youths, and usually they have earned a bachelor's degree in the behavioral or social sciences (often in psychology, sociology, social work, or education) prior to receiving specific training to prepare them to become teaching-parents.

The Teaching-Parent Training Program

The Teaching-Parent Training Program places great emphasis on the practical skills involved in successfully directing a Teaching-Family home. To achieve these goals a 1-year training sequence was developed, the heart of which is a supervised, in-service practical experience received while actually directing the operation of a group home. The first step in this training sequence in an initial 1-week intensive teaching-parent workshop at the University of Kansas. There the trainees acquire the basic organizational, motivational, teaching, social, and relationship-building skills necessary to carry out the treatment program in their local community group home. These skills are taught by members of the training staff who present sections of the workshop based on their own specific areas of experience, interest, and expertise. Many of these presentations are organized to include reading material specifically designed to enhance the acquisition of these skills. One book in particular, *The Teaching-Family Handbook* (Phillips, Phillips, Fixsen, & Wolf, 1974), provides a detailed, technical description of many aspects of the treatment program. The handbook was written as a manual or textbook to be used in conjunction with lecture material, demonstrations, or videotaped supplementary examples and, whenever possible, role-playing opportunities to rehearse these skills in simulations with staff and other trainees. During these simulations, the couples receive detailed information and suggestions (i.e., "feedback") concerning their performance, along with many opportunities to practice until they have mastered the skill.

The couples attending the workshop learn how to observe, define, and respond to ongoing behavior. The subtleties of behavioral observation are described, and the trainees are asked to practice these skills in response to specific behavioral situations. They are also taught basic counseling skills; how to help their youths with their problems, how to help them acquire problem-solving strategies, and how to develop a positive, mutually satisfying relationship with each youth. Counseling is presented as one aspect of the relationship-building process and as a prototype of the desired teaching-parent-youth style of interaction. Other aspects of and methods for developing a positive, mutually satisfying relationship are discussed. For example, the teaching-parents also learn the importance of being able to provide explanations and make requests that are seen as fair, reasonable, and acceptable by the youths. The trainees also learn how to teach a variety of new skills to their youths in a pleasant, youth-preferred manner. These include teaching youths supervisory and peer leadership skills, negotiation and group decison-making skills, and skills involved in running an effective, stimulating family conference.

Legal and ethical issues are examined in the workshop as they relate to the operation of the treatment program. The couples are sensitized to the issues of informed consent, parental rights, release of information (i.e., confidentiality), and treatment responsibilities of the program (i.e., both obligations and limitations). The procedural rights of juveniles under the judicial system and the teaching-parent's role as youth advocate are also discussed.

The couples in training learn how to develop good community relations with neighbors, program sponsors, service organizations, community agencies, and the local news media; productive working relationships with parents and families; and relationships with teachers and school administrators, which are essential to achieving social and academic problem remediation in the classroom. The trainees also discuss a variety of personal and professional issues related to being a teaching-parent. These topics include marital working relationships, personal social life requirements, organizational notions relative to easing the workload and maximizing existing resources, and the training and use of the alternate teaching-parent (i.e., relief personnel). In addition, the workshop includes a detailed description and discussion of the consumer and professional evaluation procedures and their implications regarding certification.

During the course of the workshop, the trainees visit one of the local Teaching-Family homes for an afternoon and evening practicum. There they have an opportunity to observe experienced teaching-parents interact with their youths, demonstrate methods of teaching complex skills, and respond to various prestaged "problem situations." The trainees are then asked to try out their own skills in similar situations and, following each one, receive comments and suggestions from both the teaching-parents and the youths. The couple is invited to stay for dinner, observe a family conference, and conduct their own simulated family conference with the youths. At the conclusion of the practicum, they meet informally with the teaching-parents to discuss their overall performance and any other issues of interest to the trainees.

The schedule of the workshop is organized in such a manner as to maximize the couples' opportunities for learning a great deal of material in a relatively short period of time. The skills acquired in earlier sections are elaborated, emphasized and re-employed in later sections, building on the level of sophistication and behavioral repertoire of the trainees.

The initial teaching-parent training workshop is followed by a 3-month practicum period. During this time the couples are beginning to implement their programs in their own communities and are in frequent contact with training staff consultants. This period of intensive consultation (by telephone and in-home training visits) provides the couple with direction, advice, support, and encouragement.

At the end of this practicum period, the program's consumers are asked to complete written evaluations describing their satisfaction with the trainees' performance and with the program. The consumers of the program consist of the youths residing in the home, their parents, personnel from the social welfare department, juvenile court, schools, and the board of directors. In addition to this consumer evaluation, a professional evaluator from the training staff conducts an on-site evaluation of the program. A summary report is then prepared by the training and evaluation staff. This report gives the couple detailed feedback on their results and suggestions as to how they might improve their performance in areas where they receive a low evaluation. This feedback is given in a manner that protects the anonymity of the individual respondents (i.e., consumers).

Following this first evaluation, the trainees participate in a second practicum and evaluation period that extends until the end of the year-long training sequence. During this period telephone consultation continues, and a second evaluation is conducted covering those areas in which the couple had received low ratings. This evaluation helps the couples and training staff determine if the weak areas have been sufficiently improved. Early in this second practicum and evaluation period the couples attend the advanced training workshop, a second 3-day workshop at the University of Kansas, designed to further extend and refine their skills.

The advanced training workshop differs from the initial workshop in several respects. First, it tends to be more responsive to problem-solving issues rather than being didactic in nature. In fact, many of the presentation topics change from one advanced workshop to another, depending on the specific problem areas (i.e., determined from evaluation results) and the expressed needs and interests of those attending. Second, these workshops tend to focus on more individualized program concerns and problem solving, where each couple can discuss their first private professional and consumer evaluation with a staff consultant. The second workshop is also an important medium through which the couples begin to develop personal and professional contacts as they acquaint one another with their own particular programs, discuss various issues and problems, and share ideas and mutual concerns.

At the end of the first year, the first in a series of annual evaluations is conducted. The results of this evaluation are shared with not only the couple in training, but also with their board of directors and the agencies involved in placing youths in their home and funding their program (i.e., juvenile court, social welfare department). The results of this annual evaluation determine whether the couple will be certified as professional teaching-parents. Gaining and retaining certification requires high evaluations in all consumer areas on the first and subsequent annual evaluations. In this manner certification procedures are designed to provide for the ongoing quality control of the teaching-parent profession and to hold the individual teaching-parents accountable as professionals who are fully responsive and acceptable to their consumers.

Another professional and educational linkage to the Teaching-Family Model is the availability of a graduate level M.A. program for selected teaching-parents. This master's program in Human Development requires the successful completion of training and certification, a detailed study of several core topic areas, and finally, the careful design, implementation, authorship, and defense of an experimental thesis. This graduate-level speciality in group-home research and development is offered through the Achievement Place Research Project by the Department of Human Development at the University of Kansas.

Training Effectiveness

Each presentation in the workshop is designed to teach specific skill competencies relevant to the operation of the program. With this goal in mind, each section of the workshop is evaluated as to the quality of that training. The evaluation is carried out along a wide spectrum of dimensions (e.g., effectiveness, usefulness, and pleasantness of instruction) by asking the trainees to answer several questions related to each of these dimensions (as well as offer suggestions for improvement). This assessment takes place immediately after each section of the workshop has been presented in order to obtain the couples' most vivid, detailed reactions.

In addition to asking workshop participants to assist us in the evaluation of our training, the effectiveness of the training procedures are also specifically examined vis-a-vis changes in trainee skill level. Careful research has been conducted on a variety of workshop training procedures, including the use of rationales (Braukmann, Kirigin, Braukmann, Willner, & Wolf, Note 4), accurate observing and defining of ongoing behavior (Dancer, Braukmann, Schumaker, Willner, Kirigin, & Wolf, in press), and procedures that produce effective teaching (Kirigin, Ayala, Brown, Phillips, Fixsen, & Wolf, 1975). An example of the training effectiveness data resulting from the study of teaching interaction procedures is displayed in Figure 1.[3]

A third set of evaluations are also administered to the couples 8 to 10 weeks after the workshop. These are obtained by mailing questionnaires to each couple to determine their satisfaction with the workshop, given their more seasoned perspective as implementers of the model within their community. The ratings, comments, and suggestions received from these evaluations provide an invaluable source of information to the staff in their continuing attempt to improve and refine the quality of the training program.

Another criterion of training effectiveness and success is the degree to which training prepares the teaching-parents to survive on the job and satisfy the recipients of their program services. In fact, some experimental evidence has been offered (Braukmann, Fixsen, Kirigin, Phillips, Phillips, & Wolf, 1975) suggesting the importance of consumer satisfaction as a predictor of program success in the community. As described earlier, consumer evaluation provides a formal means of assessing the extent to which the youths, their parents, personnel in the juvenile court, schools, welfare department, and the board of directors are satisfied with the service

TEACHING INTERACTION
Behavioral Components

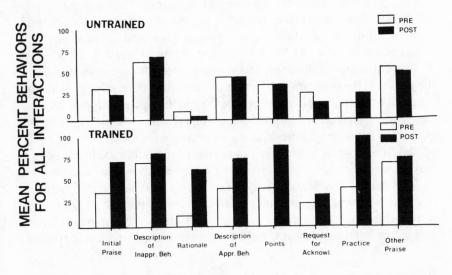

Figure 1

Mean percent of the behavior components of the teaching interaction engaged in by the trained and untrained couples before and after the teaching-parent workshops.

provided by the teaching-parents, their effectiveness in correcting problems, and the pleasantness of the program. This method of program assessment has the advantage of providing relatively immediate, economical, and sensitive feedback to the couple operating the program and to their training staff. In this manner the consumer evaluation can help the couple become aware of the strengths and weaknesses in their program as well as provide us with information concerning areas where training needs to be improved.

The results of the consumer and professional evaluation must be *formal*. In early attempts to place teaching-parents in community-based group homes (i.e., before the evaluation procedures were developed), couples were not always able to respond successfully to weaknesses in their program because they were often unaware of them. Formal feedback allows a social service program to be maximally responsive to the individuals and agencies it is designed to serve.

The consumer and professional evaluations also serve to protect the rights of those involved with the program. For example, through these evaluations, the youths in the program have the opportunity to express their satisfaction (or dissatisfaction) with the program anonymously. And because their views are presented anonymously, made public to the community, and protected by an independent evaluation group (i.e., independent of the teaching-parents), the youths have the safeguards and security necessary to assure meaningful input into their program. The youths are protected further by the openness of the homes to informal public scrutiny and by their ongoing participation and interaction in the local community (i.e., with teachers, parents, social workers, etc.).

The consumer-evaluation process also protects the agencies that place the youths in the program. The results of the annual evaluation provide the agencies with information concerning the quality of the program and the degree to which it is currently serving community needs. Ongoing program evaluation is a necessary prerequisite for being part of the Teaching-Family Model. If a program is unwilling to participate in public evaluations, this may be an indication of an attempt to disguise failure or abuse.

The annual certification evaluation is the heart and quality-control basis of the teaching-parent profession. It establishes standards of responsibility and accountability for an emerging profession which has as its goal the humane, pleasant, and effective treatment of youths in trouble.

Program Refinement in the Teaching-Family Model

The Teaching-Family Model is much different today than it was 7, 5, or even 2 years ago. The treatment program, training workshops, and evaluation procedures have continually evolved, changing in complexion, nuance, and emphasis. This gradual process of change has come about by closely examining trial-and-error attempts to solve difficult and often discouraging problems. The results of these attempts begin to take on meaning as we try to scientifically, objectively examine the reasons (i.e., independent variables) that affect these outcomes and try to replicate the procedures that have brought us success. In addition, there is another very fruitful procedure we have acquired along the way and which has become an important, ongoing theme in this process of discovery: that of responsiveness to consumers.

Our consumers, we have found, are an extremely important key to program refinement. Learning to listen to consumers may sound simple, but it is also often very painful. You hear things that you may not wish to hear, and you become aware of problems that you have no technology (presently) of solving. Nevertheless, it occasionally offers the perspective needed for overcoming a difficult problem. In our model, we have found it helpful to listen carefully (and to try to be responsive) to our consumers— the youths, the communities, and the teaching-parents. In the remaining portion of this chapter we would like to examine each of these three important consumer groups, and discuss some of the ways in which their input has contributed toward the solution of many significant problems and toward the refinement of the Teaching-Family Model. We also describe some of the problems whose solutions yet escapes us, and examine some preliminary notions and possible strategies for attacking these as well.

Youths as Program Consumers

Before examining *how* youths are important consumers and how their role has helped to achieve program improvement, a preliminary question might well be asked: *Should* youths be viewed as program consumers? For what reasons are they, the recipients of treatment, to be consulted regarding the delivery of these services? After all, one might argue, does the surgeon ask his patient which clamp, suture, or probe the patient would *like* to be used on his body during the course of the operation? And is not (to employ the medical model further) an effective treatment program for youths essentially a "social rehabilitation operation," in which the operator has the knowledge, training, and expertise to deliver treatment, and the patient, a victim of fate (or to be more precise, his environment), in helpless need of professional treatment?

The medical model analogue will probably not hold up very well in this case, and for largely *practical* reasons. For a treatment program to be successful with youths, it most probably must exhibit two specific, yet complementary, characteristics. The first is that the program staff must be *effective*, for example, in teaching their youths alternative, appropriate social, academic, vocational, and self-help behavior. The second characteristic is that the staff's interactions with the youth's must be liked or *preferred* by the youths. The second program characteristic (i.e., youth preference for staff interactions), is important for several reasons. Recent research has suggested that the presence of an adult model, who is positive and rewarding, is more likely to have a beneficial effect on the youths' participation in treatment (Jesness, 1974) as well as facilitate learning and identification with that adult (Bandura, 1969). Hirshi (1969) presents some interesting data suggesting that the strength of youth "attachments" for significant adults (i.e., parents, teachers, etc.) may be inversely related to delinquent behavior. A second consideration regarding youth satisfaction with treatment and subsequent willingness to participate bears on current legal and ethical guidlines. There is a growing recognition of the rights of youths, the importance of initial and ongoing informed consent, and the right to refuse treatment (Federal Register, 1973). This voluntary aspect of participation in treatment means, essentially, that the youth must be satisfied with the program and desire to remain in it. This is particularly true of a program located in an unlocked, community-based, residential setting, where a youth may easily walk away or formally withdraw from treatment at any time.

The youth evaluation aspect of the program evaluation has often been instrumental in identifying critical problems. These evaluations have not only been helpful with respect to correcting problems within a particular group home, but have also served to provide information concerning deficits in the teaching-parent training program. In its early stages of development, the training program placed great emphasis on the token economy and the point-transactions associated with youth motivation. Little emphasis was placed on other moment-by-moment, personal interactions between the youth and teaching-parents. Consequently, the level of interaction in some of the early replications of the Achievement Place program was less than satisfactory. The teaching-parents were described (by the youths and others) as cold, uncaring, indifferent, and unpleasant. The youths in this program were upset, the people in the community were concerned, and the teaching-parents were very unhappy. It became obvious that the focus of training needed to be shifted to that of providing the teaching-parents with the kind of interaction skills that the youths would like and to which they would be responsive.

A research investigation was conducted to determine youth preferences for various teaching-parent interaction styles (Willner, Braukmann, Kirigin, Fixsen, Phillips, & Wolf, 1977) with the eventual goal of training teaching-parents to use these preferred interaction skills and assessing if the youths enjoyed these interactions more once the teaching-parents were so trained. Our purpose in describing this study in some detail is two fold. The first is to demonstrate the critical role of youth input and preference throughout the research (i.e., problem-solving) endeavor. Youth satisfaction was the foundation of each step of the research as well as the total final goal. The second purpose of this detailed description is to give the reader an appreciation for how research plays a critical role in the Teaching-Family Model as it ties treatment to training, to improve the quality of both.[5]

The study was initiated by asking nineteen youths, eleven boys and eight girls residing in three Teaching-Family group homes, if they were willing to participate in a study. Their participation was completely voluntary and those who consented were paid for their time. The boys and girls were asked to look at a series of videotaped interactions between a teaching-parent (not their own) and a youth. These interactions covered many topics and types of teaching-parent behavior that might occur in a group home. As they looked at these, they were asked to write specific teaching-parent behaviors which they liked or disliked. At the conclusion of this exercise, the youths had written a total of approximately 790 comments concerning liked and disliked behavior. Many of these comments were similar to one another and some were identical. To reduce this "overlap" and bring these comments down to a more manageable number of catergories of liked and disliked (teaching-parent) interaction behavior, the comments were sorted down (by independent observers) to twenty-nine behavioral categories. The youths in the homes were then asked to rate each of these categories (i.e., assign a letter grade to them A, B, C, D, or F) according to how well they would like these social behaviors in their interactions with teaching-parents. This rating technique validated and qualified the relative importance of these social behaviors for the youths.

The results of this rating procedure yielded a wide range of ratings for these categories. Categories rated as most liked included teaching-parents speaking in a calm, pleasant tone of voice, offering to help the youth (with a problem, activity or task); joking and using humor with the youth; providing positive feedback (i.e., praise or recognition) for some accomplishment; being fair with and expressing concern for the youth; giving positive, tangible consequences (i.e., points) for a youth's efforts; giving informative explanations; using rationales for why a request was being made; using polite language; being brief and consise. Categories rated as disliked by youths included the use of blaming, accusing statements; shouting or raising their voice at a youth; not allowing a youth the opportunity to speak or clarify a situation; insulting the youth; being arbitrary and unfair; demanding rather than requesting that a youth do something; using profanity as an expression of anger; dwelling on only what the youth did wrong (i.e., talking only about errors); being negativistic, unfriendly or unpleasant.

Once defined (and rated), these categories of interaction behavior could be examined in ongoing interactions between teaching-parents and youths. The second aspect of the study involved the training of teaching-parent couples in the use of these youth-preferred (i.e., liked) interaction behaviors and the examination of a sample of their interactions with a youth prior to and following training to determine if: (a) they had in fact acquired these new interaction skills with training, and (b) if their behavior following training was more highly preferred by the youths (than before training).

Using a multiple-baseline design across trainees (Baer, Wolf, & Risley, 1968) three married couples (i.e., six trainees) received training in the use of youth-preferred interaction behaviors. Videotaped pre-training and post-training samples of their interaction behavior were taken over a five-month period of time. These were later analyzed by observers for the presence of youth-preferred behavior, and rated by the youths in the group homes.

Following training, the use of youth-preferred interaction behavior and the youth ratings of these social interactions were compared to the interactions of three successful, professional teaching-parents role playing similar situations. These teaching-parents, unlike the trainees, had been successfully operating a Teaching-Family program for some time in their local community. The data (i.e., level of preferred behavior and youth ratings) taken from their interactions was employed as a "normative sample" and used as a basis for making comparisons between their behavior and that of the trainees. This comparison sample was useful in determining if the changes in trainee behavior were "socially significant" changes (i.e., comparable to what one would expect of well-liked and highly skilled teaching-parents).

The results of the youth ratings of trainees interaction behavior are graphically displayed in Figure 2.[4] The results seem to indicate that the boys' and girls' ratings of the trainees' interactions were generally in the "C" and "D" range prior to the training workshops (i.e., to the left of the heavily dashed lines), but these youth ratings improved with training (i.e., to the right of the dashed lines) and increased to the "A" to "B-" range.[5] These post-treatment youth ratings correspond to the

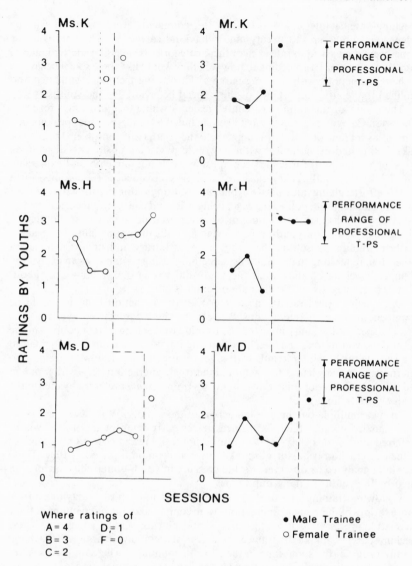

SESSIONS

Where ratings of
A = 4   D = 1
B = 3   F = 0
C = 2

● Male Trainee
○ Female Trainee

RATINGS OF TRAINEE SOCIAL BEHAVIOR

Figure 2

Youth ratings of trainee interaction behavior along a five-point grading scale of least- to most-liked behavior. Ratings of trainee performance are compared to the rated performance of professional teaching-parents. The heavily dashed vertical lines indicate the point at which training occurred, whereas the lightly dashed vertical line for trainee Ms. K represents an unscheduled prior exposure to training.

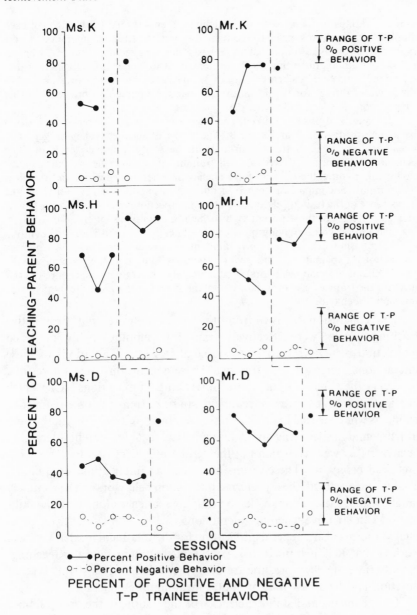

Figure 3

The percentage of positive and negative teaching-parent trainee behavior for each trainee across training sessions. Percentages of trainee behavior are compared to range of positive and negative behavior for professional teaching-parents. The heavily dashed vertical lines indicate the point at which training occurred, whereas the lightly dashed vertical line for trainee Ms. K represents an unscheduled prior exposure to training.

range of ratings of the professional teaching-parents (noted to the right of each graph). In other words, prior to receiving training, the trainees' interactions were rated by the youths as "not liked" or, at best, "neither liked nor disliked," whereas following training, the ratings of their interactions were meaningfully increased to the "liked" and "really liked very much" range. These increases corresponded to the range of ratings for the normative comparison sample and provided further support for the social validity of these changes.

Percentages of positive ("liked") and negative ("disliked") trainee interaction behavior are displayed in Figure 3. The levels of disliked behavior generally remained low for each trainee throughout the study, however levels of liked behavior did appear to increase with training of four of the six participants. Following training, these levels of liked behavior generally fell within or just below the normative comparison range, lending some additional validity to the importance of the training effect. The training procedure appeared to have had its greatest effect on those interaction behaviors involving offering or providing help to a youth, giving positive feedback (i.e., praise and recognition of accomplishment), smiling, providing motivational incentives (i.e., points), instructional explanations, and giving rationales to a youth (explaining why he should change specific behaviors). Unfortunately, the training procedure did not increase the trainees' use of humor (as joking is one of the most highly preferred interaction behaviors).

The conclusions drawn from this research were that prospective teaching-parents were effectively trained to employ highly preferred interaction behaviors with youths, and that youth evaluations of these interactions increased with training. These conclusions were interesting, however they have even more interesting implications. One such implication is that youths in treatment can be of tremendous assistance in telling us what we need to achieve in the training program. The youths were instrumental in specifying and defining critical teaching-parent interaction behaviors, as well as evaluating the results of our efforts to train these preferred behaviors. These results also carry an implication for training. That is, once defined, these preferred interaction behaviors can be routinely taught within the existing workshop training sequence along with the skills involved in effective teaching interactions (see Kirigin et al., 1975). And finally, there is also a general implication for the treatment model. We have learned that it is helpful to ask youths in treatment how the teaching-parents (i.e., and how *we*, the trainers) are doing. It is just this type of question and feedback that promotes meaningful change.

The problems and skill deficiencies of the youths in the group homes have also encouraged the research project to examine solutions to a variety of frequently occurring youth problems. Specific teaching procedures have been experimentally investigated and applied to such problems as learning to accept criticism and correction (Timbers, Timbers, Fixsen, Phillips & Wolf, Note 3), learning to respond well in stressful situations with police officers (Werner, Minkin, Minkin, Fixsen, Phillips, & Wolf, 1975), acquiring negotiation skills in interactions with parents (Kifer,

Lewis, Green, & Phillips, 1974), acquiring academic study and homework skills (Kirigin, Phillips, Timbers Fixsen, & Wolf, 1975), acquiring employment interviewing skills (Braukmann, Maloney, Fixsen, Phillips, & Wolf, 1974), gaining employment-maintaining skills (Ayala, Minkin, Phillips, Fixsen, & Wolf, in press), and improving youth-adult conversational skills (Maloney, Harper, Braukmann, Fixsen, Phillips, & Wolf, 1976; Minkin, Braukmann, Minkin, Timbers, Fixsen, Phillips, & Wolf, 1976). The impetus for these and other research endeavors has arisen from the needs and problems of the youths. As consumers of our program, they have contributed in many important respects toward its refinement.

The Community as Program Consumer

When a Teaching-Family Model program is established, its goal is to serve the needs of the community as well as those of the youths in the program. Most communities have their own unique characteristics, expectations, resources, and difficulties. However, many communities do have problems in common. The problem of establishing a new treatment facility within a community (e.g., purchasing and renovating the group home, zoning, funding, marshaling community support, incorporation) is, fortunately, not one of the most difficult. Starting up a new program entails a lot of effort and thankless hard work, but the specifics involved in carrying it out are fairly well identified at this point. Less ardous, but also less well specified, are the factors involved in optimal personnel selection. To assist boards in selecting effective, satisfied, and long-tenured couples, the Achievement Place Project is conducting a number of questionnaires polling teaching-parents about demographic data, job setting characteristics, job benefits, and the like, in an effort to determine which variables are associated with effectiveness of performance, length of tenure, and job satisfaction. The project is also currently conducting research involving an intensive pretraining interview to assess other characteristics (e.g., marital working relationship, pretraining skill level) which might relate to those variables. The results of this research will, one hopes, offer data-based suggestions to the local boards interviewing teaching-parent applicants.

The community has also helped to sensitize us to the importance of another problem: brevity of teaching-parent tenure. We find that we share this problem with a number of other residential care treatment programs, and although we may do better than some of these programs, teaching-parent length of stay in the group home is still far too brief. This problem is undoubtedly one of our most difficult, yet critically important problems to solve. Currently, the average length of tenure is 18 months. This situation is a difficult one for the community. Replacement of personnel requires additional training costs, presents a certain degree of program instability in the eyes of the community, and most importantly, interferes with the continuity of long-term, positive relationships between youths and their teaching-parents.

The problem of long-term program effectiveness is also one of primary concern. According to community reports and treatment outcome research, it appears as though the youths in the program do very well while they are in treatment, but that once they leave the program their difficulties in the community (e.g., police and court contacts) often increase. There is also an interesting trend in the outcome data which suggests greater long-term program effectiveness for those youths who have remained in treatment for a longer period of time (Kirigin, Braukmann, & Wolf, Note 6). In an attempt to arrive at a means of preserving this "in-treatment effect" (after a youth leaves the program), the Achievement Place Project is preliminarily examining the functional value of a relatively undisruptive, inexpensive supplement to the existing treatment model. This supplement would provide for the addition of a third person, the aftercare advocate, to carry on the efforts of the teaching-parent couple from the time that a youth is approaching the termination of in-home treatment through the next year or two. The aftercare advocate's role would involve a positive, supportive relationship with the youth, helping him to maintain the skills and success already achieved in the group home. The advocate would be available to help the youth solve problems with school personnel, family, employers and, if necessary, with police and court personnel. The amount of advocate contact would vary, depending on the needs of the youth. For a youth who is having no major problems, supervision would be less frequent and less intensive than for a youth whose problems are more severe. If the aftercare advocacy supplement is found to be effective in maintaining the child's in-program success, it will be well worth the additional personnel cost involved in providing such a service to the youth and to the community.

The Teaching-Parent as Program Consumer

The role of the teaching-parent in the delivery of child-care services seldom receives the attention and recognition that it deserves. There are few, for example, who appreciate the enormity and complexity of their daily professional responsibilities, or the tremendous physical and emotional energy required in the constant daily (i.e., 24 hours per day) challenge of providing for the needs of their youths. The pace is exhausting, and the demands to respond to diverse problem situations in the home, at school, in the community, in the natural home, on weekends, at night—is constant and probably unequaled in any other profession (i.e., even the good doctor, we understand, no longer makes house calls after hours).

The teaching-parent couple is undoubtedly the most essential, irreplaceable element in the Teaching-Family Model. Their perspective provides for unique input (i.e., suggestions, impetus for change) which greatly enhances the ongoing development and refinement of the model. Their importance as program consumers may be seen both in terms of sensitizing us to existing problems and actively participating in the examination of possible solutions to these problems.

In an effort to come to terms with the problem of tenure longevity, teaching-parents have been asked to pinpoint areas of current job satisfaction and dissatisfaction. Those who have left the profession have also been polled to determine the primary factors influencing their decisions to terminate. The results of these studies have indicated that various aspects of their current working conditions and lack of adequate financial remuneration are often important variables in teaching-parent job dissatisfaction. The teaching-parents often reported that they have very little personal privacy for themselves and for their family, very little time off to recuperate, and a social life which is severly limited (or nonexistent). In many communities, the group home purchased and renovated by the local board is carefully selected on the basis of how well it will provide for the needs of the youths, but the needs of the teaching-parents are often not considered and financial arrangements for relief staff (i.e., alternative teaching-parents) not provided.

This information has been shared with communities, and they are being encouraged to help teaching-parents hire alternates to work full or half-time under the direction of the teaching-parents so they can have more time off. Some local boards are also beginning to build private, comfortable living quarters onto their group homes and are reassessing their salary pay scales to provide a minimum salary of $15,000 per year per couple (i.e., $7,500 per person plus room and board). These changes reflect the type of living quarters that approximate what the teaching-parents could obtain in the community and a salary that is commensurate with their professional skills and responsibilities. But changing these conditions is a slow and arduous process. Boards and funding agencies change their policies slowly and cautiously, and so although improvements in living conditions, salaries and fringe benefits are occurring, it will take some time to see the results.

An interesting alternative to the situation where group home staff must negotiate for improved working conditions is the possibility of teaching-parents owning their own group home. This private-enterprise, entre-preneur model would probably increase the investment of the staff in the program and would hold more long-term rewards for them. Unfortunately, such a program is complicated by some state social service regulations, which make it difficult to purchase services from other than a nonprofit organization. However, the little experience we have had with this model to date is encouraging.

There are several other factors which are probably related to the longevity problem (i.e., in addition to working conditions and salary). These include the apparent lack of opportunities for advancement within the teaching-parent profession and the relative isolation of each teaching-parent couple within their own locality. The *Teaching-Family Newsletter* was developed in partial response to the desire for greater social and professional contact between teaching-parents. The *Newsletter*, mentioned earlier, provides a medium through which teaching-parents, trainees, and others in the child-care field can communicate, share ideas, pass along suggestions, provide resources (e.g., reprints of written materials and reports; techniques for solving problems), and make general announcements (e.g., regarding job opportunities, certification, availability of local funding, developments within the profession). It is also a medium for educating the local communities regarding the needs, problems, and achievements of the teaching-parents. Most importantly, however, it is a vehicle through which teaching-parents can speak to one another about issues of concern to them.

Greater opportunities for advancement within the teaching-parent profession are also beginning to present themselves. This is occurring in the form of a newly developing teaching-parent "career ladder," up which the couples may ascend toward greater responsibility and status within the profession. In the last few years, replications of the teaching-family training program have been initiated on a regional basis. Each of these regional training programs is directed by one or more Ph.D. graduates, trained in the Achievement Place Teaching-Family Model at the University of Kansas. Currently there are (or will soon be) regionalized training centers in North Carolina, Texas, Nebraska, Nevada, and New York. Each program focuses on providing training services for their own region and, consequently, seeks the employment of skilled, proven (i.e., certified) teaching-parents who can provide meaningful assistance in the training of group-home personnel for these new areas. Their skills in consultation, practicum-based training, evaluation, and administration of group homes are becoming highly marketable, and it is hoped that these new professional opportunities and increased job mobility (along with improved working conditions and salaries in the group homes) will provide sufficient personal and professional incentives to remain in the teaching-family profession and continue to provide meaningful service to youths.

There is probably one additional factor worth mentioning with regard to teaching-parent satisfaction, and that is their desire for the growth and visbility of the profession. Many teaching-parents are actively interested in many professional and organizational issues concerning quality child care.

They express an interest in maintaining standards and quality controls for the profession, especially in the face of rapid national growth. In view of these concerns, a National Association of Teaching-Family Programs is currently being established. Similar to practitioners (and associations) in other human service fields, this association will consider and develop policy regarding ethical standards, evaluation standards, accreditation, resource sharing, and issues regarding child care concerns and political/legislative impact. Increased interest and participation at these levels may not only solidify individual and collective teaching-parent involvement, but will potentially benefit the entire field of child care as well. Most certainly over the next few years, if we can maintain the involvement of well-trained, certified teaching-parents, they will undoubtedly have an important impact upon the growth and maturity of this young profession.

It is obvious that many of the problems discussed in this chapter have not yet been satisfactorily solved. There are perhaps partial solutions worked out for some; however, many difficult problems remain with us (and will probably continue to do so for some time to come). In retrospect, however, one can ascribe whatever limited success or improvement the model has experienced to the sensitivity of our program consumers in identifying problems and their potential solution, and to a careful experimental approach in trying to be responsive to these problems. It is hoped that the gradual evolution and refinement of these attempts will serve the goal of providing for meaningful, quality child-care services.

Conclusion

In reflecting on the themes developed in this chapter, the reader may recall several notions presented for consideration. One such notion was the demonstrated need for effective, economical, and humane treatment alternatives to the institutionalization of court-adjudicated youths. The Achievement Place program has been described as one such alternative which serves as a community-based, family-style, group-home treatment model for youths in trouble. This treatment model (The Teaching-Family Model) focuses on providing youths with social, academic, self-care, and prevocational skills critical to their survival and success in the community. These skills are taught by professionally-trained teaching-parents, whose concern, dedication, and training help their youths achieve maximal success at home, in school, on the job, and in the community. As directors of the treatment program, the teaching-parents' performance is carefully evaluated by a variety of program consumers. This consumer feedback allows the teaching-parents to provide maximally responsive and quality treatment programs to their youths and their communities. These

Teaching-Family programs have been adapted to serve various age groups, treatment settings, and populations.

The ongoing development and refinement of the treatment model and the teaching-parent profession are intimately tied to procedural research, program evaluation, and careful attention to the needs, ideas, and opinions of the model's consumers—the youths, the teaching-parents, and their communities. If there is one implication to be drawn from the developmental experiences described in this chapter, it is that a truly consumer-sensitive orientation is essential to the continued delivery of quality, professional child-care services.

REFERENCE NOTES

1. Wolf, M. M., Fixsen, D. L., & Phillips, E. L. *Some suggestions for accountability procedures for behavior modification treatment programs.* Prepared for the meeting of the National Institute of Mental Health concerning the development of guidelines for policy makers and program administrators regarding behavior modification programs. (Department of Human Development, University of Kansas, Lawrence), 1974.
2. Baron, R. L., Daly, P. S., Fixsen, D. L., & Phillips, E. L. *The Teaching-Family Model in a residential institutional setting.* Paper presented at the meeting of the American Psychological Association, Chicago, 1975.
3. Timbers, G. D., Timbers, B. J., Fixsen, D. L., Phillips, E. L., & Wolf, M. M. *Achievement Place for pre-delinquent girls: Modification of inappropriate emotional behaviors with token reinforcement and instructional procedures.* Paper presented at the meeting of the American Psychological Association, Montreal, Canada, 1973.
4. Braukmann, P. D., Kirigin, K. A., Braukmann, C. J., Willner, A. G., & Wolf, M. M. *The analysis and training of rationales for child-care personnel.* Unpublished manuscript, University of Kansas, 1976.
5. Kirigin, K. A., Braukmann, C. J., Fixsen, D. L., Phillips, E. L., & Wolf, M. M. *Is community-based corrections effective: An evaluation of Achievement Place.* Paper presented at the meeting of the American Psychological Association, Chicago, 1975.
6. Kirigin, K. A., Braukmann, C. J., & Wolf, M. M. *Achievement Place: The researchers' perspective.* Paper presented at the meeting of the American Psychological Association, Washington, D.C., 1976.

REFERENCES

Ayala, H. E., Minkin, N., Phillips, E. L., Fixsen, D. L., & Wolf, M. M. Achievement Place: The training and analysis of vocational behaviors. *Journal of Applied Behavior Analysis*, in press.
Baer, D. M., Wolf, M. M., & Risley, T. R. Some current dimensions of applied behavior analysis. *Journal of Applied Behavior Analysis*, 1968, *1*, 91–97.
Bailey, J. S., Wolf, M. M., & Phillips, E. L. Home-based reinforcement and modification of pre-delinquents' classroom behavior. *Journal of Applied Behavior Analysis*, 1970, *3*, 223–233.

Bandura, A. *Principles of behavior modification.* New York: Holt, Rinehart, & Winston, 1969.

Braukmann, C. J., Fixsen, D. L., Kirigin, K. A., Phillips, E. A., Phillips, E. L., & Wolf, M. M. Achievement Place: The training and certification of teaching-parents. In W. S. Wood (Ed.), *Issues in evaluating behavior modification.* Champaign, Ill.: Research Press, 1975.

Braukmann, C. J., Maloney, D. M., Fixsen, D. L., Phillips, E. L., & Wolf, M. M. An analysis of a selective interview training package for pre-delinquent youths at Achievement Place. *Criminal Justice and Behavior,* 1974, *1,* 30–42.

Dancer, D. D., Braukmann, C. J., Schumaker, J. B., Willner, A. G., Kirigin, K. A., & Wolf, M. M. The training and validation of behavioral specification skills. *Behavior Modifications,* in press.

Edwards, G. Penitentiaries produce no penitents. *Journal of Criminal Law, Criminology and Police Science,* 1972, *63,* 158–161.

Eitzen, S. D. The effects of behavior modification on the attitudes of delinquents. *Behaviour Research and Therapy,* 1975, *13,* 295–299.

Empey, L. T. *Studies in delinquency: Alternatives to incarceration.* Washington, D.C.: U.S. Department of Health, Education, and Welfare, Office of Juvenile Delinquent and Youth Development, Publication No. 9001, 1967.

Federal Register. *HEW guidelines on protection of human subjects.* Volume 38, No. 221, Part II, 1973.

Fixsen, D. L., Phillips, E. L., & Wolf, M. M. Achievement Place: Experiments in self-government with pre-delinquents. *Journal of Applied Behavior Analysis,* 1973, *6,* 31–47.

Goffman, E. *Assylums: Essays on the social situations of mental patients and other inmates.* Garden City, N.Y.: Anchor Books, 1961.

Hirishi, T. *The cause of delinquency.* Richmond: University of California Press, 1969.

James, H. *Children in trouble: The national scandal.* New York: Pocket Books, 1971.

Jesness, C. F. *Comparative effectiveness of behavior modification and transactional analysis programs for delinquency.* Sacramento: California Youth Authority, 1974.

Keller, O. J., & Alper, B. S. *Halfway houses: Community-centered correction and treatment.* Lexington, Mass.: D. C. Heath, 1970.

Kifer, R. E., Lewis, M. A., Green, D. R., & Phillips, E. L. Training pre-delinquent youths and their parents to negotiate conflict situations. *Journal of Applied Behavior Analysis,* 1974, 7, 357–364.

Kirigin, K. A., Ayala, H. E., Brown, W. G., Braukmann, C. J., Fixsen, D. L., Phillips, E. L., & Wolf, M. M. Training teacher-parents: An evaluation and analysis of workshop training procedures. In E. A. Ramp and G. Semb (Eds.), *Behavior analysis: Areas of research and application.* Englewood Cliffs, N.J.: Prentice-Hall, 1975.

Kirigin, K. A., Phillips, E. L., Timbers, G. A., Fixsen, D. L., & Wolf, M. M. Achievement Place: The modification of academic behavior problems of youths in a group home setting. In B. Etzel, J. M. LeBlanc, & D. M. Baer (Eds.), *New developments in behavioral research: Theory, method and application.* Trenton, N. J.: Lawrence Erlbaum Associates, 1975.

Maloney, D. M., Harper, T. M., Braukmann, C. J., Fixsen, D. L., Phillips, E. L., & Wolf, M. M. Teaching conversation-related skills to predelinquent girls. *Journal of Applied Behavior Analysis,* 1976, *9,* 371.

Minkin, N., Braukmann, C. J., Minkin, B. L., Timbers, G. D., Timbers, B. J., Fixsen, D. L., Phillips, E. L., & Wolf, M. M. The social validation and training of conversation skills. *Journal of Applied Behavior Analysis*, 1976, *9*, 127–139.

Phillips, E. L. Achievement Place: Token reinforcement procedures in a home-style rehabilitation setting for "pre-delinquent" boys. *Journal of Applied Behavior Analysis*, 1968, *1*, 213–223.

Phillips, E. L., Phillips, E. A., Fixsen, D. L., & Wolf, M. M. Achievement Place: The modification of the behaviors of pre-delinquent boys within a token economy. *Journal of Applied Behavior Analysis*, 1971, *41*, 45–59.

Phillips, E. L., Phillips, E. A., Fixsen, D. L., & Wolf, M. M. *The teaching family handbook*. Lawrence: University of Kansas Printing Service, 1974.

Phillips, E. L., Phillips, E. A., Wolf, M. M., & Fixsen, D. L. Achievement Place: Development of the elected manager system. *Journal of Applied Behavior Analysis*, 1973, *6*, 541–561.

Stuart, R. B. *Trick or treatment*. Champaign, Ill.: Research Press, 1970.

Werner, J. S., Minkin, N., Minkin, B. L., Fixsen, D. L., Phillips, E. L., & Wolf, M. M. "Intervention package": An analysis to prepare juvenile delinquents for encounters with police officers. *Criminal Justice and Behavior*, 1975, *2*, 55–83.

Willner, A. G., Braukmann, C. J., Kirigin, K. A., Fixsen, D. L., Phillips, E. L., & Wolf, M. M. The training and validation of youth-preferred social behaviors of child-care personnel. *Journal of Applied Behavior Analysis*, 1977, *10*, 219–230.

Wolfensberger, W. The principle of normalization and its implications to psychiatric service. *American Journal of Psychiatry*, 1970, *3*, 291–296.

NOTES

1. The Achievement Place Research project has been supported through grants from the National Institute of Mental Health, Center for Studies of Crime and Delinquency (MH20030; MH13644; and NIMH3881). The interested reader may request reprints of published material or further information by writing to the Achievement Place Research Project, 111 Haworth Hall, University of Kansas, Lawrence, Kansas, 66045. The authors wish to express their appreciation to Dr. Carol S. Willner for her critical reading of the manuscript.

2. The interested reader may contact the regional training center nearest them concerning further information regarding training. Current regional Teaching-Family Training Centers are located in Morganton, North Carolina (Dr. Gary Timbers, Director, Bringing it All Back Home Project; Houston, Texas (Dr. Hector Ayala, Director, Houston Achievement Place); Boys Town, Nebraska (Dr. Elery Phillips, Director, Father Flanagan's Home for Boys); Omaha, Nebraska (Drs. Dean Fixsen, Karen and Dennis Maloney, Co-Directors, Boys Town Center for Youth Development); Las Vegas, Nevada (Drs. Willie Brown and Hewitt Clark, Children's Behavioral Services); and Lawrence, Kansas (the authors, Achievement Place Research Project).

3. Kirigin, K. A., Ayala, H. E., Brown, W. G., Braukmann, C. J., Fixsen, D. L.,

Phillips, E. L., & Wolf, M. M. Training teaching-parents: An evaluation and analysis of workshop training procedures. In E. A. Ramp & G. Semb (Eds.), *Behavior analysis: Areas of research and application*, 1975, pp. 161–174. Reprinted by permission of Prentice-Hall, Inc., Englewood Cliffs, N.J.

4. The lightly dashed line in the upper left-hand corner of the figure (labeled "Ms. K.") represents Ms. K's probable prior exposure to treatment. Following the study, it was discovered that Ms. K. had made several unscheduled visits to a Teaching-Family program and had probably received some informal training in youth-preferred interaction behaviors during these visits. Reprinted with the permission of the editors, *Journal of Applied Behavior Analysis*.

5. Reprinted with the permission of the editors, *Journal of Applied Behavior Analysis*.

10

Behavioral Treatment of Anxiety States and Avoidance Behaviors in Children

C. Steven Richards and Lawrence J. Siegel

INTRODUCTION

Envision the following scenes. Susan is a 10-year-old girl with a severe dog phobia.[1] When a loose dog ventures by, she will climb her mother like a tree, trembling all the while. Her mother is not amused by this. The most mild-mannered dogs, even at distance, petrify her. Susan's constant effort to avoid all dogs results in a withdrawal from many social activities and a collapse into tears if she is not chauffeured to school. Previous analytic therapy has left Susan frustrated and phobic as ever, leaving her parents disgruntled and broke. Although life is difficult for Susan, it is worse for Amy. Amy is in the third grade, and she has never spoken to a teacher in the school setting. However, she talks at home with fluency and gusto, and she will even talk to her teacher there. Amy's academic future is bleak: either she talks or she flunks. With her academic performance dragging more than a year below the norm, school authorities have decided that if Amy's elective mutism continues, she will have to repeat the third grade or be sent to an "adjustment class" (the first step toward a psychiatric school placement). Teachers and school psychologists have repeatedly sallied forth with attempted cures such as explanations, threats, punishments, one-shot rewards, and tender loving care. Nothing has worked. Amy is headed for a nose-dive into academic failure and social gloom. A school administrator concludes that Amy is retarded and feels that, since she is generally cooperative, no one should "rock the boat."

We rocked the boat and successfully treated both of these children with behavior therapy techniques. Following treatment, Susan was able to handle friendly dogs with equanimity, and Amy became one of the most talkative members of her class. This chapter discusses therapy techniques and issues that pertain to the behavioral treatment of children who, like Susan and Amy, have problems with severe anxiety and avoidance behaviors. Several debilitating fear and withdrawal behaviors have an alarmingly high incidence among children. Fortunately, a number of behavior therapy techniques have evidenced therapeutic promise in this area. This chapter focuses on these techniques.

Scope, Style, and Emphasis

Some comments about the scope, style, and emphasis of this chapter are in order. The scope is purposely quite limited. The chapter is primarily an excursion into descriptive and "how-to-do-it" aspects of the particular behavioral techniques that can be applied to the treatment of anxiety states and avoidance behaviors in *children*. We feel that such a chapter is a needed and useful addition to the literature in this area. There are several things this chapter is not: it is not an encyclopedic literature review; it is not a discourse on thorny issues in theory and research methodology; and it is not a review of the many descriptive and epidemiological facets of the behavior disorders in question. Many splendid reviews exist that dwell on the things this chapter bypasses; they are cited later in the chapter.

The style of this chapter is rather informal and nontechnical. We think that an introductory chapter like this one, organized around techniques and studded with case examples and how-to-do-it suggestions, is best presented in a less constipated fashion than is typical of scientific writing.

The emphasis in this chapter is on behavior therapy techniques that are practical, empirically supported, and open to replication. The support usually includes at least one within- or between-group controlled outcome investigation, although in a few instances the sole support is from case studies. Recent and especially promising approaches, such as behavioral self-control techniques and preventative endeavors, are also given considerable play in the chapter. We conclude the chapter with a commentary on critical therapeutic issues and trends in the area.

A Few Comments on Anxiety States and Avoidance Behaviors

To the chagrin of numerous scientists and therapists, defining anxiety states and withdrawal behaviors in a suitable fashion is a difficult task (Gelfand, in press; Marks, 1969; McReynolds, 1976; Miller, Barrett, & Hampe, 1974; Quay, 1972; Ross, 1974). For anxiety states such as phobias, we like the definitional approach of Miller et al. (1974). Their tentative definition (p. 90) describes a phobia as a special form of fear that: (1) is out of proportion to demands of the situation, (2) cannot be explained or reasoned away, (3) is beyond voluntary control, (4) leads to avoidance of the feared situation. (5) persists over an extended period of time, (6) is unadaptive, and (7) is not age or stage specific.

Avoidance and social withdrawl behaviors are reasonably self-descriptive, and whether they are considered a behavior disorder requiring professional attention rests on points similar to those defining a phobia, especially points 1, 5, 6, and 7. There is a good deal of overlap between anxiety states and avoidance behaviors, of course, with the choice of one or the other labels frequently reflecting a matter of emphasis. Anxiety states usually involve avoidance, and avoidance behaviors usually involve anxiety, but negative emotional states are more pronounced in the anxiety disorders. In turn, withdrawal behaviors and social or intellectual skill deficits are more pronounced in the avoidance disorders. This chapter moves among related terms such as fear, anxiety, phobia, and avoidance in a manner that may well horrify purists; nevertheless, beyond mirroring the shifts of emphasis noted above, the promising behavioral treatment procedures for these overlapping behavior disorders are overlapping themselves and therefore warrant this style of presentation and organization.

A few more comments about these forms of psychopathology are in order. Social withdrawal and the shyness frequently accompanying it are common childhood problems. This shyness can persist into adulthood for an alarmingly high number of individuals, as indicated by the finding that 40% of a large sample of California high school and college students labeled themselves as shy, and 25% stated they were shy most of their lives (Zimbardo, Pilkonis, & Norwood, 1975, Note 1). Problems associated with their shyness included a reported inability to make friends, express opinions, or enjoy social events. Only 1% of the sample reported never having experienced shyness. Fortunately, shyness often attenuates with age, as evidenced by 41% of the sample reporting they were shy children but are not now shy adults.

Informal efforts to help shy and withdrawn children have met with little success. For instance, Bonny (1971) reported that a number of socialization experiences—such as enrolling children in nondirective play therapy, immersing withdrawn children in collaborative projects with other children, and providing advice to their parents—yielded meager improvements in social isolation. Treatment interventions that do not recognize, assess, and directly cope with the withdrawn child's *social skill deficits* are also unlikely to be successful (Gelfand, in press). Indeed, because socially isolated children frequently have socially awkward parents (Sherman & Farina, 1974), the entire *family* of a withdrawn child might profit from some social skills training.

More exhaustive reviews and theoretical discourses on avoidance behaviors in children are available in the following: Achenbach (1974), Clarizio and McCoy (1976), Gelfand (in press), Quay (1972), and Ross (1974).

Among the anxiety states of childhood, school phobia seems to be the only condition that has been studied extensively, with the ratio of professional papers on it outdistancing other phobias by at least 25 to 1. Not surprisingly, school phobia also seems to concern parents and professionals much more than other childhood phobias. Indicative of this, a treatment outcome investigation of phobias (Miller, Barrett, Hampe, & Noble, 1972a) garnered a treatment population where 69% of the children were school phobics; this occurred despite an enthusiastic 3-year effort to enlist all types of phobias in the client sample.[2]

Perhaps as many as 9 out of 10 children develop concrete fears sometime during their childhood (MacFarlane, Allen, & Honzik, 1954), Fears of physical injury (e.g., being wounded), natural events (e.g., storms), and social situations (e.g., class recitation) appear to be particularly common and identifiable (Miller et al., 1974; Miller, Barrett, Hample, & Noble, 1972b; Scherer & Nakamura, 1968). However, simple monophobias such as a fear of storms are rare in clinical populations (Miller et al., 1974). Some of these fears, of course, dissipate with age. For example, a fear of dogs is prominent among many 3-year-olds, but usually disappears by the age of 8 (MacFarlane et al., 1954).

Miller et al. (1974) have even argued that phobias in young children may sometimes reflect a desirable developmental process. They draw on the work of Piaget and other child development experts in their elaboration of this intriguing idea:

Thus according to developmental theory objects as perceived by children are age- and state-dependent, as the child's constructions and schema about the nature of reality evolve. Although we have no empirical evidence, we would postulate that a precondition for phobia is a construction of the object as dangerous, and that phobias that occur frequently at certain ages reflect the structuring process typical for that stage in development. Far from being pathognomonic, such fears would be considered a necessary and *desirable* aspect of development (Miller et al., 1974, p. 117, emphasis added).

Whether professional intervention is called for requires a weighing of the predicted duration and potential seriousness of the phobia against the likely cost and benefit of intervention. Tenacious or severely debilitating fears (e.g., school phobia) often necessitate and justify therapeutic interventions. Given that the prognosis for children who develop specific phobias is apparently rather good, treatments that are short-term, inexpensive, and practical are especially desirable. Fortunately, behavior therapy fits the bill here: it tends to be inexpensive to implement and rapid in its effects.

Numerous interesting literature reviews, clinical discussions, and theoretical essays exist on phobias in general and child phobias in particular. Some of the better ones are Achenbach (1974), Berecz (1968), Bernstein (1976), Borkovec (1976), Davison and Neale (1974), Gelfand (in press), Hersen (1971), Kelly (1973), Leitenberg (1976), Marks (1969), Miller et al. (1974), O'Leary and Wilson (1975), Rachman (1968), Ross (1974), and Yates (1970).[3]

Special Issues Regarding Children

Psychotherapy with children often presents special assessment and treatment problems peculiar to this age group, and some of the assessment problems are well illustrated in work with phobic children. Miller et al. (1974), in their review of childhood phobias, note that "determining the presence and intensity of a phobia is a difficult undertaking if one goes beyond a verbal report" (p. 96). Although behavior therapists have emphasized *in vivo* (i.e., carried out in the natural environment) behavioral measurement procedures in the assessment process, the classical literature on phobias gives the impression that phobias are such obvious phenomena that behavioral measures are unnecessary. For instance, it did not seem to perturb Freud that he never determined whether his classic child client, Little Hans, was *really* afraid of horses! Direct observations often involve salient practical problems, of course, so retrospective ratings are frequently used as indirect but more economical assessment methods. In addition to 5- or 7-point Likert-type scales for specific fears, two inventories for children's fears are available (Miller et al., 1972b; Scherer & Nakamura, 1968).

The most widely used method for obtaining assessment information here, as with many clinical problems, is the interview. Its flexibility, economy, and relationship-enhancing properties make it very useful, despite its well-known vulnerability to bias and distortion. Interviewing young children is usually tricky, however, and many clinicians caution against becoming too committed to the set of stimuli that the children report as crucial. Children's self-reports are frequently unreliable; they will often try to say what they believe adults want to hear, and sometimes they assign different meanings to words than adults do.

Smith and Sharpe (1970) provide a good example of the difficulties present in assessing children's phobias. They found that a standard interviewing technique failed to isolate the stimuli involved in a 13-year-old boy's school phobia. Shifting gears, they asked the boy to visualize and carefully describe a typical school day. They noted at which stages of his description he evidenced behavioral indications of anxiety (flushing of the skin, vocal tremors, etc.). This behaviorally oriented assessment procedure suggested that he became highly anxious at the prospect of having to speak in his math and literature classes. In contrast, his visualizations of his home and mother did not evoke signs of anxiety. The utilization of detailed visual imagery and the corresponding nonverbal cues it evoked helped to clarify the phobic stimuli in this case, and later this information was used to develop a hierarchy for implosive therapy.

In addition to special assessment considerations with children, special treatment considerations (e.g., age appropriateness, language barriers, and requisite skills) are also called for, but they are not dealt with here. Some of them are discussed as we cover specific techniques later in the chapter. Discussions of special assessment and treatment considerations with children include the following: Bijou and Redd (1975), Clarizio and McCoy (1976), Gardner (1974), Gelfand and Hartmann (1975), Krumboltz and Krumboltz (1972), O'Leary (1972), Palmer (1970), and Ross (1974).

Behavioral Assessment and Therapy

At this point some brief comments about behavioral assessment and therapy are in order. Assessment in behaviorally oriented interventions focuses on what the client is *doing*, the *content validity* of the test items, and a *sampling* interpretation of the test responses (Goldfried & Kent, 1972; Goldfried & Sprafkin, 1974; O'Leary, 1972). In contrast, traditionally oriented assessment places emphasis on what the client "has" (e.g., traits), downplays content validity (e.g., projectives), and utilizes a sign interpretation of test responses (e.g., the test response is a sign of an underlying personality disposition). Behavioral assessment assumes low cross-situational consistency in behavior (in contrast to a trait approach) and deals with the concept of "personality" as a convenient metaphor, rather than as an entity. Behavioral assessment considers the situational context of behavior as being crucial and therefore attempts to sample real-life situations. The idea of a direct sampling approach is central to any behaviorally oriented assessment. In short, behavior therapists, especially when dealing with children, like to focus their assessment effort on responses in the natural environment they can see and count.

By behavior therapy we generally mean therapy that bears the dual emphasis of empiricism and applied experimental psychology (cf. Bandura, 1969; Krasner, 1971; Rimm & Masters, 1974). Actual techniques that have a developmental history and current status reflecting these emphases include positive reinforcement, shaping, modeling, systematic desensitization, extinction, self-monitoring, punishment, and progressive relaxation training (this is only a partial list). Most behavioral interventions have the flavor of a definite learning—education approach and focus on increasing or decreasing measurable behaviors. In contrast, techniques such as nondirective play therapy tend to focus on the modification of underlying personality structures and are not considered behavioral.

With the literature on behavior therapy mushrooming like an explosion of the hydrogen bomb, the following reviews and treatment guides can aid readers in their attempt to explore and keep up with this field: Bandura (1969), Bergin and Suinn (1975), Gelfand and Hartmann (1975), Goldfried and Davison (1976), Graziano (1975), Kanfer and Goldstein (1975), Kazdin (1975), Krumboltz and Thoresen (1976), Mahoney (1974), O'Leary and Wilson (1975), Rimm and Masters (1974), Thoresen and Mahoney (1974), Ullmann and Krasner (1975), and Yates (1970, 1975).

BEHAVIORAL TECHNIQUES

This section of the chapter deals with the behavioral treatment procedures that have been frequently used with anxious and withdrawn children. In addition, some recently developed procedures that have not yet experienced widescale use, but that evidence considerable promise, are also discussed. Each technique section is introduced by a brief informal definition, followed by a detailed example of the technique in use, and concluded by a short commentary on the technique. It must be acknowledged that authors with different predilections might end up with quite different jargon and with a somewhat different list, but the major behavioral techniques used with anxious and withdrawn children are represented here.

Positive Reinforcement

Definition. This procedure entails giving positive reinforcers to the child contingent on the emission of a desired, specifiable behavior. For instance, praise or candy could be given to the child contingent on the child going to school.[4] This technique has been used for thousands of years, of course, but the realization and systematic application of its potential is a recent phenomenon (cf. Ullmann & Krasner, 1975). Positive reinforcement is perhaps the most basic technique of behavior therapy. It is closely related to and often profitably combined with several other procedures, including shaping, stimulus fading, physical prompting, and operant extinction (these are discussed later). In addition, a number of rubrics have sprung up with a similar meaning, such as contingency management (which often includes punishment) and external reward techniques.

Case Example. Ayllon, Smith, and Rogers (1970) presented an interesting instance of the behavioral management of school phobia, which relied in part on positive reinforcement procedures. Valerie, an 8-year-old black girl from a low-income area, started to exhibit episodes of gradually increasing absences from school in the second grade. This continued into the third grade and became quite extreme. Whenever Valerie's mother attempted to take her to school, Valerie threw violent temper tantrums. Her mother eventually took her to a local hospital to "get some 'pills for her nerves' " (Ayllon et al., 1970, p. 127), and the hospital pediatric staff diagnosed her as school phobic. A behavioral assessment indicated that Valerie's school phobia was, in part, maintained by several positive consequences (e.g., extra contact with her mother, fun at a neighbor's house) that accrued to her if she avoided school. By and large, what Ayllon and his colleagues attempted to do amounted to providing more positive reinforcement to Valerie for school attendance and less for school avoidance (along with some punishment for school avoidance). A summary of their procedures and results is provided in Table 1.

One facet of their intervention involved a home-based motivational system. Some of the things (positive reinforcers) Valerie liked most were chewing gum, ice cream, soda pop, and having her cousin stay overnight with her. The mother, with the therapists' assistance, implemented a charting system in which each day of voluntary school attendance by Valerie was noted with a star. Each such day resulted in several pieces of candy, and a week of these days resulted in an additional special treat. This is a good example of positive reinforcement: positive reinforcers (candy and trips) were given to Valerie contingent on the emission of a desired, specifiable behavior (voluntary school attendance). (For a while, the mother also reinforced Valerie immediately at the school door each morning.) At the same time, the mother attempted to provide as little positive reinforcement as possible for nontarget behaviors—excuses of sickness, complaining, and other aspects of nonvoluntary school attendance. As is evident in Figure 1, the results of this intervention were dramatically successful. Follow-up assessments done 6 and 9 months after

Table 1
**Procedural (Including Positive Reinforcement) and Behavioral
Progression During the Treatment of School Phobia**[a]

Temporal sequence	Procedure	Valerie's behavior
Baseline observations Days 1–10	Observations taken at home and at the neighbor's apartment where Val spent her day.	Valerie stayed at home when siblings left for school. Mother took Val to neighbor's apartment as she left for work.
Behavioral assessment Days 11–13	Assistant showed school materials to Val and prompted academic work.	Val reacted well to books; she colored pictures and copied numbers and letters.
Behavioral assessment Day 13	Assistant invited Val for a car ride after completing academic work at neighbor's apartment.	Val readily accepted car ride and on way back to neighbor's apartment she also accepted hamburger offered her.
Procedure 1 Days 14–20	Taken by assistant to school. Assistant stayed with her in classroom. Attendance made progressively earlier while assistant's stay in classroom progressively lessens.	Val attended school with assistant. Performed school work. Left school with siblings at closing time.
Day 21	Assistant did not take Val to school.	Val and siblings attended school on their own.
Procedure 1 Day 22	Val taken by assistant to school.	Val attended school with assistant. Performed school work. Left with siblings at school closing time.
Return to baseline Observations Days 23–27	Observations taken at home.	Val stayed at home when siblings left for school. Mother took Val to neighbor's apartment as she left for work.
Procedure 2 Days 28–29	Mother left for work when children left for school.	Val stayed at home when children left for school. Mother took her to neighbor's apartment as she left for work.
Procedure 3 Days 40–49	Taken by mother to school. Home-based motivational system.	Val stayed at home when siblings left for school. Followed mother quietly when taken to school.
Procedure 4 Days 50–59	On day 50, mother left for school *before* children left home. Home-based motivational system.	Siblings met mother at school door. Val stayed at home.

Temporal sequence	Procedure	Valerie's behavior
Procedure 4 Days 50–59	After 15 minutes of waiting in school, mother retured home and took Val to school.	Val meekly followed her mother.
	On day 51, mother left for school *before* children left home.	Val and siblings met mother at school door.
	On day 52, mother left for school before children left home.	Siblings met mother at school door. Val stayed at home.
	After 15 minutes of waiting in school, mother returned home and physically hit and dragged Valerie to school.	Valerie cried and pleaded with her mother not to hit her. Cried all the way to school.
	On day 53–59, mother left for school before children left home.	Val and siblings met mother at school door.
Fading procedure Days 60–69	Mother discontinued going to school before children. Mother maintained home-based motivational system.	Val and siblings attended school on their own.
Fading Procedure Day 70	Mother discontinued home-based motivational system.	Val and siblings attended school on their own.

aFrom "Behavioral Management of School Phobia" (p. 131) by T. Ayllon, D. Smith, and M. Rogers, *Journal of Behavior Therapy and Experimental Psychiatry*, 1970, *1*, 125–138. Copyright 1970 by Pergamon Press. Reprinted by permission.

treatment indicated that Valerie was voluntarily attending school, with no fuss, every day. She was now enjoying school a great deal and getting As and Bs, whereas before treatment her average grade had been C. Despite what was, from a behavioral perspective, a rosy outcome, part of the psycho-diagnostic evaluation from the pediatric department of the local hospital read as follows:

Her emotional development is characterized by deviations in the area of maturity and aggression. Her reality testing is marred by an extreme concern over sexuality and men, whom she sees as attacking, ever fighting animal-like creatures. On the basis of the recent results, without considerations to results previous to behavioral management, it would seem that the school phobia may have been treated successfully, but it has not meant anything to this girl (Quoted in Ayllon et al., 1970, p. 136).

Ayllon and his colleagues argued, of course, that since chronic absence from school is the major functional characteristic of school phobia,

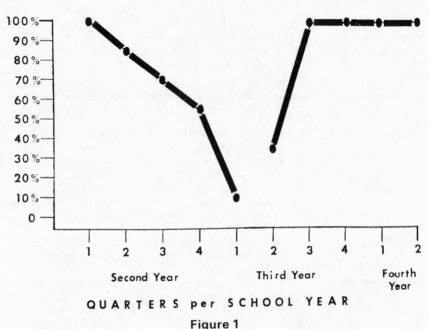

Figure 1

Valerie's voluntary school attendance. Each dot represents the percentage of voluntary attendance per school quarter (45 days). The behavioral intervention (including positive reinforcement) was initiated during the second quarter of the third year of school. (From "Behavioral Management of School Phobia" [p. 135] by T. Ayllon, D. Smith, and M. Rogers, *Journal of Behavior Therapy and Experimental Psychiatry*, 1970, *1*, 125–138. Copyright 1970 by Pergamon Press. Reprinted by permission.)

reinstating Valerie's school attendance constituted the only relevant criterion of successful cure and, therefore, *she was cured*!

Commentary. Positive reinforcement is one of the most powerful, consistent, and efficient behavioral techniques available. Especially when combined with techniques such as shaping and stimulus fading, positive reinforcement is an excellent procedure for increasing desired behaviors. It can also be used indirectly to decrease undesirable behaviors, by rewarding behavior that is incompatible with the undesirable behavior. In addition, positive reinforcement is a procedure that most therapists feel comfortable with and most parents and children quickly grasp and appreciate. It has the asset of emphasizing the positive (desired behavior) rather than dwelling on the negative.

Nevertheless, positive reinforcement is not without its limitations and, like *any* tool, it can be mindlessly used and abused. Concerns about bribery, enforcement of unreasonable rules, undermining intrinsic motivation, materialism, withholding love, coaxing, unrealistic goals, seamy manipulation, overuse, and counter-control via the same methods can in some cases become justified when the technique is thoughtlessly abused. However, when used appropriately, these concerns have generally been found to be the result of misunderstandings of the technique or misinterpretations of its effects (cf. Bandura, 1969; Krasner & Richards, 1976; Krumboltz & Krumboltz, 1972; O'Leary, Poulos, & Devine, 1972; O.Leary & Wilson, 1975; Ullmann & Krasner, 1975). The key phrase, of course, is "when used appropriately." Thus it may be beneficial to discuss a few rules of thumb for the appropriate and effective use of positive reinforcement.

One of the most important rules of thumb is that positive reinforcement works best if it immediately follows the target behavior. In addition, therapists should recognize that what is positively reinforcing is largely an individual matter and even the most effective reinforcers can be overused (hence, vary the reinforcers). Some potential reinforcers are best left out of positive reinforcement treatment programs; for instance, "love" is an inadvisable reinforcer in such programs, just as it is inadvisable to withold it if the target behavior is not emitted (cf. Krumboltz & Krumboltz, 1972). Selective praise and special attention from adults who are prestigious from the child's viewpoint are, however, very appropriate and effective reinforcers. It is usually a good idea to carefully verbalize the reinforcers and contingencies (i.e., rules for when the reinforcers will be given and for what behaviors) to the child and to be as explicit as possible here. A slow change in behavior may often be the fault of unclear contingencies (see Mahoney [1974, pp. 163–164] for a cute story on misunderstood contingencies). A sluggish beginning may also indicate more serious problems, of course, and the change agent (teacher, parent, therapist, etc.) may need to stop and re-evaluate the entire enterprise. The schedule on which the reinforcers are delivered is a critical variable, and once a target behavior is established, the change agent may want to gradually switch from a schedule in which every instance of the target behavior is rewarded to an intermittent schedule in which, for example, every 10 instances of the target behavior are rewarded (Bandura, 1969; Gelfand & Hartmann, 1975; Karoly, 1975). In turn, once natural contingencies gain more control of the target behavior and start to maintain it, the positive reinforcement program used to initiate the target behavior can be faded out altogether, but such fading should be done slowly and cautiously, with regular evaluation of its effects (cf. O'Leary & Wilson, 1975).

In part because of its powerful effects, positive reinforcement has sometimes been used when it was not necessary, and there is some concern that overuse of some positive reinforcement programs such as token economies may sap intrinsic motivation and lead to only short-term gains that will deteriorate once the token economy is withdrawn (cf. Ford & Foster, 1976; Keeley, Shemberg, & Carbonell, 1976; Levine & Fasnacht,

1974; O'Leary & Wilson, 1975; Turkewitz, O'Leary, & Ironsmith, 1975). Although the effect of extrinsic reinforcement on intrinsic motivation is still unclear, it does seem wise to balance carefully the costs and benefits of a positive reinforcement program before implementing it. Change agents should also endeavor to negotiate reasonable and fair target behaviors and contingencies with children. Reinforcement programs that are draconian or that fail to take factors such as maturation into account will fail, as indeed they should. No reinforcement program can teach a snake to read or a 4-year-old child to do calculus. Finally, adult change agents should remember that children use these same techniques with *adults*!

Other intriguing case or controlled studies using positive reinforcement techniques (sometimes in combination with other techniques) with phobic and withdrawn children include: Bauermeister and Jemail (1975), Freeman, Roy, and Hemmick (1976), Lazarus, Davison, and Polefka (1965), Leitenberg and Callahan (1973), Miller and Miller (1976), Obler and Terwilliger (1970), Walker and Hops (1973), and Wulbert, Nyman, Snow, and Owen (1973).

Shaping

Definition. Closely related to positive reinforcement is the technique of shaping. Shaping entails reinforcing successive approximations to the target behavior, with each approximation being slightly closer to the final target behavior (cf. White, 1971). For instance, a school phobic child might be rewarded for walking halfway to school, then three-fourths of the way, then all the way, then all the way plus staying there 5 minutes, then all the way plus staying there a half-hour, and so on until this gradual process leads to the child walking to school and staying there all day. Good coaches of athletic teams make extensive use of shaping; a basketball coach teaches beginning players how to hold the ball before he (or she) teaches them how to shoot it. Many positive reinforcement programs utilize shaping. Hence, rather than demanding the complete target behavior immediately, they allow for successive approximations to it.

Case Example. Semenoff, Park, and Smith (1976) provide a good example of shaping in the treatment of a 6-year-old electively mute child named Roger. Roger only talked with his parents and a few close relatives and child friends, and he would not talk at all in the classroom. He was very shy and dependent on his mother. He was cooperative and followed directions in the classroom, but he would not ask for help if he had a problem and would become frustrated and cry instead. Teachers and speech therapists in the school collaborated in a behavioral treatment program, after deciding that the counseling Roger and his family were receiving in a local mental health agency was not affecting Roger's elective mutism.

The therapy program entailed several facets, but a major component was a shaping procedure that moved all the way from imitating actions and simple sounds in a speech therapy room with a couple children present to speaking in whispers to speaking words aloud to speaking to his teacher alone in class, and after several more successive approximations, to speaking spontaneously before the whole class. It should be noted that the shaping program did suffer some setbacks, in large part resulting from a transfer to a strange school during one summer session. The flavor of this program can be gathered from the following quote, which represents a section in the middle of the shaping program:

Step 2: Eliciting Nonverbal Responses

Roger nodded "yes" and "no" to questions. In class he would raise his hand for roll call. I [first-grade teacher] would acknowledge responses with a wink. . . .

I continued to emphasize that we were "secret pals" and that some day he would share some of his secrets with me. He committed himself with a nod that some day he would. . . . I always prepared Roger for his next step by eliciting a nonverbal commitment to agree to do something in the future. . . .

Step 3: Verbal "Mumbles"

After about a week I warmed up by flashing the alphabet cards very fast. Roger nodded if he knew the letters. He began to giggle and nod his head as fast as he could. I indicated that this was the day we had prepared for, that he would tell me the names of the letters he knew, and that he could leave for lunch as soon as he told me the letters. The session took thirty minutes for one mumble. I told him I accepted what he said and trusted he was telling me the right letter (although I could not distinguish what he said). I indicated that tomorrow I would have to hear more. He left for lunch.

Step 4: Speaking in Whispers

I continued to use humor and to joke with him. The next day he began to mumble the answers. I indicated that it was unacceptable. He then responded in a low whisper. I accepted the whisper response, stressing that someday he would have to talk in a clear, loud voice. I also indicated that from now on, when he needed something he was to come up and ask me for it. . . . I gave hin his lunch bucket with a smile and a pat and said, "Have a good lunch" (Semenoff et al., 1976, pp. 93–94).

Roger continued to show progress through the rest of the first-grade school year, did not deteriorate over the summer, and bimonthly follow-up assessments of his second-grade performance indicated that Roger was respondingly verbally to 100% of the questions directed at him and that the frequency of his spontaneous or initiating remarks was equivalent to the classroom average. He was still quieter than some of the students in the class, but he was more talkative than many other students. His parents, in turn, reported that he was considerably more comfortable with strangers at home and was talking to a wide variety of people.

   Commentary. Shaping is a versatile and powerful behavior change procedure. It can be used to acquire responses in new environments gradually, and to reward the child for gradually approaching feared objects. Eventual exposure to phobic stimuli appears to be a key component of successful treatment programs for phobic children, as indicated by Miller et al.'s (1974) statement that:

> The last essential element in the treatment of phobia is stimulus confrontation. All research and clinical experience suggests that confrontation is an absolutely necessary aspect of treatment, as well as a measure of its success. In the presence of the stimulus, the child *learns* how not to be afraid or *learns* that he is no longer anxious (p. 125, emphasis added).

Because of the small steps involved, shaping places reasonable demands on the child, and it can often be associated with pleasant conditions, as the previous case example illustrates. Another asset of shaping is that the child may quickly grasp the technique himself and use it to gradually learn to approach things himself, thus developing a form of self-control that enables him to become his own therapist and teacher. Shaping is not always an easy technique to learn, however, and judging how to break up the target behavior into progressive steps and how rapidly to progress from one step to the next is somewhat of an art. If the change agent tries to progress too rapidly the child will repeatedly fail and one of the greatest assets of shaping, namely the lack of repeated failures that arise when the entire perfected target behavior is attempted on the first try, will be lost. If, on the other hand, the change agent tries to move through the hierarchy of steps too slowly, both he and the child will become frustrated and bored. Achieving an effective middle ground within these two extremes is often a tricky skill in itself. In light of the foregoing, a few suggestions may be called for.

   If in doubt about the size of steps you should use, always opt for smaller ones, especially in the early stages of the program. The child should experience clear success (and positive reinforcement) at one step before progressing onto the next one. Rearrangement of the hierarchy of steps is often needed; you should constantly evaluate the child's progress as he moves through the hierarchy, and if progress seems sluggish or if failure experiences are frequent, then consider rearranging the steps in the hierarchy or making them larger or smaller (cf. Gelfand & Hartmann, 1975; Karoly, 1975; Krumboltz & Krumboltz, 1972; Rimm & Masters, 1974). The essential concept of shaping is useful in most therapeutic work with children: do not wait for the perfect behavior—reward successive approximations to it.

Other interesting case studies utilizing shaping interventions for treating anxiety states and avoidance behaviors in children include the following: Allen, Hart, Buell, Harris, and Wolf (1964), Bauermeister and Jemail (1975), Miller and Miller (1976), Rasbury (1974), and Reid, Hawkins, Keutzer, McNeal, Phelps, Reid, and Mees (1967).

Stimulus Fading

Definition. Stimulus fading entails gradually changing the stimulus controlling a child's performance to another stimulus, usually with the intention of maintaining the performance without a loss or alteration under the new conditions (cf. White, 1971). For instance, Amy, the electively mute child discussed in the beginning of the chapter, was treated principally through a stimulus-fading procedure. The following brief description of Amy's treatment program should give readers the flavor of stimulus fading techniques (combined with some shaping procedures):

The most interesting aspect of the treatment procedure was a stimulus fading technique, with the fading done simultaneously across several stimulus and response dimensions. The therapy program started in a situation where Amy regularly talked (i.e., at home) and, through very gradual approximations, moved to a situation where Amy had never talked (i.e., at school with the teacher and entire class present). This technique bears some resemblance to those used successfully by Conrad et al. (1974) and Wulbert et al. (1973). The *teacher* implemented this technique daily and consulted with the author 2-3 times a week for advice and support. The therapy program lasted 3 months; it required considerable patience and persistence on the part of the teacher.

The stimulus and response dimensions used to successively approximate speaking in the classroom environment included the following: location, number of children present, response difficulty, response magnitude, and response frequency. The location hierarchy went from home to the school route to the school playground to the classroom. The number of children present hierarchy went from none to a close friend to a group of friends to the entire class. The response difficulty hierarchy went from one word responses (e.g., "Yes") to short answers (e.g., "Today is Friday") to short declarative statements (e.g., "I would like to go to the gym") to long spontaneous questions and statements (e.g., "I wonder why I am having so much trouble with this set of long division problems. Will you help me with this one?"). The response magnitude hierarchy went from whispers to normal conversation to loud statements. The response frequency hierarchy went from one answer or statement a day to several to several dozen. Thus, stimuli were gradually faded and responses were gradually shaped to resemble normal speech in a normal classroom.

The stimulus fading procedure was supplemented with a contingency contracting system. Both social and tangible rewards were used. Amy received these rewards contingent on her progress through the hierarchy of approximations to speaking in class. Amy's parents also provided intermittent rewards contingent on reports of her progress at school.

Outcome Results

The therapy program was a dramatic success. At the end of treatment Amy was talking frequently, fluently, and spontaneously in the classroom. Classroom observations by the author confirmed the teacher's optimistic reports. A group-administered IQ test, which was given post-treatment, yielded an IQ score of 117 for Amy. Some school personnel who had previously assumed Amy was retarded were now heard commenting on how bright she was. Everyone was pleased with the outcome.

A 15—month follow-up indicated Amy was still talking regularly in class. Her fourth grade teacher even complained that she talked *too* much! Furthermore, Amy had volunteered to play the part of Betsy Ross in a school play. She got the part and did a fine, verbose job (Richards, Note 2, pp. 3–5).

Stimulus fading shares shaping's gradual approach. In shaping the *response* requirements are gradually changed, whereas in stimulus fading the *stimulus* conditions controlling a response are gradually changed. When stimulus fading is used in the treatment of an anxiety state, extinction may play a role: the gradual approximation to stimuli that more and more resemble the condition eliciting anxiety may allow the child's fear to extinguish to each stimulus condition in the fading procedure (cf. the later section on systematic desensitization). Stimulus fading is one of several treatment procedures that could fit under the broader rubric of stimulus control (cf. Rimm & Masters, 1974; Thoresen & Mahoney, 1974; White,1971). Stimulus-fading procedures are often profitably (and sometimes necessarily) combined with positive reinforcement or punishment procedures, as the following case example illustrates.

Case Example. Wulbert, Nyman, Snow, and Owen (1973) detailed an interesting case of elective mutism treated by stimulus fading and contingency management. Emma was a 6-year-old electively mute child who had been in kindergarten for 8 months when the study began. Emma had not spoken in kindergarten, 1 year of preschool, or 3 years of Sunday school. "Although she lived just across the street from the school and played actively there, she had only to cross the street to become a pliable mannequin" (Wulbert et al., 1973, p. 436). At home Emma was fluent and would eagerly relate to her mother what had gone on during the day at school. Subtests of the WISC administered by her parents (under supervision) in the clinic and other related assessments indicated that Emma had the prerequisite skills for school, but was not implementing all of these skills in the presence of teachers, strangers, or most children.

This study investigated whether positive reinforcement for verbal behavior and time-out (having to sit in a time-out room for 1 minute—a mild punishment procedure) for nonresponse to requests for verbal behavior would be sufficient to generate verbalization in the presence of a stranger, or whether a stimulus fading procedure would be a necessary addition to the treatment package. Two alternating conditions were used in treating Emma. In one condition she received positive reinforcers for responding to requests for verbalizations and motor responses in the presence of someone (e.g., her mother) who already had stimulus control of these behaviors, while a stranger (e.g., a therapist) was gradually *faded into stimulus control*. In the other condition, a stranger imposed the same response requests and reinforcement contingencies, but the fading procedure was not used (and the mother was absent). Three 10-minute periods of both the fading and no-fading conditions were alternated in each treatment session. The steps used in fading the first therapist (experimenter) into stimulus control of Emma's verbal behavior are presented in Table 2.

Gradually, several other therapists, children from Emma's class, and her first-grade teacher were faded into stimulus control for Emma's verbal and motor behavior (both at the clinic and later at Emma's school). In addition, a time-out contingency for not responding to requests for verbalization was instituted (across both conditions) later in the treatment program.

The treatment program was quite successful, but the results indicated that the stimulus-fading procedure was a necessary component of the treatment package. The time-out contingency for nonresponding facilitated treatment when combined with stimulus fading, but was ineffective without stimulus fading. Following the treatment program, Emma would raise her hand when the teacher asked a question of the class and, if called on, would give a loud, clear verbal response.

Commentary. Stimulus fading can be very effective, but it is slow. The above study demonstrated that stimulus fading was an effective and necessary component of the treatment program for a behavior disorder— elective mutism—that is notoriously refractory to treatment (Reed, 1963; Yates, 1970). At the same time, several hundred trials were required to fade successive strangers into stimulus control for Emma's verbal behavior (see Figure 3, p. 441, in Wulbert et al., 1973). This takes patience!

Many of the comments made about shaping techniques apply here also. For instance, as with shaping, effective use of stimulus fading is in part an art: fading too quickly leads to child failures and setbacks; fading too slowly leads to discouragement for everyone. As with shaping, the steps in a stimulus-fading program should be gradual, and the child should experience success at one step before moving onto the next step (Gelfand & Hartmann, 1975; Krumboltz & Krumboltz, 1972). And finally, as with shaping, it may be profitable to associate pleasant conditions (e.g., having the mother present and providing praise and tangible rewards) with a stimulus fading program (particularly during the initial phase).

Other interesting references in this area include: Conrad, Delk, and Williams (1974), Jackson and Wallace (1974), Leitenberg and Callahan

Table 2
Graded Steps of Closeness Used in Fading an Experimenter into
Stimulus Control in a Stimulus Fading Program[a]

0. *Neither visible nor audible*
    A. Neither visible nor audible
    B. Not visible but audible over radio
        (saying, "ask Emma question#1 or give Emma direction#17")
    C. Not visible but audible both over radio and from hall
1. *Visible at door*
    A. Visible and audible standing in hall, turned 180° away from Emma
    B. Visible and audible standing in doorway, turned 180°
    C. Visible and audible standing inside room, with door closed, turned 180°
    D. Visible and audible inside room, door closed, turned 135°
    E. Visible and audible inside room, door closed, turned 90°
    F. Visible and audible inside room, door closed, turned 45°
    G. Visible and audible facing with dark glasses on
    H. Inside room with door closed, facing, radio off
2. *Inside room halfway to chair*
3. *Inside room standing at chair*
4. *Inside room sitting in chair*
5. *Reading questions in unison with person already in stimulus control*
    A. Inside room reading task items in unison with mother and/or handing cards
        together
    B. Inside room reading the critical element of the task item alone and/or
        handing cards together except mother drops hand before Emma takes
    C. Inside room reading the critical element of task alone, handing cards alone
6. *Reading questions alone while person in stimulus control remains seated at table*
    A. Inside room reading all the directions alone, holding and handing cards
    B. Inside room mother silent, but watching
    C. Inside room mother reading at table
7. *Reading questions alone while person in stimulus control moves away from the*
    table
    A. Inside room mother reading with chair away from table
    B. Inside room mother reading with chair beside door
    C. Inside room mother in doorway
    D. Inside room mother in hallway
8. *Inside room mother absent*

[a]From "The Efficacy of Stimulus Fading and Contingency Management in the Treatment of Elective
Mutism: A Case Study" (p. 437) by M. Wulbert, B. A. Nyman, D. Snow, and Y. Owen, *Journal of
Applied Behavior Analysis*, 1973, *6*, 435–441 Copyright 1973 by the Society for the Experimental
Analysis of Behavior, Inc. Reprinted by permission.

(1973), Montenegro (1968), Neisworth, Madle, and Goeke (1975), and
Reid et al. (1967).

Modeling

Definition. Therapeutic modeling entails demonstrating an appropriate
response to a child and then asking the child to imitate the performance.

The therapist (or whoever is demonstrating the target behavior) is designated as the model, and the child is said to be modeling or imitating. Modeling is successfully accomplished when the child's behavior reliably matches that of the model. For instance, a therapist might demonstrate fearless and competent dog-handling skills while a child who was dog phobic and deficient in dog-handling skills stood nearby and watched. Later the child might be asked to imitate gradually the therapists' performance with the dog. This technique has been around for a while, and it will seem familiar to most parents and teachers who have, for example, taught teenagers how to drive. Yet the last 15 years have witnessed an enormous increase in the systematic research on modeling, the development of effective procedural variations and adjuncts, and the application of modeling to the treatment of anxious and withdrawn children (Bandura, 1969, 1971a, 1976; Flanders, 1968; Gelfand, in press; Kirkland & Thelen, in press; Krasner, 1971; Marlatt & Perry, 1975; Rachman, 1972; Rimm & Masters, 1974; Rosenthal, 1976; Ross, 1974).

A large number of technical variations, procedural adjuncts, and terminological synonyms are available for modeling techniques. Some of the technical variations include live modeling versus symbolic modeling (via films, videotapes, or imagery), coping versus mastery models, gradual versus sudden exposure, *in vivo* versus contrived situations, and guided versus autonomous participation (by the child). Some of the treatment procedures used in an adjunctive fashion with modeling are positive reinforcement, shaping, physical prompting, immediate behavioral rehearsal, role playing, systematic desensitization, and self-control techniques. The terminological synonyms for modeling include observational learning, vicarious learning, and imitation. Modeling can be a very powerful behavior change procedure, as the following case example illustrates.

Case Example. Melamed and Siegel (1975) explored the effectiveness of filmed modeling as a therapeutic method for reducing the anxiety that children frequently experience when they are admitted to a medical hospital. Given that anxiety-based behavior disorders are often observed in hospitalized children and that such disorders are prognostic of additional difficulties in recovering from surgery, it does not require a polemic to be convinced this is a very important treatment area.

The participants in this investigation were 60 children between the ages of 4 and 12 who were admitted to pediatric hospitals for elective surgery. These children had no prior history of hospitalization and were scheduled for tonsillectomies, hernia operations, or urinary-genital tract surgery. Thirty children matched for age, sex, race, and type of operation were assigned to the experimental and control groups. Numerous self-report, physiological, and behavioral outcome measures were used "in order to assess the various response classes considered to reflect the multidimensional nature of anxiety" (Melamed & Siegel, 1975, p. 513). Prior to their admission to the hospital, children in the experimental and control groups viewed one of the two films described below:

The experimental film, entitled *Ethan Has an Operation*, depicts a 7-year-old white male who has been hospitalized for a hernia operation. This film, which is 16 minutes in length, consists of 15 scenes showing various events that most children encounter when hospitalized for elective surgery from the time of admission to time of discharge including the child's orientation to the hospital ward and medical personnel such as the surgeon and anesthesiologist; having a blood test and exposure to standard hospital equipment; separation from the mother; and scenes in the operating and recovery rooms. In addition to explanations of the hospital procedures provided by the medical staff, various scenes are narrated by the child, who describes his feelings and concerns that he had at each stage of the hospital experience. Both the child's behavior and verbal remarks exemplify the behavior of a coping model so that while he exhibits some anxiety and apprehension, he is able to overcome his initial fears and complete each event in a successful and nonanxious manner. Meichenbaum (1971) has shown that film models who are initially anxious and overcome their anxiety (coping models) result in greater reduction in anxiety than models who exhibit no fear (mastery models).

The subjects in the control group were shown a 12-minute film entitled *Living Things are Everywhere*. The control film was similar in interest value to the experimental film in maintaining the children's attention but was unrelated in content to hospitalization. It presents the experiences of a white preadolescent male who is followed on a nature trip in the country (Melamed & Siegel, 1975, pp. 514–515)[5]

Later in the day, following formal admission to the hospital, *all* children were given preoperative instruction by the hospital staff, a common procedure at pediatric hospitals. This instruction consisted of a nurse explaining, via pictures and demonstrations, what would happen to the child on the day of surgery.

To evaluate the modeling and control films, the childrens' anxiety was assessed at several points during and following their hospitalization. State measures of anxiety revealed a significant reduction of preoperative and postoperative fear arousal for the children who observed the peer-modeling film, but not for the children who observed the control film. Children in the modeling group evidenced lower sweat-gland activity, fewer self-reported medical fears, and less anxiety-related behavior than children in the control group, and these results were obtained both the night before surgery and at a 1-month post-surgical examination. Figure 2 clearly illustrates the effectiveness of the modeling film in alleviating anxiety as assessed by a physiological measure—the palmar sweat index. Moreover, only parents of control group children reported a significant increment in the frequency of child behavior problems following hospitalization.

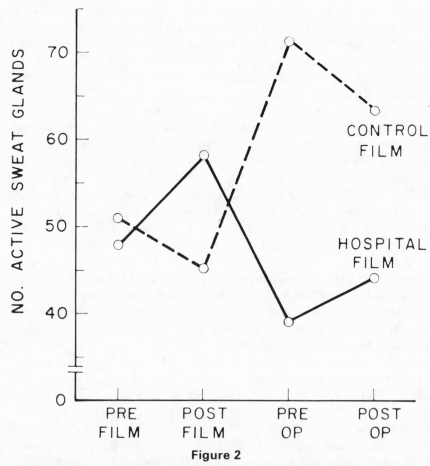

Figure 2

Number of active sweat glands for the experimental and control groups across the four measurement periods. Children about to undergo elective surgery were shown either a relevant peer modeling film of a child being hospitalized and receiving surgery or an unrelated control film. (From "Reduction of Anxiety in Children Facing Hospitalization and Surgery by Use of Filmed Modeling" [p. 516] by B. G. Melamed and L. J. Siegel, *Journal of Consulting and Clinical Psychology,* 1975, *43,* 511–521. Copyright 1975 by the American Psychological Association. Reprinted by permission.)

This study demonstrates that (a) post-hospital traumatization, as reflected in psychological disturbances, may occur unless extensive pre-operative preparations are administered and (b) filmed modeling is one highly effective preoperative preparation. The results also have preventative implications: filmed modeling may be used as a prevention method to help children cope with upcoming stress situations and thus avoid the development of debilitating fears.

Commentary. Modeling is a powerful treatment intervention for anxious and withdrawn children, especially when used in concert with other behavioral techniques such as positive reinforcement, shaping, and immediate behavioral rehearsal. Witness a recent statement by Albert Bandura, an internationally recognized authority on modeling research and procedures: "Regardless of whether deficits or defensiveness is the problem of concern, modeling, supplemented with guided performance and reinforcing consequences, is the *most* powerful means of effecting psychological change" (Bandura, 1976, p. 264, emphasis added). Strong words! We do not have to accept Bandura's seemingly effusive enthusiasm for modeling to acknowledge that optimistic reviews of the technique abound and evidence for its effectiveness is overwhelming (Bandura, 1969, 1971a, 1976; Gelfand, in press, Gelfand & Hartmann, 1975; Kirkland & Thelen, in press; Krasner, 1971; Marlatt & Perry, 1975; Rachman, 1972; Rimm & Masters, 1974; Rosenthal, 1976; Ullmann & Krasner, 1975). Modeling is effective, efficient, and versatile—useful for both reducing anxiety states and increasing social behaviors. There are some instances (usually involving shy and withdrawn children; see Gelfand, in press) of treatment failures where modeling was used, however, and therefore, some guidelines for the therapeutic use of modeling would seem apropos here.

The choice of a model is very important. Although live models may increase the attention, involvement, and motivation of the observer, symbolic models offer the advantages of efficiency, practicality, standardization, and increased therapist control over presentation (Marlatt & Perry, 1975). Tapes, after all, afford the opportunity for editing, narration, and repeated use. The lack of therapist control implied by live modeling could be troublesome: "Of course it would prove therapeutically disastrous should the [live] animal confirm the fearful observer's apprehensions by snarling at or biting one of the models" (Gelfand, in press, p. 12).[6] Competent and fearless models—who are very skilled at handling the phobic stimuli—are critical when live modeling is being attempted. Symbolic modeling has many assets, and it has often been found to be about as effective as live modeling; but, we should remain cognizant of the admonition by Miller et al. (1974) that with phobic children "confrontation [with the real phobic stimuli] is an absolutely necessary aspect of treatment, as well as measure of its success" (p. 125).

The characteristics of a model are also an important consideration. Models that are prestigious, pleasant, competent, and of an appropriate age usually enhance the modeling effect (Gelfand, in press; Krumboltz & Krumboltz, 1972; Marlatt & Perry, 1975; Thelen & Kirkland, 1976). Perceived similarity between the observer and the model also generally increases modeling effects (Flanders, 1968), as does the use of multiple models (Bandura, 1971b; Rachman, 1972). Coping rather than mastery models are probably preferable. With shy and withdrawn children, "effective modeling demonstrations have presented peer models as initially highly similar to the unskilled observers, but as increasingly assertive and successful" (Gelfand, in press, p. 38). Meichenbaum (1971) has found that coping models, who initially display anxiety but subsequently overcome their fears and complete a task in a competent manner, are more therapeutically effective than mastery models who never displayed any anxiety or ineffectiveness in the first place. Finally, Gelfand (in press) suggests that shy children are best treated (when using modeling techniques) in groups with normally assertive peers rather than in groups consisting solely of social isolates.

How the model is presented also has treatment implications:

> The model should be presented so as to maximize the observer's *attention* to and *retention* of the model's behavior. Attention may be aided by choosing an appropriate context free from distraction, and by highlighting the model's behavior through the use of preliminary instructions and narration of the key features of the model's performance, If the model is engaging in behaviors which are likely to make the observer anxious, supplementary instructions in relaxation may enhance attention to the model. The observer is also more likely to attend to the model if he is *uncertain* about how to perform the behavior himself and needs information in order to respond appropriately (Marlatt & Perry, 1975, p. 153).

Indeed, an important function of modeling is the information that it provides to the child. Modeling provides information regarding the exact nature of the feared situation and suggests alternative patterns of responding to such situations.

One of the best ways to inject modeling treatments with a high degree of potency is to include guided practice of the target behavior during or immediately following the model's performance. Bandura (1976) has argued that the combination of modeling and guided reinforced practice (which he calls "participant modeling") is *the* most powerful modeling treatment, and he has marshalled considerable evidence to support his claim. Participant modeling is a carefully structured and graduated process in which modeled performances by the therapist (or some other model) are immediately imitated and practiced by the child under gradually more difficult and real-life conditions, with the therapist initially providing extensive encouragement, physical or verbal prompts, information feedback, and positive reinforcement for the child's practice attempts:

> Desired activities are repeatedly modeled, preferably by different models, who demonstrate progressively more difficult performances. In competence training, complex patterns of behavior are broken down into requisite subskills and organized hierarchically to ensure optimal progress. To eliminate inappropriate fears and inhibitions, anxious individuals observe models engaging in threatening activities without experiencing any adverse consequences. . . .
> After the demonstration, individuals are provided with necessary guidance and ample opportunities to enact the modeled behaviors under favorable conditions at

each step until they perform them skillfully and spontaneously. Various response-induction aids are used whenever needed to assist participants through difficult performances (Bandura, 1976, p. 248).

Positive reinforcement and graduated situations likely to produce success experiences are also carefully programmed into this process. Finally, Bandura and his associates have found that behavior change can be accelerated and generalization can be enhanced via the adjunctive procedures of "response-induction aids" (e.g., prompts, joint performance with the therapist, and protective gear [gloves, etc.]) and "self-directed performance" (e.g., additional self-directed practice with a variety of situations, following the initial participant modeling treatment; see Bandura, 1976; Bandura, Jeffery, & Gajdos, 1975; Bandura , Jeffery, & Wright, 1974).

We would like to conclude this section of the chapter with the caveat that modeling processes are inevitable and that incidental modeling effects will occur in any treatment situation. Often, therapists (and teachers, parents, peers, etc.) serve—unwittingly at times—as "role models" for children, and therefore, special attention should be given to the therapeutic ramifications of this phenomenon (Krumboltz & Krumboltz, 1972; Marlatt & Perry, 1975).

There are a lot of investigations and case studies on therapeutic modeling, other than those already mentioned. Some of the better ones relevant to anxiety and withdrawl disorders follow: Bandura, Grusec, and Menlove (1967), Bandura and Menlove (1968), Evers and Schwarz (1973), Higgins, Sawtell, Simon, and Simeonsson (1973), Hill, Liebert, and Mott (1968), Hosford (1969), Keller and Carlson (1974), Kornhaber and Schroeder (1975), Lewis (1974), Melamed, Hawes, Heiby, and Glick (1975), O'Connor (1969, 1972), Ritter (1968), Vernon (1974), and Weissbrod and Bryan (1973).

Systematic Desensitization

Definition. Systematic desensitization is comprised of three basic steps. First, the client is trained to relax, usually through some form of progressive relaxation training (cf. Bernstein & Borkovec, 1973; Rimm & Masters, 1974). Second, a hierarchy of stimuli is compiled representing the stimuli that elicit the anxiety, phobia, or withdrawal behavior. Stimuli in the hierarchy are ordered from least to most anxiety producing. Third, while in a state of deep muscle relaxation, the client imagines the scenes in the hierarchy, starting with the least provoking one and gradually progressing through the hierarchy to the most provoking one. Usually, the client is not allowed to progress to a new hierarchy item until feeling comfortable with the previous one. Hence, the rapidity of progress through the hierarchy is largely governed by the client (cf. Bandura, 1969; Goldfried & Davison, 1976; Morris, 1975; Wolpe, 1973). Systematic desensitization is frequently studied and frequently used (Krasner, 1971). Variations of the systematic desensitization procedure are common, especially in terms of hierarchy formation and stimulus presentation. With children, alternative forms of relaxation induction, such as emotive imagery, are also common. (Emotive imagery is essentially a story-telling technique directed by the therapist, with the child imagining pleasant scenes from the story; see Lazarus & Abramovitz, 1962; Ploeg, 1975.) Finally, systematic desensitization bears some relation to several other fear-reduction procedures, such as extinction, symbolic modeling, and implosive therapy. (Implosive therapy is also sometimes referred to as "flooding" and entails immediate and repeated exposure to extreme forms of the feared stimulus; see Smith & Sharpe, 1970.) This section of the chapter focuses on systematic desensitization only, but some references relevant to emotive imagery and implosion will be provided at the end of the section. Although outcome research on the use of systematic desensitization with children is not as extensive or optimistic as that available for adults (see Miller et al., 1974; Morris, 1975; O'Leary & Wilson, 1975; Ross, 1974), and although systematic desensitization often must undergo procedural modifications (e.g., regarding relaxation training and imagery utilization) before it can be used with young children (Gelfand, in press), there are still some instances in which systematic desensitization can be profitably applied to the treatment of phobic or withdrawn children. The following case example is one such instance.

Case Example. Stedman (1976) provides an interesting case study of systematic desensitization with a school phobic child. Alice, a 9-year-old girl, became extremely anxious in any school situation requiring her to perform a new or poorly mastered academic task in front of a class. Reading class and music class were two such situations, and she was avoiding these anxiety-producing situations by leaving school before these classes. This had been occurring for several weeks when the therapist became involved. Additionally, it became clear that Alice's mother reinforced both Alice's school-leaving behavior and her dependent behavior in general. Alice's father punished her nightly for her school phobia, and he was rapidly taking on aversive properties for Alice.

Behavioral interventions for Alice's school phobia included two desensitization programs, a standard systematic desensitization program using an imagined hierarchy and an *in vivo* desensitization program implemented by a teacher in the school setting. A contingency contracting system was also implemented, by the parents, to reinforce Alice's school attendance. Treatment entailed 16 face-to-face meetings with Alice and her family and 2 meetings with school personnel.

The systematic desensitization program followed the standard procedure outlined in the foregoing definition section and was aimed at the main precipitant of Alice's present school avoidance—music class. Alice was successfully trained in deep muscle relaxation, and a hierarchy was developed that focused on music class, but had a general theme on performance of unfamiliar or complex school work in front of peers and teachers. Excerpts from this hierarchy are presented in Table 3. Systematic desensitization was begun in the third therapy session and continued through the fourteenth session, with Alice progressing through the hierarchy while deeply relaxed from the muscle-relaxation procedures. This program followed conventional desensitization lines, and Alice reported progressive anxiety reduction as she moved through the hierarchy.

Starting conjointly with the eighth therapy session, Alice's teachers were incorporated in an *in vivo* desensitization program, which ran concurrently with the imagery-based systematic desensitization program. This *in vivo* program, carried out in (or near) the school setting, had the following steps: (1) Alice's music teacher would tutor her outside the school setting until she reached a level equal to that of the class. (2) Alice would reenter music class for 20-minute periods but would not be required to play her recorder. (3) Alice would remain in music class for the full time and would play the recorder (Stedman, 1976, p. 285).

Table 3
Excerpts from a Music Class and Academic Hierarchy
used in a Systematic Desensitization Program[a]

1. I am at home at night thinking about sitting in music class watching the others play their recorders . . .
5. I am in music class with the teacher by herself. I am playing an easy, familiar tune on my recorder, and the teacher looks pleased . . .
9. I am in music class with the teacher by herself. I am playing a hard tune on which I make many mistakes, and the teacher looks slightly displeased . . .
14. I am in music class with the teacher and all the students. I am playing an easy tune in front of the class, with the teacher watching me . . .
18. I am in front of the music class, playing a fairly hard tune on which I make many mistakes, and several students smile and laugh . . .
22. I have played poorly in front of the music class, and the teacher corrects me after class for a poor performance . . .
26. I am in reading class, and the teacher calls on me to stand up and read. I stumble over words, while several students laugh at me and the teacher looks impatient . . .
29. I am in reading class, and the teacher calls on me to stand up and read. I stumble over words, and the teacher asks me to sit down and comments that I should know the work. The whole class laughs.

[a]From "Family Counseling with a School-Phobic Child" by J. M. Stedman, in J. D. Krumboltz and C. E. Thoresen (Eds.), *Counseling methods* (p. 285). New York: Holt, Rinehart & Winston, 1976. Copyright 1976 by Holt, Rinehart & Winston. Reprinted by permission.

This multifaceted treatment program was successful, and Alice started attending all classes regularly and reported little further anxiety in doing so. A 2-year follow-up indicated that this successful outcome had been maintained and Alice was even leading her classmates in singing at the school mass.

Commentary. Systematic desensitization enjoys considerable case-study support for use with anxious and withdrawn children, but, unfortunately, controlled experimental studies with children are almost as rare as snow in August. The few controlled studies that do exist do not argue strongly for the superiority of systematic desensitization over other therapeutic procedures or even over control groups.[7] However, systematic desensitization's gradual nature, imagery-based hierarchies, and the pleasant conditions that are usually associated with it (muscle relaxation, attention from the therapist, praise, etc.), all yield a fear-reduction procedure that children find fairly nonthreatening and palatable. When combined with other techniques such as positive reinforcement, and when tied to eventual real-world (*in vivo*) confrontation and practice with the fear-provoking stimuli, systematic desensitization is a useful technique in the child clinician's armamentarium.

This clinical procedure is not without problems, however. Sometimes it is difficult to teach young children the muscle relaxation and imagery control aspects of the treatment procedure. It is partly with this in mind that related but alternative fear-reduction techniques such as emotive imagery, *in vivo* desensitization, and implosive therapy are utilized with children. Some therapists find the desensitization procedure boring, and some adolescents find it absurd (Miller et al., 1974). Systematic desensitization requires a degree of client cooperation and enthusiasm that children may not always be inclined to give. Therapists who are enamored with systematic desensitization procedures occasionally down-play or even ignore skill deficits; this would be a blunder in most severe cases of social withdrawal. Indeed, in the case study described above, clear improvements in Alice's reading and music classes resulted from some rather adventitious skill training that occurred during the systematic desensitization program (see Stedman, 1976, pp. 284, 286). Finally, systematic desensitization may be overly elaborate and inefficient for treating most phobias in *young* children, given the efficiency and high cure rates of other procedures (such as positive reinforcement and *in vivo* modeling) with this population (Gelfand, in press; Miller et al., 1974). Lest the reader decide that the happy solution to all of this is to switch to implosive therapy, it should be pointed out that experts have their qualms about this technique also:

We imploded three adolescent school-phobics with one success, one partial success, and one failure. For reasons other than the outcome of these efforts, we discontinued our program, but these results do not point to implosion as a panacea. *Where systematic desensitization is dull, Implosive Therapy is nerve-wracking when it works well.* Once, during the implosion of a case, the therapist broke off the procedure and recommended to observing colleagues that the implosion be stopped and the child hospitalized. He was urged to continue, however, and did so with a successful outcome (Miller et al., 1974, pp. 122–123, emphasis added).

Systematic desensitization may be slow and a bit boring, but it is safe, and little advice beyond that implied above is needed. Hierarchy construction should be done very carefully,[8] and if difficulties with relaxation training or imagery control develop, the therapist should move on to alternative procedures. Finally, with phobic children the therapy program at some point should always include confrontation and practice with the actual phobic stimuli in real-world settings (Miller et al., 1974).

Other useful illustrations of systematic desensitization and related procedures with children include: Barabasz (1973), Croghan and Musante (1975), Garvey and Hegrenes (1966), Kelley (1976), Kondas (1967), Lazarus et al. (1965), Miller (1972), Montenegro (1968), Ritter (1968), and Tasto (1969) for systematic desensitization; Kissel (1972), Lazarus and Abramovitz (1962), Ploeg (1975), and Weinstein (1976) for emotive imagery;[9] and Hersen (1968), Ollendick and Gruen (1972), and Smith and Sharpe (1970) for implosive therapy.

Punishment

Definition. Punishment involves presenting an aversive stimulus (negative reinforcer) contingent on the emission of an undesirable response or removing a pleasant stimulus (positive reinforcer) contingent on the emission of an undesirable response.[10] For instance, a child could temporarily lose customary privileges contingent on refusing to go to school. A mild punishment procedure, 1-minute isolation periods or "time-out," was utilized in the Wulbert et al. (1973) study described in the stimulus-fading section. It may be recalled that they found time-out facilitated treatment when combined with stimulus fading (and positive reinforcement for correct responding) but was ineffective when used by itself. Punishment is one of several potential aversive conditioning procedures. (See Halpern, Hammond, & Cohen, 1972, for an example of another aversive technique—an escape conditioning procedure with highly aversive overtones.) Along with positive and negative reinforcement, punishment is also one of several possible contingency management procedures. Punishment has been used (probably overused) for thousands of years; nevertheless, when combined with other procedures, such as positive reinforcement for appropriate behavior, punishment will often effectively suppress inappropriate behavior (Bandura, 1969; Gelfand, in press). The following case example illustrates such a procedural combination.

Case Example. Tobey and Thoresen (1976) described a multifaceted treatment program, including punishment, for a boy with multiple problems, including school avoidance and withdrawn behavior toward verbal interactions with adults. Bill was a 9-year-old ward of the juvenile court and was referred to a family-style residential treatment facility for delinquent and emotionally disturbed children, directed by Tobey and Thoresen. Their treatment facility was called "Learning House." Bill had just spent 3 months in a local juvenile detention facility, and he had been in trouble with juvenile authorities since the age of 6. He was aggressive with peers, he rarely attended school, he was difficult to control, and he spoke in nearly inaudible tones and evidenced considerable fear when dealing with most adults.

The treatment program at Learning House included contingency contracting via a refined point system (somewhat like a "token economy"), detailed behavioral observation, teacher consultation, and parent counseling. Professionally trained married couples served as "teaching parents" at Learning House (cf. Fixsen, Phillips, Phillips, & Wolf, 1976).

The point system provided explicit measures and consequences for important child behaviors. The first section of Table 4 indicates a small sample of the behaviors that were recorded and the consequences they received. Notice that points could be earned *or* lost; the point system thus included provisions for both positive reinforcement and punishment. The second part of Table 4 protrays a typical daily point card, indicating the points earned and lost for that day. The final section of Table 4 presents a small sample of the privileges for which the points could be exchanged.

Bill's school avoidance and related behavior brought the punishment aspects of this point system into play. When school started after Christmas, Bill reluctancly agreed to attend, but he never actually showed up at school. The teaching parents were immediately informed of this and therefore knew Bill was lying when he came home an hour later and said "he had been 'sent home by the principal' " (Tobey and Thoresen, 1976, p. 167). Bill was then told how many points he lost for lying and for not attending school. A rather extensive temper tantrum then ensued on Bill's part, which resulted in further fines and use of a time-out room with the instructions that " 'when you can be quiet, that means no noise at all, for at least three minutes, then you can come out' " (Tobey and Thoresen, 1976, p. 168). Bill had a couple more outbursts, but he soon settled down and he returned to school the same day. He apparently had learned that the teaching parents words and deeds were consistent and that they were not going to be manipulated by his tantrum behavior—they would just calmly and consistently punish it (as would his school teacher). Bill rarely missed school after this, and follow-ups during and after his stay at Learning House indicated he was doing well at school; his teacher eventually even made the comment that " 'he serves as an excellent role model for many of my problem children' " (Tobey & Thoresen, 1976, p. 173). This was no small improvement![11]

Commentary. Punishment can be a powerful and rapid procedure for suppressing behavior. For both practical and ethical reasons, however, it should usually be a method of last resort, and it should always be combined with other procedures, particularly positive reinforcement for incompatible or alternative behavior (Gelfand & Hartmann, 1975; Krumboltz & Krumboltz, 1972). Aversive conditioning procedures may account for much of the ethical turbulence surrounding behavior therapy (cf. Bandura, 1969; Krasner, 1971; Stolz, Wienckowski, & Brown, 1975). Such procedures may be particularly uncalled for in treating children suffering from anxiety states and avoidance behaviors, since they can actually *produce* or *exacerbate* anxiety and avoidance (Gelfand, in press; Krumboltz & Krumboltz, 1972; Miller et al., 1974). The debatable assets of punishment are even reflected in an editors' footnote to the foregoing Tobey and Thoresen (1976) case example: "*Editors' note*: A controversial feature of this point system is that points are subtracted for undesired behavior, thus introducing a mild form of punishment of the child" (Krumboltz & Thoresen, 1976, p. 165). Another drawback of punishment

Table 4
Outline of a Contingency Contracting System
Including Punishment Procedures[a]

SAMPLE OF OBSERVED BEHAVIORS AND THEIR POINT CONSEQUENCES

Behavior	Points Earned or Lost
Social	
cooperative play	+1000/30 minutes
temper (slamming objects, voice out of control)	−500
interrupting another	−500
volunteering to help	+500
lying	−1000
good hygieve (washing face, hands, brushing teeth)	+1000
Maintenance	
setting table	+500
putting groceries away	+300/sack
vacuuming	+1000–2500
washing dishes	+3000–4000
Academic	
late leaving for school	−100/minute
homework (at home)	+5000/hour
trouble call from school	−10,000

THE DAILY POINT CARD

Points Made	Code	Description of Behavior	Points Giver	Points Lost	Code	Description of Behavior	Points Taker
1250	A	Reading	KT	400	S	Late to bed	KJ
1000	S	Quiet bedtime	KT	300	S	Neg comment	BJ
500	M	Good manners	KT	300	A	Being mean	BJ
500	S	Neat appearance	KT	300	S	Name calling	KJ
1000	S	Early to school	KT	500	S	Back talk	KJ
4000	A	Good school report	KT	1000	S	Swearing	KJ
2500	A	Reading	KT	1000	S	Lying	KJ
500	A	Homework	KT	500	S	Back talk	KJ
5000	A	Reading	KT				
500	M	Making rice	BJ				
200	S	Answering phone	BJ				

PARTIAL LIST OF PRIVILEGES ON WEEKLY SYSTEM

Privilege	Weekly Point Exchange
"Basics" (care privileges)	1,500
going outdoors on Learning House property	
using telephone to call friends in the	
local area (all calls to parents must	
be approved by teaching parent)	
using house games in study room and sports	
equipment on Learning House grounds	
using radio and record player	
Bedtime stories	1,500
Television time	5,000
Use of bicycles	4,000
Allowance $.50/week	5,000
$1.00/week	10,000

[a]From "Helping Bill Reduce Aggressive Behaviors: A Nine-Year-Old Makes Good" by T. S. Tobey and C. E. Thoresen, in J. D. Krumboltz and C. E. Thoresen (Eds.), *Counseling methods* (pp. 164–165). New York: Holt, Rinehart & Winston, 1976. Copyright 1976 by Holt, Rinehart & Winston. Reprinted by permission.

involves the somewhat unpredictable effects and side-effects it may have (especially physical punishment); these side-effects can include the *punisher* becoming aversive to the child because of his association with the aversive stimuli or the punishment process becoming *rewarding* to the child because of all the extra adult and peer attention it entails.

If punishment techniques are used, a few more rules of thumb deserve mention. First, many of the suggestions made for positive reinforcement contingency systems (e.g., immediate consequences) apply to punishment contingency systems also. Second, trying to teach *new* behaviors via some punishment system will be an unpleasant exercise in futility; punishment can suppress present behaviors, but it cannot systematically develop new desirable behaviors. Tobey and Thoresen (1976, p. 172) clearly understood this, for although they used punishment to reduce critical behaviors like school avoidance and temper outbursts, they used procedures such as modeling, role playing, and positive reinforcement to increase and improve Bill's verbal interactions with adults. Try to use alternatives to physical punishment such as "time-out" from positive reinforcement (cf. Krumboltz & Thoresen, 1976, p. 168, footnote 8). Try to eliminate any positive reinforcers for inappropriate behavior (Karoly, 1975; Rimm & Masters, 1974). Do not threaten to punish unless you really will. Be suspicious if punishment does not evidence rapid effects, for when it works at all, it tends to work quickly. Finally, and most important, *always* provide alternatives that can be positively reinforced when using punishment procedures.

Other case studies demonstrating the use of aversive conditioning techniques with phobic or withdrawn children include: Halpern et al. (1972) and Kooy and Webster (1975).

Physical Prompting

Definition. Physical prompting entails the provision of physical guidance and cues for teaching the progressive steps of a target behavior (Gelfand, in press; Ullmann & Krasner, 1975). For instance, Buell and her colleagues (Buell, Stoddard, Harris, & Baer, 1968) used physical prompting in teaching a preschool girl to use outdoor play equipment. They prompted this girl by lifting her onto the play equipment and holding her there briefly. Once the girl was in the appropriate position she received praise and other positive reinforcers from her teachers. Physical prompting is almost always combined with procedures such as positive reinforcement, shaping, and *in vivo* modeling. In most cases physical prompts are gradually withdrawn after the target behavior has been established and has received some reinforcement. Physical prompting is particularly useful with very young children or institutionalized children (e.g., retarded and autistic children) who are socially withdrawn. The following case nicely exemplifies the use of physical prompting and shaping to develop hand waving, a worthwhile social greeting, in four retarded children.

Case Example. Stokes, Baer, and Jackson (1974) utilized a multiple-baseline design to investigate both the training effects of prompting and shaping and the generalization effects of multiple trainers; their goal was to teach a greeting response to retarded children. The four children in the study, ages 10 to 13, were severely retarded and were permanent residents of a state institution. These children had no useful form of social greeting behavior at the initiation of the study. Stokes et al. (1974) decided the hand wave would be a useful social greeting to teach these children. The following operational definition of a hand wave illustrates the explicit, specifiable target response definitions that are a typical and commendable characteristic of the operant literature. It also provides a good example (in emphasis) of a physically prompted response:

A response was scored as a wave if it met the following criteria: (1) the hand, which had to be empty, was raised above elbow level; and (2) there were at least two back-and-forth motions, either of a single arm from the shoulder or elbow, or a single hand from the wrist, mainly in the vertical plane, which did not contact any part of the subject's body or any other person or object.

Two specific exclusions were made: pointing responses in which a single finger was outstretched, and fending-off responses resembling the gesture of a police officer halting traffic.

All responses were classified in one of three ways: (1) *spontaneous* response: a correct response emitted within 10 sec of the trainer or prober and the subject coming within 3 ft (0.9 m) of one another; or (2) *prompted* response; a correct response emitted only after some visual and/or manipulative prompt by the trainer, such as holding the reinforcer in front of the subject, or *taking his arm and moving it through the motions of the defined wave response*; or (3) *incorrect* response: any response within the specified 10 sec that did not meet the definition requirements (Stokes et al., 1974, p. 600, emphasis added).

Training was carried out in several settings. Initial sessions were in a small room where a large number of responses were prompted, reinforced, and shaped to successively approximate the greeting response. Latter sessions were in a dormitory playroom, corridor, and courtyard. About 20 training contacts were made each day, and each contact adhered to the following conditions:

The subject was approached within 3 ft (0.9 m) at times when he was standing or sitting, but not lying or running. The trainer or prober always stood within the subject's field of vision. A contact lasted for 10 sec, or until a greeting response was given, whichever was first (Stokes et al., 1974, p. 601).

There were no time limits governing the frequency of contacts during the first training day, and the breaks between contacts ranged from a few seconds to a few minutes, with these breaks becoming progressively longer (eventually over 15 minutes) as training continued.

As is often the case with physical prompting interventions, prompts were gradually faded and positive reinforcement was provided for successive approximations to the target behavior. Physical prompts were used very liberally during the first few days of training and then were gradually decreased. Prompts were not used at all once the greeting response was fully developed. Potato chips, candy, smiles, verbal responses (e.g., "Hello Wayne"), and physical contact (e.g., a pat on the head) were used as positive reinforcers and were delivered on a continuous schedule (i.e., after each spontaneous or prompted greeting response).

This behavioral intervention had clear and dramatic effects, as is evident in Figure 3. The multiple-baseline design demonstrated a reliable training effect, which took place dramatically when and only when the first trainer intervened with each child (see "E_1 TRG" in Figure 3). Figure 3 also demonstrates, however, that high levels of generalization to about 20 staff members who had not participated in training the response (see "Probers" in Figure 3) only occurred *after* a second trainer taught and maintained the response in conjunction with the first trainer (see "$E_1 + E_2$TRG" in Figure 3). This programmed generalization occurred over measurement periods ranging from 1 to 6 months. One of the children ("Kerry" in Figure 3) never received training from the second trainer but, nevertheless, evidenced similar generalization results following a second intensive training phase by the first trainer.

This study is a good example of the utility of physical prompting (plus shaping) with retarded children, and it is a beautiful example of a multiple-baseline design in applied research. As the authors succinctly summarize:

> No shift from near-zero baseline levels was seen in any subject before training; no subject failed to shift promptly after the training; three of four subjects required two trainers' input before extensive generalization, yet training by one or two trainers occurred at different times and after different numbers of baseline days for each subject (Stokes et al., 1974, p. 608).

Perhaps the most important implication of this study is that generalization can be enhanced considerably by training with a few trainers, rather than with just one.

Commentary. Physical prompting, its uses, potential, and abuses, may appear so straightforward as to defy meaningful commentary. Nevertheless, we offer a few laconic remarks. Physical prompting should only be used when it is obviously necessary, and if some minimal prompting and cueing is all that is needed, verbal and visual prompts are usually preferable to physical ones. The prompt should be simple and clear. One very important recommendation is that physical prompts be gentle and done in as pleasant a manner and context as possible. Children often want to be independent and will readily interpret a therapist's deliberate physical prompts as an effort to over control, perhaps even "coerce." Adolescents may be particularly sensitive to physical and verbal prompts and may perceive them as a challenge to their identity and personal judgement. Finally, physical prompting should always be meshed with other therapeutic procedures such as positive reinforcement, shaping, and modeling, with the prompting gradually faded out as the target behavior becomes established and reinforced.

Other valuable references on this topic include the following: Kennedy (1965), Lovaas (1976), and Whitman, Mercurio, and Caponigri (1970).

Self-Control

Definition. Unlike the behavioral techniques discussed so far in this chapter, behavioral self-control embodies more of a general approach and

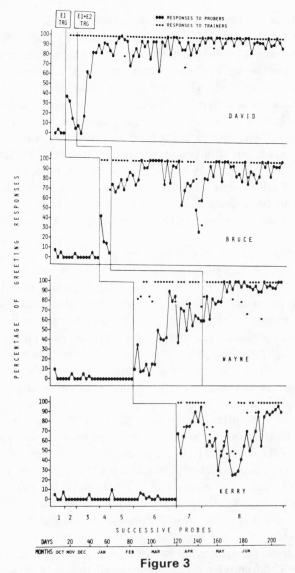

Figure 3

Generalization of greetings to probers, and maintenance by trainers (who employed prompting and shaping procedures to develop a hand-waving greeting response), as a percentage of contacts made, across the four subjects of the study. In the case of Bruce, two probe points just subsequent to Day 140 are not connected to the other points. These represent two probes conducted during a 3-day period of increased drug administration aimed at controlling disruptive behavior. (From "Programming the Generalization of a Greeting Response in Four Retarded Children" [p. 603] by T. F. Stokes, D. M. Baer, and R. L. Jackson, *Journal of Applied Behavior Analysis*, 1974, *7*, 599–610. Copyright 1974 by the Society for the Experimental Analysis of Behavior, Inc. Reprinted by permission.)

treatment strategy, rather than a specific technique. A simple (perhaps overly simple) definition of self-control was provided by Richards (1976): "Developing behavioral self-control entails learning to become one's own therapist and teacher by making specific responses that modify other personal responses" (p. 462). Thus self-control is not so much identified with a particular technique as it is with a treatment *strategy* that endeavors to teach clients how to think and behave like therapists and how to apply these thoughts and behaviors to their self-improvement. A nice example of self-control interventions with young children was provided by Schneider and Robin (1976, Note 3). They taught emotionally disturbed children—who were in an adjustment school—distraction, progressive relaxation, and problem-solving techniques to help these children assess, cope with, and control their *own* impulsive and aggressive responses to provocations in the classroom.

More elaborate and precise definitions of self-control, along with thorough reviews of the literature, can be found in: Goldfried and Merbaum (1973), Kanfer (1975), Mahoney (1974), Mahoney and Thoresen (1974), and Thoresen and Mahoney (1974).[12] Particular techniques that are frequently taught to clients within a self-control framework include self-monitoring, stimulus control, progressive relaxation, self-reinforcement, self-punishment, self-instruction, and problem solving. The two case examples presented below illustrate versions of these last two techniques, which were taught to children in a self-control context, with self-control objectives.

Case Example 1. Kanfer, Karoly, and Newman (1975) carried out an excellent investigation of verbal self-control procedures for reducing children's fear of the dark. Forty-five male and female children in the 5-to 6-year-old age range who evidenced a strong fear of the dark participated in their study. The study was conducted in a schoolroom equipped with rheostat illumination controls, covered windows, intercoms, and all the other paraphernalia that would allow for precise control and measurement of critical variables. Two treatment groups and one control group were utilized, each entailing a different set of self-instructions for darkness tolerance. Thus children were randomly assigned to one of three groups and were taught one of the following three types of verbal cues: (a) sentences that emphasized the child's active control or competence of the dark (competence group), (b) sentences that focused on reducing the aversive qualities of the dark (stimulus group), and (c) sentences that had a neutral content (neutral or control group). The children were trained in a well-lit room and then were tested in a totally dark room, with duration of darkness tolerance and terminal light intensity (children could increase the illumination) serving as the outcome measures.

For our purposes the training phase of Kanfer et al.'s study deserves more attention. The children were trained one at a time in the experimental room, with the trainer communicating to them from another room via an intercom. Children were instructed to listen to and repeat exactly what the trainer said. The self-instruction flavored sentences were called *special words* and were learned to a criterion of three consecutive errorless repetitions. The sentences were as follows:

> In the *competence group* the children were told to say "I am a brave boy (girl). I can take care of myself in the dark." In the *stimulus group* the special words were, "The dark is a fun place to be. There are many good things in the dark." In the *neutral group* they were "Mary had a little lamb. Its fleece was white as snow." (Kanfer et al., 1975, p. 253).

Once the child had learned the appropriate sentence the trainer returned to the room, praised the child, and gave further instructions for elaborating statements to accompany the initial sentences. Then the trainer left the room, and the appropriate elaborating statements for each treatment group were read to the child. After reading each elaborating sentence the trainer asked the child to repeat the initial sentence. This procedure was repeated for a second trial. The elaborating statements were as follows:

> [Competence group] When you are in the dark you know that you can turn on the light when you feel like it. In your room, when it's dark, you know exactly where everything is—your bed, your dressers, your toys. When you are in the dark if you felt like talking to someone you could always talk to your parents and they could hear you. Even though you are in the dark, when the door is closed you know that nobody can come in that you would not know.
> [Stimulus group] The dark is the best place to go to sleep and have good dreams. The dark is a special place where you can play games. It is more fun to watch a movie or the TV in the dark because you can see the picture better. When it is dark it is nice to cuddle up with stuffed animals.
> [Neutral group] Mary took a lamb to school with her one morning. That day, when she was finished with school, Mary played with the lamb in the garden behind her house. Mary was very careful and made sure that she fed the lamb every day. Sometimes Mary would run with the lamb up to the top of the hill (Kanfer et al., 1975, p. 253).

As is evident in Figure 4, the competence-focused treatment group was superior to the stimulus and neutral-verbalization groups. Self-instructional sentences that emphasized the child's competence to cope with the anxiety-inducing experience of being in a dark room resulted in the longest tolerance times. Self-instructional sentences that emphasized the positive aspects of the dark were less effective, whereas neutral sentences had no appreciable effect. Hence, self-instructions focusing on active coping and competence with the feared stimulus seem to be the most effective self-instructional treatment for young children. Another note-worthy finding of this study was the success of training children under *nonthreatening* conditions to cope effectively with a fear-provoking situation that was

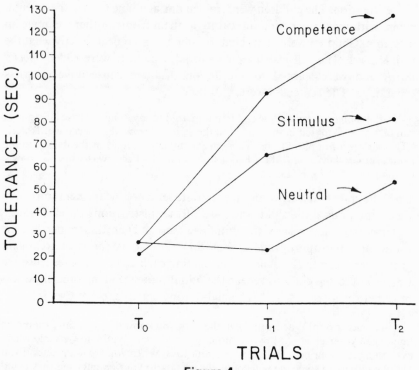

Figure 4

Mean time for tolerance of the dark in the competence, stimulus, and neutral verbalization groups during pretest baseline (T_0) and the two test trials (T_1 and T_2). Children were trained in the use of one of three types of verbal controlling response for darkness tolerance: (a) sentences emphasizing the child's active control or *competence*, (b) sentences concentrating on reducing the aversive qualities of the *stimulus* situation, and (c) *neutral* sentences. (From "Reduction of Children's Fear of the Dark by Competence-Related and Situational Threat-Related Verbal Cues" [p. 254] by F. H. Kanfer, P. Karoly, and A. Newman, *Journal of Consulting and Clinical Psychology,*, 1975, *43*, 251–258. Copyright 1975 by the American Psychological Association. Reprinted by permission.)

presented at a later point in time; several implications about prevention surface from these results. If anxiety problems can be treated without discomfort, the procedure should allow for eventual application to prophylaxis or immunization, a point we have more to say about later.

Case Example 2. Russell and Thoresen (1976) presented a clever extension of problem-solving training to the neglected, predelinquent, and acting-out children at Learning House, the residential family-style treatment program described previously in the punishment section of this chapter (see Tobey & Thoresen, 1976). These children typically lack effective problem-solving skills, and when describing troublesome situations from their past they often make statements such as " 'It was the first thing I thought to do, so I did it,' 'I didn't know what else I *could* do,' [or] 'I didn't know *that* [result] would happen' " (Russell & Thoresen, 1976, p. 377). Russell and Thoresen referred to problem solving as "decision making" and attempted to teach decision making to these children, viewing it as an important self-control skill. Steps in their decision-making process included identifying the problem, collecting information, generating alternatives, recognizing personal values, anticipating probable consequences, making the best decision, and evaluating the decision at a later date.[13] These self-management skills would presumably help the child cope with problems at Learning House and later on with problems that occur after returning to his family; it is hoped these skills would also afford the opportunity for generalization and *maintenance* of the appropriate behaviors taught at Learning House and allow the child to effectively contend with the relapses and new problems that inevitably arise.

Russell and Thoresen incorporated what they thought were the critical steps in decision making into the *Decision-Making Book for Children* (D.M.B.C.), a self-contained program of written materials, integrated with an audiotape, that was aimed at children 8 to 12 years old. The book was developed in alignment with the concept of self-pacing, wherein the child progresses through the training program at his own rate.

One facet of the D.M.B.C. was a decision chart like the one displayed in Table 5. The decision chart included all components of the decision-making process, and the child had to learn and complete each step in sequence. Children had to fill out several charts correctly for both simulated and real personal problem situations before they completed the training program.

The teaching strategy and format used with the D.M.B.C. was an interesting one:

> To allow maximum individualization with minimal staff monitoring, the D.M.B.C. uses an informal, programmed text structure. First, the child reads a simple explanation for each step of the problem-solving process with examples, pictures, and a cartoon character who "thinks out loud" for the reader. The child then listens to a story on the audiotape demonstrating an application of the step by another child or posing a problem for the listener to solve. In this way the child listens to a social model using the decision process and then obtains practice in applying each of the decision steps to a problem situation himself. At the conclusion of each section the child completes a brief quiz requiring knowledge of all the steps taught in previous sections (Russell & Thoresen, 1976, p. 379).

The results of this decision-making skills program were tentative but encouraging. First, five children participating in a preliminary treatment outcome study clearly learned the decision-making steps. On the average they were able to recall 90% of the decision-making sequence, and they were able to reproduce 90% of the decision chart from memory. Second, following training with the D.M.B.C., these children demonstrated significant improvement in their ability to generate possible alternative

Table 5
A Decision Chart Used in Teaching Decision-Making
and Problem-Solving Skills to Children[a]

Name_____
Date _____

DECISION CHART

My problem is: I don't know what to do _____
_____
_____

1.   I could _____
     good point _____
     bad point _____
2.   I could _____
     good point _____
     bad point _____
3.   I could _____
     good point _____
     bad point _____

Before I decide I will need to know _____
_____

My decision is # _____, because I value _____

THE NEXT DAY. . . .
after I carried out my decision.

A GOOD result of my decision was: _____
A BAD result of my decision was: _____

NEXT TIME I have the same problem I think I will: _____
_____
_____

[a]From "Teaching Decision-Making Skills to Children" by M. L. Russell and C. E. Thoresen, in J. D. Krumboltz and C. E. Thoresen (Eds.), *Counseling methods* (p. 379). New York: Holt, Rinehart & Winston, 1976. Copyright 1976 by Holt, Rinehart & Winston. Reprinted by permission.

solutions and to anticipate probable consequences for their actions when presented with simulated problem situations (e.g., avoidance-avoidance or double-bind conflicts). For instance, the average number of alternative solutions given by the children almost doubled pre- to post-treatment, going from 4.8 to 7.6. Since adequate control groups were lacking, however, these results are suggestive rather than definitive. Third, in alignment with the foregoing results, anecdotal reports from the staff at Learning House contributed supportive information about the decision-making program. The children were using their newly learned skills to tackle daily, real-world problems. Don, a 12-year-old boy at Learning House, even led an impromptu decision-making session one evening during a family group meeting, when it became all too obvious that the group needed to decide what to do about a recent increase in runaways. Don lead the group through the decision-making sequence with vigor and proficiency.

Commentary. It is easy to be enthusiastic about self-control techniques. They have so many things going for them, and although there is hardly a plethora of controlled group outcome studies with children, there is, plainly, enough documentary evidence to suggest that they are teetering on the precipice of success. The use of self-control interventions with children is growing rapidly, especially with children who are verbally adept. Children often like both the idea of self-control techniques (with their implied sense of autonomy, etc.) and the techniques themselves (e.g., they often report that self-monitoring, problem solving, and relaxation training are "interesting" and "fun" things to do). The versatility of self-control techniques is an especially attractive feature: they can be used to increase or decrease a tremendous variety of behaviors, and they have promising implications for the prevention of behavior disorders and for the maintenance of treatment effects over time and place. (We have more to say about these implications later.) In spite of all these assets, it must be admitted that self-control techniques are sometimes complex and difficult to teach and learn, that implementing them for certain limited anxiety and withdrawal problems may be therapeutic "overkill," and that an inept utilization of them can easily wrench defeat from the jaws of victory. Because implementing self-control procedures requires considerable savvy, let us move on to some suggestions for their use.

Therapy can be conceptualized as an apprenticeship in problem solving (Mahoney, 1974), and if this is the orientation a therapist plans to take, it should be made very explicit to the child. The child must be reasonably motivated and see the treatment goals as desirable if self-control training is not to become an exercise in frustration. A trusting relationship between therapist and child is, therefore, a necessary prerequisite for effective self-control training. Because such relationships often take considerable time to bloom and because self-control endeavors require initial support and assistance from the environment, self-control programs are frequently implemented as the *last* step of a treatment program. Thus environmentally-based interventions may be the initial focus, and the child may then gradually move along a continuum of more responsibility for assessment, intervention, and maintenance that ends with a full-fledged self-control program enabling him to truly be his *own* therapist and teacher. The case of Susan, mentioned at the beginning of the chapter, exemplifies this sort of sequencing. Susan's severe dog phobia was treated initially through a sequence consisting primarily of (a) systematic desensitization, (b) discrimination training for recognizing friendly versus unfriendly dogs, and (c) *in vivo* participant modeling with successively more threatening dogs and surroundings (and with extensive positive reinforcement from the therapists). Toward the end of the treatment program Susan was taught a self-control technique, self-instruction, as a supplement to the other therapist-based procedures. Self-instruction focuses on the cognitive factors in behavior modification and teaches children to self-monitor and revise their internal monologues, that is, what they say to themselves in stressful situations (see Goldfried & Goldfried, 1975; Kanfer, 1975; Mahoney, 1974; Meichenbaum, 1974, 1975; Meichenbaum & Cameron, 1974; Meichenbaum & Turk, 1976; Meichanbaum, Turk, & Burstein, 1975; Meichenbaum, Note 4). Meichanbaum's version of self-instructional training dovetailed nicely with the therapist-controlled participant modeling that preceded it and involved the following five steps: (1) We modeled adaptive self-verbalizations by talking out loud and administering task-relevant instructions to ourselves while we performed the task (e.g., saying "Relax; take a slow, deep breath; I'm doing fine; this dog is obviously friendly; notice his wagging tail; pet him softly; nothing to worry about," while petting the dog appropriately). (2) We then asked Susan to perform the task while we instructed her aloud. (3) Susan then performed the task and instructed herself out loud. (4) Susan performed the task and whispered the instructions to herself. (5) And finally, Susan interacted with dogs while using entirely covert self-instructions.

Steps 2–5 included extensive performance feedback and positive reinforcement from the therapists to Susan, and she progressed through the program beautifully. Let the reader beware, however, that she never would have participated in this self-control program in the first place without the therapist-controlled treatment procedures that preceded it and the partial successes, skill improvements, and rapport enhancements that they entailed.

Kanfer (1975), among others, has argued for the inclusion of thorough self-reinforcement programs in all intensive self-control endeavors. Not only is this suggestion intuitively appealing and logically sound, there is even empirical evidence to back it up. In a study with 96 adults, which nevertheless has implications for children, Perri and Richards (1977) found strong empirical support for the foregoing recommendation. Their study was an interview investigation of naturally occurring (i.e., self-initiated) attempts at self-control. The subjects had made sincere and sustained attempts to self-control one of several adult problem behaviors (e.g., dating or overeating problems). One of the most, if not *the* most, dramatic factors differentiating successful from unsuccessful self-controllers was the use of self-reinforcement techniques. Across all problem behaviors, the use of self-reward procedures was more than three times as frequent among successful self-controllers than unsuccessful ones (67% versus 19%). Perri and Richards (1977) speculated that "the efficacy of self-reward procedures may derive in part from the consequence that, when used in combination with other techniques, self-rewards probably tend to strengthen and lengthen the entire self-control attempt". In this and a related investigation (Perri, Richards, & Schultheis, in press), it was also found that successful self-controllers used more techniques for longer periods of time and varied their techniques according to the problem with which they were dealing.

As others have acknowledged, there are a number of common pitfalls with self-control programs. For instance, Watson and Tharp (1972) enumerate several problems that can sink a self-control program. Poorly defined target behaviors and faulty record keeping are two such problems. Record keeping via self-monitoring is often the first step in a self-control program (Kanfer, 1975), and despite its conceptual simplicity, self-monitoring must be taught carefully and thoroughly if it is to be effective (Richards, 1976; Thoresen & Mahoney, 1974). Further impediments to successful self-control programs include noncontingent use of self-reinforcement, long delays between target behaviors and self-reinforcement, improper shaping and fading, insufficient control of and support from the immediate environment, and procedures whose technical components (e.g., intricate verbal components) exceed the skills and capabilities of the client. Finally, we would like to add that both the therapist and the client should be prepared to do some tinkering and adjustment with a self-control program: observe, record, intervene, and *try, try again*!

We are extremely optimistic about the future of self-control interventions with children. Some (e.g., Glaser, 1972) have argued for massive self-control training in education, and self-control treatment procedures are a good example of therapy as a psychoeducational, self-managed, learning process. Self-control interventions even offer the possibility of enhancing personal freedom in an age obsessed by the spectre of ever-increasing authoritarian control:

> ... the truly "free" individual is one who is in intimate contact with himself and his environment (both internal and external). He knows "where he's at" in terms of the factors influencing both his actions and his surroundings. Moreover, he has acquired technical skills that enable him to take an active role in his own growth and adjustment. He is no mechanical automaton, passively responding to environmental forces. He is a personal scientist—a skilled engineer capable of investigating and altering the determinants of his actions (Mahoney & Thoresen, 1974, pp. 71–72).

Other useful reviews, investigations, and case studies on behavioral self-control, especially as it might apply to anxious and withdrawn children, include: Bernstein and Borkovec (1973), D'Zurilla and Goldfried (1971), Goldfried and Davison (1976), Kanfer and Goldstein (1975), Krumboltz and Thoresen (1976), Kunzelmann (1970), Linden (1973), Shure, Spivack, and Gordon (1972), Spivack and Shure (1974), Weil and Goldfried (1973), and Shure and Spivack (Note 5).

Multiple Techniques

Definition. By multiple techniques we mean a multifaceted treatment program in which all of the facets are carefully coordinated with one another and implemented in a planned, sequential fashion. We have frequently mentioned profitable technique combinations in this chapter, and we have generally advocated their use. This section deals with *elaborate* multifaceted treatment programs, which are most often called for when the behavior disorder in question is particularly vexatious, refractory to treatment, or multiform. For example, Susan, the severely dog-phobic girl mentioned in the beginning of the chapter, was treated via an integrated multiple technique program wherein each step both tackled some aspect of Susan's phobia and facilitated implementation of the next step. The steps in Susan's treatment program were: (1) systematic desensitization (plus emotive imagery adjuncts), (2) discrimination training vis-à-vis friendly versus unfriendly dogs, (3) withdrawal of social reinforcement for avoidance, (4) guided participant modeling with a live dog in the clinic, (5) extensive positive reinforcement for advancement through a hierarchy of progressively stressful interactions with the dog, (6) guided participant modeling outside of the clinic building, with the mother as therapist, (7) Meichenbaum's (1974, 1975, Note 4) self-instruction technique (plus extensive teaching adjuncts for getting Susan to relabel herself as "not afraid"), and (8) guided participant modeling involving numerous dogs in Susan's neighborhood, with Susan's mother and sister acting as therapists. This coordinated and interlocking therapy program was developed in careful alignment with a planned treatment rationale such that, for example, steps 1 and 2 made step 4 possible, steps 3 and 5 made step 4 durable, and steps 6, 7, and 8 made for the persistence and generalization that is incumbent on any serious therapy effort. We now turn to another example of a multiple technique treatment program.

Case Example. MacDonald (1975) described an elegant therapy program that utilized multiple techniques to treat an onerous and complex dog phobia in an 11-year-old boy. The boy had been dog phobic for 8 years, and his extreme fear and consequent adaptations to that fear had clearly set him apart from normal children:

By and large his peers excluded him from their interactions. He participated in none of the school physical activity programs, in part because they were typically held in locations where dogs might be found; consequently, he had developed no group game skills or outdoor solitary play skills such as swimming and bicycle riding. In general, then, both his social and personal development had been markedly restrained by his phobia (MacDonald, 1975, p. 317).

A series of assessment sessions indicated that the boy's dog phobia was maintained by multiple supports, including conditioned anxiety to dogs, parental expectations and prompting of dog avoidance, and the boy's discretionary use of these parental expectations to engineer things to suit his fancy. MacDonald (1975) succinctly detailed the rationale and goals of the multifaceted treatment program she developed for this child:

> Because of the intricate interplay between the phobia's various mutually supportive elements, a "multiple" treatment strategy was indicated—a combination of learning—based procedures used in concert to alter a specified set of targets and induce a specified set of interdependent outcomes. The targets included the child's conditioned emotional reaction to dogs, his deficit in appropriate animal handling skills, his social supports for fearful behavior, and his rather general social skill deficiency resulting from the prolonged role of "dog phobic." The goals included unemotional and skillful interactions with dogs, a social environment supportive of non—fearful behavior, an increase in the amount of emotionally uneventful time spent outdoors, and the development of solitary and group outdoor play skills (p. 318).

By perusing Table 6, the reader can gain a feel for the complexity and planned sequential nature of this treatment program. The program began with relaxation training and hierarchy construction. A skyscraper analogy was used to explain hierarchy procedures to the child, and over a period of 11 treatment sessions a 37-item hierarchy was constructed. As is reflected by the sample of excellent hierarchy items in Table 7, extensive item prompts were used to increase therapist control over visualized scenes. Systematic desensitization ran from the eighth to seventeenth treatment sessions. Desensitization adjuncts, such as emotive imagery style procedures and clever homework assignments involving relaxation practice and concomitant exposure to tape recordings of barking dogs, were implemented in a sequentially planned fashion during the course of therapy (sessions 5, 8, 10, & 12). Training in dog handling skills was initiated early in the therapy program (sessions 4–7). The boy learned how to interpret dog body language, he read several dog handling manuals, and he engaged in a participant modeling sequence (with a stuffed animal) aimed at teaching him dog petting skills (e.g., back-patting). Modeling procedures were employed during the middle and latter stages of the treatment program (sessions 5, 8, and 10–17), affording the opportunity for graduated exposure to the phobic stimulus and further instruction in dog handling skills.[14] Social environmental restructuring (sessions 5, 6, 8, 10, and 11; e.g., teaching the parents not to prompt avoidance behaviors) and

Table 6
Summary of Treatment Procedures Used in a Multifaceted
Therapy Program for a Child's Dog Phobia[a]

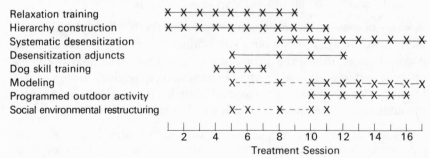

Procedure	
Relaxation training	X X X X X X X X X
Hierarchy construction	X X X X X X X X X X X
Systematic desensitization	X X X X X X X X X X X
Desensitization adjuncts	X X X X
Dog skill training	X X X X
Modeling	X----- X - - X—X—X—X—X—X—X—X
Programmed outdoor activity	X X X X X X X
Social environmental restructuring	X X- - - - X - - -X X

```
      2      4      6      8     10     12     14     16
                        Treatment Session
```

[a]From "Multiple Impact Behavior Therapy in a Child's Dog Phobia" (p. 319) by M. L. MacDonald, *Journal of Behavior Therapy and Experimental Psychiatry*, 1975, *6*, 317–322. Copyright 1975 by Pergamon Press. Reprinted by permission.

programmed outdoor activity (sessions 10–16; e.g., assignments to walk progressively greater portions of the route to school) were implemented toward the middle and latter portions of the treatment program, respectively.

The treatment program worked:

At the sixth treatment session, the child reported staying outdoors without worrying about dogs for the first time in his memory. At the eleventh session he spontaneously stated that he had told his classmates he had "gotten over his problem." He and his parents were reporting appropriate reactions in benign as well as threatening dog encounters regularly by the fourteenth treatment session. Just prior to termination, the child demonstrated his mastery and skill to his family at an outdoor "recital" (MacDonald, 1975, pp. 321–322).

In addition, a 2-year follow-up indicated that these treatment effects had been maintained. This treatment program probably owed much of its success to the comprehensive nature and careful intertwining of the therapy procedures. The program was comprehensive in that the multiple therapy procedures addressed the multiple elements supporting the child's phobia. The program demonstrated careful coordination of therapy procedures in that the procedural arrangement reflected a well-planned sequencing and overlapping of techniques. So, for example, (a) systematic desensitization was overlayed with facilitative adjuncts, (b) some dog skill training preceded—and therefore facilitated—the implementation of live modeling, and (c) some live modeling and social environmental restructuring preceded—and therefore facilitated—the programmed outdoor activities.

Commentary. The pros and cons of complex multifaceted treatment programs like the one described above are rather transparent, so we make this commentary brief. Very severe, complex, or multiply supported anxiety and withdrawal problems often require multiple treatment techniques. Some anxiety and withdrawal problems do *not* require such complex treatment packages, however, and it behooves the therapist to ascertain whether multiple techniques are clearly called for. Sometimes they are not. The following questions should help decide the issue: Will a simpler and cheaper treatment program clearly fail? Will a multiple technique program's benefit clearly justify its cost? Is the therapist clearly competent with all of the procedures in the multiple technique program? Is there a clear rationale for each step in the planned sequencing and overlapping of techniques? Is the multiple technique program well-enough planned and staffed so that it will not sink under the weight of its own complexity?

Lest the therapist drift into preposterous instances of therapeutic "overkill," he should be able to answer these questions in the affirmative before implementing a multiple technique treatment program. Although we have argued for technique combinations at several points in this chapter, this was not meant as an endorsement of wholesale therapeutic "shotgunning" or mindless eclecticism. A wise therapist is often a parsimonious therapist and a simple treatment program is often a good treatment program.

Other examples of multiple technique programs for the behavioral treatment of anxiety states and avoidance behaviors in children include:

Table 7
Illustrative Imaginal Desensitization Hierarchy Items Used in a
Multifaceted Therapy Program for a Child's Dog Phobia[a]

Item No	Item[b]
2	Standing on the front porch in the late afternoon with your Dad, about ready to go inside, looking down the block and seeing a Beagle three houses away minding his own business and trotting towards you.
10	Sitting in the family's kitchen with the rest of your family, hearing Mr. say, "He surely was a hard egg, wasn't he?" and watching Dumplin', who's lying down at the kitchen entrance, look at you, get up, and trot around the table to a spot three feet from you.
11	Standing in your Gramma and Grampa's front yard playing ball with your Dad and Sister and watching a Schnauzer exploring about fifty feet away.
31	Sitting in your back yard, alone, playing with your G. I. Joe and looking up to see an unfamiliar Collie running down your driveway and past the garage.

[a]From "Multiple Impact Behavior Therapy in a Child's Dog Phobia" (p. 319) by M. L. MacDonald, *Journal of Behavior Therapy and Experimental Psychiatry*, 1975, *6*, 317–322. Copyright 1975 by Pergamon Press. Reprinted by permission.
[b]All items were introduced with the phase "Alright, (name), I'd like you to imagine . . ."

Keat (1972), Kooy and Webster (1975), Lazarus et al. (1965), and Patterson and Brodsky (1966).

Prevention Techniques

Definition. This definition is easy. By prevention techniques we mean any technique that is aimed at behavioral "immunization" (or "prophylaxis" or "inoculation") for anxiety states and avoidance behaviors in high-risk children. The work of Poser and King (Note 6) is a good example of prevention technique research. Their project is exciting and ambitious: In the first phase of the project they are attempting to identify high school students who are very susceptible to behavior disorders, but who are still functioning normally. In latter phases of the project, Poser and King hope to determine the types and parameters of maladaptive reactions that are likely to occur in this high-risk group. Finally, in careful alignment with the results of the previous project phases, these investigators plan to develop and evaluate prevention techniques. Some of the research discussed in the modeling and self-control sections of this chapter has implications for the prevention of behavioral problems (e.g., Kanfer et al., 1975; Melamed et al., 1975; Melamed & Siegel, 1975). The following case example goes beyond implications; it reflects a direct attempt at developing a preventative mental health program for young children.

Case Example. Spivack and Shure (1974) have developed an elaborate research and training program for teaching young children cognitive problem-solving skills. Their program endeavored to teach preschool and kindergarten children techniques for assessing, coping with, and solving their own personal and interpersonal problems. Problems involving anxiety and social withdrawal were among those addressed by the program. Although much of their work was with relatively normal children, they have extended their research to include most possible treatment settings, age ranges, and levels of adjustment. Indeed, their project is an impressive example of applied programmatic research.

Previous research on their part had consistently indicated that children's (and adult's) problem-solving abilities were related to social adjustment. They isolated two critical problem-solving abilities in particular: "It is clear that two key abilities across all ages are the ability to imagine alternative solutions to problems and the ability to conceptualize means and potential obstacles in moving toward a goal" (Spivack & Shure, 1974, p. 20). They determined that these abilities were not merely one aspect of "intelligence" (as measured by IQ tests), nor were they the same as abilities required to solve impersonal, intellectual problems.

Spivack and Shure were well aware that their research had immediate application to the goal of behavioral immunization:

> The background research provided us with a springboard from which to test our hypothesis that certain cognitive problem-solving skills are a prerequisite condition for behavioral adjustment. If it could be shown that intervention which enhances these thinking skills also improves adjustment, then it would be possible to offer a new approach to the *prevention* and handling of behavioral problems (Spivack & Shure, 1974, p. 22, emphasis added).

Spivack and Shure set out to test their hypothesis in day-care, nursery, and kindergarten settings by using a training program that followed 7 fundamental principles:

(1) To teach prerequisite language and thinking skills before teaching problem-solving strategies.
(2) To teach new concepts in the context of familiar content.
(3) To base program content on people and interpersonal relations rather than objects and impersonal situations.
(4) To teach generally applicable concepts rather than correct grammar.
(5) To teach the habit of seeking solutions and evaluating them on the basis of their potential consequences rather than the absolute merits of a particular solution to a problem.
(6) To encourage the child to create his own ideas and offer them in the context of the problem.
(7) to teach problem-solving skills not as ends in themselves but in relation to the adaptiveness of overt behavioral adjustment (Spivack & Shure, 1974, p. 29).

They developed, evaluated, and modified elaborate training scripts to meet these program goals. The scripts consisted primarily of structured games and dialogues between children and adults; these were aimed at teaching children the necessary word concepts and cognitive skills. The flavor of these scripts can be gleaned from the short example in Table 8. Entire training program scripts and details for their implementation are available in Spivack and Shure (1974) and Shure and Spivack (Note 5).

As with all good programmatic research, Spivack and Shure carefully evaluated major facets of their training program and collected reams of data. (See Chapters 7, 8, and 12 of their book for a discussion of their evaluation measures and results.) Their results were very encouraging, especially for socially withdrawn children:

> We do know that the program is feasible for child-care centers, is well received by teachers, and works. Current research is evaluating the effect of extending the program into kindergarten.
> The research data also indicate that the program does something for children with behavioral problems, especially those who are inhibited. Practical questions are often asked by teachers and administrators about who needs the program and

who does not. The answer is that *as a secondary preventive program it works most efficiently for children who are inhibited, socially withdrawn, or afraid to express themselves.* . . . But the program also works for the impulsive and impatient child and apparently *has a preventive effect on the behaviorally adjusted child* (Spivack & Shure, 1974, pp. 105–106, emphasis added).

Consonant with the above, reports from teachers and parents were extremely positive.

Table 8
Illustrative Portion of a Training Program Script for Teaching Problem-Solving Techniques to Young Children[a]

OVERVIEW:
Solutions and Consequences Pairing

For Problems 9 through 12 the goal is to teach the child to think of a solution and then think immediately of its consequence. Ultimately it is hoped that the child will learn to think of a solution, weigh its pros and cons, and then decide which alternative is most appropriate before taking action.

Place the picture in the upper left-hand corner of the board and present the problem. You can now use the word *problem* with the children. The problem today is _____ . Have the children repeat the problem as usual. Then draw a line in the middle of the board. Say: "After we have an idea, I'm going to ask you about what might happen next. I'm going to put what might happen next over here." Point dramatically to the right side of the line. This visual distinction will help clarify the difference between a solution and a consequence.

After eliciting one solution ask immediately what might happen next as a consequence to that solution. To elicit consequences ask one of the following questions until one consequence is given: "What might happen next?" "What might B do if A _____ ?" "What might B say if A _____ ?" "How might B feel if A _____ ?"

Ask for one consequence only. Then go to the second solution. After one new solution has been given switch to eliciting a consequence. Occasionally call on one child at a time and ask: "What's your idea, Shelly?" Let Shelly respond. "Shelly, if (*repeat Shelly's response*) what might happen next?" Occasionally follow with: "Is that a good idea?" Let the child respond. "Why is (is that not) a good idea?" Treat enumerations, acceptable and questionable responses, and chaining as for alternative solutions and alternative consequences.

SCRIPT
Day 43
Problem 9

A girl on a bike wants a boy on a wagon to get out of her way. Use the picture of a girl and boy riding in a play-ground from the My Community set.

The problem today is: This girl on the bike (*point*) wants this boy (*point*) on the wagon to get out of her way.

What is the problem? What does the girl want the boy to do? *Children repeat the problem.*

Today we're going to play our game in a new way. I'm going to ask you for one idea. I'm going to write it over here. *Draw a line down the middle of the board and point dramatically to the left side of the line.*

OK. Who has an idea of what this girl (*point*) can do so this (*point*) boy will get out of the way?

After one solution has been offered say: OK. Now listen carefully. This is a hard question. If (*repeat the solution*) then what MIGHT happen next? *If a consequence is not offered follow with the remaining questions, such as*: What might B do (say) if   ? *As soon as one consequence is offered say*: OK, that might happen. I'm going to put all the things that might happen next over here. *Point dramatically to the right side of the line.*

Now listen again. I'm back to this side of the board (*point to the left side of the line*). Now we need an IDEA again, something the girl can DO or SAY so the boy will get out of the way. Ralph, what's your idea? *Let Ralph respond.* OK, if the girl (*point to the girl and repeat Ralph's idea*), then what might happen next? What can I write on this side of the board? *Point to the right side of the line.*

Repeat this line of questioning, always alternating solution and consequence, intermittently asking: Is that a good idea? Why is that a good idea? *Such questions should be asked for nonforceful ("ask him") as well as forceful ("hit him") solutions.*

In trying to help children with problems such as anxiety and social withdrawal, adults too often do the thinking for a child or assume that he has a sophisticated language system for dealing with interpersonal problems and emotions. The approach of Spivack and Shure circumvented these errors by teaching children how to solve their *own* problems within a language system they could really understand. Their program is logical in its conception, broad in its potential application, and exciting in its implications. In summary, they hypothesized and then demonstrated that cognitive interpersonal problem-solving skills mediate behavioral adjustment in young children. They then set about developing a program to train young children in these skills. Evaluation of this program indicated that change in problem-solving skills as a function of training led to enhanced social adjustment, which in turn generalized over time and place. Particularly interesting, and consonant with the above, they found that the degree of cognitive and behavioral change correlated highly, such that children who improved most in trained cognitive skills also evidenced the greatest overt behavioral adjustment. Finally, they found that initially well-adjusted children who participated in the program maintained their adjustment significantly better than similar children who did not participate. The conclusion is straigtforward: Spivack and Shure's training package constitutes a program of primary prevention in the mental health area.

Commentary. The research on prevention is promising, but it is still in its infancy. Until it grows up, there is not much we can say. A great deal more research is needed. Much of this chapter has been festooned with how-to-do-it suggestions, but we will not give any for prevention techniques, because it is not yet particularly clear how-to-do-it. There are several other recent developments that dovetail nicely with prevention endeavors; they include self-control training (Spivack & Shure as a case in point), use of peers and paraprofessionals as therapists (Guerney, 1969; Miller & Miller, 1976), large-scale interventions in school settings (Glaser, 1972; Spivack & Shure, 1974), and efficient treatment delivery systems— filmed modeling for instance (Melamed & Siegel, 1975). Some might argue that mental health professionals should first make sure they have found the "cures," and then focus on prevention research. From our perspective, such conservatism can get a bit wearisome, and we think prevention research on anxiety and withdrawal disorders is long overdue.

Other interesting examples and discussions of prevention techniques for anxiety and avoidance include the following: Gelfand (in press), Kanfer et al. (1975), Krumboltz and Krumboltz (1972), Meichenbaum and Turk (1976), Melamed et al. (1975), and Shure et al. (1972).

ISSUES, TRENDS, AND FUTURE NEEDS

It is now appropriate to close this chapter with a general commentary. The behavioral treatment of anxiety states and avoidance behaviors in children is a fascinating topic—important, complex, exciting, and optimistic—and by this point in the chapter we have touched on most of its applied aspects. Several nagging issues remain, however. Important trends are on the horizon, and several needs remind us that we have to do more thinking and research if substance is to outweigh hope in the future. These issues, which deserve more attention, are discussed here in an admittedly terse, critical, and slightly cavalier fashion.

Assessment. This area, like many, begs for empirically evaluated and sophisticated assessment procedures. We have a number of behavior-change techniques. But how do we rationally decide which techniques are most appropriate for the particular case that confronts us? How do we decide which facets of the child's anxiety and withdrawal are most important to change? What behavior should be changed first? What technique should be used first? When should we give up on one technique and try another? Well, dear reader, the fact of the matter is that we do not yet have scientifically supported answers to most of these questions. Clinicians out there in the "real world" *have* to come up with answers, of course, and right now their answers tend to be based on personal experience, competence, preference, simple logic, and hope. It is ironic that behavior therapists pride themselves on their empirical underpinnings, yet they have developed change techniques that are much more sophisticated than the assessment techniques which supposedly predicate change (cf. Anastasi, 1976; Goldfried & Sprafkin, 1974). Those who are not so generous might call this putting "the cart before the horse" (McFall, 1976,

p. 246). Those who are generous might call behavioral assessment an "emerging discipline."

Social Skills. Several experts (e.g., Gelfand, in press) have cautioned that social skill deficits can play a prominent role in anxiety and withdrawal disorders. Many researchers and clinicians have not heeded their advice. The primary thrust of research and practice in the area is still towards anxiety, with social skills riding in the back seat. Yet, many anxious and withdrawn children do *not* possess the social skills necessary to effectively deal with their problems, and, unless they are systematically taught these skills, they are doomed to wallow in failure.

Outcome Studies. Does this stuff really work? Sometimes. A more positive and definitive answer can be given for some procedures (e.g., positive reinforcement, participant modeling). But several of the techniques discussed in this chapter (e.g., systematic desensitization, self-control) desperately need further testing in outcome studies that are well-controlled, large-scale, long-term, and carried out in real-life settings with seriously disturbed children (cf. Bergin & Suinn, 1975; Ross, 1974). Good models for such outcome research are provided by the work of Kent and O'Leary (1976) with conduct problem children and the work of Sloane and his colleagues with adult neurotics (Sloane, Staples, Cristol, Yorkston, & Whipple, 1975). Although we are very enthusiastic about behavior therapy and eager to laud its assets, it would be less than good scholarship to ignore the dearth of controlled research on some behavioral techniques.

Treatment Maintenance. Treatment effects often do not persist. In many outcome studies, "follow-up data indicate that clients have abandoned treatment procedures and their initial progress has deteriorated" (Richards, Perri, & Gortney, 1976, p. 405). The area reviewed in this chapter is not an exception. Speaking for behavior modification and psychotherapy in general, Atthowe (1973) claims "we lack a technology of behavioral persistence. Until this . . . technology develops, our credibility will be in question" (p. 40). This technology has a ways to go! It is not unusual to find contemporary reviewers making statements such as "the maintenance problem remains an almost totally uninvestigated area" (Thoresen & Mahoney, 1974, p. 134). Why such an important area has received so little research attention is a question beyond the scope of this chapter, and the fact that such research is expensive, risky, and long-term may just be a coincidence, of course. A few researchers have started to attack this problem, and some promising maintenance strategies are appearing. Examples include self-control training, faded therapist contact, booster sessions, training in behavioral problem solving, use of "natural" reinforcers, permanent environmental changes, and more extensive treatment (cf. Richards et al., 1976). It is possible that the durability of treatment effects will share the stage with ethics as the prime therapeutic issues of the upcoming decade. It is *inevitable* that therapists who do not address this issue will often find themselves meandering in the bush, rather than on the road to therapeutic success (Gelfand & Hartmann, 1975; Keeley, Shemberg, & Carbonell, 1976; O'Leary & Wilson, 1975). Conclusion: treatment effects will frequently deteriorate if therapists do not supplement their treatments with procedures supporting behavioral persistence.

The Future. The area has some trends, but we acknowledge that this commentary reflects our hopes as much as the trends. We hope that increased attention will be given to assessment, social skills, outcome studies, and treatment maintenance. There are several other promising trends in the behavioral treatment of anxious and withdrawn children that we would like to see blossom. Further development of multiple techniques is one example. Expansion of interdisciplinary approaches is another; behavioral intervention in medical settings, such as the work of Melamed and Siegel (1975), gives a glimmer of what might come of this trend.[15] The research on prevention that is beginning to sprout up here and there is a welcome trend (see Gelfand). Finally, the expansion of theory, research, and practice on behavioral self-control offers a trend with the promise that children can learn to be their own therapists, a trend with the possibility that they will thereby maintain improvements and cope with new problems, and a trend with the hope that such learning will not only lessen their anxiety and withdrawal but also carry them a long way toward true maturity.

REFERENCE NOTES

1. Zimbardo, P., Pilkonis, P., & Norwood, R. *The silent prison of shyness.* Unpublished manuscript, Department of Psychology, Stanford University, Stanford, California, 1974.
2. Richards, C. S. *Behavior modification of elective mutism: Technical, paraprofessional, and political considerations.* Unpublished manuscript, Department of Psychology, University of Missouri, Columbia, Missouri, 1976.
3. Schneider, M., & Robin, A. *Turtle manual.* Unpublished manuscript, Department of Psychology, State University of New York at Stony Brook, New York, 1973.
4. Meichenbaum, D. *Therapist manual for cognitive behavior modification.* Unpublished manuscript, Department of Psychology, University of Waterloo, Waterloo, Ontario, Canada, 1973.
5. Shure, M. B., & Spivack, G. *Problem-solving techniques in child rearing: A training script for parents.* Unpublished manuscript, Hahnemann Medical College and Hospital, Philadelphia, Pennsylvania, 1975.
6. Poser, E. G., & King, M. C. *Primary prevention of fear: An experimental approach.* Unpublished manuscript, Department of Psychology, McGill University, Montreal, Canada, 1975.

REFERENCES

Achenbach, T. M. *Developmental psychopathology.* New York: Ronald, 1974.

Allen, K., Hart, B., Buell, S., Harris, R., & Wolf, M. Effects of social reinforcement on isolate behavior of a nursery school child. *Child Development,* 1964, *35,* 511–518.

Anastasi, A. *Psychological testing* (4th ed.). New York: Macmillan, 1976.

Atthowe, J. M. Behavior innovation and persistence. *American Psychologist,* 1973, *28,* 34–41.

Ayllon, T., Smith, D., & Rogers, M. Behavioral management of school phobia. *Journal of Behavior Therapy and Experimental Psychiatry,* 1970, *1,* 125–138.

Bandura, A. *Principles of behavior modification.* New York: Holt, Rinehart & Winston, 1969.

Bandura, A. Psychotherapy based upon modeling principles. In A. E. Bergin & S. L. Garfield (Eds.), *Handbook of psychotherapy and behavior change.* New York: Wiley, 1971a.

Bandura, A. Vicarious and self-reinforcement processes. In R. Glaser (Ed.), *The nature of reinforcement.* Columbus, Ohio: Merrill, 1971b.

Bandura, A. Effecting change through participant modeling. In J. D. Krumboltz & C. E. Thoresen (Eds.), *Counseling methods.* New York: Holt, Rinehart & Winston, 1976.

Bandura, A., Grusec, E., & Menlove, F. L. Vicarious extinction of avoidance behavior. *Journal of Personality and Social Psychology,* 1967, *5,* 16–23.

Bandura, A., Jeffery, R. W., & Gajdos, E. Generalizing change through self-directed performance. *Behaviour Research and Therapy,* 1975, *13,* 141–152.

Bandura, A., Jeffery, R. W., & Wright, C. L. Efficacy of participant modeling as a function of response induction aids. *Journal of Abnormal Psychology,* 1974, *83,* 56–64.

Bandura, A., & Menlove, F. L. Factors determining vicarious extinction of avoidance behavior through symbolic modeling. *Journal of Personality and Social Psychology,* 1968, *8,* 99–108.

Barabasz, A. F. Group desensitization of test anxiety in elementary school. *The Journal of Psychology,* 1973, *83,* 295–301.

Bauermeister, J. J., & Jemail, J. A. Modification of "elective mutism" in the classroom setting: A case study. *Behavior Therapy,* 1975, *6,* 246–250.

Berecz, J. M. Phobias of childhood: Etiology and treatment. *Psychological Bulletin,* 1968, *70,* 694–720.

Bergin, A. E., & Suinn, R. M. Individual psychotherapy and behavior therapy. *Annual Review of Psychology,* 1975, *26,* 509–556.

Bernstein, D. A. Anxiety management. In W. E. Craighead, A. E. Kazdin, & M. J. Mahoney (Eds.), *Behavior modification: Principles, issues, and applications.* Boston: Houghton Mifflin, 1976.

Bernstein, D. A., & Borkovec, T. D. *Progressive relaxation training.* Champaign, Ill.: Research Press, 1973.

Bijou, S. W., & Redd, W. H. Behavior therapy for children. In S. Arieti (Ed.), *American handbook of psychiatry,* Vol. 5. New York: Basic Books, 1975, pp. 319–344.

Bonny, M. E. Assessment of effort to aid socially isolated elementary school pupils. *Journal of Educational Research,* 1971, *64,* 359–364.

Borkovec, T. D. Physiological and cognitive processes in the regulation of anxiety.

In G. E. Schwartz & D. Shapiro (Eds.), *Consciousness and self-regulation*: *Advances in research* (Vol. 1) New York: Plenum, 1976.

Buell, J., Stoddard, P., Harris, F. R., & Baer, D. M. Collateral social development accompanying reinforcement of outdoor play in a pre-school child. *Journal of Applied Behavior Analysis*, 1968, *1*, 167–173.

Clarizio, H. F., & McCoy, G. F. *Behavior disorders in children* (2nd ed.). New York: Crowell, 1976.

Conrad, R. D., Delk, J. L., & Williams, C. Use of stimulus fading procedures in the treatment of situation specific mutism: A case study. *Journal of Behavior Therapy and Experimental Psychiatry*, 1974, *5*, 99–100.

Croghan, L., & Musante, G. L. The elimination of a boy's high-building phobia by in vivo desensitization and game playing. *Journal of Behavior Therapy and Experimental Psychiatry*, 1975, *6*, 87–88.

Davison, G. C., & Neale, J. M. *Abnormal psychology: An experimental clinical approach*. New York: Wiley, 1974.

D'Zurilla, T. J., & Goldfried, M. R. Problem solving and behavior modification. *Journal of Abnormal Psychology*, 1971, *78*, 107–126.

Evers, W. L., & Schwarz, J. C. Modifying social withdrawal in preschoolers: The effects of filmed modeling and teacher praise. *Journal of Abnormal Child Psychology*, 1973, *1*, 248–256.

Fixsen, D. L., Phillips, E. L., Phillips, E. A., & Wolf, M. M. The teaching-family model of group home treatment. In W. E. Craighead, A. E. Kazdin, & M. J. Mahoney (Eds.), *Behavior modification: Principles, issues, and applications*. Boston: Houghton Mifflin, 1976.

Flanders, J. A review of research on imitative behavior. *Psychological Bulletin*, 1968, *69*, 316–337.

Ford, J. R., & Foster, S. L. Extrinsic incentives and token-based programs: A reevaluation. *American Psychologist*, 1976, *31*, 87–90.

Freeman, B. J., Roy, R. R., & Hemmick, S. Extinction of a phobia of physical examination in a seven-year-old mentally retarded boy—A case study. *Behavior Research and Therapy*, 1976, *14*, 63–64.

Gardner, W. I. *Children with learning and behavior problems*. Boston: Allyn & Bacon, 1974.

Garvey, W. P., & Hegrenes, J. R. Desensitization techniques in the treatment of school phobia. *American Journal of Orthopsychiatry*, 1966, *36*, 147–152.

Gelfand, D. M. Behavioral treatment of avoidance, social withdrawal and negative emotional states. In B. B. Wolman, J. Egan, & A. O. Ross (Eds.), *Handbook of treatment of mental disorders in childhood and adolescence*. Englewood Cliffs, N.J.: Prentice-Hall, in press.

Gelfand, D. M., & Hartmann, D. P. *Child behavior analysis and therapy*. New York: Pergamon, 1975.

Gittleman-Klein, R., & Klein, D. School phobia: Diagnostic considerations in the light of imipramine effects. *Journal of Nervous and Mental Disease*, 1973, *156*, 199–215.

Glaser, R. Individuals and learning: The new aptitudes. *Educational Researcher*, 1972, *1* (6), 5–13.

Goldfried, M. R., & Davison, G. C. *Clinical behavior therapy*. New York: Holt, Rinehart & Winston, 1976.

Goldfried, M. R., & Goldfried, A. P. Cognitive change methods. In F. H. Kanfer & A. P. Goldstein (Eds.), *Helping people change*. New York: Pergamon, 1975.

Goldfried, M. R., & Kent, R. N. Traditional versus behavioral personality assessment: A comparison of methodological and theoretical assumptions. *Psychological Bulletin*, 1972, *77*, 409–420.

Goldfried, M. R., & Merbaum, M. (Eds.). *Behavior change through self-control.* New York: Holt, Rinehart & Winston, 1973.

Goldfried, M. R., & Sprafkin, J. N. *Behavioral personality assessment.* Morristown, N.J.: General Learning Press, 1974.

Graziano, A. M. (Ed.). *Behavior therapy with children* (Vol. 2). Chicago: Aldine, 1975.

Guerney, B. G. (Ed.). *Psychotherapeutic agents: New roles for non-professionals, parents, and teachers.* New York: Holt, Rinehart & Winston, 1969.

Halpern, W. I., Hammond, J., & Cohen, R. A therapeutic approach to speech phobia: Elective mutism reexamined. In S. Chess & A. Thomas (Eds.), *Annual progress in child psychiatry and child development,* 1972. New York: Brunner/Mazel, 1972.

Hersen, M. Treatment of a compulsive and phobic disorder through a total behavior therapy program: A case study. *Psychotherapy: Theory, Research and Practice,* 1968, *5*, 220–224.

Hersen, M. The behavioral treatment of school phobia: Current techniques. *Journal of Nervous and Mental Disease,* 1971, *153*, 99–107.

Higgins, R. W., Sawtell, R. O., Simon, J. F., Jr., & Simeonsson, R. J. Effect of behavior modification, modeling or desensitization on the child's dental behavior. *Journal of Dental Research,* 1973, *52* (special issue), 115. (Abstract No. 225, February).

Hill, J. H., Liebert, R. M., & Mott, D. E. W. Vicarious extinction of avoidance behavior through films: An initial test. *Psychological Reports,* 1968, *22*, 192.

Horan, J. J. Coping with inescapable discomfort through *in vivo* emotive imagery. In J. D. Krumboltz & C. E. Thoresen (Eds.), *Counseling methods.* New York: Holt, Rinehart & Winston, 1976.

Hosford, R. E. Overcoming fear of speaking in a group. In J. D. Krumboltz and C. E. Thoresen (Eds.), *Behavioral counseling.* New York: Holt, Rinehart & Winston, 1969.

Jackson, D. A., & Wallace, R. F. The modification and generalization of voice loudness in a fifteen-year-old retarded girl. *Journal of Applied Behavior Analysis,* 1974, *7*, 461–471.

Kanfer, F. H. Self-management methods. In F. H. Kanfer & A. P. Goldstein (Eds.), *Helping people change.* New York: Pergamon, 1975.

Kanfer, F. H., & Goldstein, A. P. (Eds.). *Helping people change.* New York: Pergamon, 1975.

Kanfer, F. H., Karoly, P., & Newman, A. Reduction of children's fear of the dark by competence-related and situational threat-related verbal cues. *Journal of Consulting and Clinical Psychology,* 1975, *43*, 251–258.

Karoly, P. Operant methods. In F. H. Kanfer & A. P. Goldstein (Eds.), *Helping people change.* New York: Pergamon, 1975.

Kazdin, A. E. *Behavior modification in applied settings.* Homewood, Ill.: Dorsey Press, 1975.

Kazdin, A. E., & Wilcoxon, L. A. Systematic desensitization and non-specific treatment effects: A methodological evaluation. *Psychological Bulletin,* 1976, *83*, 729–758.

Keat, D. B. Broad-spectrum behavior therapy with children: A case presentation. *Behavior Therapy,* 1972, *3*, 454–459.

Keeley, S. M., Shemberg, K. M., & Carbonell, J. Operant clinical intervention:

Behavior management or beyond? Where are the data? *Behavior Therapy*, 1976, *7*, 292–305.

Keller, M. F., & Carlson, P. M. The use of symbolic modeling to promote social skills in preschool children with low levels of social responsiveness. *Child Development*, 1974, *45*, 912–919.

Kelley, C. K. Play desensitization of fear of darkness in preschool children. *Behaviour Research and Therapy*, 1976, *14*, 79–81.

Kelly, E. W. School phobia: A review of theory and treatment. *Psychology in the Schools*, 1973, *10*, 33–42.

Kennedy, W. A. School phobia: Rapid treatment of fifty cases. *Journal of Abnormal Psychology*, 1965, *70*, 285–289.

Kent, R. N., & O'Leary, K. D. A controlled evaluation of behavior modification with conduct problem children. *Journal of Consulting and Clinical Psychology*, 1976, *44*, 586–596.

Kirkland, K. D., & Thelen, M. H. Uses of modeling in child treatment. In B. B. Lahey & A. E. Kazdin (Eds.), *Advances in child clinical psychology* (Vol. 1). New York: Plenum, in press.

Kissel, S. Systematic desensitization therapy with children: A case study and some suggested modifications. *Professional Psychology*, 1972, *3*, 164–169.

Kondas, O. Reduction of examination anxiety and "stage fright" by group desensitization and relaxation. *Behaviour Research and Therapy*, 1967, *5*, 275–281.

Kooy, D., & Webster, C. D. A rapidly effective behavior modification program for an electively mute child. *Journal of Behavior Therapy and Experimental Psychiatry*, 1975, *6*, 149–152.

Kornhaber, R., & Schroeder, H. Importance of model similarity on extinction of avoidance behavior in children. *Journal of Consulting and Clinical Psychology*, 1975, *43*, 601–607.

Krasner, L. Behavior therapy. *Annual Review of Psychology*, 1971, *22*, 483–532.

Krasner, L., & Richards, C. S. Issues in open education and environmental design. *Psychology in the Schools*, 1976, *13*, 77–81.

Krumboltz, J. D., & Krumboltz, H. B. *Changing children's behavior*. Englewood Cliffs, N.J.: Prentice-Hall, 1972.

Krumboltz, J. D., & Thoresen, C. E. (Eds.). *Counseling methods*. New York: Holt, Rinehart & Winston, 1976.

Kunzelmann, H. D. (Ed.). *Precision teaching*. Seattle, Wash.: Special Child Publications, 1970.

Lazarus, A. A., & Abramovitz, A. The use of "emotive imagery" in the treatment of children's phobias. *Journal of Mental Science*, 1962, *108*, 191–195.

Lazarus, A. A., Davison, G. C., & Polefka, B. A. Classical and operant factors in the treatment of school phobia. *Journal of Abnormal Psychology*, 1965, *70*, 225–229.

Leitenberg, H. Behavioral approaches to the treatment of neuroses. In H. Leitenberg (Ed.), *Handbook of behavior modification and behavior therapy*. Englewood Cliffs, N.J.: Prentice-Hall, 1976.

Leitenberg, H., & Callahan, E. J. Reinforced practice and reduction of different kinds of fears in adults and children. *Behaviour Research and Therapy*, 1973, *11*, 19–30.

Levine, F. M., & Fasnacht, G. Token rewards may lead to token learning. *American Psychologist*, 1974, *29*, 816–820.

Lewis, S. A comparison of behavior therapy techniques in the reduction of fearful avoidance behavior. *Behavior Therapy*, 1974, *5*, 648–655.

Linden, W. Practicing of meditation by school children and their levels of field dependence—independence, test anxiety, and reading achievement. *Journal of Consulting and Clinical Psychology*, 1973, *41*, 139–143.

Lippman, H. S. The phobic child and other related anxiety states. In M. Hammer & A. M. Kaplan (Eds.), *The practice of psychotherapy with children*. Homewood, Ill.: Dorsey Press, 1967.

Lovaas, O. I. Behavioral treatment of autistic children. In J. T. Spence, R. C. Carson, & J. W. Thibaut (Eds.), *Behavioral approaches to therapy*. Morristown, N.J.: General Learning Press, 1976.

MacDonald, M. L. Multiple impact behavior therapy in a child's dog phobia. *Journal of Behavior Therapy and Experimental Psychiatry*, 1975, *6*, 317–322.

MacFarlane, J. W., Allen, L., & Honzik, M. P. *A developmental study of the behavior problems of normal children between 21 months and 14 years*. Berkeley: University of California Press, 1954.

Mahoney, M. J. *Cognition and behavior modification*. Cambridge, Mass.: Ballinger, 1974.

Mahoney, M. J., & Thoresen, C. E. (Eds.). *Self-control: Power to the person*. Monterey, Calif.: Brooks/Cole, 1974.

Marks, I. M. *Fears and phobias*. New York: Academic, 1969.

Marlatt, G. A., & Perry, M. A. Modeling methods. In F. H. Kanfer & A. P. Goldstein (Eds.), *Helping people change*. New York: Pergamon, 1975.

McFall, R. M. Behavioral training: A skill-acquisition approach to clinical problems. In J. T. Spence, R. C. Carson, & J. W. Thibaut (Eds.), *Behavioral approaches to therapy*. Morristown, N.J.: General Learning Press, 1976.

McReynolds, W. T. Anxiety as fear: A behavioral approach to one emotion. In M. Zuckerman & C. D. Spielberger (Eds.), *Emotions and anxiety: New concepts, methods, and applications*. Hillsdale, N.J.: Lawrence Erlbaum & Associates, 1976.

Meichenbaum, D. Examination of model characteristics in reducing avoidance behavior. *Journal of Personality and Social Psychology*, 1971, *17*, 298–307.

Meichenbaum, D. *Cognitive behavior modification*. Morristown, New Jersey: General Learning Press, 1974.

Meichenbaum, D. Self-instructional methods. In F. H. Kanfer & A. P. Goldstein (Eds.), *Helping people change*. New York: Pergamon, 1975.

Meichenbaum, D., & Cameron, R. The clinical potential of modifying what clients say to themselves. In M. J. Mahoney & C. E. Thoresen (Eds.), *Self-control: Power to the person*. Monterey, Calif.: Brooks/Cole, 1974.

Meichenbaum, D., & Turk, D. The cognitive-behavioral management of anxiety, anger and pain. In P. Davidson (Ed.), *Behavioral management of anxiety, depression and pain*. New York: Brunner/Mazel, 1976.

Meichenbaum, D., Turk, D., & Burstein, S. The nature of coping with stress. In I. Sarason & C. Spielberger (Eds.), *Stress and anxiety* (Vol. 2). New York: Wiley, 1975.

Melamed, B. G., Hawes, R. R., Heiby, E., & Glick, J. The use of filmed modeling to reduce uncooperative behavior of children during dental treatment. *Journal of Dental Research*, 1975, *54*, 797–801.

Melamed, B. G., & Siegel, L. J. Reduction of anxiety in children facing hospitalization and surgery by use of filmed modeling. *Journal of Consulting and Clinical Psychology*, 1975, *43*, 511–521.

Miller, L. C., Barrett, C. L., & Hampe, E. Phobias of childhood in a prescientific era. In A. Davids (Ed.), *Child personality and psychopathology: Current topics.* New York: Wiley, 1974.

Miller, L. C., Barrett, C. L., Hampe, E., & Noble, H. Comparison of reciprocal inhibition, psychotherapy, and waiting list control for phobic children. *Journal of Abnormal Psychology*, 1972a, *79*, 269–279.

Miller, L. C., Barrett, C. L., Hampe, E., & Noble, H. Factor structure of childhood fears. *Journal of Consulting and Clinical Psychology*, 1972b, *39*, 264–268.

Miller, N. B., & Miller, W. H. Siblings as behavior-change agents. In J. D. Krumboltz & C. E. Thoresen (Eds.), *Counseling methods.* New York: Holt, Rinehart & Winston, 1976.

Miller, P. M. The use of visual imagery and muscle relaxation in the counterconditioning of a phobic child: A case study. *Journal of Nervous and Mental Disease*, 1972, *154*, 457–460.

Montenegro, H. Severe separation anxiety in two preschool children: Successfully treated by reciprocal inhibition. *Journal of Child Psychology and Psychiatry*, 1968, *9*, 93–103.

Morris, R. J. Fear reduction methods. In F. H. Kanfer & A. P. Goldstein (Eds.), *Helping people change.* New York: Pergamon, 1975.

Neisworth, J. T., Madle, R. A., & Goeke, K. E. "Errorless" elimination of separation anxiety: A case study. *Journal of Behavior Therapy and Experimental Psychiatry*, 1975, *6*, 79–82.

Obler, M., & Terwilliger, R. F. Pilot study on the effectiveness of systematic desensitization with neurologically impaired children with phobic disorders. *Journal of Consulting and Clinical Psychology*, 1970, *34*, 314–318.

O'Connor, R. D. Modification of social withdrawal through symbolic modeling. *Journal of Applied Behavior Analysis*, 1969, *2*, 15–22.

O'Connor, R. D. Relative efficacy of modeling, shaping, and the combined procedures for modification of social withdrawal. *Journal of Abnormal Psychology*, 1972, *79*, 327–334.

O'Leary, K. D. The assessment of psychopathology in children. In H. C. Quay & J. S. Werry (Eds.), *Psychopathological disorders of childhood.* New York: Wiley, 1972.

O'Leary, K. D., Poulos, R. W., & Devine, V. T. Tangible reinforcers: Bonuses or bribes? *Journal of Consulting and Clinical Psychology*, 1972, *38*, 1–8.

O'Leary, K. D., & Wilson, G. T. *Behavior therapy: Application and outcome.* Englewood Cliffs, N.J.: Prentice-Hall, 1975.

Ollendick, T., & Gruen, G. E. Treatment of a bodily injury phobia with implosive therapy. *Journal of Consulting and Clinical Psychology*, 1972, *38*, 389–393.

Palmer, J. O. *The psychological assessment of children.* New York: Wiley, 1970.

Patterson, G. R., & Brodsky, G. A behavior modification programme for a child with multiple problem behaviors. *Journal of Child Psychology and Psychiatry*, 1966, *7*, 277–295.

Perri, M. G., & Richards, C. S. An investigation of naturally occurring episodes of self-controlled behaviors. *Journal of Counseling Psychology*, 1977, *24*, 178–183.

Perri, M. G., Richards, C. S., & Schultheis, K. R. Behavioral self-control and smoking reduction: A study of self-initiated attempts to reduce smoking. *Behavior Therapy*, in press.

Ploeg, H. M. Treatment of frequency of urination by stories competing with anxiety. *Journal of Behavior Therapy and Experimental Psychiatry*, 1975, *6*, 165–166.

Quay, H. C. Patterns of aggression, withdrawal, and immaturity. In H. C. Quay & J. S. Werry (Eds.), *Psychopathological disorders of childhood*. New York: Wiley, 1972.

Rachman, S. *Phobias: Their nature and control*. Springfield, Ill.: Charles C Thomas, 1968.

Rachman, S. Clinical applications of observational learning, imitation and modeling. *Behavior Therapy*, 1972, *3*, 379–397.

Rasbury, W. C. Behavioral treatment of selective mutism: A case report. *Journal of Behavior Therapy and Experimental Psychiatry*, 1974, *5*, 103–104.

Reed, G. R. Elective mutism in children: A reappraisal. *Journal of Child Psychology and Psychiatry*, 1963, *4*, 99–107.

Reid, J. B., Hawkins, N., Keutzer, C., McNeal, S. A., Phelps, R. E., Reid, K. M., & Mees, H. L. A marathon behavior modification of a selectively mute child. *Journal of Child Psychology and Psychiatry*, 1967, *8*, 27–30.

Richards, C. S. The politics of a token economy. *Psychological Reports*, 1975, *36*, 615–621.

Richards, C. S. Improving study behaviors through self-control techniques. in J. D. Krumboltz & C. E. Thoresen (Eds.), *Counseling methods*. New York: Holt, Rinehart & Winston, 1976.

Richards, C. S., Perri, M. G., & Gortney, C. Increasing the maintenance of self-control treatments through faded counselor contact and high information feedback. *Journal of Counseling Psychology*, 1976, *23*, 405–406.

Rimm, D. C., & Masters, J. C. *Behavior therapy: Techniques and empirical findings*. New York: Academic, 1974.

Ritter, B. The group desensitization of children's snake phobias using vicarious and contact desensitization procedures. *Behaviour Research and Therapy*, 1968, *6*, 1–6.

Rosenthal, T. L. Modeling therapies. In M. Hersen, R. M. Eisler, & P. M. Miller (Eds.), *Progress in behavior modification* (Vol. 2). New York: Academic, 1976.

Ross, A. O. *Psychological disorders of children*. New York: McGraw-Hill, 1974.

Russell, M. L., & Thoresen, C. E. Teaching decision-making skills to children. In J. D. Krumboltz & C. E. Thoresen (Eds.), *Counseling methods*. New York: Holt, Rinehart & Winston, 1976.

Scherer, M. W., & Nakamura, C. Y. A fear survey schedule for children (FSS–FC): A factor analytic comparison with manifest anxiety (CMAS). *Behaviour Research and Therapy*, 1968, *6*, 173–182.

Schneider, M., & Robin, A. The turtle technique: A method for the self-control of impulsive behavior. In J. D. Krumboltz & C. E. Thoresen (Eds.), *Counseling methods*. New York: Holt, Rinehart & Winston, 1976.

Semenoff, B., Park, C., & Smith, E. Behavioral interventions with a six-year-old elective mute. In J. D. Krumboltz & C. E. Thoresen (Eds.), *Counseling methods*. New York: Holt, Rinehart & Winston, 1976.

Sherman, H., & Farina, A. Social inadequacy of parents and children. *Journal of Abnormal Psychology*, 1974, *83*, 327–330.

Shure, M. B., Spivack, G., & Gordon, R. Problem-solving thinking: A preventive mental health program for preschool children. *Reading World*, 1972, *11*, 259–273.

Sloane, R. B., Staples, F. R., Cristol, A. H., Yorkston, N. J., & Whipple, K.

Psychotherapy vs. behavior therapy. Cambridge, Mass.: Harvard University Press, 1975.

Smith, R. E., & Sharpe, T. M. Treatment of a school phobia with implosive therapy. *Journal of Consulting and Clinical Psychology*, 1970, *35*, 239–243.

Spivack, G., & Shure, M. B. *Social adjustment of young children: A cognitive approach to solving real life problems.* San Francisco: Jossey-Bass, 1974.

Stedman, J. M. Family counseling with a school-phobic child. In J. D. Krumboltz & C. E. Thoresen (Eds.), *Counseling methods.* New York: Holt, Rinehart & Winston, 1976.

Stokes, T. F., Baer, D. M., & Jackson, R. L. Programming the generalization of a greeting response in four retarded children. *Journal of Applied Behavior Analysis*, 1974, *7*, 599–610.

Stolz, S. B., Wienckowski, L. A., & Brown, B. S. Behavior modification: A perspective on critical issues. *American Psychologist*, 1975, *30*, 1027–1048.

Tasto, D. L. Systematic desensitization, muscle relaxation and visual imagery in the counterconditioning of four-year-old phobic child. *Behaviour Research and Therapy*, 1969, *7*, 409–411.

Thelen, M. H., & Kirkland, K. D. On status and being imitated: Effects of reciprocal imitation and attraction. *Journal of Personality and Social Psychology*, 1976, *33*, 691–697.

Thoresen, C. E., & Mahoney, M. J. *Behavioral self-control.* New York: Holt, Rinehart & Winston, 1974.

Tobey, T. S., & Thoresen, C. E. Helping Bill reduce aggressive behaviors: A nine-year-old makes good. In J. D. Krumboltz & C. E. Thoresen (Eds.), *Counseling methods.* New York: Holt, Rinehart & Winston, 1976.

Turkewitz, H., O'Leary, K. D., & Ironsmith, M. Generalization and maintenance of appropriate behavior through self-control. *Journal of Consulting and Clinical Psychology*, 1975, *43*, 577–583.

Ullmann, L. P., & Krasner, L. *A psychological approach to abnormal behavior* (2nd ed.). Englewood Cliffs, N.J.: Prentice-Hall, 1975.

Vernon, D. T. A. Modeling and birth order in response to painful stimuli. *Journal of Personality and Social Psychology*, 1974, *29*, 794–799.

Walker, H. M., & Hops, H. Group and individual reinforcement contingencies in the modification of social withdrawal. In L. A. Hamerlynck, L. C. Handy, & E. J. Mash (Eds.), *Behavior change: Methodology, concepts, and practice.* Champaign, Ill.: Research Press, 1973.

Watson, D. L., & Tharp, R. G. *Self directed behavior: Self modification for personal adjustment.* Monterey, Calif.: Brooks/Cole, 1972.

Weil, G., & Goldfried, M. R. Treatment of insomnia in an eleven-year-old child through self-relaxation. *Behavior Therapy*, 1973, *4*, 282–284.

Weinstein, D. J. Imagery and relaxation with a burn patient. *Behaviour Research and Therapy*, 1976, *14*, 481.

Weissbrod, C. S., & Bryan, J. H. Filmed treatment as an effective fear-reduction technique. *Journal of Abnormal Child Psychology*, 1973, *1*, 196–201.

White, O. R. *A glossary of behavioral terminology.* Champaign, Ill.: Research Press, 1971.

Whitman, T. L., Mercurio, J. R., & Caponigri, V. Development of social responses in two severely retarded children. *Journal of Applied Behavior Analysis*, 1970, *3*, 133–138.

Wolpe, J. *The practice of behavior therapy* (2nd ed.). New York: Pergamon, 1973.

Wulbert, M., Nyman, B. A., Snow, D., & Owen, Y. The efficacy of stimulus fading and contingency management in the treatment of elective mutism: A case study. *Journal of Applied Behavior Analysis*, 1973, *6*, 435–441.

Yates, A. J. *Behavior therapy*. New York: Wiley, 1970.

Yates, A. J. *Theory and practice in behavior therapy*. New York: Wiley, 1975.

Zimbardo, P., Pilkonis, P., & Norwood, R. The social disease called shyness. *Psychology Today*, 1975, *8*, 69–72.

NOTES

We appreciate the assistance and thoughtful advice on this manuscript that was provided by Bette L. Ham, Michael G. Perri, Carol J. Richards, and Jonalee M. Slaughter. Preparation of this chapter was facilitated by National Institute of Mental Health Grant MH 28576, awarded to the first author.

1. The names used in these case studies are ficticious.
2. Surveys indicate that school phobia occurs in less than 1% of the general population.
3. The reader might consult Lippman (1967) if he or she would like to peruse a "traditionally" oriented chapter on phobias of childhood.
4. For more elaborate definitions of behavioral techniques, see White's (1971) excellent dictionary of behavioral terminology.
5. *Ethan Has an Operation* may be obtained from the Health Sciences Communication Center, Case Western Reserve University, Cleveland, Ohio 44106. *Living Things are Everywhere* may be obtained from *Encyclopaedia Britannica*.
6. In this regard it might be noted that live modeling, including a very *friendly* dog, was one of the treatment interventions used for Susan, the dog-phobic girl mentioned in the beginning of this chapter. It was fortunate that the dog had a pleasant disposition—for at one point in the treatment program a therapist inadvertently stepped on the dog's foot! Thankfully, this *faux pas* on the part of the therapist was forgiven by the dog with a mild whimper, rather than a nasty snarl.
7. Relevant studies and reviews of this issue include: Davison and Neale (1974), Gelfand (in press), Gittleman-Klein and Klein (1973), Miller et al.(1974), Miller, Barrett, Hampe, and Noble (1972a), Obler and Terwilliger (1970), O'Leary and Wilson (1975), and Ross (1974). The work of Gittleman-Klein and Klein (1973) is particularly interesting in that it represents a rare example of a controlled study on combining behavioral and pharmacological interventions for a childhood problem (in this case for school phobia). It should also be mentioned that evaluative and methodological commentaries on some of these studies (and systematic desensitization research in general) are sometimes as negative as the results of the studies themselves (e.g., see commentaries by O'Leary & Wilson, 1975, p. 81; Kazdin & Wilcoxon, 1976). Finally, it should be noted that controlled, group outcome studies of emotive imagery and implosive therapy with children are apparently nonexistent.
8. See Stedman (1976, pp. 284–285) for a nice example of hierarchy adjustment following further assessment.
9. For a heuristic extension of this procedure to adults, that also has implications for the treatment of children, see Horan (1976).

10. Punishment should not be confused with negative reinforcement, which has the opposite effect (i.e., negative reinforcement increases the probability of responding). Negative reinforcement entails removing an aversive stimulus contingent on the emission of a response (cf. White, 1971). Recalling that a reinforcer is a stimulus, whereas reinforcement is a procedure, should help the reader cope with this jargon jungle.
11. Bill had several other problems that are not discussed here.
12. White (1971) gives the following, rather dry, definition of self-control: "The emission of behaviors by an organism for the express purpose of producing a change in the environment which will in turn alter the frequency of certain behaviors in its own repertoire" (p. 159).
13. Decision-making or problem-solving steps may follow numerous schemata. For instance, in a provocative article on problem solving and behavior modification, D'Zurilla and Goldfried (1971) proposed a five-step treatment model for problem solving: (1) general orientation or "set," (2) problem definition and formulation, (3) generation of alternatives, (4) decision making, and (5) verification. Both the therapeutic permutations and the potential of this treatment approach are considerable (Goldfried & Davison, 1976; Goldfried & Goldfried, 1975; Krumboltz & Thoresen, 1976; Mahoney, 1974; Schneider & Robin, 1976; Spivack & Shure, 1974).
14. Actually, the modeling and social environmental restructuring procedures were interspersed among the clinic treatment sessions (i.e., before or after the clinic sessions). This is indicated by a dotted line in Table 6.
15. We should caution, however, that interdisciplinary programs can be fraught with difficluties, such as political complications. Indeed, the interpersonal and institutional politics inherent in many behavioral programs has received too little attention from behavior therapists (Richards, 1975).

11

Behavioral Intervention with Somatic Disorders in Children

Lawrence J. Siegel and C. Steven Richards[1]

INTRODUCTION

Picture the following children. Steven, an 11-year-old boy, was brought to the hospital emergency room by his parents for the second time in a month. As in prior visits to the emergency room, Steven was having an acute asthmatic attack. After hospitalization for several days and remission of symptoms, he returned home. Steven has suffered from chronic asthma since he was 2 years old. A highly restricted diet, various medications (including hyposensitization therapy for multiple allergies), and restricted contact with allergic substances has offered little relief for Steven's asthmatic condition. Both he and his parents live in constant fear that, when the next attack occurs, they will not be able to reach the hospital in time for medical assistance.

Betsy, an 8-month-old female, was admitted to the hospital with symptoms of extreme weight loss, dehydration, malnutrition, and a decreased responsiveness to environmental stimulation. Two months prior to her admission to the hospital, Betsy had begun to vomit immediately after each feeding. In addition, she was often observed to regurgitate shortly after sucking her fingers. When this behavior occurred, there was no indication of gagging or choking, and she did not cry or appear to be in any discomfort. Extensive medical tests, physical examinations and developmental history did not suggest any physical or organic basis for the vomiting. A number of different medical, nursing, and feeding procedures were tried without success in an attempt to eliminate this life-threatening behavior.

Steven and Betsy present physical disorders and symptomatic behavior that have traditionally been primarily the purview of medical practitioners. However, when various medical interventions failed to decrease the frequency of the problem behaviors in these cases, behavior therapists were consulted and asked to develop treatment programs. Behavioral techniques were used successfully in both cases: Steven's asthmatic attacks were reduced considerably, and he was no longer dependent on medication for his breathing difficulties, whereas Betsy's vomiting was rapidly eliminated—resulting in a significant improvement in her physical health and social development. This chapter presents other success stories such as those of Steven and Betsy, in which various disorders of bodily dysfunction have been effectively treated with behavior therapy techniques. The results of a number of behavioral treatment programs discussed later in this chapter are particularly encouraging, given the debilitating and sometimes life-threatening nature of the physical disorders to which these treatment approaches have been applied.

Scope of the Chapter

The purpose of this chapter is to acquaint the reader with the major behavioral treatment approaches that have been used with various somatic disorders in children. Considerations of space do not permit a discussion of all disorders of the body that have been treated with behavioral techniques (other reviews of this topic include Gentry, 1976; Katz & Zlutnick, 1975; Knapp & Peterson, 1976; and Price, 1974). Also, some of the general problems often related to somatic disorders are not covered; for example, this chapter does not touch on the areas of general patient management or rehabilitation. The proliferation of literature in this area makes it impossible to provide a comprehensive review in one brief chapter. Finally, the chapter is not intended as a review of theoretical or methodological issues.

The disorders presented in this chapter have been selected to illustrate the wide range of bodily dysfunctions in children that have been treated by behavioral techniques. In this selected review an emphasis is placed on problems of bodily functioning that have traditionally been referred to as psychosomatic disorders. Particular attention is given to recent developments in the area and to some of the more innovative procedures that have been used by behavioral practitioners for the treatment of somatic problems in children.

Defining the Problem Area

With a growing interest in the study and treatment of bodily dysfunctions, referred to as "psychosomatic" disorders (also known as "psychophysiological" disorders), it has become evident that an interaction of multiple, complex factors (physical, constitutional, environmental, psychological, and social) contribute to the development and maintenance of most physical disorders (Kimball, 1970; Lipton, Sternschneider, & Richmond, 1966; Schwab, McGinnis, Morris, & Schwab, 1970). Psychosomatic or psychophysiological disorders refer to disorders in which:

There is a significant interaction between somatic and psychological components, with varying degrees of weighting in each component. Psychophysiological disorders may be precipitated and perpetuated by psychological or social stimuli of stressful nature. Such disorders ordinarily involve those organ systems that are innervated by the autonomic or involuntary portion of the central nervous system . . . Structural change occurs . . ., continuing to a point that may be irreversible and that may threaten life in some cases (Group for the Advancement of Psychiatry, 1966, p. 258).

The concept "psychosomatic" is generally considered to be of limited usefulness. This is a result of the increasing evidence for the role of psychosocial factors in contributing to the development or exacerbation of most physical illnesses. In this regard, Davison and Neale have remarked that:

Many diseases are viewed as being partially caused by emotional or psychological factors. The list, a long one, includes multiple sclerosis, pneumonia, cancer, tuberculosis and the common cold. In fact, the emotional state of the patient is now recognized as playing an important role in the precipitation or exacerbation of many illnesses (Davison & Neale, 1974, p. 152).

Given the somewhat artificial distinction between "psychosomatic" disorders and other health problems, we prefer using the term "somatic" disorders to refer to any dysfunction of the body, regardless of the presumed etiology.

Behavioral Model of Somatic Disorders

Regardless of the specific etiology of the bodily dysfunction, recent research provides evidence that learning or conditioning mechanisms can be a significant factor in somatic disorders. Research has demonstrated, for example, that autonomic (visceral) reponses can be affected and modified by both respondent (classical) or operant (instrumental) conditioning (Blanchard & Young, 1974; Miller, 1969; Schwartz, 1973). Until recently, it was believed that autonomic responses were "involuntary" and, therefore, could be modified only through respondent conditioning. However, clinical and research evidence accumulated over the last decade indicates that autonomic responses such as heart rate (Bleecker & Engle, 1973; Engle, 1972), Blood pressure (Elder, Ruiz, Deabler, & Dillenkoffer, 1973; Shapiro, Tursky, & Schwartz, 1970), and skin temperature (Sargent, Greene, & Walters, 1973; Peper & Grossman, Note 1) may be subject to voluntary control through operant conditioning mechanisms.

Davison and Neale (1974) have further suggested that "both classical and instrumental conditioning may play a role in psychophysiological disorders, although conditioning is probably best viewed as a factor that can exacerbate an already existing illness rather than cause it" (p. 157). In Chapter 1 of this book the theoretical basis for operant and respondent conditioning was briefly discussed. Through the process of respondent conditioning, involuntary or reflexive behaviors can be made to occur in the presence of a previously neutral stimulus (a stimulus that does not naturally elicit the physiological response). After repeated pairings of the neutral stimulus with the unconditioned or natural stimulus, the neutral stimulus itself acquires the ability to elicit the physiological response. Consider, for example, the case of an 8-year-old child who experienced abdominal pain for several days as a result of gastrointestinal symptoms developed during a viral infection. The child's drinking of milk during the illness appeared to worsen the stomachaches, and the pain became more intense. As a result of the learned association between the abdominal pain and the milk, the act of drinking milk alone was sufficient to elicit the stomach pains, even after the virus was no longer present. That is, each time the child attempted to drink milk, the pains appeared for a short period of time.

Stomach pains can also be shaped and maintained by operant conditioning mechanisms. In the process of operant conditioning, a response occurs and is affected by the consequences that contingently follow it. The response is then more or less likely to occur in the future, depending on whether the consequences were reinforcing, punishing, or neutral. For example, a number of positive consequences, sometimes referred to as secondary gains (or secondary reinforcers), may follow the occurrence of stomachaches. The child may receive considerable adult attention and comfort for the reported pain. In addition, when the stomachache occurs, he may stay home from school or avoid unpleasant activities such as completing his household chores. These consequences can function as reinforcers that maintain the symptomatic behavior, despite the possibility that the illness, which may have originally precipitated the abdominal pain, no longer exists. More comprehensive discussions of somatic disorders within a behavioral framework can be found in Davison and Neale (1974) and Ullmann and Krasner (1975).

Implications for Treatment

Evidence for the interaction between environmental and psychological factors, on the one hand, and the physiological state of the body, on the other, suggests that, at least for some illnesses, methods of intervention beyond traditional medical approaches may be appropriate. Because multiple factors contribute to the development of many health problems, a *collaborative* treatment approach between medical and behavioral practitioners is indicated.

With somatic disorders, knowledge of etiology is not necessarily essential for developing a behavioral treatment program. Similarly, the efficacy of a treatment approach does not necessarily provide information about the etiology of the particular disorder treated by that approach (cf. Davison & Neale, 1974). Because factors in the child's environment may currently maintain the problem behavior, regardless of the original cause, it is important to assess the relationship between environmental stimuli and the disordered behavior. This is accomplished by performing a functional analysis of the behavior, which Kanfer and Saslow (1969) define as "an attempt to identify classes of dependent variables in human behavior which allow inferences about the particular contemporary controlling factors, the social stimuli, and the reinforcing stimuli of which they are a function" (p. 419). (See Chapters 2 and 3 for a more detailed description of a functional analysis of behavior.)

Within the foregoing context, behavior therapy has emerged as a treatment approach for a wide range of illnesses or dysfunctions of the body. Disorders of both an organic and nonorganic origin have been successfully treated with behavioral procedures. Behavioral techniques used for the treatment of somatic disorders in children have focused primarily on two areas: (1) the modification of autonomic or visceral responses through both operant and respondent conditioning and (2) the modification of overt somatic responses through operant conditioning (e.g., by altering social and environmental contingencies; see Price, 1974). Other learning-based treatment procedures, such as modeling, have received less emphasis in this area.

At this point, it is important to stress that in many somatic disorders, particularly the so-called psychosomatic illnesses, physical changes or tissue damage to the body's organ systems may occur (e.g., ulcers, hives). This is true regardless of the etiology (e.g., organic *vs.* environmental). A related issue involves the possibility of there being clear organic causes for a somatic disorder that typically has a nonorganic etiology. For instance, enuresis or bedwetting, to be discussed later in this chapter, can be caused by physical defects in the urinary-tract, by neurological disorders, or by urinary tract infections. Although less than 10% of enuresis in children can be attributed to these organic factors, such factors obviously work against the successful treatment of enuresis with behavioral procedures that are used in *isolation* from medical interventions. Therefore, where any physical or somatic complaints are presented as the problem, a thorough medical examination should always be completed prior to using behavior therapy techniques, so as to rule out (or not rule out) the need for medical treatment. Of course, even when medical interventions are called for, behavioral techniques can serve a useful collaborative or adjunctive role in treatment: despite the probable involvement of medical treatment (chemotherapy, surgery, etc.) in some somatic disorders, the simultaneous use of behavioral methods has been shown to be effective in reducing or eliminating the factors that exacerbate the symptomatic behavior and in alleviating the discomfort that often results from the somatic disorder. In addition, behavioral approaches have been useful in changing any dysfunctional behavior patterns that may have developed while the medical problem was in existence.

TREATMENT OF SOMATIC DISORDERS

We now turn to a presentation of several somatic disorders in children that have been treated (at least in part) by behavioral techniques. For purposes of organization, the various disorders covered in this chapter are grouped under organ systems of the body. Thus the somatic problems presented in this section represent disorders of the respiratory, nervous, genitourinary, and gastrointestinal systems. Each somatic disorder is briefly defined, and a few relevant demographic and epidemiological factors are noted. Following a discussion of the major treatment approaches used with each disorder, a brief commentary is presented to highlight some of the critical treatment issues for that disorder.

Respiratory System: Asthma

Asthma is a condition in which the individual experiences difficulty breathing because of constriction of the bronchial passages. Breathing becomes labored when the person inhales and is particularly difficult when he exhales. Wheezing, coughing, gasping for air, and—during a severe attack—a feeling of suffocation are common symptoms of asthma.

For children who suffer from asthma—and there are many who do—it can be a very debilitating disorder. Purcell and Weiss (1970) report that approximately 60% of the individuals who have asthma are under 17 years of age; among these asthmatic children there are twice as many boys as girls. Statistics also indicate that as many as 7000 deaths a year can be attributed to asthma (Gottlieb, 1964).

Research with asthmatic children suggests that they are not a homogeneous group and that multiple factors can contribute to the development of asthma (Purcell, 1975; Rees, 1964). Three etiological factors, allergies, infections and emotional variables, have been identified as stimuli that are capable of precipitating an asthmatic attack. It is widely accepted that the precipitant of most relevance to this discussion, emotional arousal (e.g., anxiety, fear, excitement), can consistently trigger asthmatic symptoms. For instance, when the child's breathing becomes seriously impaired, regardless of the original precipitating event, the experience can evoke a high level of anxiety. If the anxiety becomes associated on repeated occasions with the stimuli that precipitate the asthmatic attacks, it is possible, based on a respondent conditioning paradigm, that the experience of anxiety alone can come to elicit the respiratory behavior that is characteristic of asthma. Operant factors can also play an important role in asthma. Once the asthmatic breathing pattern occurs at a high frequency, it becomes likely that environmental consequences (particularly attention from significant others) will consistently follow the asthmatic attacks. Therefore, from an operant conditioning framework, the pattern and frequency of the asthmatic respiratory responses may be maintained by their effect on the social environment of the child. In summary, although sensitizations to allergens and bronchial infections may initially cause the respiratory tract to respond with abnormal breathing patterns, the asthmatic behavior may be further affected and maintained in some children by conditioning processes. The theoretical formulation for the role of conditioning mechanisms in the development of asthma is presented in more detail by Turnbull (1962) and Wohl (1971).

Both operant and respondent behavioral techniques have been used in the treatment of childhood asthma. When it has been determined that psychological factors are primary determinants of the asthmatic disorder, a number of behavioral treatment approaches have been used, without concomitant medical interventions, to reduce the frequency or severity of the asthmatic behavior. Even in those situations in which medical treatment was necessary, the concurrent use of behavioral techniques has been effective in providing symptomatic relief and in reducing factors that might exacerbate the abnormal responding of the respiratory tract during an asthmatic attack. The specific behavioral procedure used depends to some extent on whether the asthmatic behavior is regarded as an operant response maintained by its environmental consequences or as a respondent behavior elicited by various antecedent environmental stimuli. Hence a careful assessment, through a functional analysis, of those factors that contribute to the asthmatic behavior is important if the treatment procedures are to be effective—different assessment results will call for different treatments. Assessment may be accomplished through a detailed clinical interview with the parents and child and through behavioral observations in the natural environment. During the evaluation process information is gathered about physical (i.e., biological) and psychological (i.e., emotional) stimuli that may precipitate an asthmatic attack. Contingent environmental events that typically follow the asthmatic behavior are also pinpointed during the evaluation. Purcell and Wiess (1970) have reviewed numerous methods for evaluating the variables that may affect asthmatic behavior. They also made the interesting comment that, in some cases, a controlled setting such as a hospital may be useful for isolating critical variables. Now it is appropriate to discuss some specific treatment examples.

Changing Social and Tangible Reinforcement Contingencies. Parents were trained to modify the asthmatic respiratory pattern of their 7-year-old son in a case study reported by Neisworth and Moore (1972). The child had evidenced asthma since early infancy, and frequent medical treatment had failed to control the asthmatic behavior. An analysis of the problem indicated that the asthma (coughing and wheezing) was most severe at bedtime. It was also at bedtime that the child received the most medication and attention from his parents, suggesting that this parental behavior might be reinforcing and maintaining the asthmatic attacks. Following a baseline measurement period, during which the attacks were observed to last more than an hour each evening, the parents were instructed to ignore the asthmatic behavior and discontinue all medication once the child had gone to bed. The treatment program also had the parents reinforcing the boy with lunch money for coughing less frequently on each successive evening. A reversal design clearly demonstrated that this combination of operant extinction and positive reinforcement significantly reduced the duration of asthmatic behavior at bedtime. (It was reduced to approximately 5 minutes.) These treatment effects were maintained at an

11-month follow-up assessment. The effects of these treatment conditions on the child's asthmatic behavior are summarized in Figure 1.

Punishment Procedures. Creer (1970) presents a case study of two 10-year-old boys who had a history of repeated admissions to the hospital because of frequent asthmatic attacks. Preliminary assessment suggested that the hospital setting had become very reinforcing for the boys, because it afforded the opportunity for special activities and attention from the medical staff. It was discovered that the children intentionally exacerbated their asthmatic symptoms by hyperventilation and by not seeking medical assistance during the early stages of the attacks (when the symptoms were less severe). They presumably did this to seek admission to the hospital. A treatment procedure was implemented in the hospital, entailing the use of time-out from positive reinforcement. Each time the boys were admitted to the hospital, they were placed in a private room and permitted to leave only for eating and trips to the bathroom. Contacts with people other than the hospital staff were highly restricted and privileges such as access to

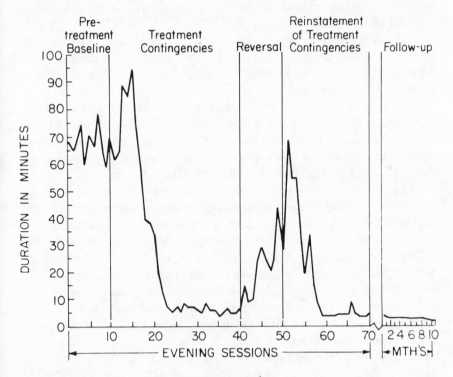

Figure 1

Duration of bedtime asthmatic responding as a function of contingency changes. (From "Operant Treatment of Asthmatic Responding with the Parent as Therapist" by J. T. Neisworth and F. Moore, *Behavior Therapy*, 1972, *3*, 95–99. Copyright 1972 by Academic Press, Inc. Reprinted by permission.)

television and comic books were removed. Subsequent to their discharge from the hospital (after the initial treatment period), the results indicated that the time-out procedure was effective in significantly reducing both the number of asthma-related hospital admissions and the length of time the boys remained in the hospital.

Relaxation Training. Systematic relaxation training has been used to modify successfully the dysfunctional respiratory pattern in asthmatic children, particularly in cases in which emotional arousal has been found to precipitate or exacerbate the asthmatic attacks. In relaxation training the child is instructed to alternately tense and relax various muscle groups in the body. During this process the child focuses his attention on the contrast between the muscles in their tense and relaxed states; he thereby learns to discriminate when his muscles are deeply relaxed. Through daily practice the child learns to produce a deeply relaxed body state that can be rapidly and easily induced in stressful situations (cf. Bernstein & Borkovec, 1973; Jacobson, 1938). Relaxation training has also been conceptualized within a self-control framework and may be viewed as a direct coping skill for use in stressful situations (Goldfried, 1971).

Alexander and his colleagues (Alexander, 1972; Alexander, Miklich, & Hershkoff, 1972) compared the effects of systematic relaxation training versus instructions to sit quietly for treating chronic asthmatic children between the ages of 10 and 15. Systematic relaxation training was shown to improve significantly respiratory behavior (increased rates of air flow), compared with the condition in which children were simply asked to sit quitely. Also worthy of note, the effect of the relaxation training was greatest with children for which it had been determined that emotional arousal was a key determinant of the asthmatic behavior.

Systematic Desensitization. Moore (1965) compared the effects of (a) relaxation training alone, (b) relaxation training combined with the suggestion that there would be some improvement in the asthma, and (c) systematic desensitization on the asthmatic behavior of children and adults. In the systematic desensitization condition, relaxation was paired with imagining several hierarchies of items related to anxiety-producing stimuli that were associated with the asthmatic attacks. Systematic desensitization is a procedure whereby an individual learns to respond to his imagination of a stressful situation with relaxation, a response that is incompatible with anxiety. A hierarchy of items related to the anxiety evoking situation is constructed, ranging from the least to most stressful events. Following training in deep-muscle relaxation, the individual is gradually exposed to the feared situation by imagining progressively stressful scenes in the hierarchy while remaining relaxed. Beginning with the least stressful situation, the person imagines each scene until he is able to remain completely relaxed during its presentation. With this procedure it is hoped that relaxation will generalize to the real-life situation, so that the person will respond with relaxation instead of anxiety in the presence of the previously stressful events (cf. Rimm & Masters, 1974; Wolpe, 1969). An example of a hierarchy that Moore presented to all subjects is given in Table 1. Although all three treatment conditions in Moore's study resulted in reports of subjective improvement (decrease in the reported number of wheezing episodes each day), only the systematic desensitization group significantly improved on the objective measure (increased respiratory function).

Biofeedback. Several studies report the use of biofeedback procedures with asthmatic children. Biofeedback training teaches an individual to become aware of internal body sensations so that he can control the internal physiological responses of his body. This is accomplished by means of highly specialized equipment, which converts physiological activity into a bioelectric signal, which in turn provides the individual with continuous external feedback regarding a particular visceral response. When a person alters a visceral state so that it correctly matches a given criterion, he is immediately provided with visual or auditory feedback indicating he has responded appropriately. Social or tangible reinforcers may also be used when the correct visceral response occurs. Although the reasons why this procedure works are not entirely understood, it is clear that people can learn to monitor and alter certain visceral responses by receiving precise information from biofeedback techniques.

A program training asthmatic children to relax, via biofeedback procedures, is reported by Davis, Saunders, Creer, and Chai (1973). They found that children with less severe asthma showed improved respiratory airflow responses in both the relaxation-alone condition and the

Table 1
Details of a Hierarchy Based on an Asthmatic
Attack Presented to All Subjects[a]

1. Very slight wheeze
2. Just a bit more wheezy
3. Wheezy, uncomfortable lying down
4. Very wheezy and have to sit up
5. Quite wheezy even sitting up in bed
6. Very wheezy even sitting up
7. Difficult to get the breath
8. Feel you cannot breathe
9. Fighting for breath
10. Cannot go on fighting, feel as if you are going to die

[a]From "Behavior Therapy in Bronchial Asthma: A Controlled Study" by N. Moore, *Journal of Psychosomatic Research*, 1965, *9*, 257–276. Copyright 1965 by Pergamon Press. Reprinted by permission.

biofeedback-facilitated relaxation condition, but the greatest improvement occurred in the biofeedback condition. However, children with more severe asthma, who were dependent on continuous medication therapy (steroids), did not evidence significant improvement with any of the behavioral treatment procedures.

Biofeedback techniques have also been applied directly to the respiratory tract for improving dilation of the airways and thereby increasing the amount of airflow. Kahn, Staerk, and Bonk (1973) treated asthmatic children between the ages of 8 and 15 by using "counter–conditioning" via biofeedback. That is, the children were trained to give responses that are *incompatible* with asthmatic constriction of the airways. Following experimentally induced constriction of the airways, biofeedback was used for training the children to dilate their bronchial passages. Respiratory function of the airways was electronically measured by the biofeedback apparatus. A red light was activated and praise was delivered when the child was responding with relaxed and dilated bronchial airways. Following 15 training sessions, there was significant improvement in the experimental group compared with the control group. Furthermore, a follow-up assessment conducted 8 to 10 months after treatment indicated that the control group had significantly more asthmatic attacks, used more medication, and had more visits to the hospital emergency room than the experimental group. Using a similar biofeedback procedure, Feldman (1976) reports an improvement in airway obstruction (equivalent to that produced by medication) for four chronic asthmatic children.

Commentary. Bronchial asthma has traditionally been regarded as a classic example of a psychosomatic disorder. Therefore, the short-term successes of behavioral interventions in this area are noteworthy. The short-term efficacy of both operant and respondent treatment approaches to childhood asthma is supported by case studies and several controlled-outcome investigations. Nevertheless, long-term improvement in this disorder following behavioral treatment *remains* to be documented. Evidence does indicate that behavioral techniques can produce beneficial changes in the physiological functioning of the respiratory tract. These changes are reflected in both subjective measures (self-reported ease of breathing) and objective measures (increased airflow through the bronchial passages). In addition, the successful treatment of asthmatic behavior through altering reinforcement contingencies has demonstrated the significant role that environmental consequences may play in the maintenance of asthmatic symptoms. Finally, these behavioral procedures have been used successfully both by themselves and in conjunction with various medical interventions.

One of the more promising areas of research with asthmatic children has been the identification of various clinical subgroups, for example, those in which emotional versus physical factors critically affect the disorder (Purcell, 1975). These investigations have important implications for treatment, since various subgroups of asthmatics have been found to respond *differentially* to behavioral procedures (e.g., Alexander et al., 1972; Davis et al., 1973). Further research in this area would permit the clinician to maximize the treatment effects of different behavioral approaches by enabling him to select the most effective method of intervention for a particular clinical subgroup of asthmatic children.

Nervous System: Seizure Disorders

Seizures constitute several different disorders of the nervous system. They may be the result of brain lesions, injuries, or infections and can be associated with a disturbance in the electrochemical activity of the brain. Many seizures have no known etiology, however. Seizures manifest themselves in a number of forms and vary from a momentary interruption of consciousness to a prolonged loss of consciousness combined with convulsive movements of the body. Most individuals with seizures require regular medical care, including drug therapy. Despite the significant reduction in seizures often produced by anticonvulsant drugs, as many as 50% of the children who take this medication continue to have occasional seizures. In addition, nearly 20% of the children who have a seizure disorder are completely refractory to drug treatment (Carter & Gold, 1968).

It is estimated that 7 out of every 100,000 school-age children have seizures (Bakwin & Bakwin, 1972). Approximately 90% of all seizure disorders are developed before 20 years of age (Livingston, 1972). When the seizures cannot be adequately controlled, the condition can seriously disrupt the individual's activities. In addition, because seizure disorders often result in a loss of consciousness, there is the potential of physical injury, for example, from a fall.

Behavioral procedures have been successfully applied to the treatment of both organically-based seizures and nonorganic (psychogenic) seizures. A number of case reports suggest the efficacy for a variety of behavioral techniques. These techniques can apparently reduce the frequency and severity of a wide range of seizure disorders (Mostofsky & Balaschak, 1977). These procedures have also been used concurrently with anticonvulsant medication and have even demonstrated therapeutic effects in some cases where pharmacological intervention has failed to adequately control the seizures.

As a final introductory note, we would like to apprise readers of the fact that a primary focus of behavioral treatment has been on the antecedent stimuli that may precede (and in some cases trigger) the onset of a seizure.

For some children an aura or warning period may occur and can serve as a cue that a seizure is imminent. In some instances children are even able to self-induce seizures by engaging in certain behaviors that precipitate seizure episodes.

Positive Reinforcement. A seizure disorder in an 11-year-old girl was treated by Balaschak (1976), using positive reinforcement for exhibiting nonseizure behaviors. At the age of 2 the girl began having several types of seizures, at which time she was diagnosed as having organically based epilepsy. Medication did not completely control her seizures and as a result they occurred at a sufficiently high frequency to interfere with her classroom performance. Baseline records indicated that she had approximately three seizures in school each week. As a result, the teacher was instructed to implement a contingency management program, in which the child was reinforced for seizure-free school periods. The teacher made a "good time" chart on which she kept a record of the number of seizures that occurred each day. If the child was able to complete a week at school without having a seizure, she was reinforced with praise and candy. During the 4 months that the treatment program was in effect, the frequency of seizures was reduced to approximately one incident each week. Improvement was also evident in the child's general attitude towards school and in her feeling of greater control over seizures. However, later, following the child's long absence from school because of an illness, the teacher was unwilling to continue the reinforcement program. The result was an increase to the baseline level in the number of classroom seizures, suggesting that the reinforcement contingencies were, in fact, responsible for the previous reduction in the child's seizure activity.

Gardner (1967) reports the use of a similar reinforcement program that was implemented by the parents of a 10-year-old girl with nonorganic seizures. By ignoring the seizures (extinction) and socially reinforcing nonseizure activities such as playing with her siblings, the parents were able to completely eliminate the seizure behavior. A 26-week follow-up indicated that the treatment effects were maintained, with no seizures reported after the termination of the treatment program.

Finally, in a case reported by Zlutnick, Mayville, and Moffat (1975), the preseizure behavior of a 17-year-old mentally retarded female was treated using a differential reinforcement procedure. Prior to each seizure, her body would tense and she would raise her arms in the air. The treatment program consisted of the experimenter placing her arms at her side or in her lap, waiting 5 seconds, and then reinforcing her with praise and tangible reinforcers for keeping her hands down. Seizures were reduced from an average of 16 per day to nearly zero, and this was maintained at a 9-month follow-up.

Punishment Procedures. Self-induced seizures in a 5-year-old male were treated by Wright (1973a) using a punishment procedure. The child was able to precipitate seizures by quickly moving his hand in front of his eyes and by blinking his eyes while staring at a light. Seizure activity manifested itself as a trancelike state that lasted approximately 10 seconds and occurred several hundred times per day. During a 3-hour daily baseline period, the child was observed to induce 53 seizures by waving his hand in front of his eyes. Treatment consisted of applying electric shock contingent on efforts at seizure inducement; it was administered by an electrode attached to the child's thigh during five 1-hour sessions over a 3-day period. When the child began to move his hand before his eyes, a brief, low-voltage shock was delivered. By the second day of treatment, the hand-waving-induced seizures had been eliminated. This punishment procedure was also used to treat the same child for seizures that were induced by eye blinking. Using this treatment approach, seizures were decreased by the fourth day of treatment from a baseline frequency of 407 per hour to 36 episodes per hour. A 7-month follow-up revealed that the hand-induced seizures no longer occurred, and there was only a slight increase from the post-treatment level in the frequency of the blinking induced seizures. In another case Wright (1973b) was also able to significantly reduce organically based seizures of a 14-year-old male by delivering shock at the onset (e.g., dropping eyelids and head nodding) of the preseizure behavior. During 3 days of treatment, these high-frequency seizures (as many as 30 an hour—they had prevented his going to school) were decreased to nearly 75% of their baseline rate.

Zlutnick et al. (1975) also used a punishment procedure to treat four children with major and minor motor seizures. Their seizures were occurring at a baseline rate of 2 to 12 per day. The punishment procedure was used to suppress certain behaviors that preceded the occurrence of seizures, such as staring at a flat surface and certain movements of the head and arms. When the parents and teachers observed these preseizure behaviors, they were instructed to shout "No!" in a loud voice and then to grasp the child by the shoulders and shake him in a vigorous (and hence aversive) manner. Using this procedure, the frequency of seizures in the four children was reduced from 40 to 100% of the baseline rate. In each case a reversal design demonstrated that the punishment contingencies were indeed responsible for controlling the seizure behavior.

Using time-out from reinforcement, Balaschak (Note 2) was able to decrease the frequency of self-induced seizures in an 11-year-old boy. Despite medication, he was having an average of 3·5 seizure episodes each day. This child precipitated seizures by looking at a bright light and blinking his eyes rapidly. Therefore, both the child's mother and teacher were trained to use a time-out treatment procedure. Each time they observed the boy blink his eyes, he was required to stand up, close his eyes, and count to 60. Praise and tangible reinforcement for nonseizure behavior were also used. This procedure reduced the number of seizures to an average of less than 1 per day. Improvement in the child's electroencephalogram (a precise measure of electrical activity in the brain, also often referred to as an EEG) was also reported. We cannot help observing at this point that punishment procedures appear particularly well-suited to the treatment of seizure disorders that are *self*-induced.

Self-control. Ince (1976) used relaxation training, systematic desensitization, and a self-control procedure to interrupt the preseizure behavior of a 12-year-old boy. The child had several types of seizures (grand mal and petit mal), which medication had failed to control adequately. The high frequency of seizures also interferred with his performance in school. Following training in relaxation, he was desensitized to several hierarchies that related to his anxiety about having seizures in school. A more direct intervention for the seizures consisted of the following: the child was instructed to repeat the cue word "relax" 10 times while he was in a completely relaxed state. He was also instructed to practice this at home. Once the cue word "relax" had become firmly associated with a relaxed body state, he was told to repeat it several times when a preseizure aura indicated that a seizure was about to occur. Hence the boy was practicing behavioral self-control by initiating and monitoring certain responses (the cue word "relax" and subsequent relaxation) that in turn altered other personal responses (seizures). It was assumed that a relaxed state was inimical to seizure precipitation: "The rational for this was explained to him [the boy], namely to associate a cue word with the relaxed body state so as to create a conditioned stimulus which could be used to produce the desired calm" (Ince, 1976, p. 41). Results of this treatment program are presented in Table 2. Systematic desensitization for seizure-related anxiety had a negligible effect on the frequency of seizures. However, using the cue word "relax" to interrupt the onset of the seizures produced a complete cessation of both the grand mal and petit mal episodes. Moreover, no seizures were reported for 9 months following termination of the treatment program.

Biofeedback. Another behavioral technique that has been used with some success in treating child seizure disorders is biofeedback. Utilizing operant conditioning, the child is trained to produce a brain wave (EEG) pattern that is incompatible with a seizure EEG pattern. The child is given corrective feedback and is rewarded with social and tangible reinforcers when he shows EEG activity of a desired form. Finley, Smith, and Etherton (1975) used biofeedback training with a 13-year-old male who had a long history of seizures that were refractory to medication. Baseline records indicated that he was having as many as eight seizures an hour; these seizures were both the grand mal and petit mal types. Biofeedback training was conducted in three 1-hour weekly sessions over a period of 6 months. During the first phase of treatment a blue light and an auditory signal were activated when the patient was producing a pattern of EEG activity that supposedly inhibits seizure behavior. He was also reinforced with one point for each 5 seconds of this brain wave pattern that he could produce. Accumulated points could then be exchanged for money. The second phase of the treatment program, which began at session 35, involved providing him with additional feedback when he was emitting an EEG pattern *associated* with seizure activity. When this occurred, a red light was activated and he was instructed to turn it off. While the red light was on, he could not earn any points (i.e., he was punished mildly by time-out from positive reinforcement). Both biofeedback procedures produced an increase—from 10 to 65%—in the frequency of EEG patterns that are incompatible with seizure activity. There was a concurrent significant reduction in the number of seizures that were observed at home. Similar results using biofeedback training with children are reported by Sterman (1973) and Sterman, MacDonald, and Stone (1974).

Stimulus Fading and Extinction Procedures. Finally, we describe a technique used by Forster (1967) and his associates. They implemented a stimulus fading plus extinction procedure to treat sensory-evoked seizures. Sensory-evoked seizures are seizures precipitated by a variety of sensory stimuli, such as flashing lights, certain visual patterns, and noises. In their procedure children were repeatedly but gradually exposed to increasingly noxious levels of the stimulus (stimulus fading) until they were able to tolerate a particular stimulus intensity or duration. This continued until the criterion stimulus failed to elicit a seizure (extinction). During this process,

Table 2
Number of Epileptic Seizures per Week[a]

	Weeks	FREQUENCY Grand mal	Petit mal
Pretreatment	1–4	9–10	25–26
Treatment for anxiety	5–9	8–9	24–25
Treatment for seizures	10–13	1–2	3–4
	14–17	0	3–4
	18–21	3–4	3–4
	22–25[b]	3–4	5–6
Follow-up	26–29	0	0
	30–33	0	0
	34–37	0	0
	38–63	0	0

[a]From "The Use of Relaxation Training and a Conditioned Stimulus in the Elimination of Epileptic Seizures in a Child: A Case Study" by L. P. Ince, *Journal of Behavior Therapy and Experimental Psychiatry*, 1976, *7*, 39–42. Copyright 1976 by Pergamon Press. Reprinted by permission.
[b]Patient seen for only one therapy session during the 4-week period.

the EEG was continuously monitered to determine the stimulus level at which a seizure was imminent. Presentation of the stimulus was discontinued at the point at which a seizure was about to occur and was later reintroduced on repeated extinction trials. (This is a nice example of the value of precise monitoring procedures—such as EEG data-collection equipment—in the implementation and evaluation of behavioral treatment programs.)

Forster (1967) presents a case of a 13-year-old girl who had a pattern-evoked seizure disorder. Her seizures were elicited when she stared at patterned surfaces such as lined upholstery and radiators (including both vertically and horizontally lined patterns). Treatment consisted of lowering the lights in a room to the point where patterns were barely visible. The room light was then gradually increased until an abnormal EEG configuration was elicited, at which point the light was immediately reduced. Through this repeated, gradual stimulus fading plus extinction process, the child was eventually able to look at patterns in normal room light without a seizure occurring. It is noteworthy that periodic booster treatments proved necessary in this case for the conditioning effects to be maintained.

Commentary. Seizure disorders represent one of the newest areas where behavioral procedures have been applied. It is only within the last few years that behavioral treatments of seizure disorders in children have been reported, and these reports are all single-case studies. Preliminary results are highly encouraging and suggest that learning-based treatment procedures hold promise as a means of reducing or eliminating a very serious disorder—seizure behaviors. These case studies also indicate that environmental conditions (both antecedent and consequent events) can affect organically based seizures. It is interesting to note that various behavioral techniques have been used successfully in cases where chemo-therapy (the primary medical intervention) has *not* been effective in controlling the seizures. Furthermore, this area is particularly significant in its demonstration that behavioral treatment procedures may be safely and successfully used with a clinically diagnosed neurological disorder. We hasten to add, however, that this area serves as a superb illustration of our caveat that behavioral treatment of somatic disorders should always be preceeded by and done in careful alignment with a thorough medical evaluation.

Genitourinary System: Enuresis

A common problem of childhood which may continue into adolescence is nocturnal enuresis or bedwetting. Enuresis is defined as a disorder that meets two conditions: (a) the involuntary discharge of urine during sleep after an age at which children usually gain nocturnal bladder control (typically 3 to 4 years old) and (b) the absence of any organic causes for this behavior. There are several forms of childhood enuresis. In primary enuresis the child has never attained nighttime bladder control. Secondary enuresis, on the other hand, refers to the loss of previously acquired nocturnal bladder control.

Approximately one out of five children continue to wet their bed at the age of 5. Fifty percent of these children still remain enuretic at age 10. Nocturnal enuresis also occurs twice as often in boys as girls (Oppel, Harper, & Rowland, 1968). Despite the fact that organic causes account for less than 10% of the enuretic behavior in children (Pierce, 1967), a medical examination should be conducted to rule out possible anatomical problems, neurological disorders, or urinary-tract infections. Should any of these organic conditions exist, the effectiveness of behavioral interventions could be impeded, and the disorder might even worsen if treatment was pursued in the context of inadequate medical evaluation.

From a behavior therapist's perspective, enuresis is regarded as a behavioral deficit that results from faulty learning histories. The acquisition of nocturnal bladder control is viewed as a high-level skill that may not develop because the particular behaviors necessary for remaining dry while asleep were not learned. An enuretic child has not learned to exercise adequate control of the bladder's sphincter muscles and, therefore, fails to inhibit the bladder reflex controlling urination under conditions of bladder distension.

Bell-and-pad. To date, the most frequently used and researched behavioral method for treating enuresis in children is the bell-and-pad conditioning method. Although this procedure was originally based on a respondent-conditioning paradigm (Mowrer & Mowrer, 1938), the exact mechanism by which it works remains to be clearly determined (Lovibond, 1963). In the bell-and-pad method, the child sleeps on a specially constructed pad. (These pads can be purchased at several chain department stores for a modest price, but they should not be used without professional consultation.) As soon as he (or she) begins to urinate, the urine completes an electric circuit that activates a bell (or buzzer). The noise serves to inhibit further urination in bed by causing the bladder muscles to reflexively (automatically) contract. Because the noise awakens the child at the time when his bladder is full, after a number of pairings of the noise with the full bladder the child learns to wake up to the cues for bladder fullness and the need to urinate. Eventually, he learns to respond to the bladder cues without the assistance of the bell-and-pad, so that bladder distension automatically elicits contraction of the sphincter muscles and awakening of the child.

The child *is* encouraged to drink fluids before bedtime to ensure that sufficient pairings of the bell and the act of urination will occur. In addition, the child is asked to sleep without pajama bottoms so that the bell is triggered at the exact moment urination starts. When the bell is sounded, the child is instructed to turn it off and go to the bathroom to finish urinating. If the child has difficulty awakening or is reluctant to go to the bathroom, the parents are asked to arouse him, making sure that he is completely awake before he turns off the switch and goes to the bathroom. The instrument is then reset, the pad is wiped off, and a dry sheet is placed on the pad. If the child is old enough, he is often asked to take the responsibility for changing the sheets. The parents are asked to keep a record of the time that the bell rings and the diameter of the wet spot on the sheet. As the procedure begins to take effect, the size of the spot and the number of times the bell rings should decrease. The child is rewarded with praise and sometimes with tangible reinforcers for each dry night. To maintain parental motivation and to ensure that the procedure is being followed correctly, weekly contact with the parents and child (particularly during the first few weeks) is highly recommended. Use of the bell-and-pad is typically discontinued following 14 consecutive dry nights. Parents are told that relapses (typically defined as two or more wet nights in a week) may occur and are asked to reinstate treatment procedures if this happens. Most enuretic children require 4 to 8 weeks with the bell-and-pad method before treatment can be terminated. More detailed descriptions of this procedure are presented in Lovibond and Coote (1970) and Werry (1967).

The bell-and-pad conditioning procedure has been found superior to traditional psychotherapy (DeLeon & Mandell, 1966; Werry & Cohressen, 1965) and drug therapy (Forrester, Stein, & Susser, 1964; Young & Turner, 1965) for the treatment of childhood enuresis. This behavioral method has demonstrated an initial success rate of approximately 80% (Lovibond & Coote, 1970), with a relapse rate around 20% following the termination of treatment (O'Leary & Wilson, 1975). Few psychotherapeutic interventions, including several other behavioral techniques, can claim as dramatically positive results! The relatively low relapse rate can be improved further if the treatment is reintroduced immediately after the relapse occurs. An overlearning procedure, in which treatment continues for a period beyond the criterion point where the bell-and-pad apparatus is normally withdrawn, has also evidenced success in reducing the relapse rate (Young & Morgan, 1972). Reinforcement for dry nights with social reinforcers (e.g., praise) or programmed self-reinforcement (e.g., by regularly noting and self-monitoring a sense of pride for no longer wetting the bed) are also suggested as means of maintaining the treatment effect (Ross, 1974). We feel obliged to conclude with the observation that this is currently one of the best researched and documented procedures for the behavioral treatment of somatic disorders in children.

Bladder Retention Control Training. Based on the observation that enuretic children tend to urinate more frequently during the day and with a smaller volume of urine than nonenuretic children, Muellner (1960) suggested a treatment program to increase bladder capacity and reduce the frequency of urination to weak bladder cues. Kimmel and Kimmel (1970) have systematized a treatment program, similar to that proposed by Muellner, in which the child is taught to increase his bladder capacity through a daytime shaping procedure. At the point where bladder tension is sufficiently strong to stimulate urination, the child is taught to voluntarily delay urination for increasingly longer periods of time. It is assumed that increased bladder control during the waking hours will generalize to nighttime retention of urine.

Specifically, the child is encouraged to drink as many liquids as he wants during the day. When he feels the need to urinate, he is asked to "hold it in" for an initial 5-minute period, and then he is permitted to go to the bathroom. This withholding period is gradually increased several minutes each day until he is able to delay urination for 30 to 45 minutes. Most chidren are able to reach this criterion in 3 weeks or less. Following each withholding period, parents are instructed to reinforce the child with praise and with tokens that the child can later exchange for a variety of other reinforcers. Parents are also asked to keep records for the child of the frequency of daytime urinations, the volume of urine, and the number of dry nights.

Paschalis, Kimmel, and Kimmel (1972) investigated the use of the daytime retention control training procedure with children, between 6 and 11 years of age, who had never experienced a dry night. Most of these children decreased their nighttime bedwetting considerably, and the improvements were maintained at a 3-month follow-up assessment. This procedure also receives some support from a case study with an enuretic adolescent that was reported by Stedman (1972). Parental involvement was not required since the adolescent was able to follow the procedure and keep records of her own behavior without any assistance.

Similarly, Miller (1973) was able to completely eliminate bedwetting in two adolescents using retention-control training. Both adolescents had become enuretic several years prior to treatmemt. During a 3-week baseline period, the adolescents kept a record of the number of times that they wet their beds each week and the frequency of daytime urinations. Retention control training was instituted subsequent to the baseline condition. The adolescents delayed urination an additional 10 minutes each week, so that by the third week of the treatment they had held back urination for 30 minutes. Fluid intake was also increased during this treatment period. Following 3 weeks of treatment, the baseline condition was reinstated (i.e., the urination-delay procedure was discontinued). In the final phase of the program, the adolescents returned to the retention control training, which continued until they achieved 3 consecutive weeks of dry nights. A 7-month follow-up revealed that both adolescents were remaining dry at night with no relapse reported. Figure 2 demonstrates the frequency of bedwetting incidents and the frequency of daytime urinations for one of the adolescents during each phase of the treatment program. This figure also illustrates the use of an ABAB reversal design in an applied setting. As can be seen in Figure 2, there was a concomitant decrease in both the frequency of enuretic episodes and daily urinations when retention control training was in effect. These results suggest that this technique increased bladder capacity, since fewer urinations occurred during the waking hours.

Dry-bed Training. Recently, Azrin, Sneed, and Foxx (1974) introduced

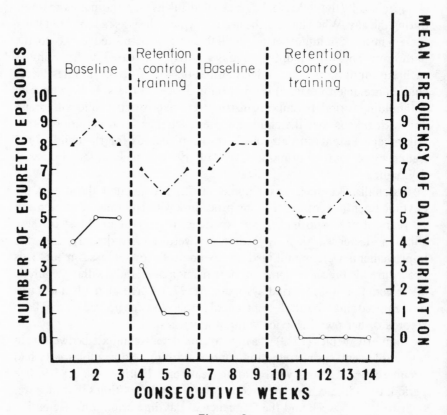

Figure 2

Number of enuretic episodes per week (represented by open circles) and mean number of daily urinations per week (represented by triangles) for subject 1. (From "An Experimental Analysis of Retention Control Training in the Treatment of Nocturnal Enuresis in Two Institutionalized Adolescents" by P. M. Miller, *Behavior Therapy*, 1973, *4*, 288–294. Copyright 1973 by Academic Press, Inc. Reprinted by permission.)

a treatment procedure for enuresis which they refer to as dry-bed training. This method includes the use of both the bell-and-pad and retention-control training procedures. In addition, a number of other techniques, primarily operant procedures, are incorporated into the treatment program; these include hourly wakenings, positive practice in going to the toilet, punishment for wetting the bed, and positive reinforcement for going to the bathroom at night. Table 3 presents a detailed outline of the dry-bed treatment procedure. Azrin et al. (1974) found dry-bed training to be more effective in reducing or eliminating enuresis than the bell-and-pad apparatus alone. Furthermore, dry-bed training required a much shorter treatment period than the bell-and-pad procedure. Children in the dry-bed training group needed only *one* evening of the intensive training program (all components, including the bell and pad); the bell and pad remained in use until the child achieved one week of dry nights. For most children, bedwetting was eliminated in a few days, with no substanial relapses reported during a 6-month follow-up. Given these impressive results, further evaluation of this procedure is warranted, including replication of the initial research findings.

Commentary. Since several techniques have been shown to be effective in decreasing the frequency of bedwetting, a question arises regarding the choice of a particular method to use with a given child. Ciminero and

Table 3
Dry-Bed Procedure[a]

I.   *Intensive training (one night)*
    (A)   *One hour before bedtime*
        1.   Child informed of all phases of training procedure
        2.   Alarm placed on bed
        3.   Positive practice in toileting (20 practice trials)
            (a)   child lies down in bed
            (b)   child counts to 50
            (c)   child arises and attempts to urinate in toilet
            (d)   child returns to bed
            (e)   steps (a), (b), (c), and (d) repeated 20 times
    (B)   *At bedtime*
        1.   Child drinks fluids
        2.   Child repeats training instructions to trainer
        3.   Child retires for the night
    (C)   *Hourly awakenings*
        1.   Minimal prompt used to awaken child
        2.   Child walks to bathroom
        3.   At bathroom door (*before* urination), child is asked to inhibit urination for one hour (omit for children under 6)
            (a)   if child could not inhibit urination
                (i)   child urinates in toilet
                (ii)   trainer praises child for correct toileting
                (iii)   child returns to bed

        (b)   if child indicated that he could inhibit urination for 1 hour
            (i)   trainer praises child for his urinary control
            (ii)   child returns to bed

4. At bedside, the child feels the bed sheets and comments on their dryness
5. Trainer praises child for having a dry bed
6. Child is given fluids to drink
7. Child returns to sleep

  (D) *When an accident occurred*

1. Trainer disconnects alarm
2. Trainer awakens child and reprimands him for wetting
3. Trainer directs child to bathroom to finish urinating
4. Child is given cleanliness training
    (a)   child is required to change night clothes
    (b)   child is required to remove wet bed sheet and place it with dirty laundry
    (c)   trainer reactivates alarm
    (d)   child obtains clean sheets and remakes bed
5. Positive practice in correct toileting (20 practice trials) performed immediately after the cleanliness training
6. Positive practice in correct toileting (20 practice trials) performed the following evening *before* bedtime

II. *Post training supervision (begins the night after training)*

  (A) *Before bedtime*

1. Alarm is placed on bed
2. Positive practice given (*if* an accident occurred the previous night)
3. Child is reminded of need to remain dry and of the need for cleanliness training and positive practice if wetting occurred
4. Child is asked to repeat the parent's instructions

  (B) *Nighttime toileting*

1. At parents' bedtime, they awaken child and send him to toilet
2. After each dry night, parent awakens child 30 minutes earlier than on previous night
3. Awakening discontinued when they are scheduled to occur within 1 hour of child's bedtime

  (C) *When accidents occurred, child receives cleanliness training and positive practice immediately upon wetting and at bedtime the next day*

  (D) *After a dry night*

1. Both parents praise child for not wetting his bed
2. Parents praise child at least 5 times during the day
3. Child's favorite relatives are encouraged to praise him

III. *Normal routine—initiatited after 7 consecutive dry nights*

  (A) *Urine-alarm is no longer placed on bed*

  (B) *Parents inspect child's bed each morning*

1. If bed is wet, child receives cleanliness training immediately and positive practice the following evening
2. If bed is dry, child receives praise for keeping his bed dry

  (C) *If two accidents occur within a week, the post-training supervision is reinstated*

[a]From "Dry-Bed Training: Rapid Elimination of Childhood Enuresis" by N. H. Azrin, T. J. Sneed, and R. M. Foxx, *Behaviour Research and Therapy*, 1974, *12*, 147–156. Copyright 1974 by Pergamon Press. Reprinted by permission.

Doleys (1976) propose a number of guidelines to consider in selecting a treatment approach for enuresis. One of the most important factors is the degree of motivation and cooperation that can be expected from the parents and child, since the success of treatment depends on how accurately the procedures are followed. For example, retention-control training places fewer demands on the parents or child, and it might, therefore, be used where cooperation of the participants is less than optimal; in contrast, dry-bed training requires a great deal of parental involvement and is more difficult to implement. The age of the child should also be taken into account when determining an appropriate treatment strategy. Younger children may have more difficulty understanding the retention-control procedure than the other approaches, which depend to a greater extent on parental management. For older children who can monitor their own voiding behavior and for whom parental involvement can be minimal, retention control or the bell-and-pad methods may be preferable. Finally, where motivation is assessed to be high, and where the severity of the problem seems to warrant it, several procedures may be used simultaneously.

Gastrointestinal System: Vomiting and Rumination

Vomiting and rumination, the latter defined as the voluntary or self-induced regurgitation of previously ingested food, are problems that occur periodically in most young children. Although it is usually an infrequent condition, in some infants and children vomiting or rumination may persist for extended periods of time. These problems typically occur shortly after the child has eaten and in extreme cases may produce a life-threatening situation for the child, because of inordinate weight loss, malnutrition, and dehydration (Bakwin & Bakwin, 1972).

Since vomiting or rumination may result from organic problems, a thorough medical examination should be completed prior to any form of treatment. When it has been determined that chronic vomiting or rumination have no physical basis, the children exhibiting these problems (many of whom were in a critical physical condition) have been successfully treated with behavioral techniques. Because of the life-threatening nature of these conditions, punishment procedures have been the most frequently used behavioral approach; this is due to punishment's potential for rapidly eliminating such troublesome behaviors.

Punishment Procedures. A very dramatic demonstration of the behavioral treatment of a child with chronic rumative vomiting is presented by Lang and Melamed (1969). Four months before the behavioral intervention, this 9-month-old boy had begun to vomit shortly after each feeding. Three previous hospitalizations and extensive medical tests, including exploratory surgery, had failed to reveal any organic basis for the vomiting. A number of medical procedures, such as changes in the diet and feeding positions, antinauseant medications, and substantial individualized nursing care were tried without success. At the time that Lang and Melamed became involved in the case, the child was in a critical physical condition, weighing only 12 pounds and being fed by means of a tube inserted through the nose into his stomach. Behavioral treatment consisted of delivering a brief and mild electric shock to the child's leg as soon as there was evidence that reverse paristalsis and, therfore, vomiting was about to occur. Physiological recordings of the muscular activity in the child's neck and throat area were taken to determine with greater accuracy when reverse peristalsis was beginning. Precise physiological assessment afforded several assets to the treatment program, including (a) an accurate differentiation of vomiting from normal feeding and sucking behaviors and (b) a temporally precise execution of the punishment contingencies. A loud tone was also paired with the shock, so that the tone subsequently acquired aversive properties and was able to be used by itself. To facilitate generalization of the treatment, sessions were conducted at different times throughout the day and while the child was engaged in different activities. The shock was needed only infrequently after the first two feeding sessions it was used. Vomiting no longer occurred by the sixth feeding session. Five days after treatment had been initiated, the child was discharged from the hospital and was continuing to eat without vomiting. Follow-up assessments at 1 and 5 months indicated that he weighed 21 pounds and 26 pounds, respectively. At a 1-year follow-up, the child continued to gain weight, with no recurrence of the vomiting. Furthermore, his social development was significantly improved, and he was more responsive to his environment.

Toister, Condron, Wooley, and Arthur (1975) and Cunningham and Linscheid (1976) also report the rapid elimination of vomiting and rumination, and the concomitant improvement in physical health and social behavior, for young children treated with contingent electric shock.

Lemon juice, as an aversive stimulus, was used by Sajwaj, Libet, and Agras (1974) to treat ruminative vomiting in a seriously malnourished and physically ill 6-month-old girl. Medical tests revealed that there was no organic cause for the vomiting. Observations of the child indicated that the vomiting behavior occurred immediately after each feeding. Several behaviors consistently preceded the rumative vomiting: the child would "open her mouth, elevate and fold her tongue, and then vigorously thrust her tongue forward and backward" (Sajwaj et al., 1974, p. 558). When these tongue and mouth movements occurred after the child had eaten, a small amount of lemon juice was squirted into her mouth. The lemon juice was reapplied to her mouth until the tongue movements ceased. Treatment continued for 8 weeks, after which the child was discharged from the hospital. A reversal design clearly demonstrated that the lemon juice was responsible for the decrease in vomiting. Two instances of rumination occurred while the child was at home. The parents were instructed to place lemon juice in her mouth at these times, and this resulted in an immediate suppression of the problem behavior. (One of the assets of this "lemon juice therapy" is that it can be easily applied by change agents—parents for example—in the natural environment; cf. the Commentary section.) The child continued to gain weight and develop normally at a 1-year follow-up. No further episodes of the vomiting behavior were reported.

Changing Social Reinforcement Contingencies. Manipulating the social contingencies for a 9-year-old mentally retarded girl was found effective in eliminating her daily vomiting behavior in the classroom (Wolf, Brinbrauer, Williams, & Lawler, 1965). Observations suggested that the vomiting was being reinforced and maintained by reinforcement contingencies— permitting the child to leave the classroom and return to her dormitory every time the vomiting occurred. The teacher was instructed to ignore the vomiting (extinction) and have the child remain in the classroom until school ended (contingency change). A reversal procedure, in which baseline conditions were temporarily reinstated, demonstrated that the vomiting behavior was maintained by allowing the child to leave the classroom after each vomiting episode. Using the extinction-contingency-change procedure, the vomiting was completely eliminated within 30 class days. Although changing social contingencies is often a very effective treatment procedure, the reader may notice that the change in behavior with this procedure tends to be slower than that resulting from punishment techniques.

Finally, the contingent withdrawal of social attention was used by Alford, Blanchard, and Buckley (1972) in the treatment of a hospitalized adolescent female with a long history of vomiting after meals. No physical cause could be found for the vomiting, and medication had failed to alleviate the problem behavior. It was noted that the girl frequently sought attention from the hospital staff and other patients, suggesting that this attention from others might be used as a positive reinforcer. Therefore, during the first phase of treatment, two hospital staff members sat alone with her in her room; they interacted with her while she ate each of her daily meals. If she vomited, the staff members immediately left the room and did not return during the meal. In the second phase of treatment, the girl was permitted to eat with the other patients in the dining room. With her knowledge, the other patients were instructed to ignore her discussions of nausea or vomiting and to move away from her table if she actually vomited. By the fourth meal following the initiation of the treatment program, the girl had ceased to vomit. She was discharged from the hospital after 12 consecutive meals evidenced no vomiting episodes. Only one incident of vomiting was reported at a 7-month follow-up assessment.

Combined Treatment Procedures. Murray, Keele, and McCarver (1976) combined the use of punishment with the manipulation of social reinforcement in the treatment of a 6-month-old boy who was hospitalized; the boy was in a seriously malnourished condition as a result of ruminative vomiting. Following each feeding he was observed to protrude his tongue repeatedly and make chewing like movements with his jaw. Shortly thereafter, he would regurgitate the previously swallowed food, until no food remained in his stomach. It was also noted that when the vomiting occurred he received considerable attention and comforting from his mother and the nursing staff, and this attention was seen by Murray et al. as reinforcing the ruminative behavior. Treatment was established during the early stages of the vomiting behavior and was conducted by the nursing staff. During feeding the child was held in an affectionate manner. If the tongue movements that signaled the onset of the ruminative behavior were observed, he was immediatly placed in his crib, and several drops of highly seasoned tabasco sauce (an aversive stimulus) were placed on his tongue. If the tongue rolling continued to occur, the use of tabasco sauce was repeated. As soon as the tongue movements stopped, the child was immediately removed from the crib and held while he received attention and affection. This procedure quickly decreased the frequency of the vomiting episodes and the volume of material regurgitated. (The combination of reinforcement and punishment procedures, as illustrated in this case, is regarded by many behavior therapists as an unusually powerful and efficient behavior change procedure; cf. the Commentary section.) No further instances of the tongue movements and resulting ruminations occurred by the tenth day of treatment. After 3 weeks in the hospital, during which time the boy had gained a significant amount of weight, he was discharged home. The child's weight at a 10-month follow-up was nearly double his hospitalization weight, and there were no further episodes of ruminative vomiting.

Commentary. Chronic vomiting and rumination in children have been treated primarily with operant conditioning procedures. The case studies presented in this section indicate that vomiting and rumination can be eliminated rapidly and effectively by behaviorial techniques and that the effects of treatment are long-term. In most instances the treatment was effective in only a few days, and improvements in the child's physical condition were usually apparent soon thereafter.

There is evidence to suggest that these disorders may often be learned behaviors and, in some cases, they certainly can be modified by changing environmental contingencies. Several case studies report a particularly powerful change procedure in which the undesirable behavior (vomiting or rumination) is punished, while alternative competing behaviors are simultaneously reinforced. Avoidance conditioning, using mild electric shock as an aversive stimulus, has also been effective in rapidly eliminating these potentially life-threatening conditions. Despite the possible ethical and esthetic concerns that may exist when shock is used with very young children, no adverse consequences have been reported in the avoidance-conditioning treatment of vomiting and rumination. In most instances, this procedure was used only for a short period of time because of its immediate effectiveness, permitting it to be discontinued after a few sessions. (At worst, a "lesser of evils" issue may be involved here, and brief professional use of contingent electric shock [e.g., Lang & Melamed, 1969] seems much less "evil" than, say, the child being left to die from chronic ruminative vomiting!) Other aversive stimuli such as lemon juice and tabasco sauce have shown promise for permanently suppressing these problem behaviors. These latter negative reinforcers offer several advantages when compared with electric shock. First, they, probably, are regarded by most people as less objectionable than electric shock. Second, in part because they are more acceptable, they are more likely to be used appropriately and consistently—an important requirement of effective punishment procedures. Most significantly, they can be used in the natural environment by parents, teachers, and others who have regular contact with the child, and they do not require the type of professional supervision that is necessary with contingent electric shock. This is an important consideration, especially if the vomiting behavior reoccurs after the child has been discharged from the hospital and thereby necessitates reinstatement of the treatment program in the natural environment.

Gastrointestinal System: Anorexia and Food Refusal

Eating problems in children, particularly poor appetites, limited food preferences, and refusal to eat certain foods, are a frequent concern of parents; these concerns are often brought to the attention of the pediatrician or family physician (Bakwin & Bakwin, 1972). Evidence suggests that eating difficulties in children represent a significant clinical problem, with the incidence in young children reported to be as high as 45% (Bentovim, 1970). Although most eating problems in children are alleviated without professional assistance, some feeding disturbances require special attention and may in some instances even present a life-threatening situation.

The most serious form of food refusal is known as anorexia nervosa. This disorder is characterized by a refusal to eat food of any kind and by extreme weight loss, all without any known organic causes. The onset of this disorder is typically during adolescence and occurs most frequently in females. In addition to malnutrition, there may also be a cessation of menstruation in female cases. Because this disorder can be fatal, treatment usually occurs in the hospital. A complete medical evaluation is needed to rule out any physical basis for weight loss.

Both operant and respondent behavioral treatment approaches have been used to modify various forms of food refusal in children and adolescents. The most frequently used procedure has been the manipulation of environmental contingencies in order to maximize caloric intake, food consumption, and weight gain. These procedures have been effective in cases where other methods of intervention (including tube feeding, insulin, tranquilizers, and traditional psychotherapy) have failed to modify the symptomatic behavior.

Operant Techniques. Bernal (1972) describes the treatment of a 4-year-old girl who insisted on eating only strained baby foods and refused any of her mother's efforts to feed her regular table foods. Earlier attempts, some as extreme as withholding all baby foods until she hopefully became hungry enough to eat other foods, had failed. A medical examination was completed prior to behavioral treatment, and it indicated that there was no physical cause for the eating problem. During the behavioral program she was maintained on multivitamins prescribed by her physician. Treatment consisted of a gradual shaping procedure, where preferred foods were used to reinforce the eating of foods that she disliked. As previously nonpreferred foods acquired desirable properties, they too were used as reinforcers for eating new table foods. Social reinforcement, such as praise and attention, and T.V. viewing were also used contingent on eating small amounts of table food. Within a period of 4 months, she had added 50 new table foods to her diet—foods that she previously had absolutely refused to eat.

Combined Operant and Respondent Techniques. Siegel and Lehrer (Note 3) used operant and respondent techniques to eliminate a 6-year-old boy's aversion to most table foods, a behavior that had resulted in a highly restricted diet. A developmental and medical history indicated that the child had experienced several illnesses that had resulted in temporary gastrointestinal symptoms; these required that he be placed on a soft food diet. However, when he was returned to his normal diet of solid foods, he refused to eat anything but a limited number of soft foods. If his mother attempted to feed him table foods, he would gag and vomit, even if the food was barely placed in his mouth. In addition, he often became nauseated while sitting at the table as other members of the family were eating. This necessitated that he eat his meals at different times from the other family members. On the advice of several pediatricians a number of interventions were tried, including changes in the feeding routine such as withholding all foods but those prepared for the family; interventions involving medication were also tried, but these interventions all failed to alter the child's eating pattern. A thorough medical examination, including metabolic and blood tests, revealed that there was no known organic factor that could account for the boy's eating problem. In the first phase of the behavioral treatment program, changing environmental contingencies for eating table food proved ineffective for modifying the maladaptive eating pattern. Although the boy attempted to eat several new foods, he either gagged or vomited and refused to continue. Because his strong avoidance behavior to trying new foods appeared to result from the occurrence of physiological responses (i.e., vomiting and gagging), a second phase of treatment was designed to address the respondent components of his eating behavior. A general shaping program was employed, wherein the eating response was broken down into its tactile, olfactory, and gustatory components, and response requirement hierarchies reflecting these components were developed. The *gradual* steps toward the terminal response of swallowing regular table food were reinforced, thus affording the opportunity for gradual extinction of his dysfunctional respondent behaviors. First, the child was asked to smell a plate of table food that had been prepared for the family. After he was able to successfully complete this first task for several days, he was reinforced for touching a small piece of food to his tongue and returning it to the plate. Next, he was reinforced for placing the food in his mouth, chewing several times, and then removing the food from his mouth. Because the gagging behavior began to reappear during this phase, he was asked to perform the chewing task while engaged in a pleasurable activity; such activities included watching television, and it was assumed that these activities would distract him from the anticipatory anxiety that presumedly elicited gagging behavior. It was also assumed that the pleasurable activity would become associated with the act of chewing food, so that chewing would no longer be anxiety provoking. This procedure was effective the first day it was instituted, and no further episodes of the gagging or vomiting were reported. During the remainder of the treatment program the child was reinforced for gradually increasing the amount of table foods he would eat, and by the twentieth week of the program he was eating a complete meal, including most of the table foods that were eaten by the family. Once he was able to swallow several table foods without any adverse consequences occurring, there was a rapid increase in the number of table foods he elected to eat.

Figure 3 illustrates the cumulative number of new foods eaten by the child during each phase of the treatment program. Contact with the family at a 6-month follow-up revealed that the child was continuing to eat regular table food at each meal and that he had continued to increase the number of new foods he would eat.

Token Economy. A token reinforcement program was used by Azerrad and Stafford (1969) to increase the weight of a 13-year-old anorexic girl.

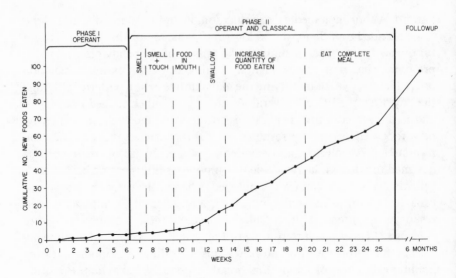

Figure 3

Cumulative number of new foods eaten during each week of the treatment program.

During succeeding phases of treatment, points were earned first for daily weight gain, second for the amount of food eaten, and finally for the specific kinds of foods eaten. Initially the points could be used to purchase various items or access to special activities, and later they could be used to earn extra home visits. There was a consistent increase in the girl's weight, with the reinforcement of increased food consumption becoming more effective than the reinforcement of daily weight gain. (Behavior therapists usually recommend reinforcing responses that are temporally and topographically as close as possible to the target response. In this case, increased food consumption is much closer to the target response than weight gain.) At a 5-month follow-up there continued to be a weight gain of approximately 1 pound per month.

Premack Principle. Based on their observation that some anorexic patients maintain a high-activity level, Blinder, Freeman, and Stunkard (1970) used access to physical activity as a reinforcer for weight gain in several adolescent females with anorexia nervosa. Use of a high-frequency behavior—physical activity—as a positive reinforcer in this case is supported by research evidence demonstrating that access to high-frequency behaviors can be used to reinforce contingently low-frequency behaviors (Premack, 1965). Previous treatment with medication and traditional psychotherapy had not produced any improvement in these girls' physical condition. In the behavioral treatment program, each patient was permitted 6 hours outside the hospital on those days that her morning weight indicated she was at least one-half pound above the previous day's weight. Using this treatment approach, a rapid weight gain (approximately 4 pounds per week) was obtained for all patients in 4 to 6 weeks. This weight gain was maintained or increased over time, as indicated by a follow-up assessment done 8 to 10 months after discharge from the hospital. Similar results with adolescent patients, using a variety of reinforcers for food consumption and weight gain, are reported by Banji and Thompson (1974), Garfinkel, Kline, and Stancer (1973), Halami, Powers, and Cunningham (1975), Leitenberg, Agras, and Thomson (1968), and Werry and Bull (1975).

Multiple Techniques. In a series of single-case studies, Agras, Barlow, Chapin, Abel, and Leitenberg (1974) systematically investigated several variables to determine their relative importance in the behavioral treatment of anorexia nervosa. Their first study investigated the effects of reinforcing weight gain on several adolescents. The patients recorded the number of mouthfuls eaten and calories consumed at each meal. They were also informed of their daily weight and asked to keep records of their progress (self-monitoring). Daily weight gain of a specified amount was reinforced with access to various activities in the hospital. This resulted in a rapid increase in weight. Using a reversal procedure, contingent reinforcement was discontinued, but the patients continued to show a weight gain. Although suggestive rather than definitive, these results indicated that reinforcement was instrumental in initiating the weight gain, but that the maintenance and additional increase in weight was due to other variables. In a second experiment, reinforcement (without self-monitoring) was delivered contingent on weight gain; this resulted in an increase in daily caloric intake and weight. However, when reinforcement was provided noncontingently, there was a decline in the rate of weight gain along with a marked decrease in caloric intake. Finally, when reinforcement was again made contingent on weight gain, there was a significant increase in both caloric intake and weight. The results of manipulating one patient's reinforcement contingencies are presented in Figure 4; the dependent variables are daily caloric intake and weight gain.

In the third series of experiments Agras et al. (1974) systematically examined the effects of reinforcement and information feedback. During all phases of treatment, reinforcement contingencies similar to those of earlier experiments remained in effect. Information feedback, which consisted of providing the patient with information about the number of calories and mouthfuls eaten at each meal and information about daily weight, was introduced for several days, discontinued, and then reintroduced. Maximal increases in caloric intake and weight gain were obtained only when the information feedback condition was in effect. Agras et al. suggested that information regarding caloric intake and weight

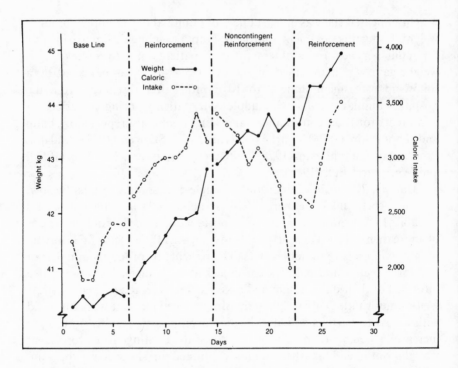

Figure 4

Data from an experiment examining the effect of positive reinforcement in the absence of negative reinforcement (patient 3). (From "Behavior Modification of Anorexia Nervosa" by W. S. Agras, D. H. Barlow, H. N. Chapin, G. G. Abel, and H. Leitenberg, *Archives of General Psychiatry*, 1974, *30*, 279–286. Copyright 1974 by the American Medical Association. Reprinted by permission.)

may enhance the effectiveness of reinforcement because it provides a cue for the patient that reinforcement is forthcoming.

The last experiment by Agras et al. (1974) demonstrated that the size of the meal given to an anorexic patient may affect the quantity of food eaten. When a large meal was provided, the patient's caloric intake increased (even if they did not eat all of it), whereas when the size of the meal was decreased, there was a concomitant decrease in the calories consumed.

Systematic Desensitization. As a final example, we describe a study by Hallsten (1965). Using a respondent conditioning approach, Hallsten treated a 12-year-old anorexic girl by systematic desensitization. Several years prior to treatment she had been teased for being overweight and then went on a diet, losing an excessive amount of weight. She expressed a fear of being fat and as a result would periodically induce vomiting. After training in deep-muscle relaxation, a hierarchy of items was constructed that related to her fears of becoming fat and of being teased by her peers for being overweight. Hierarchy items included visualizing herself being called to the table, eating at the table, eating fattening foods, standing in front of the mirror observing that she was gaining weight, and so on. Treatment continued for 12 sessions, during which time she began to eat complete meals. This resulted in a concomitant increase in her weight. These improvements in her eating pattern and weight were still evident at a 5-month follow-up.

Commentary. Taken together, the available data suggest that behavioral techniques provide a useful strategy for rapidly restoring children's eating behavior and weight in extreme cases of food refusal.' Although these procedures have shown particular effectiveness in the short run for cases in which the child is in critical physical condition and requires immediate intervention, the *long-term* treatment results for food intake and weight gain have been disappointing. These poor follow-up results may be attributed in part to the fact that, in most cases, treatment has occurred in the hospital setting. There have been few reports in which the therapeutic contingencies have been extended to the natural environment of the child. As a result, the treatment gains were not supported after the child was discharged from the hospital.

The predominant technique in the behavioral treatment of food refusal has been the contingent reinforcement of increases in food consumption, caloric intake, and weight gain. A critical factor in the success of these treatment programs has been the selection of potent reinforcers that can supersede the strong avoidance-of-eating behaviors often present in anorexia and related disorders. The observation that high-frequency behaviors may be used as reinforcers for low-frequency behaviors (Premack, 1965) provides a useful mechanism for selecting effective reinforcers to reinstate eating and accelerate weight gain.

Research efforts such as those of Agras et al. (1974), which have attempted to isolate the essential treatment variables in the behavior modification of anorexic patients, appear to offer the most promise for the development of maximally effective intervention programs. Although definitive conclusions regarding the behavioral treatment of these disorders cannot be made at this time, the extant results suggest the following tentative strategies: (a) make access to desired or high-frequency activities contingent on food consumption and weight gain of a specified amount; (b) provide the patient with detailed information regarding caloric intake, number of mouthfuls eaten at each meal, and daily weight; (c) have the patient self-monitor their caloric intake, etc.; and (d) serve meals that are large.

Gastrointestinal System: Obesity

Childhood obesity is a disorder in the regulation of body weight, where the intake of food is greater than the expenditure of energy. Contrary to popular beliefs about obesity, research evidence suggests that it is not a homogeneous disorder. A number of complex factors are implicated in the etiology of obesity; they include genetic, metabolic, physiological, and psychological influences (Quay & Werry, 1972).

Obesity in children is an important focus of concern for the pediatric practitioner, not only because of its effects on the physical health of the child, but also because of the ensuing psychosocial problems that often result. In addition, and perhaps more important, data indicate that 85 to 99% of overweight children and adolescents are also overweight as adults (Abraham & Nordseick, 1960). Furthermore, obese adults who were also overweight as children tend to be more resistant to intervention for their weight problem than those for whom obesity developed in adulthood (American Academy of Pediatrics, 1967).

Behavior techniques have only recently been applied to the treatment of obesity in *children*. A primary emphasis of these programs has been the development of eating habits that are more conductive to maintaining an appropriate body weight. Since the child's eating patterns are developed within the context of the family and are controlled to a large extent by parental attitudes about food consumption and nutrition, most treatment programs have been designed to insure parental cooperation and involvement.

Operant Techniques plus Additional Procedures. Argona, Cassady, and Drabman (1975) investigated the effects of several parental training programs on the weight loss of 15 overweight girls between the ages of 5 and 10. The girls were randomly assigned to either a response-cost plus reinforcement group, a response-cost only group, or a no-treatment control group. In both treatment groups, which only parents attended, various topics were discussed during 12 weekly sessions; these topics included instructions for daily exercise, nutritional information, and techniques of stimulus control—such as eating slowly, eating only in specific locations (e.g., the dining room), and so forth. Prior to the commencement of treatment, parents in both treatment groups gave a monetary deposit to the experimenter; they also contracted to keep records of daily caloric intake, weight and the kinds of food eaten by the child. In addition, they agreed to assist the child in following the exercise program and the stimulus control procedures. Finally, they determined weekly weight loss goals for their child of between 1 and 2 pounds. Over a period of 12 weeks, the parents could earn back their deposit as determined by the following criteria: 25% for attendance, 25% for bringing their completed records to the group, and 50% for the child losing the contracted weight.

Children were weighed on a weekly basis by the experimenter. The unearned deposit money was divided among the parents whose children lost their predetermined weight goal. The only difference between the two treatment groups was that parents in the response-cost plus reinforcement group also received information about using reinforcement and contracted to reinforce their child for exercising, following the self-control procedures, and reducing caloric intake.

Following the 12-week program, both treatment groups had lost significantly more weight than the control group. Children in the response-cost plus reinforcement group lost an average of 11.3 pounds, whereas children in the response-cost only group lost an average of 9.5 pounds. A 0.9 pound weight gain was reported for the control group. There was no significant difference between the weight loss of the two treatment groups. Although all groups gained back some weight by an 8-week follow-up, the response-cost plus reinforcement group remained significantly lighter than the control group, with the response-cost group just missing a significant level of difference. No differences were obtained between groups at a 7-month follow-up, although the response-cost plus reinforcement group regained weight more slowly than the response-cost group.

Enviromental Restructuring. Using an individualized treatment approach, Wheeler and Hess (1976) focused on changing the eating habits of overweight children between the ages of 2 and 11. Forty children with no known medical or psychological problems were assigned to a treatment or control group. Children in the treatment group were seen with their mothers for a detailed evaluation; this evaluation assessed several facets of the specific eating pattern for each family. Assessment foci included where and when food was eaten, the amount and kinds of food eaten, and the social situations in which food was eaten. Based on this information, a treatment program was established that was tailored to the home environment of each child. Particular emphases were placed on (a) changing environmental stimuli that maintained overeating and (b) altering aspects of the child's social environment that reinforced overeating. Table 4 lists the most common problems presented by these children and presents some of the strategies used to change their eating habits. During the early phase of treatment the mother and child were seen every 2 weeks for half-hour sessions. The interval between sessions was gradually increased when indicated by the child's progress. At each session the child's height, weight, and skin-fold thickness (a measure of body fat) were recorded, and changes in the program were implemented as needed. Concern was also taken to actively involve the mother and child in planning the treatment procedures, in an effort to increase their motivation and commitment to the program. Therapeutic contact continued until (a)

Table 4
Changes in Eating Made During Treatment[a]

PROBLEM BEHAVIORS[b]	SITUATIONS			CONSEQUENCES
	Eliminate inappropriate	Control inappropriate	Provide appropriate	Provide positive
1. Child consumes large amounts of candy, cookies, and ice cream	Eliminate such foods from home	Buy food in portion-controlled sizes for clear record of amount	Less-caloric but attractive snacks	Select one food as daily treat for appropriate eating
2. Child eats "on the run"—snacking from kitchen	Kitchen off bounds Tempting foods locked away or eliminated	Set times for snack same time every day	Bin of snacks easily accessible and of low calorie	Occasional favored snack placed in bin
3. Child eats overly large quantities of food at meals	Mother dishes up plates in kitchen	Mother provides seconds of vegetables and salads first	Meal begins with child's less favored food (salad first)	Child gets money or token for leaving food on plate
4. Child must prepare own food (changes difficult)	Child's responsibilities change	Mother prepares frozen dinners or buys low-calorie ones child cooks with sibling	Child cooks low-calor foods	Reward mother for following suggestions and devising her own
5. Child consuming food for which less caloric substitutes are available	End purchases of high caloric foods		Buy lower-calorie foods Educate concerning the problems or possibilities of alternate foods	Make treat contingent upon certain "countable" activities Involve parent in shared activity
6. Child gets no exercise	Curtail television and other sedentary activities	Schedule television viewing	Develop new exercise child enjoys Revise family activities	
7. Parents are "fair" and share with child their inappropriate eating	Eliminate inappropriate food from child's world	Parents inappropriate eating changed to outside home	Parent cooks special treat for special child Incorporate low-risk foods into family diet	Reinforce "different treatment"
8. High incidence of party or outside home eating (baby-sitter)	Restrict parties	Have mother inform others about child's difficulty or have office visit Request limitations of availability of inappropriate food	Select and save for treat at home one special food	

aFrom "Treatment of Juvenile Obesity by Successive Approximation Control of Eating" by M. E. Wheeler and K. W. Hess, *Journal of Behavior Therapy and Experimental Psychiatry*, 1976 7. 235–241. Copyright 1976 by Pergamon Press. Reprinted by permission.
bThe problems listed are the eight most frequent problems listed in all records, both treatment and dropout.

the child's weight was within a satisfactory range for his age and height and (b) the records indicated that the child's eating patterns were conductive to maintaining an appropriate weight. Treatment success was defined as "being closer to mean weight for age, sex, and height at the end of the study period than at the begining" (Wheeler & Hess, 1976, p. 239). The results indicated a significant difference between the treatment and control groups, with the treatment group showing a highly significant improvement in approximating their age-appropriate weight. In addition, most of the children who dropped out of treatment (attended 4 sessions or less) continued to lose weight, even though they had only limited exposure to the intervention program. Unfortunately, no long-term follow-up data were reported regarding the maintenance of these treatment effects beyond the period of active participation in the program.

Treatment Group Membership Manipulations. Finally, Kingsley and Shapiro (1977) examined the effects of treatment group membership on a behavioral weight-reduction program. They asked whether the weight loss of children and their mothers would vary depending on whether they attended the groups alone or together. Forty 10- and 11-year-old overweight children were assigned to one of three treatment groups or a control group: (a) mother and child treated together, (b) mother only, (c) child only, and (d) control. All children were above the 90th percentile in weight for children in their age group. The three therapy groups received the same treatment package, which consisted of a behavioral program similar to that described in detail by Stuart and Davis (1972). A signifcant emphasis of this weight-loss program was on restructuring environmental factors that control eating behavior (i.e., stimulus control); examples included restricting food consumption to specific times and places, interrupting the meal for a short period of time, and not engaging in other activities while eating such as watching television. In addition, the program stressed increasing the nutritional value of foods eaten and monitoring caloric intake. Detailed records of food consumption and weight were also encouraged. Parents were asked to implement a token economy program that reinforced the child for adequatley following the treatment procedures. Parents in the child-only group received information about the treatment procedures discussed at each session by means of a handout that the children took home. All treatment groups met for eight weekly sessions.

Following treatment, there was no significant difference between the three treatment groups in weight lost by the children. However, the treatment groups did lose significantly more weight than the control group. Although the treatment program focused on helping *children* to lose weight, mothers in the mother-only group were found to lose significantly more weight than mothers in the other groups. Follow-ups done at 6 and 20 weeks posttreatment revealed that weight gains for children in all three treatment groups were occurring at a rate consitent with that of normal children their age: that is, normal children should show some physical growth and weight gain during this period, and Kingsley and Shapiro took this into account. Mothers in the mother-only group evidenced significantly better maintenance than the other groups at the 6-week follow-up, but no group differences for the mothers were obtained at the 20-week follow-up. Information from a posttreatment questionnaire suggested that improvements in weight were the result of better eating habits rather than dieting per se. Finally, although mother's attendance in the therapy groups was apparently not a significant factor in their child's weight loss, there were differential satisfaction ratings as a function of group membership. Children in the mother-only group indicated dissatisfaction with not being allowed to attend the group sessions, whereas mothers in the mother-only group felt it was unlikely that treatment would be effective without their children being present at the sessions. The highest ratings of treatment satisfaction were given by participants in the groups where the child and mother attended together.

Commentary. Although childhood obesity is a disorder of diverse origins, the efficacy of behavioral techniques for producing short-term weight loss has been demonstrated in several investigations. However, the effects of treatment are highly transitory! These results are consistent with the literature on behavioral treatment of obesity in adults, which indicates that individuals generally regain weight to near-baseline levels within 1 to 2 years of treatment termination (cf. Hall & Hall, 1974; Mahoney & Mahoney, 1976). In contrast to the extensive research done on the behavioral management of obesity in adults (cf. Abramson, 1973; Leon, 1976), there is a dearth of such research with children. Furthermore, although the magnitude of weight loss produced by these procedures is usually statistically significant, the clinical significance of this weight loss is more dubious. For example, Kingsley and Shapiro (1977) report an average weight loss of only 3.5 pounds for the children who participated in their behavioral treatment groups. However, as these authors sagaciously note, because children continue to develop physically, they *should* gain some weight as they grow. This expected increase in weight needs to be taken into account when evaluating treatment effectiveness for child clients.

Given the wide variability in the response of overweight adults to behavioral treatment programs, Stunkard and Mahoney (1976) have questioned the use of standardized treatment packages that are assumed to be equally effective with all individuals. For instance, the overweight condition of each person may be maintained by different factors, such as exessive food consumption, inadequate nutritional information, and lack of physical activity. In their study with overweight children, Wheeler and

Hess (1976) have attempted to design a treatment program that takes into account the diverse conditions affecting the weight problem of each child. Based on a careful assessment of the child's environment and events related to his or her eating behavior, they developed individualized treatment programs tailored to each child's needs. Although we must await further research to corroborate the effectiveness of this approach, the available data suggest that the recent focus on individualized treatment is a wholesome trend.

A final area of investigation holding promise for the treatment of obesity is the descriptive study of factors that differentiate eating patterns of obese and nonobese children (Coates, 1976; Epstein, Parker, McCoy, & McGee, 1976). Knowledge of the variables that contribute to differences in food intake might provide numerous heuristic and therapeutic benefits—for instance, it might help clinicians develop more effective treatment strategies to permanently modify the food consumption of overweight children.

Gastrointestinal System: Encopresis and Constipation

Encopresis is defined as any voluntary or involuntary passage of feces that results in soiled clothing (Wright, 1973b). A second problem involving bowl elimination is chronic constipation or retention of fecal matter for excessive periods of time.

Encopresis and constipation are frequently associated with each other in children and, therefore, are presented together in this section. Stool retention for prolonged periods can result in relaxed sphincter muscles and a distended colon. As a result, periodic involuntary passage of fecal matter into the clothing may occur (Levine, 1975). Because encopresis and chronic constipation can be the result of physical or organic problems, a thorough medical examination should be completed prior to treatment with any behavioral procedure.

Operant techniques (particularly changing positive reinforcement contingencies) have been used as the main behavioral treatment approach with childhood encopresis and constipation. A number of adjunctive medical and psychological techniques have also been used on occasion to induce appropriate defecation.

Operant Techniques. Young and Goldsmith (1972) described the case of an 8-year-old boy who had been encopretic for approximately 1 year. Long-term traditional one-to-one psychotherapy had failed to eliminate this behavior problem. A behavioral program for this boy was established in a day-treatment center for problem children; he was reinforced with a small toy car at the end of each day if his clothing was unsoiled and if he defecated in the toilet at least once. Within 3 weeks he was not soiling and he was having an average of one bowel movement each day. One month after the program was initiated the child stated that he "got the habit" and no longer needed to be reinforced with a toy for appropriate defecation. These results generalized to the child's home situation, despite the fact that the treatment program was in effect only at the day-treatment school. We hasten to comment, however, that such unprogrammed generalization of treatment effects is the exception rather than the rule in behavior therapy.

Praise, a token economy program, and punishment were used by Plachetta (1976) to eliminate the soiling behavior of a 6-year-old boy. The child had begun soiling 4 months prior to treatment, with an average of two incidents each day. Treatment consisted of having the child sit on the toilet four times a day. For each 10-minute period he remained on the toilet he received a penny, and if he had a bowel movement he received a nickel. His parents were instructed to ignore any soiling and not to spank him as they had in the past. (Parents might be well-advised to generally avoid physical punishment in such cases, since some of the inevitable side effects of physical punishment—such as anxiety—are inimical to voluntary sphincter relaxation and control.) An emphasis was placed on actively involving the child in the program. A self-charting system was established whereby the child made stars that he pasted on a chart each soil-free day. Finally, a mild punishment procedure was used; he was required to wash his clothing each time he soiled it. By the sixth week he was completely free of soiling, and the program was discontinued by the eighth week. The child continued to display appropriate defecation at a 2-year follow-up. A similar token program was instituted with a 7-year-old boy who was a chronic soiler in both the home and school (Ayllon, Simon, & Wildman, 1975). The child received a star for each day he did not soil. If he completed a week without soiling, he was given an outing of his choice with the therapist. Soiling was eliminated by the fourth week of treatment, at which time the token system was gradually faded out. (Gradual fading rather than abrupt termination of the reinforcement contingencies will usually enhance generalization in such cases.) Following this treatment phase, the mother continued to praise the child and special trips were provided on an informal basis. An 11-month follow-up indicated no further instances of soiling.

Another relevant case involved a 9-year-old boy who soiled as much as four times each day (Conger, 1970). He was treated by changing the social consequences that his mother provided for encopretic behavior. Observations indicated that the mother made sympathetic statements and attempted to comfort him each time he soiled. She also changed his soiled pants, which he found aversive, and washed them immediately upon his demands to do so. Soiling was rapidly eliminated when the mother discontinued (a) changing his pants and (b) attending to him when he soiled (this probably amounted to a mild form of punishment). During the 90 days that the treatment program was in effect, soiling occurred only twice. The child continued to remain soil-free at a 3-month follow-up.

Lal and Lindsley (1968) used reinforcement and the changing of social contingencies to eliminate chronic constipation in a 3-year-old boy. Since the first months of life, the child required a suppository to defecate. Home observations indicated that the parents had the child sit on the toilet for as much as 2 hours at a time and they would plead with him to have a bowel movement. When he then began to cry, he received considerable attention and affection from his parents. Treatment consisted of permitting the child to engage in a favorite activity, playing in the bathtub with toys, if he had a bowel movement. The parents were instructed to place the child on the toilet and *leave* the bathroom. (Notice the low-pressure approach here.) They periodically checked to see if he had defecated. If a bowel movement occurred, the child was hugged, praised and immediately placed in the bathtub; if not, the parents left the bathroom at once. This treatment program was immediately effective in eliminating the constipation and in producing regular bowel movements. These treatment results were still in effect at an 8-month follow-up.

Punishment and reinforcement were used to eliminate soiling in a 13-year-old boy who had remained encopretic since birth (Gelber & Meyer, 1965). He soiled from one to three times daily. Treatment was conducted in the hospital with the staff inspecting the child's underpants four times each day. For each instance that his underpants were clean, he was given one-half hour free-time on the hospital grounds. If the soiling occurred, 15 minutes were deducted from previously earned time off the hospital ward. Positive reinforcement, entailing an additional one-half hour off the ward each time he defecated in the toilet, was also provided. Once soiling was significantly decreased, random pants checks were instituted and gradually faded out. During a 6-month follow-up period, only 2 episodes of soiling were reported, and even these were probably a result of not having access to a bathroom when he had to defecate.

Combined Operant and Medical Techniques. The most systematic program for treating children with encopresis is presented by Wright (1973b). This program combines the use of reinforcement and punishment techniques with medical procedures. During the first several days an enema is used to clear the colon completely. Following this phase, the parents have the child go to the bathroom to attempt defecation as soon as he awakens in the morning. If a bowel movement occurs, praise and tangible reinforcers are given to the child. When the child does not defecate, a suppository is given and the child then eats breakfast. After breakfast, the child is again taken to the bathroom, and if he now defecates he is reinforced. If he is still not able to have a bowel movement, an enema is given (this is probably aversive per se!). Should an enema be needed to induce defecation, no positive reinforcement is used. Before bedtime, the parents check the child's clothing, and he is reinforced if it is clean. If soiling has occurred, the child loses access to various reinforcing activities (punishment). Weekly contact with the therapist is used to help ensure that the parents consistently follow this multi-faceted procedure, and detailed record keeping is stressed. Following 2 consecutive weeks with no soiling, the treatment program is gradually discontinued, and the use of suppositories and enemas are gradually withdrawn. Utilizing this program, Wright (1973b, 1975) reports the successful treatment of encopresis in all but 1 out of 36 children. In most cases, soiling was eliminated in 15 to 20 weeks, and follow-up assessments as much as 4 years after treatment indicated that the children continued to remain free of the encopretic behavior.

Tomlinson (1970) treated a case of chronic constipation in a 3-year-old boy through an operant plus medical technique combination. He used a mild laxative to decrease the pain of having a bowel movement after a long period of stool retention, and he used bubble gum as a reinforcer for defecating; this procedure eliminated the chronic constipation. A 2-year follow-up evaluation showed that the child continued to defecate an average of six times each week.

Biofeedback or Hypnotic Suggestion. Finally, several cases of soiling and constipation have been treated using either a biofeedback procedure or "hypnotic suggestion." Biofeedback was used to treat a 6-year-old girl with a life long history of soiling and chronic constipation (Schuster, 1974). A special balloon was inserted in her rectum that recorded the internal and external pressure of the sphincter muscles. When her sphincter muscles responded correctly, she received visual feedback and verbal praise. In addition, for every three consecutive correct responses she was given a felt-tip pen. Training sessions lasted 2 hours; during each session she received 50 trials that were each 50 seconds in duration. This is a lot of trials! We cannot help but notice that the child may have found this procedure very unpleasant. She was able to develop more refined sphincter control in four sessions. A 1-year follow-up indicated that she was no longer encopretic and was continuing to have regular bowel movements.

"Hypnotic suggestion" to induce defecation and reinforcement for having a bowel movement in the toilet were used by Peterson and London (1964) to modify chronic constipation in a $3\frac{1}{2}$-year-old boy. Because he would only have one bowel movement every 5 days, defecation was painful, and as a result he avoided going to the bathroom. In a "relaxed state" the child was presented with a posthypnotic suggestion that "going to the potty" would feel good and not hurt. This hypnotic suggestion was presented during three sessions over an 8-day period. [We will be the first to admit that (a) "hypnotic suggestion" is not usually considered a behavioral technique and that (b) some readers may harbor considerable skepticism about such an elaborate verbal procedure being necessary or crucial in this case.] When he arrived home following the first therapy session, the boy immediately went to the bathroom and had a bowel movement. (A pretty quick cure!) His mother then praised him and gave him a popsicle. Positive reinforcement for defecation was continued for approximately 75 days and then terminated. A follow-up 1-year after termination of treatment revealed that the child continued to have a daily bowel movement without any difficulty. Perzan, Boulanger, and Fischer (1972) described a similar treatment program that included the use of laxatives and suppositories to facilitate defecation in a 4-year-old boy. Treatment was immediately effective and the boy had regular bowel movements thereafter.

Commentary. Taken together, the results presented in this section indicate that operant conditioning procedures are a viable treatment approach for encopresis and chronic constipation in children. For the most part, these behavioral treatment programs have resulted in rapid modification of long-standing elimination problems. The durability of these treatment effects with encopresis and constipation is also encouraging— something we cannot say for behavioral treatment of some of the other gastrointestinal disorders, childhood obesity for instance. We should caution, however, that most of the supportive evidence is from case studies and is, therefore, suggestive rather than definitive.

The primary focus of behavioral treatment has been the contingent reinforcement of appropriate defecation. In addition to positive reinforcement, several treatment programs have included mild punishment procedures such as response-cost and unpleasant natural consequences (e.g., cleaning soiled clothing). Most treatment programs have been conducted in the natural environment by the parents, with minimal professional involvement. This use of natural change agents in the natural environment may account, in part, for the encouraging treatment maintenance results in this area. Many authors, however, also stress the importance of regular therapist contact with the parents to ensure that the treatment procedures are being followed properly and to maintain parental motivation. The parents should be given substantial feedback and reinforcement for their efforts with the child.

This treatment is also noteworthy because of the integration of behavioral and medical techniques. Several medical procedures (e.g., suppositories, laxatives, enemas) have been used as prompts to initiate a bowel movement and thereby increase the probability that an appropriate elimination response can be reinforced. Such prompts, however, are *not* consistently required and should be used only in very circumscribed situations. For example, some children may not have regular bowel movements in an effort to avoid the pain that results from impacted feces; impacted feces are often associated with chronic constipation. Medical prompts such as laxatives would be appropriate in *this* instance, to ensure painless defecation and to allow sufficient opportunity for reinforcement. Nevertheless, frequent use of such medical prompts may be *highly aversive* for the child and may lead to the development of additional avoidance behaviors and other undesirable side effects that sometimes result from punishment procedures. For this reason, it would seem that the treatment program described by Wright (1973b), which included extensive use of medical prompts, should be implemented only after other procedures have failed. If medical prompts do indeed prove necessary, they should only be used in conjunction with a physician's supervision.

ISSUES AND FUTURE DIRECTIONS

Significant Others as Therapeutic Agents

Given the complex nature of the disorders presented in this chapter, it is interesting to note the extent to which significant others (parents, teachers, etc.) in the child's environment were enlisted as the primary change agents. Under the professional guidance of behavior therapists, significant others were trained to modify successfully a variety of somatic disorders in the natural environment of the child. Since it was clearly demonstrated in some cases that social contingencies perpetuated the somatic disorder, the success of behavioral procedures was very dependent on the participation of significant members of the child's environment in the treatment program. Such individuals have been trained in a wide array of behavioral techniques—including techniques to modify dysfunctional somatic behaviors and maintain newly acquired desirable behaviors. This model of intervention—based on natural change agents in the natural environment—has received considerable attention in the behavioral treatment of numerous childhood disorders (cf. Berkowitz & Graziano, 1972; O'Dell, 1974; Patterson, 1971). In part because behavior therapy provides explicit and systematic treatment procedures, a treatment program designed by a behavior therapist *can* be effectively implemented by people who have no previous experience with the techniques. This is not to say, of course, that regular supervision and evaluation by the professional behavior therapist will not be needed in such cases. Training significant members of the child's environment to serve as "co-therapists" with the professional behavior modifier in a consultant-mediator model of treatment (Tharp & Wetzel, 1969) has important implications for the *maintenance* of behavior change following treatment termination. Finally, the potential for *preventing* the development of further somatic disorders, by training these individuals in behavioral techniques, cannot be overemphasized.

Behavioral Medicine—A New Discipline

The emergence of behavior therapy as a viable treatment approach with a wide range of bodily disorders has brought with it the development of a new discipline that may be referred to as *behavioral medicine*. Behavior therapists have broadened the scope of their treatment procedures to include not only psychiatric disorders but also physical and other health-related problems as well. Our current knowledge of the multiple factors that contribute to problems of health and illness underscores the need for a multifaceted treatment approach that integrates medical and behavioral methods of treatment. The merits of this interdisciplinary approach have important implications for the quality and comprehensiveness of treatment available to children with somatic disorders. In this regard, Katz and Zlutnick (1975) have aptly noted that:

> In conjunction with already established medical technology, behavioral techniques allow for a more comprehensive approach to patient care. In contrast, lack of attention to the environmental, behavioral, and social components of health problems may result in a less than satisfactory treatment outcome. Clearly, the patient profits from the *collaboration* between medical practitioners and behavioral scientists (p. XV, emphasis added).

It is noteworthy that some somatic disorders that have not yielded to medical treatment have been successfully treated with behavioral procedures. Furthermore, in many cases behavioral treatment programs have resulted in rapid and dramatic changes in the symptomatic behavior. This latter finding is of particular importance because some childhood somatic disorders have serious consequences for the physical health of the child and may actually generate a life-threatening condition that requires immediate amelioration. In light of this, it is somewhat surprising—perhaps even amazing—that behavioral procedures have often been used only "as a last resort," after other treatment approaches have failed to alleviate the problematic behavior.

As an alternative treatment approach or as an adjunctive procedure to augment medical intervention, behavior therapy offers several advantages in the area of health care. Behavioral techniques afford the opportunity of avoiding the persistent use of other procedures that have serious drawbacks or that can be very unpleasant for the child. For example, tube feeding, which is often required in cases of anorexia nervosa, carries with it the risk of infection and the potential for aspiration of food into the lungs (Browning & Miller, 1968). More important, in a number of somatic disorders effective behavioral treatment programs have enabled the physician to reduce significantly or to discontinue the use of medication the child was taking for the disorder. These findings have far-reaching implications, because of the problems that may result from the repeated use of some medications with children. For instance, several drugs used in treating the disorders presented in this chapter can result in undesirable physical side effects that may in some cases be of a permanent nature. Furthermore, there is evidence to suggest that the learning process may be adversely affected by certain drugs; learning that occurs while the individual is taking the drug may not transfer to the nondrug state (Overton, 1966; Turner & Young, 1966). These suggestive findings are of particular concern to the behavior therapist, given his treatment goal of having the child *learn* more appropriate and adaptive behaviors. That is, the gains obtained in a behavioral treatment program while the child is on medication may not persist following the withdrawal of medication. Further research is warranted in this area to increase our understanding of various drug effects on the learning process in children, particularly as these effects relate to the acquisition of new behaviors through learning-based treatment programs.

Summary and Future Perspectives

The efficacy of any treatment approach must be judged not only for its ability to *initiate* behavior change but also for its potential to promote the *maintenance* of behavior change following termination of the formal treatment program (O'Leary & Wilson, 1975). Evidence presented in this chapter supports the efficacy of behavioral techniques for producing short-term changes in a number of childhood somatic disorders. However, once the desired changes in behavior have been achieved, these gains often do not persist for long periods of time after treatment:

> The durability of behavior change continues to be of particular concern to behavior modifiers as well as more traditionally oriented therapists interested in behavior change. Unfortunately, research directed at providing techniques to assure transfer and maintenance has lagged significantly behind efforts to demonstrate the functional relationships between behavior change and the manipulation of pertinent variables in the treatment setting (Marholin, Siegel, & Phillips, 1976, p. 331).

In addition, there are few long-term follow-up studies reported in this area. It is hoped we will soon see more research endeavors aimed at developing methods for achieving long-term changes in behavior.

Also notably lacking are systematic, well-controlled research efforts directed at isolating the critical variables in the behavioral treatment of childhood somatic disorders. Most of the treatment programs reported in this chapter represent single-case studies, and many of these do not even include systematic single-case study methodology—reversal or multiple baseline designs for example. Although single-case studies using within-subject research designs can provide useful information about a treatment technique (cf. Lazarus & Davison, 1971; Leitenberg, 1973), they do not permit a clear evaluation of the comparative effectiveness of several treatment procedures; in addition, their results tend to be more heuristic and suggestive than definitive regarding the effects of a procedure across a broad population of children. Unfortunately, many childhood somatic disorders are not readily amenable to the group research designs needed to assess *clearly* the comparative effects of various behavioral techniques. For example, several of the disorders presented in this chapter do not occur with sufficient frequency in children for group studies to be performed. Furthermore, several disorders are highly disruptive or present life-threatening conditions for the child that require immediate and complete intervention, often at the expense of an adequate experimental design.

Despite the problems and limitations noted above, behavior therapy holds promise as a therapeutic approach in the area of childhood health and illness. The preliminary results are sufficiently encouraging to warrant continued efforts in the behavioral treatment of somatic disorders. There has been an increasing trend toward the integration of behavior therapists into health care settings, with the result that a number of somatic disorders have become a legitimate domain for behavioral intervention. In our opinion the behavioral treatment of somatic disorders represents one of the most innovative developments in the field of behavior therapy. This innovative approach has also been addressed to certain somatic disorders in adults (e.g., cardiovascular disorders, headaches, chronic pain, sleep disorders), providing heuristic possibilities for extension to similar disorders in children.

We hope we will witness a systematic expansion of theory, research, and practice in this area. We will probably witness more collaboration between medicine and behavioral science. And we will inevitably witness some change during the next few years in one of the most exciting fields in contemporary behavior therapy—behavioral medicine. If readers feel disenchanted at this point in the chapter because they do not have black-and-white answers to all their questions, their disenchantment just reflects the reality of a field that is hardly black and white: there are many shades of gray indeed! Rather than go out on a limb and attempt a mass of bombastic and definitive statements about a field that is really new and in flux, we have opted for a conservative approach that attempts a sagacious compromise between harsh skepticsm and naive optimism. If the final taste left in the reader's mouth is one of a field with great potential—most of which is still unfulfilled—then the reader has consumed our message.

REFERENCE NOTES

1. Peper, E., & Grossman, E. *Preliminary observation of thermal biofeedback in children with migraine.* Paper presented at the annual meeting of the Biofeedback Research Society, Colorado Springs, Colorado, 1974.
2. Balaschak, B. A. *Behavior modification with epileptic children: Preliminary case reports.* Paper presented at the American Psychological Association, Washington, D.C., August 1976.
3. Siegel, L. J., & Lehrer, P. M. *Classical and operant procedures in the treatment of a case of food aversion in a child with a history of gastrointestinal disorders.* Unpublished manuscript, Department of Psychiatry, Rutgers Medical School, Piscataway, N.J., 1975.

REFERENCES

Abraham, S., & Nordseick, M. Relationships of excess weight in children and adults. *Public Health Reports,* 1960, *75,* 263–273.

Abramson, E. E. A review of behavioral approaches to weight control. *Behaviour Research and Therapy,* 1973, *11,* 547–556.

Agras, W. S., Barlow, D. H., Chapin, H. N., Abel, G. G., & Leitenberg, H. Behavior modification of anorexia nervosa. *Archives of General Psychiatry,* 1974, *30,* 279–286.

Alexander, A. B. Systematic relaxation and flow rates in asthmatic children: Relationship to emotional precipitants and anxiety. *Journal of Psychosomatic Research,* 1972, *16,* 405–410.

Alexander, A. B., Miklich, D. R., & Hershkoff, H. The immediate effects of systematic relaxation training on peak expiratory flow rates in asthmatic children. *Psychosomatic Medicine,* 1972, *34,* 388–394.

Alford, G. S., Blanchard, E. B., & Buckley, T. M. Treatment of hysterical vomiting by modification of social contingencies: A case study. *Journal of Behavior Therapy and Experimental Psychiatry,* 1972, *3,* 209–212.

American Academy of Pediatrics: Obesity in childhood. *Pediatrics,* 1967, *40,* 455–467.

Argona, J., Cassady, J., & Drabman, R. S. Treating overweight children through parental training and contingency contracting. *Journal of Applied Behavior Analysis,* 1975, *8,* 269–278.

Ayllon, T. A., Simon, S. J., & Wildman, R. W. Instructions and reinforcement in the elimination of encopresis: A case study. *Journal of Behavior Therapy and Experimental Psychiatry,* 1975, *6,* 235–238.

Azerrad, J., & Stafford, R. L. Restoration of eating behavior in anorexia nervosa through operant conditioning and environmental manipulation. *Behaviour Research and Therapy,* 1969, *7,* 165–171.

Azrin, N. H., Sneed, T. J., & Foxx, R. M. Dry-bed: Rapid elimination of childhood enuresis. *Behaviour Research and Therapy,* 1974, *12,* 147–156.

Bakwin, H., & Bakwin, R. M. *Behavior disorders in children.* Philadelphia: Saunders, 1972.

Balaschak, B. A. Teacher-implemented behavior modification in a case of organically based epilepsy. *Journal of Consulting and Clinical Psychology,* 1976, *44,* 218–223.

Banji, S., & Thompson, J. Operant conditioning in the treatment of anorexia nervosa: A review and retrospective study of 11 cases. *British Journal of Psychiatry*, 1974, *124*, 166–172.

Bentovim, A. The clinical approach to feeding disorders of childhood. *Journal of Psychosomatic Research*, 1970, *14*, 267–276.

Berkowitz, B. P., & Graziano, A. M. Training parents as behavior therapists: A review. *Behaviour Research and Therapy*, 1972, *10*, 297–317.

Bernal, M. E. Behavioral treatment of a child's eating problem. *Journal of Behavior Therapy and Experimental Psychiatry*, 1972, *3*, 43–50.

Bernstein, D. A., & Borkovec, T. D. *Progressive relaxation training*. Champaign, Ill.: Research Press, 1973.

Blanchard, E. B., & Young, L. D. Clinical applications of biofeedback training: A review of evidence. *Archives of General Psychiatry*, 1974, *30*, 573–589.

Bleecker, E. R., & Engle, B. T. Learned control of cardiac rate and cardiac conduction in Wolff-Parkinson-White syndrome. *Seminars in Psychiatry*, 1973, *5*, 475–479.

Blinder, B. J., Freeman, D. M., & Stunkard, A. J. Behavior therapy of anorexia nervosa: Effectiveness of activity as a reinforcer of weight gain. *American Journal of Psychiatry*, 1970, *126*, 1093–1098.

Browning, C. H., & Miller, S. I. Anorexia nervosa: A study in prognosis and management. *American Journal of Psychiatry*, 1968, *124*, 1128–1132.

Carter, S., & Gold, A. Convulsions in children. *New England Journal of Medicine*, 1968, *278*, 315–317.

Ciminero, A. R., & Doleys, D. M. Childhood enuresis: Considerations in assessment. *Journal of Pediatric Psychology*, 1976, *4*, 17–20.

Coates, T. J. *The efficacy of multicomponent self-control program in modifying the eating habits and body dimensions of three obese adolescents*. Unpublished doctoral dissertation, Stanford University, 1976.

Conger, J. C. The treatment of encopresis by the management of social consequences. *Behavior Therapy*, 1970, *1*, 386–390.

Creer, T. L. The use of time-out from positive reinforcement procedure with asthmatic children. *Journal of Psychosomatic Research*, 1970, *14*, 117–120.

Cunningham, C. E., & Linscheid, T. R. Elimination of chronic infant rumination by electric shock. *Behavior Therapy*, 1976, *7*, 231–234.

Davis, M. H., Saunders, D., Creer, T., & Chai, H. Relaxation training facilitated by biofeedback apparatus as a supplemental treatment in bronchial asthma. *Journal of Psychosomatic Research*, 1973, *17*, 121–128.

Davison, G. C., & Neale, J. M. *Abnormal psychology: An experimental clinical approach*. New York: Wiley, 1974.

DeLeon, G., & Mandell, W. A. A comparison of conditioning and psychotherapy in the treatment of functional enuresis. *Journal of Clinical Psychology*, 1966, *22*, 326–330.

Elder, S. T., Ruiz, Z. R., Deabler, H. L., & Dillenkoffer, R. L. Instrumental conditioning of diastolic blood pressure in essential hypertensive patients. *Journal of Applied Behavior Analysis*, 1973, *6*, 377–382.

Engle, B. T. Operant conditioning of cardiac functioning: A status report. *Psychophysiology*, 1972, *9*, 161–177.

Epstein, L. H., Parker, L., McCoy, J. F., & McGee, G. Descriptive analysis of eating regulation in obese and nonobese children. *Journal of Applied Behavior Analysis*, 1976, *9*, 407–415.

Feldman, G. M. The effects of biofeedback training on respiratory resistance of asthmatic children. _Psychosomatic Medicine_, 1976, _38_, 27–34.

Finley, W. W., Smith, H. A., & Etherton, M. D. Reduction of seizures and normalization of the EEG in a severe epileptic following sensorimotor biofeedback training: A preliminary study. _Biological Psychology_, 1975, _2_, 189–203.

Forrester, R., Stein, Z., & Susser, M. A. A trial of conditioning therapy in nocturnal enuresis. _Development Medicine and Child Neurology_, 1964, _6_, 158–166.

Forster, F. M. Conditioning of cerebral dysrythmia induced by pattern presentation and eye closure. _Conditioned Reflex_, 1967, _2_, 236–244.

Gardner, J. E. Behavior therapy treatment approach to a psychogenic seizure case. _Journal of Consulting Psychology_, 1967, _31_, 209–212.

Garfinkel, P. E., Kline, S. A., & Stancer, H. C. Treatment of anorexia nervosa using operant conditioning techniques. _Journal of Nervous and Mental Disease_, 1973, _157_, 428–433.

Gelber, H., & Meyer, V. Behavior therapy and encopresis: The complexities involved in treatment. _Behaviour Research and Therapy_, 1965, _2_, 227–231.

Gentry, W. D. Behavioral treatment of somatic disorders. In J. T. Spence, R. C. Carson, & J. W. Thibaut (Eds.), _Behavioral approaches to therapy_. Morristown, N.J.: General Learning Press, 1976.

Goldfried, M. R. Systematic desensitization as training in self-control. _Journal of Consulting and Clinical Psychology_, 1971, _37_, 228–234.

Gottlieb, R. M. Changing mortality in bronchial asthma. _Journal of the American Medical Association_, 1964, _187_, 276–280.

Group for the Advancement of Psychiatry. _Psychopathological disorders in childhood: Theoretical considerations and a proposed classification_, 1966, _6_ (Report No. 62).

Halami, K. A., Powers, P., & Cunningham, S. Treatment of anorexia nervosa with behavior modification. _Archives of General Psychiatry_, 1975, _32_, 93–96.

Hall, S. M., & Hall, G. R. Outcome and methodological considerations in behavioral treatment of obesity. _Behavior Therapy_, 1974, _5_, 352–364.

Hallsten, E. A. Adolescent anorexia nervosa treated by desensitization. _Behaviour Research and Therapy_, 1965, _3_, 87–91.

Ince, L. P. The use of relaxation training and a conditioned stimulus in the elimination of epileptic seizures in a child: A case study. _Journal of Behavior Therapy and Experimental Psychiatry_, 1976, _7_, 39–42.

Jacobson, E. _Progressive relaxation_. Chicago: University of Chicago Press, 1938.

Kahn, A. V., Staerk, M., & Bonk, C. Role of counter conditioning in the treatment of asthma. _Journal of Psychosomatic Research_, 1973, _17_, 389–392.

Kanfer, F. H., & Saslow, G. Behavioral diagnosis. In C. M. Franks (Ed.), _Behavior therapy: Appraisal and status_. New York: McGraw-Hill, 1969.

Katz, R. C., & Zlutnick, S. (Eds.) _Behavior therapy and health care: Principles and applications_. New York: Pergamon, 1975.

Kimball, C. P. Conceptual developments in psychosomatic medicine: 1939-1969. _Annals of Internal Medicine_, 1970, _73_, 307–316.

Kimmel, H. D., & Kimmel, E. An instrumental conditioning method for the treatment of enuresis. _Journal of Behavior Therapy and Experimental Psychiatry_, 1970, _1_, 121–123.

Kingsley, R. G., & Shapiro, J. A comparison of three behavioral programs for the control of obesity in children. _Behavior Therapy_, 1977, _8_, 30–36.

Knapp, T. T., & Peterson, L. W. Behavioral management in medical and nursing practice. In W. E. Craighead, A. E. Kazdin, & M. J. Mahoney (Eds.),

Behavior modification: Principles, issues, and applications. Boston: Houghton Mifflin, 1976.

Lal, H., & Lindsley, O. R. Therapy of chronic constipation in a young child by rearranging social contingencies. *Behaviour Research and Therapy*, 1968, *6*, 484–485.

Lang, P. J., & Melamed, B. G. Avoidance conditioning therapy of an infant with chronic ruminative vomiting. *Journal of Abnormal Psychology*, 1969, *74*, 1–8.

Lazarus, A. A., & Davison, G. C. Clinical innovations in research and practice. In A. E. Bergin & S. L. Garfield (Eds.), *Handbook of psychotherapy and behavior change.* New York: Wiley, 1971.

Leitenberg, H. The use of single-case methodology in psychotherapy research. *Journal of Abnormal Psychology*, 1973, *82*, 87–101.

Leitenberg, H., Agras, W. S., & Thomson, L. E. A sequential analysis of the effect of selective positive reinforcement in modifying anorexia nervosa. *Behaviour Research and Therapy*, 1968, *6*, 211–218.

Leon, G. R. Current directions in the treatment of obesity. *Psychological Bulletin*, 1976, *83*, 557–578.

Levine, M. D. Children with encopresis: A descriptive analysis. *Pediatrics*, 1975, *56*, 412–416.

Lipton, E. L., Sternschneider, A., & Richmond, J. B. Psychophysiological disorders in children. In L. W. Hoffman & M. L. Hoffman (Eds.), *Review of child development research* (Vol. 2). New York: Russell Sage, 1966.

Livingston, S. Epilepsy in infancy, childhood, and adolescence. In B. Wolman (Ed.), *Manual of child psychopathology.* New York: McGraw-Hill, 1972.

Lovibond, S. H. The mechanism of conditioning treatment of enuresis. *Behaviour Research and Therapy*, 1963, *1*, 17–21.

Lovibond, S. H., & Coote, M. A. Enuresis. In C. G. Costello (Ed.), *Symptoms of psychopathology.* New York: Wiley, 1970.

Mahoney, M. J., & Mahoney, K. Treatment of obesity: A clinical exploration. In B. J. Williams, S. Martin, & J. P. Foreyt (Eds.), *Obesity: Behavioral approaches to dietary management.* New York: Bruner/Mazel, 1976.

Marholin, II, D., Siegel, L. J., & Phillips, D. Treatment and transfer: A search for empirical procedures. In M. Hersen, R. M. Eisler, & P. M. Miller (Eds.), *Progress in behavior modification* (Vol. 3). New York: Academic, 1976.

Miller, N. E. Learning of visceral and glandular responses. *Science*, 1969, *163*, 434–445.

Miller, P. M. An experimental analysis of retention control training in the treatment of nocturnal enuresis in two institutionalized adolescents. *Behavior Therapy*, 1973, *4*, 288–294.

Moore, N. Behavior therapy in bronchial asthma: A controlled study. *Journal of Psychosomatic Research*, 1965, *9*, 257–276.

Mostofsky, D. I., & Balaschak, B. A. Psychobiological control of seizures. *Psychological Bulletin*, 1977, *84*, 723–750.

Mowrer, O. H., & Mowrer, W. M. Enuresis: A method for its study and treatment. *American Journal of Orthopsychiatry*, 1938, *8*, 436–459.

Muellner, S. R. The development of urinary control in children: A new concept in cause, prevention and treatment of primary enuresis. *Journal of Urology*, 1960, *84*, 714–716.

Murray, M. E., Keele, D. K., & McCarver, J. W. Behavioral treatment of rumination. *Clinical Pediatrics*, 1976, *7*, 591–596.

Neisworth, J. T., & Moore, F. Operant treatment of asthmatic responding with the parent as therapist. *Behavior Therapy*, 1972, *3*, 95–99.

O'Dell, S. Training parents in behavior modification: A review, *Psychological Bulletin*, 1974, *81*, 418–433.

O'Leary, K. D., & Wilson, G. T. *Behavior therapy: Application and outcome.* Englewood Cliffs, N.J.: Prentice-Hall, 1975.

Oppel, W., Harper, P., & Rowland, V. The age of attaining bladder control. *Journal of Pediatrics*, 1968, *42*, 614–626.

Overton, D. A. State-dependent learning produced by depressant and atropine-line drugs. *Psychopharmacologia*, 1966, *10*, 6–31.

Paschalis, A., Kimmel, H. D., & Kimmel, E. Further study of diurnal instrumental conditioning in the treatment of enuresis nocturna. *Journal of Behavior Therapy and Experimental Psychiatry*, 1972, *3*, 253–256.

Patterson, G. R. Behavioral intervention procedures in the classroom and in the home. In A. E. Bergin & S. L. Garfield (Eds.), *Handbook of psychotherapy and behavior change.* New York: Wiley, 1971.

Perzan, R. S., Boulanger, F., & Fischer, D. G. Complex factors in inhibition of defecation: Review and case study. *Journal of Behavior Therapy and Experimental Psychiatry*, 1972, *3*, 129–133.

Peterson, D. R., & London, P. Neobehavioristic psychotherapy: Quasi-hypnotic suggestion and multiple reinforcement in the treatment of a case of post infantile dyscopresis. *Psychological Record*, 1964, *14*, 469–474.

Pierce, C. M. Enuresis. In A. M. Freedman & H. I. Kaplan (Eds.), *Comprehensive textbook of psychiatry.* Baltimore: Williams and Wilkins, 1967.

Plachetta, K. E. Encopresis: A case study utilizing contracting, scheduling and self-charting. *Journal of Behavior Therapy and Experimental Psychiatry*, 1976, *7*, 195–196.

Premack, D. Reinforcement theory. In D. Levine (Ed.), *Nebraska symposium on motivation: 1965.* Lincoln: University of Nebraska Press, 1965.

Price, K. P. The application of behavior therapy to the treatment of psychosomatic disorders: Retrospect and prospect. *Psychotherapy: Theory, Research, and Practice*, 1974, *11*, 138–155.

Purcell, K. Childhood asthma: The role of family relationships, personality, and emotions. In A. Davids (Ed.), *Child personality and psychopathology: Current topics* (Vol. 2). New York: Wiley, 1975.

Purcell, K., & Weiss, J. Asthma. In C. G. Costello (Ed.), *Symptoms of psychopathology.* New York: Wiley, 1970.

Quay, H. C., & Werry, J. S., (Eds.) *Psychopathological disorders of childhood.* New York: Wiley, 1972.

Rees, L. The significance of parental attitudes in childhood asthma. *Journal of Psychosomatic Research*, 1964, *7*, 253–262.

Rimm, D. C., & Masters, J. C. *Behavior therapy: Techniques and empirical findings.* New York: Academic, 1974.

Ross, A. O. *Psychological disorders of children: A behavioral approach to theory, research and therapy.* New York: McGraw-Hill, 1974.

Sajwaj, T., Libet, J., & Agras, S. Lemon-juice therapy: The control of life-threatening rumination in a six-month-old infant. *Journal of Applied Behavior Analysis*, 1974, *7*, 557–563.

Sargent, J. D., Greene, E. E., & Walters, E. D. Preliminary report on the use of autogenic feedback training in the treatment of migraine and tension headaches. *Psychosomatic Medicine*, 1973, *35*, 129–135.

Schuster, M. M. Operant conditioning in gastrointestinal dysfunction. *Hospital Practice*, 1974, *9*, 135–143.

Schwab, J. J., McGinnis, N. H., Morris, L. B., & Schwab, R. B. Psychosomatic medicine and the contemporary social scene. *American Journal of Psychiatry*, 1970, *126*, 1632–1642.

Schwartz, G. E. Biofeedback as therapy: Some theoretical and practical issues. *American Psychologist*, 1973, *28*, 666–673.

Shapiro, D., Tursky, B., & Schwartz, G. E. Control of blood pressure in man by operant conditioning. *Circulation Research* (Supplement 1), 1970, *27*, 27–32.

Stedman, J. M. An extension of the Kimmel treatment method for enuresis to an adolescent: A case report. *Journal of Behavior Therapy and Experimental Psychiatry*, 1972, *3*, 253–256.

Sterman, M. B. Neurophysiological and clinical studies of sensorimotor EEG biofeedback training: Some effects on epilepsy. *Seminars in Psychiatry*, *1973, 5*, 507–525.

Sterman, M. B., MacDonald, L. R., & Stone, R. K. Biofeedback training of the sensorimotor electroencephalogram rhythm in man: Effects on epilepsy. *Epilepsia*, 1974, *15*, 395–416.

Stuart, R. B., & Davis, B. *Slim chance in a fat world: Behavioral control of obesity.* Champaign, Ill.: Research Press, 1972.

Stunkard, A. J., & Mahoney, M. J. Behavioral treatment of eating disorders. In H. Leitenberg (Ed.), *Handbook of behavior modification and behavior therapy.* Englewood Cliffs, N.J.: Prentice-Hall, 1976.

Tharp, R. G., & Wetzel, R. J. *Behavior modification in the natural environment.* New York: Academic Press, 1969.

Toister, R. P., Condron, C. J., Wooley, L., & Arthur, D. Faradic therapy of chronic vomiting in infancy: A case study. *Journal of Behavior Therapy and Experimental Psychiatry*, 1975, *6*, 55–59.

Tomlinson, J. R. The treatment of bowel retention by operant procedure: A case study. *Journal of Behavior Therapy and Experimental Psychiatry*, 1970, *1*, 83–85.

Turnbull, J. W. Asthma conceived of as a learned response. *Journal of Psychosomatic Research*, 1962, *6*, 59–70.

Turner, R. K., & Young, G. C. CNS stimulant drugs and conditioning treatment of nocturnal enuresis: A long-term follow-up study. *Behaviour Research and Therapy*, 1966, *4*, 225–228.

Ullmann, L. P., & Krasner, L. *A psychological approach to abnormal behavior* (2nd ed.). Englewood Cliffs, N.J.: Prentice-Hall, 1975.

Werry, J. Enuresis nocturna. *Medical Times*, 1967, *95*, 985–991.

Werry, J. S., & Bull, D. Anorexia nervosa—A case study using behavior therapy. *Journal of the American Academy of Child Psychiatry*, 1975, *14*, 646–651.

Werry, J., & Cohressen, J. Enuresis—An etiologic and therapeutic study. *Journal of Pediatrics*, 1965, *67*, 423–431.

Wheeler, M. E., & Hess, K. W. Treatment of juvenile obesity by successive approximation control of eating. *Journal of Behavior Therapy and Experimental Psychiatry*, 1976, *7*, 235–241.

Wohl, T. H. Behavior modification: Its application to the study and treatment of childhood asthma. *The Journal of Asthma Research*, 1971, *9*, 41–45.

Wolf, M. M., Brinbrauer, J. S., Williams, T., & Lawler, J. A. A note on apparent extinction of the vomiting behavior of a retarded child. In L. P. Ullmann

& L. Krasner (Eds.), *Case studies in behavior modification.* New York: Holt, Rinehart & Winston, 1965.

Wolpe, J. *The practice of behavior therapy.* New York: Pergamon, 1969.

Wright, L. Aversive conditioning of self-induced seizures. *Behavior Therapy,* 1973, *4,* 712–713. (a)

Wright, L. Handling the encopretic child. *Professional Psychology,* 1973, *4,* 137–144. (b)

Wright, L. Outcome of a standardized program for treating psychogenic encopresis. *Professional Psychology,* 1975, *6,* 453–456.

Young, G. C., & Morgan, R. T. T. Overlearning in the conditioning treatment of enuresis: A long-term follow-up study. *Behaviour Research and Therapy,* 1972, *10,* 419–420.

Young, G. & Turner, R. CNS stimulant drugs and conditioning treatment of nocturnal enuresis. *Behaviour Research and Therapy,* 1965, *3,* 93–101.

Young, I. L., & Goldsmith, A. O. Treatment of encopresis in a day treatment program. *Psychotherapy: Theory, Research, and Practice,* 1972, *9,* 231–235.

Zlutnick, S., Mayville, W. J., & Moffat, S. Modification of seizure disorders: The interruption of behavioral chains. *Journal of Applied Behavior Analysis,* 1975, *8,* 1–12.

FOOTNOTE

1. The authors express their appreciation to Nancy P. Davidson, Kay Kline, Maxine Little and Jonalee M. Slaughter for their assistance and valuable comments on this manuscript.

Part III
Current Issues

12

Beyond the Law of Effect

PROGRAMMING FOR THE MAINTENANCE OF BEHAVIORAL CHANGE

David Marholin II and Lawrence J. Siegel

As documented in earlier chapters, many learning-based treatment approaches have been used effectively with a broad range of behavior problems in children (Bijou & Redd, 1975; Graziano, 1971, 1975). Anyone trying to modify dysfunctional or disordered behavior in children, regardless of the therapeutic intervention he uses, is faced with the problem of maintaining the treatment effects when the child returns to his or her natural environment. Available evidence indicates that the effective transfer and maintenance of behavior change does not *automatically* occur after the termination of treatment (Allyon & Azrin, 1968; Marholin, Siegel, & Phillips, 1976; Burchard, Note 1), an observation that has led Baer, Wolf, and Risley (1968) to conclude that transfer of newly acquired behaviors must be specifically programmed into the therapeutic process and not left to chance.

Those who treat children's behavior problems too often assume that changes in behavior effected in the treatment environment will automatically generalize to other settings; for example, they expect a child whose stuttering has been eliminated in the clinic to speak fluently in the home and classroom. They may also assume that when a child is reinforced for new behaviors, similar behaviors will occur with a greater frequency in the treatment environment; for instance, they expect that a child who is reinforced for the purpose of increasing his social interaction with peers in a preschool setting will develop a more complex repertoire of social skills without being directly reinforced for these new behaviors. Finally, they sometimes take for granted the maintenance of behavior change after termination of treatment; a child whose tantrums have been eliminated during treatment is expected to remain free of such behavior.

Despite these assumptions, however, research evidence (Redd, 1969; Redd & Birnbrauer, 1969) points to the fact that human learning tends to be situationally specific. That is, behavior tends to occur in those situations or settings where the treatment or training has been conducted. Newly acquired behaviors may transfer to other settings, but unless the contingencies are compatible with those in the training environment, the behavior may extinguish (Wahler, 1969b).

Behavioral treatment approaches for a number of behavior problems in children have proved efficacious when the contingencies are present in the treatment setting; however, empirical support for the transfer of these treatment effects to other settings remains to be clearly demonstrated. This discrepancy led Burchard (Note 1) to conclude that "it is time for those involved in behavior modification programs to move beyond the repeated demonstration of the Law of Effect and to focus on building increasing resistance to those effects."

A number of strategies that appear to be functionally related to the transfer and durability of behavioral changes with children have been conceptualized within three frameworks: behavioral (Skinner, 1953), mediational (Kanfer, 1971), or cognitive-personality (Rotter, 1966). The first of these strategies is that *contingencies of reinforcement in the extra-treatment setting should be consistent with contingencies present in the treatment environment.*

For treatment effects to transfer across environments, the training contingencies must be established in both settings. If the contingencies in the post-treatment environments are not appropriate, it is likely that the newly acquired behaviors, although they may be exhibited for a while, will eventually extinguish, because discrimination rather than generalization will occur. In other words, the child will discriminate that he is paid off or reinforced for different behaviors in the post-treatment environment than he was in the training environment.

The situation-specific dependence of behavior on treatment contingencies present in a given setting has been demonstrated in a number of studies (Becker, Madsen, Arnold, & Thomas, 1967; Broden, Hall, Dunlap, & Clark, 1970). O'Leary, Becker, Evans, and Saudargas (1969), for example, have clearly demonstrated that a child's behavior tends to conform to the contingencies present in a given setting. They found that although a token program with back-up reinforcers was effective in reducing disruptive behaviors of second-grade children during afternoon class periods when the token program was in effect, the control over disruption did not generalize to the morning session when the token program was not in effect. The frequency of disruptive behavior was reduced in the morning during the first several days of the program; then there was a rapid increase in the target behaviors to earlier levels. These results suggest that the children had learned to discriminate that appropriate classroom behavior was reinforced only in the afternoon. This failure of afternoon behavior to transfer to the morning session appears to be the result of different contingencies of reinforcement, since observations of the teacher's behavior indicated that he delivered a high frequency of contingent social reinforcement in the afternoon, but delivered little reinforcement in the morning.

Wahler (1969b) also presents evidence that if newly-acquired behaviors are to occur in new settings, the treatment contingencies must be established in those settings. He investigated specific behaviors of two children in the home and school. Concurrent observations indicated that each child's behavior was a function of the short-term environmental consequences, with appropriate behavior at home resulting from differential attention from the parents. Appropriate behaviors at home concurrently produced appropriate behavior for a brief period at school; however, with no contingencies to maintain the behavior at school, there was a rapid extinction of the behavior. As predicted, the appropriate school behavior remained near baseline levels until similar differential attention procedures were instituted in the school. Observations of the attention-giving behavior of the parents and teachers clearly indicated a functional relationship between the frequencies of appropriate child behavior and the teacher and parent attention that was given for appropriate behavior.

This strategy for facilitating the transfer of treatment effects was utilized in the case of a 7-year-old child, John, who was referred to a mental health center by his school because of a problem of selective mutism. Although his language development was within normal limits, from the age of 5 he spoke only at home when his immediate family was present. He refused to speak at school or outside the home with strangers. John was admitted to a day-care school program at the mental health center which provided a controlled setting. To deal with his problem behavior the day-care staff established a token program whereby John earned points for verbalizing with the teacher and other students. The points were exchangeable for back-up reinforcers (e.g., time with adults, use of record player, time with bicycle) in the classroom and at home. Within several months, he was speaking in the classroom at a frequency similar to the other children. At this point, John was gradually introduced back into his regular public school classroom for several days a week while remaining in the day-care program for the remainder of the week. The same contingencies of reinforcement that were present in the day care school program were also in effect when he entered the public school classroom. That is, his regular classroom teacher continued to reinforce John with points and social praise whenever he spoke to the teacher or other children. Within a period of several weeks he was attending public school full time, and the frequency of his verbal behavior was measured at a level appropriate for his peers in the classroom. During the next several weeks the token program was gradually faded out of the classroom entirely, while his verbal behavior with the teacher and other children remained at a similar level to that measured when the treatment program was in effect. Had the contingencies for speaking in the public school classroom not been the same as those that were present in the treatment setting of the day-care program it is unlikely that the child would have spoke at all when he had returned to his regular classroom.

The second strategy related to the transfer and durability of behavior changes is to *teach significant others to provide appropriate contingencies in the natural environment.*

Maintenance and transfer of treatment effects may be enhanced by training significant others in the natural environment of the child. Tharp and Wetzel (1969) have developed a model of intervention whereby significant others—parents, teachers, siblings, peers—are instructed in strategies of behavior change. They suggest that the main requirement for a change agent is that he is able to contingently provide reinforcement. A child's behavior is, in large part, a result of consequences of his behavior in the real world. Therefore, training significant members of the child's environment to provide contingencies that are sensitive to the desired behavior is likely to facilitate maintenance of behavior change. Parents (Hawkins, Peterson, Schweid, & Bijou, 1966; Patterson, McNeal, Hawkins, & Phelps, 1967), teachers (Lovitt & Curtiss, 1969), and peers (Siegel & Steinman, 1975; Solomon & Wahler, 1973) have been trained to successfully modify various problem behaviors in children. Such training is particularly important in light of the research that indicates that contingencies in the natural environment are often incompatible with treatment goals (Hall, Lund, & Jackson, 1968; Walker & Buckley, 1972). In other words, contingencies in the real world often occur that reinforce deviant rather than desired behavior.

Training significant individuals to consistently reinforce appropriate behavior and punish inappropriate behavior has been shown to help the child maintain his newly acquired behaviors after treatment programs have ended. Furthermore, when these significant others applied the reinforcement procedures to additional appropriate behaviors, they were found to expand the child's prosocial repertoire. These points are well illustrated by the research of Lovaas, Koegel, Simmons, and Long (1973) with autistic children. Follow-up measures assessed from 1 to 4 years after an intensive treatment program revealed significant differences between groups of children whose parents were trained in behavior modification techniques compared with a second group of children who remained in residential facilities after treatment. The authors note that parents who were trained in behavioral techniques provided sufficient contingent positive reinforcement to maintain the appropriate behaviors. On the other hand, the institutional environment apparently failed to reinforce the newly acquired behaviors—for example, appropriate speech and social behaviors—while intermittently reinforcing inappropriate behavior like echolalia and self-destructive behaviors.

Finally, Patterson, Cobb, and Ray (1972) describe a classroom program that utilized the peer group to modify and maintain the behavior of a deviant child. Additional time at recess for the entire class was made contingent on the total number of points earned by a target child. Initial contingencies were established so that the child would earn extra recess time for his classmates during the early stages of the program. The amount of appropriate behavior required for reinforcement was gradually increased, and the results showed a substantial increase in appropriate classroom behavior that was maintained at the time of a follow-up assessment. Such a treatment program enhances the probability that the peer group will support the desired behavior of the target child. Since the child seeks reinforcement rather than punishment from his classmates, he will most likely continue to behave appropriately in their presence, which then leads to additional peer-delivered reinforcement. The likelihood is that members of the child's peer group will continue to associate with him outside of the classroom, so that the probability that the treatment effects will transfer to the new environment is also enhanced.

In the case of a 9-year-old child, Michael, who refused to get ready for school in the morning, his parents were trained to provide appropriate contingencies in the home to overcome this behavior problem. Each school morning the home became a battleground in which the parents argued and nagged at their eldest child, Michael, to get out of bed, and get ready for school on time. Because both parents were required to supervise several younger children who also attended school and had to leave the house early themselves for work, the disruptive and uncooperative behavior displayed by Michael was particularly annoying for the entire family. Careful observation suggested that the parents were probably reinforcing much of Michael's oppositional behavior in giving him all their attention by constantly nagging at him every few minutes when he refused to get ready for school.

Subsequently a program was set up with the parents whereby they were trained to ignore any behavior on the part of Michael that indicated his unwillingness to get out of bed or to get dressed for school. They were instructed to awake him 1 hour before he was to leave for school and then to inform him when there were only 15 minutes left before they were to drive him to school. No further interactions with the child were to occur other than in the daily routine of the morning. They were not to plead with him about getting dressed or eating breakfast. When they were ready to drive the children to school, they were to inform him that it was time to go. If he was not dressed, his clothes were to be placed in a bag and he was to finish getting dressed at school. The parents were also instructed not to wait if he had not eaten breakfast, and he was to go to school without eating. On the other hand, if Michael had gotten completely ready for school by the time that his parents were ready to leave the house, he earned television viewing for that evening.

As anticipated, on the day the program was started, Michael tested the new rules to see if his parents would follow through with the stated consequences. Michael failed to dress on time, and he had to go to school in his pajamas and dress upon his arrival at school. In addition, he missed breakfast that morning. Since he had not gotten completely ready for school, he was not permitted to watch television that evening. On all subsequent days during the next several months that the parents maintained contact with the psychologist who had helped them set up the program, Michael had managed to get dressed for school on time. Only on several mornings did he miss breakfast. As a result of the new contingencies the parents were instructed to provide at home, it was no longer necessary for them to nag and argue with their son about his being late for school. Furthermore, the atmosphere in the home during the morning was more relaxed and pleasant for the entire family.

A third strategy is to *establish social stimuli as functional reinforcers for the child.*

The "relevance of behavior rule" proposed by Ayllon and Azrin (1968) which states that one should "teach only those behaviors that will continue to be reinforced after training" (p. 56) suggests that behavior should be taught only if it will eventually come under the control of naturally occurring reinforcers. This further implies that the environment must contain reinforcers of sufficient strength and frequency to maintain the target behavior. Establishing praise and other social stimuli (e.g., eye contact, physical contact) as functional reinforcers for a child will greatly increase the number of reinforcers available to maintain behavior change following treatment. In addition, social reinforcers are more readily available and easier to provide in the natural environment than tangible reinforcers.

For some children a social stimulus such as praise does not function as a reinforcer (Lovaas, Freitag, Kinder, Rubenstein, Schaeffer, & Simmons, 1966; Quay & Hunt, 1965; Wahler, 1969a). Therefore, before a treatment program begins, the reinforcing value of verbal statements or praise should be established or increased. For example, Lovaas et al. (1966) paired food with verbal praise when praise alone failed to increase the prosocial behavior of schizophrenic children. Similarly, Wahler (1969a) increased the functional value of praise by pairing it with tokens after praise alone was found to be ineffective in modifying the uncooperative behavior of oppositional children. In both cases, the tokens or food were gradually withdrawn, and behavioral change was eventually maintained by praise alone.

Nolan, Mattis, and Holliday (1970) report 12-month follow-up assessment data for six children with "learning disabilities" who had been in an operant program to develop appropriate classroom behaviors. Although the effects of treatment were maintained for all children, based on behavioral observations and interviews with the teachers, those children who had been gradually faded from food to social reinforcers were found to exhibit additional improvements in behavior beyond those changes obtained in the target behaviors. In contrast, those children who had not been graduated to social reinforcement at the time formal treatment was terminated showed no further improvements in behavior.

The pairing of praise and food was used in a treatment program to establish eye contact as a prerequisite behavior necessary to teaching verbal behavior to a 3-year-old child, Nancy, who was delayed in language development. In the assessment process it was determined that Nancy was unresponsive to most social stimuli, including any form of approval or praise. Since it was hoped that praise could eventually function as a naturally occurring reinforcer in the child's environment to maintain the behaviors learned in the speech program, it was necessary systematically to develop praise as a functional reinforcer early in therapy. Each time Nancy maintained eye contact for 2 seconds when she was asked to look at the therapist a variety of food reinforcers were immediately delivered. At the same time she received food contingent on appropriate responding, the speech therapist also used a number of verbal statements of praise such as "good looking" or "good work" and made physical contact by touching her on the arm or hugging her. This pairing of food and social praise continued over a period of several weeks, until the therapist was confident that the social praise alone could function as a reinforcer for the child. The food reinforcers were then gradually faded from the training sessions until praise and other social reinforcers alone were able to maintain the responses developed during the training sessions.

The fourth strategy is to *provide discriminative stimuli in the treatment setting that have a high probability of occurring in the post-treatment environment.*

A discriminative stimulus is defined as the stimulus with which reinforcement becomes associated during training (Whaley & Malott, 1971). Subsequently, a stimulus that consistently precedes reinforcement during training acts as a signal that reinforcement is available if the proper response is emitted (e.g., a prompt; see Burleigh & Marholin, 1977). By teaching a child that reinforcement is forthcoming only when he responds in the presence of a particular stimulus (e.g., a specific person) it is possible to gain control over a child's behavior in the presence of that same stimulus. In this manner at least the short-term transfer of treatment effects to the post-treatment environment may be achieved in the presence of a stimulus that signals the availability of reinforcement.

A primary goal of behavioral intervention programs is to develop discriminative stimulus control over the individual's behavior through differential training experiences. This stimulus control must shift to additional settings if the treatment effects are to occur beyond the treatment environment. However, this shift in stimulus control beyond the treatment setting is often not programmed into the treatment process, with the inadvertent result that the therapist is programmed as the principal discriminative stimulus for the desired behavior. In other words, a child will act appropriately in the presence of his therapist, who has become a discriminative stimulus for reinforcement, but he is less likely to act appropriately in the therapist's absence (Marholin & Hall, in press). The decrease in the frequency of the newly-acquired behavior which often occurs following treatment may, therefore, be because the primary discriminative stimulus for this behavior has remained in the treatment environment (Redd, 1970; Redd & Birnbauer, 1969; Risley, 1968).

To maximize the probability of transfer, it is useful to minimize discrimination by varying the stimulus conditions of the training environment. This can be facilitated by conducting training in several different settings (Griffiths & Craighead, 1972), or by having more than one person provide appropriate contingencies (Barrett & McCormack, 1973). Reiss and Redd (1970) investigated the treatment of self-injurious behavior in a young girl. The child's maladaptive behavior was eliminated by an initial therapist through time-out and reinforcement of incompatible behaviors. However, when the original therapist was replaced by a second therapist, the child resumed her self-injurious behavior. The new therapist was able to eliminate the self-injurious behavior by re-establishing the contingencies used by the first therapist. When the second therapist was replaced by a third therapist, the self-injurious behavior reappeared, but was again eliminated upon the reinstatement of the previous treatment program. Finally, there was no reappearance of the undesirable behavior with the subsequent introductions of both a fourth and a fifth therapist.

Transfer of treatment may also be achieved by providing discriminative stimuli during the treatment program that have a high probability of occurring in the post-treatment environment (Johnston & Johnston, 1972; Marholin & Steinman, 1977; Marholin, Steinman, McInnis, & Heads, 1975). Johnston and Johnston (1972) investigated promoting the transfer of training by programming stimuli into the treatment setting that are discriminative for appropriate behavior. Two children were trained to monitor and reinforce the appropriate speech of each other in such a way that each child became discriminative for peer-delivered reinforcement; this demonstrated the specificity of stimulus control that can result from differential reinforcement in the presence of specific stimuli. As a result of this training program, the two children responded appropriately only when they were together.

Another study found that a teacher's presence in or absence from a classroom for conduct-problem children developed discriminative stimulus control over several social behaviors (Marholin, Steinman, McInnis, & Heads, 1975). The effect of the teacher's presence or absence on task-oriented and disruptive behavior was evaluated under three contingencies: (1) reinforcement delivered noncontingently by the teacher, (2) reinforcement delivered by the teacher for on-task and nondisruptive behavior, and (3) reinforcement delivered by the teacher for academic rate and accuracy. Transfer of training was assessed by programming the teacher's absence from the classroom. The data indicated that discriminative control by the teacher's presence was established when on-task behavior was reinforced; that is, substantial increases in disruptive behavior and concurrent decreases in on-task behavior were observed when the teacher was absent from the classroom. When accuracy and rate of academic performance were reinforced, however, during the teacher's absence, the academic materials were found to exert stimulus control, with less decrease of on-task behavior and less increase in disruptive behavior from the teacher-present to the teacher-absent condition.

In the speech program with the 3-year-old child, Nancy, whose delay in language development was described previously, the child's mother sat next to the therapist throughout the treatment program. This was done to ensure that the speech therapist would not be the sole discriminative stimulus for appropriate speech and to increase the probability that the newly acquired verbal behavior would occur outside the treatment setting in the presence of significant others. Once the therapist gained control over the child's attending behavior and began to develop simple verbal skills in the child, the mother was trained to deliver reinforcement contingently in therapy. During the early stages of the treatment program, the mother reported that her child was exhibiting appropriate speech at home similar to that learned in therapy. This would suggest that the mother's presence during the training sessions and her association with reinforcement for appropriate responding facilitated the transfer of the child's appropriate speech outside the treatment setting.

A fifth strategy is to *fade reinforcement gradually during training to an intermittent schedule that is consistent with schedules in the post-treatment environment.*

When the treatment program is designed to establish a new response or to increase the strength of an already existing response, continuous reinforcement (i.e., after every response) is necessary during the initial phase of treatment. However, once the response is appearing at a desired frequency, there must be a gradual fading of reinforcement to increasingly thinner schedules (i.e., after some set number of responses or time between responses) if the newly acquired behavior is to be maintained when the child returns to the post-treatment environment.

Animal research provides much data on various schedules of reinforcement which have implications for modifying human behavior. These data consistently point to an increased resistance to extinction with carefully planned intermittent schedules of reinforcement (Ferster & Skinner, 1957). Resistance to extinction may be a significant factor in facilitating both transfer and maintenance of treatment effects, since the reinforcement provided in the natural environment closely approximates increasingly intermittent schedules of reinforcement.

Kazdin and Polster (1973) studied the effects of intermittent and continuous schedules of token reinforcement on maintaining social interaction in retarded children. In an initial training phase, continuous reinforcement was used to establish a high frequency of social interaction with other children, and a substantial decrease was observed when reinforcement was later withdrawn. During the second phase of the program, one child was reinforced on a continuous schedule, as in the earlier condition, whereas a second child was reinforced on a gradually increasing variable-ratio schedule. The results indicated that the child who had been faded to an intermittent schedule of reinforcement maintained a level of social interaction similar to that when continuous reinforcement was used. On the other hand, a significant decrease in social interaction was observed for the child who had been maintained on a continuous reinforcement schedule. The difference in the rate of social interaction was maintained at a 5-week follow-up assessment, with intermittent reinforcement proving to be more effective than continuous reinforcement.

The treatment of a 10-year-old child, Jimmy, with the problem of encopresis or soiling illustrates the use of this procedure, whereby reinforcement was gradually faded from a continuous to intermittent schedule of reinforcement. A treatment program was set up in the home, where Jimmy earned a quarter, a reinforcer he had selected, at the end of each day he had clean pants. When he had achieved 2 consecutive weeks with no soiling, the contingency for reinforcement was changed slightly; he received a quarter for every 2 days that no soiling had occurred. Following 2 weeks of clean pants on this new schedule of reinforcement, the contingency was again changed so that reinforcement was delivered for 4 days of not soiling. Again, following 2 weeks of clean pants, the contingency was changed; he received one dollar at the end of the week for not soiling. Finally, after 2 consecutive weeks of earning a dollar, he was graduated from the treatment program, and monetary reinforcement was discontinued. A follow-up assessment at 1 month and again at 6 months revealed that he had not soiled since the treatment program had been terminated. The results suggest that naturally occurring reinforcers (e.g., social praise, the opportunity to participate in varied activities that were previously unavailable because of his frequent soiling) in Jimmy's environment were maintaining soil-free behavior, despite the fact that the money reinforcement had long been discontinued.

The sixth strategy is to *train the child on a schedule of reinforcement that approximates the delays found in the natural environment.*

Because numerous rewards in the real world are delayed—grades, for example, or television privileges—in teaching children it seems desirable to use a schedule of reinforcement that closely approximates these naturally occurring delays. If a child is taught to expect delayed rewards rather than immediate gratification, extinction should also be delayed. Two types of delay procedures have been used (O'Leary & Becker, 1967; Schwartz & Hawkins, 1970). The first increases the time period between the response and contingent feedback. Schwartz and Hawkins (1970) employed this technique in modifying face-touching, posture, and voice-loudness of a sixth-grade child. They used a videotape delayed-feedback system that allowed for contingencies to be evoked for behavior occurring before the child viewed the videotape. O'Leary and Becker (1967) used a second delay procedure, involving a progressive increase in time between token reinforcement and the exchange of tokens for back-up reinforcers. In another classroom study (Colter, Applegate, King, & Kristal, 1972) the delay between token acquisition and exchange was progressively extended to 4 days, with little decline in the reinforced target behaviors. In each of the studies using delayed reinforcement, behavior was maintained at times during the day other than that devoted to treatment.

The seventh strategy is to *teach behaviors that are incompatible with the undesirable behaviors.*

A treatment program devoted exclusively to the reduction of inappropriate behavior is not likely to be successful. If a child employs a particular behavior or set of inappropriate behaviors before treatment in order to acquire various reinforcers from his environment, he will eventually try the same behavior again unless he has been taught incompatible behaviors that provide the same opportunity for reinforcement in the real world. In the strictest sense, incompatible behavior is defined as any behavior that cannot physically be emitted at the same time as another response. Several classroom studies found that disruptive behaviors decreased as a function of reinforcing academic quality alone (Ayllon & Roberts, 1974; Marholin & Steinman, 1977; Marholin, Steinman, McInnis, & Heads, 1975). In each of these studies, rather than merely punishing disruptive behaviors, the authors chose to reinforce an incompatible behavior that was likely to be reinforced in other classrooms by other teachers. Results suggest that not only did the incompatible behavior (i.e., academic performance) increase, but the decreased frequency of disruptive behavior and the increase in academic performance were generalized to other periods of the school day, when systematic contingencies were not in effect. It is likely that the children were intermittently reinforced for being academically productive in their regular nontreatment classrooms, and that this maintained the newly learned behavior and made disruption unnecessary as their source of reinforcement.

The reinforcement of incompatible behavior was used by a teacher to eliminate aggressive behavior exhibited by a 7-year-old child, Ron. A token program was established, in which Ron could earn the opportunity to engage in free-time activities in school for cooperative play. Appropriate play was selected as the target behavior to be reinforced by the teacher because it provided him with the opportunity to teach Ron a behavior that was incompatible with the aggressiveness that he wished to decrease. Each time the teacher observed Ron interacting appropriately with another child, a marble was placed in a container on his desk. During specified periods of the day Ron could exchange each marble for 10 minutes of time in a favorite activity in school. By the fifth week of the program Ron's level of aggressiveness had decreased to a near zero level, even though the teacher had not provided any specific consequences for aggressive behavior. The tokens were gradually withdrawn from the classroom, with little effect on the gains achieved during the treatment program. It was felt that naturally occurring reinforcement from peers (e.g., peer attention, increase in classroom status) served to maintain the appropriate play behavior once token reinforcement had been discontinued.

The eighth strategy is to *teach behaviors that permit the child to enter an environment that naturally reinforces and maintains responses associated with the target behavior.*

Once the target has been firmly established, a child may exhibit additional changes in behavior beyond those specifically programmed by the treatment procedures. A newly learned behavior may facilitate additional behavior change by permitting the child to enter environments that support the acquisition of behaviors functionally related to the newly-acquired behavior. This increased potential for reinforcement enhances the opportunity for the transfer and maintenance not only of the target response but also of related nontarget behaviors.

The process whereby the newly-acquired entry behaviors allow for the reinforcement of similar behaviors has been termed a "behavioral trap" (Baer & Wolf, 1970). This concept is illustrated (Allen, Hart, Buell, Harris, & Wolf, 1964) by a treatment program designed to decrease the social withdrawal and solitary play of a young girl. Teacher attention was used as a reinforcer to shape her behavior so that she would remain close to other children. Six days after treatment had begun, the child was observed interacting with other children in the classroom in a way not previously observed. The shaping of an initial entry response—physical proximity to peers— established social interactions with the peer group, which then shaped additional behavioral changes in the child.

A ninth strategy is to *teach the child to control the contingencies and antecedent conditions of his own behavior.*

As previously stated, sometimes the post-treatment environment fails to maintain behaviors acquired during treatment because it does not provide appropriate contingencies of reinforcement. It is possible to enhance the probability that the newly acquired behavior will be maintained after treatment by teaching the individual to control the available reinforcers by making them contingent on his behavior (Kanfer, 1975). Research has shown that a child can be taught to control the consequences of his own behavior through self-reinforcement or self-punishment (Bandura & Perloff, 1967; Drabman, Spitalnik, & O'Leary, 1973) and to control the antecedent events of his behavior through self-instructions (Hartig & Kanfer, 1973; Meichenbaum & Goodman, 1971).

Self-reward or self-reinforcement may take the form of self-administered consequences, such as being able to watch television after cleaning one's room, or it may take the form of verbal-symbolic self-reinforcement, such as self-praise for completing a homework assignment. Several studies have demonstrated that self-imposed contingencies are at least equally as effective as reinforcement delivered by another person in increasing the frequency of behavior (Felixbrod & O'Leary, 1973; Lovitt & Curtiss, 1969). Self-reinforcement and self-instructional training, therefore, appear to offer a practical method for facilitating the long-range maintenance of behavior change.

Glynn, Thomas, and Shee (1973) taught second-grade children to use self-management techniques to produce high levels of appropriate social behavior in the classroom. Each child was trained to monitor his own behavior to determine if he had met an on-task criterion, to record his own behavior, and, finally, to provide reinforcement contingent on his behavior. A 2-month follow-up assessment indicated that the self-management program was successful in maintaining the on-task behavior at a level similar to that obtained when external reinforcement procedures were used.

A self-control procedure utilizing self-instructions was used by Meichenbaum and Goodman (1971) to modify the behavior of impulsive children. The children were trained to self-administer instructions to direct themselves to perform a variety of tasks in a systematic and methodical manner. A gradual fading procedure was used in which overt and finally covert (subvocal) instructions were used to guide the child's behavior. First, an adult, using overt verbal instructions, modeled how to perform a task. The child then attempted the task while repeating the instructions aloud. In the next step the child whispered the instructions to himself. Finally, covert self-verbalizations were used by the child to guide his performance of the task. During each step of the procedure the child was trained to reinforce his behavior through statements of self-praise. Improved performance on a number of measures of impulsivity was maintained at a 1-month follow-up assessment period.

A final strategy is to *provide treatment conditions that permit the child to attribute both success and failure to his own behavior.*

Evidence from research on several cognitive-personality variables (Crandall, Katkovsky, & Crandall, 1965; Rotter, 1966) suggests that behavior change which the individual attributes to his own efforts will be maintained to a greater extent than behavior changes attributed to external factors. This research has particular implications for developing intervention programs for children who have learned to be "helpless," that is, to give up in the face of failure because they perceive their failure to be the result of some external force or agent. The child gives up after the first experience of failure because he believes that he is helpless to affect the outcome of a particular situation (Hiroto & Seligman, 1975). Dweck and Reppucci (1973), for example, have shown that two children who receive the same number and sequence of success and failure trials during a task will respond differently, depending on whether they are instructed to interpret the failure to mean that they have or do not have control over what occurs.

Procedures that provide the child with sucess-only experiences during training may, therefore, be short-sighted if they do not teach the child to deal with subsequent failure in the post-treatment environment, where immediate success and subsequent frequent reinforcement are unlikely. Teaching the child to handle failure through the programming of nonreinforced trials into treatment would increase the probability of persistence in the face of failure and thereby increase the likelihood that the behavior would eventually be reinforced and thus maintained after treatment.

These theoretical notions have been incorporated into a reattribution training program described by Dweck (in press) in which children were taught to try harder when they experienced failure. The result was that they viewed success as due to their own efforts and thus under their control. Children were selected for the training program who characteristically gave up on academic tasks when they failed. During training sessions, in which children worked on math problems, one group received success-only training; they were given problems they could easily complete correctly, thus guaranteeing reinforcement. A second group of children were exposed to failure by increasing the level of difficulty of the problems. Following failure, the experimenter indicated to the child that he had nearly reached the criterion for reinforcement and that he needed to try harder to succeed. This procedure taught the children to attribute their failure to complete the math problems correctly to insufficient effort rather than to lack of skill. Although both groups evidenced improvement in the rate and accuracy of their work when faced with failure experiences (difficult math problems), children who had received success-only training deteriorated significantly in their performance on the task; whereas children in the attribution retraining condition maintained or improved their task performance when exposed to failure. Thus teaching children to handle failure can produce increased persistence, enabling them to persevere in situations in which reinforcement may not be immediately forthcoming.

In summary, empirical evidence clearly supports the efficacy of operant treatment procedures in the modification of children's behavior when the contingencies are present in the treatment environment. However, if the post-treatment contingencies are not compatible with the contingencies provided during the training program, the treatment effects may not be maintained, if indeed they transfer at all to the natural environment.

The final criterion for assessing the efficacy of any treatment approach is whether the treatment effects extend beyond the setting in which the behavior was changed. To ensure that the gains obtained in treatment will be maintained once the treatment program has ended, we need to understand which variables mediate the transfer of training to other environments.

The procedures described above have been successfully used to enhance response maintenance and transfer of treatment effects. However, this research has received far less attention than work dealing with functional relationships between behavior change and the manipulation of specific variables in the treatment environment. Post-hoc analysis of the data, as often reported in behavioral research programs, does not provide an understanding of the mechanisms for response maintenance and transfer. For that we must systematically evaluate how each variable contributes, both alone and in combination, to the durability and transfer of the target behaviors beyond the treatment setting.

Appropriate behaviors acquired during the therapy program are of no use to a child if they do not occur in the natural environment. If behaviors that have been taught in a therapeutic environment do not appear in at least one other setting, they will have no lasting value. If we fail to keep this fact in mind, we are likely to develop highly transitory behavioral change techniques that will have little or no utility for the child once he has left the structured therapy setting.

REFERENCE NOTE

1. Burchard, J. D. Behavior modification with delinquents: Some unforeseen contingencies. Paper presented at the American Orthopsychiatric Association, New York, April, 1971.

REFERENCES

Allen, K. H., Hart, B. M., Buell, J. S., Harris, F. P., & Wolf, M. M. Effects of social reinforcement on isolate behavior of a nursery school child. *Child Development*, 1964, *35*, 511–518.

Ayllon, T., & Azrin, N. H. *The token economy: A motivational system for therapy and rehabilitation.* New York: Appleton-Century-Crofts, 1968.

Ayllon, T., & Roberts, M. D. Eliminating discipline problems by strengthening academic performance. *Journal of Applied Behavior Analysis*, 1974, *7*, 71–76.

Baer, D. M., & Wolf, M. M. The entry into natural communities of reinforcement. In R. Ulrich, T. Stachnik, & J. Mabry (Eds.), *Control of human behavior—from cure to prevention*, Vol. II. Glenview III: Scott, Foresman, 1970, pp. 319–324.

Baer, D. M., Wolf, M. M., & Risley, T. R. Some current dimensions of applied behavior analysis. *Journal of Applied Behavior Analysis*, 1968, *1*, 91–97.

Bandura, A., & Perloff, B. Relative efficacy of self-monitored and externally imposed reinforcement systems. *Journal of Personality and Social Psychology*, 1967, *7*, 111–116.

Barrett, B. H., & McCormack, J. E. Varied-teacher tutorials: A tactic for generating credible skills in severely retarded boys. *Mental Retardation*, 1973, *11*, 14–19.

Becker, W. C., Madsen, C. H., Arnold, C. R., & Thomas, D. R. The contingent use of teacher attention and praising in reducing classroom behavior problems. *Journal of Special Education*, 1967, *1*, 287–307.

Bijou, S. W., & Redd, W. H. Child behavior therapy. *In American Handbook of Psychiatry*, Vol. 5. New York: Basic Books, 1975, pp. 319–344.

Broden, M., Hall, R. V., Dunlap, A., & Clark, R. Effects of teacher attention and a token reinforcement system in a junior high school class. *Exceptional Children*, 1970, *36*, 341–349.

Burleigh, R. A., & Marholin II, D. Don't shoot until you see the whites of his eyes— An analyses of the adverse side effects of verbal prompts. *Behavior Modification*, 1977, *1*, 109–122.

Cotler, S. B., Applegate, G., King, L. W., & Kristal, S. Establishing a token economy system in a state hospital classroom: A lesson in training student and teacher. *Behavior Therapy*, 1972, *3*, 209–222.

Crandall, V. C., Katovsky, W., & Crandall, V. J. Children's beliefs in their own control of reinforcement in intellectual-academic achievement situations. *Child Development*, 1965, *36*, 91–109.

Drabman, R. S., Spitalnik, R., & O'Leary, K. D. Teaching self-control to disruptive children. *Journal of Abnormal Psychology*, 1973, *82*, 10–16.

Dweck, C. S. The role of expectations and attributions in the alleviation of learned helplessness. *Journal of Personality and Social Psychology*, in press.

Dweck, C. S., & Reppucci, N. D. Learned helplessness and reinforcement responsibility in children. *Journal of Personality and Social Psychology*, 1973, *25*, 109–116.

Felixbrod, J. J., & O'Leary, K. D. Effects of reinforcement on children's academic behavior as a function of self-determined and externally imposed contingencies. *Journal of Applied Behavior Analysis*, 1973, *6*, 241–250.

Ferster, C. B., & Skinner, B. F. *Schedules of reinforcement*. New York: Appleton-Century-Crofts, 1957.

Glynn, E. L., Thomas, J. D., & Shee, S. M. Behavioral self-control of on-task behavior in an elementary classroom. *Journal of Applied Behavior Analysis*, 1973, *6*, 105–113.

Graziano, A. M. *Behavior therapy with children* (Vol. 1). Chicago: Aldine-Atherton, 1971.

Graziano, A. M. *Behavior therapy with children* (Vol. 2). Chicago: Aldine-Atherton, 1975.

Griffiths, H., & Craighead, W. E. Generalization in operant speech therapy for misarticulation. *Journal of Speech and Hearing Disorders*, 1972, *37*, 485–494.

Hall, R. V., Lund, D., & Jackson, D. Effects of teacher attention on study behavior. *Journal of Applied Behavior Analysis*, 1968, *1*, 1–12.

Hartig, M., & Kanfer, F. H. The role of verbal self-instructions in children's resistance to temptation. *Journal of Personality and Social Psychology*, 1973, *25*, 259–267.

Hawkins, R. P., Peterson, R. F., Schweid, E., & Bijou, S. W. Behavior therapy in the home: Amelioration of problem parent-child relations with the parent in a therapeutic role. *Journal of Experimental Child Psychology*, 1966, *4*, 99–107.

Hiroto, D. S., & Seligman, M. E. P. Generality of learned helplessness in man. *Journal of Personality and Social Psychology*, 1975, *31*, 311–317.

Johnston, J. M., & Johnston, G. T. Modification of consonant speech-sound articulation in young children. *Journal of Applied Behavior Analysis*, 1972, *5*, 233–246.

Kanfer, F. H. The maintenance of behavior by self-generated stimuli and reinforcement. In A. Jacobs & L. B. Sachs (Eds.), *The psychology of private events*. New York: Academic, 1971.

Kanfer, F. H. Self-management methods. In F. H. Kanfer & A. P. Goldstein (Eds.), *Helping people change: A textbook of methods*. New York: Pergamon, 1975, pp. 309–356.

Kazdin, A. E., & Polster, R. Intermittent token reinforcement and response maintenance in extinction. *Behavior Therapy*, 1973, *4*, 386–391.

Lovaas, O. I., Freitag, G., Kinder, M. I., Rubenstein, B., Schaeffer, B., & Simmons, J. W. Establishment of social reinforcers in schizophrenic children using food. *Journal of Experimental Child Psychology*, 1966, *4*, 109–125.

Lovaas, O. I., Koegel, R., Simmons, J. O., & Long, J. S. Some generalization and follow-up measures on autistic children in behavior therapy. *Journal of Applied Behavior Analysis*, 1973, *6*, 131–165.

Lovitt, T. C. and Curtiss, K. A. Academic response rate as a function of teacher and self-imposed contingencies. *Journal of Applied Behavior Analysis*, 1969, *2*, 49–53.

Madsen, C. H., Becker, W., & Thomas, D. R. Rules, praise and ignoring: Elements of elementary classroom control. *Journal of Applied Behavior Analysis*, 1968, *1*, 139–151.

Marholin II, D., & Gray, D. Effects of group response cost procedures on cash shortages in a small business setting. *Journal of Applied Behavior Analysis*, 1976, *9*, 57–63.

Marholin II, D. & Hall, K. From institution to community: A behavioral approach to contracting, advocacy, and staff training. *Adolescence*, in press.

Marholin II, D., Siegel, L. J., & Phillips, D. Transfer and treatment: A search for empirical procedures. In M. Hersen, R. M. Eisler, & P. M. Miller (Eds.), *Progress in Behavior Modification* (Vol. 3). New York: Academic, 1976, pp. 293–343.

Marholin II, D., & Steinman, W. M. Stimulus control as a function of the behavior reinforced. *Journal of Applied Behavior Analysis*, 1977, *10*, in press.

Marholin II, D., Steinman, W. M., McInnis, E. T., & Heads, T. B. The effect of a teacher's presence on the classroom behavior of conduct-problem children. *Journal of Abnormal Child Psychology*, 1975, *3*, 11–25.

Meichenbaum, D., & Goodman, J. Training impulsive children to talk to themselves: A means of developing self-control. *Journal of Abnormal Psychology*, 1971, *77*, 115–126.

Nolan, J. D., Mattis, P. R., & Holliday, R. C. Long-term effects of behavior therapy: A 12-month follow-up. *Journal of Abnormal Psychology*, 1970, *76*, 88–92.

O'Leary, K. D., & Becker, W. C. Behavior modification of an adjustment class: A token reinforcement program. *Exceptional Children*, 1967, *33*, 637–642.

O'Leary, K. D., Becker, W. C., Evans, M. D., & Saudargas, S. A. A token reinforcement program in a public school: A replication and systematic analysis. *Journal of Applied Behavior Analysis*, 1969, *2*, 3–13.

Patterson, G. R., Cobb, J. A., & Ray, P. S. Direct intervention in the classroom: A set of procedures for the aggressive child. In F. Clark, D. Evans, & L. Hamerlynck (Eds.), *Implementing behavioral programs for schools and clinics: The proceedings of the Third Banff International Conference on*

Behavior Modification. Champaign, Ill.: Research Press, 1972.

Patterson, G. R., McNeal, S., Hawkins, N., & Phelps, R. Reprogramming the social environment. *Journal of Child Psychology and Psychiatry*, 1967, *8*, 181–195.

Quay, H. C., & Hunt, W. A. Psychopathy, neuroticism and verbal conditioning: A replication and extension. *Journal of Consulting Psychology*, 1965, *29*, 283.

Redd, W. H. Effects of mixed reinforcement contingencies on adults' control of children's behavior. *Journal of Applied Behavior Analysis*, 1969, *2*, 249–254.

Redd, W. H. Generalization of adults' stimulus control of children's behavior. *Journal of Experimental Child Psychology*, 1970, *9*, 286–296.

Redd, W. H., & Birnbrauer, J. S. Adults as discriminative stimuli for differential reinforcement contingencies with retarded children. *Journal of Experimental Child Psychology*, 1969, *7*, 440–447.

Reiss, S., & Redd, W. H. Suppression of screaming behavior in an emotionally disturbed, retarded child. *Proceedings of the American Psychological Association*, 1970, 741–742.

Risley, T. R. The effects and side effects of punishing the autistic behavior of a deviant child. *Journal of Applied Behavior Analysis*, 1968, *1*, 21–34.

Rotter, J. B. Generalized expectancies for internal versus external control of reinforcement. *Psychological Monographs*, 1966, *80*, Whole No. 609.

Schwartz, N. L., & Hawkins, R. P. Application of delayed reinforcement procedures to the behavior of an elementary school child. *Journal of Applied Behavior Analysis*, 1970, *3*, 85–96.

Siegel, L. J., & Steinman, W. M. The modification of a peer observer's classroom behavior as a function of his serving as a reinforcing agent. In E. Ramp & G. Semb (Eds.), *Behavior analysis: Areas of research and application*. Englewood Cliffs, N.J.: Prentice-Hall, Inc., 1975, pp. 321–340.

Skinner, B. F. *Science and human behavior*. New York: Macmillan, 1953.

Solomon, R. W., & Wahler, R. G. Peer reinforcement control of classroom problem behavior. *Journal of Applied Behavior Analysis*, 1973, *6*, 49–56.

Tharp, R. G., & Wetzel, R. J. *Behavior modification in the natural environment*. New York: Academic, 1969.

Wahler, R. G. Oppositional children: A quest for parental reinforcement control. *Journal of Applied Behavior Analysis*, 1969a, *2*, 159–170.

Wahler, R. G. Setting generality: Some specific and general effects of child behavior therapy. *Journal of Applied Behavior Analysis*, 1969b, *2*, 239–246.

Walker, H. M., & Buckley, N. K. Programming generalization and maintenance of treatment effects across time and across settings. *Journal of Applied Behavior Analysis*, 1972, *5*, 209–224.

Whaley, D., & Malott, D. *Elementary principles of behavior*. New York: Appleton-Century-Crofts, 1971.

13

Ethical and Legal Considerations in Behavior Therapy

Tom B. Heads

Several years ago the author received a request to be a consultant to a residential treatment facility for children and adolescents whose behavior problems were of a magnitude that prevented placement in less restrictive settings. The program director, recently graduated with a master's degree, introduced the author to several staff members and residents, described the kinds of problems that the residents presented, and gave a brief tour of the physical plant. Finally, the time came to discuss the role of the consultant. The director wanted help in setting up a token economy to modify the residents' more objectionable behaviors. He confidently announced that although he had not had much time for planning, he had "placed an order for 3000 tokens, and as soon as they arrive in the mail, we're going to start handing them out."

The anecdote illustrates an old axiom that applies to any approach to treatment: a little bit of knowledge is a dangerous thing. At first glance, implementation of behavioral principles seems relatively easy. To modify a person's behavior, you reinforce more desirable behaviors, ignore those behaviors you want to decrease, and perhaps use an aversive event as a consequence of highly maladaptive or inappropriate behavior. What could be simpler or more clear cut? However, as with any treatment approach, taking a few courses in college, reading relevant journals and books, and visiting facilities to observe the treatment procedures in operation barely provides an individual with the rudimentary skills necessary to deliver successful and competent treatment (Bijou, 1970). In the example above, the program director's statement that he was ready to begin as soon as the tokens arrived was as appalling to the author, whose orientation is behavioral, as would be a novice's statement to a group therapist that the group would meet as soon as enough chairs could be found.

The program director or behavior therapist who possesses a superficial knowledge of behavioral principles and has limited experience in their application not only poses a danger to his clients, but may also place himself in legal jeopardy by unwittingly violating client's rights (Friedman, 1975; Wexler, 1973). The purpose of this chapter is to provide the reader with information about the ethical and legal issues that are associated with the practice of behavior therapy. Having achieved a familiarity with possible ethical and legal pitfalls, the practitioner is more likely to anticipate and avoid them, thereby preserving the rights and dignity of his clients. Following a discussion of the criticism of behavioral approaches to treatment and the resultant developments in regulation of behavior therapy, aspects of relevant court decisions concerning the right to treatment are reviewed. Criteria are then offered to assist the therapist, client, and parent or guardian in selecting target behaviors. Finally, the issues surrounding informed consent are examined, and a treatment contract is described.

CRITICISM AND REGULATION

Behavior therapy has been the subject of severe criticism in recent years, in spite of its demonstrated effectiveness (O'Leary & Wilson, 1975). The criticism generally falls into one of three categories: (1) opposition from those who are theoretically or philosophically opposed to the behavioral approach to treatment, (2) confusion of behavioral with nonbehavioral procedures, and (3) reactions to the misuse of behavioral principles. According to Roos (1974), much of the criticism in the first category stems from concerns that behavior therapists and the procedures they employ are cold, manipulative, and exploitative. This stereotype is usually a result of the critic's superficial understanding of behavioral approaches to treatment and a strong allegiance to a nonbehavioral treatment orientation

(Marholin, Taylor, & Warren, in press). The validity of the stereotype has never, to the author's knowledge, been demonstrated.

The high degree of specificity in defining objectives and the emphasis on the manipulation of the client's physical and interpersonal environment elicit fears that the behavior analyst has an unwarranted amount of control over the client, who thus loses his freedom to make choices without coercion (Kazdin, 1975). Although all treatment strategies that are successful in effecting permanent changes in behavior have the potential of being misused by the therapist, "approaches which strive to accomplish such vague or ill-defined objectives as fostering self-actualization, fulfilling human potentials, or serving society are much less vulnerable to this criticism" (Roos, 1974, p. 5). Thus the strengths of behavior analysis—clear specification of goals and procedures, as well as quantitative evaluation of outcomes—result in criticism. If adequate precautions are taken to ensure that the client fully understands and freely consents to the goals of treatment, the techniques used to attain the goals, and the risks involved, then fears that the therapist is unduly controlling and influencing the client are unjustified (Kazdin, 1975; Skinner, 1971).

The field of behavior modification has received criticism from various sources for methods that are not even employed in behavioral treatment programs. For example, the Senate Judiciary Committee (United States Congress, 1974) contributed to the general public's confusion by including under the heading "behavior modification" such diverse procedures as electroconvulsive shock, drug injections, physical punishment, psycho-surgery, group encounters, and physical deprivation. As a result the public's fears of an array of nonbehavioral methods become linked with behavioral treatment approaches. Rather than encompassing *any* technique designed to modify human behavior, behavior modification is the "explicit and systematic application of principles and technology derived from research in experimental psychology" (Stolz, Wienckowski, & Brown, 1975, p. 1029). Systematic monitoring and continuous evaluation of effectiveness are integral components of a behavioral approach to treatment.

Criticism of behavior therapy is justified when it is in reaction to evidence that the therapist, through ignorance, negligence, or malice, has misused the techniques. Reports of the gross misuse of behavior therapy carried by the national news media have stirred public alarm, have made "behavior modification" unacceptable both as a concept and a practice in numerous communities, and have stimulated a lengthy investigation by the United States Senate Judiciary Committee (United States Congress, 1974). For example, two special education teachers placed an asthmatic, 12-year-old, retarded child in a small, unventilated box as a punishment for disrupting classroom activities. Moreover, they failed to obtain parental consent and defended the practice as a legitimate "time out" procedure (Langworthy, Note 1). Token economies in prisons have involved the unlawful deprivation of basic necessities such as nutritious food, a bed, appropriate clothing, and the right to communicate with others (United States Congress, 1974). Delinquent and retarded youth in a residential institution were subjected to as much as 4 hours of solitary confinement and to public humiliation, ridicule, and embarrassment in a progam that was labeled "behavior modification" (May, Note 2).

Pressures from public organizations and individuals to regulate or even to outlaw behavioral treatment have been the result of these and other unfortunate incidents, even though they are numerically insignificant when compared with the many conscientious and effective applications of behavioral procedures. Behavioral practitioners themselves, outraged by flagrant abuses of behavior therapy and apprehensive about the negative effects of adverse publicity or their professional reputation, have begun to advocate for the regulation of behavior therapy from within the profession (Agras, 1973; Stolz, in press). They realize that severe restrictions imposed by well-intentioned but naive critics of behavior therapy might result in the denial of treatment to clients who sincerely desire to alter aspects of their behavior that are maladaptive and ineffective.

Regulations that protect clients from negligent treatment but still allow competent practitioners to treat them are currently being developed. In response to the need for guidelines for the ethical practice of behavior therapy, the Association for the Advancement of Behavior Therapy (1976) and the Commission on Behavior Modification of the American Psychological Association (Note 3) have proposed a checklist for ethical practice. The checklist is composed of a series of questions regarding goals, treatment methods, consent, evaluation of outcome, referral practices, confidentiality, and therapist competence. Specific prescriptive and proscriptive statements ("shalls" and "shall nots") have been avoided in favor of a format that functions to remind the practitioner of his responsibility in crucial areas of ethical concern.

In addition to guidelines developed by professional organizations, at least nine states have passed or have proposed statutes that place restrictions on treatment procedures which are intrusive in nature, in order to protect the constitutional rights of the client. The Florida guidelines (National Association for Retarded Citizens, 1975), formulated by a task force of persons with recognized expertise in behavior therapy, law, and advocacy, are perhaps the best administrative regulations currently available for the use of behavioral procedures. Emphasis is placed on increasing the involvement of the client and his advocate in treatment planning and obtaining their informed consent prior to behavioral intervention. Review committees are established to monitor the intervention and to ensure that staff are trained to a level of competence which makes effective treatment possible and reduces the chance of abusive treatment.

Some professionals (e.g., Stolz, in press) have opposed specific guidelines, fearing that they will result in a denial of the benefits of behavior therapy to clients. It is predicted that this denial would occur because guidelines would cause lengthy bureaucratic delays and would force institutional staff to avoid behavioral methods, instead using other treatment approaches that are not regulated. Whether these concerns are justified is an empirical question that has yet to be answered. The benefit of specific, comprehensive, well-formulated guidelines is that they can direct the therapist toward more ethical practices and that they increase the probability that the rights of his clients will be safe-guarded. Although guidelines cannot prevent the intentional misuse of behavioral procedures, they can provide essential direction for the conscientious behavior therapist.

RIGHT TO TREATMENT

Although most behavioral practitioners have routinely considered the ethical and legal implications of their activities and have taken pains to evaluate the effectiveness of the treatment they provide, recent court decisions have begun to define standards for treatment quality and effectiveness (Ennis & Friedman, 1973; Mental Health Law Project, Note 4). Specifically, seven recent court decisions, in defining and elaborating the concept of the "right to treatment," have delineated the boundaries of adequate treatment. These decisions have considerable relevance for the practice of behavior therapy (Goldiamond, 1974; Martin, 1975; Wexler, 1973).

The first legal decision affirming the right to treatment, *Rouse v. Cameron* (1966), established the right of persons involuntarily confined to public mental hospitals (in this case, convicted criminals in a psychiatric facility) either to receive adequate and appropriate treatment or to be released. The plaintifs' arguments were based on the constitutional guarantees, from the Fifth and Fourteenth Amendments, of due process and equal protection under the law, as well as the Eighth Amendment prohibition against cruel and unusual punishment. Prior to the *Rouse* decision, courts had not been involved in evaluating the conditions in institutions where convicted persons had been placed to see if treatment was actually being provided to them. Rather, the administrator of the institution had complete authority in deciding whether therapy would be provided and, if so, the nature and quality of that therapy (Halpern, 1976).

The right to treatment for juveniles involuntarily committed to an institution was established in *Morales v. Turman* (1974). Particularly relevant to those who work with children removed from the natural family is the federal court's warning that "it is not sufficient . . . to contend that merely removing a child from his environment and placing him in a 'structured' situation constitutes constitutionally adequate treatment." The court set a precedent by ruling that adequate habilitation requires an individualized plan of treatment. Thus, practices such as establishing a token economy with the same goals and criteria for each person or systematically structuring the interpersonal environment and labeling it a "therapeutic mileu" do not meet the standards for adequate treatment. In addition, the court insisted on well-trained and supervised staff as a prerequisite for treatment, equating "treatment" administered by an untrained and/or poorly supervised staff with cruel and unusual punishment. Finally, periodic reviews of progress were demanded as an integral component of treatment.

Donaldson v. O'Connor (1975) established the principle that persons who are diagnosed "mentally ill' and are placed in an institution involuntarily on a civil commitment (not accused or convicted of a crime) must either receive treatment or be released. Depriving a person of liberty because he is a danger to himself or others is justifiable only when treatment is provided. Notable in this case is the court's ruling that staff members in a mental health facility can be held personally liable for depriving an individual of his liberty, manifested in this case by fines being levied against two of the institution's psychiatrists.

Standards for adequate treatment that were suggested in only general terms in *Morales* were elaborated in *Wyatt v. Stickney* (1972; later *Wyatt v. Aderholt*, 1974) and the "Willowbrook" consent decree (*New York Association for Retarded Children v. Rockefeller*, 1973). Although the standards developed in these cases apply to retarded persons living in institutions, the principles can be readily extrapolated to children in other treatment settings. The courts in both cases reaffirmed that an individual plan of care and a well-trained and supervised staff are required for the provision of adequate treatment. Client progress must be evaluated periodically. The minimal conditions for a humane psychological and physical environment are described, including a listing of constitutionally protected rights that must be respected and which cannot be used as privileges that are given contingently to reinforce desired behaviors. Adequate food, comfortable and appropriate clothing, a bed, and privacy are among the items mentioned as basic rights. The *Wyatt* decision ordered the formation of a human rights committee mandated to protect the clients who receive treatment. Also established was a professional review board, to evaluate the overall quality of treatment and the progress of each client.

The *Wyatt* decision provided one basis for the Federal Intermediate Care Facility standards (Federal Register, 1974), which are now being implemented nationally to upgrade services to retarded persons in residential facilities. Significant portions of the *Wyatt* decision can be found in Ennis and Friedman (1973).

The agreement in the Willowbrook case, endorsing essentially the same standards of treatment as *Wyatt v. Stickney*, is notable for several reasons. First, although court decisions in other right-to-treatment cases were based on the constitutional guarantees of equal protection of all citizens under the law and due process before a right can be abridged, the Willowbrook decision was founded on the Eighth Amendment prohibition against cruel and unusual punishment. Courts in the past have derived the concept of "protection from harm" from this amendment but have used it conservatively, intervening only when conditions were found to be "shocking to the conscience" or "barbarous." The present decision utilizes a broad, comprehensive definition of "harm," asserting that "harm can result not only from neglect but from conditions which cause regression or which prevent development of an individual's capabilities" (President's Committee on Mental Retardation, 1975, p. 5). In other words, if a client's level of adaptive functioning deteriorates or even remains unchanged over time, he is being harmed, and his constitutional right to protection from harm is being denied. Thus the only acceptable situation for a client in a residential treatment program is one in which he continues to develop and to improve his level of functioning.

Two court decisions have addressed themselves to the client's right to refuse treatment and to be treated in the least restrictive setting possible. The *Kaimowitz v. Michigan Department of Mental Health* decision (1973) suggests that a client in an institution cannot be forced to undergo a type of treatment that is experimental in nature and that exposes him to a great degree of risk. The client must furnish voluntary consent that is based on complete and valid information. Furthermore, because of the inherently coercive nature of a closed institution (such as a prison or locked psychiatric facility), valid consent may be impossible to obtain, and thus some aversive, experimental, and intrusive types of treatment cannot be used. The concept of "least restrictive alternative" was established in *Lake v. Cameron* (1966). When an individual is committed by the state for the purpose of protection, the least restrictive alternative, both in terms of the general environment and the type of treatment provided, must be utilized. It is the state's obligation to show that less risky, drastic, and intrusive treatment measures and a lesser infringement of the client's liberty would not be effective.

Although most of the court decisions reviewed above address the situation of individuals who are involuntarily confined in an institution for treatment, the decisions and standards promulgated apply to all clients residing in institutions, regardless of their legal status at the time of admission. The distinction between "voluntary" and "involuntary" commitment is invalid, because once clients are admitted, the staff of the institution generally provide the same quality of treatment to all of them, with no distinctions made on the basis of the client's legal status (Halpern, 1976). The court in the Willowbrook agreement ruled that all institutionalized persons should receive adequate treatment and live in an environment that fosters continuing development.

For the behavior therapist, the right to treatment rulings imply responsibility both for the development of formal treatment programs and for a general restructuring of the physical environment and the interpersonal contingencies experienced by the client. Treatment programs must be individualized, must be implemented by trained and supervised staff, and must be evaluated periodically. The client may not be deprived of basic necessities to increase their value as reinforcers, even though this may at times seem very desirable from a therapeutic point of view. Voluntary consent for treatment must be obtained from the client or his guardian.

SELECTION OF TARGET BEHAVIORS

Prior to initiating treatment, the therapist, the client, and his parents or guardian must reach agreement concerning the behaviors to be modified. The target behaviors, behavioral objectives, or goals selected for intervention should meet the five conditions discussed below. If they do not, the responsible behavior therapist should refuse to work toward them, but should continue to meet with the client and parents until goals acceptable to all parties are identified.

The target behaviors that are selected must be *ethical*. That is, they must result in long-term, positive consequences for the client and must be in his best interest. Goals such as gaining independence in toileting, bathing, and dressing, acquiring reading and numerical skills, learning to ride a bicycle, and playing cooperatively with peers are generally acceptable and rarely raise serious questions about whether they are in the child's best interest. Other goals that parents, school personnel, or community staff might propose cannot be so easily identified as "ethical." Should the behavior analyst, at the parent's request, develop a program to train the child to use his right hand for writing, rather than the preferred and dominant left hand? What if a single parent wants the child to change the quality of his interaction with a recently separated spouse? Should a child be trained to engage in academic tasks 10 hours per day, when the behavior therapist can predict that the gains in academic performance will be at the expense of other experiences that will foster the child's social, emotional, and physical development? What if both parents and child select goals that seem to be unethical?

As with all ethical problems, there are few, if any, universally right and wrong answers. Each target behavior has to be examined separately. The behavior therapist has to look at the function of the proposed change. Does it really lead to positive, long-range consequences, or is the client being taught to fit into a system (e.g., school, family, classroom) that is abnormal or oppressive and should itself be changed? Winett and Winkler (1972) correctly question the blind enthusiasm of some professionals to devise procedures to motivate children to "be still, be quiet, be docile" in the classroom, satisfying the values and goals of some school administrators and teachers. The responsible change agent is obligated to ask "Am I being asked to fit a child into a situation that is not in his best interest?" The goals and values of the institution or system, rather than the behavior of the client, might be the correct target of intervention. If the child is the client, then interests of the institution or system that conflict with those of the child must be questioned. Also, the therapist should not hesitate to question the "best interest" decisions of the parents and to discuss possible alternative goals with them.

Goals must be *stated behaviorally* and must include a *quantitative criterion* for the attainment of the goal. As discussed elsewhere in this book (Marholin & Bijou, Chapter 2), target behaviors must be defined in such a way that they are observable, measurable, and quantifiable. It is not sufficient to know that the parents and school want the client to "respond better to authority" and to "improve his classroom behavior." Rather than accepting statements employing abstract ideas, traits, and personality characteristics, the behavior therapist must continue to question the persons who have referred the child for service until he knows what behaviors are to be eliminated, what behaviors are to be developed or strengthened, with what frequency and under which conditions (Bijou & Peterson, 1971). When the initial referral involves a request for improved response to authority and better classroom behavior, it is incumbent upon the therapist to question his informants until he can formulate goal statements such as "follows directions given by parents and teachers 90% of the time within 1 minute" and "obtains a 3.5 average in arithmetic, reading, and composition, with no grade lower than 1.0; and displays classroom study behaviors (in seat, on task, no disruption) equal to or better than the mean for the entire class." Note that these goal statements include numerical criteria, so that attainment of the goal can be determined. To arrive at quantified criteria, it is necessary to have baseline observations of the frequency of occurrence of the target behaviors. Thus, when parents or other referral sources present a complaint based on subjective and informal observation, reliable information must be collected before quantified criteria for successful change can be established.

The goals must be *realistic*, in terms of the expected quality and quantity of the behavior and the amount of time it will take for change to occur. For example, although parents might want to eliminate sexual exploration behaviors of their developing adolescent, it is highly unlikely that this goal could be attained without very drastic measures. Eliminating all the behaviors of a 5-year-old that the parents might find annoying, besides being ethically questionable, would be an unrealistic goal. Rather than devising a program to teach a young, severely retarded child to attain advanced academic skills, a goal that might be possible only over a period of many years, selecting short-range goals that have a reasonable probability of being reached is more sensible. Choosing realistic goals that have a good probability of being attained will provide more reinforcement to the client, the parents, and the therapist.

The goals must be ones that can be *realized with available resources*. Even if a goal is behaviorally defined, ethical, and realistic, resources such as staff and parent time, materials, and adequate physical facilities may be lacking. The goal of elimination of self-injurious behavior in a large custodial institution is an unfortunate example. The technology to eliminate self-injury is available (Bachman, 1972; Baumeister & Rollings, 1976; Smolev, 1971), but if the institution is not able to afford the tremendous short-term investment of staff time that is required, the goal is unattainable. Similarly, even if the goal of elimination of a client's sexual activity were found to be ethical, it is unlikely that suitable incompatible behaviors and reinforcers of sufficient potency would be available to reach the goal. When acceptable behavioral goals cannot be reached because of inadequate resources, the behavior therapist must decide if his professional role includes advocacy. If it does, then he is obligated to attempt to influence administrators to find necessary resources so that treatment can commence.

The goals selected for intervention must be ones that can be *maintained by naturally occuring reinforcers* (see Marholin & Siegel, Chapter 12). This is the "Relevance of Behavior Rule" discussed by Ayllon and Azrin (1968, p.49): "Teach only those behaviors that will continue to be reinforced after training." If the new behaviors do not result in positive consequences outside of the training situation, this nonreinforcement or extinction will negate any changes that have been accomplished (Marholin, Siegel, & Phillips, 1976). The example of elimination of self-injury within a custodial institution illustrates this principle of goal selection. A child who bangs his head with his fists has to be taught new behaviors that are incompatible with using his hands to injure himself. Whereas it might be relatively easy to teach the child to manipulate toys, draw with a crayon, and play catch with a ball, these and other activities which involve the use of hands must be maintained and strengthened by the child's environment if they are permanently to replace banging the head with fists. In the typically understaffed residential institution, even the most well-meaning staff person may be too occupied with other responsibilities to see that the child has access to play materials and is reinforced for using them appropriately. Selection of target behaviors that meet with positive consequences in the child's various settings will ensure that they will be maintained.

In summary, target behaviors must be ethical in nature, be stated behaviorally, be realistic and attainable with available resources, and be capable of being maintained by naturally occurring reinforcers. Three precautions must be mentioned with regard to these requirements. First, the behavior therapist has to guard against being so ethically conservative and so limited in the range of target behaviors that he accepts for treatment that a sizable percentage of referrals are turned away as "untreatable." The therapist, the client's parents or guardian, and review committees must find a reasonable balance between cautious protection of the client's rights and provision of needed treatment. Second, the behavior therapist is cautioned against the tendency to identify as targets those behaviors with which he has had success in the past, to the neglect or exclusion of other behaviors which cause equal or greater difficulties for the child. Finally, the author feels obligated again to mention that targets should be selected that are of greatest benefit to the client and not primarily for the benefit of persons who have contact with that child.

INFORMED CONSENT

The concept of informed consent in behavior therapy is derived from medical practice. A visit to a physician for a simple medical procedure (e.g., a physical examination, an injection) does not require that the patient give written permission for the doctor to treat him. Instead, a treatment contract is implied; the patient expects that the physician will treat him in a competent manner, and the physician expects that the patient will be cooperative and informative. However, prior to beginning a more complex medical procedure which carries greater risk (e.g., a series of X-rays, an operation), the patient is required to sign a consent form. Essential features of such a consent form are (1) the diagnosis, (2) an explanation of the nature of treatment, (3) a statement of the risks involved, (4) the probability of successful outcome, (5) the prognosis if the treatment is not performed, and (6) alternative methods of treatment (Schwitzgebel, 1975). Prior to a complex operation that is experimental and involves great risk, such as a heart transplant, approval from a board of physicians and community representatives is also required.

To qualify as valid informed consent, the person who signs the statement must be intellectually capable of giving consent, must be acting in a voluntary manner free from coercion and duress, and must be fully informed regarding the nature and consequences of the proposed treatment. Elkin (1976) observes that a parent or guardian may "hesitate to question the quality of a service, be it educational, health, or residential, because of the threat (real or imagined) of exclusion or retaliation" (p. 89). Thus parental consent for use of a particular treatment procedure, given at the request of a therapist or administrator who subtly implies that the child might be transferred to a less desirable program or living situation if consent is not obtained, is involuntary. Consent cannot be truly voluntary if a consequence, either reward or the avoidance of punishment, is associated with the consenting.

The complex issue of whether a person in a "closed" institution, such as a prison or security hospital, is capable of giving truly voluntary consent to participate in behavioral procedures is beyond the scope of this chapter. Interested readers are directed to discussions of consent in closed institutions by Friedman (1975), Martin (1975), and Stolz, et al. (1975).

The presence of a client in a residential institution, a classroom, a day-treatment program, or similar setting does not give the superintendent, principal, chief medical officer, administrator, or staff member the authority to select goals and implement treatment procedures without the consent of the client or a guardian acting in his behalf. In the past a program administrator was often allowed to give consent on behalf of clients. His authority for this came from state statute or administrative guidelines, from interpretation of his mandate to provide all necessary care, or from a blanket authorization form signed by the client's parents at the time of admission. The practice of administrative consent is of questionable validity and may be increasingly restricted in the future (Martin, 1975).

Obtaining consent becomes a particularly complex issue when a client is unable to give the consent for himself. Children, emotionally impaired children and adults, and severely retarded persons are generally assumed to be legally incompetent, and thus they require a parent or guardian to act in their best interest. Courts of law usually assume that parents are sufficiently dedicated to their child's welfare to be allowed to exercise the power of consent for medical and psychological interventions, even though the parents are rarely held accountable for responsibility in making decisions for their child (Price & Burt, 1976). Parents are restrained, however, from giving consent for the child to undergo a procedure that is clearly illegal or that places the child in great danger, unless the potential benefit is great enough to justify the risk (Martin, 1975).

A difficult dilemma arises when a client who is legally incompetent to consent as a result of age or functional level is nonetheless able to express a strong preference. For example, an adolescent who is sexually active may desire contraceptive information and devices in the absence of or contrary to the wishes of the parents. The degree to which the child's rights can supercede the parent's authority is an issue that is not fully resolved by the courts. When a parent consents to a procedure for his child and the child expresses an unwillingness to participate, the behavior therapist must decide whether to implement the treatment in spite of the client's objections. Although not legally required, it is recommended that consent be obtained whenever possible for all clients, regardless of their legal status, both to satisfy ethical standards and to take advantage of the therapeutic effects of having the client express commitment to the goals and procedures of the intervention.

No simple rules are available to aid the therapist in deciding what degree of rigor in consent and review procedures is adequate for different behavior techniques. Each case has to be judged on its own. A categorization of common behavioral techniques is offered in Table 1 as a rough guide to determine the stringency of consent and review that should be required (Miller, Thomas, & Heads, Note 5). The techniques are grouped according to several factors. As one moves from group A downward, the potential for misuse of the technique, for physical injury, and for aversiveness to the client increases. The techniques in the lower categories are generally more unacceptable to the public, are more physically intrusive, and have effects that are more likely to be irreversible. Because of these characteristics, the more aversive techniques require that the therapist have more advanced training and experience to implement them.

As previously mentioned, physicians require implied or verbal consent for routine office procedures, formal written consent for operations, and a complex review for operations that carry a high degree of risk. There is a similar progression in consent and review procedures in the proposed state policy from which Table 1 is taken (Miller, et al., Note 5). Consent for category A techniques is obtained by means of a standard consent form at the time the client enters treatment. Implementation of techniques in categories B–E is contingent on prior approval of the client, parent or guardian, and the agency's human rights committee. In addition, techniques in category E require prior approval of the agency administrator, a consultant with recognized competency in behavioral analysis, the state agency director, and the state human rights committee.

If formal standards for consent and review are not available, it is the responsibility of the behavior therapist to formulate his own guidelines, both to protect the rights of his clients and to protect himself from charges of malpractice. It is strongly recommended that the review of techniques that are aversive or have not been thoroughly evaluated in controlled empirical studies include, at a minimum, one or more professional peers, a consultant who is not an integral part of the system in which the therapist practices, and a group whose responsibility it is to protect the rights of clients.

Table 1
Behavioral techniques categorized according to the stringency of consent and review required

Group A
    Positive reinforcement
    Social disapproval
    Token economy (positive reinforcement only)
    Time out I (within view)
    Extinction of *non*-health-threatening behaviors
    Graduated guidance
    Redirection
    Response cost I (removal of toy, etc.)
    Modeling
Group B
    Time out II (removed from view or room)
    Response cost II (restriction from activity)
    Overcorrection
    Restitution
    Positive practice
    Token economy (with response cost)
Group C
    Required relaxation
    Response cost III (removal of food tray)
    Time out III (time out room)
Group D
    Contingent use of physical restraint
    Extinction of health-threatening behavior
    Application of noxious stimuli
    Satiation
    Contingent physically intrusive stimuli
Group E
    Electric shock
    Food or water deprivation
    Physical striking
    Contingent environmental extremes

TREATMENT CONTRACT

Once target behaviors have been selected and the therapist has determined what techniques and procedures will be used to reach the behavioral goals, a treatment contract can be written. The purpose of the contract is twofold: (1) to clarify and formalize the expectations of the client and therapist regarding treatment, and (2) to satisfy the need for written consent. Furthermore, a properly written contract can serve to increase the accountability of the therapist and client to each other (Kanfer, 1975).

The treatment contract is developed by the therapist with the assistance of the child and his parents and is signed prior to the initiation of treatment. It should contain, at a minimum, the following information: (1) a description of the target behaviors, (2) an explanation of the nature of the treatment, including the techniques and the reinforcers that will be used, (3) the behavioral criteria for the attainment of each target behavior, (4) an estimate of the duration of treatment, (5) an explanation of how progress will be assessed, (6) a statement of the behaviors expected of the parents and others who interact with the child, (7) the fee for service (if any), (8) a statement that the parent has read the treatment contract, understands it, and has been informed that it can be terminated or renegotiated at the request of either parent, client, or therapist, (9) the signatures of the client, parents and therapist; also if applicable, the signatures of the supervisor, agency head, or representative from the human rights committee.

CONCLUSION

The chapter began with an anecdote about a program director who was ready to implement a treatment program without first considering the ethical and legal implications of his actions. The remainder of the chapter can be viewed as a discussion of what a conscientious behavior therapist should consider before initiating treatment. Target behaviors are selected in a meeting with the client and his parents. Care is taken to choose targets that are ethical, stated in behavioral terms with quantitative criteria, realistic, attainable with available resources; and capable of being maintained by naturally occurring reinforcers. A decision is made about the least intrusive and restrictive treatment techniques necessary to reach the behavioral objectives. The treatment program is individualized for each client. Training is conducted with staff and a supervisory plan is developed. Periodic reviews of progress are scheduled. The therapist discusses the treatment program with peers, consultants, and a human-rights committee. Finally, a treatment contract is written and is signed by the client, the parents, and the therapist.

Although the ideas in this chapter may prompt the reader to consider the ethical and legal implications of behavior therapy, they will not necessarily change his behavior. The best that might be accomplished is to increase the number and the quality of the questions the reader asks himself about his professional activities. With an increase in such self-examination, a few potential instances of misuse of behavior therapy will be anticipated and avoided.

REFERENCE NOTES

1. Langworthy, R. Butte-Boulder box battle is a bomb for "be-mod." *Boulder Behaviorist*, 1975, *3*, 1–2. Boulder River School and Hospital, Boulder, Montana.
2. May, J. G. Ethical and legal contingencies in and upon behavior modification programs. Unpublished manuscript, Florida State University, May 1974.
3. American Psychological Association, Commission on Behavior Modification, Open Meeting, September 1976, Washington, D.C.
4. Mental Health Law Project. *Basic rights of the mentally handicapped*, 1973. Available from Mental Health Law Project, 1751 N Street N.W., Washington, D.C., 20036.
5. Miller, D., Thomas, C., & Heads, T. Development of a state policy for the regulation of behavioral procedures. Paper presented at Region 10 A.A.M.D. meeting, October, 1976. Available from Dr. Donald Miller, North Central Regional Center, Bloomfield, Connecticut, 06002.

REFERENCES

Agras, W. S. Toward the certification of behavior therapists? *Journal of Applied Behavior Analysis*, 1973, *6*, 167–173.

Association for the Advancement of Behavior Therapy. Ethical practice guidelines. *AABT Newsletter*, 1976, *3*, 2.

Ayllon, T., & Azrin, N. H. *The token economy: A motivational system for therapy and rehabilitation.* New York: Appleton-Century-Crofts, 1968.

Bachman, J. A. Self-injurious behavior: A behavioral analysis. *Journal of Abnormal Psychology*, 1972, *80*, 211–224.

Baumeister, A. A., & Rollings, J. P. Self-injurious behavior. In N. R. Ellis (Ed.), *International review of research in mental retardation* (Vol. 8). New York: Academic, 1976.

Bijou, S. W. What psychology has to offer education—now. *Journal of Applied Behavior Analysis*, 1970, *3*, 65–71.

Bijou, S. W., & Peterson, R. F. Psychological assessment of children: A functional analysis. In P. McReynolds (Ed.), *Advances in psychological assessment* (Vol. 2). Palo Alto, Calif.: Science and Behavior Books, 1971.

Donaldson v. O'Connor, 95 S. Ct. 2486 (1975).

Elkin, E. S. Reaction comment. In M. Kindred, J. Cohen, D. Penrod, & T. Shaffer (Eds.), *The mentally retarded citizen and the law*. New York: Free Press, 1976.

Ennis, B. J., & Friedman, P. R. (Eds.). *Legal rights of the mentally handicapped* (Vols. 1–3). New York: Practising Law Institute, 1973.

Federal Register, 1974, *39* (12), 2220–2235.

Friedman, P. R. Legal regulation of applied behavior analysis in mental institutions and prisons. *Arizona Law Review*, 1975, *17*, 39–104.

Goldiamond, I. Toward a constructional approach to social problems. *Behaviorism*, 1974, *2*, 1–84.

Halpern, C. R. The right to habilitation. In M. Kindred, J. Cohen, D. Penrod, & T. Shaffer (Eds.), *The mentally retarded citizen and the law*. New York: Free Press, 1976.

Kaimowitz v. Michigan Department of Mental Health, Civil No. 73–19434–AW, (Cir. Ct. Wayne Co., Mich., July 10, 1973), 575.

Kanfer, F. H. Self-management methods. In F. H. Kanfer & A. P. Goldstein (Eds.), *Helping people change*. New York: Pergamon, 1975.

Kazdin, A. E. *Behavior modification in applied settings*. Homewood, Ill.: Dorsey Press, 1975.

Lake v. Cameron, 364 F. 2d. 657 (D. C. Cir. 1966).

Marholin, D., Siegel, L. J., & Phillips, D. Treatment and transfer: A search for empirical procedures. In M. Hersen, R. M. Eisler, & P. M. Miller (Eds.), *Progress in behavior modification* (Vol. 3). New York: Academic, 1976.

Marholin II, D., Taylor, R. L., & Warren, S. A. A report on attitudes toward behavior modification as a function of knowledge, coursework, and experience. *Teaching of Psychology*, in press.

Martin, R. *Legal challenges to behavior modification*. Champaign, Ill.: Research Press, 1975.

Morales v. Turman, 383 F. Supp. 53 (E. D. Texas, 1974).

National Association for Retarded Citizens. Guidelines for the use of behavioral procedures in state programs for retarded persons. *M. R. Research*, 1975, *1* (1).

New York Association for Retarded Children v. Rockefeller, 357 F. Supp. 752 (E.D.N.Y. 1973).

O'Leary, K. D., & Wilson, G. T. *Behavior therapy: Application and outcome*. Englewood Cliffs, N.J.: Prentice-Hall, 1975.

President's Committee on Mental Retardation. New York signs far-reaching consent decree in the "Willowbrook" case. *Mental Retardation and the Law*, June 1975, 1–7.

Price, M. E., & Burt, R. A. Nonconsensual medical procedures and the right to privacy. In M. Kindred, J. Cohen, D. Penrod, & T. Shaffer (Eds), *The mentally retarded citizen and the law*. New York: Free Press, 1976.

Roos, P. Human rights and behavior modification. *Mental Retardation*, 1974, *12*, 3–6,

Rouse v. Cameron, 373 F. 2d 451 (D.C. Cir. 1966).

Schwitzgebel, R. K. A contractual model for the protection of the rights of institutionalized mental patients. *American Psychologist*, 1975, *30*, 815–820.

Skinner, B. F. *Beyond freedom and dignity*. New York: Knopf, 1971.

Smolev, S. R. Use of operant techniques for the modification of self-injurious behavior. *American Journal of Mental Deficiency*, 1971, *76*, 295–305.

Stolz, S. B. Why no guidelines for behavior modification? *Journal of Applied Behavior Analysis*, 1977, *10*, in press.

Stolz, S. B., Wienckowski, L. A., & Brown, B. S. Behavior modification: A perspective on critical issues. *American Psychologist*, 1975, *30*, 1027–1048.

United States Congress, Senate Committee of the Judiciary, Subcommittee on Constitutional Rights. *Individual rights and the federal role in behavior modification*. Washington, D.C.: U.S. Government Printing Office, 1974.

Wexler, D. B. Token and taboo: Behavior modification, token economies, and the law. *California Law Review*, 1973, *61*, 81–109.

Winett, R. A., & Winkler, R. C. Current behavior modification in the classroom: Be still, be quiet, be docile. *Journal of Applied Behavior Analysis*, 1972, *5*, 499–504.

Wyatt v. Aderholt, 368 F. Supp. 1382, 1383 (M.D. Ala. 1974).

Wyatt v. Stickney, 344 F. Supp. 373, 344 Supp. 387 (M.D. Ala. 1972).

14

Training and Motivating Staff Members

Titus McInnis

This chapter deals with some of the factors important in the sucessful operation of a residential treatment or educational program. Factors discussed include the organization and structure of the program, initial training of staff members, incentive programs for staff members, and the role of evaluation of treatment as it relates to incentive programs. Persons being treated are referred to as "students," although in other contexts they might be referred to as "clients," "residents," or "patients." Those conducting the treatment or educational programs are called "staff members," and their activities are labeled as "treatment," even though the activities may be primarily directed to normal rather than "clinical" populations.

ORGANIZATIONAL AND STRUCTURAL FACTORS

Underlying successful treatment programs are a good organizational structure and carefully specified staff duties. Elements of a good organization have been discussed by Glaser and Taylor (1973), Friedlander and Brown (1974), McInnis (1976), and Whittington (1973). Whittington (1973) noted that two factors seem to stand out when attempting to improve morale of staff members, (1) improved communications and (2) clarification of roles and responsibilities. Glaser and Taylor (1973) listed full and open discussions among staff members about treatment issues, a search for criticism, maximization of formal and informal communication, and sharing of all problems with all staff members as some of the features of successful programs. Friedlander and Brown (1974) listed such factors as sharing of information, solving interpersonal staff problems through discussion of them, full participation in decision making, decentralization of authority, and job enrichment. Glaser and Taylor (1973) also mentioned that a successful program was not likely to be a placid one, but rather that "stormy" interactions would be likely to occur among staff members as the program's problems were solved.

The papers mentioned above, especially the one by Whittington (1973) dealing with general administration of a treatment program, can be consulted for full discussions of organizational factors in treatment programs. The present author would like to focus here on a few aspects of an organization that may be of crucial importance.

Information and its dissemination within a treatment program seems to be very important to any organization. For an information program to work the administrators of the program must be willing to share information and seek advice from staff members. Once policies are decided on, the administrators face the problem of getting the policy details to all staff members. Several "mechanical" rules may help in this regard. The program should have a treatment manual, and each staff member should have a copy of it. Changes in manuals and the addition of new policies require some means of making sure that all staff members know of them. The staff meeting is the basic mechanism for imparting information. Although rules for meetings might sound simplistic, they are necessary. It is suggested that meetings last for at least $1\frac{1}{2}$ hours, that they occur regularly, and that an agenda and minutes be prepared. Meetings should be supplemented with a memo system, so that those who miss meetings receive all information. Staff members could be asked to sign or initial the memos as a check on their having read them. Any written policies must be reviewed, changed, or discarded periodically. Whittington (1973) has warned of the ". . . inexorable accretion of policies and procedures accumulated over the years, which come to have the force, first, of tradition, and then of immutable law . . . (p. 73)."

There is a feature of successful treatment programs that has implications for the areas of staff motivation and program effectiveness and survival. Glaser and Taylor (1973) concluded that successful programs tended to seek and maintain contact with outsiders, including expert advisors. Public exposure of a treatment program may help in its maintaining high technical and ethical standards. Many treatment programs are vulnerable to misunderstanding of good, but apparently harsh, procedures that can be justified if an attempt is made. In the absence of public scrutiny, some programs may drift into unethical and shoddy procedures. An excellent way to prevent such a situation from occurring would be to subject the program to inspection and critique not only by scientific experts but also by laymen. In regard to visits by laymen, it is suggested that the general public, those closely associated with the program (e.g., relatives of students), and the press be invited and encouraged to visit the program regularly. These visits should be guided ones accompanied by explanations of the program procedures. Nothing at all should be hidden from inspection, and reactions from visitors should be solicited.

Whittington (1973) has noted that professional staff members have a reputation for wanting to "do their own thing" but, in fact, begin eventually to seek structure in their jobs. Even in a dynamic, democratic, organization it seems necessary to specify staff members' work schedules and duties. Not only do staff members seek such structure, but it is also necessary if the program's administrators want some assurance that what they consider to be good treatment is actually being performed.

The difference between a structured and an unstructured program can be illustrated by looking at the work of an individual staff member. At one extreme a staff member may be instructed to "do psychotherapy" with a child, whereas at the other extreme the staff member may be provided with a lesson plan that specifies the specific goal of the treatment and detailed instructions for achieving the goal. Either of these teachers may succeed or fail in his goal of helping the child. However, the detailed procedures set down for the second staff member offer several advantages to the administrators and employees of the treatment program. First, when training a new employee in the procedure, the completely specified treatment procedure can serve as a lesson plan. Second, once the employee is trained, his work can then be checked by a supervisor, who can visit the treatment situation to see if the specified plan is (or is not) being followed. Third, since the employee knows exactly what the procedure is and keeps a running record of steps completed, he has a good check on his own performance. Fourth, with a record of what actually happened in the treatment situation along with a record of the child's progress, the administrators and the teacher can evaluate the procedure and, perhaps, improve it. With such specification of treatment procedures comes the opportunity to evaluate the effectiveness or ineffectiveness of treatment procedures. Without specification, as with the instruction, "do psychotherapy," one cannot evaluate.

Other types of specifications are important in a treatment program. Staff activities should be scheduled so that supervisors will know where staff are and what they should be doing. Recording forms should be designed not only to record student progress but also to include cues or reminders to staff members of such things as times activities should start and stop, which staff member should perform each type of activity, lists of criteria against which to judge students' response to treatment, and the like. Recording forms can be used as a means of directing and "supervising" the actions of staff members.

STAFF TRAINING

Several authors have addressed themselves to the issue of whether on-the-job training is superior or inferior to academic instruction in training staff members (Cone & Sheldon, Note 1; Gardner, 1972; Paul & McInnis, 1974; Paul, McInnis, & Mariotto, 1973). Without going into details of studies, it may be suggested that evidence tends to support on-the-job training over academic instruction. However, there is suggestive evidence that at least some behaviors can be taught in an academic situation (Cone & Sheldon, Note 1). In spite of the evidence, academic instruction in the principles of treatment and how the principles can be applied probably should be given in addition to on-the-job training. There are always situations wherein any employee must make independent decisions, and it is important that he know the proper guiding principles on which to base his actions. One way to help ensure that an employee knows how to apply principles is to show him and explain to him how they are applied during the on-the-job phase of instruction. One must not assume that an employee will transfer principles taught in a classroom to the actual treatment situation.

The literature on staff training contains several training programs that seem to have merit (Goldstein & Goedhart, 1973; Martin, McDonald, & Murrell, Note 2; Paul & McInnis, 1974; Watson, Gardner, & Sanders, 1971). Good training programs have several features in common, including (1) use of verbal and written instructions, (2) discussions, (3) presentation of models, and (4) role playing exercises. In addition, during on-the-job instruction good training programs include (1) modeling by experienced employees of treatment procedures followed by try-out of the procedures by trainees, (2) regular review and critique of the on-the-job performance of trainees, and (3) additional academic instruction briefly presented as needed. These features of good training programs do not seem to be unusual or novel ones. What characterizes such training progams is the thoroughness with which they are implemented. Objectives are clearly specified in great detail, and these objectives are taught rigorously. Any staff trainer might consider himself to be thorough, but good training programs tend to be almost compulsive in this respect.

Since it is not necessarily the case that a freshly trained staff member will do good work, even if he is given refresher courses (Quilitch, 1975), all training programs should be supplemented with regular supervision and motivational procedures to ensure continued good performance. Motivational techniques are discussed in the following section.

INCENTIVE METHODS

Several investigators have questioned the use of extrinsic "rewards" to motivate employees on the grounds that such rewards tend to decrease overall motivation by lessening "intrinsic motivation" (e.g., Notz, 1975). Most of the supporting evidence for this theory has come from short-term, laboratory studies, and results of some of these studies are contradictory. Until the evidence for the theory is stronger, it can be assumed that in real life work situations over a lengthy period of time employees will tend to perform more satisfactorily if they are openly and explicitly rewarded for good work. Certainly the literature cited below tends to show that employees respond favorably to extrinsic rewards.

In this section the use of the structure of the program itself and of praise in motivating staff members is discussed. In addition, a list of extrinsic rewards used by various investigators is presented. All this material represents a summary of many articles dealing with these matters. Many of the articles have been summarized in some detail by McInnis (1976). Although the reader might take the ideas presented in this section as a starting point for his own development of an incentive system, and might find more specific suggestions in the McInnis (1976) paper, he probably should consult the original articles for very specific details which he might adopt in his own situation. To this end, a long list of relevant articles is presented here (see Barton, Guess, Garcia, & Baer, 1970; Bricker, Morgan, & Grabowski, 1969; Colman & Boren, 1969; Cossairt, Hall, & Hopkins, 1973; Favell, Note 3; Hermann, de Montes, Dominquez, Montes, & Hopkins, 1973; Katz, Johnson, & Gelfand, 1972; Loeber, 1971; Loeber & Weisman, 1975; Martin, McDonald, & Murrell, Note 2; McInnis, 1976; Panyan, Boozer, & Morris, 1970; Patterson, Cooke, & Liberman, 1972; Pomerleau, Bobrove, & Smith, 1973; Pommer & Streedbeck, 1974; Watson, Gardner, & Sanders, 1971; Wolf, Giles, & Hall, 1968).

One method of influencing the work behaviors of staff members is to specify their work tasks carefully, as described in an earlier section of this chapter, so that they themselves can know when they deviate from ideal performance standards. Inspections by supervisors can help the employee determine if he is adhering to specified work procedures and can provide the employee with helpful feedback. To the extent that the supervisor has power by virtue of his position as a "boss," his feedback can be a form of extrinsic motivation to the staff member.

Verbal praise may be the most important incentive one can use. This is not because it is more powerful than food for a hungry person, for example; but, because most people are "conditioned" to respond to it, it seems like a natural incentive, and it is easy to administer. A verbally reinforcing milieu should be established within the treatment program. Since many of us have to learn how to notice and praise "good" behavior, it is important that praising skills be taught. An appropriate teacher in a treatment program would be the program director who can explain that he wants the staff members to praise each other's work and who can model the behavior. At first, praise might actually have to be scheduled. Such scheduling may seem a cold-blooded thing to do, but it is no more a calculated action than a mother's admonishing her child to say "thank you" in an attempt to make the child a "naturally" charming person. Praise should never be dishonest. A program director must establish a reputation for honesty, for only then will his praise (and criticism) be truly meaningful. One should praise behavior that is ordinarily expected of an employee, and not reserve it for outstanding performances.

It may be necessary to use motivators other than praise. Use of "material" rewards is certainly not novel in treatment situations, though rewards are frequently not administered fairly. Awarding of days off, for example, is typically contingent on some performance criterion. If material rewards are used, it is particularly important that a formal system of observation and recording of staff members' work behaviors be established, although such a system can never be a perfect one (see the following discussion). Various authors (see long list above) have recommended a number of consequences that can be used in an incentive program. On the positive side there are (1) letters of recommendation, (2) "employee of the week" awards, public recognition through plaques, posted photographs, and news reports, (3) assignment to desired work shifts, work schedules, work areas, vacation times and lengths, lunch time, co-workers, and even parking spaces, (4) opportunity to leave early from work, (5) increased responsibility, authority, and freedom, (6) raises in pay, and (7) bonus money or trading stamps. On the negative side can be listed (1) letters of reprimand, (2) suspension without pay, and (3) dismissal. Awarding of positive consequences can be more or less public, and, if public, may result in competition for the awards. Some of the positive awards can also be given to groups rather than to individuals, possibly resulting in competition between groups of employees. To save money, monetary awards can be given periodically to one or a few employees in a competitive situation.

Finally, as noted in an earlier section, public and professional scrutiny of a treatment program can have good effects on the program staff. Staff members who are frequently observed by outsiders may be inclined to do their best work.

RELATION OF EVALUATION STRATEGIES
TO MOTIVATING STAFF

How treatment programs are evaluated is intimately related to staff motivational programs and to the improvement of larger treatment systems such as hospitals and schools. The relationship between evaluation and administration of programs has not always been clearly seen. A discussion of evaluation in large treatment systems is tangential to the focus of this chapter; however, some discussion of it is necessary to clarify the role of evaluation in staff incentive programs. In this section two general types of program evaluation, process and outcome evaluation, are defined, an overemphasis on process evaluation is discussed, and negative aspects of process evaluation are presented. The application of the process-outcome evaluation distinction to small treatment programs and staff incentive programs is then presented, showing that outcomes of treatment must be at least one criterion for rewarding staff members for good work. In these discussions the term "outcome monitoring" is used to describe, simply, the measurement of changes in students. The term "outcome evaluation" is used to describe the monitoring of changes in students in the context of an experimental design, which makes it possible to choose between alternative treatment strategies. Process evaluation is defined below.

Processes can be defined as all those predetermined features of a treatment program, for example, treatment plans and staff-student ratios, which are thought to contribute to success of the program. Macmahon, Pugh, and Hutchison (1969) defined the evaluation of processes as efforts to ". . . find out whether a supposedly therapeutic or preventive practice is in fact being carried out within specified limits . . . " (p. 52).

Process evaluation has been overemphasized in large programs, probably because of pressures from governmental agencies and insurance companies for documentation of treatment procedures, the relative ease of conducting process evaluation as opposed to outcome evaluation, and assumptions by treatment planners that good treatment outcomes follow automatically from what they consider to be "ideal" treatment procedures (Ellsworth, Note 4; McInnis & Kitson, in press; McLean, 1974).

Process evaluation is necessary, since program administrators cannot and should not avoid an attempt to implement and maintain the best possible treatment programs. However, process evaluation has several negative features. First, elaborate process evaluation systems such as utilization review and peer review are expensive (Ellsworth, Note 4). Second, process evaluation, because it can only ensure that predetermined "ideal" procedures are being followed, can maintain only the *status quo*. There is no mechanism in process evaluation for evaluating "ideal" processes and for modifying them (Ellsworth, Note 4; McInnis & Kitson, in press, Paul, 1956). The predetermined procedures may not be ideal ones after all, and in fact, are not likely to be at the present time, because so little is known about what processes contribute to good outcomes (Ellsworth, Note 4; Lawton & Cohen, 1975).

In large treatment systems, outcome evaluation, if added to process monitoring, can help motivate administrators to change aspects of the treatment process so as to improve outcomes. For example, in a mental hospital an assumption might be that electroshock therapy, if performed according to certain rules, would be beneficial to some patients. Process evaluation would only ensure that the rules for the therapy were being followed. Outcome evaluation would determine, in addition, if the therapy were actually working and if it could lead to modification of the procedures or abandonment of that kind of therapy.

Now, how do these considerations apply to staff motivational systems in small treatment units? Even in small treatment programs, including behavioral ones, there seems to have been an overemphasis on process evaluation in conduct of staff incentive programs. This is true, for example, of most of the staff motivation studies listed above. In most of those studies a treatment process, that is, adherence to a treatment plan, was used as the basis for staff rewards.

There is evidence that monitoring of outcomes enhances improvement of students, but that evaluation of processes alone does not. In one of the staff motivation studies, not only were the staff's actions monitored, but also progress with individual students (Martin, McDonald, & Murrell, Note 2). In one condition in the latter study, staff members were rewarded for adhering to a treatment plan (process evaluation), whereas in another condition they were rewarded for producing positive changes in their students (outcome evaluation). In the former condition the staff members' work performance significantly improved, but only in the latter condition did the students improve. The authors of the study noted that in the latter condition the staff members not only worked harder than in the first condition, but also showed more initiative in assembling necessary training materials, paid more attention to their students, and paid more attention to charts of their students' progress. The lesson to be learned from this study is that only if outcomes are monitored will the staff be motivated to actually give treatment plans a full try-out. Thus it seems necessary, in small treatment programs, to base staff rewards at least partly on the results they obtain with their students. However, it is still desirable to check the work of staff members directly.

In some treatment programs a point system could be used, wherein some points were awarded for staff members' obtaining good results with students and some points for their carefully following treatment procedures. The proportion of points to be awarded for improvement of students would depend on a judgement of how long it would reasonably be expected for the students to begin to respond to the treatment procedures. With some students improvement could be slow in coming, and an incentive program based only on improvement of students would be quite frustrating to the staff members. However, it should be possible to assign students with good as well as poor chances for quick response to treatment to each staff member, thus ensuring that every staff member has an equal chance to receive rewards for helping his students. An additional reason for not basing rewards solely on treatment outcomes is that the treatment plans themselves may be poor ones. If treatment plans are poor, it would be unfair to expect staff members to get good results using them.

Using treatment outcomes as a basis for staff rewards is a form of process evaluation, since the purpose is to ensure that predetermined treatment plans are followed. Outcome evaluation involves not only assessing outcomes but also using experimental controls. Although sheer monitoring of outcomes is not, in itself, outcome evaluation, use of outcomes as a basis for staff rewards can improve outcome evaluation in an interesting manner. If all possible favorable factors seem to be operating in a treatment program, there can still be a crucial failure of staff members to show initiative and determination in fully carrying out treatment plans. Even careful observation and supervision, as pointed out, may fail to detect this failure. If the program fails, an erroneous conclusion may be made that the treatment plan was at fault when the fault was actually in the implementation of the treatment plan. If staff members were rewarded for achieving good results with their students, one could more accurately credit treatment failures and successes to the treatment plans themselves.

SUMMARY

Organizational and structural elements of treatment programs that underlie successful treatment programs have been discussed. In general, successful programs tend to have at least the following features: (1) full sharing of information and problems with all staff members, (2) openness to criticism and scrutiny, (3) decentralization of authority and job enrichment, and (4) careful structuring of staff roles and responsibilities.

Recommendations for staff training programs include the suggestion that an emphasis be placed on on-the-job training, with careful attention being paid to teaching staff members how to actually apply treatment principles. Recommended training techniques include: (1) academic instruction, (2) discussions, (3) presentation of models, (4) role playing, and (5) supervised on-the-job training, employing experienced staff members as teachers and models. Although these techniques are not unique or novel, it is suggested that good results can be obtained if they are applied in a very rigorous manner.

Several incentive methods have been presented, ranging from the relatively unobtrusive use of the structure of the program itself as a motivating device to use of explicit "material" rewards. A number of "material" rewards are listed, and it is suggested that the reader consult original articles describing use of such rewards before developing his own incentive system.

Finally, it is suggested that staff rewards be based not only on direct observations of the work behaviors of staff members but also on the results the staff members obtain with their "own" students. Using only adherence to predetermined treatment plans as the basis for rewards can lead to apparent but not actual good work performance. These conclusions regarding the basis for staff rewards are presented in the context of a general discussion of the role of process and outcome evaluation as it relates to administration of large treatment systems as well as to administration of staff incentive programs in small treatment programs. A final conclusion is that basing staff rewards on their results with their students enhances the accuracy of outcome evaluation of treatment programs.

REFERENCE NOTES

1. Cone, J. D., & Sheldon, S. S. Training behavior modifiers: Getting it going with remote auditory prompting. Paper presented at the meeting of the American Psychological Association, Montreal, Canada, August 1973.
2. Martin, G. L., McDonald, L. & Murrell, J. Developing and maintaining behavior modification skills of psychiatric nurses, aides, and attendants working with institutionalized retardates. Paper presented at the meeting of the American Psychological Association, Montreal, Canada, August 1973.
3. Favell, J. E. Reduction of staff tardiness by a feedback procedure. Paper presented at the meeting of the American Psychological Association, Montreal, Canada, August 1973.

4. Ellsworth, R. B. A developing imbalance in the evaluation of mental health programs. Paper presented at the meeting of the American Psychological Association, Chicago, August 1975.

REFERENCES

Barton, E. S., Guess, D., Garcia, E., & Baer, D. M. Improvement of retardates' mealtime behaviors by timeout procedures using multiple-baseline techniques. *Journal of Applied Behavior Analysis*, 1970, *2*, 77–84.

Bricker, W. A., Morgan, D. G., & Grabowski, J. C. Development and maintenance of a behavior modification repertoire of cottage attendants through TV feedback. *American Journal of Mental Deficiency*, 1972, *77*, 128–136.

Colman, A. D., & Boren, J. J. An information system for measuring patient behavior and its use by staff. *Journal of Applied Behavior Analysis*, 1969, *2*, 207–214.

Cossairt, A., Hall, R. V., & Hopkins, B. L. The effects of experimenter's instructions, feedback, and praise on teacher praise and student attending behavior. *Journal of Applied Behavior Analysis*, 1973, *6*, 89–100.

Friedlander, F., & Brown, L. D. Organization development. *Annual Review of Psychology*, 1974, *25*, 313–341.

Gardner, J. M. Teaching behavior modification to nonprofessionals. *Journal of Applied Behavior Analysis*, 1972, *5*, 517–521.

Glaser, E. M., & Taylor, S. H. Factors influencing the success of applied research. *American Psychologist*, 1973, *28*, 140–146.

Goldstein, A. P., & Goedhard, A. The use of structured learning for empathy enhancement in paraprofessional psychotherapist training. *Journal of Community Psychology*, 1973, *1*, 168–173.

Hermann, J. A., de Montes, A. I., Dominquez, B., Montes, F., & Hopkins, B. L. Effects of bonuses for punctuality on the tardiness of industrial workers. *Journal of Applied Behavior Analysis*, 1973, *6*, 563–570.

Katz, R. C., Johnson, C. A., & Gelfand, S. Modifying the dispensing of reinforcers: Some implications for behavior modification with hospitalized patients. *Behavior Therapy*, 1972, *3*, 579–588.

Lawton, M. P., & Cohen, J. Organizational studies of mental hospitals. In M. Guttentag & E. L. Struening (Eds.), *Handbook of evaluation research* (Vol. 2). Beverly Hills, Calif.: Sage Publications, 1975.

Loeber, R. Engineering the behavioral engineer. *Journal of Applied Behavior Analysis*, 1971, *4*, 321–326.

Loeber, R., & Weisman, R. G. Contingencies of therapist and trainer performance: A review. *Psychological Bulletin*, 1975, *82*, 660–688.

Macmahon, B., Pugh, T. F., & Hutchinson, G. B. Principles in the evaluation of community mental health programs. In H. C. Schulberg, A. Sheldon, & F. Baker (Eds.), *Program evaluation in the health fields*. New York: Behavioral Publications, 1969.

McInnis, T. Training and maintaining staff behaviors in residential treatment programs. In R. L. Patterson (Eds.), *Maintaining effective token economies*. Springfield, Ill.: Charles C Thomas, 1976.

McInnis, T., & Kitson, L. Process and outcome evaluation in mental health systems. *International Journal of Mental Health*, in press.

McLean, P. D. Evaluating community-based psychiatric services. In P. O. Davidson & L. A. Hamerlynck (Eds.), *Evaluation of behavioral programs.* Champaign, Ill.: Research Press, 1974.

Notz, W. W. Work motivation and the negative effects of extrinsic rewards: A review with implications for theory and practice. *American Psychologist*, 1975, *30*, 884–891.

Panyan, M., Boozer, H., & Morris, N. Feedback to attendants as a reinforcer for applying operant techniques. *Journal of Applied Behavior Analysis*, 1970, *3*, 1–4.

Patterson, R., Cooke, C., & Liberman, R. P. Reinforcing the reinforcers: a method of supplying feedback to nursing personnel. *Behavior Therapy*, 1972, *3*, 444–446.

Paul, B. D. Social science in public health. *American Journal of Public Health*, 1956, *46*, 1390–1396.

Paul, G. L., & McInnis, T. L. Attitudinal changes associated with two approaches to training mental health technicians in milieu and social-learning programs. *Journal of Consulting and Clinical Psychology*, 1974, *42*, 21–33.

Paul, G. L., McInnis, T. L., & Mariotto, M. J. Objective performance outcomes associated with two approaches to training mental health technicians in milieu and social-learning programs. *Journal of Abnormal Psychology*, 1973, *82*, 523–532.

Pomer, D. A., & Streedbeck, D. Motivating staff performance in an operant learning program for children. *Journal of Applied Behavior Analysis*, 1974, *7*, 217–221.

Pomerleau, O. F., Bobrove, P. H., & Smith, R. H. Rewarding psychiatric aides for the behavioral improvement of assigned patients. *Journal of Applied Behavior Analysis*, 1973, *6*, 383–390.

Quilitch, H. R. A comparison of three staff-management procedures. *Journal of Applied Behavior Analysis*, 1975, *8*, 67–75.

Watson, L. A., Gardner, J. M., & Sanders, C. Shaping and maintaining behavior modification skills in staff members in an MR institution: Columbus State Institute Behavior Modification Program. *Mental Retardation*, 1971, *9*, 39–42.

Whittington, H. G. People make programs: personnel management. In S. Feldman (Ed.), *The administration of mental health services.* Springfield, Ill.: Charles C Thomas, 1973.

Wolf, M. M., Giles, D. K., & Hall, R. V. Experiments with token reinforcement in a remedial classroom. *Behaviour Research and Therapy*, 1968, *6*, 51–64.

15

Intra-Institutional "Roadblocks" to Behavior Modification Programming

W. Robert Nay

Although the efficacy of institutional behavior modification programs in changing an array of academic, social, and task-related behaviors has frequently been reported within the literature (Kazdin & Bootzin, 1972; O'Leary & Drabman, 1971), interest has been increasingly directed toward an explication of those variables that predict the outcome of such intervention and the methodology used to evaluate such outcome (e.g., Davidson & Seidman, 1974). Although particular investigators have noted the important role of staff resistances, community constraints, institutional traditions, and so forth as potential delimiters of program success (e.g., Kuypers, Becker, & O'Leary, 1968; Repucci & Saunders, 1974; Tharp & Wetzel, 1969), most treatment-oriented researchers have ignored (if by omission only) the role of such factors as potential independent variables that may very well predict the outcome of intervention. The goals of this chapter are to define an array of institutional phenomena that can serve as delimiters or "roadblocks" to any effort at imposing a system of behavioral change in a therapeutic environment. The author has employed his own experiences as a behavioral "consultant" to an array of child and adolescent treatment agencies (Kendall, Nay, & Jeffers, 1975; Nay, 1974; Nay & Legum, 1976; Nay, Schulman, Bailey, & Huntsinger, 1976) as well as the reports of others as a source for the ideas presented. This is not to imply that the author has mastered the role of consultant. In fact, this presentation is more a testimonial to the myriad of problems he has faced in devising schemes of institutional change. Although much could be said about the potential role of social and political variables within the community as predictors of institutional policy (as nicely detailed by Repucci & Saunders, 1974), this presentation focuses on in-house, staff-related phenomena while underscoring the obvious interdependence of client, staff, and community variables within a general systems orientation (Katz & Kahn, 1966; Thompson, 1967).

ASSIGNMENT OF STAFF TO CLIENTS

Quite often, the behavioral change agent (BCA) has little or no control over the manner in which clients are assigned to certain physical locations within an institution or, more specifically, are assigned to staff members. Although the goals of a behavioral change program might rely on the ability of staff members across institutional settings to apply some treatment of interest (e.g., socially rewarding some particular targeted behavior) in a coordinated, systematic fashion, a number of factors may make such a combined staff effort impossible or unfeasible. For example, if one places the job descriptions of staff on a dimension of role permeability (e.g., the degree to which a given role such as aide or cottage parent is free to assume divergent functions), one can readily see that institutions that adopt a relatively impermeable array of job descriptions restrict the potential roles of staff as agents of treatment. Within such an "impermeable" system of role assignation, the operations of staff members remain quite fixed and unchanging. Thus in a school setting, a "teacher's" job would be to teach and not to deal directly with "emotional" (e.g., behavior management) problems that are within the province of the "school psychologist." A "nurse" on a psychiatric ward would administer certain medications within her role, but might never design a treatment plan for a client, which, of course, would fall within the pervue of the "psychiatrist" or "psychologist."

Thus impermeability implies that the functions of one's job role are relatively impermeable to the functions of some other job role. The client is viewed as a compendium of needs, and members of an array of different job descriptions are assigned to meet each of these specific needs. Because these specialists perform a specific and unique task and in many cases vary in their appearance (i.e., long white coat, short white coat, smock), each may be viewed much differently by both clients and staff members, and often such staff categories are explicitly or implicitly assigned a differing degree of status by all parties involved. An impermeable model often restricts communication among staff members, as there is little practical need for them to interact in carrying out their very unique functions. In addition, staff members representing different roles may reside in geographically different places within the institution, thus further increasing the communicative distance between staff. Communication may take place by writing notes in charts, reports, or completing staff logs, thus making it quite difficult to coordinate an individual client's treatment plan, make changes, or even gather assessment information as a prelude to treatment planning. This author vividly remembers the disastrous and inefficient outcome when some 13 professionals (e.g., social worker, welfare worker, psychiatrist, neurologist, psychologist, teacher, visiting teacher) independently attempted to assess and alter a child's "hyperactivity" within a classroom setting. The author and his colleagues were well along the way to developing a program of behavior modification when it was found that two such programs had been previously tried and were unsuccessful, because of the poor coordination of staff members involved, and one program was currently being developed.

Rogers (1975) nicely relates the notion of role impermeability to the various "units" of staff members who function within the "hospital."

A third factor that affects the organizational structure and policies of state mental hospitals is the perhaps overrated prestige of the clinical specialties. This tends to shape the institution's structure into the form of a "federal" system, in which various units strive to be independent of one another rather than fitting into well-structured institutional policies. In "the Hospital," there is a tendency for each unit to favor its autonomy whether in research, treatment or education. Professional courtesy helps this makeshift system work after a fashion, but it experiences critical difficulties when the question of the patients' interest in quality care arises. In addition, administrators are frustrated when they try to devise and implement important institution-wide policies (p. 14).

Perlman and Tornatzky (1975) argue that "the excessive form of professional and task specialization" (p. 30) seen in community mental health and other treatment agencies should not be permitted. Rather, they suggest that our current lack of knowledge regarding optimum client treatment combinations can best be overcome by organizing staff members "around broad problem areas with specialization occurring when genuine knowledge of the problem is developed" (p. 30). In addition, they point out that the "medical model" which implies a uniform treatment for specific "mental disease" processes (spawning the "specialist") should be cast aside in favor of increased role permeability and the informal communication channels that this predicts.

The foregoing suggests that the BCA would do well carefully to assess those avenues of communication and coordination which exist among staff members prior to treatment planning. A preliminary analysis of what each staff member specifically does with clients and other staff within and across days and an evaluation of the relative discreteness of such activities can provide an assessment of the degree of role permeability to be found within an agency. Individualized verbal exploration of how each potential change agent views his role and definition of those activities that are valued/disliked further define the BCA's options in encouraging multiple staff to participate in a treatment program. Such options are obviously restricted in certain extremely role-impermeable settings, and when this is the case the BCA might consider requesting that administrators and staff reassess existing job descriptions and communication media (e.g., frequency of staff meetings; means of communicating treatment plans) *prior* to requesting staff participation.

EXTRA-PROGRAM CONSTRAINTS

The BCA should carefully examine the working environment of proposed treatment agents to determine whether existent "treatment" settings, equipment, and supplies (if relevant) or other aspects of the tangible environment are facilitative of the kind of treatment that is proposed. One of the major problems this author has faced in assigning staff members to one-to-one interactions with clients (e.g., interviewing, modeling, shaping), is that physical space which is free from interruption and distraction is often difficult to locate. Although many newer facilities provide individual therapy rooms equipped with one-way mirrors, videotape equipment, and so forth, many institutions require staff-client interactions to take place within an open cottage, ward, or other such setting. In some cases the requirements that staff members maintain eye-level supervision of a larger population of clients while attempting to work with an individual client dramatically restrict treatment possibilities. A systematic observational analysis of the number of staff and clients assigned to each potential treatment space (e.g., offices, classrooms, television/recreation room) within daily time blocks and across days may permit the BCA to optimally propose settings for treatment. Those staff-client dyads or groupings that require a restricted setting may thus be given priority to particular settings.

Along these lines, the availability of equipment and/or supplies required by a proposed treatment program (e.g., for record keeping;

material and activity reinforcers) should be systematically assessed. In providing material "backup" reinforcers for token earning within an institution-wide token economy for adolescent delinquents, this author found his program budget "strained" after a few months and began looking for alternative sources of funds.

A "night-spot" was created for the girls in the basement of one of the cottages. Representative subjects decorated the setting to suit their tastes. At specified point cost a soda counter supplied subjects with a variety of desirable food and material items. Since the provision of such material items becomes expensive, regular allotments of canteen funds provided by the state purchased many of the items— with donations and some limited program funds purchasing the remainder. Wise incorporation of existing recreational funds, training funds, and canteen allotments within a token program becomes a necessity when program funds are limited. Moreover, by requiring the program to make use of existing funds within the institution, the program is not dependent on external grants, which may vanish as state and federal budgets are altered. Since trips to the night spot were limited to two each week for each cottage, privileges, cottage activities, and off-campus events stressing social interaction and exposure to the community were emphasized (Nay, 1974, p. 220).

The BCA should keep in mind that the employment of community-based activities, although certainly facilitating reintegration back into the natural setting for impatient clients, often requires a consideration of existing legal and "customary" policies. This is particularly true for most "total," relatively closed institutions (Goffman, 1961) or for client populations institutionalized for legal reasons (e.g., delinquents).

Many of the privileges and activities chosen, such as off-campus trips, additional canteen allowances, and activities calling for staff supervision, required extensive planning by the institutional administration. In some cases approval at the level of state supervisory agencies was necessary. To incorporate an extensive array of highly valued reinforcers within a treatment program, sufficient time and manpower to carry out the planning necessary is an obvious requirement for success (Nay, 1974, p. 212).

TRAINING VARIABLES

Although most BCAs are very clearly in the business of training staff members as well as clients to alter their behavior in desired directions, very few provide a detailed explication of staff-training mechanisms, frequency and characteristics of staff evaluation, and incentive systems directed at promoting behavioral change on the part of staff members (Grabowski & Thompson, 1972; Kazdin & Bootzin, 1972; Poser, 1972). A cataloguing of training procedures is beyond the scope of this presentation, but the BCA might do well to evaluate the *possibilities* for informal and formal systematized training within the setting of interest. First, an evaluation of how new staff members are introduced into the institutional treatment program as well as the frequency and characteristics of ongoing, "in-service" training might be investigated by comparing "published" accounts of training mechanisms with institutional records, administrator and staff self-reports, and observational data. This author has found that an elaborate and complex daily schedule for staff (particularly teachers) often severely limits potential training sessions. Often, staff members must be trained on their "own" time or while carrying out an array of other obligatory and preprogrammed duties, with training taking a back-seat to other role requirements of staff positions. The implicit communication to staff members in such a situation is that program procedures are less important than other duties, and they often respond (or fail to) accordingly. A careful evaluation of staffing schedules and a determination of the degree to which such schedules may be altered for training sessions should be undertaken by the program designer. When insufficient staff time is available, the BCA should carefully define training time requirements for administrators. Too often the BCA is willing to initiate an individual or group management program prior to staff displaying competency in employing program procedures to, in effect, work "around" existing staff schedules and institutional policy. Unfortunately, when the program fails to achieve its desired outcome with clients or extinguishes itself in a veritable sea of staff incompetence, program procedures are often blamed. This author has found that "some kind of program" is *not* better than none at all, and has become increasingly assertive in outlining for administrators the basic training requirements (contingencies) for a successful program.

Although most BCAs readily suppose that client efforts at changing behavior must be carefully monitored, with appropriate positive and negative feedback provided for participation, very few investigators report on procedures for differentially reinforcing staff members for their efforts at behavioral change. Particularly within the most impermeable role model, it is most difficult systematically to monitor precisely what staff members do (or fail to do) with clients, and this lack of a data base makes any kind of differential feedback dependent on a host of subjective and nonspecific factors. Although monitoring approaches have ranged from self-reports within staff meetings (e.g., Brierton, Garms, & Metzger, 1969; Pizzat, 1973) to publicly displayed charts of client progress as an indicator of staff effectiveness (e.g., Panyon, Boozer, & Morris, 1970), it would seem that the utility of any supervisory system depends on the ability of program administrators to set explicit goals and to provide contingent negative and positive feedback (see Kim & Hamner, 1976). Unfortunately, particularly within many public facilities, the almost exclusive incentives of salary, pay raise, and promotion are dependent on a host of factors (e.g., length of

452 W. Robert Nay

tenure; grievance procedures) other than operationally defined staff performance. Often, program administrators tend to emphasize these material incentives, which cannot be differentially administered (e.g., Ayllon & Azrin, 1968; Martin, 1972) in lieu of an array of other items that may hold powerful incentive properties.

For example, institutional prerequisites such as access to time off, choice of working schedule and co-workers, choice and length of vacation times, choice of space within the setting, quality/decoration of space, access to desirable staff parking, choice of lunch time, early daily dismissal (e.g., one-half hour), and choice of client are ignored in favor of the obvious material categories of incentives. Alternative social options might include the public posting of "outstanding" staff names; posting of charts depicting staff and/or client behavior; citation of achieving staff members in institutional magazines, newspapers, or other media; laudatory letters placed in a staff member's permanent folder; letters of commendation for outstanding efforts; or reinforcing dinners, get-togethers, parties, or other social activities, which are based upon an array of often powerful social/affectional relationships that ordinarily exist within the agency. Finally, differential assignment of responsibility, change of job descriptions, "levels" that define staff members at various positions of responsibility, access to seminars and academic courses within the community, and access to supervisory roles are among responsibility incentives that can provide feedback to staff members regarding their progress.

"RESISTANCES"

Whereas many BCAs speak of the "resistances" to change that in-house staff as well as outside "consultants" meet when proposing an alternative way of doing things, the idea of resistance is rarely talked about within the clinical intervention literature, perhaps because of the difficulty in operationalizing the array of variables that fall within this rather crude descriptive dimension. The literature documenting those systems that operate within businesses and other organizations, with its reliance upon the noninstitutional "consultant" as a primary data collector, has often documented and attempted to define the nature of resistance to change (e.g., Coch & French, 1968; Falck & Barnes, 1975). Unfortunately, this "organizational" literature is seemingly ignored by many "clinically" oriented change agents who meet resistance as if it were some novel phenomenon directed singularly toward their efforts.

This author has heard a number of research-minded BCAs complain that an individual client or group program was not effective, because staff members "resisted" any efforts at changing their behavior with clients. It is most unfortunate that the failure of institutional behavior modification programs is rarely reported in the literature, because an explication of the kinds of variables which "on the face of it" promote institutional resistance might lead to more systematic speculations and ultimate attention to the factors that could predict failure as well as success.

Although resistances to behavioral change may be directly related to the specific demands that a treatment plan imposes on participating staff members (e.g., time demands, demanding skills beyond the staff member's behavioral repertoire, staff disagreement with the treatment strategy, staff incompetence) it is this author's opinion that such resistance is a general phenomenon that is certainly not the exclusive characteristic of staff members of institutions, and certainly, individuals vary in the degree to which they can accept direction from others (e.g., Pines & Julian, 1967; Rotter & Mulry, 1962) as well as divergent role behavior (e.g., Kelly, 1955). Many popular writers have attempted to document the effects of change on our behavior and the manner in which individuals attempt to deal with rapid change (e.g., Toffler, 1970). To the extent that repetitive behavioral patterns, traditions, and customs become positively valued over time, the BCA must expect that any proposal for alternative, novel behavior may generate anxiety on the part of staff members and subsequent patterns of behavior which are viewed by the consultant as "resistant." As an example, Tharp and Wetzel (1969) describe the case of a school guidance counselor who had achieved little success in his individual efforts in altering a client's behavior. The author describes what occurred when a team approach to the client's behavioral problems was suggested:

"In a conference among school counselors, administrators, and behavioral research program staff, called for the purpose of discussing several cases which had counselor involvement, one counselor stated his position honestly and boldly: "I know counseling hasn't helped with . . ., but this is my case and I don't want to turn it over to anybody" (p. 40).

In proposing a new treatment strategy that violates the traditions of a setting, the BCA might alleviate much of the resistance generated by "the unknown" by expending time to educate those staff members as to the rationale and expected results of the proposed treatment. Staff members should be given a role in determining the way the clients are to be treated, and whenever possible, customary patterns of behavior that are not dissonant with the goals of treatment should be permitted and encouraged rather than viewed as antiquated and "resistant." In their account of the change agent within the mental health organization, Falck and Barnes (1975) emphasize the importance of being tolerant of custom.

Often overlooked are the traditions and history of the organization. Some practices and procedures within every organization are important to its maintenance, morale, stability, values, and the very life or *esprit de corps* of the organization itself. In examining the present and past history of an organization, the change agent will no doubt discover that some traditions appear to make little or no sense. However, unless he concerns himself with how people feel about traditions, he may find that his tampering will arouse great anger and resistance. A change agent must determine which traditions can be ignored or buried and which must be handled gently. More than one change agent has been impaled or run out of town because he failed to understand the traditions and history of the organization (p. 8).

Often, objections to a BCA's plans to introduce novel treatments or data collection schemes are couched in vague terms by staff members asked to participate.

A number of the tenured staff members see themselves as captives of their pension rights or other benefits, or of personal concerns such as children's schooling. Both staff and patients to a large extent, believe they are victimized by an unidentified "them," those in control of the establishment and the "system." The result is a feeling of powerlessness and the need to exercise one's wits, to play up to the "power structure" in order to be able to do "his own thing." While carefully testing the limits of institutionally acceptable behavior, staff and patients seem routinely to behave in an apathetic manner. Yet, close to the surface, there is a lack of security and strong feelings of frustration, discontent, rage and guilt (pp. 17–18).

Those factors that promote staff insecurity or general dissatisfaction must, obviously, be understood and dealt with if the BCA is to expect active and attentive participation in carrying out treatment procedures. Regardless of the soundness of a proposed treatment program, it is unlikely to be successful if overlaid on an institutional entity (e.g., ward, cottage) that is beset by general dissatisfaction and apathy among staff members.

In some cases resistances may be generated by the negativistic views that staff members and administrators hold regarding "behavior modification." The words "behavioral" and "modification" may suggest or connote certain forms of control, mechanization or "bribery" to staff. Although the systematic and data-supported criticism of behavior modification programs has increasingly been reported within the academic as well as popular media (Davison & Wilson, 1973; Goodall, 1972; Wheeler, 1973) the operational definition of what "behavior modification" is has become clouded. Because of its semantic breadth, the term could, justifiably, describe any form of change procedure that "modifies" client behavior. Thus although behavior modification most often involves attempts at employing social learning principles (e.g., Bandura, 1969) and is certainly nonmedical/biological in orientation, electro-convulsive shock, aversive chemical agents, surgical intervention, and brain stimulation are among treatments termed "behavior modification" in the recent media. Many behavioral BCAs have exacerbated this problem by employing a technical language (e.g., "operants," "schedules," "reinforcers") with staff members who do not understand the meaning of certain words (why *should* they) and respond only to the connotative meaning (e.g., harsh, mechanistic, inhuman) the words evoke.

Because of the myriad of procedures that seem to fall within a "behavioral" orientation (e.g., Kazdin, 1975; Rimm & Masters, 1974), it would seem that the BCA should carefully describe, in language that is meaningful and appropriately geared to a given staff member or grouping, the rationale for and specific operations of the proposed treatment. This author avoids using the term "behavior modification" in consulting with institutional staff because of its imprecision and obvious surplus value, holding the use of technical jargon to a minimum. If presented in terms of clearly defined operations, staff members can evaluate proposed treatments based on their specific merits. Jargon-laden phrases and banner-waving, proselytizing polemics only serve to emphasize how "behavior modification" is somehow different from (and superior to!) other conceptual and procedural points of view. Such an approach often "backfires" and only serves to hamper the communication of ideas, almost *forcing* staff members to defend existing avenues of treatment in which an investment has been made.

Repucci and Saunders (1974), in their account of problems in implementing behavioral programs within "delinquent" populations, support the need for BCAs to use understandable operational language in interacting with staff.

For some, the concept, and consequently the language, of behavior modification may provoke a clash of values; for others, the particular words just may not "catch on." The point is that choosing *meaningful* and *acceptable* words to convey the general principles and to pinpoint specific concepts is an important aspect of planning for change and preparing for new ways of thinking.

In most cases, the problem of language can be surmounted if the behavior modifier is sensitive to the issues involved and does not insist that his vocabulary is always the right and only one. There are usually several words that can be used to convey the same idea (e.g., *reward* and *positive reinforcement*), and it is necessary to choose the one that will be acceptable and meaningful to most people in the particular setting (p. 653).

Another phenomenon that cannot be described in very specific terms, yet may contribute to staff resistance, is the idea that new programs and procedures may come and go, but things will ultimately change very little. In a sense this syndrome implies that the status quo has a momentum of its own. Unfortunately, new programs often do "come and go" with great alacrity, which perhaps serves to reinforce this notion. The BCA should ensure that those staff members who will reside in the setting on a permanent basis are thoroughly trained in program mechanisms and can thus "direct" and supervise the program when extrinsic consultants leave. Institutional administrators must ensure that adequate positive feedback is provided for such staff efforts, so that the program continues to have an advocate as contemporary and novel problems develop. One of the major predictors of negative outcomes for programs is the incidence of high levels of yearly staff turnover within an agency, such that well-trained and competent staff members are not available to train incoming members who are not invested in current programs. This author has attempted to implement treatment programs within agencies displaying turnover rates approaching 100% per year. Needless to say, at the outset the potential goals of intervention were most delimited and positive outcomes quite restricted as a result of the transitory state of things that staff turnover predicts. Systematic avenues of reinforcement for staff members along the material, prerequisite, social, and responsibility dimensions would seem to decrease the possibility of turnover, thus ensuring the availability of competent program advocates.

The introduction of a new program implicitly suggests that certain staff members will be asked to change or expand on current repertoire behaviors. The foregoing discussion has suggested that change may well provoke staff attempts at resistance and that resistance to change must be actively dealt with by the BCA rather than used as a post-hoc explanation for program failure. Falck and Barnes (1975) offer a number of suggestions to the change agent to enhance the probability of program acceptance. They emphasize that the BCA should adopt a "non-normative" approach, neither totally committing himself to current staff norms nor assuming the role of a markedly different or "deviant" staff member. The first approach does not permit the change agent to induce change (without violating group norms), whereas the second will likely promote massive resistance while relegating the BCA to a "very restricted area of influence" (p. 5). The recommended non-normative style is summarized by the authors.

The non-normative person does not meet the standards and norms of the organization on the one hand, but neither does he put himself in a position where he openly or even covertly opposes them. He stands in the middle, neither supporting the current ideology nor fighting it. He represents a third option, one that initially may be unsupportive of current normative standards but which in the long run turns out to be suggestive of a new synthesis between the old ideologies and his new ones. He promotes the survival of both the old and the new in a new synthesis and context (p. 5).

The idea here is for the BCA to introduce change in a gradual manner, establishing his own credibility as a loyal yet independent, thinking, staff-group member. In this role, the BCA, presumably, can learn enough about current channels of communication, define those persons in a position of power, and understand customs and traditional ways of viewing clients as well as treatment methods. The BCA is then able to construct strategies for client intervention that are both effective *and* have some likelihood of being accepted and employed. In addition, the BCA is in a position to know which staff members/supervisors are most likely to be receptive to a proposed program strategy. Instituting a program with maximally responsive staff under low-threat conditions may ensure program success that, once demonstrated, takes on a momentum of its own.

SUMMARY AND CONCLUSIONS

Among many potential problems that the BCA may be confronted with in instituting behavior modification programs, this presentation has emphasized certain in-house, staff-related dimensions. A careful assessment of each "problem" domain prior to treatment planning is heartily encouraged. The author's underlying assumption is that although careful consideration is often paid to program-related variables, little systematic attention is directed at the institutional milieu within which the program must be carried out. The fact that the foregoing account might best be described as the author's phenomenal view of the institution as a medium for treatment reflects the lack of interest shown within the literature for such variables. Perhaps the treatment-oriented investigator would do well to peruse the industrial/organizational literature (e.g., Haas & Drabek, 1973; Katz & Kahn, 1966, provide excellent textbook reviews) or the diagnostic schemes of writers such as Levinson (1972) to obtain an overview of certain intra-organizational variables related to administrator-staff-client interactions that may be relevant to "mental health" settings.

The systematic definition and clarification of the "roadblocks" to behavioral change will certainly increase the probability of positive program outcome and will predictably expand the horizon of the treatment agent to include an array of variables that are now rather nonspecific and vague in character, but potentially powerful in their effect.

REFERENCES

Ayllon, T., & Azrin, N. *The token economy: A motivational system for therapy and rehabilitation.* New York: Appleton-Century-Crofts, 1968.

Bandura, A. *Principles of behavior modification.* New York: Rinehart & Winston, 1969.

Brierton, S., Garms, R., & Metzger, R. Practical problems encountered in an aide-administered token reward cottage program. *Mental Retardation*, 1969, *7*, 40–43.

Coch, L., & Rench. J. Overcoming resistance to change. In D. Cartwright & A. Zander (Eds.), *Group dynamics: Research and theory*. New York: Harper, 1968.

Davidson, III, W. S., & Seidman, E. Studies of behavior modification and juvenile delinquency: A review, methodological critique and social perspective. *Psychological Bulletin*, 1974, *81*, 998–1011.

Davison, G., & Wilson, G. T. Attitudes of behavior therapists toward homosexuality. *Behavior Therapy*, 1973, *4*, 686–699.

Falck, H. S., & Barnes, R. E. The change agent in the organization. *Administration in Mental Health*, 1975, *3*, 3–11.

Goffman, E. *Asylums*. New York: Doubleday, 1961.

Goodall, K. Shapers at work. *Psychology Today*, 1972, *6*, 53–63.

Grabowski, J., & Thompson, T. A behavior modification program for behaviorally retarded institutionalized males. In J. Grabowski & T. Thompson (Eds.), *Behavior modification of the mentally retarded*. New York: Oxford University Press, 1972.

Haas, E. J., & Drabnek, T. E. *Complex organizations*. New York: Macmillan, 1973.

Katz, D., & Kahn, R. L. *The social psychology of organization*. New York: Wiley, 1966.

Kazdin, A. *Behavior modification in applied settings*. Homewood Ill.: Dorsey Press, 1975.

Kazdin, A., & Bootzin, R. The token economy: An evaluative review. *Journal of Applied Behavior Analysis*, 1972, *5*, 343-372.

Kelly, G. A. *The psychology of personal constructs*. New York: Norton, 1955.

Kendall, P. C., Nay, W. R., & Jeffers, J. Timeout duration and contrast effects: A systematic evaluation of a successive treatment design. *Behavior Therapy*, 1975, *6*, 609–615.

Kim, J. S., & Hamner, W. C. Effects of performance feedback and goal setting on productivity and satisfaction in an organizational setting. *Journal of Applied Psychology*, 1976, *61*, 48–57.

Kuypers, D. S., Becker, W. C., & O'Leary, K. D. How to make a token system fail. *Exceptional Children*, 1968, *35*, 101–109.

Levinson, H. *Organizational diagnosis*. Cambridge, Mass.: Harvard University Press, 1972.

Martin, G. Teaching operant technology to psychiatric nurses, aides, and attendants. In F. W. Clark, D. R. Evans, & L. A. Hamerlynck (Eds.), *Implementing behavioral programs for schools and clinics: Proceedings of the Third Banff International Conference on Behavior Modification*. Champaign, Ill.: Research Press, 1972.

Nay, W. R. Comprehensive behavioral treatment in a training school for delinquents. In K. Calhoun, H. Adams, & K. Mitchell (Eds.), *Innovative treatment methods in psychopatholgy*. New York: Wiley, 1974.

Nay, W. R., & Legum, L. Increasing generalization in a token program for adolescent retardates: A methodological note. *Behavior Therapy*, 1976, *7*, 413–414.

Nay, W. R., Schulman, J. A., Bailey, K. G., & Huntsinger, G. M. Territory and classroom management: An exploratory case study. *Behavior Therapy*, 1976, *7*, 240–246.

O'Leary, K., & Drabman, R. Token reinforcement programs in the classroom: A review. *Psychological Bulletin*, 1971, *75*, 379–398.

Panyon, M., Boozer, H., & Morris, N. Feedback to attendants as a reinforcer for applying operant techniques. *Journal of Applied Behavior Analysis*, 1970, *3*, 1–4.

Perlman, B., & Tornatzky, L. G. Organizational perspectives on community mental health centers. *Administration in Mental Health*, 1975, (Fall), 27–31.

Pines, H. A., & Julian, J. W. Effects of task and social demands on locus of control differences in information processing. *Journal of Personality*, 1967, *40*, 407–416.

Pizzat, F. *Behavior modification in residential treatment for children: A model program*. New York: Behavioral Publications, 1973.

Poser, E. Training behavior change agents: A five-year perspective. In F. W. Clark, D. R. Evans, & C. A. Hamerlynck (Eds.), *Implementing behavioral programs for schools and clinics: Proceedings of the Third Banff International Conference on Behavior Modification*. Champaign, Ill.: Research Press, 1972.

Repucci, N. D., & Saunders, J. T. Social psychology of behavior modification: Problems of implementation in natural settings. *American Psychologist*, 1974, *29*, 649–660.

Rimm, D., & Masters, J. C. *Behavior therapy: Techniques and empirical findings*. New York: Academic, 1974.

Rogers, K. State mental hospitals: An organizational analysis. *Administration in Mental Health*, 1975, *3*, 12–20.

Rotter, J. B., & Mulry, R. C. Internal versus external control of reinforcement: A major variable in behavior theory. In E. Washburn (Ed.), *Decisions, values and groups*. New York: Pergamon, 1962.

Tharp, R., & Wetzel, R. *Behavior modification in the natural environment*. New York: Academic, 1969.

Thompson, J. D. *Organizations in action*. New York: McGraw Hill, 1967.

Toffler, A. *Future shock*. New York: Random House, 1970.

Wheeler, H. (Ed.). *Beyond the punitive society*. San Francisco: Freeman, 1973.

NOTE

1. The author wishes to thank Mr. James C. Melvin for his advice and criticism.

Author Index

Subject Index